Of Papers and Protests:
Hong Kong responds to Occupy Central
Volume 2

Guy Breshears

<Published by Guy Ruben Breshears>
<2016>

Copyright © <2016> by <Guy Breshears>

All rights reserved. Any portion of this book may not be reproduced or used in any manner whatsoever without the written permission of the publisher. Book reviews, scholarly journals or the Government of the Hong Kong Special Administrative Region need no special permission as long as credit is given to the author. Press reports, Hong Kong government blogs and court injunctions are copyrighted and are used with the kind permission of the Government of the Hong Kong Special Administrative Region.

Cover photo: Protesters and Supporters prepare to open their umbrellas for 87 seconds in silence. 87 was the number of tear gas canisters fired on the first official day of Occupy Central. October 28, 2014, Admiralty. Copyright © 2014 by the author. All rights reserved.

First Printing: <2016>

ISBN <978-988-77039-1-4>

Other books by the author:
Loyal till Death: A Diary of the 13th New York Artillery
Major Granville Haller: Dismissed with Malice
To Seize Their Lands: Manifest Destiny in Washington State
Visit http://www.heritagebooks.com for more information of these books

For more information about this book contact the publisher:

Breshears, Guy Ruben
PO Box 88409
Sham Shui Po Post Office
Kowloon
Hong Kong

Dedication

To my wife who has stood by me ever since I have arrived in Hong Kong. I could not have survived without her continuing support.

Also, to Our Lady of China: Pray for all that live here so that those who govern will do so with equal justice for all. Finally, pray for the faithful who live here and have recourse to thee.

Table of Content

November 2014	1
December 2015	203
January 2015	293
May 2015	303
June 2015	313
February 2016	333
March 2016	353
Mong Kok Court Injunctions	
October 20, 2014	359
November 10, 2014	369
November 13, 2014	399
August 11, 2015	405
CITIC Towers Court Injunctions	
October 20, 2014	411
November 10, 2014	413
Admiralty Court Injunctions	
December 1, 2014	443
December 1, 2014	463
US-China Economic and Security Review Commission Report	483
US Congressional-Executive Commission on China Annual Report 2015	507

Introduction

Contradiction and struggle are universal and absolute, but the methods of resolving contradictions, that is, the forms of struggle, differ according to the differences in the nature of the contradictions. Some contradictions are characterized by open antagonism and others are not. In accordance with the concrete development of things, some contradictions, which were originally non-antagonistic, develop into antagonistic ones, while others which were originally antagonistic develop into non-antagonistic ones.[1]

History has shown that the aspiration to select one's own leadership can be a struggle, by the people, to make their voices heard and to institute a form of government that best suits the needs of the people. While the formation of government has been in the minds of people for many centuries it is often a struggle to form the government for the people, by the people and of the people.

Therefore, it is fascinating to see Hong Kong take up this democratic struggle now since they are officially part of China. It is remarkable because that while still a colony of Great Britain they could have petitioned the British government for a new form of government but instead just accepted whomever the British government sent as governor of this "barren rock"[2].

Officially, Occupy Central only lasted from 26 September to 15 December 2014 as a protest against China's proposal on how to reform the electoral system in Hong Kong. It is also known by a number of other names such as the Umbrella Movement or the Umbrella Revolution. However, the roots and effects of it expand beyond these dates and still casts a specter of discontent to this day.

Protests in Hong Kong, since returning to China in 1997, are nothing new. Every 1 July there are planned protests that lasts most of the afternoon and evening. Various groups tend to protest just about everything from policies of China to people in Hong Kong government; from local issues to international ones. The 1 July protesters just have to apply for a protest permit, to the police, and then wait their turn to protest on that day. There are, normally, no repercussions for protesting and it is generally considered part of the Hong Kong social culture of that day.

In contrast to 1 July events protesting took a serious turn in September 2002 when the Hong Kong government released its proposals for an anti-subversion law. Among the proposals were

---

[1] Mao Tse Tung, from his work "On Contradiction" (August 1937)
[2] British Foreign Secretary Lord Henry John Temple Palmerston wrote to, then British Superintendent of Trade, Charles Elliot when it was learned that Hong Kong was acquired by Elliot. Palmerston stated that Hong Kong was "a barren rock with nary a house on it."

limiting free speech and assembly. This law would increase police powers and allow them to enter a place of residence without a court order and arresting those at the airport who are in transit just because they, or the organization they belong to, have been banned by China.

In December, of that year, people took to the streets to protest against this proposed law. People feared this law, if enacted, would do away with the many rights, and freedoms, they had while they were under British rule. The government tried to do damage control but the following year protests broke out again. Eventually, the proposal was withdrawn until further notice. The people cheered this victory with perhaps some thinking that it would send a strong message to China not to interfere with the internal affairs of Hong Kong.

Prior to the protests of 2002 the Education Bureau, in 2001, quietly started to work on a new curriculum for schools and revised it in 2008. It was announced, in 2010, that a new *moral and national education* would replace the current *moral and civic education* in the schools starting in 2013.

Once this plan was announced many groups, such as Scholarism (which would play a role in Occupy Central later on) protested this new plan. Among the things that were criticized was that China (and therefore, Communism) was treated as a great and noble country while those of the west (and hence Democracy) were viewed as less than perfect. It was also incorporated that the state who would take the responsibility of teaching students morals instead of the parents and religious groups.

During the summer, of 2010, protests were sparked again against the curriculum. At the end of July people took to the street in protest. Around 90,000 people took part demanding that this new plan be removed before it even got started or voted upon.

On August 30 members of Scholarism began an occupation outside the government's Central Government complex and some began a hunger strike. They demanded that the new education plan be dropped. A few days later the occupation ended but little did they suspect that they would be returning there again someday.

Under this new pressure, the government shelved the new education plans and is currently working with the old curriculum. While the new program may have been put aside, government observers continue to watch and see if the government will introduce this plan in a new and different packaging.

Tensions eased on both sided until the idea for Hong Kong universal suffrage was introduced in 2007. It was then the National People's Congress Standing Committee of China made the decision that the Chief Executive of Hong Kong could be selected by universal suffrage in 2017.

The question of 'how' was a matter of debate it wasn't until July 2014 that a report was made to China's National People's Congress. The report spelled out how the goal was to be achieved. The report basically kept the same requirements as the current system and that whoever was elected would be pro-Beijing and thus have China's support and approval. This decision was derided by the people of Hong Kong and the international press.

Hong Kong government knew it has to do something to show this was the best way for its citizens and the rest of the world. For the world they responded with letters to the editors and other measures to show how good it is. For its citizens they tried to advertise it and calm the anger of the people and then waited. They didn't have to wait very long.

On 22 September student groups, led by organizations like Scholarism and others, launched a protest against the white paper. Many schools joined the protests with students refusing to do any work during the school day.

On 26 September groups began protesting outside government headquarters during the day and went home for the evening. The group planned to end the protests a few days later so that the group Occupy Central could do their protest starting on 1 October. However, the Occupy Central committee decided to start their protest early and began occupying parts of Central and Admiralty on 28 September. They also abandoned their original plan of protesting for economic reasons and instead when to join the political debate.

When Occupy Central forces started their new plan it caught everyone by surprise; both the public and the police. As people came to the Central area the police, and the government began to plan on how to meet this growing sentiment of public opinion and the crowds that were starting to build because of it.

Someone, in government, brought in police teams trained to use tear gas and ordered them to fire into the crowds hoping they would disperse. Many rounds of tear gas was indeed fired into the crowds but instead of dispersing them it had the opposite effect- it made for some great photo moments as well as giving the crowds something to response to and to try and bring more people on their side and against the government.

The next day more crowds gathered around the government buildings and police erected more barracks. The feeling one got was that the Hong Kong government was under siege. Everyone waited for something to happen. When it did it wasn't what the crowds expected.

The police decided to pull back their tear gas teams and calm the situation down. This left the crowds with nothing to rally against and not sure where to go or what to do. On the second day of Occupy Central it was over and yet no one knew it at the time.

Without anything to rally the public against the Occupy Central forces gathered more public who would spend the days, and nights, in various zones in Hong Kong. The main base was in the Admiralty area, others went to Causeway Bay while some of the more radical elements went to Mong Kok. There they all waited for something to happen and for the various leaders to do something.

The days of Occupy Central continued and the leaders tried to do something. First, they tried to convince the Hong Kong government that they should change the new way of electing the Chief Executive. This failed because the leaders of Occupy Central failed to realize that Hong Kong was nothing more than a city in China and thus, were subject to the rules laid out by China.

Then they tried to go to China directly but this failed because many of the Occupy Central leaders had their travel permits revoked by China and thus failed to even enter China proper.

Finally, they tried to get help from Great Britain and even the rest of the world. This failed because China told the world that they would not tolerate international interference in what they considered to be a domestic matter. The world protested but did nothing to upset China and any trade agreements they had with them.

What finally ended Occupy Central was not an agreement because the people and the government but the courts. Various groups took different sections of Occupy Central to court for a number of reasons. Mostly, the various Occupy Central groups were blocking traffic and thus causing Hong Kong businesses to lose money.

The courts agreed with the various businesses and with the help of the police, over a period of time, managed to remove those occupying the various streets and letting businesses, and traffic move through the area again.

For the length of protest of Occupy Central both sides showed various signs of restrain. Yes, it is true that both sides escalated the protests to a point of violence over course of protest. The most infamous police example would be the arrest and beating of Civic Party member Ken

Tsang during the overnight protests on Lung Wo Road on the night of 14/15 October 2014. Several officers arrested Ken Tsang and then took him to a dark spot and hit and kicked him for several minutes. This beating was captured on video and shown to the world. This video shocked everyone and the police could not deny that his injuries were caused by them.

Also, people would be arrested based on reinterpretation of various laws. One of the better known cases happened on 18 October 2014 when a person was arrested and charged with "access to computer with criminal or dishonest intent."[3] All this person did was, from a home computer, to post on a Hong Kong internet message board which was titled *occupy MongKong on Friday, occupy Lung Wo on Saturday, and occupy Central on Sunday.*[4]

While the various protest groups didn't go around beating up people they caused the government, and the public, many problems by the whole concept of occupation. First, they split into three separate occupation zones. The main one was in the Admiralty area. It was sprawled over a large area and buffered the Central Government's offices and the People's Liberation Army Headquarters.

It is also with this zone that at least two skirmishes were fought over the occupation of Lung Wo Road. On these occasions Occupy Central people would blockade this main road and basically dared the police to do something about it. The police did (because they had to get it cleared before the morning commutes) and it often ended badly for the blockaders.

Another was set up in the area of Causeway Bay. Here, it became quickly forgotten and ignored by just about everyone. It, like the one in Admiralty became a tourist area. However, the main difficulty with this zone was that it occupied a section of tram tracks which caused the trams to cut short their normal routes and to suffer from a lack of maintenance because of the occupation.

Perhaps the more notorious zone was set up in the shopping district of Mong Kok. Those who were there often stated that they recognized no leadership except their own and would do what they wanted-with or without the main leadership in Admiralty. This zone was subject to abuses by various groups that included taxi groups and the Chinese triads. Often arguments would break out, almost on a daily basis, and this would sometimes lead to fights that were started by these various groups.

---

[3] http://qz.com/285998/police-are-using-hong-kongs-computer-crime-law-to-crack-down-on-pro-democracy-organizers/ (accessed 3 January 2016)
[4] Ibid.

By Christmas the protests were over and everyone waited to see what the following year would bring. It was an uneasy holiday for all sides.

The first part of the year passed peacefully as the Occupy Central leaders said they would not repeat the occupation of the previous year. Instead, they turned their attention to the Legislative Council and their attempts to pass the law on how the Chief Executive would be selected. Tensions were high as each side tried to persuade Hong Kong that they were right and the other side was wrong.

Finally, on 18 June 2015 the Legislative Council voted on how the Chief Executive would be selected. It was defeated and no new plans have been introduced; status quo has returned and with the exception of protests in Mong Kok during Lunar New Year, 2016 both sides have been quiet.

China, for its part, has viewed the protest and an internal matter told the world not to interfere with matters that don't concern them. They have also worked, through various means, to clamp down their ownership of Hong Kong and to instruct future generations of people who will live here.

Now, with a stalemate in place all sides are watching each other and are deciding on what to do next. Somewhere, there is a powder keg with a fuse that is waiting to be lit. All sides have a match and it is only a matter of time before someone will light the fuse. Then Hong Kong will emerge as something different from what it is now. Only time will tell.

This book takes no position on which side is right or wrong. It is simply a book about a historical event that occurred and surprised the world by its execution and duration. It is up to the reader to make a decision on the protest and the various responses to them.

In several of the articles included there is mention of one or more annexes. For a variety of reasons I have not included them. It is up to the reader to look for them if they are motivated to do so.

Finally, I would like to thank the Government of the Hong Kong Special Administrative Region for their kind permission to allow me to use their material. Without them this book could not have been put together for now and future generations who wish to study these protests.

But in order that justice may be retained in government it is of the highest importance that those who rule States should understand that political power was not created for the advantage of any private individual; and that the administration of the State must be carried on to the profit of those who have been committed to their care, not to the profit of those to whom it has been committed. Let princes take example from the Most High God, by whom authority is given to them; and, placing before themselves His model in governing the State, let them rule over the people with equity and faithfulness, and let them add to that severity, which is necessary, a paternal charity. On this account they are warned in the oracles of the sacred Scriptures, that they will have themselves some day to render an account to the King of kings and Lord of lords; if they shall fail in their duty, that it will not be possible for them in any way to escape the severity of God[5]

---

[5] Pope Leo XII, *Diuturnum,* June 29, 1881

NOVEMBER 1[6]

TD reminds public to pay attention to traffic arrangement of large-scale event
****

The Transport Department (TD) said today (November 1) that in view of the occupy movement, some activities originally planned to be held in the areas being affected by the movement have to change the venues. Members of the public should pay special attention to the traffic and transport arrangements of these activities.

The venue of the annual "Wine and Dine Festival" has changed from the New Central Harbourfront to the open space outside Kai Tak Cruise Terminal this year. The TD anticipated that the traffic in the vicinity of Kai Tak Cruise Terminal will be very congested and called on members of the public who are going to take part in the event today and tomorrow to make use of the free shuttle bus services provided by the event organiser.

Members of the public are advised to take a free special circular bus service of KMB Route No. 215R (Kai Tak Cruise Terminal to Lam Tin MTR Station) (Lam Tin MTR Station Exit B) as far as possible . Other free shuttle bus services are available at Kowloon Tong Suffolk Road Public Transport Interchange (Kowloon Tong MTR Station Exit D) and East Tsim Sha Tsui Station Forecourt (East Tsim Sha Tsui MTR Station Exit K).

Participants may also take the existing public transport, including KMB Route No. 5R (Ngau Tau Kok MTR Station Exit A) and Kowloon GMB Route No. 86 (Kowloon Bay MTR Station Exit A). The services of these two routes will be strengthened to cater for the passenger demand when necessary. A taxi drop off point is temporarily designated at the lay-by on the eastern kerbside of Shing Fung Road (Kai Tak Cruise Terminal bound) outside the venue. Nevertheless, the drop off point will be suspended to facilitate the implementation of special traffic measures when the traffic in the area is congested. Members of the public are advised to attend to the announcements and take the shuttle bus services as far as possible.

In view of limited parking space and to avoid driving after drinking, participants of the event should not drive to the venue. The TD and the Police will closely monitor the traffic situation and implement appropriate traffic control measures, including setting up buffer zones to control traffic flow whenever necessary. Motorists and the public are advised to attend to the latest traffic news and take heed of the instructions from the police officers on site.

---

[6] http://www.info.gov.hk/gia/general/201411/01.htm

In addition, special traffic and transport arrangements will be implemented in So Kon Po and Causeway Bay for a football match to be held at the Hong Kong Stadium tomorrow (November 2). The TD anticipated that the traffic in the vicinity of So Kon Po and Causeway Bay will be congested. Motorists are advised to avoid driving to the affected areas. Members of the public planning to go to the affected areas are advised to use public transport as far as possible. Actual implementation of the traffic arrangements will be made depending on traffic and crowd conditions in the area.

Regarding public transport services, a total of 220 bus routes are still affected today with eight bus routes suspended and 212 bus routes diverted. Among the affected bus routes, 80 routes travelling via Mong Kok are diverted due to the closure of a number of road sections in Mong Kok. A total of 20 green minibus routes travelling via Harcourt Road, Nathan Road and Argyle Street are still diverted or suspended or with service adjusted. Currently, the tram service between Percival Street and Paterson Street is still suspended. The MTR Corporation Limited continues to increase services for all urban lines to cope with passenger demand.

The TD's Emergency Transport Co-ordination Centre will continue to monitor the road traffic situation and public transport services. For details of road closure, traffic diversion, suspension and route diversion of green minibus services, please refer to the TD's website (www.td.gov.hk). Regarding temporary traffic arrangements for bus routes, please refer to the following bus companies' websites for details:

For routes of New World First Bus and Citybus: www.nwstbus.com.hk/en/uploadedFiles/OC2014/TAA.htm

For routes of Kowloon Motor Bus: www.kmb.hk/en

As there will be updates on bus services from time to time due to traffic changes, members of the public are advised to pay attention to the latest service arrangements announced by bus companies before starting their journeys.

Issued at HKT 17:27

Opening remarks by Police Chief Superintendent at press conference
****

Following are the opening remarks by the Chief Superintendent of Police Public Relations Branch, Mr Hui Chun-tak, at the press conference today (November 1):

The first point is about offences related to illegal occupations. Police have all along expressed our concern about the growing tendency of people not abiding by the law arising from the illegal occupation and blockage of roads. The illegal acts have eroded our most treasured value of the rule of law, which is the cornerstone of the success of Hong Kong.

There are still daily occurrence of crimes and conflicts relating to the illegal occupation. At 7.30pm last evening, two cans of spray paint were dropped from height in Causeway Bay. Police later arrested four youngsters, aged between 15 and 16, on the rooftop of a building. They were suspected of allowing objects to drop from height. The case is now investigated by Wan Chai District Investigation Team.

At about 11pm yesterday, Police arrested a 46-year-old female for criminal damage. Also, at about 2am today, two police officers, when they were responding to a dispute case on Nathan Road, Mong Kok, a 35-year-old man assaulted one of the officers and pushed the other officer onto the ground. The man was arrested for assaulting police. These two cases are now handled by Mong Kok District Investigation Team.

Since the commencement of the illegal occupation, Police have arrested 319 persons, including 272 males and 47 females, for offences including unlawful assembly, disorderly conduct in a public place, assault, criminal damage, resisting arrest, assaulting police officer and obstructing police officer, etc. On the other hand, 65 police officers, including 64 male officers and one female officer, have been injured in the execution of statutory duties.

Police have repeatedly pointed out, the illegally occupied area in Mong Kok is of a higher risk of turning chaotic than other areas. There are radical protesters and troublemakers holding polarised views. The illegal occupation there is prone to disputes which could easily develop into scuffles and physical confrontations. Police are concerned about the worsening situation. We urge members of the public to remain calm and peaceful in expressing their opinions, and should under no circumstances resort to violence.

The second point is about cyber crime. I note there are some concerns and misunderstanding of Police investigation into some of the recent cyber crimes. There is also query as to whether Police are suppressing the freedom of expression on the Internet. Police reiterate our respect for the freedom of speech. However, I must point out that the Internet is not a lawless virtual world. Any illegal acts in the cyber world are sanctioned by laws, and offenders are subject to criminal liability.

The majority of the ordinances in Hong Kong are applicable in the cyber world and we advise the public to abide by the law in the virtual arena. For the purpose of carrying out our statutory duties to prevent and detect crime, Police may request Internet service providers to provide necessary information in order to assist in the investigation. All requests for information would be made in accordance with the established procedures and related ordinances or code of practice.

I would like to remind the public, it is an offence to incite others to commit criminal acts on the Internet. Police will collect evidence on any offences committed on the Internet, conduct follow up investigation and make arrest as necessary.

Since September 26, Police have arrested 12 persons including nine males and three females, aged between 13 and 39, for the offence of access to computer with criminal or dishonest intent.

The third point is about respecting the rule of law. I would like to remind the public that the Interim Injunction Orders on the illegal occupation of roads in Mong Kok and the blockage of access to CITIC Tower in Admiralty remain in force. I urge illegal road occupiers to respect the rule of law and to comply with the orders of the court and to leave the occupied areas promptly. Police stress, we are committed to preserving public peace and order and will take actions against anyone who obstructs those authorised to execute the Injunction Orders. If anyone resorts to violence against those authorised persons, Police will take resolute actions.

I urge protesters, in particular students, to stay away from radical individuals and troublemakers. Do not mix with these radicals in the crowd, do not take part or be incited to take part in any act of violence and do not charge at Police. We do not want to see anyone, especially students, being hurt when they place themselves close to the radical individuals and troublemakers during their violent acts. When Police officers are executing their duties on the ground, protesters, in particular students, should not put up resistance. They should stay calm and maintain a safe distance.

Many citizens may take part in various public activities during the weekend. I would like to remind the public to stay alert, be vigilant to their personal safety and to follow Police instructions whilst taking part in these activities, particularly in crowded places.

I would like to highlight my points again. Firstly, as there are still daily occurrence of crimes in the illegally occupied areas, particularly Mong Kok, which remains high risk, members of the public should stay away from these illegally occupied areas. All illegal occupiers are urged to leave promptly.

Secondly, members of the public, students in particular, should not commit offences on the Internet or to incite others to do so.

Thirdly, protesters should respect the rule of law. They should not obstruct those authorised to execute the Injunction Orders. Students in particular, should not be incited by radical individuals to commit illegal acts or to resort to the use of violence so as to avoid unnecessary injuries.

Please rest assured that Police will remain impartial and steadfast, and will continue to serve the public with devotion.

Issued at HKT 18:20

NOVEMBER 2[7]

Public transport services update from time to time in view of traffic situation
****

The Transport Department (TD) today (November 2) said that traffic situation on Hong Kong Island and in Kowloon continues to be unstable due to protests. The TD has frequently reminded members of the public and would like to repeat that, if they are to go to work or school, they should pay special attention to the traffic condition of working days, and plan their journey in advance, start their journey earlier and allow more time for travelling.

Commuters should stay alert to the updates on public transport information provided by the TD and bus companies in view of the traffic situation. The TD and bus companies have recently reviewed the road situation and resumed the original routing of five bus services travelling via Mong Kok since yesterday. The five bus routes, which used to be affected by the protest activities in Mong Kok, mainly provide services between Mong Kok and Tuen Mun, Tsing Yi, Tung Chung and so on. With the resumption of their original routing, the bus services make it more convenient for the passengers travelling between Kowloon and New Territories.

As affected by the "occupy movement", some events have to be relocated to districts where protest activities are not being held. The annual "Hong Kong Wine & Dine Festival" has changed its venue from the New Central Harbourfront to the open space outside Kai Tak Cruise Terminal this year. Since today is the last day of the event, it is expected that a large number of people will grasp this last chance to take part in the event. The TD anticipated that the traffic in the vicinity of Kai Tak Cruise Terminal will still be congested and called on members of the public to take the free shuttle bus services provided by the event organiser, including a free special circular bus service of KMB Route No. 215R plying between Kai Tak Cruise Terminal and Lam Tin MTR Station, as well as another two free shuttle bus services from Kowloon Tong and Tsim Sha Tsui East to Kai Tak Cruise Terminal respectively.

Due to limited parking space and to avoid driving after drinking, participants of the festival should not drive to the venue. The TD and the Police will closely monitor the traffic situation and implement appropriate traffic control measures, including setting up buffer zones to control traffic flow whenever necessary. Motorists and the public are advised to pay attention to the latest traffic news and take heed of the instructions from the police officers at the scene.

In addition, special traffic and transport arrangements will be implemented in So Kon Po and Causeway Bay for a football match to be held at the Hong Kong Stadium tonight. The TD anticipated that the

---

[7] http://www.info.gov.hk/gia/general/201411/02.htm

traffic in the vicinity of So Kon Po and Causeway Bay will be congested. Motorists are advised to avoid driving to the affected areas. Members of the public planning to go to the affected areas are advised to use public transport as far as possible. Actual implementation of the traffic arrangements will be made depending on traffic and crowd conditions in the area.

Regarding public transport services, since today is a public holiday, less bus routes are affected than on a working day. Nonetheless, a total of 138 bus routes are affected today with eight bus routes suspended and 130 bus routes diverted. A total of 20 green minibus routes travelling via Harcourt Road, Nathan Road and Argyle Street are still diverted or suspended or with service adjusted. Currently, the tram service between Percival Street and Paterson Street is still suspended. The MTR Corporation Limited continues to increase services for all urban lines to cope with passenger demand.

The TD's Emergency Transport Co-ordination Centre will continue to monitor the road traffic situation and public transport services. For details of road closure, traffic diversion, suspension and route diversion of green minibus services, please refer to the TD's website (www.td.gov.hk). Regarding temporary traffic arrangements for bus routes, please refer to the following bus companies' websites for details:

For routes of Citybus and New World First Bus:
www.nwstbus.com.hk/en/uploadedFiles/OC2014/TAA.htm

For routes of Kowloon Motor Bus: www.kmb.hk/en

As there will be updates on bus services from time to time due to traffic changes, members of the public are advised to pay attention to the latest service arrangements announced by bus companies before starting their journeys.
Issued at HKT 13:43

Opening remarks by Police Chief Superintendent at press conference
****

Following are the opening remarks by the Chief Superintendent of Police Public Relations Branch, Mr Hui Chun-tak, at the press conference today (November 2):

The first point is about the prolonged illegal occupation and blockage of roads. Police are concerned about the continued illegal occupation and blockage of major roads as well as a recent claim by protestors of having abundant supplies to sustain their prolonged occupations which have lasted for more than a month. It is regretful that the protestors continue to use illegal occupation of major roads to express their discontentment as if they are not aware that majority of the public is now suffering from the adverse consequences so created.

The fact remains that the daily lives and livelihoods of the general public have been seriously affected in the past month due to the illegal occupation. The occupation has affected various sectors either directly or indirectly. The direct impact has been reflected by the loss of business of the retail, food and transportation industries, etc. The general public have been suffering from different degrees of interruption, whether they need to go to work or go to school. Although there appears to be no large-scale confrontations in the illegally occupied areas recently, and the public have been most tolerant, it is an indisputable fact that members of the public are now really suffering from the negative impacts of the illegal occupation of major roads.

In fact, there are still daily conflicts and crimes relating to the illegal occupation. Yesterday in Mong Kok, a man positioned himself at height to express his grievances about the loss of his job as a result of the prolonged illegal occupation. Yesterday afternoon, people holding different views verbally abused one another and Police were deployed to the scene to prevent confrontations. In the early morning in Central, a couple, while walking past the junction of Connaught Road Central and Jackson Road, had a dispute with a male. The two males had a fight against each other. The female was hit by another male with a skateboard. Police arrested the two males for 'Fighting in a Public Place'. Police are concerned about the growing tendency of confrontations and people not abiding by the law. We urge members of the public to remain calm and peaceful when they are expressing their opinions, and should under no circumstances resort to violence.

As we can see, the occupation movement has deviated from its original principle and caused much disruption to the normal lives of the general public. There are increasing grievances and clear public view that the unlawful assemblies and illegal blockage of roads cannot drag on indefinitely. Various sectors of the society have clearly voiced out their views that the protestors should end the illegal occupation of major roads as soon as possible so that the roads can be re-opened and public order restored.

At the start of the illegal occupation movement, the initiators had openly called on people to come out to block the major roads. Now, while they are gradually fading into the background, they have not shown the ethics or the courage to openly call for an end to the illegal occupations. This is irresponsible and has blatantly disregarded the well being of the students as well as the interests of the general public who have to endure the serious disruption of their daily lives. The initiators and organizers should not evade their responsibilities by giving the excuses that they are incapable of calling for an end to the illegal occupation or their plea will not be heard. They should have the courage to take the lead to call for an end to the illegal occupation for the sake of the students' safety and long-term benefits of Hong Kong. I hope they have the courage to respond to the clear demands of the general public by asking the protestors to go home as this is the only way to shoulder responsibility and to truly respect the rule of law.

The second point is about the rule of law. Yesterday some representatives of the transportation industry have filed another application of Injunction Order to the Court of First Instance against the illegal occupation on Connaught Road, Harcourt Road and Cotton Tree Drive, etc. Whilst the application is still await hearing, I must point out that the Injunction Orders regarding the illegal occupation of roads in Mong Kok and the blockage of access to CITIC Tower, Admiralty are still in force. I urge the illegal road occupiers to respect the rule of law and comply with the Court orders and leave the areas soonest.

I reiterate if any person obstructs the authorized persons to execute the Injunction Orders, Police are duty bound to take action to safeguard the public safety and public order. Police will take resolute actions if anyone resorts to violence against the authorized persons in executing the Injunction Orders.

I urge the protesters, in particular students, to stay away from radical individuals and troublemakers. Do not mix with them in the crowd and do not be incited to take part in any violent acts. When Police are executing our statutory duties, do maintain a safe distance, and do not put up resistance or charge at Police. We do not want to see anyone, especially students, being hurt when they mix with radical protestors and troublemakers during confrontations.

In addition, I notice on the Internet that some people are trying to convey a very negative message about Police to young children and depict police officers as bad people. This is highly irresponsible.

The rule of law is the cornerstone supporting the success of Hong Kong and Police are under the duty to enforce the law, to maintain law and order and to safeguard public safety and public order. The good public order and low crime rate in Hong Kong depends on the joint efforts of the law abiding public, a professional police force and the good cooperation between Police and the public.

In the past month, the illegal occupiers have been flouting the law, assembling unlawfully and occupying major roads illegally. Some of the radical protestors committed criminal damage, disorderly conduct, snatched mills barriers, insulted police officers and even surrounded our officers attempting to free arrested persons forcibly. These illegal acts have seriously undermined our most core value of the rule of law. If the situation continues, can you imagine how it would affect our next generation? It is now the right time to tell the next generation the need to respect the rule of law and the importance of cooperation between Police and the public. Image this, if a child faces emergency or crime, do you want to see him or her getting confused as to whether to seek Police help or not? Do you really want to see them insulting law enforcers and ignoring the rule of law? I have repeatedly urged parents not to bring their young children to the illegally occupied area, either as spectators or staying overnight, particular in Mong Kok as it remains a high risk area. Regrettably, there are still parents bringing their children to the illegal occupied areas in Mong Kok and staying overnight. This irresponsible act will expose children to unnecessary risk of getting hurt.

The endless illegal assembly and occupation of roads have caused significant adverse impacts on the daily lives of our citizens. The public safety and public order have been seriously disrupted and the rule of law undermined. I urge the initiators and organizers of these illegal occupations, for the sake of the interest of the general public, to shoulder responsibility, respect the court orders, and call on the illegal occupiers to remove the road obstacles and go home peacefully, so that traffic can be resumed and normal daily lives and public order can be restored.

Issued at HKT 18:27

NOVEMBER 3[8]

HKMA's update on the operation of the banking system and financial market
****

The following is issued on behalf of the Hong Kong Monetary Authority:

According to the reports to the Hong Kong Monetary Authority (HKMA) from banks as at 8am today (November 3), one branch of one bank was affected and temporarily closed. ATMs in the affected areas have largely resumed normal operation. The HKMA has requested banks to resume normal services as soon as circumstances permit. Customers should pay attention to the relevant banks' announcements regarding affected branches and ATMs. The HKMA will also publish on its website relevant updates from time to time.

Issued at HKT 09:28

Guided tours and education service of the LegCo Complex partially resumed
****

The following is issued on behalf of the Legislative Council Secretariat:

The Legislative Council (LegCo) Secretariat announces today (November 3) that, with immediate effect, guided tours and education service of the LegCo Complex have partially resumed. Depending on the circumstances, the LegCo Secretariat will revise the arrangements for such services.

Issued at HKT 09:47

Speech by SFST at HKIFA 8th Annual Conference
****

Following is the speech by the Secretary for Financial Services and the Treasury, Professor K C Chan, at the Hong Kong Investment Funds Association (HKIFA) 8th Annual Conference today (November 3):

Mr (Bruno) Lee, distinguished guests, ladies and gentlemen,

Good morning. It is a great pleasure to join you today at the HKIFA Annual Conference. I last spoke to you, to this conference, in 2010. My focus then was on the "strong confidence" - the "excitement" - the

---

[8] http://www.info.gov.hk/gia/general/201411/03.htm

world had in Hong Kong, the health of our finance market and the new opportunities we offered the world.

Well, four years later, it's fair to say that some of you might be wondering about the state of Hong Kong, given the continuing protests. To that, let me say that we are working hard to bridge the political divide that exists in our community. And I believe that the decency and mutual respect Hong Kong has long been known for will help us find a way forward.

At heart, I am a pragmatist. While there can be honest differences in politics among the people of Hong Kong, that need not - and will not - impinge on what Hong Kong does best: create business opportunities here in Asia and around the world. With that in mind, I'm pleased to tell you what we've been up to in financial services - what we've accomplished and what we've set our targets on.

Allow me to begin with Hong Kong's asset management industry, which has been growing from strength to strength. According to the Fund Management Activities Survey conducted by SFC (Securities and Futures Commission), the total combined fund-management business reached a record high at the end of last year, topping HK$16 trillion. That's a growth of more than 27 per cent, year on year.

Our deepening economic integration with Mainland China makes Hong Kong the ideal testing ground for measures designed to gradually open the country's capital markets. The rapid growth of the offshore Renminbi (RMB) market over the past 10 years certainly showcases the role Hong Kong can play.

Perhaps most relevant to the asset management industry is the RQFII (Renminbi Qualified Foreign Institutional Investor scheme). Launched in 2011, the arrangement allows holders of offshore RMB to invest in Mainland equities and bonds. Under the RQFII, the range of products available to offshore RMB holders has vastly increased, promoting the RMB as an international investment currency.

At the end of August, 74 Hong Kong financial institutions were qualified under the scheme, with approved quotas reaching RMB265 billion. Some 55 fund products have been approved by the SFC, including 16 exchange traded funds (ETF). At the end of June, RMB63 billion was managed under RQFII products. It's fair to say they are now an integral part of our asset management industry.

It's important here to note that the capital flow is a two-way street. After years of rapid growth and wealth accumulation, Chinese companies and individuals are increasingly seeking to invest their capital offshore. And Hong Kong's asset management industry is uniquely positioned to serve this ever-growing need.

In this regard, we provide a competitive tax and regulatory framework to help our asset management industry meet the challenges and opportunities. Public consultation on our plan to introduce an open-ended fund company, or OFC, as a fund vehicle, ended in June. We believe that the OFC will attract more funds to Hong Kong; that it will help us develop a more comprehensive asset management industry, one that encompasses registration, investment, and sales and marketing of fund products.

We are also planning extra support for the private equity industry. This will be in the form of a profits tax exemption on transactions in private companies incorporated or registered outside Hong Kong, and those neither hold properties in Hong Kong nor carry out business here.

The ETF is a product popular among those investing overseas for the first time. To promote their use, we will waive the stamp duty for the dealing of all ETFs.

We've also been working closely with the Mainland authorities on the proposed mutual recognition and cross-boundary offering of funds. Once implemented, the range of fund products available to investors in the Mainland and Hong Kong will expand significantly.

Then of course there's the Shanghai-Hong Kong Stock Connect, which will allow Mainland investors to invest directly in 266 stocks listed in the Hong Kong market. The scheme will also open Shanghai's stock market to international RMB investors using Hong Kong's trading infrastructure. Although the launch date has not yet been fixed, we will continue to work hard to bring about the successful launch of the scheme. Once launched, it will bring unprecedented opportunities to the financial world. Indeed, in a recent New York Times feature on the initiative, a senior Western banker in Asia called it "the single most important development in China's intention to internationalise this market".

Industry growth, of course, is not without challenges. As a good global citizen, Hong Kong has been a supporter of international efforts to promote tax transparency and combat cross-border tax evasion. We are pursuing comprehensive avoidance of double-taxation agreements and tax-information-exchange agreements with other jurisdictions. We have also been an active participant in the OECD's Global Forum on Transparency and Exchange of Information for Tax Purposes.

Recently, we indicated our support for the new global standard on the automatic exchange of information with appropriate partners on a reciprocal basis. Indeed, we hope to have legislation in place by 2017. With that, we would begin the first information exchanges by the end of 2018. Our next step would be to engage local stakeholders and to address relevant policy and legal issues before seeking our legislature's approval.

On this, we look forward to your support and input. The key here is in protecting Hong Kong's status as an asset management centre.

The Government is also keenly aware of the talent shortage in the industry. According to a survey by the Vocational Training Council, there is a general need for qualified professionals in all areas. After engaging the industry in various ways, we found that there is a need to raise the awareness of the spectrum of career opportunities available in the financial industry. It is also important for practitioners to continue to upgrade their skills.

To solve the human resource challenge, I ask the industry to join us in making the development of talent a priority. This can be in the form of increased hiring at the university graduate level and additional training and mentoring for junior staff. After all, human resources are our most important asset.

Ladies and gentlemen, as Mainland China continues to move forward with its opening up and reform policies, it opens up tremendous opportunities for our asset management industry. I trust that you will make the most of your annual conference to explore ways of taking full advantage of these opportunities - in Mainland China and throughout Asia.

Thank you.
Issued at HKT 11:16

LegCo to consider a motion under the Legislative Council (Powers and Privileges) Ordinance
****
The following is issued on behalf of the Legislative Council Secretariat:

The Legislative Council (LegCo) will hold a meeting on Wednesday (November 5) at 11am in the Chamber of the LegCo Complex. During the meeting, Members will consider a motion under the Legislative Council (Powers and Privileges) Ordinance.

The motion, to be moved by Ms Claudia Mo, states: "That this Council appoints a select committee to inquire into the allegation of the Chief Executive of the Hong Kong Special Administrative Region Mr Leung Chun-ying receiving the benefits of UGL Limited, an Australian corporation; and that in the performance of its duties the committee be authorised under section 9(2) of the Legislative Council (Powers and Privileges) Ordinance (Cap. 382) to exercise the powers conferred by section 9(1) of that Ordinance."

Meanwhile, Mr Michael Tien will move a motion on returning a happy childhood to students. The motion states: "That the majority view of society has all along held that 'pressure leads to progress'; nowadays, there are many books and discussions available at the market about 'tiger moms and dads', 'helicopter parents' and 'monster parents', etc. for boosting children's learning, but excessive boosting may likely increase pressure on children and dampen their learning interests; the results of a survey conducted by the Programme for International Student Assessment show that some Hong Kong parents excessively intervene in children's learning and drill them by being over-anxious for results, rendering a decline of children's motivation to learn and a negative impact on their academic results; quite a number of media reports have also pointed out that some Hong Kong students have emotional problems because of heavy study pressure, and they become easily anxious and have symptoms such as insomnia, loss of appetite and irritability, etc.; all these problems are attributable to the education system which emphasises solely on examination results; at the stage of kindergarten education, parents have already enrolled their children in many types of interest classes and request them to do dictation and spelling exercises, etc.; at the stage of primary education, students need to participate in the Territory-wide System Assessment, the Internal Assessments for Secondary School Places Allocation purpose that take place at the end of Primary Five and both in mid-year and at the end of Primary Six, and the Pre-Secondary One Hong Kong Attainment Test; at the stage of secondary education, students are faced with a shortage of university places and the 'die or live' pressure from the Hong Kong Diploma of Secondary Education Examination; in contrast, the education systems and teaching modes in many advanced places are better able to provide students with room for exploring their interests to enhance their creativity development; in this connection, this Council urges the Administration to:

(1) assess afresh the pressure and psychological impact of the existing education system on students, and comprehensively review the examination system, the curriculum contents and the mechanism for progression in education;

(2) enhance parental education to avoid parents from excessively boosting children's learning; and

(3) enhance the support for school social workers and teachers to facilitate them to early identify whether or not students are under excessive pressure."

Dr Helena Wong, Ms Alice Mak, Mr Ip Kin-yuen, Dr Priscilla Leung and Mr Charles Peter Mok will move separate amendments to Mr Michael Tien's motion.

Mr Kenneth Leung will also move a motion on reorganising the Government's structure to improve its policy implementation. The motion states: "That the current-term Government has repeatedly committed blunders in its policy implementation, and the policies as implemented are not in place and unable to respond to people's demands, coupled with the situations where a number of officials successively committed scandals and serious dereliction of duty, resulting in serious doubts about the Government's ability to govern and implement policies; in this connection, this Council urges the Government to examine afresh its operating structure, and after consulting the Legislative Council and the public, to effect improvement, adjustment and division of labour in respect of the functions, objectives and policy portfolios of various policy bureaux, and to conduct structural reorganisation on a need basis for enhancing the quality and competence of various policy bureaux and the departments under their purview in policy formulation and execution, making the Government's policy implementation more open, closely follow public opinions, integrated and consistent."

Ms Emily Lau, Dr Elizabeth Quat and Mr Charles Peter Mok will move separate amendments to Mr Kenneth Leung's motion.

Moreover, Mr Wong Yuk-man will move a motion for the adjournment of the Council under Rule 16(4) of the Rules of Procedure. The motion states: "That this Council do now adjourn for the purpose of debating the following issue: the security arrangements adopted by the Legislative Council in respect of large-scale public events."

During the meeting, Members will also ask the Government 22 questions on various policy areas, six of which require oral replies.

The agenda of the above meeting can be obtained via the LegCo Website (www.legco.gov.hk). Please note that the agenda is subject to change, and the latest information about the agenda could be found in the LegCo Website.

Members of the public are welcome to observe the proceedings of the meeting from the public galleries of the Chamber of the LegCo Complex. They may reserve seats by calling 3919 3399 during office hours. Members of the public can also watch or listen the meeting via the web broadcast system on the LegCo Website.

Issued at HKT 17:27

TD reminds members of the public to be patient in case of traffic congestion
****

The Transport Department (TD) today (November 3) said that because major trunk roads on Hong Kong Island are still illegally occupied and two traffic accidents occurred on Connaught Road Central near Exchange Square in Central during morning peak hours today, there was very serious traffic congestion in the vicinity. As a number of road sections are closed due to the occupation movement, the impact on traffic and public transport services would be considerable if there are any unforeseen incidents on roads. The TD reminded members of the public and motorists to exercise patience in case of traffic congestion, and pay attention to road safety at all times.

Since major trunk roads on Hong Kong Island such as Harcourt Road are yet to be re-opened, motorists could only continue to use Lung Wo Road and inner Gloucester Road to travel between the eastern and western parts of Hong Kong Island. Hence, traffic congestion continued on Lung Wo Road eastbound while vehicles were found moving slowly on inner Gloucester Road westbound heading for Central during peak hours this morning. The two traffic accidents in Central this morning respectively resulted in temporary closures of the middle and slow lanes of Connaught Road Central (Wan Chai bound), and the slow lane of Connaught Road Central (Central bound), seriously intensifying traffic loads on Hong Kong Island.

As public transport services affected by the traffic situation are still unstable, the TD again reminded members of the public that they should start their journeys early and allow more time for travelling. Police will also continue to implement temporary traffic control measures according to the traffic situation to divert traffic flow. Motorists should pay attention to the arrangements and follow the instructions of the Police at the scene.

Regarding public transport services, a total of 221 bus routes are still affected today, with eight bus routes suspended and 213 bus routes diverted. Among the affected bus routes, 80 routes travelling via Mong Kok are diverted due to the closure of a number of road sections in Mong Kok. A total of 20 green minibus routes travelling via Harcourt Road, Nathan Road and Argyle Street are still diverted or suspended or with service adjusted. Currently, the tram service between Percival Street and Paterson Street is still suspended. The MTR Corporation Limited continues to increase services for all urban lines to cope with passenger demand.

The TD's Emergency Transport Co-ordination Centre will continue to monitor the road traffic situation and public transport services. For details of road closure, traffic diversion, suspension and route diversion of green minibus services, please refer to the TD's website (www.td.gov.hk). Regarding temporary traffic arrangements for bus routes, please refer to the following bus companies' websites for details:

For routes of Citybus and New World First Bus: www.nwstbus.com.hk/en/uploadedFiles/OC2014/TAA.htm

For routes of Kowloon Motor Bus: www.kmb.hk/en

As there will be updates on bus services from time to time due to traffic changes, members of the public are advised to pay attention to the latest service arrangements announced by bus companies before starting their journeys.
Issued at HKT 18:13

Opening remarks by Police Senior Superintendent at press conference
****

Following are the opening remarks by the Senior Superintendent of Police Public Relations Branch, Mr Kong Man-keung, at the press conference today (November 3):

I will first respond to some individuals alleging publicly that Police had used excessive force during the confrontation on Lung Wo Road in the early morning of October 15. These individuals claimed that they have not lodged any complaint against Police due to their own concerns.

I would like to draw your attentions and memories back to the night of the confrontations. As can be seen on the television and newspaper reports, on the night of the incident, some radical protesters who were assembling unlawfully ignored public safety, dashed onto Lung Wo Road, and threw objects like water bottles on the road. Some protesters even blocked the east and west bound lanes there with water barriers which resulted in a chaotic situation. During the incident, a large crowd of radical protesters surrounded and charged police officers. They verbally abused and humiliated our officers, stirred up others' emotion and even attempted to stop officers from escorting the arrested persons away. Despite repeated Police advice and warnings, they continued their illegal acts. Under such circumstances, Police had used minimum level of force to restore public order. On that night, Police arrested 45 persons, including 37 males and 8 females, aged 17 to 54, for offences including 'Unlawful Assembly'.

I need to point out that Police have been handling the illegal acts in a professional, highly restrained and impartial manner. Police would take resolute actions commensurate with the circumstances at scene to preserve public peace and public safety. During the confrontation at Lung Wo Road, five officers were injured during their execution of duty.

I reiterate that the Complaints Against Police Office (CAPO) will handle all complaints related to the unlawful assembly impartially and in accordance with established mechanism. All such Reportable Complaints would be passed to the Serious Complaint Committee of Independent Police Complaints Council for review. The one-sided allegation on police excessive use of force is unfair and those in doubt are advised to approach CAPO as soon as possible.

The second point is about cyber crime. Last night, a report was made to Aberdeen Police Station that messages were found on social media threatening to commit violent acts in Admiralty. The case has been classified as 'Access to Computer with Criminal and Dishonest Intent' and is currently investigated by Technology Crime Division. No arrest has been made at this stage.

I want to remind the public that the Internet environment is not a lawless virtual world. Illegal acts in the cyber world are sanctioned by laws and offenders are subject to criminal liability. The majority of the laws of Hong Kong are equally applicable to the cyber world. Inciting others to commit criminal acts on the Internet is also illegal. We advise the public to abide by the law in the virtual arena. Police will collect evidence on offences committed on the Internet, conduct follow-up investigation and make arrest as necessary.

In fact, since September 26, Police have arrested 13 persons, including 10 males and 3 females, aged 13 to 39, for the offences of 'Access to Computer with Criminal and Dishonest Intent' and 'Criminal Intimidation'.

The last point is about Injunction Orders. I would like to remind the public that the Injunction Orders on the illegal occupation of roads in Mong Kok and access into CITIC Tower in Admiralty are still valid. I urge the illegal road occupiers to respect the rule of law, to comply with the court orders and to leave the occupied area as soon as possible.

I reiterate that if any person obstructs the authorized persons in executing the Injunction Orders, Police are duty bound to take action to safeguard public safety and public order. Police will take resolute actions if anyone resorts to violence against these authorized persons in executing the Injunction Orders.

I urge the protesters, students in particular, to stay away from radical individuals and troublemakers. Do not mix with them in the crowd or be incited to take part in any violent acts. When Police are taking enforcement actions, do maintain a safe distance with them. Do not put up resistance or charge at Police. We do not want to see anyone, especially students, getting hurt when they mix with radical protestors and troublemakers during confrontations.

To conclude, I need to point out that the endless unlawful assemblies and extensive illegal occupation of roads have harmed the interest of the majority of our society. I hope the students illegally occupying the roads, would be sensible enough to consider the sufferings and disruptions that were caused to the general public. For the overall benefits of the Hong Kong society, and in respecting the court order, I hope the initiators, organizers and illegal occupiers would have the courage to cease the illegal occupation, so that the citizens' normal daily lives can resume and public order restored.

Lastly, I would like to sum up today's messages. Firstly, Police have all along been highly restrained in the use of force and would only use the minimum level of force commensurate with the situation as necessary. I urge those who have made allegations on the use of excessive force by Police to approach CAPO.

Secondly, I urge members of the public not to commit any illegal acts on the Internet, in particular not to threaten or incite anyone in the use of violence. Police will no doubt take follow-up investigation on such cases.

Thirdly, for the overall benefits of Hong Kong, I urge the illegal road occupiers to respect the rule of law, to comply with the Court orders and to cease the illegal occupation soonest.

Issued at HKT 19:18

NOVEMBER 4[9]

HKMA's update on the operation of the banking system and financial market
****

The following is issued on behalf of the Hong Kong Monetary Authority:

According to the reports to the Hong Kong Monetary Authority (HKMA) from banks as at 8am today (November 4), one branch of one bank was affected and temporarily closed. ATMs in the affected areas have largely resumed normal operation. The HKMA has requested banks to resume normal services as soon as circumstances permit. Customers should pay attention to the relevant banks' announcements regarding affected branches and ATMs. The HKMA will also publish on its website relevant updates from time to time.

Issued at HKT 09:55

Pedestrian precincts at Chater Road and East Point Road on Hong Kong Island suspended
****

The Transport Department (TD) today (November 4) said that the traffic situation continues to be affected by the closures of a number of roads in Central district and Causeway Bay due to the occupation movement. In order to alleviate traffic congestion on Hong Kong Island, the pedestrian precincts at Chater Road in Central and East Point Road in Causeway Bay are suspended to allow traffic flow until further notice. The TD reminded members of the public and motorists to pay attention to the arrangements.

To improve the pedestrian environment, the TD set up various pedestrian precincts in the territory. A section of Chater Road between Pedder Street and Jackson Road in Central was originally a pedestrian precinct from 7am to midnight on Sundays and public holidays. To alleviate traffic congestion caused by the occupation movement in Central district, the Chater Road pedestrian precinct has been suspended to allow traffic flow.

The section of Yee Wo Street eastbound between East Point Road and Sugar Street in Causeway Bay has been illegally occupied over the past month, seriously affecting public transport services and traffic. To lessen traffic load in the vicinity, the arrangements of the pedestrian precinct in Causeway Bay at Lockhart Road east of Cannon Street, East Point Road, and Great George Street west of Paterson Street

---

[9] http://www.info.gov.hk/gia/general/201411/04.htm

originally from 4pm to midnight on Mondays to Fridays and from noon to midnight on Saturdays, Sundays and public holidays, is suspended to allow traffic flow.

Yee Wo Street in Causeway Bay and Harcourt Road in Central district are both major trunk roads in their respective areas, and Yee Wo Street is also part of the tramway. The blockage of the tram line severs the tramway service between the eastern and western parts of Hong Kong Island and prevents passengers from commuting between the two sides of Hong Kong Island conveniently. Currently, the tram service between Percival Street and Paterson Street is still suspended. Hong Kong Tramways has already taken measures proactively, including operating tram services in sections, providing a free circular tram route in the section near Victoria Park and offering free same-day tram transfer service, to minimise any inconvenience caused to passengers by the currently hampered service. Even so, blockages of roads still severely affect the already bustling traffic in Hong Kong. Protesters are urged again to peacefully retreat from illegally occupied roads to let the public transport services and traffic return to normal.

Regarding public transport services, a total of 221 bus routes are still affected today with eight bus routes suspended and 213 bus routes diverted. Among the affected bus routes, 80 routes travelling via Mong Kok are diverted due to the closure of a number of road sections in Mong Kok. A total of 20 green minibus routes travelling via Harcourt Road, Nathan Road and Argyle Street are still diverted or suspended or with service adjusted. The MTR Corporation Limited continues to increase services for all urban lines to cope with passenger demand.

The TD's Emergency Transport Co-ordination Centre will continue to monitor the road traffic situation and public transport services. For details of road closure, traffic diversion, suspension and route diversion of green minibus services, please refer to the TD's website (www.td.gov.hk). Regarding temporary traffic arrangements for bus routes, please refer to the following bus companies' websites for details:

For routes of Citybus and New World First Bus: www.nwstbus.com.hk/en/uploadedFiles/OC2014/TAA.htm

For routes of Kowloon Motor Bus: www.kmb.hk/en

As there will be updates on bus services from time to time due to traffic changes, members of the public are advised to pay attention to the latest service arrangements announced by bus companies before starting their journeys.

Issued at HKT 18:42

Opening remarks by Police Chief Superintendent at press conference
****

Following are the opening remarks by the Chief Superintendent of Police Public Relations Branch, Mr Hui Chun-tak, at the press conference today (November 4).

First of all, I would like to talk about the ongoing conflicts and offences arising from the illegal occupation of major roads. Hong Kong has all along been a law abiding and orderly society and the citizens have been proud of our low crime rate and good public order. Regrettably, we note a growing tendency of people not abiding by the law arising from the prolonged illegal occupation. There is a gradual erosion of our treasured value of the rule of law. The situation is worrying.

In fact, there are still daily occurrence of crimes and conflicts relating to the illegal occupation. Yesterday, in the illegally occupied area in Mong Kok near the junction of Nathan Road and Argyle Street, individuals attempting to remove the obstacles confronted with the illegal occupiers. Someone had attempted to set fire on a paper figure with a lighter. The situation turned chaotic with physical confrontations. After enquiry at the scene, Police arrested a 31-year-old man for the offence of 'common assault'.

Last night, near the same location in Mong Kok, a confrontation between two disputing parties attracted a large crowd of onlookers. Police officers had to separate the parties and eventually arrested a 47-year-old male for 'common assault'. The above two cases are now being investigated by Mong Kok District Investigation Team.

At about the same time last night, a 38-year-old man holding a folding knife was seen wandering on Legislative Council Road near the illegally occupied area in Admiralty. A member of the public reported that the same man had also threatened him on October 29. Police responded to the scene and seized a five-inch long folding knife from the man. He was arrested for 'possession of offensive weapon' and 'criminal intimidation'. The Central Police District Investigation Team is currently investigating the case.

I need to stress that the illegally occupied area in Mong Kok remains a high risk area. There are radical individuals, troublemakers and people holding polarised views. There are frequent disputes between supporters and opponents of the illegal occupation. The risk of confrontation keeps escalating as the illegal occupation drags on. I urge members of the public and students in particular to stay away from these areas. Parents should not bring their children to the illegally occupied area to avoid unnecessary injuries.

I notice that confrontations in other areas of illegal occupation have become more frequent. I hope members of the public would not underestimate the risk in these areas. The risks of disputes and confrontations are on the rise. I urge people with different views to express their opinions in a peaceful and rational manner. Police will not tolerate any violence and will take resolute actions against anyone using violence.

The second point is about the adverse impacts of the prolonged illegal occupation. I notice that different sectors of the society, including the transportation, tourism, retail and food industries, had a public meeting yesterday to express their grievances about the prolonged illegal occupation. Coach drivers, tram drivers and salespersons spoke about how the illegal road occupation had substantially affected their livelihoods.

In fact, the illegal occupation and blockage of roads have created serious traffic congestions and even paralysed the traffic flow in many areas. They have also adversely affected the daily life of the public, the income of drivers and business of small shops. No doubt, the illegal occupation has harmed the overall interests of the society, undermined the rule of law and stirred up resentment and grievances.

In the past month, different sectors of the community, including Government officials, Vice Chancellors, religious leaders, doctors, lawyers, retired judge and academia have issued appeals to persuade the illegal occupiers to respect the rule of law and leave the occupied areas promptly. Regrettably, all these efforts were in vain. However, Police will continue to deploy negotiators and Police Community Relations Officers to persuade protesters to remove the obstacles and clear the roads, which would allow the restoration of public order and resumption of the normal daily life of the public.

The third point is about respecting the rule of law. Police have all along emphasised the importance of the rule of law, which is the cornerstone of the success of Hong Kong. I would like to remind the public that the Interim Injunction Orders on the illegal occupation of roads in Mong Kok and the blockage of access to CITIC Tower in Admiralty remain in force. I urge illegal road occupiers to respect the rule of law and to comply with the court orders to leave the occupied areas promptly. Police are committed to preserving public peace and public order. We will take resolute actions against people who obstruct those authorised to execute the Injunction Orders or radical individuals who charge at Police with violence.

I stress that Police have the statutory duties to maintain law and order, to preserve public peace and ensure public safety. I urge protesters, students in particular, to stay away from radical individuals and troublemakers. Do not mix with these radicals in the crowd. Do not take part or be incited to take part in any act of violence and do not charge at Police. When Police are taking enforcement actions, do not put up resistance. Protesters should stay calm and maintain a safe distance from the officers. We do not want to see anyone, especially students, getting hurt when they place themselves close to radical individuals and troublemakers during confrontations.

I would like to sum up today's messages. Firstly, members of the public should stay away from the illegally occupied areas, as there are still daily occurrence of conflicts and crimes. Mong Kok remains a high risk area. People with different views should express their opinions in a peaceful and rational manner.

Secondly, the endless illegal occupation of roads has created significant adverse impacts on the daily life of our citizens. I urge the illegal road occupiers to remove the road obstacles and leave peacefully, so that the public can resume their normal life and public order restored.

Thirdly, the illegal road occupiers should respect the rule of law and not to interfere with those authorised to execute the injunction orders. Students should not be incited by radical individuals to commit illegal acts and should not resort to the use of violence so as to avoid unnecessary injuries. Police will remain impartial and steadfast, and will continue to serve the public faithfully and diligently.

Issued at HKT 19:26

NOVEMBER 5[10]

HKMA's update on operation of banking system and financial market
****

The following is issued on behalf of the Hong Kong Monetary Authority:

According to the reports to the Hong Kong Monetary Authority (HKMA) from banks as at 8am today (November 5), one branch of one bank was affected and temporarily closed. ATMs in the affected areas have largely resumed normal operation. The HKMA has requested banks to resume normal services as soon as circumstances permit. Customers should pay attention to the relevant banks' announcements regarding affected branches and ATMs. The HKMA will also publish on its website relevant updates from time to time.

Issued at HKT 09:19

Special arrangements on submission of tenders arising from temporary closure of Government Secretariat Tender Box
****

Owing to the special access arrangements at the Central Government Offices (CGO) in Tamar, the Government Secretariat Tender Box (GSTB) located on the ground floor of the East Wing of CGO is closed for tender deposit temporarily.

All tenders that should originally be deposited into the GSTB are instead requested to be deposited into the Government Logistics Department Tender Box (GLDTB) located on the ground floor of North Point Government Offices at 333 Java Road, North Point. This special arrangement came into effect on September 30 this year until further notice.

Tenderers may wish to check in advance their route to the GLDTB and allow sufficient time to make arrangements to deposit their tenders into the GLDTB before the respective closing time of tenders. Late tenders will not be accepted.

For enquiries, please call 2810 2497 or 2231 5288 between 9am and 6pm from Mondays to Fridays (except public holidays).

Issued at HKT 11:32

---

[10] http://www.info.gov.hk/gia/general/201411/05.htm

LCQ3: Police complaints mechanism
****

Following is a question by Professor Hon Joseph Lee and a reply by the Secretary for Security, Mr Lai Tung-kwok, in the Legislative Council today (November 5):

Question:

In the early hours of the 15th of last month, a local news agent recorded a video footage of a subdued participant in an assembly being allegedly kicked and punched by police officers in Tamar Park, Admiralty. Regarding the use of force by police officers, will the Government inform this Council:

(1) as the Police guidelines on the use of force stipulate that police officers may use minimum force as appropriate only when such an action is absolutely necessary and there are no other means to accomplish the lawful duty, of the meaning of "minimum force", and whether it includes kicking and punching persons who have been subdued; if it does not, of the level of force to which such an action belongs; of the respective forms of force and weapons involved in the "minimum force" that may be appropriately used under different circumstances;

(2) as the Police said on the same day after the occurrence of the aforesaid incident that the Complaints Against Police Office had received a relevant complaint and would handle it in accordance with the established procedures, of the details of the "established procedures"; and

(3) of the number of complaints received by the Police in the past three years about police officers having allegedly assaulted other people while on duty and the details of such complaints, including whether the complaints were substantiated in the end and the penalties imposed on the police officers involved in the substantiated cases?

Reply:

President,

Regarding a case of police officers' suspected assault of a protester in Admiralty on October 15, given that the Police have received formal complaints and reports about the case and that the case is under criminal investigation, the Administration considers that, as a matter of fairness, it is inappropriate to provide comment in public, lest the investigation be affected.

The Administration's reply to the Hon Lee's question is as follows:

(1) The Police have the responsibility to maintain public safety and public order, as well as to safeguard life and property in accordance with the law. On occasions where an act causing danger to others is occurring or is about to occur, the Police shall, based on the circumstances at scene, make assessments and exercise professional judgment to take appropriate actions, which include using the minimum force required for public safety and public order. Police officers maintain self-discipline with a high degree of restraint in the discharge of duties. The Police have very clear guidelines and rigorous training to instruct their officers not to use force unless it is necessary and there are no other alternatives to accomplish their lawful duties. The level of force to be used shall be minimal and reasonably required under the prevailing circumstances. Prior to the use of force, police officers shall, as far as circumstances permit, give warnings while the person(s) involved shall be given every opportunity, whenever practicable, to obey police orders before force is used. The use of force shall cease once the purpose of which has been achieved. Generally speaking, the force to which the Police may resort includes the use of empty-hand control, OC foam, batons and firearms. The meaning of "minimum force" depends on the prevailing circumstances at scene and no particular decision would fit all cases.

(2) Public complaints against police officers are handled under a statutory two-tier police complaints mechanism. According to section 11 of the Independent Police Complaints Council Ordinance (the Ordinance) (Cap. 604), a complaint received by the Hong Kong Police Force (HKPF) must be categorised as a reportable complaint if the complaint relates to the conduct of a member of the police force while on duty or in the execution or purported execution of his duties, whether or not he identified himself as such a member, and, at the same time, meets other conditions that make it a reportable complaint under the Ordinance in that, for instance, it is made by a complainant directly affected by the police conduct, irrespective of whether the allegation involves any criminal elements. Such a complaint shall be investigated by the Complaints Against Police Office (CAPO) with the investigation report submitted to the Independent Police Complaints Council (IPCC) for examination in accordance with the statutory requirements under the Ordinance.

The CAPO under the HKPF is specifically responsible for handling and investigating public complaints against police officers, including general complaints as well as the criminal investigations involved. To ensure that complaints are handled in a fair and impartial manner, the CAPO is independent of other Police units. In the course of the investigation of a complaint case, if criminal elements are detected, the CAPO shall instigate criminal investigation and may consider classifying the case as "sub-judice" in which case the involved criminal allegations shall be handled first, and, where necessary, advice from the Department of Justice shall be sought. Only upon completion of the criminal investigation and the related judicial proceedings shall CAPO re-institute the mechanism of the complaint investigation.

The person concerned in the suspected case of unnecessary use of force by police officers mentioned in the question, in reporting his case to the Police, had indicated that it was a complaint against police officers. As the allegations were related to the complainees' conduct in the discharge of duties, the case was referred to the CAPO for following up. A dedicated special investigation team has been set up under the CAPO to handle the case under the established mechanism and procedures. The CAPO has decided to commence criminal investigation towards the case and has classified the case as "sub-judice". The CAPO shall re-institute the mechanism of the complaint investigation only upon completion of the criminal investigation and the related judicial proceedings. A complaint investigation report shall also be submitted to IPCC for examination in accordance with the statutory requirements under the Ordinance. The complaint is related to the "Occupy Central" (or referred to as the "Occupation Movement"). Given that the IPCC has decided to refer all reportable complaints arising from the "Occupy Central" to the Serious Complaints Committee (SCC) for monitoring, the CAPO shall, in accordance with SCC's requirement, report the investigation progress of such reportable complaints on a monthly basis.

(3) According to the CAPO, a total of 829 complaint cases involving allegations of assault by police officers were handled between 2011 and 2013. Of the allegations involved, over 84% were endorsed by IPCC as "not pursuable" or "withdrawn", while the remaining 16% were mostly classified as "no fault", "false" or "unsubstantiated" upon thorough investigation, without any case being classified as "substantiated".

Upon analysis of the statistical data, the CAPO pointed out that a substantial number of complainants alleging that they had been assaulted by police officers were themselves involved in some criminal cases while lodging such complaints to the Police. The complainants or their legal representatives generally used the substance of their complaints as defence in the criminal trial. Once the criminal cases were closed, the complainants would often take the initiative to withdraw their complaints or refuse to contact or respond to the CAPO. As a result, a considerable number of complaints involving assault were eventually classified as "not pursuable" or "withdrawn" every year.

Between 2011 and 2013, a total of three allegations involving assault were endorsed and classified as "not fully substantiated" by IPCC, i.e. there was some reliable evidence to support the complainants' allegation but such evidence was insufficient to fully substantiate the complaint. Upon examination, the Police considered that the cases were stand-alone incidents involving individual officers' integrity, and was unrelated to Police's procedures and guidelines. To follow up, the Police took disciplinary actions against the three officers involved, including warnings and disciplinary proceedings.

Thank you, President.
Issued at HKT 15:03

LCQ6: Involvement of external forces in internal affairs of Hong Kong
****

Following is a question by Dr Hon Kenneth Chan and a reply by the Secretary for Security, Mr Lai Tung-kwok, in the Legislative Council today (November 5):

Question:

The Chief Executive (CE) said earlier in a media interview that external forces were involved in the Occupy Central movement. CE subsequently indicated that he would duly consider at appropriate time whether to disclose the related evidence. In this connection, will the Government inform this Council:

(1) whether it has conducted any form of intelligence gathering or investigation on the alleged involvement of external forces in the Occupy Central movement, and whether it has gathered intelligence in collaboration with the State security organs of the Central People's Government or overseas intelligence agencies; if so, of the details; if it has not conducted any investigation or gathered intelligence, the basis for CE's comment that external forces were involved in the Occupy Central movement;

(2) whether it has concrete evidence on hand at present about the involvement of external forces in the Occupy Central movement; if so, of the details (including the overseas countries or organisations involved), and the reasons for the Government not making public such evidence at present; of the circumstances under which it would be appropriate time to consider whether to disclose the related evidence; and

(3) whether it will take any form of follow-up action on the alleged involvement of external forces in the Occupy Central movement; if so, of the details?

Reply:

President,

Since the beginning of the "Occupy Central" (OC) movement, different analyses have been made and views expressed by Hong Kong and overseas communities, politicians and media on whether external forces have been involved in or have influenced the movement directly or indirectly. The issue has aroused concerns locally and overseas. In response to a question raised by the programme host at a TV interview on October 19, 2014 and when speaking at a media stand-up on October 21, 2014, the Chief Executive (CE) pointed out that the involvement of external forces in the OC movement was not a mere speculation. Hong Kong, as part of China and itself a highly open city, has been operating within a rather complicated international environment and exposed to the influence of external forces.

At a regular press conference on October 20, 2014, the spokesperson of the Ministry of Foreign Affairs remarked that some foreign individuals and forces attempted to interfere with Hong Kong affairs, exert influence on Hong Kong's development, and even side with or incite illegal activities such as the OC movement. The Ministry of Foreign Affairs also reiterated that Hong Kong affairs fell entirely within China's internal affairs, and the Chinese side resolutely opposed the intervention in Hong Kong affairs by any external forces in any form.

We believe that our community and the general public do not wish to see, and will not accept, any direct or indirect involvement of external forces in the internal affairs of Hong Kong or our nation, not to mention in such activities as the OC movement which disrupts social order and breaks the law. Nor do they wish to see any change in the nature of Hong Kong's political or social activities or their complication as a result of influence of external forces. We understand that the general public and the Legislative Council are concerned about how external forces get involved in and have influenced the OC movement, and the impact so caused. However, the issue involves national and local security as well as a lot of other complicated and sensitive information. In dealing with matters of this kind, we consider it inappropriate for the HKSAR Government, as for any other governments, to conduct an open discussion. Having said that, the HKSAR Government will face and deal with the intervention of any external forces, to ensure that Hong Kong's constitutional reform may proceed within the framework of the Basic Law and on the basis of the decisions of the Standing Committee of the National People's Congress. As far as the OC movement is concerned, the HKSAR Government will restore social order in accordance with the law as soon as possible. The CE has also indicated that the HKSAR Government would consider, at an appropriate time, how to disclose details of external forces' involvement and influence on the OC movement.

It has been more than a month since the beginning of the OC movement. Large-scale road blockage and acts of charging have adversely affected people's daily life and posed great pressure on Police work. Worse still, OC participants have not only tried to rationalise their unlawful activities such as road blocking and charging on the pretext of "civil disobedience", they have recently also acted in open defiance of the temporary court injunctions. The spread of this sense of lawlessness and its erosion of Hong Kong's rule of law are truly worrying. Whether participants are joining the movement of their own volition or with the benefit of assistance from external forces, the continuation of the movement will only cause grave and long-lasting damage to the community of Hong Kong as a whole.

OC is an unlawful gathering. The Government will deal with this illegal activity, including its organisation, planning and funding, in a serious manner. I must stress that Hong Kong is a city of rule of law. The law enforcement agencies will deal with the illegal activities in accordance with the law. Once again, I appeal to all organisers and participants to leave peacefully and stop obstructing the roads as soon as possible, so that social order and people's life may return to normal as early as possible.

Thank you, President.
Issued at HKT 15:27

LCQ5: Prosecution matters involving public order events
****

Following is a question by Dr the Hon Elizabeth Quat and a reply by the Secretary for Justice, Mr Rimsky Yuen, SC, in the Legislative Council today (November 5):

Question:

The Department of Justice (DoJ) added a Public Order Events section to its newly revised Prosecution Code (the new Code) released in September last year to provide guidelines and pointers to prosecutors. The section states that as there are provisions in the Basic Law guaranteeing Hong Kong residents freedoms in respect of speech, association, assembly, procession and demonstration, etc., "[o]ffences alleged to have been committed in conjunction with the exercise of these constitutionally guaranteed freedoms may give rise to special considerations" (special considerations). I have learnt that regarding this type of cases, the Police need to await DoJ's consent before they may institute prosecutions even if they have got sufficient evidence. In this connection, will the Government inform this Council:

(1) whether DoJ has issued to the prosecutors specific working guidelines on how they should make the special considerations, and what measures it has put in place to ensure that making the special considerations will not complicate and lengthen the prosecution procedures;

(2) of the total number of cases involving public order events handled by DoJ since the issuance of the new Code and, among such cases, the respective numbers of those for which prosecutions have been and have yet to be instituted; the average time taken by the authorities for making prosecution decisions for such cases, and how it compares with the time taken for other cases in which the Police may institute prosecutions directly; and

(3) given comments that despite a number of people having been arrested at the assembly venues of the recent occupation movement for alleged breaches of the law, the authorities have not, after a long time, instituted prosecutions against such people because the Police have to gather substantial evidence for such cases to enable prosecutors to make the special considerations, resulting in the public misunderstanding that persons breaching the law at the assembly venues will neither be prosecuted nor incur criminal liabilities, of DoJ's remedial measures to clear such public misunderstanding?

Reply:

President,

Article 63 of the Basic Law of the Hong Kong Special Administrative Region (HKSAR) provides that the Department of Justice (DoJ) shall control criminal prosecutions, free from any interference. The DoJ has always been controlling criminal prosecutions on behalf of the HKSAR on that basis so as to ensure that justice is done. A decision on whether to prosecute any individual or organisation is just as important for the suspect and the victim as it is for the community as a whole. Hence, with public interest in mind, prosecutors must act without fear or favour, and in accordance with the relevant law and evidence. The DoJ will treat all implicated parties equally and in accordance with the law, irrespective of their background, identity and social status.

Prosecution should only be brought when there is cogent and credible evidence in support. According to paragraph 5.3 of the current Prosecution Code, when considering whether to prosecute, prosecutors must first consider whether there is sufficient evidence. If so satisfied, prosecutors should next consider and balance all issues of public interest. A prosecution shall not be commenced or continued unless there is a reasonable prospect of conviction. A prosecution which is not supported by evidence will not only be unfair to the defendant(s), but will also lead to a waste of court resources. Prosecutors have always acted in strict compliance with the Prosecution Code in handling prosecutions and incidental works to ensure that an effective and fair criminal justice system is maintained.

All prosecution decisions are made in accordance with the law, the Prosecution Code and the evidence, totally free from any political, media or public pressure. In considering whether or not to prosecute an alleged breach of criminal law during a public order event, the DoJ will adopt the same principles as those adopted when handling other criminal cases, i.e. to consider whether there is sufficient evidence in support of the charge, and whether it is in the public interest to prosecute.

The DoJ's reply to the three-part question raised by Dr the Hon Elizabeth Quat is as follows:

(1) Taking into account the circumstances in which prosecutors operate and operational need, the DoJ published the latest Prosecution Code in September last year. The Prosecution Code covers specific offences in the form of dedicated sections. In the section on Public Order Events, it makes references to the Basic Law, the Hong Kong Bill of Rights and landmark court decisions, including the judgment delivered by the Court of Final Appeal in Yeung May-wan v HKSAR (2005) 8 HKCFAR 137, so as to remind prosecutors of the well established legal principles applicable to the handling of cases related to public order events.

The Prosecution Code also reminds prosecutors that offences alleged to have been committed in conjunction with the exercise of constitutionally guaranteed freedoms may give rise to special considerations. The purpose is to ensure that in handling such cases, prosecutors will strike an appropriate balance between the interest of society and maintaining public order on the one hand, and the right of individuals to lawfully and peacefully exercise their constitutionally guaranteed freedoms on the other.

In fact, prosecutors have all along made references to the relevant statutory provisions, judgments and principles involved when handling cases involving public order events. It should be pointed out that the Prosecution Code does not prescribe any special procedures to be followed before the prosecution of cases involving public order events can be commenced. The new Prosecution Code does not complicate or lengthen the prosecution procedures. Nor is there any need for more specific working guidelines for prosecutors in the handling of these cases.

(2) The Prosecution Code took effect on September 7, 2013. The DoJ has not, whether before or after this date, kept figures about the number of legal advices rendered in relation to public order events or the number of cases involved, or any breakdown as to the number which have recommended prosecution and

the number which have yet to. We also have not maintained statistics on the average time taken for making prosecution decisions for such cases.

Based on the figures on prosecutions involving public order events maintained by the Police, for the period between September 2013 and June 2014, the number of public order events is 5,529. As at 8 September 2014, the number of public order events involving prosecutions is 12, and the number of protestors prosecuted is 16.

(3) As I have pointed out in part (1) of the reply, the section on Public Order Events added to the latest edition of the Prosecution Code only serves to remind prosecutors of the basic legal principles applicable to the handling of cases concerning public order events. Hence, there is no question of imposing new requirements on the gathering of evidence by law enforcement agencies, nor resulting in any more time spent by the Police in gathering evidence or delaying the decision to institute prosecution. The DoJ will at all times seek to provide legal advice to law enforcement agencies including the Police as expeditiously as possible, and the actual time that it takes to provide legal advice on each case depends on various factors, including mainly the nature and complexity of the case. Among cases submitted to the DoJ for legal advice, the number of suspects and the complexity of the cases may also vary. The responsible prosecutor may require more time to go through the evidence, analyse the facts of the case, and, where necessary, advise on the appropriate manner to handle the case.

In order to achieve better efficiency in the handling of cases concerning public order events and with a view to ensuring consistency of approach as far as possible, the DoJ has set up a small dedicated team of prosecutors within the Prosecutions Division to handle such cases, so that professional legal advice can be provided to the Police as expeditiously as possible so as to enable early referral of cases which merit prosecution to the courts for adjudication.

Lastly, I hope to take this opportunity to emphasise that the DoJ will continue to maintain communication with the Police in respect of any illegal acts involved in the "Occupy Central" activities, and will handle relevant prosecution work in a timely manner.

Issued at HKT 15:51

LCQ 21: Injunctions
****

Following is a question by the Hon Ng Leung-sing and a written reply by the Secretary for Justice, Mr Rimsky Yuen, SC, in the Legislative Council today (November 5):

Question:

On October 20 this year, the High Court granted interim injunctions restraining participants of the assemblies triggered by the Occupy Central movement from continued occupation of certain passageways in Mong Kok and obstruction of the entrance to the car park, the fire access and emergency vehicular access of a building in Admiralty. Protesters are also forbidden to obstruct the plaintiffs from removing the obstacles in question. However, some protesters refused to obey the injunctions. In this connection, will the Government inform this Council:

(1) whether it knows the total number of interim and formal injunctions granted by the High Court in the past five years, and the enforcement situation of such injunctions; and

(2) as some protesters refused to obey the aforesaid injunctions, what actions the law enforcement agencies intend to carry out; whether, in the light of this incident, the authorities will consider comprehensively reviewing and improving the mechanism for enforcing injunctions?

Reply:

President,

The rule of law is the cornerstone of Hong Kong's success and the Government places great importance in upholding the rule of law. Amongst others, respect for the authority of the Court is a fundamental aspect of the concept of the rule of law. Court orders, including injunction orders (whether interim or permanent), should be fully respected and strictly followed. Even if a party does not agree that an injunction should be granted, the party should lodge an appeal or make other appropriate application to the relevant Court pursuant to the relevant procedure instead of deliberately acting in breach of the injunction. Loss of respect for the Courts and the orders they make will erode the rule of law, which in turn will cause harm to our society.

The Government's reply to the Member's question is as follows:

(1) Application for injunction is a type of civil proceeding dealt with by the Courts. We have consulted the Judiciary on this part of the question. We have been advised that the Judiciary does not have readily available statistics on the number of injunctions granted by the Courts in the past five years.

Enforcement of injunctions is generally dealt with by the parties to the relevant civil proceedings, although the Bailiffs will render assistance as and when appropriate and Judges will deal with such applications as may be incidental to the enforcement of injunctions. According to its records, the Judiciary has received a total of six applications in the past five years requesting the assistance of the Bailiffs in the serving of injunction orders. All of the orders in these six requests have been duly served.

(2) Since applications for injunction are civil (as opposed to criminal) in nature, they are generally and mostly handled by private litigants. Accordingly, in the absence of specific Court direction or order, the Police are generally not involved in the enforcement of an injunction order. However, the Police have a statutory duty under the Police Force Ordinance, Cap 232 to take appropriate actions if a breach of the peace occurs or when suspected criminal acts have been committed. If the relevant Court order expressly directs the Police to perform certain specified acts for the purpose of assisting a party to enforce an injunction, the Police will provide such assistance as is specified in the relevant Court order.

An injunction is a solemn order made by the Court and that it is in the overall and long-term interests of the rule of law and the proper administration of justice that all injunction orders should be complied with. With a view to protecting the due administration of justice (which is fundamental to the upholding of the rule of law), the Government (through the Police or otherwise) is ready and willing to assist in the enforcement of the injunction orders in such ways as the Court may find it appropriate to direct.

As regards the specific cases referred to in the question, before the Court hands down its judgments, the Police will continue to dispatch appropriate manpower and make appropriate deployment to maintain public order and protect public safety. The Government also urges those who are unlawfully blocking the roads should strictly and fully observe the relevant Court orders as soon as possible.

On the mechanism for enforcing injunctions, the Government will, as usual, keep the relevant law under review and will consider the need of any reform as and when necessary.

Issued at HKT 16:01

LCQ22: Residential requirement for registered electors
****

Following is a question by the Hon Emily Lau and a written reply by the Secretary for Constitutional and Mainland Affairs, Mr Raymond Tam, in the Legislative Council today (November 5):

Under section 28(1) of the Legislative Council Ordinance (Cap. 542), one of the eligibility criteria for registration as an elector in the register of geographical constituencies is that the person must ordinarily reside in Hong Kong. The authorities conducted a public consultation from January to March 2012 on the improvement measures of the voter registration (VR) system. In April of the same year, the authorities indicated in the consultation report that during the consultation, they had received public views on the definitions of "ordinarily reside in Hong Kong" and "principal residential address" in relation to VR, but such definitions were outside the scope of the consultation exercise and were complicated issues that had to be handled carefully by the fourth-term Government. Meanwhile, it was reported in May this year that a member of the public had complained to the Registration and Electoral Office (REO) that there were a number of suspected vote rigging cases in his constituency during a District Council (DC) by-election. Upon investigation, REO found that in those cases, some electors were currently not residing in their registered addresses due to various reasons, and REO indicated that it was taking follow-up actions. In this connection, will the Government inform this Council:

(1) whether the fourth-term Government has handled the aforesaid issue regarding the definition of "ordinarily reside in Hong Kong"; if it has, of the details; if not, the reasons for that; and

(2) if it has assessed whether electors no longer residing or working in their registered constituencies but continuing to vote in that constituency will render it impossible for elected members (especially DC members) to effectively take care of the interests of electors; if the assessment outcome is in the affirmative, whether the Government has put in place any improvement measure; if the assessment outcome is in the negative, of the reasons for that?

Reply:

Mr President,

(1) According to section 28(1) of the Legislative Council Ordinance (Cap. 542), a person is not eligible to be registered as an elector in the register of geographical constituencies unless, at the time of applying for

registration, the person satisfies the Electoral Registration Officer (ERO) that he/she ordinarily resides in Hong Kong and that the residential address provided is the person's only or principal residence in Hong Kong.

The Government has repeatedly pointed out in the relevant discussions at the Panel on Constitutional Affairs of the Legislative Council that the definition of "ordinarily resides in Hong Kong" is a complicated issue: the definition of "ordinarily resides in Hong Kong" is not set out in the existing legislation; whether a person "ordinarily resides in Hong Kong" depends on the facts of each case and is a matter involving judgment on the specific circumstances of an individual case and the relevant previous court judgments.

In processing applications for voter registration (VR), the ERO will decide whether the applicant ordinarily resides in Hong Kong by taking into account the specific situation of an individual case and referring to the previous court judgments. If the Registration and Electoral Office (REO) receives a concerned enquiry or complaint, it will carefully examine the details of the case and, where necessary, seek legal advice on the specific situation and/or refer the case to the law enforcement agencies for follow-up investigation. Besides, the REO publishes the provisional registers of electors, the omissions lists and the final registers of electors each year for public inspection to ensure that a highly transparent VR system is maintained. During the period when the provisional registers of electors and the omissions lists are published, the public may make objections or claims to the ERO against the entries on the registers and the lists. Such cases will then be referred to the Revising Officer and a determination will be made after representations from both parties are heard at an open hearing. Hence, a mechanism is already in place in the VR system to handle applications under various situations and to allow for public monitoring.

(2) The Government attaches great importance to maintaining the fairness, openness and integrity of the electoral system, and adopts various measures to ensure a high degree of transparency, the integrity and accuracy of the VR system. On the one hand, the Administration actively encourages the public to register as electors; on the other hand, we have repeatedly reminded applicants that they have to provide true and accurate information. Any person who makes a false statement in an application for VR or change of his residential address violates the electoral law. The Government has also reminded electors through various publicity channels to fulfill their civic responsibility to notify the REO to update their registered addresses after moving home.

Besides, to maintain the credibility of the VR system and to enhance the accuracy of the information in the registers of electors, the REO has launched a series of improvement measures from 2012, including verification checks on electors' registered residential addresses through cross-matching of data with the Housing Department and the Home Affairs Department; checks on multiple electors or multiple surnames of electors registered with the same residential address; random sample checks on the existing electors; checks on addresses with incomplete information, commercial addresses or suspected non-residential addresses; as well as checks on addresses in buildings that have already been demolished or that have already been vacated pending demolition, etc. If the REO receives a complaint against a suspected false registered address of an elector, it will check against the relevant registration record and whenever necessary, request the elector concerned to confirm the relevant registered address and/or refer the case to the law enforcement agencies for follow-up investigation. In addition, the REO will continue to strengthen education and publicity to remind electors to fulfill their civic responsibility to ensure that the registration particulars are accurate. Electors should, upon moving home, notify the REO to update their residential addresses as soon as possible before the statutory deadlines so that they can vote in the constituency they are currently residing.

The VR arrangements mentioned above aims to ensure that, on the one hand, the system is convenient to the public to register as electors and, on the other, a high degree of transparency, integrity and accuracy of the VR system, and striking a right balance between the two.

Regarding the complaint in May 2014 concerning a suspected case of individual electors providing false residential addresses, the REO, upon receiving the complaint, wrote to the electors concerned immediately and requested them to confirm in writing the relevant information about their registered residential addresses. It was confirmed that some of the electors had passed away and some of them had moved while some of the electors had not replied. As a result, the REO updated the relevant registration particulars in accordance with the relevant legislation when compiling the 2014 final register and deleted the electors who could not confirm their registered residential addresses.
Issued at HKT 16:02

LCQ4: Access to computer with criminal or dishonest intent
****

Following is a question by the Hon Charles Peter Mok and a reply by the Secretary for Security, Mr Lai Tung-kwok, in the Legislative Council today (November 5):

Question:

When the authorities amended the Crimes Ordinance in 1993, section 161 was added to provide for the offence of "access to computer with criminal or dishonest intent" (section 161). The then Secretary for Security explained that the new section 161 was aimed at "penalising access to a computer for acts preparatory but falling short of the commission of a fraud. Examples would include someone obtaining access to computerised bank records to obtain details of credit balances for later fraudulent use". Last month, the Police noted that some persons had posted messages on the Internet to incite members of the public to take part in the unlawful assemblies in Mong Kok and Admiralty. After investigation, the Police arrested a man for allegedly committing the offence under section 161 and that of "unlawful assembly". Regarding the scope of application of section 161, will the Government inform this Council:

(1) of the details of the cases in which prosecutions were instituted by the authorities under section 161 in the past three years, including case numbers, other charges in the same case (if applicable), sentencing outcome, appeal outcome (if applicable), and case type (e.g. criminal intimidation, blackmail, indecent assault, theft, deception, criminal damage, public safety, soliciting for an immoral purpose, sale or use of non-compliant electronic products and network attacks), and set out such information in a table; among such cases, the number of those involving fraud or acts preparatory of the commission of a fraud and their case numbers; and

(2) as most of the laws for prevention of crimes in the physical world apply equally to the cyber world, whether the authorities have planned to review and amend section 161 to bring its scope of application more in line with its legislative intent, that is focusing on tackling crimes such as computer frauds and network attacks, instead of imposing criminal liabilities on people posting on the Internet messages which are not in violation of other legislative provisions?

Reply:

President,

According to section 161 of the Crimes Ordinance (Cap 200)(i.e. access to computer with criminal or dishonest intent), any person who obtains access to a computer with any of the following intention or purpose:

(a) with intent to commit an offence;
(b) with a dishonest intent to deceive;
(c) with a view to dishonest gain for himself or another; or
(d) with a dishonest intent to cause loss to another,

whether on the same occasion as he obtains such access or on any future occasion, commits an offence.

The above section aims at combating acts of "access to computer with criminal or dishonest intent", such as technology crimes like online fraud and illegal access to a computer system, urging or inciting others to engage in illegal activities, as well as other crimes committed through the use of computer. Any persons who commit such an offence are subject to a maximum penalty of five-year-imprisonment on conviction upon indictment.

Between 2011 and 2013, there were a total of 128 prosecution cases pertaining to section 161 of the Crimes Ordinance (Cap 200). During the same period, there were 114 convicted cases. Detailed figures of prosecution cases, convicted cases and non-convicted cases between 2011 and 2013 are at Annex[11]. The Administration, however, did not have any information on whether the charges in prosecution cases were laid as alternative charges, whether the cases involved "access to a computer for acts preparatory of the commission of a fraud", or other categories of crimes involved in such cases.

In early October this year, a hacker group threatened to launch cyber attacks on the network systems of Hong Kong government departments, and even incited others to join in the attacks by using hackers' websites or software. Meanwhile, the Police found that some people, via social networking platforms on the Internet, were inciting members of the public to take part in the attacks, as well as making available certain tools for such attacks. Despite that the Police had required the Internet Service Providers concerned to delete those messages inciting others to commit crime, some members of public, taking no heed of their criminal liabilities, responded to the appeals on the social networking platforms by participating in the illegal cyber attacks. The Police have, since early October, received a number of reports of "Denial of Service Attacks" on the network systems of Hong Kong government departments and private organisations. Some of their websites experienced an unusually high hit rate, leading to network congestion and intermittent service disruption. Upon in-depth investigation, the Technology Crime Division under the Commercial Crime Bureau of the Police launched a number of actions, in which 11 persons were arrested for suspected "access to computer with criminal or dishonest intent" under section 161 of the Crimes Ordinance, with two arrested persons being charged by the Police, while the remaining nine were released on police bail pending further investigation. These persons were arrested for having been incited to join the cyber attacks by using the hackers' websites or software.

The case mentioned in the Hon Mok's question was about a man urging members of the public to participate in the unlawful assemblies at Mong Kok and Admiralty. On an Internet discussion forum, the person in question incited others to join the unlawful assembly at Mong Kok and to storm the Police, suggesting protesters to paralyse the railway system by gathering on railway platforms in an attempt to create chaos, in case Mong Kok could not be successfully taken back. Upon investigation, the Police arrested

---

[11] To view: http://gia.info.gov.hk/general/201411/05/P201411050605_0605_136809.pdf

the man on October 18 for having involved in the acts of "access to computer with criminal or dishonest intent" and "unlawful assembly".

As another issue, during "Occupy Central" or "Occupation Movement", a person uploaded the personal data of a police officer, and even those of his family members and children, onto the Internet. Apart from incessant personal attacks via social media, the person posted messages on an online discussion forum, claiming that somebody had been directed to assault the police officer's family members. The police officer and his family members were consequently subject to unnecessary nuisances and personal safety concerns. Upon in-depth investigation, the Police arrested the man on October 22 for suspected "criminal intimidation".

I have to stress that it is an act of extreme irresponsibility by inciting others to participate in illegal activities and making threatening remarks on the Internet. The Police and I severely condemn such acts. As legal proceedings for the cases that I just mentioned have commenced or are going to commence, I am not in a position to make further comments. However, as seen from the above cases, any persons committing unlawful acts in the real world or cyber world, like launching cyber attacks on network systems, inciting others through online platforms to conduct illegal activities, and making remarks that put others' personal safety at risk, shall be criminally liable and be brought to justice.

The Police shall, in consideration of the nature of individual crimes, take enforcement actions in accordance with relevant laws. The Police have internal guidelines in which police officers are instructed to seek advice from the Department of Justice (DoJ) before pressing charges against any persons arrested for having involved in public order events. Police officers will also seek DoJ's advice as to which legal provisions shall be invoked when pressing charges. In handling other types of cases, including internet-related cases, the Police shall determine the charge(s) to be laid with regard to the evidence of individual cases, and, where necessary, DoJ's advice shall also be sought before prosecution. Whether a person is to be convicted is a matter of which the court shall pass a fair and impartial judgment upon considering all evidence available.

The Police always remind the public that the Internet is not an unreal world that is beyond the law. As far as the existing legislation in Hong Kong is concerned, most of the crime-prevention laws in the real world are applicable to the Internet world. As reminded by the Police, the public should not risk breaking the law. They are also advised to use the Internet properly and lawfully, while refraining from sending any irresponsible messages and inciting others to engage in illegal activities. The Police shall definitely collect evidence on any illegal online activities for follow-up investigations and take arrest actions where necessary.

The Administration considers that the law in place is effective in meeting the demand for combating technology crime and safeguarding cyber security and there is no plan for legislative amendments at this stage.

Issued at HKT 17:09

Over 200 complaints related to public transport services and traffic affected by occupation movement received

****

The Transport Department (TD) today (November 5) said that the occupation movement, which has lasted for over a month, has resulted in road closures, traffic congestion and route adjustments of public transport services, causing great inconvenience to the daily life of members of the public. The 1823 Hotline has so far received more than 270 complaints related to public transport services and traffic affected by the illegal occupation of roads.

The complaints are mainly related to adjustments of public transport services, including change, truncation and suspension of routes; insufficient public transport services, lost trips and unstable frequencies; relocation of bus stops and requests for additional bus stops; and road closures due to blockage and traffic congestion.

During the illegal occupation of major trunk roads for over a month, the TD and public transport operators have constantly reviewed the road situation and have resumed public transport services as far as possible to minimise the impact on members of the public. However, routings and frequencies of public transport services have inevitably become unstable when being affected by the traffic situation. Meanwhile, the TD and the Police have been closely monitoring the traffic situation and have implemented a number of temporary traffic control measures to alleviate congestion. Nevertheless, if the major trunk roads such as Harcourt Road being illegally occupied by protesters cannot be reopened, traffic congestion cannot be improved.

Under the current circumstances, the TD continues to call on members of the public going to work and school to start their journeys early and plan their journeys in advance. They are also advised to allow more time for travelling. Motorists should avoid driving to Hong Kong Island as far as possible. They should also pay attention to the arrangements of temporary traffic control measures and related temporary traffic signs, and follow the instructions of the Police at the scene.

Regarding public transport services, a total of 221 bus routes are still affected today with eight bus routes suspended and 213 bus routes diverted. Among the affected bus routes, 80 routes travelling via Mong Kok are diverted due to the closure of a number of road sections in Mong Kok. A total of 20 green minibus routes travelling via Harcourt Road, Nathan Road and Argyle Street are still diverted or suspended or with service adjusted. Currently, the tram service between Percival Street and Paterson Street is still suspended. The MTR Corporation Limited continues to increase services for all urban lines to cope with passenger demand.

The TD's Emergency Transport Co-ordination Centre will continue to monitor the road traffic situation and public transport services. For details of road closure, traffic diversion, suspension and route diversion of green minibus services, please refer to the TD's website (www.td.gov.hk). Regarding temporary traffic arrangements for bus routes, please refer to the following bus companies' websites for details:

For routes of Citybus and New World First Bus: www.nwstbus.com.hk/en/uploaded-Files/OC2014/TAA.htm .

For routes of Kowloon Motor Bus: www.kmb.hk/en .

As there will be updates on bus services from time to time due to traffic changes, members of the public are advised to pay attention to the latest service arrangements announced by bus companies before starting their journeys.
Issued at HKT 17:57

LCQ7: Impact of "Occupy Central"
****

Following is a question by Dr Hon Lam Tai-fai and a written reply by the Secretary for Security, Mr Lai Tung-kwok, in the Legislative Council today (November 5):

Question:

The Chief Executive (CE) indicated earlier that external forces were involved in the Occupy Central movement, and that Hong Kong, being a part of China and a highly open city, was caught in a complicated international environment. When asked about whether he would disclose related evidence, CE indicated that he would duly consider the matter at appropriate time. In addition, during the period when the assemblies triggered by the Occupy Central movement (Occupy Central assemblies) were being held, physical confrontations occurred from time to time among assembly participants, people opposing the assemblies and police officers, causing injuries to many people of various sides. It was even reported that such confrontations involved triad members. In this connection, will the Government inform this Council:

(1) whether it has assessed if the fact that the evidence relating to the involvement of external forces in Hong Kong's affairs is not disclosed immediately will adversely affect national security and the stability of Hong Kong society; how the authorities will guard against the involvement of external forces in Hong Kong's affairs;

(2) whether it knows if persons advocating independence of Xinjiang, Xizang and Taiwan as well as Falun Gong have participated in the Occupy Central movement and are involved in Hong Kong's internal affairs; if it knows, of the details;

(3) as it has been reported that the National Endowment for Democracy (NED) of the United States has provided funds for pan-democratic organisations in Hong Kong in recent years for promoting the development of democracy in Hong Kong, whether it has taken the initiative to find out or investigate if NED has participated in the Occupy Central movement; if investigation has been conducted and the outcome is in the affirmative, of the details, including the political parties or organisations in Hong Kong which have received such funds and the amount of funds involved; if investigation has not been conducted, the reasons for that;

(4) whether it knows if triad members have participated in activities of organising, planning, commanding and funding assemblies in support of and opposing the Occupy Central assemblies; if the triad members have done so, of the details; the number of related triad members arrested by the Police so far, and whether prosecution will be instituted against them;

(5) whether it knows if personnel from the Ministry of State Security have participated in organising, planning, commanding and funding actions to charge at the participants of the Occupy Central assemblies by people opposing such assemblies; if such personnel have done so, of the details;

(6) since the occurrence of the Occupy Central assemblies, of the police manpower deployed by the Police for maintaining public order at assembly venues, and how the numbers of crimes such as robbery, theft, indecent assault, etc. in each District Council district compare with the corresponding numbers in the same period of the year before;

(7) since the occurrence of the Occupy Central assemblies, of the number of police officers who received psychological counselling due to excessive pressure, tendered resignation or refused to perform duty at areas where the assemblies were held;

(8) since the occurrence of the Occupy Central assemblies, of the respective maximum daily numbers of persons participating in such assemblies and those assemblies opposing the Occupy Central movement in Mong Kok, Causeway Bay, Admiralty and Central;

(9) of the total number of canisters of tear gas that the police officers handling the Occupy Central assemblies in the area around Admiralty on the 28th of September this year were equipped with; whether it has assessed if that number is adequate;

(10) whether it has assessed if the Police have adequate equipment (e.g. anti-riot shields, protective helmets, extendable batons and pepper spray, etc.) for handling the Occupy Central assemblies; if it has, of the outcome;

(11) whether it has compiled statistics on the number of canisters of pepper spray used by the Police since the occurrence of the Occupy Central assemblies; whether it has reviewed if any police officer had used pepper spray inappropriately; if it has conducted such a review, of the outcome;

(12) since the occurrence of the Occupy Central assemblies, of the respective response time performance of ambulances and fire appliances in each of the divisions under the Ambulance/Fire Commands, and the number of service calls attended at venues of such assemblies (set out in a table);

(13) according to the data obtained by the authorities, of the number of persons injured or feeling unwell in the Occupy Central assemblies so far, with a breakdown by the identity of such persons (i.e. assembly participants, police officers, tourists, journalists and other persons); among them, the number of persons who required hospital treatment;

(14) whether it has compiled statistics on the number of public properties (such as mills barriers, water barriers, rubbish bins, 3-coloured recycling bins, etc.) being damaged or stolen at venues of the Occupy Central assemblies so far, and the number of persons arrested by the Police for alleged vandalism of government properties; and

(15) given that in reply to a question raised at the meeting of this Council on the 15th of last month regarding whether the three initiators of the Occupy Central movement would be prosecuted, the Secretary for Security indicated that the Police would definitely conduct in-depth investigations into illegal acts and

would take appropriate actions in due course, whether related investigations have been initiated by the Police, and of the circumstances under which it would be the appropriate time to institute prosecutions against the initiators, organisers and assembly participants of the Occupy Central movement?

Reply:

President,

Following a spate of unlawful acts by radical protesters, the public meeting on the pavement outside the Central Government Offices since September 26 has developed into an unlawful assembly affecting various areas on Hong Kong Island and in Kowloon. Protesters, staging large-scale unlawful assemblies in the areas of Admiralty, Mong Kok and Causeway Bay in recent days as well as in Tsim Sha Tsui previously, have blocked a number of major trunk roads in an illegal manner. "Occupy Central" or the occupation movement has persisted for over a month, causing extremely widespread, serious and substantive impact on traffic and transport, emergency rescue services, Government operation, daily life of the community and even various kinds of economic activities. The Government severely condemns such irresponsible and illegal acts.

Our consolidated reply to Dr Hon Lam Tai-fai's question is as follows:

External Forces

Since the beginning of "Occupy Central", different analyses have been made and views expressed by Hong Kong and overseas communities, politicians and media on whether external forces have been involved in or have influenced "Occupy Central" directly or indirectly. The issue has aroused concerns locally and overseas. In response to a question raised by the programme host at a TV interview on October 19, 2014 and when speaking at a media stand-up on October 21, 2014, the Chief Executive (CE) pointed out that the involvement of external forces in "Occupy Central" was not a mere speculation. Hong Kong, as part of China and itself a highly open city, has been operating within a rather complicated international environment and exposed to the influence of external forces.

At a regular press conference on October 20, 2014, the spokesperson of the Ministry of Foreign Affairs remarked that some foreign individuals and forces attempted to interfere with Hong Kong affairs, exert influence on Hong Kong's development, and even side with or incite illegal activities such as the "Occupy Central". The Ministry of Foreign Affairs also reiterated that Hong Kong affairs fell entirely within China's internal affairs, and the Chinese side resolutely opposed the intervention in Hong Kong affairs by any external forces in any form.

We believe that our community and the general public do not wish to see, and will not accept, any direct or indirect involvement of external forces in the internal affairs of Hong Kong or our nation, not to mention in such activities as "Occupy Central" which disrupts social order and breaks the law. Nor do they wish to see any change in the nature of Hong Kong's political or social activities or their complication as a result of influence of external forces. We understand that the general public and the Legislative Council are concerned about how external forces get involved in and have influenced "Occupy Central", and the impact so caused. However, the issue involves national and local security as well as a lot of other complicated and sensitive information. In dealing with matters of this kind, we consider it inappropriate for the HKSAR Government, as for any other governments, to conduct an open discussion. Having said that, the HKSAR Government will face and deal with the intervention of any external forces, to ensure that Hong Kong's constitutional reform may proceed within the framework of the Basic Law and on the basis of the decisions of the Standing Committee of the National People's Congress. As far as "Occupy Central" is concerned, the HKSAR Government will restore social order in accordance with the law as soon as possible. The CE has also indicated that the HKSAR Government would consider, at an appropriate time, how to disclose details of external forces' involvement and influence on "Occupy Central".

Demonstrations triggered by "Occupy Central"

Over the past month, "Occupy Central" has turned from a student assembly to an unlawful assembly with a mix of participants including a large number of people of different backgrounds and from different radical organisations, with some protesters forced their way into government buildings, violently charged the police cordon, seized mills barriers, assaulted police officers, occupied major trunk roads and paralysed the traffic. Their illegal occupation of roads is an act of deliberate contravention of the law in that they have blocked the roads with stolen government properties including mills barriers, rubbish bins and recycling bins, and have even put up large barricades with bamboo poles, wooden planks and plastic straps to reinforce their road blockage. As a result, emergency vehicles can neither gain direct access to nor pass through the illegally occupied areas, posing unnecessary safety risk to people in the neighbouring areas. We condemn such acts.

In recent days, there have been confrontations and crimes of different scales in various illegally occupied areas or in other "Occupy Central"-related public order events. In crowded areas, there is always a risk of confrontation. Gatherings of people holding different views are prone to verbal disputes and scuffles, which may end in chaos with physical confrontations. As at November 3, the Police have arrested 324 persons in total for illegal acts directly related to "Occupy Central". The alleged offences include unlawful assembly, disorderly conduct in a public place, common assault, criminal damage, assault occasioning actual bodily harm, resisting arrest, assault on a police officer, obstructing a police officer in the execution of his duties, indecent assault and so forth. Some of the arrested persons have triad backgrounds. The cases involved in such arrests are currently under police investigation, and prosecution shall not be ruled out where sufficient evidence is available.

As crime figures are classified by police region and such figures for September and October this year are still under compilation, a comparison between the crime figures since the launch of "Occupy Central" for all districts and those in the same period of last year, as requested in the question, is not available.

The Police have stressed repeatedly their utter intolerance of illegal conduct. Where there is evidence for the alleged offences, the Police shall definitely take follow-up actions in accordance with the law, and seek advice from the Department of Justice when necessary for consideration of prosecution.

Handling of large-scale unlawful assemblies by the Police

As a law enforcement department, the Police have the statutory duties to maintain law and order, as well as to safeguard life and property. In the face of a considerable number of large-scale unlawful assemblies for more than a month, frontline police officers have been in full gear around the clock to deal with such assemblies and storming by groups of protesters, which involves substantial police manpower and resources, and they are, at the same time, well-equipped for the handling of such assemblies and the relevant police operations. To maintain day-to-day police services, the Police have allocated sufficient manpower to every region through resource and manpower deployment. However, the manpower and equipment utilised by the Police in the operation are not to be disclosed, as they were a matter of operational particulars. In addition, as the unlawful assemblies associated with "Occupy Central" are still on-going, the figure on the use of Oleoresin Capsicum foam in the operation is subject to verification.

The Police do not have any daily figures of people participating in assemblies for and against "Occupy Central" at various locations of unlawful occupation. As "Occupy Central" is still on-going, statistical information on stolen or damaged public property is not available at this point of time.

"Occupy Central" is still going on in different districts where large-scale unlawful assemblies have been involved. The complexity of Police's operations in response to "Occupy Central" is unprecedented. Police officers are facing immense challenge and are under enormous stress. The Force management has been maintaining close liaison and communication with officers of different ranks, rendering them support and encouragement, as well as listening to their views on the operations. Police Clinical Psychologists are assigned to visit police officers at the frontline to understand their needs and the state of their morale. Since the onset of "Occupy Central", the Police have received requests for psychological counselling from a total of five police officers and immediate assistance has been provided by the Psychological Services Group. Moreover, Force Welfare Officers have offered welfare support to those wounded in the operation. Up to now, the Police do not have any reports of resignation or refusal to perform duty at areas of assemblies from regular police officers due to stress.

During the operations in recent weeks, Hong Kong Police have stood fast to their posts and performed their duties with perseverance and untiring devotion in a professional and impartial manner while exercising a high level of restraint. The HKSAR Government fully supports the Police in their continued efforts to handle with professionalism such extremely difficult tasks.

Number of casualties

The storming and confrontations at different locations of unlawful assemblies in recent days have resulted in the injury of 65 police officers. According to the records of the Fire Services Department (FSD), as at November 3, a total of 262 persons, including 40 police officers, were sent to hospital by FSD ambulances due to injury or not feeling well during the protest assemblies. FSD does not have any breakdown of other categories of persons being sent to hospital.

The impact of "Occupy Central" on emergency rescue services

The illegal occupation of a number of major trunk roads by assembly participants on Hong Kong Island and in Kowloon during "Occupy Central" has resulted in serious traffic congestion. Emergency vehicles often need to detour. Although various Government departments have been monitoring and assessing the development with a view to making corresponding arrangements, responses to some emergency calls have inevitably been delayed.

FSD has not compiled the statistics of the response time performance (RTP) of every individual ambulance/fire division since the start of "Occupy Central". Nonetheless, the department releases the RTPs of emergency ambulance services and building fire calls of the three affected areas on a daily basis. From the onset of "Occupy Central" up to November 3, the RTPs for emergency ambulance services in the three affected areas, i.e. Central (including Admiralty), Causeway Bay and Wanchai, and Mong Kok were 81.1%, 90.1% and 95.1% respectively, while the RTPs for building fire calls in Central, Causeway Bay and Wanchai, and Mong Kok were 84%, 94.1% and 86.5% respectively. The RTPs for emergency ambulance services and building fire calls in these three areas have dropped as compared to those before "Occupy Central".

The Administration reiterates that time is of vital importance in fire-fighting and rescue services as well as in emergency ambulance services. A small fire may turn into a disaster with severe loss of life and property because of a few minutes' delay. To those injured persons and patients requiring emergency ambulance services, one minute of delay can mean a difference between life and death. Hence, the Administration urges all protesters, who have illegally occupied the roads for a long span of time, to remove their obstacles as soon as possible and to leave in an orderly manner, so that the roads can be reopened to emergency vehicles for provision of timely emergency rescue services to those in need, sparing the public from unnecessary risks.

Issued at HKT 18:59

Statement by Chief Executive's Office
****

In response to a column in Apple Daily today (November 5) on the agreement signed between the Chief Executive and UGL, the Chief Executive's Office issued the following statement:

The columnist wrote that although the Chief Executive knew well that the relevant provisions in the agreement may give rise to a conflict of interest, he did not cancel the provisions but rather he added the handwritten note "provided that such assistance does not create any conflict of interest". The columnist said it was highly possible that the note was added after Mr Leung was elected as Chief Executive as he wanted to avoid conflict of interest and, at the same time, pocket the 4 million pounds.

The above accusation on the handwritten note being added after Mr Leung was elected as Chief Executive is grossly inaccurate.

Mr Leung declared that he added the handwritten note with his signature when he was signing the agreement on December 2, 2011, which was more than three months before he was elected as Chief Executive.

Mr Leung expresses deep regret over the unfounded allegations made by the columnist.

Issued at HKT 19:02

Opening remarks by Police Chief Superintendent at press conference
****

Following are the opening remarks by the Chief Superintendent of Police Public Relations Branch, Mr Hui Chun-tak, at the press conference today (November 5):

First of all, I would like to talk about the crime situation at the illegally occupied areas. The illegal occupation has lasted for more than a month and there are still daily occurrence of crimes and conflicts relating to the illegal occupation. At around 11pm last night, a man quarrelled with the illegal occupiers on Nathan Road, Mong Kok and pushed another male, who was taking photos of the incident, onto the ground and left. Police are now locating the assailant, a male of about 50 years old, suspected of common assault.

In this early morning, the illegal occupiers in Mong Kok surrounded a man who tried to enter the area and a dispute aroused. Another man slipped and was injured during the incident. To avoid further conflicts, Police escorted the man away from the scene.

I have repeatedly pointed out that the illegally occupied area in Mong Kok remains a high risk area. Radical individuals, troublemakers and people holding different views there are pronged to disputes which could easily turn into physical confrontations. The illegal occupation is the source of various conflicts and Police hope the illegal occupiers would remove the obstacles and leave. I urge protesters to remain calm and peaceful when expressing their opinions and should not resort to violence under any circumstances. Students and members of the public should stay away from the occupied area in Mong Kok and should not bring children there to avoid any unnecessary injuries.

Besides, there appears to be more and more undesirable characters mingling in the crowd in the illegally occupied areas. There is risk of youngsters being exposed to criminals who may lure them to take part in illegal activities. Police urge members of the public, youngsters in particular, to stay vigilant and guard against any undue influence by undesirable characters to engage in illegal activities. I notice that some protesters have encouraged others to hide their identity and wear masks during protests or resistance. I have to remind these people that hiding their identities could not help them to evade legal liability. I hope they would not breach the peace or even resort to violence. Others should stay away from these radical individuals and troublemakers and do not take part or be incited to take part in any act of violence. We have deployed appropriate manpower to respective areas to protect public safety and to maintain law and order. Police will take resolute enforcement actions against anyone using violence.

The second point I would like to talk about is the rule of law. I want to remind the public that the Injunction Orders regarding the illegal occupation of roads in Mong Kok and the blockage of access to CITIC Tower, Admiralty are still in force. I urge the illegal road occupiers to respect the rule of law by complying with the court orders and leave the areas soonest.

Police are committed to preserving public peace and public order. We have the responsibility to take actions against individuals who forcefully obstruct those authorised to execute the Injunction Orders. I urge the protesters, students in particular, to stay away from radical individuals and troublemakers. Do not take part or be incited to take part in any act of violence. Police will take resolute actions if radical individuals violently charge at those authorised to execute the Injunction Orders.

Members of the public are well aware of the extensive disruptions caused by the illegal blockage of major roads. The fact remains that the daily life of the general public has been seriously affected in the past month due to the illegal occupation. The business of various sectors and the livelihoods of many workers have been adversely affected. Hong Kong is a society that upholds the rule of law, which is our long-standing and treasured core value. Regrettably, the prolonged illegal occupation of roads has not only seriously affected our citizens' daily lives and livelihoods, but has also undermined our rule of law and disrupted the public order. All these will have long-term impacts on the various sectors of our society.

Hong Kong Police Force is a professional and responsible law enforcement agency. Police are politically neutral. We are duty bound to maintain law and order and to preserve public peace and ensure public safety. We are confident and capable of enforcing the laws. Police have all along displayed utmost tolerance and restraints in handling the illegal occupation because we do not want to see a large number of persons getting injured, especially students. This is out of our care and concern for the well being of the students. However, the prolonged illegal occupation of roads and the blatant defiance of court orders are endangering our foundation of the rule of law, disrupting public peace and seriously affecting the daily life and livelihoods of the public. As such, Police have all along been urging organisers of the illegal occupation to shoulder responsibility to call for an end to the illegal blockage of roads that has lasted for more than a month.

Lastly, I would like to sum up the key messages today. Firstly, there are still conflicts and crimes occurring every day in the illegally occupied areas and members of the public are urged to stay away from these areas, particularly Mong Kok. People holding different views should express their opinions in a peaceful and rational manner. Students should be mindful of undesirable characters and not be unduly influenced by them.

Secondly, the endless illegal occupation has already adversely affected the public. In the interest of protecting the students' personal safety, respecting the rule of law, restoring public order and ceasing the disruptions to the public's daily life and livelihoods, I urge organisers and participants of the illegal occupation to stop the blockage of roads promptly and to leave the areas peacefully. At this difficult time,

Police will remain steadfast and do our very best. We appeal for public cooperation with the Police so that we can continue to provide effective service to all Hong Kong citizens.

Issued at HKT 19:47

LegCo meeting to continue tomorrow
****

The following is issued on behalf of the Legislative Council Secretariat:

As the business on the agenda of the Legislative Council (LegCo) meeting cannot be finished today (November 5), the President of LegCo, Mr Jasper Tsang has, in accordance with Rule 14(4) of the Rules of Procedure, decided that the Council meeting will resume tomorrow (November 6) at 9am.

Ends/Wednesday, November 5, 2014

Issued at HKT 20:25

NOVEMBER 6[12]

HKMA's update on the operation of the banking system and financial market
****

The following is issued on behalf of the Hong Kong Monetary Authority:

According to the reports to the Hong Kong Monetary Authority (HKMA) from banks as at 8am today (November 6), one branch of one bank was affected and temporarily closed. ATMs in the affected areas have largely resumed normal operation. The HKMA has requested banks to resume normal services as soon as circumstances permit. Customers should pay attention to the relevant banks' announcements regarding affected branches and ATMs. The HKMA will also publish on its website relevant updates from time to time.

Issued at HKT 10:16

Rising traffic flow could further congest roads
****

The Transport Department (TD) today (November 6) said that, while the occupation movement has been illegally occupying roads, traffic flow at the three harbour crossings and the Aberdeen Tunnel has been returning to normal in the past weeks. The TD urges members of the public to use public transport as far as possible, and to avoid driving if it is not necessary, particularly to areas on Hong Kong Island, to prevent further increases in traffic congestion.

The TD noted that the traffic flow at the three harbour crossings and the Aberdeen Tunnel decreased by about 10 per cent in the first two weeks after roads became illegally occupied. In the following three weeks, the traffic flow at these tunnels rose gradually, particularly at the Cross Harbour Tunnel and the Eastern Harbour Crossing, and has nearly returned to the level before the illegal occupation of roads.

The TD is concerned that since roads illegally occupied on Hong Kong Island and in Mong Kok remain closed, traffic will be more seriously congested if the number of vehicles on road returns to the normal level. Motorists are urged again to avoid driving to areas on Hong Kong Island if it is not necessary. They must also abide by traffic regulations and temporary traffic control measures to prevent the already congested traffic going from bad to worse. The TD notes that motorists, for the sake of convenience, are often found making unauthorised U-turns towards Central on Harbour Road (Causeway Bay-

---

[12] http://www.info.gov.hk/gia/general/201411/06.htm

bound) outside Shui On Centre in Wan Chai. Such behaviour affects other vehicles travelling along the road and pedestrians walking across the road using pedestrian crossings. The TD reminds motorists not to act in breach of the law and pedestrians to pay attention to road safety.

Tomorrow is the day before weekend, and traffic is usually more congested. When going out, members of the public should continue to start their journeys early to allow more time for travelling, and pay attention to the latest traffic and public transport information announced by the TD and bus companies to plan their journeys in advance.

Regarding public transport services, a total of 221 bus routes are still affected today with eight bus routes suspended and 213 bus routes diverted. Among the affected bus routes, 80 routes travelling via Mong Kok are diverted due to the closure of a number of road sections in Mong Kok. A total of 20 green minibus routes travelling via Harcourt Road, Nathan Road and Argyle Street are still diverted or suspended or with service adjusted. Currently, the tram service between Percival Street and Paterson Street is still suspended. The MTR Corporation Limited is continuing to increase services for all urban lines to cope with passenger demand.

The TD's Emergency Transport Co-ordination Centre will continue to monitor the road traffic situation and public transport services. For details of road closure, traffic diversion, suspension and route diversion of green minibus services, please refer to the TD's website (www.td.gov.hk). Regarding temporary traffic arrangements for bus routes, please refer to the following bus companies' websites for details:

For routes of Citybus and New World First Bus: www.nwstbus.com.hk/en/uploadedFiles/OC2014/TAA.htm

For routes of Kowloon Motor Bus: www.kmb.hk/en

As there will be updates on bus services from time to time due to traffic changes, members of the public are advised to pay attention to the latest service arrangements announced by bus companies before starting their journeys.
Issued at HKT 18:33

Opening remarks by Police Chief Superintendent at press conference
****

Following are the opening remarks by the Chief Superintendent of Police Public Relations Branch, Mr Hui Chun-tak, at the press conference today (November 6):

First of all, I would like to talk about a few incidents on Hong Kong Island which took place between the previous evening to this early morning. Protestors wearing masks took part in processions in Causeway Bay, Admiralty and Central areas and even dashed out onto the roads.

In this early morning, more than a hundred masked protestors gathered on Lung Wo Road, Admiralty. During the incident, about 20 protestors dashed onto the eastbound carriageway and intercepted the moving vehicles there. Some of them snatched away police mills barriers and placed them in the middle of the road with a view to blocking the traffic. Some even attempted to obstruct the traffic flow by tossing coins purposely onto the carriageway. Police issued warnings to them. After that, all the protestors left.

In another incident, an 18-year-old man was seen using a 'walkie-talkie' leading about one hundred protestors, about 50 of them wearing masks, to dash onto Queensway to block eastbound traffic. He was arrested for 'unlawful assembly' and the case is now investigated by Central Police District Investigation Team. I strongly condemn such reckless and dangerous acts, which can cause serious consequence.

Earlier in the morning, at the junction of Queen's Road Central and Ice House Street, Police stopped and questioned a suspicious male who was wearing mask. The man failed to produce proof of identity. He was arrested and then released, but will be summonsed for 'failing to produce identity document'.

I also note that some protestors who were wearing masks traveled on the MTR and caused nuisance to others. Their behaviour had caused other passengers to feel concerned and worried. Since there are large crowds traveling on the MTR, I urge protestors to stop these nuisance behaviours as they may endanger public safety and public order.

I urge protesters not to disrupt public order or even resort to violence. Other protesters should stay away from these radical individuals and troublemakers. Do not take part or be incited to take part in any act of violence.

I would like to point out that some protesters encouraged others to hide their identities and wear masks during protests or resistance. I have to remind these people that hiding their identities could not help them evade legal liability. Police are capable of enforcing the laws and we will take resolute enforcement actions if anyone resorts to violence.

Secondly, I want to talk about the violent incidents occurring in the high risk area in Mong Kok. At about 11pm, people holding polarized opinions were having a dispute in Mong Kok. Police were deployed to separate them to prevent the incident from developing into a confrontation. During the incident, a radical male protestor repeatedly used the bright flash light of his mobile phone to obscure the view of Police officers and obstructed the officers from performing their duties. Despite repeated warnings, the male continued his disruptive acts. When Police decided to arrest this man, another male, aged 33, incited other protestors to charge the Police cordon line and obstruct Police officers. After repeated warnings, this

33-year-old man was arrested for the offences of 'obstructing Police officer', 'resisting arrest' and 'disorderly conduct'. During the arrest, that male put up resistance strongly and fell to the ground, resulting injury to his mouth. He was later sent to the hospital for medial treatment.

At about the same time last night in Mong Kok, two males holding polarized views were quarrelling and one of them was not happy about being video-recorded by the other using mobile phone. During the incident, a mobile phone was reportedly hit onto the ground and damaged. A 50-year-old man was later arrested for 'criminal damage'. The above two cases are now handled by Mong Kok District Investigation Team.

At about 2.30am this morning, around 200 highly emotional illegal road occupiers gathered in Mong Kok. The scene was chaotic and Police urged the protestors to remain restrained and stay clam. During the incident, a male acted against Police advice by leading and inciting others to charge at the Police cordon line, with an attempt to dash onto the road. Police had issued multiple warnings and displayed warning banners, which were however ignored. Police had no choice but to use pepper spray to contain the situation. A 24-year-old man was arrested for the offences of 'assaulting Police officer', 'resisting arrest' and 'obstructing Police officer'. The case is now handled by Mong Kok District Investigation Team.

I trust we are all well aware of the current situation in the illegally occupied area in Mong Kok, which is still a high-risk area. There are radical protesters and troublemakers mixing with other protesters in the unlawful assemblies. They incite others to disrupt public order and even to physically charge against Police. I must emphasis that Police will not tolerate any violent charging and are duty bound to take resolute action in preserving the public peace and public order.

The third point is about the law abiding awareness. I trust all Hong Kong citizens are proud of the good public order that we are enjoying and makes other metropolitan cities envy. We are concerned about the growing tendency of people not abiding by the law arising from the illegal occupation and blockage of roads.

I notice that crimes and confrontations take place every day in the illegally occupied areas. Apart from the previously mentioned confrontations, there were individuals misappropriating government or private properties, such as mills barriers, water barriers, road signs and miscellaneous items, to build obstacles for blocking roads. There were also individuals illegally abstracting electricity. Furthermore, the surfaces of the pavement and curb along Harcourt Road and Queensway were damaged, because some 60 to 70 paving bricks there were lift simply for securing banners of protestors. These are selfish and shameful acts. Should these criminal acts and the sense of lawlessness continue, the majority of the community will suffer while offenders and criminals will benefit from the deteriorating order.

I emphasis that no one can go above the rule of law irrespective of the grounds and the general public will not accept or agree to such behaviours.

I would like to sum up the key messages today. Firstly, I have to sternly warn radical protestors, trouble makers and those mask-wearing protesters. Their attempts to hide their faces would not help them to evade legal liability. Police will not tolerate any violent behaviours. We will collect evidence and will take resolute action against any illegal acts.

Secondly, there are conflicts and confrontations in the illegally occupied areas. Members of the public should stay away from radical individuals and troublemakers. Do not take part or be incited to take part in any act of violence.

Thirdly, illegal activities are still occurring in the illegally occupied areas. The community will ultimately suffer from a persistent sense of lawlessness, which is eroding the good order of Hong Kong. I urge protestors to observe the laws and not to take part in any illegal activities.

Hong Kong Police are committed to preserving public safety and public order. We will remain steadfast and do our very best in serving all Hong Kong citizens.

Issued at HKT 21:33

NOVEMBER 7[13]

Speech by FS at Economic Freedom of World and Lion Rock Institute Gala Dinner
****

Following is the speech delivered by the Financial Secretary, Mr John C Tsang, at the Economic Freedom of the World and The Lion Rock Institute Gala Dinner at the Harbour Grand Hotel last evening (November 6):

Bill (William Stacey), distinguished guests, ladies and gentlemen,

Good evening.

I am delighted to join you all this evening for the "Lion Rock Institute Economic Freedom of the World Annual Dinner" and congratulations to the 10th Anniversary.

It is always a great pleasure for me to speak with people who appreciate the strength of economic freedom; people who understand the importance of free-market principles; people like Siegfried of the Friedrich Naumann Foundation; people like Fred McMahon of the Fraser Institute. Great to have you here with us again, Fred. As you know, Fred runs the Fraser Institute's global network, among other things.

Indeed, this is an important and opportune moment for me, the Financial Secretary or perhaps today the Acting Chief Executive of Hong Kong, to thank the Fraser Institute, on behalf of the people and the businesses of Hong Kong for bestowing on us again the honour of being the world's freest economy. I am proud to add that Hong Kong has held the number-one rating every year since the Institute's first Economic Freedom report came out back in 1996. The report tells us what we have done right. It also offers timely and valuable insights into areas on which we need to work harder if we are to reap even more of the benefits that economic freedom can bring to us in Hong Kong.

The importance of applying the free-market philosophy to the formulation of Hong Kong's economic policies cannot be over-emphasised. For us, economic freedom is our core value, the linchpin of our success and the formula of our global competitiveness. Today, amid increasing interdependence in the globalised world among economies, which in some ways, unfortunately, is driving our decision makers towards a new normal - a new normal with less freedom and more regulation. The less competitive economies of the world are urging multi-national organisations to enforce the implementation of hugely burdensome and rather imposing initiatives in the post-Lehman era, raising the level of inefficiency for

---

[13] http://www.info.gov.hk/gia/general/201411/07.htm

everyone in an effort to equalise the world of competition. That is why spreading the gospel of economic freedom has become even more important now than ever.

Hong Kong is a small and open economy. We rely, heavily, on international trade. Inevitably, that reliance makes us susceptible to external shocks. Our steadfast commitment to free-market principles has indeed guided us through a variety of challenges and crises over the years. It does so by enabling market forces to bring about fast and efficient adjustments to our economy. That's economic freedom at work. It is not an exaggeration to say that economic freedom has been the cornerstone of Hong Kong's economic stability, growth and prosperity.

So, what do we mean by economic freedom? Fred has just mentioned, in the Fraser Institute's own words, "personal choice, voluntary exchange, freedom to enter markets and compete, and security of the people and privately owned property" are the essentials of economic freedom. Accordingly, the Institute measures economic freedom in five broad areas: legal system and property rights, regulations, freedom to trade internationally, access to sound money, and size of government.

Those elements should be familiar to everyone here, familiar because they are in perfect alignment with our own free market principles and governance philosophy. Let me share with you tonight my thoughts on how Hong Kong is faring in these five areas.

First, the legal system and property rights, or more broadly speaking, the rule of law as Fred has just mentioned. It is the foundation of modern society, the key element for the smooth functioning of markets. We do take pride in the fact that the rule of law is firmly established here in Hong Kong, and that it enjoys support throughout the community.

The rights and freedoms of all - individuals, businesses and organisations - are explicitly guaranteed in our constitutional document, the Basic Law. Private property rights, including intellectual property rights, are also well protected in Hong Kong. These rights have been made possible thanks to our own concerted efforts in formulating legislation, in law enforcement as well as in public education.

Judicial independence is also guaranteed by the Basic Law. It has been - and will always be - rigorously upheld. In particular, the Judiciary of Hong Kong is free from intervention of any kind by our Administration or our Legislature. And the Basic Law provides clear rules concerning the appointment and removal of judges as well as the appointment of senior judges from other common law jurisdictions to sit and make judgments on cases in our own Court of Final Appeal. That is something unique. That no other jurisdictions have the same kind of arrangement.

The continuing protests in the past few weeks in Hong Kong have raised some concerns about our rule of law. Let me take this opportunity to share my views with you. The continuing protests clearly demonstrate the freedom of speech, freedom of assembly and other fundamental human rights are protected here and are protected by the Basic Law. We shall uphold the rule of law relentlessly because it represents our core principal and serves as the cornerstone of Hong Kong's prosperity. Moreover, our vocal and unfettered media, many of them are present here today, have always been a powerful guardian of our rule of law. They articulate their concerns without fear or favour over any apparent sign of deterioration in this area.

As to those who have been challenging the rule of law by charging the cordon line and ignoring the court injunctions in the name of civil disobedience, we shall in our usual way follow the due process in dealing with all the individual case concerned after collecting the necessary evidence.

The second area is regulation, which goes hand-in-hand with the rule of law. Without the rule of law, regulations cannot be effectively enforced, no matter how well-deliberated and how business-friendly they are. In this regard, I am pleased to note that the Institute's 2014 report ranked Hong Kong first, once again, in this area.

Hong Kong has always provided a secure and predictable regulatory environment, and a level playing field, for local and overseas companies alike. We are a faithful practitioner of the nationality-neutral principle. We treat everyone, every business, every organisation the same way, regardless of their nationality. We apply the same rules and same regulations to everyone alike. We allow everyone to enjoy the same privileges accorded by, for example, our free trade agreements and other international agreements. We operate a true level playing field, unlike other jurisdictions in our region.

We are continuing to improve our regulatory environment. Under our "Be the Smart Regulator" Programme, we promote business efficiency by cutting red tape, eliminating outdated and burdensome regulations, enhancing regulatory efficiency and transparency, and reducing business compliance costs.

Let me give you an example: we have designed a one-stop, online electronic service for company incorporation and business registration that can actually issue both of these certificates to an applicant in just 15 minutes. This is almost equivalent to the speed of Usain Bolt.

Our labour-market regulations are another example of how carefully we formulate economic policies. The statutory minimum wage, which, I believe, many of you think is totally unnecessary, came into effect in May 2011. We have been able to strike a delicate balance in the implementation of this policy. To date, the policy has been successful in forestalling excessively low wages and in helping the vulnerable, while preserving Hong Kong's virtually full employment. We may have been fortunate in introducing this policy during an up-cycle, if you really think the past few years can be so considered, but we are also mindful of the longer-term impact of minimum wage on labour-market dynamics, particularly during times of less vibrant economic performance.

Moving on to cross border trade. Even though the benefits of trade have been known since the times of Adam Smith and David Ricardo, protectionism continues to prevail, and continues to be a barrier to international trade. Our inability to conclude the Doha round with the implementation of the Bali agreement, which I think is basically a modest collection of facilitation measures, is a good example of how far some economies will go to obstruct free trade in order to protect their own national interests by leveraging on the welfare of the least developed economies. This is unacceptable and will ultimately damage the credibility as well as the effectiveness of the WTO, which is now the only multi-lateral trade organisation left.

To this end, I can proudly say that we remain a staunch supporter of free trade and open markets. A free port, Hong Kong imposes no tariff on exports or imports. We do not exercise any form of capital control, and we have no restrictions on the flow of information.

Thanks to our institutional strengths and geographical location, Hong Kong has been able to provide an unmatched environment for conducting international business. And that, together with the Mainland's rapid development, has enabled us to become a leading trade, business and services hub.

Consider the following. In 2013, our trade in goods and services totalled some 460 per cent of our GDP. That placed us among the world's top economies in terms of openness to trade. More than 7,000 overseas companies operate in Hong Kong. About 4,000 of them use Hong Kong as their regional headquarters or regional offices. This underlines Hong Kong's high degree of freedom to engage in international trade and our openness to foreign investment.

On to "sound money". We have fared less well in this area of assessment, given the criteria that the Institute has employed and the monetary system that has worked effectively for us in the last three decades. I do not want to dispute the fine points of these criteria, but I feel that the assessors should give greater consideration to our highly successful monetary system, which has brought a lot of stability to Hong Kong.

Under the Linked Exchange Rate System, prices and domestic costs in Hong Kong adjust quickly in aligning our macroeconomic conditions with external changes. This reflects, in a positive way, our economy's price flexibility, which allows for efficient adjustments in our macro-fundamentals to stay in sync with the ebbs and flows of global business. Thanks to our long-standing, transparent, rule-based currency-board system, Hong Kong is blessed with one of the world's most consistent and effective monetary policies.

Finally, let us look at the size of government. We believe in the efficiency of the private sector. We believe that the government should leave sufficient room in the economy to allow the private sector to flourish. Hong Kong has chosen to limit the size of government to accomplish this objective. We believe that, by keeping the public sector small, more resources in our community can be taken up by the private sector, the latter being more flexible and has the uncanny ability to allocate these limited resources in a more efficient manner.

Hong Kong has a simple tax system anchored by a low tax rate. Our maximum salaries tax rate is 15 per cent, while our profits tax rate is a flat 16.5 per cent - both among the lowest in the world. A simple, low tax regime minimises decision-making distortions made by companies and individuals; it also helps keep compliance and enforcement costs low.

Given our commitment to low tax rates, we need to conduct our fiscal policies with prudence. Hong Kong is virtually debt-free, with government debt at just 0.5 per cent of GDP. The debts issued in recent years under the Government Bond Programme are of my making. I need to take responsibility of that. But they are not intended for the financing of further government spending, but for promoting the development of the local bond market. We have been able to invest the money raised through the Bond issuances and keep them away from the sticky fingers of our Legislative Councillors. The rewards and the returns that we are getting will be used for worthwhile projects in the future.

Our recurrent government expenditure has remained steady over the past five years, at about 13 per cent of GDP. This low level of expenditure reflects, in part, our determination to maintain rationality and pragmatism in our policies, and not fall prey to calls for politically motivated populist measures.

We have focussed instead on fostering a favourable business environment. For Hong Kong, that means creating employment opportunities, while providing a social safety net for people who are genuinely in need. The fact that we have been able to maintain full employment in our community, currently at 3.3 per cent, and social welfare spending has continue to account for only a small share of total government expenditure in recent years are clear signs that that our policies are working effectively.

Some of you may have noted that our government expenditure related to infrastructure investment has increased in recent years. I believe that infrastructure spending, when used appropriately, represents investment that can reap significant benefits by enhancing Hong Kong's productive capacity in the longer term. It is also a useful tool to stimulate the economy during a slow down period. It is clearly the result of fiscal prudence that we have the choice and the resources to support such infrastructure spending and to roll out counter-cyclical measures to stabilise the economy when it became necessary.

Despite our solid fiscal position, we are not complacent. As mentioned, I set up a Working Group on Long-term Fiscal Planning last year. Its purpose was to assess our fiscal sustainability, given the immense challenges posed by Hong Kong's low fertility rate and aging population.

Since the release of the study's report, I have also rolled out a series of expenditure-control measures, with the aim of re-engineering and re-prioritising government department spending initiatives to help maximise the effectiveness and efficiency of our public services.

In short, Ladies and Gentlemen, our commitment to the free market is absolute. We value, and we take pride in, Hong Kong's number-one ranking in the Fraser Institute's economic freedom index. Thank you very much. But more importantly, we need to sustain and protect the market institutions that have been working effectively in Hong Kong. We need to remain committed to our core values. We need to protect these core values and there are no shortcuts to developing, and maintaining, a genuinely free economy.

We are in it for the long haul, rain or shine, for the long term benefit of the people of Hong Kong.

Thank you very much.

Issued at HKT 00:21

Special arrangements on submission of tenders arising from temporary closure of Government Secretariat Tender Box
****

Owing to the special access arrangements at the Central Government Offices (CGO) in Tamar, the Government Secretariat Tender Box (GSTB) located on the ground floor of the East Wing of CGO is closed for tender deposit temporarily.

All tenders that should originally be deposited into the GSTB are instead requested to be deposited into the Government Logistics Department Tender Box (GLDTB) located on the ground floor of North Point Government Offices at 333 Java Road, North Point. This special arrangement came into effect on September 30 this year until further notice.

Tenderers may wish to check in advance their route to the GLDTB and allow sufficient time to make arrangements to deposit their tenders into the GLDTB before the respective closing time of tenders. Late tenders will not be accepted.

For enquiries, please call 2810 2497 or 2231 5288 between 9am and 6pm from Mondays to Fridays (except public holidays).

Issued at HKT 08:31

HKMA's update on the operation of the banking system and financial market
****

The following is issued on behalf of the Hong Kong Monetary Authority:

According to the reports to the Hong Kong Monetary Authority (HKMA) from banks as at 8am today (November 7), one branch of one bank was affected and temporarily closed. ATMs in the affected areas have largely resumed normal operation. The HKMA has requested banks to resume normal services as soon as circumstances permit. Customers should pay attention to the relevant banks' announcements regarding affected branches and ATMs. The HKMA will also publish on its website relevant updates from time to time.

Issued at HKT 09:38

Avoid driving to congested roads on Hong Kong Island
****

The Transport Department (TD) today (November 7) said that the very busy traffic on Hong Kong Island this morning, with a traffic accident and a vehicle breakdown in Wan Chai, caused serious traffic congestion at Gloucester Road. Traffic is anticipated to be very congested tomorrow due to a public procession in the afternoon and a football match at Hong Kong Stadium in the evening. Members of the public should avoid driving to parts of Hong Kong Island.

Due to the traffic accident at inner Gloucester Road near Fleming Road in Wan Chai during the morning rush hours, Gloucester Road (Central bound) was very congested. About half an hour later, a bus broke down on the slow lane of Hennessy Road near Anton Street, and the slow lane of Hennessy Road towards Central was closed temporarily. The two incidents seriously affected the traffic towards Central at Gloucester Road and Hennessy Road.

While a number of roads are currently closed due to the occupation movement, and the number of vehicles on the roads is rising, any unexpected incident will disrupt further the already severely congested traffic. The TD reminds members of the public and motorists that traffic on Hong Kong Island remains unstable. They are advised to exercise patience and be mindful of road safety at all time.

Special traffic and transport arrangements will be implemented from Causeway Bay to Central tomorrow afternoon for a public procession. A total of 63 bus routes and three green minibus routes operating in the affected areas will be temporarily diverted. Due to the road closure arrangements caused by the occupation movement, the TD anticipates that the traffic from Causeway Bay to Central will be very congested.

In addition, a football match will be held at Hong Kong Stadium in the evening tomorrow, and special traffic and transport arrangements will be implemented in So Kon Po and Causeway Bay. The TD anticipates that traffic in the vicinity of So Kon Po and Causeway Bay will be congested. Motorists are advised to avoid driving to the affected areas. Members of the public planning to go to the affected areas are advised to use public transport as far as possible. Actual implementation of the traffic arrangement will be made depending on traffic and crowd conditions in the area. In case of traffic congestion, motorists should exercise tolerance and patience, and follow the instructions of the Police.

Regarding public transport services, a total of 223 bus routes are still affected today with eight bus routes suspended and 215 bus routes diverted. Among the affected bus routes, 80 routes travelling via Mong Kok are diverted due to the closure of a number of road sections in Mong Kok. A total of 20 green minibus routes travelling via Harcourt Road, Nathan Road and Argyle Street are still diverted or suspended or with service adjusted. Currently, the tram service between Percival Street and Paterson Street is still suspended. The MTR Corporation Limited continues to increase services for all urban lines to cope with passenger demand.

The TD's Emergency Transport Co-ordination Centre will continue to monitor the road traffic situation and public transport services. For details of road closure, traffic diversion, suspension and route diversion of green minibus services, please refer to the TD's website (www.td.gov.hk). Regarding temporary traffic arrangements for bus routes, please refer to the following bus companies' websites for details:

For routes of Citybus and New World First Bus: www.nwstbus.com.hk/en/uploaded-Files/OC2014/TAA.htm

For routes of Kowloon Motor Bus: www.kmb.hk/en

As there will be updates on bus services from time to time due to traffic changes, members of the public are advised to pay attention to the latest service arrangements announced by bus companies before starting their journeys.
Issued at HKT 17:31

Opening remarks by Police Senior Superintendent at press conference
****

Following are the opening remarks by the Senior Superintendent of Police Public Relations Branch, Mr Kong Man-keung, at the press conference today (November 7):

First of all, I would like to talk about the series of confrontations happened in the illegally occupied area in Mong Kok on Wednesday night. I noticed that there are various reports on the incidents. Regrettably some of them are inaccurate and may be misleading. I therefore would like to take this opportunity to provide an overall and accurate picture on what had happened.

At about 11pm on Wednesday, there were large crowds gathering in front of the barricade at the junction of Nathan Road and Argyle Street. Many of them were wearing masks and safety helmets. They disputed with another group of people holding a different view. Police separated them to prevent confrontation and protect them. However, some radical protestors repeatedly used the bright flash light of mobile phones as torches to shine on Police officers continuously to obscure their view and obstructed the officers from performing their duties. Despite repeated warnings, a male continued his disorderly act, and verbally abused and provoked Police officers.

When Police attempted to arrest this man, a 33-year-old man incited other protestors to create chaos, attemptting to charge and obstruct police officers. After giving repeated warnings, the 33-year-old man was arrested for 'obstructing police officer', 'resisting arrest' and 'disorderly conduct'. During the arrest, the man resisted and fell to the ground, resulting in injury to his mouth. He was later sent to hospital for medical treatment. Meanwhile, the man who used flashlight to obstruct Police had escaped in the middle of the chaos.

In the course of the event, some protestors, wearing masks and equipped with improvised shoulder and arm pads, hurled abuse at Police officers and had a stand off with the Police. These troublemakers subsequently backed down when Police reinforcement arrived. At about the same time, Police arrested a 50-year-old man for 'criminal damage'. Both cases are now being handled by District Investigation Team of Mong Kok District.

At about 2am yesterday, more than a hundred radical protestors and troublemakers, some wearing helmets, staged another organised confrontation with the Police line. They hurled abuse and acted provocatively, while some even threw safety helmets and miscellaneous items at Police officers. The situation was very chaotic. Despite Police's repeated warnings, the display of yellow warning banners on the possible use of force and the on guard baton position adopted by officers, these protestors continued their violent acts and repeatedly charged at Police line with umbrellas. Under such circumstances, Police used pepper spray to restore order to prevent the situation from further deteriorating. During the incident, Police arrested a 24-year-old man for 'obstructing Police Officer' and 'resisting arrest'.

During these confrontations in Mong Kok, Police had arrested three men aged from 24 to 50. We have also received two complaints against Police, including the previously mentioned 33-year-old arrested person, and a 32-year-old male who alleged being assaulted by Police. The Complaints Against Police Office will investigate these complaints in a fair and impartial manner. And we hope the complainants could provide sufficient information for the investigation.

As for another protestor who alleged being hit by Police on the head and being kicked for multiple times, when being enquired by Police, he came up with another version which is different from what he had told the media. He told Police that he was assaulted by an unidentified individual in plainclothes with a hard object. The man was later sent to the hospital for treatment, where he refused to provide any statement and did not lodge any complaint against Police. He left the hospital without receiving any medical treatment. The case was classified as 'assault occasioning actual bodily harm' and is being investigated by District Investigation Team of Mong Kok District.

The second point is about Mong Kok remains a high risk area. The chaotic situation that took place in Mong Kok on Wednesday further proved that Mong Kok remains a high risk area. Radical individuals, troublemakers and people holding polarised views are gathering there, and quarrels and physical confrontations are frequent. The risk of serious confrontation is escalating. Some radical individuals and troublemakers deliberately incited other people to provoke Police officers or to charge at Police cordon line with a view to creating chaos.

I urge protesters, students in particular, to stay away from radical individuals and troublemakers. Do not mix with these radicals in the crowd. Do not take part or be incited to take part in any act of violence and do not charge at Police. When Police are taking enforcement actions, do not put up resistance. Protesters should stay calm and maintain a safe distance from the Police officers. We do not want to see protestors, students in particular, getting hurt when they place themselves close to radical individuals and troublemakers during confrontations.

Thirdly, I would like to remind the public that the Injunction Orders regarding the illegal occupation of roads in Mong Kok and blockage of access to CITIC Tower, Admiralty, are still in force. I urge the illegal road occupiers to respect the rule of law by complying with the court orders and to leave the areas soonest.

Police are committed to preserving public peace and public order. We have the responsibility to take actions when individuals forcibly obstruct those authorised to execute the Injunction Orders. Police will take resolute actions if radical individuals violently charge at those authorised to execute the Injunction Orders.

To conclude, I would like to sum up the key messages today. Firstly, the confrontations in Mong Kok in the night of Wednesday were deliberately staged by radical protestors and troublemakers. They provoked Police officers in an organised manner and our officers had tried their very best to maintain the law and order. Confronted by repeated violent charging, officers at scene had to use the minimum level of force to restore order and to prevent the situation from further deteriorating.

Secondly, it is evident that Mong Kok remains a high risk area where large-scale confrontations can be sparked off at any moment. Members of the public should stay away from the illegally occupied areas. I urge people holding different opinions to express their views in a peaceful and rational manner. Students, in particular, should stay away from radical individuals and not be incited by them to commit illegal acts or to resort to the use of violence, so as to avoid unnecessary injuries.

Thirdly, illegal road occupiers should respect the rule of law. They should not obstruct those authorised to execute the Injunction Orders. Police will remain impartial and steadfast in maintaining law and order. We will continue do our very best in serving all citizens of Hong Kong.

Issued at HKT 20:15

NOVEMBER 8[14]

Cases arising from illegal occupation[15]
****

Police today (November 8) presented information of cases which occurred the day before arising from the illegal occupation.

The illegal occupation has lasted for more than a month. There are still daily occurrence of crimes in the illegally occupied areas. At 4am this morning, a 26-year-old man reported to Police that his mobile phone valued at $8,000 was stolen while he was sleeping underneath a footbridge near 16 to 18 Harcourt Road, Central. The "Theft" case is now being investigated by Central District Investigation Team.

A Police spokesman pointed out that more and more notorious characters are present in the illegally occupied areas. Criminals can easily take advantage of the deteriorating situation. He reminded the public to take care of their personal properties and that youngsters should be vigilant of the risk of being lured to take part in illegal activities.

On cyber crime, Police noted that there were persons inciting others on the social media platforms to participate in illegal assembly, cause obstruction and block the access to a place in Central on a specified date. Upon investigation, the Technology Crime Division of the Commercial Crime Bureau arrested a 25-year-old man, surnamed "Yau", at about 7.45pm last evening in Mong Kok. The case has now been classified as "Access to Computer with Criminal and Dishonest Intent".

Since September 26, Police have arrested 14 persons, including 11 males and 3 females, aged 13 to 39, for the offences of "Access to Computer with Criminal and Dishonest Intent" and "Criminal Intimidation".

Police remind members of the public that the Internet environment is not a lawless virtual world. Illegal acts committed in the cyber world will be sanctioned by laws and the offenders will have to shoulder the criminal liability. The majority of the laws of Hong Kong are equally applicable to the cyber world. The public should refrain from committing unlawful acts on the Internet. Inciting others to commit criminal acts on the Internet is likewise illegal. Police will collect evidence, conduct follow up investigation and make arrest when there is sufficient evidence.

At around 6pm yesterday (November 7), a male police constable, on his way to Kwai Chung Police Station to report duty, was assaulted by a man near the Kwai Fong MTR Station. He sustained injuries to his head, face and hands. After uttering intimidating remarks, the assailant fled. The police constable

---

[14] http://www.info.gov.hk/gia/general/201411/08.htm
[15] The Hong Kong Police Public Relations Bureau also announced that it will not hold any more daily press conferences about the protests starting today. From now on, press conferences will be held as needed.

gave chase but in vain. He was sent to hospital where he was treated and discharged. The case is now classified as "Assault Occasioning Actual Bodily Harm" under the investigation by Kwai Tsing District Crime Squad.

The Police spokesman stated that the police constable had been deployed to the illegally occupied areas in Mong Kok and Admiralty for duty. Police are investigating whether the motive involved in the case is related to the illegal occupation.

Police condemn such violent acts, stressing that Police will not tolerate any violence. Police will take decisive enforcement actions against illegal acts in a fair and impartial manner regardless of the background of any person involved.

Issued at HKT 16:11

Police urge protestors in Admiralty to desist from acts endangering public order
****

Police urge the protestors presently gathering on the footbridge connecting the Admiralty Centre and Central Government Offices (November 8) to remain calm and restrained. They should express their views in a peaceful and rational manner and desist from acts that endangering public order.

At about 7pm, some protestors gathered and placed mills barriers on the footbridge in an attempt to block the access to the Central Government Offices. Police took actions immediately and removed the mills barriers. Police condemned such acts of the protestors which disrupted public order.

Police appeal to the protestors at scene to adhere to the instructions of Police officers. Police reiterate that any acts endangering public order and public safety will not be tolerated. The Hong Kong community regard that individuals should express their views in a rational and peaceful manner.

Issued at HKT 22:40

NOVEMBER 9[16]

Motorists and pedestrians urged to observe road safety
****

The Transport Department (TD) today (November 9) said that the number of vehicles on roads is rising, motorists are advised to drive with extra care and pedestrians should pay attention to traffic condition to avoid accidents. People are in a hurry to reach their destinations while a number of roads are currently closed due to the occupation movement, but they should still observe road safety.

As the weather is unsettled with occasional rain patches, motorists are urged to reduce speed and to keep a distance between themselves and the vehicle in front. Pedestrians are also advised to take heed of traffic while crossing the roads, particularly at busy junctions or when their view is obstructed. Affected by the occupation movement, impact on traffic and public transport services would be considerable if there are any unforeseen incidents on roads.

Meanwhile, a public procession will be held in Central and Western District this afternoon. Traffic lanes on Queen's Road Central and Queen's Road West will be intermittently closed starting from about 2.30pm. It is anticipated that traffic in Central and Western District will be congested. Actual implementation of the traffic arrangement will be made depending on traffic and crowd conditions in the area. Motorists should drive safely, exercise tolerance and patience, and follow the instructions of the Police.

Regarding public transport services, since today is a public holiday, fewer bus routes are affected than that on a working day. Nonetheless, a total of 141 bus routes are affected today with eight bus routes suspended and 133 bus routes diverted. A total of 20 green minibus routes travelling via Harcourt Road, Nathan Road and Argyle Street are still diverted or suspended or with service adjusted. Currently, the tram service between Percival Street and Paterson Street is still suspended. The MTR Corporation Limited continues to increase services for all urban lines to cope with passenger demand.

The TD's Emergency Transport Co-ordination Centre will continue to monitor the road traffic situation and public transport services. For details of road closure, traffic diversion, suspension and route diversion of green minibus services, please refer to the TD's website (www.td.gov.hk). Regarding temporary traffic arrangements for bus routes, please refer to the following bus companies' websites for details:

For routes of Citybus and New World First Bus: www.nwstbus.com.hk/en/uploadedFiles/OC2014/TAA.htm

---

[16] http://www.info.gov.hk/gia/general/201411/09.htm

For routes of Kowloon Motor Bus: www.kmb.hk/en

As there will be updates on bus services from time to time due to traffic changes, members of the public are advised to pay attention to the latest service arrangements announced by bus companies before starting their journeys.

Issued at HKT 11:53

Transcript of remarks by CE at media session in Beijing
****

Following is the transcript of remarks by the Chief Executive, Mr C Y Leung, at a media session in Beijing today (November 9):

Reporter: You said you are going to restore the law and order in Hong Kong to develop the financial markets. Does it mean that you are clearing the scene soon? Did President Xi Jinping give you any advice on how to handle the occupy campaign?

Chief Executive: We cannot make public any Police operation, any road clearance operation of our Police Force as a result of the Occupy Central campaign. Like all Police operations, it will not be announced beforehand.

Issued at HKT 15:27

Incidents and cases relating to illegal occupation
****

Police today (November 9) provided information of incidents and cases which occurred the day before and were related to the illegal occupation.

The illegal occupation has lasted for about one and a half months. There are still daily occurrence of incidents and cases relating to the illegal occupation. Earlier, there were messages posted on the social media platforms inciting others to participate in an illegal assembly in Central. Police already arrested a man for "Access to Computer with Criminal and Dishonest Intent" in Mong Kok on November 7. Yesterday afternoon (November 8), Police spotted a suspicious man at the venue concerned. Police officers intercepted him and found about 200 stainless steel cable ties and five bicycle chain locks in his rucksack. He refused to explain the possession of the items and was arrested for "Possession of instruments fit for unlawful purpose". This 27-year-old man has been released on bail and will report back in early December. The case is being investigated by Central District Investigation Team.

At around 7pm yesterday evening, tens of protestors responded to online appeals and gathered at the footbridge connecting the Admiralty Centre and Central Government Offices. Some of them wore facemasks, goggles or surgical masks. They attempted to block the passage with mills barriers and rubbish bins. Police took immediate action to clear the mills barriers and urged the protestors to leave. They all left the scene before midnight.

Police spokesman condemned the acts of the protestors which disrupted public order. He reminded the youngsters to stay vigilant towards messages posted online. They should avoid being incited by radical individuals and troublemakers to commit any illegal acts. Members of the public should comply with the laws and social order when expressing their views. Police do not wish to see a growing tendency of people not abiding by the law in the community.

At around 12am today, a man quarrelled with illegal road occupiers at the junction of Argyle Street and Portland Street, Mong Kok. Police officers attended the scene to separate the two parties and escorted the man away.

The spokesman stated that the illegally occupied area in Mong Kok remains a high risk area, with radical individuals, troublemakers and people holding polarised views gathering there. There are frequent quarrels and disputes. There is a high possibility for more confrontations or violent acts. Members of the public and students, in particular parents with children, are urged to stay away from these illegally occupied areas to avoid unnecessary injuries.

In addition to the mobile phone theft case which happened on Harcourt Road, Central in the small hours yesterday, Police received report of another case at around 8.40am today. A man, who stole a mobile phone valued at $3,000 from a tent on Nathan Road, Mong Kok, was stopped and handed over to Police. The 41-year-old man was arrested for "Theft". The case is being handled by Mong Kok District Investigation Team.

The spokesman pointed out that more and more notorious characters are present in the illegally occupied areas. Criminals can easily take advantage of the deteriorating situation. He reminded the public to take care of their personal properties and that youngsters, in particular students, should be vigilant of the risk of being lured to take part in illegal activities.

Issued at HKT 16:43

NOVEMBER 10[17]

HKMA welcomes launch of Shanghai-Hong Kong Stock Connect
****

The following is issued on behalf of the Hong Kong Monetary Authority:

The Hong Kong Monetary Authority (HKMA) welcomes today's announcement of the launch of Shanghai-Hong Kong Stock Connect on November 17.

The Chief Executive of the HKMA, Mr Norman Chan, said "I am very pleased to see the Shanghai-Hong Kong Stock Connect coming into operation next week, following intensive discussions and preparations by the stock exchanges and authorities in the Mainland and Hong Kong. This marks an important milestone in the liberalisation of the Mainland's capital account, allowing overseas investors to invest in the Mainland A-share market through Hong Kong, and Mainland investors to trade Hong Kong shares through Shanghai. The linking of the Hong Kong and Shanghai stock markets will also propel the development of offshore renminbi (RMB) business in Hong Kong to new heights."

From November 10, the HKMA is offering intraday RMB funds of up to RMB 10 billion to authorised institutions participating in RMB business in Hong Kong. Earlier, the HKMA has designated seven banks as Primary Liquidity Providers for the offshore RMB market in Hong Kong and is providing a dedicated repo facility to each of them. With the commencement of Shanghai-Hong Kong Stock Connect, these measures will assist banks in managing their RMB liquidity.

Issued at HKT 09:42

HKMA's update on the operation of the banking system and financial market
****

The following is issued on behalf of the Hong Kong Monetary Authority:

According to the reports to the Hong Kong Monetary Authority (HKMA) from banks as at 9am today (November 10), all previously affected bank branches have resumed operation. One branch of one bank would shorten its business hours today. The HKMA has requested banks to resume normal services as soon as circumstances permit. Customers should pay attention to the relevant banks' announcements regarding affected branches and ATMs. The HKMA will also publish on its website relevant updates from time to time.

---

[17] http://www.info.gov.hk/gia/general/201411/10.htm

Issued at HKT 09:58

CE welcomes launching of Shanghai-Hong Kong Stock Connect
****

The Chief Executive, Mr C Y Leung, welcomed in Beijing today (November 10) the approval by the China Securities Regulatory Commission and the Securities and Futures Commission to the official launching of the pilot programme to provide mutual trading access between the Shanghai and Hong Kong stock markets (Shanghai-Hong Kong Stock Connect)commencing next Monday (November 17).

The Chief Executive expressed his sincere thanks to the state leaders and the Central Government for trusting and supporting Hong Kong. While wishing the Shanghai-Hong Kong Stock Connect a smooth implementation, the Chief Executive believed that Hong Kong's financial market could make greater contribution to the reform and opening up of the country as well as the stability and prosperity of Hong Kong.

Issued at HKT 10:10

HKSAR Government welcomes official launch of Shanghai-Hong Kong Stock Connect
****

The China Securities Regulatory Commission and the Securities and Futures Commission issued a joint announcement today (November 10), announcing their approval of the official launch of the Shanghai-Hong Kong Stock Connect on November 17. The Hong Kong Special Administrative Region Government welcomed the announcement.

The Shanghai-Hong Kong Stock Connect is a mutually beneficial collaboration project. Through enhancing mutual stock market access between Hong Kong and Shanghai, the programme promotes the gradual opening up of the Mainland's capital accounts as well as the internationalisation of the Renminbi (RMB). The collaboration project will reinforce Hong Kong's position as a premier international financial centre and also strengthen Hong Kong's role as an offshore RMB business centre.

The Financial Secretary, Mr John C Tsang, said, "I am very pleased that the Shanghai-Hong Kong Stock Connect is confirmed to be launched next Monday. The preparatory work of the Shanghai-Hong Kong Stock Connect has been carried out in a step-by-step manner from its conception to rollout. It is gratifying for me to note the relevant Central Authorities' staunch support for us in the process. The relevant regulatory authorities of the two sides as well as exchanges and clearing companies of Hong Kong and Shanghai have carried out tremendous preparatory work, and I would like to thank all relevant colleagues for their efforts over the past years. The Shanghai-Hong Kong Stock Connect will be implemented very soon. We will continue to exert our best efforts to carry out various monitoring and risk management work so that the Shanghai-Hong Kong Stock Connect will contribute to the economic and financial reforms of our country and reinforce Hong Kong's position as an international financial centre."

The pilot programme on mutual stock market access between Hong Kong and Shanghai was announced by Premier Li Keqiang at the opening ceremony of the Bo'ao Forum on April 10. It will allow eligible Mainland investors to trade directly for the first time in eligible stocks listed on the Stock Exchange of Hong Kong (SEHK) through the Shanghai Stock Exchange (SSE). At the same time, it will also allow Hong Kong and overseas investors to trade for the first time in eligible stocks listed on the SSE through the SEHK directly.

Since the Shanghai-Hong Kong Stock Connect is a pilot project, it will be implemented in a progressive and risk-controlled manner, and cross-border investment will be subject to quotas. The aggregate net purchase of SSE securities by Hong Kong and overseas investors will be capped by a limit of RMB300 billion and there is a daily net purchase quota of RMB13 billion. Similarly, the purchase of SEHK securities by eligible Mainland investors will be capped by an aggregate net quota of RMB250 billion and a daily net quota of RMB10.5 billion. The quotas may be subject to appropriate adjustments in accordance with the actual operational circumstances.

Issued at HKT 15:43

Transcript of remarks by SED
****

Following is the transcript of remarks by the Secretary for Education, Mr Eddie Ng Hak-kim, at a media session after attending the opening ceremony of "Making the Future of Our Younger Generation - Life Planning Education Forum" this afternoon (November 10):

Reporter: One of the reports of the Hong Kong Examinations and Assessment Authority claims that schools should go deeper into the education of the rule of law instead of just educating students about executing the law or obeying the law. How will the bureau execute later to have a better education on that?

Secretary for Education: The public examination/assessment is the responsibility of the Hong Kong Examinations and Assessment Authority. Every year, after the public examination, they would do a summary. The purpose of the summary is to share among the teachers and schools about the performance of individual subjects, without names of students, of course. By doing so, hopefully every year teachers and schools will be able to pick up whatever the learning points or lessons to learn, in order to improve further the teaching and learning process. From this particular case, my understanding is that actually the concept of the rule of law is something much broader than what it is about execution as well as the compliance of law. It is much broader than that. So the idea is to pick up this particular extreme example as a point of learning so that people understand they need to take a more multi perspective of each and every definition. This is also part of the multi-angle learning. Thank you.

Issued at HKT 17:11

Public transport services and transport trade business affected by occupy movement
****

The Transport Department (TD) today (November 10) said that a number of roads on Hong Kong Island and in Kowloon have continued to be illegally occupied by protesters for over 40 days, and this has caused a great impact on the operation of public transport services and people working in the transport trade.

The transport trade, including taxis, public light buses, trams, non-franchised buses and trucks, has repeatedly said that the occupy movement has dealt the trade a heavy blow. The road closures have resulted in traffic congestion and doubled journey time, causing members of the public to avoid using road-based public transport. Some public transport services have had to make a detour or even suspend their services, causing inconvenience to commuters and loss of business to the transport trade.

Meanwhile, if the occupy movement continues and public transport services such as bus services are still unable to resume as normal, frontline staff members will continue to work under great pressure. The TD again called on the protesters illegally occupying the roads to retreat from the carriageways of major trunk roads such as Harcourt Road, to let traffic, public transport services and the daily life of members of the public return to normal.

The TD also observed that there has recently been a growing amount of traffic flow and that serious traffic congestion occurred on inner Gloucester Road in Wan Chai this afternoon. If the traffic flow continues to rise, it may paralyse the traffic on Hong Kong Island. The TD again urged motorists to avoid driving, especially to Hong Kong Island, as far as possible to give public transport services priority over road use.

Regarding public transport services, a total of 223 bus routes were still affected today, with eight bus routes suspended and 215 bus routes diverted. Among the affected bus routes, 80 routes travelling via Mong Kok are diverted due to the closure of a number of road sections in Mong Kok. A total of 20 green minibus routes travelling via Harcourt Road, Nathan Road and Argyle Street are still diverted or suspended or with service adjusted. Currently, the tram service between Percival Street and Paterson Street is still suspended. The MTR Corporation Limited continues to increase services for all urban lines to cope with passenger demand.

The TD's Emergency Transport Co-ordination Centre will continue to monitor the road traffic situation and public transport services. For details of road closure, traffic diversion, suspension and route diversion of green minibus services, please refer to the TD's website (www.td.gov.hk). Regarding temporary traffic arrangements for bus routes, please refer to the following bus companies' websites for details:

For routes of Citybus and New World First Bus: www.nwstbus.com.hk/en/uploadedFiles/OC2014/TAA.htm .

For routes of Kowloon Motor Bus: www.kmb.hk/en .

As there will be updates on bus services from time to time due to traffic changes, members of the public are advised to pay attention to the latest service arrangements announced by bus companies before starting their journeys.
Issued at HKT 19:29

LegCo to debate motion on devising constitution by all people, making new covenant, and realizing genuine "Hong Kong people ruling Hong Kong"
****
The following is issued on behalf of the Legislative Council Secretariat:

The Legislative Council (LegCo) will hold a meeting on Wednesday (November 12) at 11am in the Chamber of the LegCo Complex. During the meeting, Members will debate a motion on devising the constitution by all people, making a new covenant, and realizing genuine "Hong Kong people ruling Hong Kong".

The motion, to be moved by Mr Wong Yuk-man, states: "That this Council requests the Chief Executive and all accountability officials to resign en masse with civil servants maintaining the daily operation of the SAR Government, to be followed by immediately establishing a constitutional amendments convention on Hong Kong Affairs to amend the Basic Law; based on the Universal Declaration of Human Rights and the Hong Kong Bill of Rights Ordinance, the new constitution should precisely determine the scope of Hong Kong's right of autonomy and the definition of defence and foreign affairs; a referendum law should be enacted to give Hong Kong people the right of initiative and referendum of laws; a political party law to regulate the operation of political parties and a political donations law to require political parties to disclose their received political donations should also be enacted; candidates for the office of the

Chief Executive should be permitted to have political party background, and Legislative Council Members should be allowed to introduce bills relating to government policies without the written consent of the Chief Executive; and after the passage of a new constitution by referendum of Hong Kong people, dual universal suffrage for the Chief Executive and the Legislative Council elections should be conducted with nominations jointly endorsed by citizens, so as to manifest 'direct democracy' and realize genuine 'Hong Kong people ruling Hong Kong'."

Mr Lee Cheuk-yan will move an amendment to Mr Wong Yuk-man's motion.

Mr James To will move a proposed resolution under section 34(4) of the Interpretation and General Clauses Ordinance to seek the Council's approval to extend the period for amending the Inland Revenue (Double Taxation Relief and Prevention of Fiscal Evasion with respect to Taxes on Income) (Republic of Korea) Order and the Inland Revenue (Double Taxation Relief and Prevention of Fiscal Evasion with respect to Taxes on Income) (Socialist Republic of Vietnam) (Amendment) Order 2014 laid on the table of the Council on October 22, 2014 to the meeting of December 10, 2014.

Mr Dennis Kwok will also move a proposed resolution under section 34(4) of the Interpretation and General Clauses Ordinance to seek the Council's approval to extend the period for amending the Overseas Lawyers (Qualification for Admission) (Amendment) Rules 2014 (Commencement) Notice laid on the table of the Council on October 22, 2014 to the meeting of December 10, 2014.

Ms Cyd Ho will move a proposed resolution under section 37B(4) of the Air Pollution Control Ordinance to seek the Council's approval to extend the period for amending the Fourth Technical Memorandum for Allocation of Emission Allowances in Respect of Specified Licences laid on the table of the Council on October 22, 2014 to the meeting of December 10, 2014.

On bills, Members will resume Second Reading debate on the Competition (Amendment) Bill 2014. If the Bill is supported by Members and receives its Second Reading, it will then go through the Committee stage and be read the third time.

n addition, Members will ask the Government 22 questions on various policy areas, six of which require oral replies during the meeting.

The agenda of the above meeting can be obtained via the LegCo Website (www.legco.gov.hk). Please note that the agenda is subject to change, and the latest information about the agenda could be found in the LegCo Website.

Members of the public are welcome to observe the proceedings of the meeting from the public galleries of the Chamber of the LegCo Complex. They may reserve seats by calling 3919 3399 during office hours. Members of the public can also watch or listen the meeting via the web broadcast system on the LegCo Website.

Issued at HKT 19:51

Injunction orders should be respected and complied with
****

In response to media enquiries about Au J's Judgment delivered this afternoon in respect of the three injunction applications concerning the obstruction of certain roads in Mong Kok and also the obstruction at the entrance and exit of CITIC Tower, a spokesman for the Department of Justice (DoJ) said today (November 10) that the DoJ welcomes the exposition of the concept of the rule of law in paragraphs 137 to 150 of the Judgment and invites those who are still acting in breach of the injunction orders to respect the rule of law. The spokesman further said that the DoJ takes note of paragraph 152 of the Judgment, which states as follows:

(1) The bailiff do take all reasonable and necessary steps to assist the plaintiff and its agents to effect the clearance and removal of the obstructions.

(2) The bailiff be authorised and directed to request the assistance of the Police where necessary.

(3) Any police officer be authorised to arrest and remove any person who the police officer reasonably believes or suspects to be obstructing or interfering any bailiff in carrying out his or her duties in enforcing the terms of the injunction order, provided that the person to be arrested has been informed of the gist of the terms of the court order and that his action is likely to constitute a breach of the order and obstruction of the administration of justice, and that he may be arrested if he does not desist.

(4) Any person so arrested by the police shall be brought before the court as soon as practicable for further directions.

The spokesman said that the Police are willing and ready to provide such assistance regarding the enforcement of the injunction orders as stated in the Judgment.

"As highlighted in paragraphs 123 and 124 of the Judgment, attempts to obstruct bailiffs in their execution of duties may constitute criminal contempt, which is a common law offence. Whilst the Police will provide assistance in respect of the enforcement of the injunction orders, the Secretary for Justice may also consider taking appropriate action against persons who may have committed the offence of criminal contempt.

"We fully understand that people have different views on Hong Kong's constitutional development. However, irrespective of one's views, one should act in accordance with the law and comply with court order, or else there would be negative impact on the rule of law. We urge all the relevant persons to respect and comply with the court order and take immediate action to remove all the obstructions. The rule of law is the cornerstone of the success of our society and we should do our utmost to uphold and defend this important value," the spokesman said.

Issued at HKT 21:04

NOVEMBER 11[18]

HKMA's update on the operation of the banking system and financial market
****

The following is issued on behalf of the Hong Kong Monetary Authority:

According to the reports to the Hong Kong Monetary Authority (HKMA) from banks as at 8am today (November 11), all previously affected bank branches have resumed operation. One branch of one bank would shorten its business hours today. The HKMA has requested banks to resume normal services as soon as circumstances permit. Customers should pay attention to the relevant banks' announcements regarding affected branches and ATMs. The HKMA will also publish on its website relevant updates from time to time.

Issued at HKT 10:15

Transcript of remarks by Acting CE at media session before ExCo meeting (with video)
****

Following is the transcript of remarks by the Acting Chief Executive, Mrs Carrie Lam, at a media session before the Executive Council meeting today (November 11):

Acting Chief Executive: I just want to say a few words in English. Yesterday afternoon the High Court, having heard representations from various parties, has decided to continue the injunction orders with regard to certain occupied areas at Admiralty and also in Mong Kok.

I believe we all agree that the rule of law is the cornerstone of Hong Kong's success, the foundation of our democracy and an important core value of Hong Kong. The Hong Kong SAR Government is committed to safeguarding the rule of law, and members of public have always respected court decisions.

An injunction is a solemn order made by the court which should be fully respected and strictly followed by all. So I strongly urge protesters who are still staying in the occupied areas, whether the areas are covered by the injunctions or not, they should voluntarily and peacefully leave the areas as soon as possible so that the roads as well as the building entrances could be reopened.

The court has already authorised the bailiff to request Police assistance where necessary and has authorised the Police to arrest and remove anyone obstructing or interfering with any bailiff in enforcing the

---

[18] http://www.info.gov.hk/gia/general/201411/11.htm

terms of the injunction orders. So, with a view to protecting the due administration of justice and upholding the rule of law, the Police will give full assistance, including making arrest where necessary to enforce the injunction orders in such ways as the court instructs.

So I call on those who are still unlawfully blocking the roads in Hong Kong to leave the occupied areas peacefully of their own accord and end the occupy movement as soon as possible.

Issued at HKT 11:18

Speech by Commissioner of Police at the Force Remembrance Day
****

The following is the speech delivered by the Commissioner of Police, Mr Tsang Wai-hung, at the Force Remembrance Day today (November 11):

We are gathered here today to pay tribute to both the Regular and Auxiliary members of the Hong Kong Police Force who have given their lives in the line of duty. This solemn ceremony is also a fitting tribute to the dedication and fortitude of all members of staff who have served with the Force over the past 170 years.

Today, we honour the memory of those who, whilst performing their sworn duty, have made the ultimate sacrifice by giving their lives in the service of the people of Hong Kong. Time and time again, we police officers confront danger and continually face the uncertainty of whether our duty to protect and serve will place us in harm's way. For the sake of the safety and stability of our community, we will never flinch from this challenge.

And, this promise has particular resonance this year. Over the last six weeks, the Force has faced unprecedented challenges dealing with the ongoing unlawful assembly here in Hong Kong. To date, over 60 of our officers policing these events have been injured, thankfully none too seriously. And, on a day when we are thinking of our fallen comrades, I can promise you all that we will honour their memories through continuing to rise to the current challenges facing us; through continuing to police Hong Kong with neither fear nor favour; and through continuing, as we have always done, to serve our community by upholding public order and public safety in this great city of ours.

In this ceremony, we are joined by members of the Hong Kong Police Old Comrades Association, the Royal Hong Kong Police Association and other former members of the Hong Kong Police Force. Like the many officers who came before them, they represent the finest traditions of service to the community for which the Force is both famed and justifiably proud – traditions, which are passed on from generation to generation.

To all of you present here today, may I ask that you remain standing, and following the "Last Post" join with me in observing a two-minute silence in memory of all the officers who have made the ultimate sacrifice in the line of duty.

Issued at HKT 11:41

Motorists should abide by traffic laws not to stay within yellow box marking at intersections
****

The Transport Department (TD) said today (November 11) that the busy traffic in Hong Kong has become more congested when being affected by the occupy movement. Under such circumstances, motorists are reminded that they must abide by the traffic regulations to prevent the traffic from becoming more chaotic.

The TD's Emergency Transport Co-ordination Centre (ETCC) has been closely monitoring the traffic situation and some motorists, for the sake of convenience, were found to have violated traffic regulations such as stopping illegally on yellow box marking at intersections, causing obstruction to vehicles on road sections in the vicinity and affecting the overall traffic flow. Such illegal behaviours are often found at a number of intersections in Wan Chai, including the junctions between Fenwick Street and Lockhart Road; Lockhart Road and Fleming Road; Fleming Road and Hennessy Road; as well as Harbour Road and Fleming Road, resulting in serious traffic congestion in Wan Chai North.

With a view to preventing motorists from making unauthorised U-turns towards Central on Harbour Road (Causeway Bay-bound) outside Shui On Centre in Wan Chai, the Police have placed water barriers and "No U-turn" warning signs at the scene. The TD reminds motorists not to act in breach of the law because it will affect other vehicles travelling along the road and pedestrians walking across the road at pedestrian crossings.

As for the traffic situation, since a number of roads affected by protests on Hong Kong Island are still closed and there has been a growing amount of traffic flow, traffic was busy and congested at the Island Eastern Corridor, Gloucester Road westbound towards Central, Lung Wo Road and in the vicinity of the Aberdeen Tunnel during peak hours today. The TD and the Police will continue to implement temporary traffic control measures when necessary to divert traffic. Motorists should pay attention to the temporary arrangements and follow the instructions of the Police at the scene. The TD urged motorists to avoid driving as far as possible and give the public transport services priority over road use.

As special traffic and transport arrangements will be implemented for the horse racing meeting in Happy Valley tomorrow night, it is anticipated that traffic will be very busy with increased traffic load on Hong Kong Island during peak hours in the evening and that serious traffic congestion is very likely to occur. Members of the public are advised to use public transport as far as possible and avoid driving to Hong Kong Island.

Regarding public transport services, a total of 223 bus routes were still affected today, with eight bus routes suspended and 215 bus routes diverted. Among the affected bus routes, 80 routes travelling via Mong Kok are diverted due to the closure of a number of road sections in Mong Kok.

Due to traffic congestion in the vicinity of Causeway Bay, starting from the first departure tomorrow, amendments will be made on the following routes:

- the NWFB Route No.38, 42, 42C and CTB Route No.76, 77 will omit Leighton Road, and be diverted via Canal Road West, flyover and Victoria Park Road;
- the CTB Route No. 5B will be diverted via Percival Street, Leighton Road, Hysan Avenue, Hoi Ping Road, Caroline Hill Road, Eastern Hospital Road, Tung Lo Wan Road, Irving Street, Pennington Street, Yee Wo Street and then resumed its original routing to Western District;
- the KMB Route No. 603P will be departed from Central Ferry Pier and then diverted via Man Yiu Street, Man Cheong Street, Connaught Road Central, Rumsey Street, Des Voeux Road Central, Queensway, Hennessy Road, Fleming Road, Convention Avenue, Hung Hing Road, Victoria Park Road and then resumed its original routing to Island Eastern Corridor.

A total of 20 green minibus routes travelling via Harcourt Road, Nathan Road and Argyle Street are still diverted or suspended or with service adjusted. Currently, the tram service between Percival Street and Paterson Street is still suspended. The MTR Corporation Limited continues to increase services for all urban lines to cope with passenger demand.

The TD's ETCC will continue to monitor the road traffic situation and public transport services. For details of road closure, traffic diversion, suspension and route diversion of green minibus services, please refer to the TD's website (www.td.gov.hk). Regarding temporary traffic arrangements for bus routes, please refer to the following bus companies' websites for details:

For routes of Citybus and New World First Bus: www.nwstbus.com.hk/en/uploaded-Files/OC2014/TAA.htm .

For routes of Kowloon Motor Bus: www.kmb.hk/en .

As there will be updates on bus services from time to time due to traffic changes, members of the public are advised to pay attention to the latest service arrangements announced by bus companies before starting their journeys.

Issued at HKT 20:22

Agenda of tomorrow's LegCo meeting revised
****

The following is issued on behalf of the Legislative Council Secretariat:

The agenda of the Legislative Council (LegCo) meeting, scheduled for tomorrow (November 12) at 11am in the Chamber of the LegCo Complex, has been revised. In addition to the original items, the President of LegCo has given permission for Mrs Regina Ip to move, under Rule 16(2) of the Rules of Procedure, a motion for the adjournment of the Council. The motion states: "That this Council do now adjourn for the purpose of debating the following issue: the Police's assistance in enforcing the orders issued by the High Court on November 10, 2014 in respect of the three injunction applications concerning the obstruction of certain roads in Mong Kok and that at the entrance of CITIC Tower in Admiralty."

For the latest agenda items of tomorrow's LegCo meeting, please refer to the LegCo website: www.legco.gov.hk/yr14-15/english/counmtg/agenda/cm20141112.htm .

Issued at HKT 20:40

NOVEMBER 12[19]

HKMA's update on the operation of the banking system and financial market
****

The following is issued on behalf of the Hong Kong Monetary Authority:

According to the reports to the Hong Kong Monetary Authority (HKMA) from banks as at 8am today (November 12), all previously affected bank branches have resumed operation. One branch of one bank would shorten their business hours today. The HKMA has requested banks to resume normal services as soon as circumstances permit. Customers should pay attention to the relevant banks' announcements regarding affected branches and ATMs. The HKMA will also publish on its website relevant updates from time to time.

Issued at HKT 09:56

Special arrangements on submission of tenders arising from temporary closure of Government Secretariat Tender Box
****

Owing to the special access arrangements at the Central Government Offices (CGO) in Tamar, the Government Secretariat Tender Box (GSTB) located on the ground floor of the East Wing of CGO is closed for tender deposit temporarily.

All tenders that should originally be deposited into the GSTB are instead requested to be deposited into the Government Logistics Department Tender Box (GLDTB) located on the ground floor of North Point Government Offices at 333 Java Road, North Point. This special arrangement came into effect on September 30 this year and remains in effect until further notice.

Tenderers may wish to check in advance their route to the GLDTB and allow sufficient time to make arrangements to deposit their tenders into the GLDTB before the respective closing time of tenders. Late tenders will not be accepted.

For enquiries, please call 2810 2497 or 2231 5288 between 9am and 6pm from Mondays to Fridays (except public holidays).

Issued at HKT 11:3

---

[19] http://www.info.gov.hk/gia/general/201411/12.htm

LCQ2: Selecting CE by universal suffrage

****

Following is a question by the Hon Emily Lau and a reply by the Acting Secretary for Constitutional and Mainland Affairs, Mr Lau Kong-wah, in the Legislative Council today (November 12):

Question:

According to Article 25(b) of the International Covenant on Civil and Political Rights (ICCPR), citizens shall have the right and the opportunity, without unreasonable restrictions, to vote and to be elected at elections. On the other hand, the Standing Committee of the National People's Congress (NPCSC) made a decision on August 31 this year on issues such as the selection of the Chief Executive (CE) of the Hong Kong Special Administrative Region (SAR) by universal suffrage (the NPCSC decision). The United Nations Human Rights Committee (UNHRC) convened a meeting in Geneva on the 23rd of last month to consider matters relating to the implementation of universal suffrage for the selection of CE in the Hong Kong SAR in accordance with ICCPR. It has been reported that UNHRC was of the view that Hong Kong should take all necessary measures to implement the rights of universal suffrage in conformity with ICCPR and that Hong Kong's performance in following UNHRC's recommendations was not satisfactory. In this connection, will the executive authorities inform this Council:

(1) whether they have assessed if the selection of CE by universal suffrage in 2017, conducted under the framework of the NPCSC decision, will comply with the requirement of UNHRC; if the assessment outcome is in the negative, how the authorities will deal with the issue, including how and when they will give a reply to UNHRC; whether the authorities will formulate a universal suffrage system for the selection of CE in 2017 in compliance with the requirement of UNHRC, so as to ensure that Hong Kong people will enjoy the equal right to vote and to stand for election without unreasonable restrictions; if they will, of the details; if not, the reasons for that;

(2) whether they have assessed if the Government has an obligation to ensure that the method for selecting CE by universal suffrage in 2017 complies with the relevant requirements of ICCPR; if the assessment outcome is in the affirmative, how the authorities will honour such obligation; if the assessment outcome is in the negative, of the justifications; and

(3) as officials of both the Central Government and the Hong Kong SAR Government have said that

Hong Kong shall follow the Basic Law and the NPCSC decision but not ICCPR in implementing universal suffrage and that the Government of the United Kingdom made a reservation not to apply Article 25(b) when it extended ICCPR to Hong Kong, what justifications, apart from the reservation, the authorities have in support of the statement that the universal suffrage system in Hong Kong is not regulated by ICCPR?

Reply:

President,

The Third Report of the Hong Kong Special Administrative Region (HKSAR) in the light of the International Covenant on Civil and Political Rights (Covenant) (Third Report) was submitted to the United Nations in 2011 as requested by the United Nations Human Rights Committee (UNHRC). Upon the issue of the Concluding Observations of the UNHRC on the Third Report in March 2013, the HKSAR Government submitted a follow-up response to the UNHRC in March this year as requested by the UNHRC, and provided further updated information to the UNHRC in light of a UNHRC meeting in October this year.

The Government is aware that the UNHRC has discussed at its meeting on October 23 the implementation of the Covenant in the HKSAR. However, the HKSAR Government has not yet received any official notification from the UNHRC, and hence it is inappropriate to give any specific comment at this stage. We will consider whether it is necessary to make further response upon receipt of the relevant notification from the UNHRC.

Our reply to the questions raised by the Hon Lau is as follows.

(1) and (2) The constitutional basis of the political structure of the HKSAR lies in the Constitution of the People's Republic of China (Constitution) and the Basic Law. The HKSAR was established by the decision of the National People's Congress made pursuant to Article 31 and Article 62(13) of the Constitution; the systems to be implemented in the HKSAR, including the political structure of the HKSAR, are prescribed in accordance with the Constitution and the Basic Law. According to Article 15 of the Basic Law:

"The Central People's Government shall appoint the Chief Executive and the principal officials of the executive authorities of the Hong Kong Special Administrative Region in accordance with the provisions of Chapter IV of this Law."

According to Article 25 of the Basic Law:
"All Hong Kong residents shall be equal before the law."

According to Article 26 of the Basic Law:

"Permanent residents of the Hong Kong Special Administrative Region shall have the right to vote and the right to stand for election in accordance with law."

According to Article 45 of the Basic Law:

"The Chief Executive of the Hong Kong Special Administrative Region shall be selected by election or through consultations held locally and be appointed by the Central People's Government.

The method for selecting the Chief Executive shall be specified in the light of the actual situation in the Hong Kong Special Administrative Region and in accordance with the principle of gradual and orderly progress. The ultimate aim is the selection of the Chief Executive by universal suffrage upon nomination by a broadly representative nominating committee in accordance with democratic procedures.

The specific method for selecting the Chief Executive is prescribed in Annex I: 'Method for the Selection of the Chief Executive of the Hong Kong Special Administrative Region'."

On August 31, 2014, the Standing Committee of the National People's Congress (NPCSC) adopted the Decision of the Standing Committee of the National People's Congress on Issues Relating to the Selection of the Chief Executive of the Hong Kong Special Administrative Region by Universal Suffrage and on the Method for Forming the Legislative Council of the Hong Kong Special Administrative Region in the Year 2016 (Decision), formally determining that universal suffrage for the Chief Executive (CE) election through "one person, one vote" could be implemented in the HKSAR starting from 2017. It also sets out a clear framework on the specific method for selecting the CE by universal suffrage.

In exploring the specific method for selecting the CE by universal suffrage, the Basic Law and the relevant Interpretation and Decisions of the NPCSC must be strictly adhered to, and it must be in accordance with "One Country, Two Systems" and the basic policies of the State regarding Hong Kong. As regards how to devise a specific model for implementing universal suffrage, the design of political systems in different parts of the world is different, this is because the electoral system of each country or place must be devised having regard to her own history, constitutional system and actual situations. The United Nations also recognises that internationally there is no prescribed electoral system considered to be the only one that conforms with the principles of the Covenant.

As mentioned above, the Decision of the NPCSC adopted on August 31, 2014 sets out a clear framework on the method for selecting the CE by universal suffrage. When universal suffrage for the CE election is implemented, all eligible voters in Hong Kong would have the right to vote on a "one person, one vote" basis; and the right to vote is universal and equal. Furthermore, any interested person who meets the requirements in Article 44 of the Basic Law and the relevant statutory qualifications would enjoy an equal opportunity to contend for nomination by the Nominating Committee. Persons nominated by the Nominating Committee would participate in an open election on an equal footing, seek support from five million eligible voters, and enjoy an equal right to be elected.

(3) As regards the Covenant, when the Covenant was applied to Hong Kong in 1976, a reservation was made by the British government reserving the right not to apply Article 25(b). After the establishment of the HKSAR, in accordance with the Central People's Government's notification to the United Nations Secretary-General in June 1996 and Article 39 of the Basic Law, only the provisions as applied to Hong Kong should remain in force, and their implementation has to be through the laws of the HKSAR. Hence, the basis for the ultimate aim of universal suffrage for Hong Kong's constitutional development lies in the Basic Law and the relevant Interpretation and Decisions of the NPCSC, but not the Covenant.
Issued at HKT 12:42

LCQ18: Impact of road occupation on securities market
****

Following is a question by the Hon James Tien and a written reply by the Secretary for Financial Services and the Treasury, Professor K C Chan, in the Legislative Council today (November 12):

Question:

It has been reported that since the occurrence of the road occupation movement (the occupation movement) on September 28 this year, there were some unusual fluctuations in the securities market of Hong Kong, including a significant drop in the Hang Seng Index and the more active trading activities to build stock index futures positions, etc. The reports have further pointed out that foreign hedge funds and local individuals participating in the occupation movement had seized the opportunity to make profit by block sale of index futures contracts. In this connection, will the Government inform this Council:

(1) whether the authorities concerned have conducted an investigation into the aforesaid fluctuations in the securities market; if they have, of the methods and outcome of such investigation; if not, the reasons for that;

(2) in the light of the involvement of foreign-funded institutions or local individuals participating in the

occupation movement in the aforesaid profit-making acts, how the authorities prevent market manipulation and avoid the recurrence of substantial fluctuations in the securities market due to such acts;

(3) given that the Financial Secretary remarked in his blog in August this year that "the multitude of complicated and entangled risk factors (which by themselves cannot be tackled easily), if combined with political instability locally, may trigger a perfect financial and economic storm and open up the opportunities for international speculators, with consequences too ghastly to contemplate", whether the authorities have assessed the likelihood of Hong Kong being attacked by international speculators at present; if they have, of the details; if not, the reasons for that; and

(4) whether it has assessed the impact of the occupation movement on the launch time and specific arrangements of the Shanghai-Hong Kong Stock Connect as well as the credit ratings of Hong Kong; if it has, of the details; if not, the reasons for that?

Reply:

President,

(1) and (2) Hong Kong has a robust regulatory framework for short selling. Aside from prohibiting naked short selling and imposing an uptick requirement to prevent short sales of securities at successively lower prices, a statutory short position reporting regime was also introduced in June 2012 to enhance the Securities and Futures Commission (SFC)'s monitoring of short selling activities in the market.

The SFC has been monitoring closely trading activities of the cash market, particularly short selling activities, as well as trading activities and open interests of the derivatives market, so as to assess the potential systemic risks and detect any market misconduct.

The SFC is not aware of any significant abnormalities so far. According to the SFC's analysis, in October, the average daily open interests of the Hang Seng Index (HSI) and Hang Seng China Enterprises Index futures were 122 400 and 212 766 contracts respectively, which were comparable with the average daily open interest levels during the period between January and September (i.e. 124 420 and 231 113 contracts respectively). The SFC is not aware of any signs of concentration or build-up of large positions in the futures markets.

(3) In the past month or so, together with the financial regulators, we have been monitoring closely the financial market situation and taken relevant measures to minimise the impact of the protests on the financial system. Generally speaking, Hong Kong's financial system, including the banking system, stock market and foreign exchange market, etc. have been functioning in a normal and orderly manner. The linked exchange rate system is robust, interest rates remain steady. However, any prolonged protests would give rise to more evident impact on Hong Kong, and social instability may affect the confidence of local and overseas investors. We will, together with the financial regulators, continue to monitor closely the financial market situation, and take appropriate measures as and when necessary.

(4) On November 10, 2014, the China Securities Regulatory Commission and the SFC issued a joint announcement on their approval of the official launch of the Shanghai-Hong Kong Stock Connect on November 17, 2014. The Shanghai-Hong Kong Stock Connect is a mutually beneficial collaboration project. Through enhancing mutual stock market access between Hong Kong and Shanghai, the programme promotes the gradual opening up of the Mainland's capital accounts as well as the internationalisation of Renminbi (RMB). The collaboration project will reinforce Hong Kong's position as a premier international financial centre and also strengthen Hong Kong's role as an offshore RMB business centre.

Regarding whether the protests will affect Hong Kong's credit ratings, we note that the credit rating agencies generally consider that the immediate impact of the protests on Hong Kong's economic and financial systems to be minimal. However, any prolonged protests would inevitably affect the confidence of local and overseas investors, which would in turn cause negative impact on Hong Kong's economic prospects, thereby creating downward pressure on the ratings of Hong Kong over the longer term.

The credit rating agencies maintained the credit ratings of Hong Kong in their reports published in October. Together with the financial regulators, we will continue to maintain close dialogues with credit rating agencies to ensure that they maintain a balanced and objective assessment on Hong Kong's credit ratings.

Issued at HKT 13:12

LCQ5: Submission of reports on constitutional development to the Central People's Government
****

Following is a question by the Hon Kwok Ka-ki and a reply by the Acting Secretary for Constitutional and Mainland Affairs, Mr Lau Kong-wah, in the Legislative Council today (November 12):

Question:

On July 15 this year, the Chief Executive (CE) made a report to the Standing Committee of the National People's Congress (NPCSC) on whether there is a need to amend the methods for selecting CE of the Hong Kong Special Administrative Region (HKSAR) in 2017 and for forming the Legislative Council (LegCo) of HKSAR in 2016 (the July 15 Report) in accordance with the Interpretation by NPCSC of Article 7 of Annex I and Article III of Annex II to the Basic Law of HKSAR of the People's Republic of China (the Interpretation). After considering the aforesaid report, NPCSC made a decision on August 31 on issues relating to the selection of CE by universal suffrage and the method for forming LegCo in 2016. Many members of the public have occupied roads in a number of districts since September 28 to fight for the selection of CE by universal suffrage in 2017 (the occupation movement). On October 21, government officials had a dialogue with representatives of the Hong Kong Federation of Students. At the meeting, the Chief Secretary for Administration said that the SAR Government would submit a public sentiment report regarding constitutional development to the Hong Kong and Macao Affairs Office of the State Council. In this connection, will the Government inform this Council:

(1) of the legal and policy bases for the authorities submitting the public sentiment report; whether they have assessed if such an action complies with the requirements on amending the methods for selecting CE and forming LegCo as set out in the Interpretation; if the assessment outcome is in the affirmative, of the details; what the authorities expect the submission of the public sentiment report will accomplish, including whether it will facilitate a peaceful conclusion of the occupation movement;

(2) which government officials are responsible for drafting the public sentiment report; when the report will be completed; how the authorities ensure that the report will fully reflect the public opinions in Hong Kong and NPCSC will go along with the wishes of the public when making decisions on the constitutional development of Hong Kong; and

(3) whether CE will, in response to the public aspiration for the selection of CE by universal suffrage in 2017, re-submit the July 15 Report after making amendments or a supplement to it; if he will, of the details; if not, the reasons for that?

Reply:

President,

On July 15, 2014, the HKSAR Government published the Report on the Public Consultation on the Methods for Selecting the Chief Executive in 2017 and for Forming the Legislative Council in 2016, to objectively and truthfully reflect the views received from different groups and individuals from various sectors of the community during the five-month consultation period. On the same day, the Chief Executive (CE) submitted his report to the Standing Committee of the National People's Congress (NPCSC) to invite the NPCSC to make a determination on whether there is a need to amend the methods for selecting the CE in 2017 and for forming the Legislative Council (LegCo) in 2016, and formally kick-started the "Five-step Process" of constitutional development. On August 31, 2014, the NPCSC adopted the Decision of the Standing Committee of the National People's Congress on Issues Relating to the Selection of the Chief Executive of the Hong Kong Special Administrative Region by Universal Suffrage and on the Method for Forming the Legislative Council of the Hong Kong Special Administrative Region in the Year 2016 (Decision), which marks the completion of the Second Step of the "Five-step Process" of constitutional development. The Decision formally determines that universal suffrage for the CE election through "one person, one vote" could be implemented starting from 2017.

Officials from the Central Authorities have repeatedly reiterated that they attach great importance to the constitutional development of the HKSAR, and have been keeping abreast of the opinions and sentiments of the community in Hong Kong, including the different views and opinions of different sectors of the community since the Decision was adopted by the NPCSC.

Our reply to the questions raised by Dr the Hon Kwok is as follows:

(1) Members of the Task Force on Constitutional Development (Task Force), including the Chief Secretary for Administration, the Secretary for Justice, and the Secretary for Constitutional and Mainland Affairs, together with the Director of Chief Executive's Office and the Under Secretary for Constitutional

and Mainland Affairs, had a two-hour dialogue with representatives of the Hong Kong Federation of Students on October 21, 2014. At the meeting, the HKSAR Government indicated that, without prejudice to the provisions of the Basic Law, and outside the "Five-step" constitutional process, we were willing to submit a "Public Sentiments Report" to the Hong Kong and Macao Affairs Office of the State Council, to objectively and truthfully reflect the aspirations and opinions regarding constitutional development expressed by different sectors of the community and the related social movement since August 31.

(2) The "Public Sentiments Report" will be drafted and submitted in the name of the Task Force. We will endeavour to include the different aspirations and opinions from different sectors of the community that have been publicly expressed through various channels, including relevant opinion polls and signature campaigns conducted by different organisations.

In adopting the Decision on August 31, the NPCSC had stated that the Decision was made after having considered thoroughly the report submitted by the CE, as well as the views from different sectors of the community.

(3) As mentioned above, the HKSAR Government will only submit one "Public Sentiments Report", which will not constitute a part of the "Five-step" constitutional process. For the next step, the HKSAR Government will conduct a second round public consultation in accordance with the Decision adopted by the NPCSC on August 31, and submit at an appropriate juncture to the LegCo a resolution to amend Annex I to the Basic Law, with a view to securing a two-thirds majority approval of the LegCo, so that the HKSAR could implement universal suffrage for the CE election through "one person, one vote" in 2017. Issued at HKT 14:47

LCQ15: Independent Police Complaints Council
****

Following is a question by Professor Hon Joseph Lee and a written reply by the Secretary for Security, Mr Lai Tung-kwok, in the Legislative Council today (November 12):

Question:

The Independent Police Complaints Council Ordinance (Cap. 604) (the Ordinance) came into operation on June 1, 2009 and the then existing Independent Police Complaints Council (IPCC) was also incorporated into a statutory body on the same day, with its Chinese name changed. The functions of

IPCC are to ensure that complaints against the Police are handled in a fair, impartial, effective and transparent manner, and to advise on improvement to police procedures to enhance service quality and public accountability. In this connection, will the Government inform this Council:

(1) given that section 8(1)(c) of the Ordinance provides that IPCC may identify any fault or deficiency in any practice or procedure adopted by the police force that has led to or might lead to reportable complaints, and make recommendations (as IPCC considers appropriate) to the Commissioner of Police (Commissioner) or the Chief Executive or both of them in respect of such practice or procedure, whether it knows, since the establishment of the statutory IPCC, the situations under which the aforesaid provision was invoked to identify the related faults or deficiencies, as well as the number of times in which recommendations were made to the Commissioner or the Chief Executive under that provision and the details of such recommendations; whether there were recommendations not accepted by the Commissioner; if so, of the reasons for the recommendations not being accepted;

(2) if it knows (i) the procedures adopted by IPCC for examining the practice or procedure of the police force in accordance with the aforesaid provision (e.g. site inspections and interviews with the officers concerned, etc.) and the number of times for which each of these procedures was adopted, and (ii) whether IPCC has encountered difficulties in adopting such procedures; if IPCC has encountered difficulties, of the details and the reasons for that;

(3) given that section 20 of the Ordinance provides that IPCC may, at any time after an investigation report has been submitted by the Commissioner under section 17 of the Ordinance, interview the person(s) concerned for the purpose of considering the report, whether it knows, since the establishment of the statutory IPCC, if any police officer (including complainees or witnesses, etc.) has refused to be interviewed by IPCC; if so, of the relevant figures and reasons for refusal, and whether the authorities will consider relaying such situations to the Commissioner and requesting improvement; if they will, the details; if they will not, the reasons for that; and

(4) given an upward trend in the number of complaints against the Police recently, whether the authorities have plans to enhance the image of IPCC and promote public awareness of IPCC in order to enhance its recognition, so that IPCC can monitor the Police more effectively; if they have such plans, of the details?

Reply:

President,

With the enactment of the Independent Police Complaints Council Ordinance (the Ordinance) on June 1, 2009, the Independent Police Complaints Council (IPCC) came into operation as an independent statutory body on the same day. Its daily operation, manpower arrangement and financial management are totally independent of the Government. There is a separate head of expenditure for IPCC (Head 121) in the Government's Estimates, with the Secretary-General of IPCC as the Controlling Officer. Since 2009, the Government has provided IPCC with additional annual resources and additional posts for IPCC's better discharge of its statutory function of monitoring the Police in their handling of complaints.

The Ordinance provides expressly a legal basis for a two-tier police complaints handling system. While specifying the functions, power and operation of IPCC under the above system, the Ordinance stipulates that the Police shall provide necessary assistance to IPCC and comply with the requirements set by IPCC under the Ordinance.

The Administration's reply to Professor Hon Joseph Lee's question is as follows:

(1) and (2) The Complaints Against Police Office (CAPO) has submitted over 15 000 investigation reports on reportable complaints to IPCC for examination since the latter's inception as a statutory body in June 2009. In the process of examining and endorsing investigations into reportable complaints, IPCC has from time to time, made recommendations on deficiency in practice or procedure adopted by the Police that, in its view, has led to or might lead to reportable complaints. For the purpose of complaint prevention and continuous enhancement of police service quality, CAPO studies and follows up all advice provided by IPCC, and accepts recommendations that may help improve the Force's practice, procedures and service quality, such as procedures for issuing illegal parking tickets and handling found property containing personal data, modification of procedures in notifying victims of traffic accidents for progress of the case and court hearing, installation of telephones with recording system in report rooms, and upgrading of close circuit television systems at police stations. For certain recommendations involving greater complexity or different police units, other departments or organisations, e.g. cases concerning notification and investigation of cash missing from ATM and arrangements for Police to interview persons still under their custody in hospital, CAPO needs a longer time for in-depth deliberation with IPCC, relevant police units and other departments or organisations. Advice of the Department of Justice may also be sought where necessary. CAPO does not have any statistics on the number of recommendations made by

IPCC under section 8(1)(c) of the Ordinance, nor does it have any statistical data relating to the particulars of such recommendations.

(3) According to CAPO, a total of 32 police officers were invited by IPCC for interviews from June 2009 to October 2014 during its examination of the investigation reports on reportable complaints submitted by CAPO. Among them, 27 attended the interviews, whereas five were not subsequently interviewed by IPCC. Of those five officers, two were complainees whom IPCC, after interviewing the complainants of the cases concerned, had decided that no further interviews were necessary. The other three were invited to be witnesses, of whom two had left the Force before IPCC extended its invitations. As regards the remaining officer, since his testimony was similar to that of another officer who IPCC had intended to interview, IPCC eventually decided to meet with the latter only.

(4) Annual figures of reportable complaint cases received by CAPO between 2009 and 2013 were as follows:

	2009	2010	2011	2012	2013
Number of reportable complaint cases received by CAPO each year	4 231	3 271	2 762	2 373	2 421

We understand that, IPCC, since its inception, has been deploying resources to enhance public awareness of its functions and public confidence in the two-tier police complaints handling system. A Publicity and Survey Committee was set up under IPCC to examine and advise on IPCC's publicity programmes. We note that in recent years IPCC has been committed to strengthening liaison with various stakeholders and augmenting public awareness of its role through videos and mini TV series, IPCC Quarterly Newsletters, and media conferences.

Issued at HKT 15:54

LCQ16: Police's equipment
****

Following is a question by Dr Hon Kwok Ka-ki and a written reply by the Secretary for Security, Mr Lai Tung-kwok, in the Legislative Council today (November 12):

Question:

It was reported in the press on October 28 this year that the Police had purchased arms totalling 1.4 billion pounds from the United Kingdom (UK) since 2008. Regarding the Police's purchase and use etc. of arms, will the Government inform this Council:

(1) of the countries other than UK from which the Police purchased arms in the past five years, and the criteria for choosing suppliers of arms;

(2) of the quantity, expenditure involved, closing inventory and usage of the various types of arms purchased by the Police each year from 2010 till the end of October this year, and set out such information in tables of the same format as Table 1;

Table 1

Year : _____

Type of arms	Quantity purchased	Expenditure involved	Closing inventory	Usage
A) Sniper rifle				
B) Assault rifle				
C) Machine gun				
D) Rifle				
E) Semi-automatic pistol				
F) General purpose machine gun				
G) Submachine gun				

H) Tear gas round

(3) of the respective specific criteria adopted by the Police for deciding the purchase quantity and inventory level of the arms mentioned in (2);

(4) of the guidelines issued by the Police to police officers on the use of the arms mentioned in (2), and the lowest ranks of the police officers who are authorised to approve the use of such arms respectively, and set out such information in Table 2;

Table 2

Type of arms	Guidelines on the use of arms	Lowest rank of police officers authorised to approve the use of arms
A) Sniper rifle		
B) Assault rifle		
C) Machine gun		
D) Rifle		
E) Semi-automatic pistol		
F) General purpose machine gun		
G) Submachine gun		
H) Tear gas round		

(5) of the specific occasions on which police officers used the arms mentioned in (2) in the past five years and the respective casualties inflicted by the use of such arms, and set out such information in Table 3;

Table 3

Type of arms	Specific occasions on which arms were used	Casualties inflicted
A) Sniper rifle		
B) Assault rifle		
C) Machine gun		
D) Rifle		
E) Semi-automatic pistol		
F) General purpose machine gun		
G) Submachine gun		
H) Tear gas round		

(6) of the details of the complaints received by the Police in the past five years about police officers' use of the arms mentioned in (2), including (i) the number of complaints, (ii) the number of cases substantiated among these complaints, (iii) the number of police officers involved, and (iv) the number of police officers who were disciplined for misuse of arms, and set out such information in Table 4; and

Table 4

Type of arms	(i)	(ii)	(iii)	(iv)
A) Sniper rifle				
B) Assault rifle				
C) Machine gun				
D) Rifle				
E) Semi-automatic pistol				
F) General purpose machine gun				
G) Submachine gun				
H) Tear gas round				

(7) whether the Police will review the guidelines or codes on the use of arms to ensure that the arms mentioned in (2) will not be abused as well as to reduce the casualties inflicted by the use of such arms; if they will, of the timetable?

Reply:

President,

The Administration's reply to Dr Hon Kwok Ka-ki's question is as follows:

(1) to (3) The Police procure suitable equipment for operational needs. In accordance with the established Government procurement procedures, the Police invite tenders through appropriate tender process. All tenders are subject to detailed assessment against a marking scheme, under which the one meeting all the requirements with the highest mark will be accepted.

Details, expenditure breakdown, purchase quantity, inventory level and utilisation rate with respect to the Police's procurement of various types of weapon are not to be disclosed as such data are part of particulars of their operational deployment.

(4) According to section 10 of the Police Force Ordinance (Cap 232), the Police have the responsibility to adopt lawful measures to maintain public safety and public order, as well as to safeguard life and property. On occasions where an act causing danger to others is occurring or is about to occur, the Police shall assess the circumstances on the scene and exercise professional judgment for appropriate actions, which include using the minimum force required.

There are strict Police guidelines for the use of force in that the force to be used shall be the minimum force necessary for achieving a lawful purpose. The equipment issued to police officers of different posts, including different types of arms, varies with operational needs. Field commanders shall, having made a professional assessment and judgment of the force that should be used, decide on the appropriate force to be used in the light of the overall circumstances and operational needs at the material time. Before using force, Police officers shall, when circumstances permit, give warning of their intention to use force. The person(s) involved shall be given every opportunity, whenever practicable, to obey police orders. Police officers exercise a high level of restraint at all times in the use of force, which shall cease once the purpose has been achieved.

(5) According to Police records, in the past five years, some of the arms mentioned in Table 3 of the question were used by the Police in two operations, namely an arrest operation in Kai Ching Estate, Kowloon Bay on June 1, 2014 and an anti-theft-of-vehicle operation in Tuen Mun on July 10, 2010. No casualties were inflicted by the firing of bullets from the arms used in these two operations.

When handling the violent and organised charging launched by a large number of protesters on Hong Kong Island on September 28, 2014, the Police used oleoresin capsicum (OC) foam to stop the protesters' violent acts as Police's repeated advice and warnings were given in vain. On that day, quite a number of protesters were equipped with such gear as goggles, face masks, umbrellas and cling film for eye and body protection, rendering the use of OC foam not being able to achieve the effect of counteracting the charging of the crowd. To prevent the situation from getting further out of control, the Police had no alternative but to use tear gas to put an immediate halt to the violent charging acts staged by the protesters, to create a safe distance from the protesters and to stop any acts that might threaten public safety and public order.

(6) The Police do not maintain statistics on complaint cases about the use of arms by police officers.

As at November 10, Complaints Against Police Office (CAPO) received complaints from a total of 1 362 members of the public about Police's handling of "Occupy Central". These complaints are now being processed. CAPO shall handle the allegations in a fair and impartial manner under the established procedures, and shall submit investigation reports on reportable complaints to the Independent Police Complaints Council (IPCC) for examination in accordance with the statutory requirements under the IPCC Ordinance.

(7) The Police shall review in a timely manner their training and guidelines on the use of force to ensure police officers' safe and effective discharge of duties.
Issued at HKT 16:28

Seven bus routes adjusted due to busy traffic in Causeway Bay
****

The Transport Department (TD) today (November 12) reminded members of the public that since a number of roads affected by the occupy movement on Hong Kong Island are still closed, traffic in Causeway Bay is very busy and seven bus routes travelling via Causeway Bay are adjusted starting today. As there will be updates on bus services from time to time due to traffic changes, members of the public are advised to pay attention to the latest service arrangements announced by bus companies before starting their journeys.

With effect from today, the following amendments have been made to the seven bus routes:

- NWFB Route No.38, 42, 42C and CTB Route No.76, 77 will omit Leighton Road, and be diverted via Canal Road West, flyover and Victoria Park Road;

- CTB Route No. 5B will be diverted via Percival Street, Leighton Road, Hysan Avenue, Hoi Ping Road, Caroline Hill Road, Eastern Hospital Road, Tung Lo Wan Road, Irving Street, Pennington Street and Yee Wo Street, then resume its original routing to Western District; and

- KMB Route No. 603P will depart from Central Ferry Pier and then be diverted via Man Yiu Street, Man Cheong Street, Connaught Road Central, Rumsey Street, Des Voeux Road Central, Queensway, Hennessy Road, Fleming Road, Convention Avenue, Hung Hing Road and Victoria Park Road, then resume its original routing to Island Eastern Corridor.

As special traffic and transport arrangements will be implemented for the horse-racing meeting in Happy Valley this evening, it is anticipated that traffic will be very congested in the vicinity. Members of the public are advised to use public transport as far as possible and avoid driving to Hong Kong Island, especially in the vicinity of Causeway Bay and Happy Valley to avoid increasing traffic load on Hong Kong Island during evening peak hours.

Regarding public transport services, a total of 223 bus routes were still affected today, with eight bus routes suspended and 215 bus routes diverted. Among the affected bus routes, 80 routes travelling via Mong Kok are diverted due to the closure of a number of road sections in Mong Kok. A total of 20 green minibus routes travelling via Harcourt Road, Nathan Road and Argyle Street are still diverted or suspended or have their services adjusted. Currently, the tram service between Percival Street and Paterson Street is still suspended. The MTR Corporation Limited continues to increase services for all urban lines to cope with passenger demand.

The TD's Emergency Transport Co-ordination Centre will continue to monitor the road traffic situation and public transport services. For details of road closures, traffic diversion, suspension and route diversion of green minibus services, please refer to the TD's website (www.td.gov.hk). Regarding temporary traffic arrangements for bus routes, please refer to the following bus companies' websites for details:

For routes of Citybus and New World First Bus: www.nwstbus.com.hk/en/uploadedFiles/OC2014/TAA.htm .

For routes of Kowloon Motor Bus: www.kmb.hk/en .
Issued at HKT 16:56

LCQ8: Teaching Chinese history and Moral and National Education in secondary schools
****

Following is a question by the Dr Hon Lam Tai-fai and a written reply by the Secretary for Education, Mr Eddie Ng Hak-kim, in the Legislative Council today (November 12):

Question:

On September 8, 2012, the Chief Executive announced changes to the policy on implementing the Moral and National Education (MNE) subject in secondary schools. Under the new policy, school sponsoring bodies may decide on their own whether the MNE subject should be taught and whether it should be taught as an independent subject in the curriculum of the secondary schools under their sponsorship. In view of the latest political situation in recent days, quite a number of members of the education sector have pointed out that young people in Hong Kong have inadequate understanding of our country and its situation, and they have therefore requested that the MNE subject be implemented again and the Chinese

History subject be made compulsory in the secondary school curriculum. However, in reply to my question on the 29th of last month, the Secretary for Education did not directly respond to whether he would revoke the decision on shelving the implementation of the MNE subject and said that students could learn Chinese history through the subjects of Chinese Language, Liberal Studies and Geography. In this connection, will the Government inform this Council:

(1) whether it will consider afresh requiring various secondary schools to teach Chinese History as an independent subject in the curriculum of the junior secondary level; if it will, of the details; if not, the reasons for that;

(2) whether it will make the Chinese History subject compulsory in the curricula of the junior and senior secondary levels; if it will, of the respective details; if not, the reasons for that;

(3) whether it has compiled statistics on the number of secondary schools which currently teach Chinese History as a compulsory subject in the curriculum of the junior secondary level; if it has, of the details; if not, the reasons for that;

(4) whether it has compiled statistics on the number of secondary schools which currently teach Chinese History as a compulsory subject in the curriculum of the senior secondary level; if it has, of the details; if not, the reasons for that;

(5) whether it has gauged the effectiveness of students learning Chinese history through the subjects of Chinese Language, Liberal Studies and Geography; if it has, of the details and effectiveness; if not, the reasons for that;

(6) whether it knows the respective candidates who applied to sit for the examinations of the Chinese History subject in the Hong Kong Certificate of Education Examination, the Hong Kong Advanced Level Examination and the Hong Kong Diploma of Secondary Education Examination in each year since 1997;

(7) whether it knows the number of local secondary school students admitted by each local university as undergraduates majoring in Chinese History and the total number of undergraduates majoring in Chinese History, in each year since 1997;

(8) given that following the decision of the Education Bureau in 2000 not to make the Chinese History

subject compulsory, there has been a general downward trend in the number of students sitting for the examinations of the Chinese History subject in public examinations, whether it has reviewed if the decision made in that year was wrong; if it has conducted such a review, of the details; if not, the reasons for that;

(9) whether the authorities will revoke within the current term of the Government the decision to shelve the implementation of the MNE subject; if they will, of the timetable; if not, the reasons for that;

(10) whether it has regularly and comprehensively reviewed the feasibility of revoking the decision to shelve the implementation of the MNE subject; if it has, of the details; if not, the reasons for that;

(11) whether it knows the numbers of primary and secondary schools in Hong Kong which are currently implementing the MNE subject and the relevant details (including the mode of teaching, teaching hours and qualifications of the teachers concerned); and

(12) whether it has provided guidance or support for the primary and secondary schools which are implementing the MNE subject and monitored the effectiveness of teaching and learning of the subject; if it has, of the details; if not, the reasons for that?

Reply:

President,

The political situation in recent days was brought by various factors, and it is observed that the participants come from different age groups, social strata, and with diverse backgrounds. Thus, what happens now cannot be attributed simplistically to the youngsters' inadequate understanding of our country and its situation. Since the "Curriculum Guide of the Moral and National Education subject" was shelved in early October 2012, we understand that, under the guidance of the school sponsoring bodies and curriculum leaders, schools, as in the past, continue implementing moral, civic and national education in various degrees and formats, making references to previous curriculum guides and support materials. This policy will be continued. With regard to the question about Chinese history education, in the meeting on October 29, I have stated that "Chinese History is not the only subject to help students understand the situation of our country, Chinese Language, Chinese geography, and Liberal Studies, etc., also comprise relevant knowledge, and students can also learn through various modes of learning. So there is not only one subject." The Education Bureau (EDB) attaches great importance to national education, but opines that it can be promoted through various forms and methods, so it should not depend only on the Chinese History subject. Similarly, the EDB attaches great importance to Chinese history education, which was stipulated as compulsory in junior secondary level in 2001, but opines that besides teaching Chinese history via an independent subject mode which is focusing on the rise and decline of dynastic regimes chronologically, schools should also be given flexibility to choose the most suitable and effective mode of curriculum organisation.

With regard to the twelve questions raised by Dr Hon Lam Tai-fai, the replies are as follows:

(1) Building on the Chinese history contents embedded in General Studies for Primary Schools, nearly 90% of secondary schools currently offer Chinese History as an independent subject at the junior secondary level. For the remaining schools, in order to further improve and develop Chinese history education, they adopt different curriculum modes other than the dynastic chronological approach to organise the contents of Chinese history in accordance with their schools' overall curriculum planning, the different learning needs of their students and the expertise of their teachers. For example, some adopt "the curriculum mode of linking two Histories", in which the development of Chinese history served as the backbone, making cross references to relevant topics in world history; some adopt an "integrated curriculum mode", which organises the contents of Chinese history with reference to various themes and topics. The EDB does not subscribe to the view that all schools in Hong Kong can only adopt the independent subject mode, which is focusing on the rise and decline of dynastic regimes to teach Chinese history.

(2), (3) and (4) At junior secondary level, Chinese history is taught in all secondary schools in Hong Kong, though schools may adopt different curriculum modes. In the curriculum guide "Learning to learn: The Way Forward in Curriculum Development" promulgated by the Curriculum Development Council in 2001, it is already stated that Chinese history and culture is the essential learning content at junior secondary level, and all junior secondary students must learn Chinese history. No matter what curriculum mode is adopted by schools to teach Chinese history, all schools must offer on average about 2 periods per week to teach its contents.

In the 2014/15 school year (Note 1), 392 secondary schools representing 88.29% of all the secondary schools (Note 2) offer Chinese History as an independent subject (curriculum contents adopting the dynastic chronological approach, so as to help students understand the rise and decline of major dynastic regimes in history) in junior secondary level. This includes:

(i) 350 secondary schools teaching Chinese History as an independent subject throughout the junior secondary level (i.e. Secondary One to Three), representing 78.83% of all the secondary schools, and

(ii) 42 secondary schools teaching Chinese History as an independent subject in any 1 or 2 years of the junior secondary level, representing 9.46% of all the secondary schools, e.g.

*schools that offer Chinese History in S3 as an independent subject, but link world history with Chinese history in S1 to S2;

*schools, for improving teaching effectiveness, that offer Chinese History in either S1 or S2 with double lesson time to meet the minimum lesson time requirement set by the EDB.

In this school year, 52 schools adopt other curriculum modes to offer Chinese history in junior secondary level, amounting to 11.71% of all secondary schools. Among them,

(i) 18 schools (4.05%) offer Chinese history and Culture (linking world history with Chinese history) throughout S1 to S3. The development of Chinese history served as the backbone, making cross references to world history; and

(ii) 34 schools (7.66%) offer Integrated Humanities throughout S1 to S3. They adopt a topical approach to organise the contents of Chinese history and culture.

As for the senior secondary level, Chinese History has always been an independent elective subject before and after the reunification with the Mainland. It remains unchanged after the implementation of the New Senior Secondary curriculum. According to the information collected in the 2013/14 school year, the majority of Hong Kong secondary schools (about 90%) offer Chinese History at senior secondary level.

(5) At present, students acquire knowledge of Chinese history, culture, and its current situation mainly through subjects such as Chinese Language, Chinese History, Chinese Literature, Geography, Liberal Studies, Life and Society, as well as Art and Physical Education, and also via moral, civic and national education as well as life-wide learning activities, etc. For example, the study of Chinese Language nurtures students' understanding of the Chinese culture; the study of Geography helps students understand China's agricultural, manufacturing and urban developments, and the problems faced; students can also study relevant issues about "Modern China" through the study of senior secondary Liberal Studies. For the details on the elements of Chinese history, culture, and current situation embedded in the primary and

secondary curriculum, the teaching resources and the figures of teacher professional development provided by the EDB, please refer to Annex 1[20].

There is not much research concerning the effectiveness of students learning in this area. In 2009, Hong Kong participated in the International Civic and Citizenship Education Study conducted by the International Association for the Evaluation of Educational Achievement. Among the 38 countries/places surveyed, the 15-year-old Hong Kong students ranked fifth in knowledge on civic education and citizenship. In terms of national identity, Hong Kong students possess multiple identities (Chinese, Hong Kong Chinese, Hong Kong people, global citizens), which reflect the role of Hong Kong as a part of our nation and also as a metropolitan city in the world. The survey also revealed that Hong Kong students are proud of both Hong Kong and the nation. They are proud of both national and Hong Kong's icons such as the Great Wall, the national flag, the HKSAR flag, etc. In 2011, the EDB commissioned the Chinese University of Hong Kong to carry out a survey on "the Study on School Curriculum Reform". Over 90% of the surveyed primary six students agreed that "I identify with my national identity, and I care about Hong Kong and the nation."

(6) and (8) As mentioned before, Chinese history is at present taught systematically in all secondary schools in Hong Kong at junior secondary level, though schools may adopt different curriculum modes. In fact, before the reunification with the mainland, Chinese History at junior secondary level was only an elective subject among the humanities subject group in "grammar schools" and "technical schools", while it was not offered in the "prevocational schools". (Please refer to Annex 2 for the relevant document[21]). After the reunification, the EDB attaches great importance to Chinese history education. In the curriculum document "Learning to Learn: The Way Forward in Curriculum Development" promulgated by the Curriculum Development Council in 2001, it states that: "Students in all types of junior secondary schools will study Chinese history and culture."

As for the decline in the numbers of students taking Chinese History in public examinations, on the one hand, it is because the whole student population keeps decreasing in recent years; and on the other hand, it is also because in the new senior secondary academic structure, students usually take 2 to 3 electives only. As a result, the number of students enrolled for each elective subject drop, including those enrolled for Chinese History. In my written reply to the question raised by Hon Mrs Regina Ip Lau Suk-yee dated October 29, 2014, in order to enhance students' interest in learning Chinese history so that more students will choose Chinese History as their elective subject at senior secondary level, the Curriculum Development

---

[20] To view: http://gia.info.gov.hk/general/201411/12/P201411120594_0594_137215.pdf
[21] To view: http://gia.info.gov.hk/general/201411/12/P201411120594_0594_137190.pdf

Council has set up an ad hoc Committee in May this year to review the junior secondary curricula of Chinese History and History. Moreover, the EDB is collaborating with different stakeholders to organise more teacher training programmes to enliven the learning and teaching strategies in the Chinese History classrooms, and to provide more teaching resources to improve the learning and teaching of Chinese history. These aim to enhance students' knowledge and interest in Chinese history, so as to encourage more to choose Chinese History subject at the senior secondary level.

The number of candidates who applied to sit for the examinations of Chinese History subject in the Hong Kong Certificate of Education Examination (HKCEE), the Hong Kong Advanced Level Examination (HKALE) and the Hong Kong Diploma of Secondary Education Examination (HKDSE) in each year since 1997 are listed below (information provided by Hong Kong Examinations and Assessment Authority):

Year	HKCEE	HKALE	HKDSE
1997	37 684	4 153	
1998	38 500	4 352	
1999	40 234	4 540	
2000	40 254	4 581	
2001	35 981	4 745	
2002	35 337	4 965	
2003	33 283	4 880	
2004	31 416	5 056	
2005	30 533	4 765	
2006	27 865	4 808	
2007	27 121	5 071	
2008	28 045	5 040	
2009	29 296	5 026	
2010	29 915	5 068	
2011	1 105	5 242	

(Note 3)

2012	5 058	8 596
2013	177	8 167
	(Note 4)	
2014		7 459

(7) Many History Departments in local universities offer degree programmes in History, which cover various research areas including Hong Kong history, Chinese history and world history etc. Since no undergraduate programme is exclusively allocated for students majoring in Chinese history, the EDB is not able to provide data concerning the number of students majoring in Chinese history. For the University of Hong Kong, other than the History Department in the Faculty of Arts, the School of Chinese also offers Chinese history and culture courses for the three/four year Bachelor Degree Programme. However, the School also has no data on the number of undergraduates majoring solely in Chinese history.

(9) and (10) Although the Government has shelved the Moral and National Education Curriculum Guide, the element of moral, civic and national education in the Moral and National Education (MNE) subject is not a complete novelty. Since the Curriculum Reform introduced in 2001, moral and civic education (including national education) has been made one of the four key tasks in the school curriculum. Based on the "Revised Moral and Civic Education Curriculum Framework" introduced in 2008, primary and secondary schools in Hong Kong systematically nurture students' positive values and attitudes in diversified school-based approaches, according to the school contexts and the needs of curriculum development, through various Key Learning Areas (KLAs)/subjects (for example, Chinese Language, Physical Education, General Studies, Life and Society, Liberal Studies, Chinese History, History, etc.), so as to achieve the curriculum aim. The importance of moral, civic and national education in school curriculum has not been varied though the "Moral and National Education Curriculum Guide" was shelved in 2012.

Moral, civic and national education is an important facet of school education, and should include knowledge about one's country, understanding of one's national identity and awareness of such core values as inclusiveness and diversity in the wider society. Therefore, it is natural that students have moral, civic and national education in schools. The EDB encourages, as in the past, school sponsoring bodies (SSBs) and schools to design learning experiences/activities (for example, school assembly, period for personal growth education, class teacher period, project learning, service learning, visit, etc.) for values education (including moral, civic and national education) based on schools' mission, philosophy of education and the needs of curriculum development, to promote whole person development of students. In conclusion, school has made use of the related curriculum framework to promote moral, civic and national education through a school-based approach. In view of the professional discretion already given to schools, we deem that it is not necessary to review the implementation of the MNE subject.

(11) Under the school-based policy and its regulations, the EDB respects schools' professional decisions on the choice of teaching guides and related learning and teaching resources to be adopted with reference to their schools' mission, aims of education, school contexts and students' needs, by adopting a school-based and student-centred approach when providing students with worthwhile learning experiences to develop desirable moral and civic qualities. On April 30, 2012, the Secretary for Education accepted the recommendations by the Curriculum Development Council on the refined Moral and National Education Curriculum Guide for primary and secondary schools. In consideration of public's views, the "Moral and National Education Curriculum Guide" was shelved alongside the abolition of the initiation period in early October 2012. Schools and school sponsoring bodies are given the latitude to decide whether to implement the MNE curriculum and if so, how. In view of the discretion given to SSBs and schools, the Government has not conducted and will not conduct any data collection exercise that aims specifically to gauge the number of schools and SSBs that have decided to implement the MNE initiative and the related information such as mode of implementation, length of class and teacher qualification.

As a matter of fact, schools and SSBs have made their own professional judegement to determine the pace and ways for values education (including moral, civic and national education). According to the curriculum implementation study in 2011 (Note 5), all the interviewed schools adopted different modes of implementation to promote moral, civic and national education. Around 41% of schools scheduled the periods for moral and civic education at their junior secondary levels, around 31% of schools scheduled the related periods at their senior secondary levels; around 82% of schools at their junior secondary levels scheduled the periods for religious education/ life education/ personal growth education/life and society, 63% of schools scheduled the related periods at their senior secondary levels. Besides, the importance of nurturing students' values and attitudes is highlighted by the Other Learning Experiences in senior secondary education which include moral and civic education as well as community services. The "Basic Education Curriculum Guide (P.1 – P.6)" has been updated in 2014. The updated Guide continues to strengthen and deepen the implementation of moral, civic and national education in different KLAs and subjects of both primary and secondary schools, to match with the curriculum development of primary school education and to tie in with the secondary school curriculum. It also reinforces the learning goal of "understanding our national identity, to care for our community, our nation and our world, and become a responsible citizen."

(12) All along, schools have been adopting a school-based and student-centred approach when providing students with worthwhile learning experiences to develop desirable moral and civic qualities. In addition, schools are using their professional judgement choose teaching guides and related learning and teaching resources with reference to their own mission, aims of education, school contexts and students' needs.

The EDB has continued to keep abreast of schools' development in different domains and the effectiveness of learning through a wide range of channels, such as seminars and focus group interviews. The EDB will keep in contact with SSBs and schools, listen actively to their opinions and suggestions, and respect their professional discretion in deciding whether and how they are to implement the MNE subject. The EDB respects schools' professional autonomy and, as an established practice, will continue to provide professional development programmes and school-based professional support when such needs arise.

Note 1: In October every year, all schools are required to submit to the EDB information on the subjects offered at each year of secondary education. The information submitted by the EDB this time is the latest data of the 2014/15 school year. Although there are slight differences from what was submitted on October 29 when replying to the enquiry from Hon Mrs Regina Ip Lau Suk-yee, the statistics has in general remained steady for years.

Note 2: In the 2014/15 school year, there were 444 secondary schools (including Direct Subsidy Scheme Schools, but not including special schools, private independent schools, private independent schools [non-local curriculum], private schools, international schools, senior secondary schools) offering mainstream school curriculum.

Note 3: The last HKCEE took place in 2011; the application was limited to private candidates.

Note 4: The last HKALE took place in 2013; the application was limited to private candidates.

Note 5: Based on the data of New Senior Secondary Curriculum Implementation Study (2011) collected by the EDB.

Issued at HKT 18:45

LCQ2: Selecting CE by universal suffrage
****

Following is a question by the Hon Emily Lau and a reply by the Acting Secretary for Constitutional and Mainland Affairs, Mr Lau Kong-wah, in the Legislative Council today (November 12):

Question:

According to Article 25(b) of the International Covenant on Civil and Political Rights (ICCPR), citizens shall have the right and the opportunity, without unreasonable restrictions, to vote and to be elected at elections. On the other hand, the Standing Committee of the National People's Congress (NPCSC) made a decision on August 31 this year on issues such as the selection of the Chief Executive (CE) of the Hong Kong Special Administrative Region (SAR) by universal suffrage (the NPCSC decision). The United Nations Human Rights Committee (UNHRC) convened a meeting in Geneva on the 23rd of last month to consider matters relating to the implementation of universal suffrage for the selection of CE in the Hong Kong SAR in accordance with ICCPR. It has been reported that UNHRC was of the view that Hong Kong should take all necessary measures to implement the rights of universal suffrage in conformity with ICCPR and that Hong Kong's performance in following UNHRC's recommendations was not satisfactory. In this connection, will the executive authorities inform this Council:

(1) whether they have assessed if the selection of CE by universal suffrage in 2017, conducted under the framework of the NPCSC decision, will comply with the requirement of UNHRC; if the assessment outcome is in the negative, how the authorities will deal with the issue, including how and when they will give a reply to UNHRC; whether the authorities will formulate a universal suffrage system for the selection of CE in 2017 in compliance with the requirement of UNHRC, so as to ensure that Hong Kong people will enjoy the equal right to vote and to stand for election without unreasonable restrictions; if they will, of the details; if not, the reasons for that;

(2) whether they have assessed if the Government has an obligation to ensure that the method for selecting CE by universal suffrage in 2017 complies with the relevant requirements of ICCPR; if the assessment outcome is in the affirmative, how the authorities will honour such obligation; if the assessment outcome is in the negative, of the justifications; and

(3) as officials of both the Central Government and the Hong Kong SAR Government have said that

Hong Kong shall follow the Basic Law and the NPCSC decision but not ICCPR in implementing universal suffrage and that the Government of the United Kingdom made a reservation not to apply Article 25(b) when it extended ICCPR to Hong Kong, what justifications, apart from the reservation, the authorities have in support of the statement that the universal suffrage system in Hong Kong is not regulated by ICCPR?

Reply:

President,

The Third Report of the Hong Kong Special Administrative Region (HKSAR) in the light of the International Covenant on Civil and Political Rights (Covenant) (Third Report) was submitted to the United Nations in 2011 as requested by the United Nations Human Rights Committee (UNHRC). Upon the issue of the Concluding Observations of the UNHRC on the Third Report in March 2013, the HKSAR Government submitted a follow-up response to the UNHRC in March this year as requested by the UNHRC, and provided further updated information to the UNHRC in light of a UNHRC meeting in October this year.

The Government is aware that the UNHRC has discussed at its meeting on October 23 the implementation of the Covenant in the HKSAR. However, the HKSAR Government has not yet received any official notification from the UNHRC, and hence it is inappropriate to give any specific comment at this stage. We will consider whether it is necessary to make further response upon receipt of the relevant notification from the UNHRC.

Our reply to the questions raised by the Hon Lau is as follows.

(1) and (2) The constitutional basis of the political structure of the HKSAR lies in the Constitution of the People's Republic of China (Constitution) and the Basic Law. The HKSAR was established by the decision of the National People's Congress made pursuant to Article 31 and Article 62(13) of the Constitution; the systems to be implemented in the HKSAR, including the political structure of the HKSAR, are prescribed in accordance with the Constitution and the Basic Law. According to Article 15 of the Basic Law:

"The Central People's Government shall appoint the Chief Executive and the principal officials of the executive authorities of the Hong Kong Special Administrative Region in accordance with the provisions of Chapter IV of this Law."

According to Article 25 of the Basic Law:

"All Hong Kong residents shall be equal before the law."

According to Article 26 of the Basic Law:

"Permanent residents of the Hong Kong Special Administrative Region shall have the right to vote and the right to stand for election in accordance with law."

According to Article 45 of the Basic Law:

"The Chief Executive of the Hong Kong Special Administrative Region shall be selected by election or through consultations held locally and be appointed by the Central People's Government.

The method for selecting the Chief Executive shall be specified in the light of the actual situation in the Hong Kong Special Administrative Region and in accordance with the principle of gradual and orderly progress. The ultimate aim is the selection of the Chief Executive by universal suffrage upon nomination by a broadly representative nominating committee in accordance with democratic procedures.

The specific method for selecting the Chief Executive is prescribed in Annex I: 'Method for the Selection of the Chief Executive of the Hong Kong Special Administrative Region'."

On August 31, 2014, the Standing Committee of the National People's Congress (NPCSC) adopted the Decision of the Standing Committee of the National People's Congress on Issues Relating to the Selection of the Chief Executive of the Hong Kong Special Administrative Region by Universal Suffrage and on the Method for Forming the Legislative Council of the Hong Kong Special Administrative Region in the Year 2016 (Decision), formally determining that universal suffrage for the Chief Executive (CE) election through "one person, one vote" could be implemented in the HKSAR starting from 2017. It also sets out a clear framework on the specific method for selecting the CE by universal suffrage.

In exploring the specific method for selecting the CE by universal suffrage, the Basic Law and the relevant Interpretation and Decisions of the NPCSC must be strictly adhered to, and it must be in accordance with "One Country, Two Systems" and the basic policies of the State regarding Hong Kong. As regards how to devise a specific model for implementing universal suffrage, the design of political systems in different parts of the world is different, this is because the electoral system of each country or place must be devised having regard to her own history, constitutional system and actual situations. The United Nations also recognises that internationally there is no prescribed electoral system considered to be the only one that conforms with the principles of the Covenant.

As mentioned above, the Decision of the NPCSC adopted on August 31, 2014 sets out a clear framework on the method for selecting the CE by universal suffrage. When universal suffrage for the CE election is implemented, all eligible voters in Hong Kong would have the right to vote on a "one person, one vote" basis; and the right to vote is universal and equal. Furthermore, any interested person who meets the requirements in Article 44 of the Basic Law and the relevant statutory qualifications would enjoy an equal opportunity to contend for nomination by the Nominating Committee. Persons nominated by the Nominating Committee would participate in an open election on an equal footing, seek support from five million eligible voters, and enjoy an equal right to be elected.

(3) As regards the Covenant, when the Covenant was applied to Hong Kong in 1976, a reservation was made by the British government reserving the right not to apply Article 25(b). After the establishment of the HKSAR, in accordance with the Central People's Government's notification to the United Nations Secretary-General in June 1997 and Article 39 of the Basic Law, only the provisions as applied to Hong Kong should remain in force, and their implementation has to be through the laws of the HKSAR. Hence, the basis for the ultimate aim of universal suffrage for Hong Kong's constitutional development lies in the Basic Law and the relevant Interpretation and Decisions of the NPCSC, but not the Covenant.
Issued at HKT 20:01

Letter by the Information Coordinator, Chief Executive's Office to International New York Times in response to an article "Taking back Hong Kong's future"
(Published on 2014-11-12)[22]

Hong Kong's Future Candidates
12 November 2014
Re "Taking back Hong Kong's future" (Opinion, Oct. 30): Joshua Wong Chi-fung makes a misleading statement when he writes "Beijing claims to be giving us one-person, one-vote, but a plan in which only government-approved candidates can run for election does not equal universal suffrage."
Under the Basic Law, the territory's constitutional document, all Hong Kong permanent residents who are Chinese citizens aged 40 or above with no right of abode in any foreign country and have ordinarily resided in Hong Kong for a continuous period of not less than 20 years may run for chief executive.

---

[22] http://www.isd.gov.hk/2017/eng/mr_20141112.html

The Basic Law and the decisions of the National People's Congress Standing Committee further provide that, in 2017, the chief executive will be elected by universal suffrage upon nomination by a broadly representative nominating committee in accordance with democratic procedures. The Nominating Committee that nominates the two to three candidates will have 1,200 members, the vast majority of whom will be elected by constituents in their respective sectors.

There is no question of the government approving candidates.

Andrew Fung, Hong Kong

The writer is the information coordinator for the Hong Kong government's Chief Executive Office.

NOVEMBER 13[23]

HKMA's update on operation of banking system and financial market
****

The following is issued on behalf of the Hong Kong Monetary Authority:

According to the reports to the Hong Kong Monetary Authority (HKMA) from banks as at 8am today (November 13), all previously affected bank branches have resumed operation. One branch of one bank would shorten their business hours today. The HKMA has requested banks to resume normal services as soon as circumstances permit. Customers should pay attention to the relevant banks' announcements regarding affected branches and ATMs. The HKMA will also publish on its website relevant updates from time to time.

Issued at HKT 09:45

Serious traffic congestion in Causeway Bay during road closures
****

The Transport Department (TD) today (November 13) said that a number of major trunk roads affected by the occupy movement are still closed and this has caused busy traffic on Hong Kong Island, especially in the vicinity of Causeway Bay and Wan Chai. Coupled with an event recently held by a company in Causeway Bay, involving a lot of trucks travelling on nearby roads for loading and unloading activities, the situation has resulted in serious traffic congestion in the area.

In view of the frequent loading and unloading activities in the vicinity of Lockhart Road, Percival Street and Gloucester Road in Causeway Bay, the TD called on members of the public to avoid driving to Hong Kong Island, especially in the vicinity of Causeway Bay, to avoid paralysing the traffic in the area. The Police will also continue to implement temporary traffic control measures according to the traffic situation to divert traffic flow. Motorists should pay attention to the arrangements and follow the instructions of the Police at the scene.

Since the traffic in Causeway Bay is very busy, seven bus routes travelling via Causeway Bay, namely New World First Bus (NWFB) routes No. 38, 42 and 42C; Citybus (CTB) routes No. 76, 77 and 5B; and Kowloon Motor Bus (KMB) route No. 603P, have been adjusted with effect from yesterday. As there will be updates on bus services from time to time due to traffic changes, members of the public are advised to

---

[23] http://www.info.gov.hk/gia/general/201411/13.htm

pay attention to the latest service arrangements announced by bus companies before starting their journeys.

Regarding public transport services, a total of 223 bus routes were still affected today, with eight bus routes suspended and 215 bus routes diverted. Among the affected bus routes, 80 routes travelling via Mong Kok are diverted due to the closure of a number of road sections in Mong Kok. A total of 20 green minibus routes travelling via Harcourt Road, Nathan Road and Argyle Street are still diverted or suspended or have their services adjusted. Currently, the tram service between Percival Street and Paterson Street is still suspended. The MTR Corporation Limited continues to increase services for all urban lines to cope with passenger demand.

The TD's Emergency Transport Co-ordination Centre will continue to monitor the road traffic situation and public transport services. For details of road closures, traffic diversion, suspension and route diversion of green minibus services, please refer to the TD's website (www.td.gov.hk). Regarding temporary traffic arrangements for bus routes, please refer to the following bus companies' websites for details:

For routes of CTB and NWFB: www.nwstbus.com.hk/en/uploadedFiles/OC2014/TAA.htm.

For routes of KMB: www.kmb.hk/en.

Issued at HKT 15:52

NOVEMBER 14[24]

Special arrangements on submission of tenders arising from temporary closure of Government Secretariat Tender Box
****

Owing to the special access arrangements at the Central Government Offices (CGO) in Tamar, the Government Secretariat Tender Box (GSTB) located on the ground floor of the East Wing of CGO is closed for tender deposit temporarily.

All tenders that should originally be deposited into the GSTB are instead requested to be deposited into the Government Logistics Department Tender Box (GLDTB) located on the ground floor of North Point Government Offices at 333 Java Road, North Point. This special arrangement came into effect on September 30 this year and remains in effect until further notice.

Tenderers may wish to check in advance their route to the GLDTB and allow sufficient time to make arrangements to deposit their tenders into the GLDTB before the respective closing time of tenders. Late tenders will not be accepted.

For enquiries, please call 2810 2497 or 2231 5288 between 9am and 6pm from Mondays to Fridays (except public holidays).

Issued at HKT 08:30

HKMA's update on the operation of the banking system and financial market
****

The following is issued on behalf of the Hong Kong Monetary Authority:

According to the reports to the Hong Kong Monetary Authority (HKMA) from banks as at 8am today (November 14), all previously affected bank branches have resumed operation. One branch of one bank would shorten its business hours today. The HKMA has requested banks to resume normal services as soon as circumstances permit. Customers should pay attention to the relevant banks' announcements regarding affected branches and ATMs. The HKMA will also publish on its website relevant updates from time to time.

Issued at HKT 09:3

---

[24] http://www.info.gov.hk/gia/general/201411/14.htm

Traffic in areas affected by occupy movement to be more congested before weekend
****

The Transport Department (TD) today (November 14) said that a number of roads affected by the occupy movement on Hong Kong Island and in Kowloon are still closed. As more people than usual will drive to go out tonight before the weekend, it is anticipated that the already bustling traffic in the affected areas such as in the vicinity of Causeway Bay will be even more congested. The TD called on motorists not to drive to Hong Kong Island as far as possible to avoid increasing pressure on roads on Hong Kong Island, especially in Causeway Bay.

The TD noted that the tram tracks on Yee Wo Street in Causeway Bay have been illegally occupied for over a month while very frequent loading and unloading activities in the vicinity of Lockhart Road, Percival Street and Gloucester Road in Causeway Bay have been found recently, and this has continuously caused serious congestion in the area. Affected by the occupy movement, the tram service between Percival Street and Paterson Street is still suspended and tram services connecting the eastern and western parts of Hong Kong Island are yet to resume. Tram cars on the eastern part of Hong Kong Island are also unable to return to the Whitty Street depot in Western District for inspection and maintenance. These tram cars can only undergo limited inspection at the depot in Sai Wan Ho and thus tram operations and services have been seriously affected.

Hong Kong Tramways has already taken a number of measures proactively to minimise inconvenience caused to passengers by the currently hampered service. Nevertheless, if the tram tracks cannot be reopened, members of the public would be unable to commute between the two sides of Hong Kong Island conveniently by tram, and the problems of traffic congestion, tram maintenance and decreasing patronage would not be resolved. The TD urged the protesters to peacefully retreat from the occupied roads to let services of trams and other public transport as well as the overall traffic situation return to normal.

Regarding public transport services, a total of 225 bus routes were still affected today, with eight bus routes suspended and 217 bus routes diverted. Among the affected bus routes, 80 routes travelling via Mong Kok are diverted due to the closure of a number of road sections in Mong Kok. A total of 20 green minibus routes travelling via Harcourt Road, Nathan Road and Argyle Street are still diverted or suspended or have their services adjusted. The MTR Corporation Limited continues to increase services for all urban lines to cope with passenger demand.

The TD's Emergency Transport Co-ordination Centre will continue to monitor the road traffic situation and public transport services. For details of road closures, traffic diversion, suspension and route diversion of green minibus services, please refer to the TD's website (www.td.gov.hk). Regarding temporary traffic arrangements for bus routes, please refer to the following bus companies' websites for details:

For routes of Citybus and New World First Bus: www.nwstbus.com.hk/en/uploaded-Files/OC2014/TAA.htm.

For routes of Kowloon Motor Bus: www.kmb.hk/en.

As there will be updates on bus services from time to time due to traffic changes, members of the public are advised to pay attention to the latest service arrangements announced by bus companies before starting their journeys.

Issued at HKT 19:02

Opening remarks by Police Chief Superintendent at press conference
****

Following are the opening remarks by the Chief Superintendent of Police Public Relations Branch, Mr Hui Chun-tak, at the press conference today (November 14).

Today is the 48th day since the illegal road occupations began. The daily lives and livelihoods of the general public have been seriously affected. The illegal occupiers' lack of regard to the law and prolonged unlawful assembly and blockage of roads have caused severe impact on Hong Kong's core value of the rule of law.

On November 10, the Court of First Instance decided to extend the Injunction Orders on the blockage of roads in Mong Kok and access into CITIC Tower, Admiralty. The court also authorized bailiffs to assist the plaintiffs in removing obstructions and that the bailiffs could request the assistance of Police when necessary. The court further authorized Police to arrest those who obstruct the bailiffs in performing their duties. When the parties concerned have completed the relevant procedures, Police will provide assistance at the request of the bailiffs.

I notice that on the Internet there are some people inciting illegal road occupiers to obstruct the bailiffs in executing the Injunction Orders by making various requests or doing other acts at scene with a view to causing delays. I need to point out that the bailiffs are authorized by the court to execute court orders. Any act amounts to obstruction may render one liable to the offence of 'criminal contempt of court'. Police will take resolute actions against those who violently charge the bailiffs when the bailiffs are executing their duties.

On the other hand, there are some people who incite others to re-occupy the cleared areas or other sections of roads after the bailiffs have completed the removal actions in order to continue with the illegal occupation. I must say that the general public will not accept such illegal acts in defiance of the rule of law. I reiterate that Police are duty bound to take resolute actions to preserve public order and safeguard public safety if anyone occupies new sections of roads or those that have been cleared.

Injunction Orders are solemn orders issued by the court that everyone should respect and obey. I urge the illegal road occupiers to respect the rule of law, obey the court orders, remove obstacles and personal belongings, and to leave the areas promptly and peacefully so that the roads can be re-opened and public order restored.

The second point I would like to talk about is the situation in the occupied area in Mong Kok. Police always emphasize that the illegally occupied part of Mong Kok is a high risk area. Radicals and troublemakers of different camps often provoke others to charge at Police line with a view to creating chaos.

On November 10, Police seized twelve metal planks and plastic shields at the staircase and rooftop of a building inside the occupied area. Two days ago, Police found construction waste inside a tent and some people claimed that the waste was for fixing the tent. Police at once advised those people to remove the waste but they refused. At about 10am yesterday, Police officers made enquiry in that area but could not locate owners of the waste. For the sake of public safety, Police officers seized 13 bags of construction waste containing stone and bricks and three bags of lime powder. A notice has been posted at scene to urge the owner to contact Police for collection of those items.

I must stress that Police will take resolute actions against those who obstruct Police officers in their execution of duties, or those who violently charge at Police line or use hard objects or other items to attack Police officers or others. If there is violent situation with no other alternatives, Police will use minimum level of force necessary in order to maintain law and order, to preserve public safety and public order.

I urge the illegal road occupiers not to provoke, obstruct or charge at Police. I also urge other protestors, particularly students, to stay away from radical individuals and troublemakers. Do not mix with them in the crowd and do not take part or be incited to take part in any acts of violence. When Police officers are executing duties on the ground, do maintain a safe distance from them. Do not charge at Police or put up resistance. We do not want to see anyone, especially students, being hurt when they place themselves close to radical individuals and troublemakers during violent acts.

I would like to sum up today's key messages. Firstly, the Court of First Instance has extended the Injunction Orders concerning access into CITIC Tower, Admiralty and the occupied area in Mong Kok. Police respect decision of the court and would comply with the directions accordingly. When the concerned parties have completed the relevant procedures, Police will render assistance at the request of the bailiffs. Once again, I urge protestors to respect the court orders, to remove the obstacles as soon as possible and to stop the illegal occupation.

Secondly, Mong Kok remains a high risk area. Members of the public should stay away from the occupied area. I urge illegal road occupiers not to provoke, obstruct or charge at Police. We do not want to see any confrontations leading to injuries, especially upon students. I stress that Police will take resolute actions against radicals who violently charge at Police.

Hong Kong Police is a professional law enforcement agency. We are capable and determined to preserve public safety and public order. Police will remain united and steadfast in doing our very best to serve the public.

Issued at HKT 19:19

NOVEMBER 15[25]

Remarks by Commissioner of Police at media session
****

Following are the remarks by the Commissioner of Police, Mr Tsang Wai-hung, at a media session after attending the passing-out parade of probationary inspectors and recruit constables at the Hong Kong Police College today (November 15).

The Police have tried its very best to maintain law and order in Hong Kong in the past seven weeks. I have to thank my officers for their efforts and steadfastness during this period. I also have to thank members of the community for their support. During the same period, the Police have exercised the utmost restraint in dealing with the unlawful behaviours of the protesters including those participating in unlawful assembly and those unlawfully occupying major thoroughfares in Hong Kong.

All along, we the Police hope to avoid major confrontation and to avoid bloodshed when dealing with these unlawful behaviours. As a law enforcement agency, however, the Police cannot allow these unlawful behaviours to go on indefinitely. The latest court ruling clearly directs that the Police assist the bailiffs in executing the injunction order and in reopening the blocked roads. The Police will give its fullest support and will exercise such other legal power as required to maintain public order and ensure public safety.

These protesters who have blocked our roads and those who have been taking part in these unlawful assembly have seriously disrupted the order of our society and also seriously undermined the rule of law of Hong Kong. Now I appeal again to them to immediately stop the unlawful behaviours and to immediately leave the blocked roads. I also urge them to obey the court order and not to obstruct the execution of the relevant injunction orders. For those protesters who choose to defy the law, choose to ignore the court order and obstruct the execution of the injunction order, the Police will take resolute measures to deal with them in accordance with the law.

Issued at HKT 14:55

---

[25] http://www.info.gov.hk/gia/general/201411/15.htm

NOVEMBER 17[26][27]

HKMA's update on operation of banking system and financial market
****

The following is issued on behalf of the Hong Kong Monetary Authority:

According to the reports to the Hong Kong Monetary Authority (HKMA) from banks as at 8am today (November 17), all previously affected bank branches have resumed operation. One branch of one bank would shorten their business hours today. The HKMA has requested banks to resume normal services as soon as circumstances permit. Customers should pay attention to the relevant banks' announcements regarding affected branches and ATMs. The HKMA will also publish on its website relevant updates from time to time.

Issued at HKT 09:38

Speech by CE at Shanghai-Hong Kong Stock Connect launch ceremony
****

Following is the speech by the Chief Executive, Mr C Y Leung, this morning (November 17) at the launch ceremony of the Shanghai-Hong Kong Stock Connect at the Hong Kong Exchanges and Clearing Limited:

At the Bo'ao Forum in April, Premier Li Keqiang announced that "conditions are being actively created to establish a trading mechanism between the Shanghai and Hong Kong stock markets".

After months of detailed preparation by the Central Authorities of the country and the Hong Kong SAR Government, and all other relevant parties, we are about to witness the launch of the Shanghai-Hong Kong Stock Connect.

This is a scheme of historic significance to both Hong Kong and Mainland stock markets. With the launch of Stock Connect, institutional and retail investors in Hong Kong and from overseas will be able to invest directly in eligible Mainland A-shares while eligible Mainland investors can invest in eligible Hong Kong stocks. Hong Kong banks have also implemented a new arrangement with effect from today whereby the Renminbi (RMB) daily conversion limit for Hong Kong residents has been lifted to facilitate Hong Kong residents in participating in Stock Connect and other RMB financial transactions.

The new mutual market access has special significance in two respects:

---

[26] There was no government press releases for November 16
[27] http://www.info.gov.hk/gia/general/201411/17.htm

I. The scheme creates synergy for the two stock markets by expanding the sources of investment and boosting their competitiveness;

II. Stock Connect facilitates the gradual opening of the Mainland's capital account and the internationalisation of the RMB as an investment currency for global investors, thereby reinforcing Hong Kong's position as an international financial centre and a premier offshore RMB hub.

Hong Kong has the combined advantages of "One Country" and "Two Systems". We also offer the unique feature of being part of China and yet outside the Mainland. We are therefore the "super-connector" between the rest of the country and the rest of the world. Stock Connect aligns the Mainland market with the international markets and is the upgraded version of Hong Kong as the super-connector to and from China.

The National 12th Five-Year Plan undertakes to support Hong Kong to "consolidate and enhance its status as an international financial, trade and transportation centre". Stock Connect is the latest illustration of such support. The Hong Kong SAR Government will now work with the Central Government on the next Five-Year Plan, to map out further enhancements of Hong Kong as an international financial centre. To this end, the HKSAR Government has also established the Financial Services Development Council.

I offer my sincere gratitude to all those who have put in so much effort within so short a space of time to finalise the preparation of this launch. Once Stock Connect starts, there will be close monitoring by the Government, regulators and exchanges. It is necessary to ensure that the scheme operates smoothly to meet the market needs and consider what room there is to improve the mechanism and expand the scheme in an orderly manner.

Thank you.

Issued at HKT 10:47

LegCo to consider motion under Legislative Council (Powers and Privileges) Ordinance
****

The following is issued on behalf of the Legislative Council Secretariat:

The Legislative Council (LegCo) will hold a meeting on Wednesday (November 19) at 11am in the Chamber of the LegCo Complex. During the meeting, Members will consider a motion under the Legislative Council (Powers and Privileges) Ordinance.

The motion, to be moved by Ms Cyd Ho, states: "That this Council appoints a select committee to inquire into whether the Chief Executive of the Hong Kong Special Administrative Region, Mr Leung

Chun-ying, has contravened Article 47 of the Basic Law which stipulates that the Chief Executive must be a person of integrity, dedicated to his or her duties; whether he had accurately declared his holding of shares in DTZ Japan to the Chief Justice of the Court of Final Appeal of the Hong Kong Special Administrative Region when he assumed office; and whether the gains from his shares have constituted any conflict of interest with his performance of the duties of the Chief Executive, including but not limited to not issuing a domestic free television programme service licence to Hong Kong Television Network Limited, and other related issues; and that in the performance of its duties the committee be authorised under section 9(2) of the Legislative Council (Powers and Privileges) Ordinance (Cap. 382) to exercise the powers conferred by section 9(1) of that Ordinance."

Meanwhile, Mr Ronny Tong will move a motion on constitutional reform. The motion states: "That this Council urges the Government to expeditiously put forward a practical and feasible constitutional reform package."

Ms Emily Lau will move an amendment to Mr Ronny Tong's motion.

Mr Poon Siu-ping will also move a motion on ensuring occupational safety. The motion states: "That, as the number of work injury accidents and fatal industrial accidents in Hong Kong remains high, this Council urges the Government to establish a dedicated committee for comprehensively reviewing the policies on Hong Kong employees' occupational safety and health, including the protection coverage of occupational diseases and improvement of the protection for workers in high-risk occupations (i.e. insurance, compensation, therapy and rehabilitation)."

Mr Tang Ka-piu and Mr Chan Kin-por will move separate amendments to Mr Poon Siu-ping's motion.

Moreover, Mr James To will move a proposed resolution under section 34(4) of the Interpretation and General Clauses Ordinance to seek the Council's approval to extend the period for amending the Inland Revenue (Double Taxation Relief and Prevention of Fiscal Evasion with respect to Taxes on Income) (Republic of Korea) Order and the Inland Revenue (Double Taxation Relief and Prevention of Fiscal Evasion with respect to Taxes on Income) (Socialist Republic of Vietnam) (Amendment) Order 2014 laid on the table of LegCo on October 22, 2014 to the meeting of December 10, 2014.

On bills, Members will resume Second Reading debate on the Child Abduction Legislation (Miscellaneous Amendments) Bill 2013. If the Bill is supported by Members and receives its Second Reading, it will then go through the Committee stage and be read the third time.

During the meeting, Members will also ask the Government 22 questions on various policy areas, six of which require oral replies.

The agenda of the above meeting can be obtained via the LegCo Website (www.legco.gov.hk). Please note that the agenda is subject to change, and the latest information about the agenda could be found in the LegCo Website.

Members of the public are welcome to observe the proceedings of the meeting from the public galleries of the Chamber of the LegCo Complex. They may reserve seats by calling 3919 3399 during office hours. Members of the public can also watch or listen the meeting via the web broadcast system on the LegCo Website.

Issued at HKT 17:01

Police render full assistance to bailiffs in executing Injunction Order
****

Police have met with the plaintiff of the Injunction Order on the blockage of the access into CITIC Tower, Admiralty and the bailiffs today (November 17) with regard to the execution of the order. Police are ready to give the fullest support to the bailiffs to execute the court order tomorrow (November 18).

The Court of First Instance earlier in its judgment authorised bailiffs to assist the plaintiff in removing obstructions and that the bailiffs could request the assistance of Police when necessary. The court further authorised Police to arrest those who obstruct the bailiffs in executing their duties.

Police emphasise that the bailiffs are authorised by the court to execute court orders. Any act amounts to obstruction may render one liable to the offence of "criminal contempt of court". If anyone obstructs or violently charges the bailiffs when they are executing their duties, Police will take resolute action.

Police urge the illegal road occupiers to obey the court order, remove obstacles and personal belongings, and stop the illegal occupation soonest.

Issued at HKT 20:40

NOVEMBER 18[28]

HKMA's update on operation of banking system and financial market

****

The following is issued on behalf of the Hong Kong Monetary Authority:

According to the reports to the Hong Kong Monetary Authority (HKMA) from banks as at 8am today (November 18), all previously affected bank branches have resumed operation. One branch of one bank would shorten its business hours today. The HKMA has requested banks to resume normal services as soon as circumstances permit. Customers should pay attention to the relevant banks' announcements regarding affected branches and ATMs. The HKMA will also publish on its website relevant updates from time to time.

Issued at HKT 09:33

Transcript of remarks by CE at media session

****

Following is the transcript of remarks by the Chief Executive, Mr C Y Leung, at a media session before the Executive Council meeting today (November 18):

Reporter: Mr Leung, the bailiffs are now clearing the area outside the Citic Tower. Are you worried that the demonstrators will go somewhere else and, you know, occupy somewhere else again?

Chief Executive: Well, I think it is abundantly clear by now that the occupiers are and have been breaching the law of Hong Kong. Hong Kong is a law-abiding society and the rest of Hong Kong expect the occupiers, like everyone else in Hong Kong, to follow the law. The demand on the part of the occupiers when it comes to the constitutional development, especially universal suffrage to elect the Chief Executive in 2017, is also very clear, so I don't see any point in resisting the court order.

Issued at HKT 10:49

---

[28] http://www.info.gov.hk/gia/general/201411/18.htm

Speech by FS at networking reception in Sydney (English only)
****

Following is the speech by the Financial Secretary, Mr John C Tsang, at a networking reception co-organised by the Hong Kong Economic and Trade Office (HKETO) in Sydney and the Hong Kong Australia Business Association in Sydney today (November 18):

The Honourable John Barilaro, Mr (Mark) Speakman, the Honourable Ernest Wong, President (Peter) Sinn, distinguished guests, ladies and gentlemen,

Good evening.

It is a great pleasure for me to join you all at tonight's reception co-organised by the HKETO here in Sydney and the Hong Kong Australia Business Association. It is, by the way, 11 years ago this month that I last addressed the business community in Sydney. Some things have changed since then; some have not.

Eleven years ago, I was, well, 11 years younger. Less gray hair perhaps. And, like some of you here, a few pounds, or kilos, lighter. Of course, we are all 11 years wiser. In my address here 11 years ago, I commiserated with you over the Wallabies' Rugby World Cup final loss to England.

In just 10 months, it is World Cup time again, with England hosting the eighth Rugby World Cup. If you are a rugby fan, you know that Australia is in the same pool with England, not to mention Wales. Well, no one said it would be easy - unless, of course, you are New Zealand, sitting there in Pool C, alongside rugby powerhouses like Namibia, Georgia, Tonga and Argentina.

Eleven years ago, Hong Kong was recovering from the after effects of the SARS virus outbreak earlier that year. This year, we are all pretty much healthier, thank you.

But, there is always something - something to be thankful for, and certainly something to "occupy" us as well - we now have a political situation to contend with. No doubt, you have been watching, and reading, about the protest that has gripped Hong Kong over these past seven weeks or so.

More than capturing global attention, it has taken over a few of Hong Kong's main thoroughfares. Pup tents, roadside sleepovers and impromptu entertainment may make it all look like an ambitious street carnival. But it is, of course, cause for concern for us. And we are working to bridge the divide that exists in our community, working hard to create a consensus rooted in the Basic Law, our constitution.

The divide, and hence the protests, are about the nomination procedure for the Chief Executive election in 2017. I am confident that, 11 years from now, you will not need any further updates on this issue from me or my future colleagues.

Those are a few of the differences between Hong Kong in 2003 and Hong Kong today. Mostly, however, we continue to work from longstanding strengths to create business opportunities for Australian companies, and companies around the world.

Thanks to our unparalleled location, our longstanding business connections, our professional knowledge and our deep cultural ties, Hong Kong serves as the bridge between Mainland China and the world.

We are also a major player in the ASEAN region, home to more than 600 million people, with a rapidly growing middle class. In fact, half the world's population is within a five-hour flight of Hong Kong. And we have hourly flights to a dozen major Asian destinations. About 7,500 overseas and Mainland Chinese companies have a presence in Hong Kong. More than half of them are regional headquarters or regional offices. Some 600 Australian companies do business in Hong Kong.

The attractions are many, from the free flow of capital and information, to our independent judiciary and the confidence that comes from knowing that everyone - and every business in Hong Kong - is treated equally. That Australian nationals and companies enjoy the same rights as locals do. That Hong Kong presents a truly level playing field, unlike other so-called free markets in our region.

No less important, in Hong Kong you get to keep most of your hard-earned income. Our tax regime is low and uncomplicated. The top salaries tax rate is 15 per cent; profits tax is fixed at a flat 16.5 per cent. There is no capital gains tax, no inheritance tax, and no sales tax of any kind in Hong Kong. I even eliminated the tax on wine and beer six years ago. Many people ask how do we do that. In short, we believe in small government - and big opportunities. We have managed to keep the public sector at about 20 per cent of GDP, and allow the private sector to make more efficient use of the limited resources, creating opportunities for our community.

For Australian business, Hong Kong is also the international financial centre in the Asian time zone. More than 70 of the world's largest 100 banks operate in Hong Kong, including five Australian banks. We rank first and third respectively in the World Economic Forum's Financial Development Index and the City of London's Global Financial Centres Index. We maintain a highly open and internationalised market, and our regulatory regime is aligned with major markets around the world.

As the region's international financial centre, Hong Kong is also the major provider of financial services for businesses in the Mainland. And this symbiotic relationship continues to strengthen.

Indeed, Hong Kong has a unique role to play in contributing to our nation's financial reforms. We serve as both the laboratory for China's new reform measures as well as the firewall to shield the Mainland's fledgling financial market from international volatility against the background of its fast-changing financial landscape.

And if it is changing, and changing fast, in Mainland China, the changes are no less fluid, no less promising, in Hong Kong. To take one example, there is the Shanghai-Hong Kong Stock Connect. I am pleased to tell you that it launched just yesterday. Under the programme, investors from Hong Kong, from Australia and from around the world, can trade in the Hong Kong Stock Exchange some 570 Shanghai-listed shares, directly, for the first time. Mainland China investors, meanwhile, will be able to trade in the Shanghai Stock Exchange the 270 Hong Kong-listed shares directly.

This brand-new initiative brings unprecedented opportunities to the financial world. One senior Western banker recently described it as the single most important development in China's intention to internationalise this market. The Shanghai-Hong Kong Stock Connect will also accelerate the development of our offshore Renminbi business.

That began in earnest a decade ago. Today, it is perhaps the most vivid illustration of financial co-operation between Mainland China and Hong Kong. Over the past 10 years, our offshore Renminbi business has showcased Hong Kong's unique position to contribute to, and benefit from, the continuous economic and financial reform of China.

At the end of September, our banks held 1.1 trillion yuan in deposits and certificates of deposit. In the first nine months of this year, Renminbi trade settlement handled by banks in Hong Kong totalled 4.5 trillion yuan. From 2007 to October this year, more than 460 Renminbi-denominated bond issuances had been held in Hong Kong, with an outstanding amount exceeding 360 billion yuan. Anyway you count it, it adds up to good business, and great promise, for Hong Kong - and Australia, too.

I welcome the development of Renminbi business in Australia. It can only mean wider use of and expanded convertibility for the Renminbi. And that will surely open up more business, and investment prospects, for companies in Australia, Mainland China and Hong Kong.

Ladies and gentlemen, let me close with the same ending I offered the business community here 11 years ago - and I quote, "As the old saying goes, seeing is believing. So, ladies and gentlemen, I urge you to come to Hong Kong to see for yourself, to assess the opportunities . . . to feel the pulse, the energy and the dynamism of Asia's world city. I am sure you will not be disappointed."

That was then. Let me add only that I know you will not be disappointed. Yes, I am even more confident in Hong Kong these days, in the opportunities we can offer Australian business. Today and tomorrow.

Thank you.

Issued at HKT 16:35

Agenda of tomorrow's LegCo meeting revised
****

The following is issued on behalf of the Legislative Council Secretariat:

The agenda of the Legislative Council (LegCo) meeting, scheduled for tomorrow (November 19) at 11am in the Chamber of the LegCo Complex, has been revised. In addition to the original items, the President of LegCo has given permission for Mr Dennis Kwok to ask an urgent question on "immediate measures to be taken by the Police before giving further assistance to the bailiffs in enforcing injunction orders" under Rule 24(4) of the Rules of Procedure at the meeting.

For the latest agenda items of tomorrow's LegCo meeting, please refer to the LegCo Website: www.legco.gov.hk/yr14-15/english/counmtg/agenda/cm20141119.htm.

Issued at HKT 19:30

NOVEMBER 19[29]

LegCo meeting rescheduled and tours of LegCo Complex cancelled
****
The following is issued on behalf of the Legislative Council Secretariat:

Please broadcast the following message as soon as possible and repeat it at suitable intervals:

The meeting of the Legislative Council (LegCo) Public Works Subcommittee originally scheduled for 8.30am and the Council meeting for 11am this morning (November 19) have been rescheduled.

Meanwhile, the guided educational tours of the LegCo Complex are cancelled today.

Issued at HKT 08:06

Police strongly condemn acts endangering public order
****
Police strongly condemned the acts of protesters who attempted to enter the Legislative Council (LegCo) Complex by force and endangered public order in the small hours today (November 19).

At about 1am, some protesters attempted to force their way into the LegCo Complex and caused damages to various parts of the building. Police, on the request of LegCo, provided assistance at scene.

Protesters repeatedly charged the Police cordon line. Police had to take actions including the use of OC Foam to stop them and defend against attack after advice and warnings had failed.

In the incident, Police arrested four males, aged between 18 and 24, for "criminal damage" and "assaulting police officer" respectively. Three male police officers sustained injuries and were sent to hospital for treatment.

Police strongly condemned such acts of the protesters which disrupted public order. Protesters are urged to follow Police officers' instructions and leave the scene peacefully and orderly.

Police reiterate that any acts endangering public order and public safety will not be tolerated. The Hong Kong community regard that individuals should express their views in a rational and peaceful manner.

Issued at HKT 08:12

---

[29] http://www.info.gov.hk/gia/general/201411/19.htm

HKMA's update on the operation of the banking system and financial market
****
The following is issued on behalf of the Hong Kong Monetary Authority:

According to the reports to the Hong Kong Monetary Authority (HKMA) from banks as at 8am today (November 19), all previously affected bank branches have resumed operation. One branch of one bank would shorten its business hours today. The HKMA has requested banks to resume normal services as soon as circumstances permit. Customers should pay attention to the relevant banks' announcements regarding affected branches and ATMs. The HKMA will also publish on its website relevant updates from time to time.
Issued at HKT 09:41

Special meeting of the Legislative Council Commission
****
The following is issued on behalf of the Legislative Council Secretariat:

The Legislative Council Commission will hold a closed special meeting at 11am today (November 19) in Conference Room 5 of the Legislative Council Complex.
Issued at HKT 10:3

Public services in LegCo Complex suspended
****
The following is issued on behalf of the Legislative Council Secretariat:

The Legislative Council (LegCo) Secretariat announces that the service of the LegCo Public Complaints Office is suspended today (November 19).
Meanwhile, the LegCo Library, the LegCo Archives, the Children's Corner and the exhibition area in the main lobby of the LegCo Complex continue not to be open to the public until further notice.
Issued at HKT 10:59

Special arrangements on submission of tenders arising from temporary closure of Government Secretariat Tender Box
****

Owing to the special access arrangements at the Central Government Offices (CGO) in Tamar, the Government Secretariat Tender Box (GSTB) located on the ground floor of the East Wing of CGO is closed for tender deposit temporarily.

All tenders that should originally be deposited into the GSTB are instead requested to be deposited into the Government Logistics Department Tender Box (GLDTB) located on the ground floor of North Point Government Offices at 333 Java Road, North Point. This special arrangement came into effect on September 30 this year and remains in effect until further notice.

Tenderers may wish to check in advance their route to the GLDTB and allow sufficient time to make arrangements to deposit their tenders into the GLDTB before the respective closing time of tenders. Late tenders will not be accepted.

For enquiries, please call 2810 2497 or 2231 5288 between 9am and 6pm from Mondays to Fridays (except public holidays).

Issued at HKT 11:30

Government strongly condemns LegCo break-in by violent acts of radicals
****

The Government strongly condemns the violent acts by some violent radicals who stormed the Legislative Council (LegCo) Complex early this morning (November 19).

In the course of forcing themselves into the LegCo Complex, violent radicals repeatedly charged the Complex by using mills barriers and bricks to smash the glass doors at different places and damage the building facade, resulting in severe damage to various parts of the Complex. The radicals also attempted to obstruct police officers at the scene from carrying out their duties and provoked them. After repeated appeals and warnings, which turned out to be futile, police officers adopted the minimum force to counteract and stop the protesters from continued charging. In the incident, three police officers sustained injuries and six persons have been arrested so far. The Police are conducting a thorough investigation into the incident and further arrests will be made.

Due to the violent acts by the radical protesters, the meetings of the LegCo Public Works Subcommittee and the Council meeting originally scheduled for this morning were forced to be rescheduled. The operation of the LegCo was once again disrupted.

A government spokesman stressed that members of the public shall observe the law when expressing views or aspirations. The spokesman added that the Government would not tolerate any violent acts.

Issued at HKT 15:25

Legislative Council Commission strongly condemns storming of LegCo Complex
****

The following is issued on behalf of the Legislative Council Secretariat:

The Legislative Council Commission (the Commission) strongly condemns the violent acts of storming the Legislative Council (LegCo) Complex (the Complex) early this morning (November 19) causing severe damage to various parts of the Complex. The Commission urges the law-enforcing bodies to take prompt and decisive actions to arrest the culprits and bring them to justice.

Anyone who obstructs a LegCo Member going to or from the precincts of the Chamber commits an offence. The Commission has instructed the LegCo Secretariat to step up liaison with the Police and take appropriate measures to ensure the safety of LegCo Members and staff of the Secretariat entering and leaving the Complex, and the smooth conduct of meetings.

Issued at HKT 18:44

LegCo meeting to be held tomorrow
****

The following is issued on behalf of the Legislative Council Secretariat:

The Legislative Council (LegCo) meeting originally scheduled for today (November 19) has been rescheduled for tomorrow (November 20) at 9am in the Chamber of the LegCo Complex.

Issued at HKT 19:19

Opening remarks by Police Chief Superintendent at press conference
****

Following are the opening remarks by the Chief Superintendent of Police Public Relations Branch, Mr Hui Chun-tak, at the press conference today (November 19):

First of all, Police strongly condemned the violent acts of some radical protestors who stormed the Legislative Council (LegCo) Complex in the early hours of today. The riotous acts had seriously disrupted public order and public safety and led to damage in various parts of the LegCo Complex.

At about 1am this morning, a group of radical individuals and troublemakers wearing helmets, goggles, surgical masks or facemasks repeatedly charged the glass doors of the Complex. They used mills barriers, bricks, concrete drainage covers and rubbish bins to smash the glass doors and damage the building facade.

At about 1.05am, Police received a request for assistance from the LegCo. Police promptly arrived at scene and set up a cordon line outside the Complex to prevent violent radicals and troublemakers from further damaging the building and to preserve public safety and public order. Regrettably, some protestors obstructed Police reinforcements and led to serious confrontations. These radical protestors continued to incite others to charge Police. They verbally abused and provoked Police through loudhailers at close range and used flashlight to obscure the view of officers. They even threw umbrellas, plastic bottles and helmets at Police or charged Police officers resulting in violent confrontations. Some officers were pushed onto the ground and sustained injuries.

Police issued multiple warnings through announcement and display of warning banners at scene. These radical individuals and troublemakers ignored the warnings and continued to charge Police violently. Police had no alternative but to take resolute action and use minimum level of force by using pepper spray and batons to stop the violent acts. At the request of LegCo Secretariat, Police inspected the Complex to ensure that no radical individuals remained thereat.

Police have so far arrested six males, aged between 18 and 24, for 'criminal damage' and 'assaulting police' in connection with the violent incident. Three Police officers were injured and required medical treatment.

I notice that some people incited others to block access to the LegCo Complex on the Internet in an attempt to prevent LegCo members from entering the building for meetings. I have to point out that there are many rumours and inaccurate information being circulated on the Internet. Members of the public have to make careful judgment to avoid being incited or used for illegal acts. I have to remind the public that anyone who obstructs LegCo members from attending LegCo meetings may be criminally liable. On the other hand, it is against the law to incite others on the Internet to commit illegal acts. The rule of law is the cornerstone of Hong Kong's success and everyone should obey the law. Anyone who commits an illegal act, be it in the real world or cyber world, has to bear criminal liability and be subject to legal sanction. Police will continue to investigate the case and may make further arrests.

Police stress that we will not tolerate any acts of violence. Police have commenced a thorough criminal investigation and will bring those criminally liable to justice.

The second point concerns the Injunction Order on the blockage of roads in Mong Kok. The Court of First Instance has authorized bailiffs to assist the plaintiffs in removing obstructions and that the bailiffs can request the assistance of Police when necessary. The court has further authorized Police to arrest those who obstruct the bailiffs in executing their duties. Today, Police had a meeting with the plaintiffs and bailiffs in respect of the Injunction Orders relating to the blockage in Mong Kok. When the relevant parties have finalized the preparation, Police will assist the bailiffs to execute the Injunction Orders.

Police stress that the bailiffs are authorized by the court to execute court orders. Any acts amounting to obstruction may render one liable to the offence of 'criminal contempt of court'. I appeal to protestors not to be incited by radical individuals and troublemakers to obstruct or violently charge the bailiffs. Police will take resolute actions against those who obstruct or violently charge the bailiffs who are executing their duties. When necessary, Police will use other powers conferred by the law to preserve public order and public safety. Police will also reclaim government property, such as mills barriers and water barriers, which have been illegally taken by the illegal road occupiers.

Police once again urge the illegal road occupiers to obey the court orders, remove obstacles and personal belongings, and to leave in a peaceful and orderly manner so that the roads can be re-opened and public order restored.

I want to emphasize that the illegally occupied part of Mong Kok remains a high-risk area. There are radicals and troublemakers of different camps provoking others in the illegally occupied areas. There is also a large assembly of people with different views who often dispute with each other in an emotional state, thereby increasing the chance of confrontation. Large-scale confrontations may be sparked off any time in Mong Kok. At about 2.15am this morning, Police arrested a 52-year-old man for 'common assault' and the case is now being handled by District Investigation Team of Mong Kok District. Members of the public, especially students, are urged to stay away from these areas and parents should not bring children there to avoid any unnecessary injuries. I notice that some radical individuals and troublemakers have incited others to commit illegal acts of violence on the Internet or at scene, and even provided supplies to facilitate the violent charging actions. However, these people left at once when violent confrontations were sparked off to avoid criminal liability and to shed the responsibility to others. I wish to remind the public that anyone taking part in such violent acts will have to bear the criminal liability. As such, do not be incited or used by others to commit illegal acts of violence.

I would like to sum up the two key messages today. Firstly, Police strongly condemned the violent radicals for storming and damaging the LegCo Complex. Police will not tolerate any acts of violence in breach of public order and public safety. Such violent acts are not acceptable in society. Secondly, when the relevant parties have finished their preparation, Police will assist the bailiffs in executing the Injunction Orders concerning the blockage of roads in Mong Kok. Police are prepared and will take resolute actions against those who obstruct or violently charge the bailiffs who are executing their duties. Members of the public should not be incited or used by radical individuals or troublemakers to commit acts of violence. Police also urge the illegal road occupiers to obey the court orders, remove obstacles and personal belongings, and to stop occupying the roads to allow daily life of the general public to resume normal.

Issued at HKT 20:12

NOVEMBER 20[30]

HKMA's update on the operation of the banking system and financial market
****

The following is issued on behalf of the Hong Kong Monetary Authority:

According to the reports to the Hong Kong Monetary Authority (HKMA) from banks as at 8am today (November 20), all previously affected bank branches have resumed operation. One branch of one bank would shorten their business hours today. The HKMA has requested banks to resume normal services as soon as circumstances permit. Customers should pay attention to the relevant banks' announcements regarding affected branches and ATMs. The HKMA will also publish on its website relevant updates from time to time.

Issued at HKT 09:45

LCQ17: Impact of Occupy Central movement on staging of events and tourism industry
****

Following is a question by the Hon Wong Ting-kwong and a written reply by the the Secretary for Commerce and Economic Development, Mr Gregory So, in the Legislative Council today (November 20):

Question:

The Secretary for Commerce and Economic Development told the media earlier that since its occurrence, the Occupy Central movement had affected the events staged in Hong Kong and the desire of travellers to visit Hong Kong. For example, the Hong Kong Wine and Dine Festival (the Festival) was re-sited, with 10 per cent of its exhibitors having withdrawn from the event; the international Gran Fondo Hong Kong cycling race (the cycling race) originally scheduled for December this year was cancelled. Moreover, some members from the information technology sector indicated that individual staff members of overseas companies had cancelled their trips to Hong Kong for attending meetings due to the Occupy Central movement. The number of non-Mainland travellers to Hong Kong in the first 28 days of last month dropped by 3.7 per cent compared to the same period last year. In this connection, will the Government inform this Council:

---

[30] http://www.info.gov.hk/gia/general/201411/20.htm

(1) whether it has assessed the economic losses suffered by Hong Kong as a result of the re-siting of the Festival and the cancellation of the cycling race; whether it knows the respective numbers of events which were re-sited, suspended or even cancelled due to the Occupy Central movement, and whether it has quantified the economic losses so incurred;

(2) whether, in the light of the drop in the number of non-mainland travellers due to the Occupy Central movement, it has assessed the resultant economic losses suffered by the tourism industry; if it has, of the details; if not, the reasons for that; whether it has assessed how long it will take for the tourism industry to recover after the Occupy Central movement ends; and

(3) as the Occupy Central movement is still going on at present, whether it knows if the Hong Kong Tourism Board (HKTB) has assessed the impact of the movement on its planning and promotion of tourism activities; if HKTB has assessed, of the outcome?

Reply:

President,

The Government has been closely monitoring the impact of the Occupy Movement on different sectors. Since the start of the Occupy Movement, the Commerce and Economic Development Bureau has met with representatives of the travel and hotel trades for several times to understand the impact of the Occupy Movement on the tourism industry in Hong Kong.

Our replies to the questions raised by Hon Wong Ting-kwong are as follows:

(1) The Hong Kong Wine & Dine Festival was organised by the Hong Kong Tourism Board (HKTB) from October 30 to November 2 at the former Kai Tak Runway. As quite a number of expenses and income items are incurred in the event, the final results of the event can only be assessed when the report is completed.

The HKTB has decided to postpone the Hong Kong Cyclothon originally scheduled for December 2014. Since most of the promotional work for the event has not yet been launched, the HKTB is not able to assess the economic impact brought about by the postponement of the event at this stage.

The events that the HKTB will organise in 2014/15 are set out in the Annex[31].

There is no sign showing that the events set out in the Annex[32] would be affected by the Occupy Movement at this stage.

(2) and (3) According to the statistics of the Immigration Department, the number of non-Mainland visitor arrivals in October this year has decreased by 3.5 per cent as compared to that of the same period last year, while the number of non-Mainland visitor arrivals from November 1 to 17 has decreased by 7.5 per cent as compared to that of the same period last year. All these indicate a tendency towards a bigger drop in arrival figures. Some trade representatives expressed that since the start of the Occupy Movement, there has been cancellation of bookings for over 1 000 hotel rooms every day. The percentage of rooms with advance bookings from mid-October to November has dropped from 60 to 70 per cent over the same period last year to 40 to 50 per cent only this year. Besides, some representatives of the retail industry indicated that the business of some shops locating in nearby areas of the Occupy Movement has dropped by 30 to 70 per cent. The travel trade is worried that if the Occupy Movement continues, it would affect the livelihood of frontline employees of the tourism industry and give a blow to the tourism industry in Hong Kong.

The overall actual impact can only be assessed upon the release of relevant economic data. The Government and the HKTB will co-operate and work hand-in-hand with the trade to step up tourism promotional efforts immediately after the Occupy Movement has ended.

Issued at HKT 11:11

LCQ11: Measures against "Occupy Central"
****

Following is a question by the Hon Ng Leung-sing and a written reply by the Secretary for Security, Mr Lai Tung-kwok, in the Legislative Council today (November 20):

Question:

Last month, the British Broadcasting Corporation reported that human rights activists from around the world attended this year's conference of the Oslo Freedom Forum (OFF) held in Norway last month. The topics discussed at the meeting included the Occupy Central movement which occurred in Hong Kong, and that plans for the occupation of roads (the occupation) were hatched by initiators of the movement

---

[31] To view: http://gia.info.gov.hk/general/201411/20/P201411200285_0285_137601.pdf
[32] ibid

and human rights activists from around the world as far back as January 2013, with more than 1 000 Hong Kong people having received specific training, including how to speak to the Police and how to manage their action, etc., prior to the initiation of the occupation. In this connection, will the Government inform this Council:

(1) whether it has grasped the planning of the occupation; if it has not, of the reasons for that; if it has, whether it has taken targeted measures to prevent the occurrence of the occupation; and

(2) whether it has assessed if OFF's conduct of activities related to Hong Kong has constituted a threat to the security of Hong Kong; if it has assessed, of the outcome; if it has not assessed, the reasons for that?

Reply:

President,

The Administration's reply to the Hon Ng Leung-sing's question is as follows:

(1) In January 2013, a scholar advocated non-violent civil disobedience in a newspaper article as a means to fight for implementation of genuine universal suffrage in Hong Kong, by rallying up to 10 000 protesters to unlawfully occupy the major trunk roads in Central for a long span of time (hereinafter, the "Occupy Central"), with the aim of paralysing Hong Kong's political and economic hub, whereby forcing the Central Government to accede to their demand. In the following one year and more, the initiators of "Occupy Central" and a number of organisations kept on propagating the concept of "Occupy Central" through various channels. While keeping a close watch on the situation, the Police had conducted risk assessments and formulated plans in a timely manner, and had also set out corresponding deployment and contingency measures. The Administration could not disclose specific particulars of Police's assessments, plans and deployment as they are matters of operational details.

The SAR Government, in the past one year and more, has put in place a number of measures against the "Occupy Central" on the community front. For instance, the Administration had, on different occasions, called on persons who intend to organise public order events to notify the Police and provide details in accordance with the Public Order Ordinance. When expressing their aspirations, participants of meetings or processions were also advised to abide by the laws of Hong Kong and respect other's right so that the events could proceed in a peaceful and orderly manner without compromising the Police's efforts to maintain law and order. The SAR Government had repeatedly spelt out the potential negative impact of

"Occupy Central" on various sectors of the community in different ways and through different channels. Given that such an event might jeopardise public safety and public order, members of the public, in contemplating participation in such an event, were also reminded to take heed of its legality, the possible out-of-control situation, personal safety, legal liabilities and so on. At the briefings organised by the banking, hotel and retail sectors, the Police were invited to expound the potential negative impact of "Occupy Central" on such sectors while advising them to make contingency plans.

(2) According to media reports, participants of an overseas forum had had discussions on the planning and operation management of "Occupy Central". The Administration noted that, since the beginning of "Occupy Central", different analyses have been made and views expressed by Hong Kong and overseas communities, politicians and media on whether external forces have been involved in or have influenced "Occupy Central" directly or indirectly. The issue has aroused concerns locally and overseas. The Chief Executive pointed out that the involvement of external forces in "Occupy Central" was not a mere speculation. Hong Kong, as part of China and a highly open city, has been operating within a rather complicated international environment and exposed to the influence of external forces. However, the issue involves national and local security as well as a lot of other complicated and sensitive information. In dealing with matters of this kind, the Administration considers it inappropriate for the SAR Government, as for any other governments, to conduct an open discussion.

As far as "Occupy Central" is concerned, the SAR Government will restore social order in accordance with the law as soon as possible. Stressing that "Occupy Central" is an unlawful assembly, the Government will deal with this illegal activity, including its organisation and planning, in a serious manner. Hong Kong is a city of rule of law. The law enforcement agencies will deal with this illegal activity in accordance with the law.

Issued at HKT 12:12

LCQ9: Taxation issues
****

Following is a question by the Hon Sin Chung-kai and a written reply by the Secretary for Financial Services and the Treasury, Professor K C Chan, in the Legislative Council today (November 20):

Question:

The incumbent Chief Executive (CE) announced his resignation from DTZ in November 2011. It has recently been reported by some Australian media that in December of the same year, CE signed an agreement with UGL Limited (UGL), which was then planning to acquire DTZ, undertaking not to poach employees from or compete with DTZ as well as to act as a referee and adviser to UGL, within two years after the acquisition was completed. Under the aforesaid agreement, CE received a remuneration of £4 million in total in 2012 and 2013. In addition, according to that agreement, CE may sell at any time his shares in DTZ Japan (the Japanese branch of DTZ) to UGL fetching at least £200,000. At the meeting of this Council held on the 6th of this month, the Acting Chief Secretary for Administration cited the professional advice of a certified public accountant (practising) that according to relevant requirements under the Inland Revenue Ordinance (Cap. 112), salaries tax was applicable to income arising in or derived from Hong Kong from an office, employment and any pension only, and CE was therefore not required to pay salaries tax for the payments he received from UGL. Nevertheless, some members of the public have pointed out that the aforesaid agreement involves the provision of services and has to be carried out in Hong Kong. As such, they have queried why CE was not required to pay tax for the payments concerned. In this connection, will the Government inform this Council if it has assessed:

(1) whether the remunerations receivable by a Hong Kong resident under an agreement entered with an overseas company, under which he undertakes to act as a referee and adviser to that company, shall be deemed "income arising in or derived from Hong Kong" from an "employment of profit", and hence shall be subject to salaries tax assessment; if the assessment outcome is in the negative, of the justifications for that; if the assessment outcome is in the affirmative, whether the full amount or just part of the remunerations concerned shall be deemed assessable income; and

(2) whether, in accordance with Cap. 112, a Hong Kong resident is required to pay tax for the profits earned from the sale of the shares of an overseas company; if the assessment outcome is in the negative, of the reasons for that?

Reply:

President,

My consolidated reply to the Hon Sin Chung-kai's question is as follows:

In accordance with the requirements under section 8 of the Inland Revenue Ordinance (Cap. 112) (IRO), salaries tax is chargeable on every person in respect of his income from any office or employment or any pension arising in or derived from Hong Kong. In assessing whether an income is chargeable to tax, the assessor has to consider all details of each individual case including the territorial source of the employment and the nature of the income concerned. Generally speaking, salaries, wages and director's fees, commissions, bonuses and leave pay are chargeable income. As regards other types of income, their chargeability to tax can only be assessed on the basis of the facts involved. The assessor has to examine all details of the case before making the assessment.

As to whether profits earned from the sale of the shares of an overseas company are chargeable to tax, all relevant facts of each individual case, including the locality and nature of the profits concerned, have to be examined before an assessment can be made. Since Hong Kong adopts a territorial source principle of taxation and does not charge capital gains tax, generally speaking, if the profits concerned are sourced from Hong Kong and are of revenue nature, such profits are chargeable to tax. However, if the profits concerned are not sourced from Hong Kong or if the profits are of capital nature, they are not subject to tax. The assessor has to ascertain the locality and nature of the profits on the basis of relevant facts in deciding whether tax should be charged on the individuals concerned.

Given the official secrecy provision under section 4 of the IRO, the Inland Revenue Department will not comment or disclose any further information on individual cases.

Issued at HKT 12:20

LCQ18: Granting of legal aid to a person for institution of legal proceedings for continuation with illegal activities

****

Following is a question by the Hon Ng Leung-sing and a written reply by the Secretary for Home Affairs, Mr Tsang Tak-sing, in the Legislative Council today (November 20):

Question:

Recently, large-scale illegal occupation of roads occurred in a number of districts in Hong Kong. On the 20th of last month, the Court granted interim injunctions to a number of organisations affected by the occupation, restraining the occupants from continued occupation of the roads in Mong Kok, and from obstruction of the passageways leading to a commercial building in Admiralty. Subsequently, an occupant was granted legal aid by the Legal Aid Department (LAD) to apply to the Court for discharging the interim injunctions granted in respect of the occupied area in Mong Kok. On the other hand, under Section 10(3) of the Legal Aid Ordnance (Cap. 91) (Section 10(3)), the Director of Legal Aid (DLA) may refuse to grant legal aid where it appears to him that there are circumstances as set out in that provision in a legal aid application. As occupation of roads is illegal, some members of the public have queried why LAD approved the legal aid application. In this connection, will the Government inform this Council:

(1) given that the aforesaid legal aid applicant intends to institute legal proceedings for continuation with the illegal occupation of roads, of the reasons why, at the time when DLA vetted and approved the legal aid application concerned, it did not appear to him that there were circumstances as set out in Section 10(3) in that case, and hence he had not rejected the application;

(2) apart from considering whether the applicant could pass the means test and merits test, of the specific factors that LAD took into account in vetting and approval of the legal aid application, and of the precedent cases available for reference; and

(3) whether an independent monitoring mechanism is currently in place to ensure the vetting and approval results of similar legal aid applications are reasonable; if so, of the details; if not, the reasons for that?

Reply:

President,

Occupying roads and blocking traffic are unlawful acts. The Government is determined in safeguarding the rule of law and committed to securing public order. Legal aid is an integral part of the legal system in Hong Kong. The policy objective of legal aid is to ensure that no one with reasonable grounds for pursuing or defending a legal action in the Hong Kong courts is denied access to justice because of a lack of means. To qualify for legal aid, a person has to satisfy the means test and the merits test as provided by the Legal Aid Ordinance (LAO) (Cap. 91). The Legal Aid Department (LAD) processes legal aid applications in accordance with the established principles and procedures, and the Home Affairs Bureau will not comment on the processing of individual applications.

Our reply to the three parts of the question is as follows:

(1) and (2) To ensure that only those cases with reasonable grounds are granted legal aid, all legal aid applications are processed by Legal Aid Counsel appointed to serve in LAD. In conducting the merits test, LAD will consider the background of the case, evidence available and the legal principles applicable to the case to determine whether there are reasonable grounds for legal aid to be granted. In assessing the merits (including compliance with Section 10(3) of LAO), LAD must be satisfied that there are reasonable grounds or points of law involved for which it is desirable to grant legal aid to enable the matter to be submitted to the court for decision or judgment. For individual applications, if the available documents already demonstrate strong ground(s) for taking proceedings or that the issues raised are already covered by previous judgments or advice, legal aid may be granted to applicants who have passed the means test. If complicated legal issues are involved in the application, LAD may seek independent legal opinion from counsel in private practice on the merits of the application under Section 9(d) of LAO.

Regarding the legal aid applications for the discharge of the injunctions, in accordance with Section 24 of LAO, which imposes restrictions on the disclosure of information concerning applicants and aided persons, and the provisions of the Personal Data (Privacy) Ordinance, LAD is not at liberty to comment on any individual legal aid application nor disclose the specific merits, principles or facts of the case concerned. However, LAD can confirm that the above merits/reasonable ground tests have been applied to all cases which have been granted legal aid.

(3) Legal aid will only be granted to applicants who pass both the merits test and the means test in accordance with LAO. LAD has also put in place a monitoring mechanism to ensure that the processing of legal aid applications is reasonable and to safeguard against abuse of legal aid. If an application is refused, the applicant may appeal against the decision of the Director of Legal Aid to the Registrar of the High Court in accordance with Section 26 of LAO, for which the decision of the Registrar is final. Furthermore, if anyone believes that an applicant or aided person has provided false information on either merits or means, he/she can provide LAD with such details from which the Department will conduct an investigation into the matter. If it is found that an aided person has provided false representations or withheld material information about the facts of the case or his/her financial resources, LAD would discontinue legal aid and refer the matter to the Police for follow up action.

Issued at HKT 13:00

LCQ2: Curricula of senior secondary subjects
****

Following is a question by the Hon Ip Kin-yuen and a reply by the Secretary for Education, Mr Eddie Ng Hak-kim, in the Legislative Council today (November 20):

Question:

Recently, there have been public comments that the encouragement of students to discuss Hong Kong people's participation in socio-political affairs by the teaching and learning activities under the theme of "rule of law and socio-political participation" in the Liberal Studies (LS) subject of the New Senior Secondary Academic Structure is one of the causes for the massive turnouts of secondary students in the "occupation" movement. There have also been press reports that the Government intends to amend the LS curriculum to delete topics relating to the politics of Hong Kong and beef up the contents in areas such as the Basic Law. Some educational bodies consider that such a move is tantamount to political intervention in educational affairs. Regarding the curricula of senior secondary subjects, will the Government inform this Council:

(1) of the details of the authorities' plan to amend the LS curriculum and the justifications for that; the authorities' considerations in, and their procedure for, setting senior secondary subjects as core or elective ones, or changing the subjects as such;

(2) of the criteria and procedure for amending the curricula and assessment guides for various subjects;

the time generally required for the amendment process, and whether the subject teachers concerned will be consulted before amendments are made; if so, of the details and scale of the consultation; whether it will undertake that it will not, under any circumstances, amend the curricula of various subjects based on non-professional considerations; and

(3) as it has been reported that an incumbent Executive Council Member, who was formerly an official of the Education Bureau once promoting the LS subject, claimed that the subject had become morbid, whether the authorities have assessed if the subject has deviated from its objective; if the assessment outcome is in the affirmative, of the details; if the assessment outcome is in the negative, the justifications for that?

Reply:

President,

Our reply to Hon Ip's questions is as follows:

(1) and (2) The curriculum review of Liberal Studies is part of the New Academic Structure (NAS) Review. Since August 2012, the Education Bureau (EDB), the Curriculum Development Council (CDC) and the Hong Kong Examinations and Assessment Authority (HKEAA) have jointly launched the review of the New Senior Secondary (NSS) curriculum and assessment (including Liberal Studies). Short-term recommendations were announced in April 2013, and the first batch of medium-term recommendations as well as the fine-tuning measures on the implementation of curriculum and assessment were announced in April 2014 (for details, please see the designated page of the NAS review (334.edb.hkedcity.net/EN/334_review.php)). The second stage of the NAS Medium-term Review is now in progress, including students' learning experiences in the whole-school curriculum, the impact of the NAS on students' further studies, the implementation of curriculum and assessment at the school level (including school-based arrangements), and the implementation of curriculum and assessment of individual subjects (including Liberal Studies). The proposed recommendations would be made according to student-centered and professional principles (including considering the achievement of curriculum aims, teachers' workload, balanced breadth and depth of the overall curriculum contents, students' knowledge foundation in the junior secondary level, catering for learner diversity in curriculum and assessment, alignment between public assessment and curriculum and backwash effects etc.). We will further consult different stakeholders such as teachers, principals, tertiary institutions, employers and students through

multiple channels (e.g. questionnaire surveys, focus group meetings and forums) in end November.

The procedure and time generally required for revising the curriculum and assessment guides for various subjects would depend on subject nature and needs. When making important revisions, teachers and other stakeholders will be consulted, together with the existing committee mechanism and professionalism taking major role, for discussing and implementing the relevant revisions.

Liberal Studies is inter-disciplinary by nature and is indispensable to the curriculum as a core subject. On one hand, it allows students to study an extensive curriculum appropriate for Hong Kong through six modules, and covers personal development, society and culture (including local, national and global aspects), science and technology. On the other hand, it enables students to develop on the knowledge foundation from the basic education and utilise their interdisciplinary knowledge with an issue-enquiry approach, so as to broaden their horizons, to construct more knowledge, to think critically and rationally, and to develop multiple perspectives. It also helps students develop positive values and attitudes, so that they can better prepare themselves for the responsibilities and multiple roles in society and their future life.

Liberal Studies is complementary to the other core subjects, elective subjects and Other Learning Experiences, providing senior secondary students with diversified learning experiences suitable for their own interests and abilities.

The deliberation on whether to set an NSS subject as a core subject or an elective subject should be evidence-based. We should consider whether the change can achieve the same education aims, maintain international standard and recognition, and articulation to study and career pathways. As the implementation and effectiveness of the NSS curriculum and assessment have yet to reach a state of stability and the curriculum has just been implemented for a limited period of time, more time is needed to collect data and conduct studies for fine-tuning and updating.

(3) We respect the opinions expressed by different sectors of the community on educational issues. As I have pointed out in the reply above, the NAS Medium-term Review is still on-going. We will adhere to the student-centered professional principles, propose recommendations and consult schools, teachers and professional organisations of the relevant subjects, as well as other stakeholders. The EDB will carefully collect and listen to views from all sides in order to make the review more comprehensive. The medium-term recommendations and the long-term development direction of Liberal Studies will be announced by July 2015.

It is also noteworthy that the efforts made by the education profession on Liberal Studies deserve our recognition. According to the Progress Report on the New Academic Structure Review released in 2013, most teachers and students agreed that the curriculum aims and learning outcomes of Liberal Studies had been achieved. Most teachers also agreed that the Independent Enquiry Study was able to nurture students' problem-solving and independent thinking ability, and had a positive impact on building up students' confidence in learning.

Issued at HKT 16:25

LC Urgent Q: Police's role in enforcement of injunction orders
****

Following is an urgent question by Hon Dennis Kwok under Rule 24(4) of the Rules of Procedure and a reply by the Secretary for Security, Mr Lai Tung-kwok, in the Legislative Council today (November 20):

Question:

On the 10th of this month, the Court of First Instance (CFI) of the High Court continued the interim injunction orders it granted earlier in respect of three cases concerning the obstruction of certain roads in Mong Kok and the obstruction of the entrance and exit of CITIC Tower in Admiralty. Such injunction orders restrain the occupiers from obstructing the bailiffs in dismantling or removing the obstructions at designated locations and authorise the Police to take arrest actions where they reasonably believe that any person may obstruct or interfere any bailiff in enforcing the terms of the injunction orders, and the Police shall bring the persons so arrested before the Court as soon as practicable for further directions. On the 14th of this month, CFI granted an order which stipulates that without prejudice to the Police's enforcement of the provisions of the Police Force Ordinance (including sections 51 and 52), the Police shall bring the arrested persons before the Court as soon as possible for further directions. On the other hand, the Commissioner of Police indicated that the Police would give their full support to the plaintiffs in enforcing the civil injunction orders concerned. In this connection, will the Government inform this Council, before giving further assistance to the bailiffs in enforcing the injunction orders:

(1) of the channels through which the Police will ensure that the occupiers clearly understand the gist of the injunction orders so that they will have the opportunity to consider desisting from the acts of violating the injunction orders in order to avoid being arrested;

(2) whether the Police will immediately make public the criteria for deciding if the occupiers arrested for allegedly violating the injunction orders and committing other criminal offences at the same time are to be brought before the Court for further directions, or be detained at police stations and/or brought before a

magistrate; and

(3) whether the Police will immediately make public the measures to enable the persons who are arrested for alleged violation of the injunction orders and brought before the Court for further directions to get to know their legal rights and be legally represented?

Reply:

President,

The High Court orders issued on November 10 in relation to the three injunction applications concerning the obstruction of certain roads in Mong Kok (Mong Kok) as well as the obstruction of the entrance and exit of CITIC Tower (CITIC Tower) have given clear directions in respect of the role of police officers in the enforcement of the injunction orders. As stated in those orders:

(a) The bailiff do take all reasonable and necessary steps to assist the plaintiff and its agents to effect the clearance and removal of the obstructions.

(b) The bailiff be authorised and directed to request the assistance of the Police where necessary.

(c) Any police officer be authorised to arrest and remove any person who the Police officer reasonably believes or suspects to be obstructing or interfering any bailiff in carrying out his or her duties in enforcing the terms of the injunction order, provided that the person to be arrested has been informed of the gist of the terms of the court order and that his action is likely to constitute a breach of the order and obstruction of the administration of justice, and that he may be arrested if he does not desist.

(d) Without prejudice to the provisions of the Police Force Ordinance (Cap. 232 of the Laws of Hong Kong) (including sections 51 and 52 thereof), any person so arrested by the Police shall be brought before the court, under lawful or legal processes, as soon as practicable for further directions.

As stated in paragraphs 123 and 124 of the relevant High Court judgment, attempts to obstruct bailiffs in their execution of duties may constitute criminal contempt of court, which is a common law offence punishable by imprisonment. In addition, the Department of Justice (DoJ) also pointed out that under section 23 of the Summary Offences Ordinance (Cap. 228 of the Laws of Hong Kong), it is a criminal offence for any person to resist or obstruct a public officer or other person lawfully engaged, authorised or employed in the performance of any public duty or any person lawfully assisting such public officer or person therein. As advised by DoJ, bailiffs are public officers covered by the above Ordinance and as such, a person who resists or obstructs a bailiff lawfully engaged in the enforcement of the relevant injunction orders may also commit an offence under section 23 of the Summary Offences Ordinance. Moreover, we do not rule out the possibility that a person may also commit other offences in the course of resisting or obstructing bailiffs in their lawful enforcement of the injunction orders.

Preparation has been made by the Police with respect to the aforementioned court orders. The Police shall, in accordance with the directions of the court orders, and having regard to the actual circumstances at the time, render assistance in the enforcement of such injunction orders, and, where necessary, exercise the powers conferred upon the Force by other laws, including the power of arrest under the Police Force Ordinance. In rendering their assistance, the Police may take appropriate actions to maintain public order and public safety where there is a real need.

My reply to Hon Dennis Kwok's question is as follows:

(1) It is the responsibility of the plaintiff of an injunction order and his lawful agent to validly serve the injunction order notice issued by the court. I noted that the plaintiff of the CITIC Tower injunction order had, under the court's direction, published the notice of the injunction order in full in local newspapers on November 15 and 17, and had posted such a notice in a conspicuous position at the car park entrance of CITIC Tower. One of the plaintiffs of the Mong Kok injunction orders had also published the notice in full in newspapers on November 18 under the court's direction.

On the morning of November 18, the bailiffs commenced their enforcement of the injunction order outside CITIC Tower. Prior to the removal of obstructions, the bailiffs, using a loudspeaker, announced that the removal actions would begin in 30 minutes and urged the persons at scene to comply with the court order by leaving immediately. The plaintiff's solicitor had also clearly read out the content of the injunction order on the spot.

Since the court's delivery of its judgment of the injunction order, the Hong Kong Police Force has, through the media, declared to the general public on different occasions that any acts of any person which constitute an obstruction of a bailiff's enforcement of a court order may be liable to the offence of criminal contempt of court, and that the Police have been authorised by the court, where necessary, to arrest those who obstruct the bailiffs in their execution of duties. Resolute enforcement actions shall definitely be taken by the Police against any person who obstructs or violently charges the bailiffs during their execution of duties. The Police also called on those who had unlawfully occupied the roads to comply with the court orders by removing the obstructions and personal belongings and stopping their illegal occupation as soon as possible.

The Police have made preparation at this stage to ensure that the actions to be taken are in line not only with their enforcement guidelines but also legal requirements. Knowing that arrangements may vary from one situation to another, and that operational details are involved, I am in no position to disclose such arrangements in detail. However, I should clearly point out that the Police shall give warnings to the persons involved by appropriate means before they start their arrest actions, so that the concerned persons will clearly know the contents of the court orders and the possible criminal offences resulting from their actions, as well as the possible consequences. The Police shall, before taking further actions, give such persons every reasonable opportunity to stop their unlawful acts.

(2) As stated in the judgment of the injunction orders, anyone arrested by the Police for obstructing or interfering any bailiff in the execution of his duties to enforce the injunction orders shall be brought before the Court as soon as possible for further directions.

As to under what circumstances any person so arrested will be brought before the High Court for directions, and under what circumstances the person will be detained at police stations and/or brought before the magistrates' court for trial, the Police shall make the decision pursuant to the Police Force Ordinance (sections 51 and 52 in particular), the directions of the court orders, the acts of the person concerned and the actual situation.

In case a person commits other crimes at the same time, the Police shall, in the light of the actual circumstances, exercise the power conferred upon the Force by law to maintain public order and public safety. DoJ's advice shall also be sought where necessary.

(3) In case a person is arrested by the Police for having obstructed or interfered with a bailiff's execution of his duties to enforce an injunction order, the Police shall, in accordance with the established procedures, inform him of his lawful rights, which include meeting his legal representative and contacting his relatives/friends. Such procedures are in no way different to those for handling other arrested persons.

Persons detained by the Police for suspected violation of the injunction orders shall have the right to meet their lawyer duly instructed by them or a lawyer instructed by a third party. The Police shall, as far as possible, facilitate the requests of such persons for external communication, such as meeting with their legal representative and contacting their relatives/friends. The Police shall, taking account of the nature of the case and the progress of investigation, deal with such matters in accordance with the established procedures and criteria.

Thank you, President.

Issued at HKT 18:47

LegCo meeting to continue tomorrow
****

The following is issued on behalf of the Legislative Council Secretariat:

As the business on the agenda of the Legislative Council (LegCo) meeting cannot be finished today (November 20), the President of LegCo, Mr Jasper Tsang has, in accordance with Rule 14(4) of the Rules of Procedure, decided that the Council meeting will resume tomorrow (November 21) at 9am.
Issued at HKT 20:30

HKSARG's response to United States-China Economic and Security Review Commission 2014 Annual Report
****

In response to media enquiries on the United States-China Economic and Security Review Commission (USCC) 2014 Annual Report, a spokesman for the Hong Kong Special Administrative Region (HKSAR) Government said today (November 20) :

On Constitutional Development

"The HKSAR Government regrets that the latest report published by the USCC today is biased and the allegations on the constitutional development of Hong Kong therein unfounded and misleading. The HKSAR Government does not agree with views set out in the report. The report represents a lack of understanding of the USCC on the actual situation on the constitutional development of Hong Kong.

"The USCC's report has failed to take into consideration the constitutional set-up of the HKSAR. The HKSAR was established by the decision of the National People's Congress of the People's Republic of China (PRC) pursuant to the Constitution of the PRC. According to the Basic Law (a national law and the constitutional document of the HKSAR), the HKSAR is a local administrative region of the PRC which enjoys a high degree of autonomy and comes directly under the Central People's Government. When discussing the method for selecting the Chief Executive (CE) of the HKSAR, one must bear in mind that the CE is the head of the HKSAR as well as the head of the HKSAR Government, being accountable to both the HKSAR and the Central People's Government of the PRC. A candidate of CE returned at a local election is subject to appointment by the Central People's Government before the incumbent can assume office. The selection of the CE by universal suffrage upon nomination by a broadly representative Nominating Committee in accordance with democratic procedures has its origin in Article 45 of the Basic Law promulgated back in 1990. The method for selecting the CE by universal suffrage must therefore strictly comply with the relevant provisions of the Basic Law, accord with the principle of 'One Country, Two Systems', and befit the legal status of the HKSAR.

"The Sino-British Joint Declaration on Hong Kong's return to China makes no mention at all of universal suffrage. All it states is that the CE should be selected by election or through consultations held locally and be appointed by the Central People's Government. It is only the Basic Law that mentions, for the first time, universal suffrage as the ultimate goal. Since the PRC resumed the exercise of sovereignty over Hong Kong, the Central Authorities of the PRC, the HKSAR Government, together with the community of Hong Kong, have been working towards the ultimate goal of universal suffrage on a gradual and orderly process, taking into account the actual situation in the HKSAR.

"On August 31, 2014, the Standing Committee of the National People's Congress (NPCSC) adopted the Decision of the Standing Committee of the National People's Congress on Issues Relating to the Selection of the Chief Executive of the Hong Kong Special Administrative Region by Universal Suffrage and on the Method for Forming the Legislative Council of the Hong Kong Special Administrative Region in the Year 2016 (Decision). The Decision formally determined that universal suffrage for the CE election through 'one person, one vote' could be implemented from 2017 onwards. This is an important step forward of constitutional development of Hong Kong. If a consensus could be reached, five million eligible voters in Hong Kong could elect its next leader through 'one person, one vote' in 2017.

"To prepare for the implementation of universal suffrage for the CE election for the first time in our history, the HKSAR Government will consult the public on the specific method for selecting the CE by universal suffrage in 2017, with a view to submitting enabling legislation to the Legislative Council (LegCo) on amendments to the electoral method in Annex I to the Basic Law at an appropriate juncture. Different sectors of the community may engage in more in-depth and pragmatic discussions then on the specific arrangements for the CE election in 2017.

"It is the common aspiration of the Central Authorities of PRC, the HKSAR Government and the people of the HKSAR to successfully implement universal suffrage for the CE election in 2017 in accordance with the Basic Law and the relevant interpretation and decisions of the NPCSC. Detailed electoral methods, including the issues such as the composition of and specific nominating procedures for the Nominating Committee to nominate candidates for the CE election, are still subject to public consultation. It is unfortunate that the USCC's report has entirely overlooked the facts, but to denounce the concerted efforts of the Central Authorities of the PRC, the HKSAR Government and the community of Hong Kong to take forward democratic development of Hong Kong so as to enable about five million eligible voters in Hong Kong to elect their next leader through 'one person, one vote' in 2017 as scheduled.

On Public Order Events

"The freedom and right of procession and peaceful assembly are enshrined in the Basic Law and the Hong Kong Bill of Rights Ordinance. The Police always handle public order events in a fair, just and impartial manner in accordance with the laws of Hong Kong. When expressing their aspirations, participants of public assemblies or processions were advised to abide by the laws of Hong Kong and respect other people's rights so that the events could proceed in a peaceful and orderly manner without compromising the Police's efforts to maintain law and order.

"The HKSAR Government has repeatedly urged protesters, who have been illegally occupying the roads since late September, to remove their obstacles as soon as possible and to disperse in a peaceful and orderly manner. Hong Kong is governed by the rule of law and the HKSAR Government will deal with the illegal activities associated with 'Occupy Central' in accordance with the law so that public order is maintained and the lives of all members of the public may return to normal as soon as possible. The Police will take suitable and resolute actions at the appropriate time.

On Military Presence in the HKSAR

"Since the Reunification, the Hong Kong Garrison has been performing defence functions and responsibilities in Hong Kong in strict accordance with the Basic Law and the Law of the People's Republic of China on the Garrisoning of the HKSAR (the Garrison Law). In accordance with the Garrison Law, the Hong Kong Garrison does not interfere with the local affairs of the HKSAR. Members of the Hong Kong Garrison abide by the national laws and the laws of the HKSAR at all times.

"According to Article 14 of the Basic Law, the Government of the HKSAR shall be responsible for the maintenance of public order in the Region. The law enforcement agencies of the HKSAR Government are fully capable of handling public order situations in Hong Kong. The HKSAR Government has no intention to seek assistance from the Hong Kong Garrison in dealing with the 'Occupy Central' protest.

On Press Freedom

"The HKSAR Government is firmly committed to protecting the freedom of expression and freedom of the press. These freedoms are rights enjoyed by the people of Hong Kong as enshrined in Article 27 of the Basic Law and the Hong Kong Bill of Rights Ordinance.

"The HKSAR Government has all along been fostering an environment for the news industry to develop freely with minimum regulation. The media reports freely in Hong Kong and rigorously performs its role as a watchdog. The Government will not and cannot interfere with the internal operations of media organisations or commercial decisions of any private enterprise. As a matter of principle, we support that every endeavour should be made for journalists to report news professionally and accurately under the principle of editorial autonomy.

"At present, about 50 local newspapers and 720 periodicals are published in Hong Kong. About 90 international media organisations have offices in Hong Kong. Hong Kong is also the regional base for a number of international media.

"With reference to cases of violence against journalists, the Government strongly condemns the violent acts. The Government has always striven to maintain law and order and safeguard the personal safety of all members of the public. Every incident of violence will be tackled seriously under the law.

On USCC's Recommendation

"The HKSAR Government strongly objects to the USCC recommendation, which is made based on misguided and unfounded allegations, that the United States-Hong Kong Policy Act should be re-enacted. Foreign governments and legislatures should not interfere in any form in the internal affairs of Hong Kong."

Issued at HKT 22:40

NOVEMBER 21[33]

Special arrangements on submission of tenders arising from temporary closure of Government Secretariat Tender Box
****

Owing to the special access arrangements at the Central Government Offices (CGO) in Tamar, the Government Secretariat Tender Box (GSTB) located on the ground floor of the East Wing of CGO is closed for tender deposit temporarily.

All tenders that should originally be deposited into the GSTB are instead requested to be deposited into the Government Logistics Department Tender Box (GLDTB) located on the ground floor of North Point Government Offices at 333 Java Road, North Point. This special arrangement came into effect on September 30 this year and remains in effect until further notice.

Tenderers may wish to check in advance their route to the GLDTB and allow sufficient time to make arrangements to deposit their tenders into the GLDTB before the respective closing time of tenders. Late tenders will not be accepted.

For enquiries, please call 2810 2497 or 2231 5288 between 9am and 6pm from Mondays to Fridays (except public holidays).

Issued at HKT 08:31

HKMA's update on operation of banking system and financial market
****

The following is issued on behalf of the Hong Kong Monetary Authority:

According to the reports to the Hong Kong Monetary Authority (HKMA) from banks as at 8am today (November 21), all previously affected bank branches have resumed operation. One branch of one bank would shorten their business hours today. The HKMA has requested banks to resume normal services as soon as circumstances permit. Customers should pay attention to the relevant banks' announcements regarding affected branches and ATMs. The HKMA will also publish on its website relevant updates from time to time.

Issued at HKT 09:50

---

[33] http://www.info.gov.hk/gia/general/201411/21.htm

Response to media enquiries
****

In response to press enquiries about the remarks made by Lord Patten at the US Congressional-Executive Commission on China yesterday, a spokesman for the Hong Kong Special Administrative Region (HKSAR) Government today (November 21) has responded with the following:

"Firstly, constitutional development in Hong Kong is an internal matter for Hong Kong and an internal affair for China, in which foreign governments and legislatures should not interfere.

"Secondly, the one and only basis for Hong Kong's constitutional development is the Basic Law, not the Joint Declaration. The Joint Declaration contains no mention of universal suffrage for the selection of the Chief Executive or the formation of the Legislative Council; it is the Basic Law which provides for universal suffrage.

"Thirdly, it is clearly laid down in the Basic Law that the National People's Congress Standing Committee (NPCSC), the Chief Executive and the Legislative Council have their respective constitutional roles to play in the process to attain universal suffrage in Hong Kong. It is a plainly incorrect reading of the Basic Law to suggest, as Lord Patten did, that the NPCSC has no role to play in the constitutional development of Hong Kong.

"Fourthly, the HKSAR Government has been engaging in dialogues with various sectors of the community, including an open dialogue with the representatives of the Hong Kong Federation of Students on October 21, with a view to forging a consensus to bring forward the constitutional process to attain universal suffrage. We have repeatedly pointed out that constitutional development in Hong Kong must proceed in accordance with the Basic Law and the relevant NPCSC's interpretation and decisions. We continue to appeal to all sectors of the community to express their views in a peaceful manner and cease all illegal activities as soon as possible."

Issued at HKT 16:12

NOVEMBER 24[34][35]

HKMA's update on operation of banking system and financial market
****

The following is issued on behalf of the Hong Kong Monetary Authority:

According to the reports to the Hong Kong Monetary Authority (HKMA) from banks as at 8am today (November 24), all previously affected bank branches have resumed operation. One branch of one bank would shorten their business hours today. The HKMA has requested banks to resume normal services as soon as circumstances permit. Customers should pay attention to the relevant banks' announcements regarding affected branches and ATMs. The HKMA will also publish on its website relevant updates from time to time.
Issued at HKT 09:31

LegCo to debate motion on constitutional reform
****

The following is issued on behalf of the Legislative Council Secretariat:

The Legislative Council (LegCo) will hold a meeting this Wednesday (November 26) at 11am in the Chamber of the LegCo Complex. During the meeting, Members will debate a motion on constitutional reform.
The motion, to be moved by Mr Ronny Tong, states: "That this Council urges the Government to expeditiously put forward a practical and feasible constitutional reform package."
Ms Emily Lau will move an amendment to Mr Ronny Tong's motion.
Mr Poon Siu-ping will also move a motion on ensuring occupational safety. The motion states: "That, as the number of work injury accidents and fatal industrial accidents in Hong Kong remains high, this Council urges the Government to establish a dedicated committee for comprehensively reviewing the policies on Hong Kong employees' occupational safety and health, including the protection coverage of occupational diseases and improvement of the protection for workers in high-risk occupations (i.e. insurance, compensation, therapy and rehabilitation)."
Mr Tang Ka-piu and Mr Chan Kin-por will move separate amendments to Mr Poon Siu-ping's motion.
On bills, Members will resume Second Reading debates on the Contracts (Rights of Third Parties) Bill

---

[34] There were no government press releases concerning Occupy Central for November 22 and 23
[35] http://www.info.gov.hk/gia/general/201411/24.htm

and the Statute Law (Miscellaneous Provisions) Bill 2014. If the Bills are supported by Members and receive their Second Reading, they will then go through the Committee stage and be read the third time.

In addition, Members will ask the Government 22 questions on various policy areas, six of which require oral replies during the meeting.

The agenda of the above meeting can be obtained via the LegCo Website (www.legco.gov.hk). Please note that the agenda is subject to change, and the latest information about the agenda could be found on the LegCo Website.

Members of the public are welcome to observe the proceedings of the meeting from the public galleries of the Chamber of the LegCo Complex. They may reserve seats by calling 3919 3399 during office hours. Members of the public can also watch or listen the meeting via the web broadcast system on
Issued at HKT 17:28

Police render full assistance to bailiffs in executing Injunction Order in Mong Kok
****

Police have met with the plaintiffs of the Injunction Orders on the unlawful occupation of roads in Mong Kok and the bailiffs with regard to the execution of the orders. Police are ready to give the fullest support to the bailiffs to execute the court order on the carriageway of Argyle Street between the junction of Tung Choi Street and Portland Street in Mong Kok tomorrow (November 25).

The Court of First Instance earlier in its judgment authorised bailiffs to assist the plaintiff in removing obstructions and that the bailiffs could request the assistance of Police when necessary. The court further authorised Police to arrest those who obstruct the bailiffs in executing their duties.

Police emphasise that the bailiffs are authorised by the court to execute court orders. Any act amounts to obstruction may render one liable to the offence of "criminal contempt of court". If anyone obstructs or violently charges the bailiffs when they are executing their duties, Police will take resolute action. When necessary, Police will use other powers conferred by the law to preserve public order and public safety. Police will also reclaim government property, such as mills barriers and water barriers, which have been illegally taken by the illegal road occupiers.

In addition, Police have noticed that some people at the illegally occupied areas have prepared supplies to provoke others to put up resistance. There are also some people on the Internet claiming that they will re-occupy the cleared areas or other sections of roads after the bailiffs have completed the removal actions in order to continue with the illegal occupation. Police reiterate that we are duty bound to take resolute actions to preserve public order and safeguard public safety if anyone occupies new sections of roads or those that have been cleared.

Police point out that the illegally occupied area in Mong Kok remains a high-risk area and members of the public, especially students, should stay away from there. They should not mix with the radicals and troublemakers and be incited or used by others to commit any illegal acts. Parents should not bring children there as well to avoid any unnecessary injuries.

Police reiterate that the Injunction Orders are solemn orders issued by the court. Police urge the illegal road occupiers to obey the court orders, remove obstacles and personal belongings, and stop the illegal occupation soonest so that the roads can be re-opened and public order restored.

Issued at HKT 19:19

NOVEMBER 25[36]

HKMA's update on operation of banking system and financial market
****

The following is issued on behalf of the Hong Kong Monetary Authority:

According to the reports to the Hong Kong Monetary Authority (HKMA) from banks as at 8am today (November 25), one branch of one bank was affected and temporarily closed today. In addition, one branch of one bank would shorten their business hours today. The HKMA has requested banks to resume normal services as soon as circumstances permit. Customers should pay attention to the relevant banks' announcements regarding affected branches and ATMs. The HKMA will also publish on its website relevant updates from time to time.

Issued at HKT 10:18

Police render full assistance to bailiffs in executing Injunction Order in Mong Kok
****

Police have met with the plaintiffs of the Injunction Orders on the unlawful occupation of roads in Mong Kok and the bailiffs with regard to the execution of the orders. Police are ready to give the fullest support to the bailiffs to execute the court order on the carriageways of Nathan Road between Argyle Street and Dundas Street in Mong Kok tomorrow (November 26).

The Court of First Instance earlier in its judgment authorised bailiffs to assist the plaintiff in removing obstructions and that the bailiffs could request the assistance of Police when necessary. The court further authorised Police to arrest those who obstruct the bailiffs in executing their duties.

Police emphasise that the bailiffs are authorised by the court to execute court orders. Any act amounts to obstruction may render one liable to the offence of "criminal contempt of court". If anyone obstructs or violently charges the bailiffs when they are executing their duties, Police will take resolute action. Police will also reclaim government property, such as mills barriers and water barriers, which have been illegally taken by the illegal road occupiers.

When necessary, Police will use other powers conferred by the law to preserve public order and safeguard public safety. Police will also take actions to clear the obstructions on the blocked roads at various locations, including the road junctions at Portland Street and Argyle Street, Sai Yeung Choi Street South and Nathan Road and Shantung Street.

---

[36] http://www.info.gov.hk/gia/general/201411/25.htm

Police reiterate that we are duty bound to take resolute actions to preserve public order and safeguard public safety if anyone occupies new sections of roads or those that have been cleared.

Police point out that the illegally occupied area in Mong Kok remains a high-risk area. Members of the public, especially students, should stay away from there. They should not mix with the radicals and troublemakers and be incited or used by others to commit any illegal acts. Parents should not bring children there as well to avoid any unnecessary injuries.

Police reiterate that the Injunction Orders are solemn orders issued by the court. Police urge the illegal road occupiers to obey the court orders, remove the obstacles, take away their personal belongings, and leave the illegally occupied areas soonest so that the roads can be re-opened and public order restored.
Issued at HKT 22:43

Police appeal to the public to avoid going to Mong Kok
****

Police assisted the bailiffs to execute the Injunction Order on Argyle Street, Mong Kok today (November 25). During the operation, Police arrested a total of 23 people, including 18 males and 5 females, aged between 14 and 69, for the offences of criminal contempt of court, and resisting or obstructing public officers. Three police officers were also injured.

Later on, a large crowd of protestors gathered in the vicinity of Portland Street and scuffled with Police officers at the scene. As at 8pm, Police arrested another 57 persons for offences including unlawful assembly, assaulting Police and obstructing Police officers.

Police operation against the unlawful assembly in the vicinity of Shantung Street and Shanghai Street, Mong Kok is ongoing. Police urge the people at the scene to stay restrained, listen to the instructions of Police officers and leave immediately. They should not block the roads or obstruct the traffic. Police appeal to the public, in particular students, not to go to the above areas to avoid unnecessary injuries.
Issued at HKT 23:52

NOVEMBER 26[37]

Police appeal to people assembling unlawfully in Mong Kok to leave
****

Police assisted bailiffs to execute the Injunction Order on Argyle Street, Mong Kok yesterday (November 25). The carriageways on Argyle Street near Portland Street were re-opened yesterday afternoon.

Later on, a large crowd of protestors assembled unlawfully in the vicinity of Portland Street, Shanghai Street, Shantung Street, Reclamation Street and Ferry Street. They confronted with Police officers at the scene and attempted to obstruct the roads again with obstacles. As such, Police took resolute actions and drove them out.

During the operation yesterday, Police arrested a total of 86 people (77 males and nine females), for offences including unlawful assembly, assaulting Police, possession of offensive weapon and obstructing Police officers. Among the arrestees, a male in possession of objects including axe, iron hammer and crowbar was arrested by Police for possession of offensive weapon. Police will investigate all cases in a determined and impartial manner and take out prosecutions according to evidence collected. Nine Police officers were injured during the operation.

Police operation against the unlawful assembly in the vicinity of Shantung Street and Dundas Street is ongoing. Police urge the people assembling unlawfully at the scene to leave immediately and not to block the roads or charge Police. Police also appeal to the public, in particular students, not to go to the above areas to avoid unnecessary injuries. They should not mix with the radicals and troublemakers and be incited or used by others to commit any illegal acts.

Police again remind journalists covering the operation, in particular when they are in between Police cordon and radical protestors, to take care of their personal safety to avoid unnecessary injuries.

Police reiterate that if anyone blocks re-opened roads or other roads, Police are duty bound to take resolute actions to safeguard public order and public safety.

Issued at HKT 02:56

---

[37] http://www.info.gov.hk/gia/general/201411/26.htm

HKMA's update on the operation of the banking system and financial market
****

The following is issued on behalf of the Hong Kong Monetary Authority:

According to the reports to the Hong Kong Monetary Authority (HKMA) from banks as at 8am today (November 26), five branches of five banks were affected and temporarily closed today. The HKMA has requested banks to resume normal services as soon as circumstances permit. Customers should pay attention to the relevant banks' announcements regarding affected branches and ATMs. The HKMA will also publish on its website relevant updates from time to time.

Issued at HKT 09:40

Special arrangements on submission of tenders arising from temporary closure of Government Secretariat Tender Box
****

Owing to the special access arrangements at the Central Government Offices (CGO) in Tamar, the Government Secretariat Tender Box (GSTB) located on the ground floor of the East Wing of CGO is closed for tender deposit temporarily.

All tenders that should originally be deposited into the GSTB are instead requested to be deposited into the Government Logistics Department Tender Box (GLDTB) located on the ground floor of North Point Government Offices at 333 Java Road, North Point. This special arrangement came into effect on September 30 this year and remains in effect until further notice.

Tenderers may wish to check in advance their route to the GLDTB and allow sufficient time to make arrangements to deposit their tenders into the GLDTB before the respective closing time of tenders. Late tenders will not be accepted.

For enquiries, please call 2810 2497 or 2231 5288 between 9am and 6pm from Mondays to Fridays (except public holidays).

Issued at HKT 11:30

HKMA's update on the operation of the banking system and financial market (2)

****

The following is issued on behalf of the Hong Kong Monetary Authority:

According to the reports to the Hong Kong Monetary Authority (HKMA) from banks as at 11.30am today (November 26), 10 branches of 9 banks were affected and temporarily closed now. The HKMA has requested banks to resume normal services as soon as circumstances permit. Customers should pay attention to the relevant banks' announcements regarding affected branches and ATMs. The HKMA will also publish on its website relevant updates from time to time.

Issued at HKT 12:08

LCQ19: Flexible deployment of Police manpower and resources for handling "Occupy Central"

****

Following is a question by the Hon Jeffrey Lam and a written reply by the Secretary for Security, Mr Lai Tung-kwok, in the Legislative Council today (November 26):

Question:

It has been reported that since the occurrence of the road occupation movement (the occupation movement), most of the frontline police officers have been required to work overtime and have even been subjected to abuses hurled at them from time to time by the protesters and supporters of the occupation movement. As a result, they have become physically and mentally exhausted and even their relationship with family members has been affected. In this connection, will the Government inform this Council:

(1) since the occurrence of the occupation movement, of (i) the shift arrangements for police officers, (ii) the number of staff members of the Police who worked overtime for performing duties relating to the occupation movement and the total numbers of hours and days of such overtime work, and (iii) among these staff members, the respective numbers of those who are regular police officers, auxiliary police officers and civilian staff members; and the respective percentages of such numbers in the total numbers of the staff members concerned;

(2) how the Police compensate the staff mentioned in (1) for the overtime work performed by them;

(3) since the occurrence of the occupation movement, of the number of police officers who were injured when performing duties relating to the occupation movement, or suffered from emotional problems, fell ill or sought help from the Hong Kong Police Force because of excessive pressure; and

(4) whether it has assessed the impacts of the occupation movement on the manpower of the Police so far; if it has assessed, of the outcome?

Reply:

President,

The Administration's reply to the Hon Jeffrey Lam's question is as follows:

(1) and (4) As a law enforcement agency, the Police have the statutory duties to maintain law and order, as well as to safeguard life and property. Given the serious impact of "Occupy Central" (or "the Occupy Movement") on public safety and public order, the Police have to deploy substantial manpower and resources for handling operations related to "Occupy Central" on the one hand, and maintaining day-to-day police work and public services in various districts in Hong Kong on the other.

In the face of large-scale unlawful assemblies triggered by "Occupy Central" at a number of locations for almost two months, frontline officers have remained steadfast to their duties around the clock. Police officers involved in the handling of "Occupy Central" are required to work for a long span of time. Their duties include preventing violent incidents within the occupied areas and their vicinity; conducting mediation and separating crowds with different views to minimise confrontations and physical scuffles; taking enforcement actions against acts in serious breach of law; following up on arrests and providing other support services. The Police have flexibly deployed their internal manpower and resources to meet the operational needs arising from "Occupy Central" and, at the same time, provided various districts with sufficient manpower (including auxiliary police) to maintain day-to-day police work. The Police's deployment of manpower involves operational particulars, and is, therefore, not to be disclosed.

(2) The Hong Kong Police Force compensates police officers for their overtime work in accordance with the Civil Service Regulations. Overtime work shall normally be compensated by time-off in lieu. Disciplined services overtime allowance would be paid to an eligible police officer if granting of time-off cannot be arranged within one month after the officer has undertaken overtime work.

(3) "Occupy Central" has been going on for almost two months, coupled with large-scale unlawful assemblies in different districts at the same time. The complexity of Police's operations in response to "Occupy Central" is unprecedented. Police officers are facing immense challenge and are under enormous stress. The storming and confrontations at different locations of unlawful assemblies in recent days have resulted in the injury of 69 police officers.

The Police have been making proactive efforts to promote a caring culture and establish a well-designed information system on stress management training and education to strengthen police officers' resilience. Starting from the foundation training, new recruits are provided with courses on psychology in policing and management of stress. The Psychological Services Group (PSG) of the Police also provides officers with training on positive psychology for sustained positive work attitude and emotion. The PSG keeps abreast of the daily development of "Occupy Central"-related operations. In addition to delivering encouraging messages to colleagues through the Carelinks Cadre, which is formed by voluntary officers having completed psychological service training, and mobile phones and the Police intranet, the PSG also gives advice on self-care and emotional adjustment. To help officers in their emotional adjustment and to understand their morale, Police's senior management and Police Clinical Psychologists visit frontline officers at places including the Police Headquarters, the Central Government Offices and the Mong Kok Community Centre to communicate with them directly. As at November 24, requests for PSG's assistance were received from eight police officers on account of post-operational stress.

During the operations in the recent two months, Hong Kong Police have stood fast to their posts and performed their duties with perseverance and untiring devotion in a professional and impartial manner with a high level of restraint. The SAR Government fully supports the Police in their continued efforts to handle with professionalism such extremely difficult tasks.

Issued at HKT 12:40

HKMA's update on operation of banking system and financial market (3)
****

The following is issued on behalf of the Hong Kong Monetary Authority:

According to the reports to the Hong Kong Monetary Authority (HKMA) from banks as at 2pm today (November 26), 12 branches of 11 banks were affected and temporarily closed now. The HKMA has requested banks to resume normal services as soon as circumstances permit. Customers should pay attention to the relevant banks' announcements regarding affected branches and ATMs. The HKMA will also publish on its website relevant updates from time to time.

Issued at HKT 14:45

LCQ4: Rule of law
****

Following is a question by the Hon Tam Yiu-chung and a reply by the Secretary for Justice, Mr Rimsky Yuen, SC, in the Legislative Council today (November 26):

Question:

Some members of the public have relayed to me that the remarks about the rule of law recently made on a number of occasions by some politicians with legal background, who are also supporters of the illegal road occupation movement, may have misled the public. For instance, these politicians have claimed that even if some people have deliberately breached the law, the rule of law will not be undermined insofar as they subsequently turn themselves in to bear the legal consequences, and that the rule of law does not mean unconditional compliance with the law. In addition, these politicians have also criticised the Police for their earlier arrest of two occupiers for allegedly fighting with three other persons in a public place, claiming that these two occupiers were then merely exercising "the power of citizens to arrest" under section 101A of the Criminal Procedure Ordinance ("section 101A") to stop those three persons from throwing objects at the occupiers. In this connection, will the Government inform this Council:

(1) whether it has studied the impacts of the aforesaid remarks made by these politicians (i.e. the rule of law will not be undermined insofar as the people who have deliberately breached the law subsequently turn themselves in, and the rule of law does not mean unconditional compliance with the law, etc.) on the proper understanding of the public about the concept of the rule of law; if the study outcome indicates that there are negative impacts, how the authorities will refute such remarks; if the study outcome indicates

that there are no negative impacts, of the justifications for that;

(2) whether it will step up publicity and education to instill in members of the public the correct concept of the rule of law; if it will, of the details; if not, the reasons for that; and

(3) whether it can clearly explain "the power of citizens to arrest" under section 101A in concrete terms, including the criteria for determining whether members of the public have lawfully exercised such power, as well as the degree of force they may use in arresting suspected offenders?

Reply:

President,

The rule of law is a fundamental core value of the Hong Kong society; it is also one of the important reasons which makes Hong Kong an international city as well as an international financial and commercial centre. In order to effectively maintain the rule of law, the citizens, the government and the entire community must respect the rule of law, including paying respect to court decisions. Besides, the rule of law is the cornerstone of democracy. The aspiration to attain universal suffrage surely cannot be used as a pretext to challenge the rule of law.

The reply of the Department of Justice (DoJ) to the three-part question raised by the Hon Tam is as follows:

(1) Since the beginning of the "Occupy Central" movement, different members of the community have made remarks on the rule of law. The remarks mentioned in the Hon Tam's question have seriously distorted the spirit of the rule of law. On November 10, the Honourable Mr Justice Au of the Court of First Instance of the High Court ruled on the applications for interim injunction made in the three cases concerning the occupy movement. The relevant judgment contained a clear exposition of the concept of the rule of law. The key points include:

(i) The concept of the rule of law must include the notion that every citizen and the government alike should obey and comply with the law.

(ii) Even if the defendants are of the view that a court order is wrongly granted, instead of simply disobeying it, they should first comply with it and then seek to challenge that order pursuant to the judicial process. The law cannot allow obedience of its orders to be a matter of individual choice.

(iii) It is wrong for any suggestions that the rule of law is not undermined or under challenged if people can freely or intentionally disobey the law first and then accept the consequences of breaking the law. The rule of law cannot realistically and effectively operate in a civilised and orderly society on this basis.

(iv) The upholding of the rule of law must be built upon, among others, the due administration of justice for the enforcement of court orders and the law.

(v) Worryingly, there have been repeated open suggestions by a number of public figures (including some legally trained individuals) to the public and the protestors and demonstrators en masse to the effect that ex parte injunctions need not to be complied with until they had been determined after an inter partes hearing, and that there is no challenge to the rule of law from merely disobeying civil orders, and that the rule of law is only threatened when there is disobedience of an actual order of committal for contempt of court. These suggestions are wrong and incorrect and would cause the public and the defendants an unwarranted misunderstanding on the concept of the rule of law.

When the Court of Appeal dealt with the relevant applications for leave to appeal, it clearly stated that it echoed the above observations made by the Honourable Mr. Justice Au. The Government welcomes the courts' exposition of the concept of the rule of law. We appeal to members of the public to obey and comply with the law and court orders, and to express their views in a peaceful and law abiding manner, or else there would be profound negative impact on Hong Kong.

(2) The DoJ has all along worked closely with other government departments and bureaux to educate the public on the concept of the rule of law through various channels. For example, the DoJ organises "Prosecution Week" and actively participates in the "Law Week" organised by the Law Society of Hong Kong on an annual basis so as to enhance the understanding of students and the public in respect of the justice system and the rule of law. Further, the DoJ participates in the works of the Committee on the Promotion of Civic Education, which, inter alia, promotes education on the rule of law in various ways. Further, the Police seek to raise citizens' awareness of law abiding and crime prevention through various channels. As regards primary and secondary schools, the Education Bureau has embedded the legal and rule of law education in the current primary and secondary school curricula. Schools also foster students' values in respecting the rule of law through diversified learning experiences including court visits. The Government

will continue these works, and is proactively considering various ways to enhance this area of work.

(3) Section 101 of the Criminal Procedure Ordinance (the CPO) (Cap. 221 of the Laws of Hong Kong) sets out the circumstances where a citizen has the power to make an arrest. Section 101(2) stipulates that "[a]ny person may arrest without warrant any person whom he may reasonably suspect of being guilty of an arrestable offence", while section 101(4) states that "[e]very person who finds any person in possession of any property which he, on reasonable grounds, suspects to have been obtained by means of an arrestable offence may arrest such last-mentioned person without warrant and take possession of the property".

Thus, "the power of citizens to arrest" as referred to in the question is applicable only in circumstances involving an "arrestable offence". Under Section 3 of the Interpretation and General Clauses Ordinance (Cap. 1 of the Laws of Hong Kong), an "arrestable offence" means an offence for which the sentence is fixed by law or for which a person may under any law be sentenced to imprisonment for a term exceeding 12 months, and including any attempt to commit any such offence.

On the other hand, section 101A of the CPO stipulates that "(a) person may use such force as is reasonable in the circumstances in the prevention of crime or in effecting or assisting in the lawful arrest of offenders or suspected offenders or of persons unlawfully at large".

As a law enforcement agency, the duties of the Hong Kong Police Force include upholding the law. The police have the statutory power to arrest persons suspected of having committed an offence. Should citizens witness any person committing an offence, they should report to the Police at once. If citizens find it necessary to stop any criminal act or to subdue any suspected offender, they may only use such force as is reasonable and proportionate in the circumstances to control the suspect but they do not have the power to search. Whether the offence in respect of which an arrest is made by a citizen constitutes an "arrestable offence" and whether the force used was reasonable can only be determined after the Police have made comprehensive investigation.

Issued at HKT 16:08

LCQ22: Number of persons eligible for voter registration

****

Following is a question by the Hon Alan Leong and a written reply by the Secretary for Constitutional and Mainland Affairs, Mr Raymond Tam, in the Legislative Council today (November 26):

Question:

According to the paper submitted to the Panel on Constitutional Affairs of this Council by the Government on the 20th of last month, the 2014 Final Register of electors contained 3 507 786 registered electors for geographical constituencies, representing a registration rate of 73.5 per cent. In this connection, will the Government inform this Council:

(1) of the annual numbers of persons eligible for registration as electors from 2012 to 2014;

(2) of (i) the annual numbers of persons eligible for registration as electors in each District Council (DC) district from 2012 to 2014, and (ii) among them, the number of those who had not registered as electors, with a breakdown by the age group and gender to which they belong set out in Table 1 of the annex[38] to the question; and

(3) in respect of each of the past three DC general elections (held in 2003, 2007 and 2011), of (i) the number of persons eligible for registration as electors in each DC district and (ii) among them, the number of those who had not registered as electors, as well as (iii) the number of persons who voted in the elections, with a breakdown by the age group and gender to which they belong set out in tables of the same format as Table 2[39] of the annex to the question?

Reply:

President,

(1) The Registration and Electoral Office (REO) estimates the number of persons eligible for voter registration on the basis of the population estimates of Hong Kong compiled by the Census and Statistics

---

[38] To view: http://gia.info.gov.hk/general/201411/26/P201411250818_0818_137965.pdf
[39] ibid

Department and the number of Hong Kong permanent identity card holders. Accordingly, the estimated number of persons eligible for voter registration is 4 711 900 in 2012, 4 744 300 in 2013 and 4 773 800 in 2014 respectively.

(2) In estimating the number of persons eligible for voter registration, the REO takes the population in Hong Kong as a whole instead of using District Council delineation as the basis. Hence, we only have the estimated number of persons eligible for voter registration in Hong Kong as a whole according to age groups and gender, but not the estimated number of persons eligible for voter registration by District Council delineation.

The number of registered electors is an actual figure based on the Final Registers published by the REO annually.

The number of persons eligible for voter registration but yet to be registered is derived by subtracting the actual number of registered electors from the estimated number of persons eligible for voter registration. Hence, the number of persons eligible for voter registration but yet to be registered is an estimate as well.

According to the estimation and calculation mentioned above, in 2012-2014, the number of persons eligible for voter registration in Hong Kong, registered electors, and persons eligible for voter registration but yet to be registered according to age groups and gender, are set out in Table 1[40].

(3) Regarding the estimates of the number of persons eligible for voter registration in 2003, 2007 and 2011, similar to the reason given in the reply to part 2 of this question, the REO only has the estimated number of persons eligible for voter registration in Hong Kong according to age groups and gender but not the estimates according to District Council delineation. For the 2003, 2007 and 2011 District Council Election, the number of persons eligible for voter registration in Hong Kong, registered electors, persons eligible for voter registration but yet to be registered, as well as the statistical breakdown of electors who have cast their votes according to age groups, gender and District Council delineation are set out in Table 2[41].

Issued at HKT 16:43

---

[40] To view Table 1(a): http://gia.info.gov.hk/general/201411/26/P201411250818_0818_138040.pdf; Table 1(b): http://gia.info.gov.hk/general/201411/26/P201411250818_0818_138041.pdf; Table 1(c): http://gia.info.gov.hk/general/201411/26/P201411250818_0818_138042.pdf

[41] To view Table 2(a): http://gia.info.gov.hk/general/201411/26/P201411250818_0818_138082.pdf; Table 2(b): http://gia.info.gov.hk/general/201411/26/P201411250818_0818_138083.pdf; Table 2(c): http://gia.info.gov.hk/general/201411/26/P201411250818_0818_138084.pdf

SJ on execution of injunction orders
****

Following is the transcript of remarks by the Secretary for Justice, Mr Rimsky Yuen, SC, at a media session on the enforcement of injunction orders after attending the Legislative Council meeting today (November 26):

Reporter: ... The protesters complained that the Police took over the action this morning 10 minutes after the bailiffs moved in.

Secretary for Justice: I wasn't at the scene, so I cannot comment on exactly what the bailiffs did or did not do in the course of the explanation. But if there is any person who takes the view that the bailiffs are not performing their duty properly, I am sure they can take the matter at the appropriate venue. In relation to the second part of your question, I believe the Police would have to act according to the circumstances. As I was saying earlier in Cantonese, the court order, although it contained an authorisation granted to the Police, the court order at the same time made it clear that it is entirely without prejudice to the statutory power of the Police and also the power of the Police under the general law. In other words, in any given circumstances, the Police can, on the one hand, assist the bailiffs, at the bailiffs' request, to discharge their duties in enforcing the injunction. On the other hand, if and when the circumstances become or render it necessary, the Police can, if not duty-bound to, discharge their duties to actually exercise their statutory power to, for instance, maintain the peace as well as to prevent the occurrence of other criminal activities. Issued at HKT 17:58

Police arrest seven police officers for assault occasioning actual bodily harm
****

Regarding a case in which a man was suspectedly assaulted on Lung Wo Road in Central, a Police spokesman said that upon further investigation and seeking legal advice, Police today (November 26) arrested seven interdicted officers for "assault occasioning actual bodily harm".

The arrest action is made today in accordance with the procedures and the progress of the investigation. Police emphasised that there is no delay in the handling of the case. The complainant has confirmed his presence at an identification parade to be conducted today, but he failed to turn up. Police hope that he will assist in our investigation work soonest. The complaint is being handled by the Special Investigation Team of the Complaints Against Police Office (CAPO) in a criminal investigation. Collection of evidence and investigation of the case is ongoing. Police will seek advice from the Department of Justice when the investigation is completed.

Police also noticed that some people earlier claimed they would express their discontent towards the way Police handling the case by committing uncooperative acts to affect the service of police stations.

The spokesman pointed out that such acts show a lack of civic-mindedness and selfishness and will affect Police's normal service to the public. Police have been handling complaints related to the conduct of a Police officer while on duty or in the execution of his duties according to normal and established procedures under which the complaints are to be investigated by CAPO. For the greater interests of the general public, he appeals to those people to refrain from committing any selfish acts.

Police reiterate that if any Force member commits illegal acts, Police will handle this seriously and investigation will be conducted in a fair and impartial manner.

Issued at HKT 20:02

Opening remarks by Police Chief Superintendent at press conference
****

Following are the opening remarks by the Chief Superintendent of Police Public Relations Branch, Mr Hui Chun-tak, at the press conference today (November 26):

Yesterday and today, Police provided full assistance to the plaintiffs and bailiffs in executing the Injunction Orders along Argyle Street and Nathan Road. As mentioned in yesterday's press statement, Police also used other powers conferred by the law to clear the obstructions at various locations in Mong Kok, including the road junctions on Portland Street and Argyle Street, Sai Yeung Choi South Street and Shantung Street, and Nathan Road and Shantung Street.

As you can see from the media footages and reports, some illegal road occupiers openly defied the law and disregarded the court orders by obstructing the plaintiffs and bailiffs in the execution of the Injunction Orders. Subsequently, at the request of the bailiffs, Police assisted in the execution of the Injunction Orders, removed the obstacles, dispersed and arrested the protestors who continued to illegally occupy the roads. However, Police faced strong resistance. In the course of assisting in the execution of Court orders, Police arrested a total of 55 persons, aged between 14 and 69 for the offences of 'Criminal Contempt of Court' and 'Obstructing a Public Officer in Execution of Duty'.

Last evening, a large group of protestors unlawfully assembled on Portland Street. They then moved to the areas of Shanghai Street, Shantung Street, Reclamation Street and Ferry Street to continue with the unlawful assembly and blockage of roads. They used iron railings and wooden pellets to create barricades and created chaos. Some even threw bamboo poles and miscellaneous items at our officers and caused physical confrontations. To preserve public order and public peace, Police took resolute actions to disperse and arrest these people. As a result, 93 persons (89 males and 4 females) were arrested for the offences of 'Resisting Arrest', 'Disorderly Conduct in a Public Place', 'Possession of Offensive Weapons', 'Unlawful Assembly', 'Assaulting Police' and 'Obstructing Police' etc. In the 'Possession of Offensive Weapon' case, the arrested male was found in possession of an axe, a metal hammer and a crowbar. Police will investigate all the cases seriously and collect evidence with a view to laying criminal charges accordingly. In the operations in these two days, 22 Police officers were injured. Police condemn the violent acts of the radical protestors who disrupted public order, defied the court orders and undermined the rule of law.

I note there are misleading accusations that Police officers advanced the check lines without issuing warnings beforehand and used unnecessary force. I must clarify that these allegations are totally untrue and unfounded. In the operation yesterday, Police had issued repeated appeals, advice and warnings at scene to the protestors through making public announcements and displaying warning banners to urge them to leave. Police also provided sufficient time for the illegal road occupiers who were unlawfully assembling there to leave but they refused to comply.

I must stress that Police have made it clear on numerous occasions that if any person blocks the re-opened roads, or attempts to block other roads, Police have the responsibility to take resolute action to maintain the public order. Police have the determination and ability to restore public order and protect public safety.

Regrettably, some people put up excuses that Portland Street is not covered in the Injunction Order in an attempt to detract others from the fact that they were engaged in an unlawful assembly. They used this excuse to call on more people to occupy roads in Mong Kok and to put up strong resistance against Police enforcement actions. Such acts were totally irresponsible and full of twisted facts. Some radical protestors and troublemakers continued to incite others to charge the police cordon, verbally abuse and physically confront our officers. Some even threw umbrellas, miscellaneous objects, water bottles and unknown powders at our officers. They blatantly defied the law, disregarded the wish and interests of the general public. These radicals continued to scatter to different areas, blocked sections of roads and disrupted public order.

These radical individuals and protestors took no heed of the warnings. They continued to unlawfully assemble, block the roads and charge our officers violently. With no other alternatives, Police took resolute actions by using the minimum level of force necessary, including the use of pepper spray, pepper based solution and baton, to stop the violent and unlawful acts of these radicals and to disperse and arrest them as well.

Police reiterate that Injunction Orders are solemn orders issued by the court. Police urge all protestors not to employ illegal means to express their views. This is unacceptable to the general public. If anyone attempts to block the re-opened roads or other sections of roads, or to disrupt public order, Police are duty bound to take resolute actions and to exercise our statutory powers to safeguard the public order and public safety.

Now, the traffic lanes on Argyle Street and Nathan Road are re-opened. If any person plans or attempts to occupy other roads or places, Police will take resolute actions to restore order. If necessary, operations to re-open any blocked roads will continue.

I reiterate that Police have the determination and capability to strictly enforce the law, so as to restore public order and protect public safety.

Issued at HKT 20:35

NOVEMBER 27[42]

HKMA's update on operation of banking system and financial market
****

The following is issued on behalf of the Hong Kong Monetary Authority:

According to the reports to the Hong Kong Monetary Authority (HKMA) from banks as at 8am today (November 27), all previously affected bank branches have resumed operation. One branch of one bank would shorten its business hours today. The HKMA has requested banks to resume normal services as soon as circumstances permit. Customers should pay attention to the relevant banks' announcements regarding affected branches and ATMs. The HKMA will also publish on its website relevant updates from time to time.

Issued at HKT 09:31

Police are committed to preventing re-blockage of roads
****

In the past two days, Police assisted bailiffs in the execution of Injunction Orders on Argyle Street and Nathan Road, Mong Kok and exercised other legal powers conferred by the law to remove obstacles blocking the public thoroughfares. Argyle Street, South and North bounds of Nathan Road and other roads in the proximity are now re-opened.

Though the roads were re-opened, radicals and troublemakers still lingered in the vicinity and often provoked others, created chaos and attempted to block the roads again. Police urge members of the public not to go to Mong Kok and linger there. They should stay away from radical individuals and troublemakers, and should not take part or be incited to take part in any illegal acts. They should maintain a safe distance from police officers when the officers are executing their duties. Police do not want to see anyone, especially students, being hurt when they place themselves amongst the violent acts of radical individuals and troublemakers.

Shops in Mong Kok were forced to close their business and members of the public were forced to use indirect routes that caused inconvenience due to the unlawful acts of the people who assembled unlawfully. Their behaviours interfered with the local residents and ignored their interest. The protestors should not attempt to block the roads again as the roads belong to the general public.

---

[42] http://www.info.gov.hk/gia/general/201411/27.htm

Last evening, a group of protestors started to gather on Nelson Street and Shantung Street to block the roads. Police issued multiple appeals, advice and warnings through public announcements and displaying warning banners at scene. However, the protestors refused to comply and scattered around the area. They attempted to block the roads, incited others to provoke the officers and charged at Police check lines. To prevent the situation from further deteriorating, Police, with no other alternatives, used the minimum level of force and took resolute action, including using pepper spray and baton to stop the violent and unlawful acts, and to disperse and arrest the protestors involved.

Police dispersed all the troublemakers and resumed the traffic flow in Mong Kok at seven this morning. In the operation from last night to the early morning of today (November 27), Police arrested a total of 21 males, aged between 19 and 42, for the offences of 'Criminal Damage', 'Disorderly Conduct in a Public Place', 'Possession of Offensive Weapons', 'Unlawful Assembly', 'Assaulting Police' and 'Obstructing Police'.

In addition, at around ten last night, some protestors dashed onto Salisbury Road, Tsim Sha Tsui, attempted to block the carriageways and then fled immediately. Police swiftly deployed officers to remove the obstacles. Police pointed out that these illegal acts were highly irresponsible and endangered the safety of the protestors themselves and other road users as well. Police will not allow erection of barricades on roads that have been re-opened or other sections of roads, and will take strict enforcement actions to stop these illegal acts.

Police have always been emphasising that Mong Kok is a high risk area. We have repeatedly urged the public, in particular students, not to go there to avoid unnecessary injuries. Local residents and business operators should also be careful of their own safety to avoid injuries.

Police have deployed sufficient manpower to maintain order and prevent re-blockage of roads. Police have the responsibility to take resolute action by exercising the statutory powers conferred by the law to maintain public order and safeguard public safety.

Police have the determination and capability to restore public order and to protect public safety. We will take resolute enforcement actions if anyone resorts to violence or disrupts public order.

Issued at HKT 22:24

NOVEMBER 28[43]

Special arrangements on submission of tenders arising from temporary closure of Government Secretariat Tender Box
****

Owing to the special access arrangements at the Central Government Offices (CGO) in Tamar, the Government Secretariat Tender Box (GSTB) located on the ground floor of the East Wing of CGO is closed for tender deposit temporarily.

All tenders that should originally be deposited into the GSTB are instead requested to be deposited into the Government Logistics Department Tender Box (GLDTB) located on the ground floor of North Point Government Offices at 333 Java Road, North Point. This special arrangement came into effect on September 30 this year and remains in effect until further notice.

Tenderers may wish to check in advance their route to the GLDTB and allow sufficient time to make arrangements to deposit their tenders into the GLDTB before the respective closing time of tenders. Late tenders will not be accepted.

For enquiries, please call 2810 2497 or 2231 5288 between 9am and 6pm from Mondays to Fridays (except public holidays).

Issued at HKT 08:31

HKMA's update on operation of banking system and financial market
****

The following is issued on behalf of the Hong Kong Monetary Authority:

According to the reports to the Hong Kong Monetary Authority (HKMA) from banks as at 8am today (November 28), all previously affected bank branches have resumed operation. One branch of one bank would shorten their business hours today. The HKMA has requested banks to resume normal services as soon as circumstances permit. Customers should pay attention to the relevant banks' announcements regarding affected branches and ATMs. The HKMA will also publish on its website relevant updates from time to time.

Issued at HKT 09:40

---

[43] http://www.info.gov.hk/gia/general/201411/28.htm

Opening remarks by Police Chief Superintendent at press conference
****

Following are the opening remarks by the Chief Superintendent of Police Public Relations Branch, Mr Hui Chun-tak, at the press conference today (November 28).

On this Tuesday and Wednesday, Police assisted bailiffs in the execution of Injunction Orders on Argyle Street and Nathan Road, Mong Kok and exercised other legal powers conferred by the law to remove obstacles blocking the public thoroughfares. Argyle Street, south and north bounds of Nathan Road and other roads in the proximity are now re-opened.

Although the roads in Mong Kok have been re-opened, there were still radicals and troublemakers gathering and loitering in the area in the past few nights. These people provoked others and created chaos in an attempt to block the roads again. Police urge members of the public not to go to Mong Kok to gather and linger there. They should stay away from these radical individuals and troublemakers, and should not take part or be incited to take part in any illegal acts. When Police officers are executing their duties, members of the public are advised not to gather around as onlookers and should maintain a safe distance from Police officers. Police do not want to see anyone, especially students, being hurt when they place themselves among the violent acts of radical individuals and troublemakers.

Because of the illegal acts of those who unlawfully assembled in Mong Kok, shops in the area were forced to close their business and members of the public had to use indirect routes, causing huge inconvenience. The behaviours of these radicals have seriously disturbed the local residents and totally disregarded the public interest. These radical protesters need to realise that the roads in Mong Kok do not belong solely to any particular group of people, they are public thoroughfares for the whole community. I urge protesters not to block the roads again for the benefits of the community.

In the past two nights, there were protesters with radicals and troublemakers mixing among them. They gathered along Sai Yueng Choi Street South, Shan Tung Street and Soy Street and blocked nearby roads. Police had issued multiple advice and warnings through public announcements and display of warning banners, urging them to leave but they refused to comply. They continued to loiter around the area, blocking the roads and creating chaos. They put up excuses that they were just gathering there for shopping and watching television together, picking up dropped coins and waiting for someone else, etc. Some radicals deliberately merged themselves into the crowd and incited others to verbally abuse and provoke Police officers, to charge Police line and to obstruct Police enforcement actions. To prevent the situation from worsening, with no other alternatives, Police took resolute actions to disperse those who unlawfully assembled thereat. Because of the chaotic situation and the deliberate acts of some people to disrupt public peace, frontline officers at scene were confronted with a lot of difficulties when carrying out their duties. Some people thought that what they did could exhaust Police manpower and provoke our officers, however how could such irresponsible acts be of benefits to Hong Kong as a whole?

At around 10.30am this morning, Police intercepted five persons, including four males and one female, aged between 14 and 24, at the junction of Argyle Street and Nathan Road, Mong Kok. Police seized eleven lighters, a bottle of petroleum and a cutter on them and in two rucksacks they were carrying. They were arrested for the offences of 'possession of offensive weapons' and 'possession of instrument fit for unlawful purpose'. Mong Kok District Investigation Team is now looking into the case.

Furthermore, I noticed that some radicals called for mass gathering in Mong Kok tonight on the Internet to block the roads again and to commit further radical acts. This will undoubtedly cause unnecessary and even unreasonable adverse impacts on the Mong Kok residents. Police are sceptical of the true intentions of these radicals who disregarded the interests of the general public but are stubborn on their own way of resistance. These people constantly resort to illegal means in expressing their views, for this the community will neither accept nor agree with their behaviours.

Police have made it clear on numerous occasions that if any person blocks the re-opened roads, or attempts to block other roads, Police have the responsibility to take resolute action by exercising the legal power conferred by the law, in order to maintain public order. Police would take resolute actions against anyone who commits illegal acts, and including unlawful acts committed in the cyber world.

I also note that certain student organisations called upon members of the public to bring along different supplies, such as umbrellas, goggles and helmets, to gather at the illegally occupied area in Admiralty on the coming Sunday, and proclaimed to escalate their actions at that time. I must stress that the gathering in Admiralty is an unlawful assembly and the occupation and blockage of roads are illegal. The acts of these illegal road occupiers have disrupted public order and seriously undermined the rule of law in Hong Kong. Sadly, these organisations continued to foment members of the public to commit illegal acts and the general public would not accept these acts. I urge the illegal road occupiers to stop their illegal acts and to leave the occupied roads at once.

Police are highly concerned of a Police officer suspected to be involved in an incident of unnecessary use of force. Police have initiated follow up actions and the officer concerned has been removed from the current operation. I stress that there are stringent guidelines governing the use of force and Police will handle the case in a serious manner. I take the opportunity here to appeal to the persons concerned to come forth and provide information to Police to assist in the investigation. Police will definitely handle the case in a fair and impartial manner.

Regarding the arrest of a press photographer, Police stress that we will take enforcement actions in a fair and impartial manner regardless of the background or profession of the persons involved in the illegal acts.

Police have all along respected the freedom of the press. You can see that the situation at scene is often very chaotic. There are a lot of people holding mobile phones, cameras or small size camcorders, recording the scene in between the crowds. Some individuals even behave in a provocative manner in an attempt to obstruct Police. Police understand that it is the duty of the press to make news coverage at scene and we endeavour to facilitate the press in carrying out their duty. The Deputy Commissioner of Police (Operations) and myself met with the management of major media organisations this afternoon to reassure them of our policy of respecting the freedom of the press. We also explained the operational difficulties faced by frontline officers in the midst of chaos at scene and we appealed for mutual understanding and mutual respect. Police officers will endeavour to facilitate the works of media as much as possible. Police would continue to deploy our Media Liaison Teams at scene to provide coordination and mediation. At the same time, Police also appeal for the co-operation of frontline reporters to wear easily identifiable clothing to identity themselves, to heed Police officers' direction at scene and avoid obstructing Police operation.

In addition, Police are aware that some radicals have threatened to harm Police officers and their family on the Internet, some have incited others to block Government premises. I must point out that it is against the law to incite others to commit illegal acts on the Internet. The rule of law is the cornerstone of Hong Kong's success and all citizens should abide by the law. Regardless of whether it is in the real world or through online social media, any persons who commits illegal acts have to bear criminal liability and will be brought to justice. Police will collect evidence and to effect arrest when necessary.

Lastly, I need to point out that although the roads in Mong Kok have been re-opened, Mong Kok still remains a high-risk area as there have been a lot of radicals gathering there in the past few nights. These radicals behaved provocatively in an attempt to block the roads again. Confrontations can be sparked off at any moment. Police urge members of the public, particularly students, to avoid going to the area at night in order to avoid unnecessary injuries. Citizens should also stay away from radicals and troublemakers and not to be used or incited to commit illegal acts. Residents and business operators nearby shall be vigilant of their personal safety and prevent themselves from getting injured.

Police have deployed appropriate manpower in Mong Kok to maintain public order and prevent blocking of roads that have been re-opened or other sections of roads. Police are duty bound, and have the determination and the capability to maintain public order and protect public safety through exercising the legal powers conferred by the laws of Hong Kong. Should anyone resort to violence or illegal acts to disrupt public order, Police will take resolute enforcement actions.

Issued at HKT 20:06

NOVEMBER 29[44]

Police condemn people illegally assembled endangering public order and public safety
****

Police condemned the acts of protesters who illegally assembled in Mong Kok, blocked roads and endangered public order and public safety last night (November 28) and in the small hours of today (November 29).

Last night, a large number of protesters gathered on Sai Yeung Choi Street South, Shantung Street and Soy Street and blocked the roads. Police issued multiple appeals, advice and warnings through public announcements and displaying warning banners at scene. However, the protesters refused to comply. They scattered around the area and created chaos. Some protesters even provoked and threw hard objects at police officers and charged at police check lines. Police, with no other alternatives, used the minimum level of force and took resolute actions, including using pepper spray and batons to stop the unlawful acts, and to disperse and arrest the protesters involved.

Some protesters placed large objects such as rubbish bins and recycling bins on Dundas Street between Fa Yuen Street and Nathan Road in an attempt to block the roads. Police swiftly removed the obstacles and arrested the people concerned.

From last night to 6am today, Police arrested 27 males and one female, aged between 16 and 52, in Mong Kok for offences including "Unlawful Assembly", "Assaulting Police", "Possession of Offensive Weapons", "Possession of Instrument Fit for Unlawful Purpose", "Obstructing Police Officer", "Possession of Part I Poison", "Disorderly Conduct in Public Place". During the operation, eight police officers were injured. Two of them were hit by hard objects thrown by protesters.

Police condemned the irresponsible acts of the protesters which disregarded safety of others and seriously endangered public order. Police reiterate that resolute enforcement actions will be taken to preserve public order and safeguard public safety.

Issued at HKT 13:41

[44] http://www.info.gov.hk/gia/general/201411/29.htm

Transcript of remarks by CE and CS at media session
****

Following is the transcript of remarks by the Chief Executive, Mr C Y Leung, and the Chief Secretary for Administration, Mrs Carrie Lam, at a media session after the 15th meeting of the Commission on Poverty today (November 29):

Reporter: Chief Executive, why do you think and how do you think policy in that upward mobility will help resolve the political impasses? Some lawmakers have criticised that you shouldn't focus on these poverty issues and you should focus on political policies to help resolve the impasse and the stalemate? What do you think needs to be done?

Chief Executive: I heard that the lawmaker who made this point was actually the Honourable Mr Frederick Fung. Now you are nodding your head. The Honourable Frederick Fung did not take part in the second part of the Poverty Commission meeting just now, so he didn't make his point at the Commission's meeting. If he made his point at the Commission meeting, I have a sense that most of the Commission members will not agree with him. I think we are much better and more productive if Mr Fung had made that point at the meeting so that we can actually discuss it.

I think the answer to your question or Mr Fung's question is that it was a Poverty Commission meeting. And the point has been made that one of the reasons behind discontent amongst the new generation in Hong Kong that has led to the occupy movement, I have to say that the understanding is that this is one of the reasons, I am not saying it is a major reason or minor reason, obviously the main cause is the disagreement on constitutional development, is a lack of upward mobility. Therefore, as a responsible government, we do not want to leave any stone unturned. And therefore the Poverty Commission, being the Poverty Commission, at the request of Government, will look at the question of youth mobility or the lack of it, and that's what we are doing. This Commission is not a constitutional development commission, so it's doing its job, looking at the question of upward mobility of the young people.

Reporter: The Chief Secretary, the Chief Secretary, do you share the belief that people making less than $14,000, $15,000 Hong Kong dollars a month would potentially constitute that obstacles to the political development in Hong Kong?

Moderator: You are asking the Chief Secretary?

Reporter: Yes, the Chief Secretary. Chief Secretary. Do you share the belief that people making less than $14,000 or $15,000 Hong Kong dollars may constitute an obstacle?

Chief Secretary for Administration: As the Chief Executive has said, this is the Poverty Commission. So we gather together this morning to look at the poverty situation in 2013, and that situation and all those statistics do point to the fact that the policies introduced by this term of the SAR Government to alleviate poverty in Hong Kong have produced some early results.

Political participation is another matter. I think citizens of Hong Kong will all want to have more participation in our political system. And that is why we, the Central Government and the majority of people in Hong Kong, are so keen to see universal suffrage in the selection of the Chief Executive in 2017, and that is something that we would continue to work very hard at.

Chief Executive: Let me try to respond to this question. I am determined as the Chief Executive, and I have the power to give consent under the Basic Law the change of method of electing Chief Executive for the next term Government in 2017. I have made my decision known and so has the Central People's Government. Our determination is very clear. We want universal suffrage election, "one-man, one-vote" in Hong Kong to elect the next Chief Executive in 2017. And that change would, for the first time to give every eligible voter in Hong Kong, we are talking about over 5 million people, the chance to vote for the first time in Hong Kong's history, regardless of his or her level of income. And our determination is very clear and the fact that I take an active part in the work of the Poverty Commission, and we have been keeping close contact with members of the entire Poverty Commission, means that whatever is our method of electing the Chief Executive, whatever is our political system, we want to help the poor in Hong Kong and we are determined, we are determined to have universal suffrage election in 2017. I will repeat this point again. Whatever the level of income of voters come 2017, provided that we get two-third of the majority of LegCo to pass the Government's proposal, everyone will have a vote.

Thank you.
Issued at HKT 18:17

Police urge the public not to block the roads again

****

Police stress that Mong Kok remains a high risk area. Although Argyle Street, south and north bounds of Nathan Road and other roads in the proximity are now re-opened, in the past few nights, there were still large groups of troublemakers gathering in Mong Kok, provoking others here and there and attempting to block the roads again. Their acts caused great nuisances and adverse impacts on the local residents and business operators. They even charged the police lines. Further confrontations can be sparked off any time.

Police urge members of the public, particularly students, to avoid going to the area at night. They should also stay away from the radicals and troublemakers, and not to be used or incited to commit illegal acts, so as to avoid unnecessary injuries. Residents and business operators nearby should be vigilant of their personal safety and prevent themselves from getting injured.

Police have deployed appropriate manpower in Mong Kok to maintain public order and prevent blockage of roads which have been re-opened or other sections of roads. Police are duty bound to maintain public order and protect public safety through exercising the legal powers conferred by the laws of Hong Kong.

Police condemned the acts of protesters who illegally assembled in Mong Kok, blocked the roads and severely endangered public order and public safety last night (November 28) and in the small hours this morning (November 29).

Starting from 7 pm last evening, there were large groups of protesters illegally assembling at Sai Yeung Choi Street South and Shantung Street. The unlawful assembly was later extended to Soy Street, Sai Yee Street, Nelson Street, Dundas Street, Fa Yuen Street, and even as far as the Tsim Sha Tsui Pier. Police issued multiple advice and warnings through public announcements and display of warning banners, urging them to leave. However, they refused to comply, but dispersed into groups and continued to loiter around the area. They put up excuses, such as shopping, waiting for buses, picking up dropped money, etc., with the intent to block the roads. They crossed the roads slowly with an attempt to interfere with the traffic and jeopardise public order. Some protesters placed large objects such as rubbish bins and recycling bins in an attempt to block the roads, including the section of Dundas Street between Fa Yuen Street and Nathan Road. There were also troublemakers using different ways to disturb the shops nearby, including blocking the goldsmith shops, or interfering with their normal operation together. Some radicals and troublemakers even intentionally threw miscellaneous items such as water bottles, umbrellas, eggs and tin cans at police officers. Police had immediately made public announcement to urge them to stop these highly irresponsible and dangerous behaviours because the hard objects thrown might hurt other persons at scene including the reporters working there and pedestrians walking by. However, they took no heed.

During mid-night, when a vehicle was entering Argyle Street from Sai Yeung Choi Street South, some radical protesters dashed onto the roads to create chaos. Some troublemakers deliberately merged themselves into the crowd, incited others to provoke and verbally abused the police officers there, and to charge police lines, creating chaos intentionally to obstruct the police enforcement actions. To prevent the situation from worsening, with no other alternatives, Police took resolute actions and used minimum level of force, including pepper spray and baton, to stop these illegal acts, and to disperse and arrest those involved.

From last night to 4 pm today, Police arrested 27 males and one female, aged between 16 and 52, in Mong Kok for offences including "Unlawful Assembly", "Assaulting Police", "Possession of Offensive Weapons", "Possession of Instrument Fit for Unlawful Purpose", "Obstructing Police Officer", "Possession of Part I Poison", "Disorderly Conduct in Public Place", etc. During the operation, eight police officers were injured on the face and limbs, of whom two were hit by hard objects thrown by protesters. Besides, two police motorcycles parked in Sai Yeung Choi Street South were intentionally tampered by protesters, causing damages to the foglight, antenna, beacon, rear-mirror and radio. These serious unlawful acts were classified as a case of 'Criminal Damage' which is being investigated by Mong Kok District Investigation Team.

Police note that certain student organisations called upon members of the public to bring along different supplies and equipment to assemble at the illegally occupied areas in Admiralty tomorrow (October 30) and proclaimed to escalate their actions. Police stress that the gathering in Admiralty is an unlawful assembly, and the occupation and blockage of roads are illegal. The acts of the illegal road occupiers have disrupted public order of Hong Kong, and incessantly eroded the foundation of the rule of law. Police are regretful that these organisations continue to foment members of the public to commit illegal acts. The general public will not accept these acts. Police urge the illegal road occupiers to cease their illegal acts and leave the occupied roads immediately.

Police also urge reporters working on ground to be vigilant of their personal safety, particularly when they position themselves between police officers and radical protesters, or within close range from them, so as to avoid injuries as a result of the confrontations. Police have also deployed Media Liaison Teams to facilitate their work on ground and provide assistance to any reporters as necessary.

Ends/Saturday, November 29, 2014

Issued at HKT 21:08

NOVEMBER 30[45]

Police urge protesters not to block roads
****

A large number of protesters gathered on Sai Yeung Choi Street South and Shantung Street from last night (November 29) to the small hours of today (November 30) and they later went to Soy Street, Sai Yee Street, Nelson Street, Dundas Street, Fa Yuen Street and even as far as to the Tsim Sha Tsui area. They crossed the roads slowly by excuses such as shopping, waiting for buses, picking up dropped money and the like with the intent to block the roads and other road users; and disturbed the normal operation of the shops nearby. Some troublemakers even threw miscellaneous items and placed wooden planks and rubbish bins onto the carriageways. Police had made repeated public announcements to urge them to leave but they refused to comply. Police had to take appropriate actions to maintain public order and safeguard public safety.

During the operation, Police arrested seven men and two women, aged between 15 and 56, for offences including "Possession of Offensive Weapon", "Theft", and "Taking Conveyance Without Authority".

Police appealed to protesters not to block roads and endanger public order and condemned the irresponsible acts of the protesters which disregarded the safety of road users. Police reiterate that resolute enforcement actions will be taken to preserve public order and safeguard public safety.

Members of the public are advised that when Police officers are executing duties, they should not gather around as onlookers and should maintain a safe distance from Police officers, particularly when they position themselves between Police officers and radical protesters, or within close range from them, so as to avoid injuries as a result of the confrontations.

Issued at HKT 17:34

---

[45] http://www.info.gov.hk/gia/general/201411/30.htm

Opening remarks by Senior Superintendent at a media session
****

Following are the opening remarks by Senior Superintendent of Police Public Relations Branch, Mr Kong Man-keung, at a media session today (November 30).

I now provide the gist of the two key messages today. The first one is about the situation in Mong Kok.

Since Police have assisted bailiffs in executing injunction orders in Mong Kok and resumed the traffic and public order, Mong Kok remains a high risk area. Particularly for the past two nights, protestors gathered there, with attempt to block the roads and disrupt public order. Police strongly condemn all such acts.

In the past two nights, large groups of protestors assembled illegally on Sai Yeung Choi Street South and Shantung Street. They later moved on to other streets in Mong Kok, and even Tsim Sha Tsui slowly. They used different acts to obstruct the traffic and affect the daily lives of local residents. Some troublemakers even interfered with the nearby shops and forced them to stop business even though Police repeatedly appealed them to stop the acts. Regrettably, the protestors refused to comply.

In the early morning on November 29, some radicals and troublemakers threw miscellaneous items such as water bottles and tin cans at Police officers and incited others to charge the Police lines. To prevent the situation from deteriorating, with no other alternatives, Police took resolute actions and used minimum level of force to stop these illegal acts, and to disperse and arrest those involved.

There were also troublemakers placing large obstacles on the carriageways with attempt to block the roads, disregarding the safety of road users. Police had to take appropriate actions to restore the public order.

Since November 28, Police have arrested 42 persons (38 males and 4 females), aged between 14 and 56, for the offences of "Unlawful Assembly", "Assaulting Police", "Possession of Offensive Weapon", "Obstructing Police Officer", "Disorderly Conduct in Public Place". During the operation, eight police officers were injured.

I again urge members of the public, particularly students, not to go to the area to avoid any unnecessary injury. Local residents and business operators should be vigilant of their personal safety. Police will deploy appropriate manpower to maintain law and order as it is our statutory duty for doing so.

The second key message is about student organisations calling for the public to assemble in Admiralty this evening. They asked the public to bring along with equipment such as helmet, goggle, mask and umbrella etc. and proclaimed to escalate their actions, including to block the Central Government Offices.

Police stress that the unlawful assemblies in Admiralty have disrupted public order, and eroded the foundation of the rule of law of Hong Kong. Police are highly regretful that these organisations continue to incite members of the public to commit illegal acts.

Police have also found that some people on the Internet incite members of the public to take part in the assembly and plan for violent charging acts. From the past experience, this sort of incitement would lead more radicals and troublemaking individuals or organizations to take part, making the situation even more chaotic. There are increasing risks of the assembly this evening. Untoward incidents can be sparked off any time. Police remind the public, particularly students, should be vigilant of their personal safety, stay away from the location and do not take part in the event.

Police urge the illegal road occupiers not to do any provocative acts, obstruct or charge police officers and maintain a safe distance from our officers. Protestors, particularly students, should stay away from the radicals and troublemakers. Police do not want to see anyone, particularly students, getting hurt.

I emphasise, if anyone obstructs Police in the execution of our duties, charges Police lines violently or attempts to block the Central Government Offices, Police will take resolute enforcement actions. In case of any violence, Police, with no other alternatives, will use minimum level of force to stop any violent and illegal acts, so as to uphold the law and order.

I also urge media workers to be vigilant of their personal safety to avoid injuries. We will deploy Media Liaison Teams to facilitate their work on ground.

I reiterate, Police have the determination and the capability to take enforcement actions to maintain public order and protect public safety.

Issued at HKT 17:51

Transcript of remarks by SED
****

Following is the transcript of remarks by the Secretary for Education, Mr Eddie Ng Hak-kim, at a media session after officiating at prize presentation ceremony of "CEO Parents Election" held by the Hong Kong Institute of Family Education today (November 30):

Reporter: (On the new task force set up to follow up youth issues by the Commission on Poverty yesterday)

Secretary for Education: Yesterday the major one was on the Commission on Poverty. As far as that part is concerned, we believe that the setting up of a new subcommittee to address some particular issues faced by the youth would be one of the focuses. There would be a lot of other activities going on as reported in the summit yesterday such as education opportunities, university opportunities, vocational education and better employment in future as well.

Reporter: How about tonight's public gathering (in the vicinity of the Central Government Offices in Admiralty)?

Secretary for Education: As I said earlier, it is important for everyone to understand the whole "Occupy Central" movement has been going on for more than two months now. It has brought the public severe inconvenience and a lot of people have been suffering from the disruption of public transportation services, long travelling hours and also the chaos created that might put people's lives in danger. On this particular account, my position is that I would like to appeal to everyone including the potential organisers, please do not do that. For students, please try to stay away from all those problematic and dangerous locations.

Issued at HKT 18:21

Transcript of remarks by STH

****

Following is the transcript of remarks by the Secretary for Transport and Housing, Professor Anthony Cheung Bing-leung, at a media session after attending a public function this (November 30) afternoon:

Reporter: Do you think on Monday that the students, if they break inside the Government Offices today, do you think on Monday it would affect the work of the Administration when officers come back to the Government? How do you warn the students...

Secretary for Transport and Housing: It is not for me to speculate what might happen. But as far as I am concerned, we would continue to operate within the CGO (Central Government Offices) at Tamar. For students, I always maintain the line that while they have every right to express their views about the future, about political reform, they must at the same time respect others and we should try to foster a tolerant society that we respect others while articulating our views. I think that kind of tolerance, that kind of allowance for different views is very important for Hong Kong. I think that is what Hong Kong is good for.

Issued at HKT 20:35

DECEMBER 1[46]

CGO is temporarily closed this morning
****

Attention duty announcers, radio and TV stations:

Please broadcast the following message as soon as possible and repeat it at suitable intervals:

"As the access roads leading to the Central Government Offices (CGO), Tamar are now blocked, the Administration Wing announced that the CGO will be temporarily closed this morning (December 1). Staff working in the CGO are advised not to go to the workplace in the morning and should work in accordance with the contingency plans of their respective bureaux or departments. All visits to the CGO in the morning will be postponed or cancelled."

Issued at HKT 07:00

Rescheduling/Cancellation of LegCo committee meetings and public hearing this morning
****

The following is issued on behalf of the Legislative Council Secretariat:

The Committee meetings and public hearing of the Legislative Council (LegCo) to be held this morning today (December 1) have been rescheduled/cancelled. These are:

(1) the closed meeting of the LegCo Public Accounts Committee scheduled for 8.30am;

(2) the public hearing of the LegCo Public Accounts Committee scheduled for 9am; and

(3) the meeting of the LegCo Panel on Financial Affairs scheduled for 9.30am.

Issued at HKT 07:51

---

[46] http://www.info.gov.hk/gia/general/201412/01.htm

Public services in LegCo Complex suspended
****

The following is issued on behalf of the Legislative Council Secretariat:

The Legislative Council (LegCo) Secretariat announces that the service of the LegCo Public Complaints Office is suspended this morning (December 1). The guided educational tours of the LegCo Complex are cancelled today.

Meanwhile, the LegCo Library, the LegCo Archives, the Children's Corner and the exhibition area in the main lobby of the LegCo Complex continue not to be open to the public until further notice.

Issued at HKT 08:16

HKMA's update on operation of banking system and financial market
****

The following is issued on behalf of the Hong Kong Monetary Authority:

According to the reports to the Hong Kong Monetary Authority (HKMA) from banks as at 8am today (December 1), all previously affected bank branches have resumed operation. One branch of one bank would shorten its business hours today. The HKMA has requested banks to resume normal services as soon as circumstances permit. The HKMA would closely monitor the situation in the areas concerned including Admiralty and Mongkok and announce relevant update if necessary. Customers can also pay attention to the relevant announcements by banks.

Issued at HKT 09:47

CGO will resume operation this afternoon
****

Attention duty announcers, radio and TV stations:

Please broadcast the following message as soon as possible and repeat it at suitable intervals:

The Administration Wing has announced that the Central Government Offices at Tamar will resume operation this afternoon (December 1).

Issued at HKT 10:35

Rescheduling of LegCo committee meetings and public hearing this afternoon
****

The following is issued on behalf of the Legislative Council Secretariat:

The Committee meetings and public hearing of the Legislative Council (LegCo) to be held this afternoon (December 1) have been rescheduled. Details are at below:

(a) meeting of the LegCo Panel on Housing scheduled for 2.30pm;

(b) closed meeting of the LegCo Public Accounts Committee scheduled for 3pm;

(c) public hearing of the LegCo Public Accounts Committee scheduled for 3.30pm; and

(d) meeting of the LegCo Bills Committee on Copyright (Amendment) Bill 2014 scheduled for 4.30pm.

Issued at HKT 12:35

Government strongly condemns violent radicals storming Central Government Offices and blocking Lung Wo Road
****

The Hong Kong Special Administrative Region Government today (December 1) strongly condemned the protesters taking part in unlawful assemblies for conspiring and organising the storming of police cordon lines and blockading access to the Central Government Offices (CGO) and Lung Wo Road. Such acts show blatant disregard for the law and endanger public safety.

The Government spokesman reiterated that society would not accept the illegal acts of violent radicals who repeatedly pushed police officers and charged their cordon lines during scuffles last night and this morning. The spokesman added that these illegal acts have seriously disrupted public order and put the safety of police officers and protesters at stake.

During the jostling, the violent radicals deliberately threw objects including water bottles, helmets and pepper powder at the police officers. They also used strong flashlights against police officers and attacked them with fire extinguisher spray. The violent radicals repeatedly provoked and verbally abused police officers and continuously incited others at the scene to charge the police cordon lines. To prevent the situation from deteriorating, the Police took resolute action by using appropriate force to stop these illegal acts and disperse and arrest those involved. However, the radical protesters ignored repeated police appeals and warnings and continued to charge the police cordon lines. Eleven police officers were injured during the incident and 40 persons have been arrested so far. Further arrests will be made.

The Government strongly condemns the student groups for planning illegal assemblies and inciting protesters to charge towards the CGO repeatedly. The spokesman said a number of recent polls have revealed that the majority of the people hope that the protesters would leave the occupied sites as soon as possible and cease the blockades of roads. However, the relevant organisations went against the views of the majority and escalated the occupy actions, aggravating the damage to social order and sacrificing the overall interests of the Hong Kong people.

On claims by the student groups that the blockade of the CGO will continue until the Government responds to their demands, the Government has reiterated repeatedly that any discussion relating to constitutional reform must be guided by the Basic Law and the decision of the National People's Congress Standing Committee. Deliberate disregard for and distortion of these important legal principles through building castles in the air would only delay the constitutional and democratic development of Hong Kong.

The Government appeals to organisers of the illegal assemblies to stop their illegal acts immediately and ask all participants to remain calm and exercise restraint, stop provoking police officers and charging police check lines, and leave the scene peacefully and in an orderly manner. The Police will, in the light of the prevailing circumstances, continue to take appropriate action to restore public order and protect public safety.

Issued at HKT 13:19

Statement by ExCo Non-official Members
****
The following is issued on behalf of the Executive Council Secretariat:

The Non-official Members of the Executive Council (ExCo) today (December 1) issued the following statement on violent acts occurred outside the Central Government Offices:

The Non-official Members of the Executive Council seriously condemn the series of violent acts instigated by part of the protesters in the areas outside the Central Government Offices last night (November 30) and this morning (December 1). Members also condemn the organisers of these illegal activities for being irresponsible as they advocated public participation in these illegal activities, without regard to the safety of the participating public.

The ExCo Non-official Members call on protestors to stop blocking the access to the Central Government Offices immediately so that normal government operation could be resumed as soon as possible. They also call upon all protesters of the Occupy Central movement to leave the scene as soon as possible, in response to the wish of the great majority of the public to resume law and order in the city.

Issued at HKT 13:48

Transcript of remarks by FS at press conference on Hong Kong's latest overall economic situation
****

The Financial Secretary, Mr John C Tsang, and the Government Economist, Mrs Helen Chan, today (December 1) held a press conference on Hong Kong's latest overall economic situation at the Information Services Department Press Conference Room. Following is the transcript of remarks by the Financial Secretary at the press conference:

Reporter: Secretary, could you comment on last night's events in Admiralty at the occupy movement? And my second question is: How has the occupy movement affected economic growth in this third quarter? You mentioned that there has been double-digit growth in visitors, but you said in non-Mainland visitors there has been a drop. And looking towards the future, if the occupy movement continues, what are your concerns? Thank you.

Financial Secretary: I've already explained that earlier. I think you just want to have a - I'll just provide you with a brief English explanation. The occupy movement made some pretty violent type of move on Hong Kong Island in Admiralty, and the Police went on to enforce, which, you know, this is their job. I feel that this sort of organised movement is totally irresponsible and is totally, sort of, ruffian type of attack needs to be reprimanded.

Reporter: ... if it continues, what are your concerns? Do you think people won't invest in Hong Kong? How will it affect investors' confidence in the city?

Financial Secretary: My biggest concern is really for the middle and longer term. If the occupation were to continue, no doubt our international image could be seriously damaged, which could lead to investment confidence running down. We have already seen different examples of that recently, and if the instability were to continue, that would also affect pay level as well as new job creations. But what is more important, if that whole rule of law concept were to be damaged, that would be very difficult to repair. That is our really core value. That kind of internal damage would be very difficult to heal.

Reporter: Sir, recently several economists have come out with comments that the debt level that Hong Kong companies and households have taken on is too high and has made Hong Kong one of the most vulnerable economies in Asia from an external shock, as, for example, particularly an interest rate hike, as you have pointed out before. Would you share the opinion that the debt level in Hong Kong is too high, and what is the Government doing to prepare for possible external shock?

Financial Secretary: I don't believe our debt level is too high. I think the debt level in Hong Kong now is manageable, and our banking regulator is keeping a very close watch at all times, and as a matter of fact we've been keeping a pretty close watch since 2008 on all the overall situation, and the current situation is still manageable.

Issued at HKT 16:27

Transcript of remarks by S for S

****

Following is the transcript of remarks (the opening remarks are an English translation) by the Secretary for Security, Mr Lai Tung-kwok, at a media session today (December 1):

Secretary for Security: The unlawful assemblies and occupation activities, which have been going on for more than two months, took a sharp turn for the worse last night.

Over the past weekend, the leaders of the Hong Kong Federation of Students (HKFS) and Scholarism repeatedly made public appeals to protesters to bring their gear to Admiralty to lay siege to government buildings last night. At about 9pm, the student groups urged the protesters to head towards Lung Wo Road and surround the Central Government Offices. In the process, the protesters charged the Police cordon with shields and mills barriers intentionally and systematically. They threw objects, including bottles, helmets and pepper powder, at police officers. The protesters also projected strong flashlights onto police officers and attacked them with fire extinguisher spray. They set up obstacles to block Lung Wo Road, which is a major trunk road on Hong Kong Island. After repeated appeals and warnings, the Police took resolute enforcement actions to disperse the protesters and make arrests. Social order and traffic flow were temporarily restored.

At about 3am the protesters assembled again after an appeal from the student groups to occupy Lung Wo Road. This morning, the Police took another round of enforcement actions to disperse the protesters and restore traffic flow on Lung Wo Road. The obstacles on the footbridge connecting the Admiralty MTR Station and the Central Government Offices were also cleared. During the operation, a number of persons, including 11 police officers, were injured. Nobody would like to see that happen.

Although the leaders of the student groups announced several times before the incident that their actions would be peaceful, rational and non-violent, the latest developments show the opposite. The protesters charged the police cordon with mills barriers and tools, and also threw hard objects at the officers. Batons, bricks and other objects were found on the protesters when they were searched by the Police. The actions went way beyond their proclaimed principles of peace and non-violence. This was an organised and calculated attempt to paralyse the operation of the Government. Such behaviour would not be tolerated by any government and is not something members of the public wish to happen.

I offer the strongest condemnation of the leaders of the HKFS for staging the actions last night, which began as a siege and then turned into violent charging. It was not a peaceful assembly. After the incidents last night, I believe we all realised that the demonstration in Admiralty was on the verge of becoming uncontrollable. I appeal to all protesters to leave immediately and the public should not take part in any such activities.

The Government and the Police have been exercising the utmost restraint and tolerance towards the demonstrations in the past two months. However, time and again, the protesters have charged and provoked police officers, and recently even escalated their actions. The Police will take resolute enforcement actions to resume social order.

Reporter: Would you comment on last night's clearance after the escalation of the action? Do you think that Police were very forceful with protesters? Some people complained that some of the Police were very violent in dealing with female protesters. And you mentioned that the HKFS and Scholarism have said they would have a non-violent movement. Do you think they have gone beyond this? Do you think they have changed their plans? What do you think happened last night?

Secretary for Security: I think what happened last night fully demonstrated that it has far, far away gone beyond what they have declared. The Police, after repeated warnings, have to take resolute actions. They have no choice because it is their duty to restore law and order.

Reporter: Would you comment on last night's clearance in terms of the Police's actions? How did the protesters provoke the Police? What exactly did they do? And in terms of future actions, will the Government try to clear out Admiralty completely?

Secretary for Security: For the future actions, this is a question concerning operational details, I regret that I am not going to reveal pre-maturely. For your first question, those protesters, they systemically charged the Police cordon. I just quoted one or two scenes. They gathered together, put up their so-called defensive materials and then they said five, four, three, two, one and they charged the police cordon. This was systemic with a command. Another example, they took mills barriers and then formed a barricade, and used that to push their line forward. All these fully demonstrated that they were well prepared to block a major road on Hong Kong Island. As you could see from the live broadcast, at that time, traffic towards both sides had been suddenly stopped. It took quite a lot of effort for drivers to drive their vehicles out of this problem area. All these fully demonstrated what they have done.

Thank you.

Issued at HKT 17:36

Speech by FS at Hong Kong Exporters' Association Christmas Luncheon 2014
****

Following is the speech by the Financial Secretary, Mr John C Tsang, at the Hong Kong Exporters' Association Christmas Luncheon 2014 today (December 1):

Ivan (Ting), distinguished guests, ladies and gentlemen,

Good afternoon.

I am indeed really pleased to join you here today for the Christmas luncheon hosted by the Hong Kong Exporters' Association.

It's actually been seven years since I last had the pleasure of addressing you over Christmas lunch. I hope I did not misbehave so badly seven years ago that I was not invited again until now.

Actually, a lot has happened over those seven years. In 2008, of course, we discovered that there is really no Santa Claus. Even though our tables got Santa Claus. Or, at least, Mr Claus had taken an extended sabbatical that holiday season, leaving very little joy to the world.

It was not until 2010 when the trade engine that powers Hong Kong started to regain its momentum, thanks mainly to the strong growth of the Mainland market. Consider the numbers. In 2007, Hong Kong was the world's 11th largest trading economy. Last year, we were the eighth largest, and the ninth largest exporter in terms of merchandise trade.

In 2006, our total exports were about HK$2.5 trillion. Last year, our export figures hit HK$3.6 trillion. That's up over 40 per cent in seven years, although our exports to the US and to Europe have yet to recapture the lost ground. Our exports this year are again on the rise, up 3.8 per cent over the first 10 months, year on year, despite a much slower growth of only 2.5 per cent to the Mainland.

The journey in the last seven years has been rough. Given the challenges of the global economy, I would say those are rather comforting figures, and it reflects the hard work by you all, the export community.

Looking ahead in 2015, the external environment is still full of challenges. Europe is still suffering from high unemployment, they are still suffering from political turmoil arising from austerity measures as well as geopolitical tensions. The increase in sales tax in April has slowed down Japan's economic momentum. We have yet to see any concrete evidence to suggest that the quantitative easing measures in Europe and in Japan will put their economic growth back on track.

The US, on the other hand, seems to be making some steady and sustained recovery. However, the improved economic performance of the US has yet to be translated into strong demand for our exports. Moreover, the US labour participation rate remains on the low side. Recent signs seem to suggest that the property market is also slowing down. The political struggle between the two parties is already intense, and the President's effort to go solo on immigration will add to the problem.

The ongoing economic reform of the Mainland is necessary for healthy and sustainable economic development of our nation in the medium and longer term. However, it also means that in the short run, the Mainland market may not be able to provide our export sector with the timely cushioning effect that we saw in the last seven years.

Domestically, if the occupy movement and the irrational political behaviours were to continue, Hong Kong's international reputation and the rule of law, which is our basic core value and the foundation of our competitiveness, could be seriously damaged, making the healing process a long and painful one. Everyone in Hong Kong, including the exporter community, would be affected.

But despite all these factors, I am confident that Hong Kong will continue to be resilient and all of you would be able to meet these challenges with flying colours and the export sector would become an even stronger driver of our economy.

In terms of business establishments and employment, I cannot overstate the importance of our import-export sector. As of June, more than 100,000 companies were engaged in import-export trade in Hong Kong. Those companies employed about half a million people, which is the largest share of our total employment.

Those numbers reflect your relentless efforts over the years. Whatever the product, whatever the service, in the end it is your hard work, your dedication and your ability to seize the opportunity, wherever it may lie, that drive Hong Kong's exports and global confidence in our exports.

For that, you have my thanks and you have the gratitude of the Hong Kong people. And more than that, you can count on our continuing support.

Meanwhile, I wish you all happy holidays and a prosperous and successful New Year - with or without Santa. Thank you very much.

Issued at HKT 17:40

Opening remarks by Police Chief Superintendent at press conference
****

Following are the opening remarks by the Chief Superintendent of Police Public Relations Branch, Mr Hui Chun-tak, at the press conference today (December 1).

The first point I would like to talk about is the charging of Police check lines. Last night and this early morning, a lot of people taking part in the unlawful assembly, with radicals and troublemakers mixing among them, violently charged at Police and blocked the roads. Their acts seriously disrupted public order and public safety. Police strongly condemned these riotous acts.

At around 9pm last night, some student organizations provoked other citizens in the illegally occupied area in Admiralty to bring along different supplies, such as helmets, masks, goggles and umbrellas to surround the Central Government Offices. Radicals and troublemakers were found in between the crowd who created chaos deliberately. Some of them took command to incite others to violently charge Police in an organized manner. Some people were injured as a result. During the charging, these rioters stole materials from a nearby construction site, moved mills barriers, water barriers and bricks around and damaged government properties so as to block the roads again. It was obvious that these troublemakers committed the violent acts in a premeditated and organized manner.

You could all see from television broadcast that the violent acts of these rioters had deviated from their proclaimed 'non-violence', 'no charging of Police' and 'no vandalism' principles. It was also a complete opposite of the principle of 'peace'.

In the past few days, Police had pointed out that there was high risk of radicals and troublemakers merging into the unlawful assembly. The situation might turn chaotic and the unlawful assembly would be of very high-risk. Police had repeatedly reminded and urged members of the public, particularly students, not to participate in the unlawful assembly. We had also warned the people taking part in the unlawful assembly not to provoke and charge at Police, to maintain a safe distance from the radicals and troublemakers, and not to take part or be incited to take part in any violent acts. Police do not want to see protestors, particularly students, getting injured when they place themselves in the middle of the charging acts of radicals and troublemakers.

It is a fact that the violent charging of Police by these radicals and troublemakers was premeditated and organized. They violently advanced towards Police check lines, carrying their own shields made of wooden planks and metal nails. These people behaved in an extremely provocative manner, including the deliberate throwing of various objects at Police, such as pepper powder, powder of unknown nature, helmets, water bottles, canned drinks and eggs etc. Some of them also used strong light to obscure the views of officers, to spray officers with a fire extinguisher, to verbally abuse our officers and incite others to charge Police lines.

Police had repeatedly advised and warned the protestors through public announcements and display of warning banners at scene. However, they took no heed of our warnings. With no other alternatives, Police used the minimum level of force commensurate with the circumstances, including the spraying of water, pepper spray, pepper based solution and batons to stop the violent and illegal acts and to restore public order.

In addition, Police raided a residential flat in Tai Kok Tsui yesterday. Police seized three modified air guns and a large number of makeshift wooden shields. There were reasons to believe that these equipment would be used in the illegally occupied areas. In the operation, Police arrested four males and one female for the offences of 'possession of firearms without license' and 'possession of instruments fit for unlawful purpose'. The case is now being investigated by a Crime Wing unit.

At around 10am this morning, three plainclothes police officers walked past Admiralty Center after completing their duties in Admiralty. More than 40 protestors suddenly surrounded the three officers and attacked them. Other Police officers later came to reinforce and disperse the assailants. In the incident, six Police officers were injured, including abrasions to right eye, head, arm and limbs. One of the officers suffered serious injury, was once unconscious, and is now admitted in hospital for observation. Police arrested a 30-year-old male for 'assaulting Police'. Police strongly condemned these irrational and violent acts.

In the operation last night and this morning, 17 police officers were injured. One of the officers sustained two open wounds on his right arm as he was hit by a makeshift shield which was made of wooden planks, metal nails and screws. Other officers had fractures in finger, bleeding at eye corner after being hit by hard objects and some had sustained multiple bruises.

The second point is about the blockage of Lung Wo Road last night. You are aware that, since the illegal occupation of Harcourt Road commenced two months ago, Lung Wo Road has become the major thoroughfares connecting the east and west of Hong Kong Island and is also an emergency vehicle access route. At around 9.35pm, a large number of radicals and troublemakers suddenly dashed onto Lung Wo Road to illegally block all the four vehicle lanes. Their acts seriously disrupted the traffic flow. Some of them even pushed towards Police check lines with mills barriers and makeshift shields.

Police emphasized that these illegal acts were extremely irresponsible and dangerous, disregarding the personal safety of those involved and other road users. Police issued multiple advice and warnings but these radicals took no heed of them. To re-open Lung Wo Road, to protect public safety and maintain public order, Police took resolute actions to disperse the illegal road occupiers and remove the obstacles on Lung Wo Road by exercising the minimum level of force commensurate with the circumstances.

East and west bounds of Lung Wo Road were re-opened at 7.31am this morning. In the operation, Police arrested 40 persons, including 35 males and five females, for the offences of 'possession of offensive weapon', 'theft', 'disorderly conduct in public place' and 'unlawful assembly'. All the arrested persons are being detained for further enquiries.

I reiterate that the illegal road occupations have disrupted the public order of Hong Kong and eroded the foundation of the rule of law. The illegal road occupiers disregarded Police advice and warnings continuously and occupied Lung Wo Road twice. They behaved in a riotous manner and showed no consideration for the safety of the general public. Police strongly condemned these acts.

The third point is about the situation in Mong Kok. From last night to this early morning, a lot of radicals still gathered in Mong Kok, Yau Ma Tei and Tsim Sha Tsui in an attempt to block the roads again. Police repeatedly advised and warned these radicals to leave but they refused to comply and continued to scatter around the area. These radicals put up various excuses to block the roads, crossed the roads to and fro slowly and stood on the vehicle lanes to obstruct pedestrians and vehicles deliberately. Some of them even shouted loudly in the middle of the night to create chaos and to upset traffic flow and public order intentionally. The selfish acts of these radicals caused great disturbances and the general public would neither accept nor agree with them.

In the incident, Police arrested 12 males in Mong Kok, aged between 20 and 64, for the offences of 'obstructing Police', 'possession of offensive weapon', 'disorderly conduct in public place', 'assaulting Police' and 'resisting arrest'.

I now conclude my messages today. Police strongly condemned the acts of these rioters who surrounded the Central Government Offices and re-blocked Lung Wo Road. Their behaviors were completely irrational. Police urge members of the public, particularly students, to stay away from these people and do not commit, or be incited to commit, any radical acts.

Hong Kong society agrees with the use of rational and peaceful means to express one's views. Police will not tolerate any violent acts that disrupt public order and public safety and will take resolute actions accordingly. I emphasize that Police have the determination and capability to take stringent enforcement actions in order to protect public safety and restore public order.

Issued at HKT 20:46

DECEMBER 2[47]

HKMA's update on operation of banking system and financial market

****

The following is issued on behalf of the Hong Kong Monetary Authority:

According to the reports to the Hong Kong Monetary Authority (HKMA) from banks as at 8am today (December 2), all previously affected bank branches have resumed operation. One branch of one bank would shorten its business hours today. The HKMA has requested banks to resume normal services as soon as circumstances permit. The HKMA would closely monitor the situation in the areas concerned including Admiralty and Mongkok and announce relevant update if necessary. Customers can also pay attention to the relevant announcements by banks.
Issued at HKT 09:35

Transcript of remarks by S for S

****

Following is the transcript of remarks by the Secretary for Security, Mr Lai Tung-kwok, after attending the Legislative Council's Panel on Security meeting today (December 2):

Reporter: Mr Lai, what were your thoughts on the occupy trio planning to turn themselves in tomorrow?[48]

Secretary for Security: Any persons who intend to turn themselves in because they believed that they had breached the laws, of course, it is welcome. The Police have an established practice and procedures to handle this kind of situation. They will act accordingly.
Issued at HKT 17:48

---

[47] http://www.info.gov.hk/gia/general/201412/02.htm
[48] These would be the founders of Occupy Central; University of Hong Kong professor Benny Tai, sociologist Chan Kin-man and the Rev Chu Yiu-ming

Police committed to protecting public safety and public order
****

Police stressed today (December 2) that the assembly at the illegally occupied areas in the vicinity of Admiralty is unlawful. Troublemakers, radical individuals and organisations often infiltrate into the illegal assembly, making the situation very chaotic. The unlawful assembly in the vicinity of Admiralty is still of high risk and it is necessary to re-open the roads so as to reduce risks associated with the unlawful assembly.

Police believed that protestors who took part in the deliberate charging of Police cordon on Lung Wo Road and at the Central Government Offices on November 30 and in the early morning of December 1 had also participated in the illegal blockage of roads in Mong Kok. Some of the radicals and troublemakers took command and incited others to violently charge Police while some of them deliberately damaged government properties. Fences of about 30 metres long on Lung Wo Road near Legislative Council Road were maliciously damaged.

In addition, Police noted that some people have called for the throwing of makeshift stink bombs at Police officers on the internet and the spraying of paint on officers' helmets so as to obstruct their views. Police condemned these unlawful acts. Police reiterate that it is against the law to incite others to commit illegal acts on the internet. Hong Kong is under the rule of law and all citizens shall abide by the law regardless of whether it is in the real world or on social media platforms. Anyone who commits illegal acts have to bear criminal liability and will be brought to justice. Police will collect evidence and make arrest when necessary.

Since the illegal occupation of Harcourt Road started two months ago, Lung Wo Road has become the major thoroughfares connecting the east and west of Hong Kong Island and it also serves as an emergency vehicle access. Police have deployed appropriate manpower to prevent the re-blocking of Lung Wo Road and nearby roads. Police will not tolerate the blocking of re-opened roads or violent acts that disrupt public order or public safety. Police will take resolute enforcement actions against all unlawful acts.

Police are duty bound to take resolute enforcement actions with the powers conferred by the law in order to maintain public order and protect public safety. Police have the determination and capability to take stringent enforcement actions to re-open the roads and to restore public order. Police urge the illegal road occupiers to immediately remove the obstacles, take away personal belongings and leave in a peaceful and orderly manner.

In respect of the Injunctions Orders on Connaught Road Central and Harcourt Road, Admiralty, Police respect the judgment of the court and will comply with the court order accordingly. Depending on the circumstances, Police will render assistance as necessary.

Organisers of the illegal occupation proclaimed to turn themselves in to Police. Police will deal with this in accordance with the established procedures fairly and impartially. It is hoped that the relevant persons could follow Police arrangement so as to minimise impact on the provision of normal services to the general public.

Issued at HKT 18:37

DECEMBER 3[49]

HKMA's update on operation of banking system and financial market
****

The following is issued on behalf of the Hong Kong Monetary Authority:

According to the reports to the Hong Kong Monetary Authority (HKMA) from banks as at 8am today (December 3), all previously affected bank branches have resumed operation. One branch of one bank would shorten their business hours today. The HKMA has requested banks to resume normal services as soon as circumstances permit. The HKMA would closely monitor the situation in the areas concerned including Admiralty and Mongkok and announce relevant update if necessary. Customers can also pay attention to the relevant announcements by banks.

Issued at HKT 09:43

Agenda of today's LegCo meeting revised
****

The following is issued on behalf of the Legislative Council Secretariat:

The agenda of the Legislative Council (LegCo) meeting, scheduled for today (December 3) at 11am in the Chamber of the LegCo Complex, has been revised. In addition to the original items, the President of LegCo has given permission for Dr Kenneth Chan to move, under Rule 16(2) of the Rules of Procedure, a motion for the adjournment of the Council. The motion states: "That this Council do now adjourn for the purpose of debating the following issue: the Police's assistance in enforcing the injunction orders in Mong Kok and its handling of public assemblies since November 25, 2014."

Meanwhile, the Vice-Chairman of the Independent Police Complaints Council (IPCC), Dr Lam Tai-fai, will present the IPCC's Report 2013/14 at the meeting and address the Council on the Report.

For the latest agenda items of today's LegCo meeting, please refer to the LegCo Website: www.legco.gov.hk/yr14-15/english/counmtg/agenda/cm20141203.htm.

Issued at HKT 10:12

---

[49] http://www.info.gov.hk/gia/general/201412/03.htm

Delineation of constituencies for 2015 District Council Election
****

The Chief Executive in Council has accepted all the final recommendations in the report submitted by the Electoral Affairs Commission regarding the delineation of constituencies for the District Council election in 2015.

A government spokesman said today (December 3) that the decision of the Chief Executive in Council would be effected by way of the Declaration of Constituencies (District Councils) Order 2014, which will be published in the Gazette on December 5 and tabled at the Legislative Council on December 10 for negative vetting.

The report of the Commission, submitted to the Chief Executive on November 5, was tabled at the Legislative Council today as required by law. The report is divided into three volumes. Volume 1 is the report, setting out the Commission's recommendations and the reasons for its recommendations. Volume 2 contains 23 maps on the recommended constituency boundaries and the related boundary descriptions. Volume 3 records all the written representations. The report is available for public viewing at all Public Enquiry Service Centres of District Offices and the Registration and Electoral Office during ordinary business hours starting from today. The report can also be viewed at the Commission's website (www.eac.gov.hk).

The spokesman said that the Commission had conducted public consultation on its provisional recommendations from June 26 to July 25.

"The Commission had carefully considered all the public representations before making its final recommendations for submission to the Chief Executive. It had endeavoured to strike a fair and proper balance between the expressed wishes of the public on the one hand, and the statutory criteria for delineation on the other hand."

There will be 431 constituencies for the District Council election to be held in 2015. One District Council member will be elected for each constituency.

"The making of the Order is an important step in the preparation for the next District Council election in November 2015. In the year ahead, the Government and the Commission will put in place all necessary arrangements to facilitate the conduct of the election," the spokesman said.

Issued at HKT 12:40

LCQ7: Processing of teaching staff members' applications for suspension from teaching work and personnel policies of tertiary institutions

****

Following is a question by the Hon Tony Tse and a written reply by the Secretary for Education, Mr Eddie Ng Hak-kim, in the Legislative Council today (December 3):

Question:

It has been reported that two professors were respectively given approval by the University of Hong Kong and The Chinese University of Hong Kong, where they teach, for about one month's suspension from teaching work for the purpose of organising and participating in an illegal occupation movement. Some members of the public have pointed out that the University Grants Committee (UGC) is duty-bound to monitor the institutions funded by it (UGC-funded institutions) on matters relating to their processing of teaching staff members' applications for suspension from teaching work, as well as their personnel policies for dealing with teaching staff members who have committed criminal offences, so as to ensure that such institutions have good governance and use public money properly. In this connection, will the Government inform this Council if it knows:

(1) whether UGC has approached UGC-funded institutions to gain an understanding of their mechanisms for processing applications of teaching staff members for suspension from teaching work, including the circumstances under which such applications will be approved, the longest duration of suspension from teaching work, and the arrangements to be made by the institutions to avoid students' learning and the operation of the institutions being affected, etc.; if UGC has looked into the matter, of the details; if not, the reasons for that;

(2) whether UGC has requested UGC-funded institutions to assess the impacts of their teaching staff members suspended from teaching work on aspects such as the operation of the institutions and the use of public money, etc.; if the institutions have conducted such an assessment, of the details and the measures to reduce such impacts; if not, the reasons for that, and whether they will conduct such an assessment in future;

(3) whether UGC has requested UGC-funded institutions to review if it was appropriate for them to grant approval for teaching staff members to suspend from teaching work for the purpose of organising and participating in an illegal occupation movement, and whether this was in line with the principle of using

public money properly; if the institutions have conducted such a review, of the details; if not, the reasons for that, and whether UGC will request these institutions to conduct such a review; and

(4) whether UGC has looked into the existing personnel policies of UGC-funded institutions regarding how to deal with teaching staff members convicted of having committed criminal offences, including the arrangements pertaining to the teaching posts, remunerations and fringe benefits of the teaching staff member concerned; if UGC has looked into the matter, of the details; if not, the reasons for that?

Reply:

President,

All institutions funded by the University Grants Committee (UGC) are autonomous with their own Ordinances and governing Councils. The UGC Notes on Procedures state that institutions enjoy autonomy in the development of curricula and academic standards, selection of staff and students, initiation and conduct of researches, internal allocation of resources, etc., and are accountable for their decisions in these aspects. That said, the UGC Notes on Procedures also state that institutional autonomy does not exempt institutions from public interest and criticism. In fact, in view of the significant funding the institutions receive in the form of Government subvention and private contributions, as well as the importance of higher education to the development of society, it is incumbent upon the Government and the community at large to have a legitimate interest in the operation of the institutions. Therefore, while the Government and the UGC attach great importance to safeguarding institutional autonomy, institutions are expected to remain committed to transparency and accountability in their operation, to ensure that funding is put to appropriate uses that serve the best interests of the community and students.

Recently, there is widespread public concern about staff of universities getting involved in organising and participating in illegal activities. We stress that Hong Kong is a city of rule of law and that the law enforcement agencies will deal with the concerned illegal activities, including their organisation and planning, in a serious manner in accordance with the law. Meanwhile, the Government and the UGC have received numerous complaints that are concerned with internal management matters of an institution, including complaints about work arrangement and discipline matters of staff. We have referred the complaints to the relevant institution and requested it to handle the complaints in a serious manner and give an account of how these complaints are handled.

(1) to (3) According to the information provided by the funded institutions, they have put in place internal mechanisms, rules and procedures to deal with leave applications of staff and the corresponding work and teaching arrangements. Staff must fulfill their contractual obligations. Leave entitlements of staff should comply with the minimum requirements as stipulated in relevant labour legislation and should be set out in employment contracts. All leave applications require approval. When deciding whether to approve leave applications of a staff member, an institution will take into full account its duty-related needs and other factors, and will ensure that the department concerned will make proper corresponding work arrangements (such as supply teachers, make-up classes, reshuffle of duties or re-scheduling of timetables, co-teaching, etc.) in order to maintain normal classroom teaching activities, while minimising the impact on the teaching and learning, research and other operations of the institution as a result the staff member taking leave. Generally speaking, institutions have different leave types such as annual leave, sick leave, maternity leave, conference/working leave and no-pay leave, etc. Depending on the type of leave, different application criteria and approving procedures apply, which include seeking approval from the designated authority as well as making proper corresponding duty-related arrangements. There are limits on the number of leave days to which a staff member is entitled for each type of leave. If necessary, institutions may also grant no-pay leave to their staff having regard to individual circumstances.

On the understanding that the above-mentioned mechanisms and procedures are complied with, institutions deal with leave applications of staff and the corresponding work and teaching arrangements by themselves. The UGC does not stipulate any particular rules in this regard. That said, the UGC Notes on Procedures also provide that the UGC is responsible for providing assurance to the Government and the community on the standards and cost-effectiveness of the operations and activities of the UGC-funded institutions. Where necessary, the UGC can relay its concern regarding operational issues of the institutions, and request the institutions to look into the matters concerned and take appropriate follow-up actions.

(4) According to the information provided by the funded institutions, institutions have put in place internal mechanisms, rules and procedures to deal with staff discipline matters, including cases involving staff members convicted of criminal offences. In general, institutions will take appropriate follow-up actions having regard to the nature and seriousness of the cases. If necessary, disciplinary procedures will be initiated. Depending on the nature and seriousness of the case, the disciplinary procedures will be handled by personnel of appropriate ranks or an investigation/disciplinary panel/committee, and these include investigation and hearing. In the course of the procedures, the institutions will provide the staff concerned with

the opportunities to clarify and respond. Subject to the investigation results, institutions will take appropriate actions or impose suitable sanctions, including termination of appointment, in accordance with the established personnel policies and guidelines as well as the terms and conditions laid down in the employment contracts. Appeal mechanisms are also available in all institutions to ensure that decisions are made in a fair and impartial manner. All personnel involved are required to observe confidentiality and all disciplinary actions taken will be recorded and filed properly.

Issued at HKT 14:51

LCQ5: Freedom and privacy of communication of Hong Kong residents shall be protected by law
****

Following is a question by the Hon Cyd Ho and a reply by the Secretary for Security, Mr Lai Tung-kwok, in the Legislative Council today (December 3):

Question:

It has been reported that since the 7th of last month, nine Hong Kong residents with no criminal records either in Hong Kong or on the Mainland have been refused entry one after another by mainland border officials when they headed for the Mainland. These residents include a non-core member of Scholarism, a volunteer of Scholarism who is also an intern assistant to a Legislative Council Member, three university student union members or university students having participated in the "Umbrella Movement" (the Movement), a stewardess-on-duty who is allegedly a supporter of the Movement, and three representatives of the Hong Kong Federation of Students (HKFS) who intended to go to Beijing on the 15th of last month. The reasons given for refusing their entry include their participation in activities which violated national security or affected national diplomacy, as well as "contravention of the relevant rules". Some members of the public have expressed the concern that some law enforcement personnel from outside Hong Kong have come to the territory to monitor the activities of members of the public, with a view to restricting the freedom of Hong Kong residents to travel to and from the Mainland. In this connection, will the Government inform this Council:

(1) whether it has monitored the activities of various social movement organisations such as Scholarism and HKFS as well as their members, and the activities of those members of the public who have participated in the Movement; whether it has kept a blacklist of social activists and forwarded such a blacklist to the Mainland authorities;

(2) of the existing legislation that protects members of the public from the monitoring of their activities by law enforcement personnel from outside Hong Kong, and the channels through which members of the public may lodge complaints or seek assistance when they suspect that their activities have been monitored by law enforcement personnel from outside Hong Kong, so as to protect their privacy; and

(3) whether the existing legislation has any requirement for law enforcement personnel from outside Hong Kong to obtain the authorisation by the relevant authorities for undertaking monitoring activities in Hong Kong; if there is such a requirement, whether the authorities instituted any prosecution in the past three years against law enforcement personnel from outside Hong Kong who had undertaken monitoring activities in Hong Kong without authorisation; if there is no such requirement, whether the authorities will consider making amendments to the Interception of Communications and Surveillance Ordinance to regulate such acts of monitoring; if they will not consider, of the reasons for that?

Reply:

President,

    The Hon Cyd Ho is concerned about the recent refusal of some Hong Kong residents' entry to the Mainland by Mainland border officials. I would stress that Hong Kong and the Mainland have their own immigration clearance policies and regimes under which the immigration departments of both sides implement their respective policies. Relevant law enforcement authorities of the Mainland may, in accordance with the Mainland policies, determine the arrangements with respect to Mainland immigration matters. For some recent cases in which Hong Kong residents were denied entry to the Mainland, there are people holding the Administration responsible for providing a so-called "blacklist of social activists" to the Mainland authorities. I maintain that such accusations are totally unfounded, and are nothing more than malicious slander against the law enforcement agencies (LEAs), to which I would note with regret.
    As we all know, over the past 60 days, there have been very extensive and highlighted local media reports of the "Occupy Central" (OC) or the "Occupy Movement", together with wide coverage on the Internet and by overseas media. Presented lavishly with words and photos, those reports contain such personal data as names, identities and backgrounds of some protesters.
    Besides, by means of current social networking platforms, any person may upload their own audios and videos onto the web for sharing of opinions, stances, acts, etc. During the OC, there were also cases in which a group of people, while taking no heed of law and order, used the web media to indiscriminately incite others to commit unlawful acts. This should definitely be condemned. While posting their

opinions, photos and videos online, these people might also have disclosed their personal data. Given that the Internet is boundary-free, any information uploaded online may eventually go public.

In consultation with the Constitutional and Mainland Affairs Bureau, I give my reply to the three parts of the Hon Ho's question as follows:

(1) The Administration absolutely does not compile any so-called "blacklists of social activists", not to mention the passing of such lists to any authorities outside Hong Kong.

Under the Personal Data (Privacy) Ordinance (PD(P)O) (Cap. 486), the handling of personal data is protected by law. Always acting in a lawful manner, the Administration handles the personal data of Hong Kong residents in accordance with the law.

(2) and (3) Article 30 of the Basic Law clearly stipulates that the freedom and privacy of communication of Hong Kong residents shall be protected by law. No department or individual may, on any grounds, infringe upon the freedom and privacy of communication of residents except that the relevant authorities may inspect communication in accordance with legal procedures to meet the needs of public security or of investigation into criminal offences.

At present, no lawful channels are in place for law enforcement officers from other jurisdictions to conduct surveillance in Hong Kong.

As far as the Interception of Communications and Surveillance Ordinance (ICSO) (Cap. 589) is concerned, I have to make it clear that the purpose of the ICSO is not related to the concerns raised in the question. The purpose and designated scope of the ICSO are to regulate lawful interception of communications and surveillance by designated LEAs in Hong Kong for the prevention and detection of serious crimes and the protection of public security. In addition to a complicated and sophisticated mechanism, there are stringent provisions under the ICSO to govern LEAs' submission of applications to panel judges for the authorisation of interception of communications and surveillance according to statutory procedures and requirements. The ICSO does not apply to non-public officers. Nor is it applicable to non-governmental organisations or individuals. The Administration has no intention to amend the ICSO to cover non-public officers.

Any acts of interception of communications by non-public officers may contravene the provision of wilful interception of messages by a telecommunications officer under section 24 of the Telecommunications Ordinance (Cap. 106), or the provision of damaging, removing or interfering telecommunications with intent under section 27 of the same. Such acts shall be under the regulation of the PD(P)O if collection of personal data is involved.

Thank you, president.

Issued at HKT 15:19

LCQ4: Shanghai-Hong Kong Stock Connect
****

Following is a question by the Hon Chung Kwok-pan and a reply by the Acting Secretary for Financial Services and the Treasury, Mr James Lau, in the Legislative Council today (December 3):

Question:

The Shanghai-Hong Kong Stock Connect (S-HK SC), implemented since the 17th of last month, has widened the investment channels between Shanghai and Hong Kong. The Government envisages that driven by S HK SC, the capital markets of the two places will gradually move towards integration, enabling the finance industry of Hong Kong to expand and enhancing Hong Kong's competitiveness, thereby transforming Hong Kong into a premier gateway for international capital to make investments on the Mainland. Investors may directly invest, through the S-HK SC platform, in specified types of stocks listed in Shanghai and Hong Kong. Besides, the abolition of the daily exchange limit of Renminbi imposed on Hong Kong people also facilitates financial transactions. Nonetheless, since the launch of S-HK SC, utilisation of the investment quotas is well below market expectations, and S-HK SC has failed to boost the prices of Hong Kong stocks substantially, with investors giving lukewarm response to southbound investments on Hong Kong stocks under the Southbound Trading Link in particular. In this connection, will the Government inform this Council:

(1) as some members of the securities industry have pointed out that utilisation of the quotas in the Southbound Trading Link has lagged far behind that in the Northbound Trading Link in the first week since the launch of S-HK SC because major mainland institutional investors including public funds and insurance companies, etc. are still waiting for the publication of relevant investment guidelines by regulatory organisations, whether the authorities have examined why such investors are not yet ready given that S-HK SC was in the pipeline for a long time; whether the authorities have, in collaboration with the relevant mainland authorities, formulated any mechanism to jointly review the specific impacts of S-HK SC on the securities markets in the two places;

(2) whether the authorities have assessed if S-HK SC will lead to the situation of "southern capital being

channelled to the north", which means that a large amount of money originally invested in Hong Kong stocks is transferred to invest in Shanghai stocks; if they have assessed, of the outcome; whether the authorities will introduce more policies to attract capital inflow to invest in Hong Kong stocks, such as further cooperation with the relevant mainland departments to enable more mainland institutional investors to get familiar with the securities market in Hong Kong, as well as encourage and facilitate these investors to invest in Hong Kong stocks; and

(3) as there are differences in the law and regulations governing the securities markets in Shanghai and Hong Kong, whether the authorities will provide assistance to Hong Kong investors who have encountered legal problems or disputes when making investments in mainland stocks; if they will, from which government department(s) the investors may seek assistance; how the authorities will tackle the issues concerned so as to protect small investors and further enhance the connectivity between the securities markets in Shanghai and Hong Kong; of the measures to be put in place in future to help investors in the two places to understand the respective law and regulations governing the securities markets in the two places?

Reply:

President,

Regarding parts (1) and (2) of the question, it is generally the case that investors, in particular institutional investors, necessarily take a cautious approach when entering a new market. Institutional investors may need to conduct due diligence and risk assessment before they will consider participating in a new market. Some institutional investors such as investment funds may also need to change constitutional documents to allow them to invest in a new market. Besides, the Mainland and Hong Kong stock markets have rather different structures in terms of investor profiles, regulatory requirements as well as trading and clearing arrangements. Some Mainland institutional investors may need to obtain regulatory approval before they will consider participating in a new market.

The exchanges in the two markets have done a lot of promotional work before the launch of Shanghai-Hong Kong Stock Connect (Stock Connect), and will continue such work. They will also continue to maintain close liaison with market participants, and help them understand and participate in each other's market.

The Stock Connect is a pilot programme just launched recently. The relevant promotional work will continue. We hope that investors will gradually be familiar with this mechanism. It is too soon to do an assessment on the trading volume at this stage. In fact, the investment quota under the Stock Connect is imposed as a risk management tool for the market, not as a volume target or even an indicator. The very priority at the present stage is to ensure the smooth operation of the Stock Connect and the effective implementation of risk management and regulatory measures. Overall speaking, the Stock Connect is operating smoothly. The Administration, the relevant regulators and the exchange in Hong Kong will continue to collaborate with their Mainland counterparts in monitoring the development of the Stock Connect, and will communicate with market participants closely to assess the state of implementation.

As regards part (3) of the question on how to handle information requests from investors, the Securities and Futures Commission (SFC) and the China Securities Regulatory Commission (CSRC) have established an arrangement for handling and referring requests from investors under the Stock Connect.

Under the arrangement, requests from Hong Kong and overseas investors investing in Mainland stocks will be treated at par as Mainland investors. Investors under the Northbound Trading Link can file complaints in respect of their disputes directly with the CSRC, Shanghai Stock Exchange, the eligible Shanghai listed company or the clearing service provider for Shanghai stocks. In accordance with the principle of home supervisor regulation, requests from Mainland, Hong Kong and overseas investors on issues within the CSRC's jurisdiction will be handled by the CSRC in accordance with the relevant Mainland laws and regulations.

Hong Kong and overseas investors can also raise the above requests with the SFC, which will refer such requests to the CSRC for further handling.

Regarding investor education, Hong Kong's Investor Education Centre (IEC) is responsible for education of Northbound Hong Kong and overseas investors while the Mainland's Investor Protection Bureau targets Southbound Mainland investors.

These education initiatives aim to help investors understand this pilot programme before entering a different market and to encourage them to get well prepared and make informed investment decisions. The education initiative has focused on key issues from the perspective of retail investors, in particular the different rules and regulations, trading and settlement arrangements between Hong Kong and the Mainland, as well as the risks involved in cross-boundary investment. The IEC also reminds the public to be aware of the difference in investor protection rules, taxation and fees and charges arrangements between the two markets.

Both before and after the launch of the Stock Connect, the IEC has conducted investor education work through various channels and means, including publications, websites, seminars, media interviews and columns as well as programs and education video on television and radio.

Issued at HKT 15:57

SJ delegates authority to Deputy Director of Public Prosecutions to handle case involving Benny Tai
****

A spokesman for the Department of Justice (DoJ) said today (December 3) that regarding the fact that Mr Benny Tai has surrendered to the Police in respect of his involvement in the "Occupy Central" movement or "Occupy Movement", since the Secretary for Justice, Mr Rimsky Yuen, SC, and the Director of Public Prosecutions (DPP), Mr Keith Yeung, SC, have known Mr Tai for many years and the three of them were classmates when they studied law at the Faculty of Law of the University of Hong Kong, the Secretary for Justice and the DPP, in order to avoid any possible perception of bias or improper influence, after satisfying themselves that the Deputy Director of Public Prosecutions, Mr David Leung, has no connection with any of the persons involved in the case, have delegated to Mr Leung the authority to handle the matter including (should it become necessary to do so) considering and deciding whether any prosecution is warranted.

Having considered the circumstances of this case and the public interest, the Secretary for Justice took the view that the community should be notified as to how the DoJ will handle the matter. The Secretary for Justice, as the head of the DoJ, will ensure that due and proper processes are observed in the conduct of the case and in strict accordance with the law and prosecution policy.

Issued at HKT 16:55

LCQ19: The subject of Liberal Studies under the New Senior Secondary Academic Structure
****

Following is a question by the Hon Regina Ip and a written reply by the Secretary for Education, Mr Eddie Ng Hak-kim, in the Legislative Council today (December 3):

Question:

It has been reported that an experienced teacher of the subject of Liberal Studies (LS) for senior secondary education has pointed out that the performance samples of those candidates who achieved the excellent result of Level 5 in the LS subject of the 2014 Hong Kong Diploma of Secondary Education Examination, recently published by the Hong Kong Examinations and Assessment Authority, have displayed a distinct anti-government political attitude and showed that such candidates have failed to achieve the assessment objective that the candidates should be able "to consider and comment on different viewpoints in their handling of different issues" set out in the assessment framework of the LS subject. That teacher has also queried that the personal political stance of the markers might have influenced their assessment of the candidates. In addition, there are views that while one of the aims of the LS subject is to develop students' critical thinking skills, the term "critical thinking" has been translated into Chinese as "批判性思考" which makes students tend to be critical of others' views. Notwithstanding the recent translation of the term as "明辨性思考" by the Education Bureau (EDB), this new translation has not been adopted in the publications and web site of EDB across the board. In this connection, will the Government inform this Council:

(1) whether EDB will conduct a review to see if the assessment standards adopted for the examination of the LS subject are too vague, and whether it will take measures to prevent markers' assessment of the candidates from being affected by their personal political stance; if it will, of the timetable for conducting such a review and taking such measures; if not, the reasons for that;

(2) whether EDB will take measures to clarify further the correct Chinese translation for "critical thinking" being "明辨性思考", and request all departments under EDB and all related organisations to use this Chinese translation uniformly; if it will not, of the reasons for that; and

(3) as an Associate Professor of the Philosophy Department of the University of Hong Kong has pointed out that critical thinking should not be confused with being argumentative or being critical of other people, and that critical thinking skills should enable a person to understand the logical connections between ideas and to put the information collected into good use for analysing a subject in a comprehensive manner, whether EDB will make reference to the explanation of this scholar and review its current description of the meaning of the term "critical thinking"; if it will not, of the reasons for that?

Reply:

President,

With regard to the questions raised by Hon Regina Ip, the replies are as follows:

(1) There are clear assessment objectives for Liberal Studies. Based on the assessment requirements of each question, a level-wise marking guideline (with descriptions of the performance level and examples of answering approaches) is developed to illustrate the marking standard, and sample scripts are also provided for markers' reference. Similar to all other subjects, before and in the course of marking, the Hong Kong Examinations and Assessment Authority (HKEAA) has established rigorous procedures and mechanism for ensuring the marking standard. The Chief Examiners and the Assistant Examiners as well as the

Onscreen Marking System will closely monitor the performance of markers.

For those questions requiring candidates to express their own stance, the key marking consideration is not the stance but the sufficiency and organisation of their arguments. All appointed markers in the Hong Kong Diploma of Secondary Education (HKDSE) Examination are professional teachers. Before marking, they need to go through the training and qualifying stages. Random check-marking in the course of marking is conducted to ensure that the marking standard is adhered to. Markers' political orientation and political affiliation (if any) should not affect their professional judgement in the marking exercise.

Besides, double-marking has been adopted in Liberal Studies. Each marker is only responsible for marking one question in the paper and each question is marked separately by two markers. If the mark discrepancy between the two markers is great, the system will distribute the script to a third marker for marking. If there is a continuing discrepancy, the system will distribute the script to the Chief or Assistant Examiner for a fourth marking. Therefore, each question in an answer script might be marked up to four times by at most four markers (including the Chief or Assistant Examiner). For the Liberal Studies Examination, as each candidate has to answer four questions, his/her script will be marked up to 16 times by at most 16 markers (including the Chief or Assistant Examiner).

Moreover, the HKEAA will explain the assessment requirements, marking standard and candidates' performance through publishing the Examiner's Reports, organising briefing sessions for teachers and providing samples of different levels of performance after the examination every year. After the marking process, markers are invited to indicate their views on the question papers and the marking process in the markers' reports. The HKEAA will conduct a questionnaire survey to solicit views from schools on the examinations of different subjects every year. Besides, the HKDSE Subject Committees under HKEAA will conduct regular meetings to review the question papers and the assessment mechanisms.

The second stage of the New Academic Structure (NAS) Medium-term Review is now in progress, including students' learning experiences in the whole-school curriculum, the impact of the NAS on students' further studies, the implementation of curriculum and assessment at the school level (including school-based arrangements), and the implementation of curriculum and assessment of individual subjects (including Liberal Studies). The proposed recommendations would be made according to student-centred and professional principles.

(2) and (3) According to the Xiandai Hanyu Cidian (5th ed.) (2007) （現代漢語詞典） edited by the Lexicographic Section of the Institute of Linguistics, the Chinese Academy of Social Sciences, the meanings of "批判" are "分析判別，評論好壞" or "對錯誤的思想、言論或行為做系統的分析，加以否定

". Meanwhile, the Chinese terms of "批判思維" or "批判思考" have been widely adopted on the mainland, in Taiwan and Macau (please refer to Appendix 1 for examples). In Hong Kong, the Chinese term "批判性思考" has been commonly used by the education sector (please refer to Appendix 2 for examples).

According to our recommendation, students should master numerous skills during their learning of critical thinking, namely collating relevant information, grasping facts, distinguishing between facts and opinions, conducting objective analysis, and making well-grounded exposition and comment. However, there are some public misconceptions of the Chinese term "批判性思考" which is being perceived as negative criticisms or only for the sake of being critical. Thus, EDB agrees to adopt the Chinese term "明辨性思考" as the translation for "critical thinking", alongside the Chinese term "批判性思考" and this practice can reassure the education sector that it is not a new skill being introduced to replace the existing one. For instance, the composite term "批判／明辨性思考能力" has been extensively adopted in the Basic Education Curriculum Guide - To Sustain, Deepen and Focus on Learning to Learn (Primary 1 - 6) (2014) to facilitate educators and the public to understand the emphasis of the term.

I would like to reiterate that the above-mentioned exposition of "critical thinking" has always been adopted by the EDB in teacher training activities whenever they are related to the development of students' thinking skills. Also, teachers of Liberal Studies already have a thorough understanding of the exposition. Our description of critical thinking is no different from the view of the mentioned Associate Professor of the Department of Philosophy of the University of Hong Kong. In future curriculum documents and training activities, EDB will adopt the term "明辨（批判）性思考能力" as the Chinese translation of "critical thinking".

Issued at HKT 16:56

Police handle cases of surrender in accordance with procedures in a fair and impartial manner
****

In response to media enquiries on organisers of illegal occupation and relevant persons surrendering to Central Police Station today (December 3), a Police spokesman stated that up to 4.30 pm today, a total of 24 persons, including 18 males and six females aged between 33 and 82, attended Central Police Station and surrendered for the offence of 'taking part in an unauthorised assembly'.

In this incident of surrender by persons taking part in illegal occupation, before they left the police station, they were explicitly told by the interviewing officers that illegal occupation of public places was an unlawful act and they should stop such act immediately. Police will conduct follow-up investigations based on the information provided.

Police hope that the persons surrendered could follow Police arrangement so as to minimise the impacts on the provision of normal services to the general public.

Police emphasise that irrespective of the occupation and background of the persons involved, Police will handle every case in a fair and impartial manner.

Issued at HKT 16:58

Statement by Chief Executive's Office
****

In response to an open letter by members of Scholarism who are taking part in a hunger strike, a spokesman for the Chief Executive's Office today (December 3) replied as follows[50]:

The Chief Executive, Mr C Y Leung, has repeatedly stated that he is determined and will do his utmost to achieve selection of the Chief Executive by universal suffrage in 2017. He and the Hong Kong Special Administrative Region (HKSAR) Government are willing to communicate and conduct dialogues on constitutional reform in an appropriate manner with different sectors of the community.

However, any discussion relating to constitutional reform must be guided by the regulations set out in the Basic Law and the Interpretation and Decisions of the National People's Congress Standing Committee (NPCSC). We must follow the law in order to achieve genuine universal suffrage. Expressing views

---

[50] Scholarism's open letter:
Dear Mr CY Leung,

It is believed that when protesters are exposed to the harsh environment or even start hunger strike, you are still living in your utopia under the shelter of power by turning a cold shoulder to the reality. However, being those sacrificed for the sake of justice, we have a better life than you, even without materialistic prosperity. Protecting your own interests, you have no choice but rely on autocratic and exploitative political system, with violent police bureaucracy. What keeps our heart warm is our endless hope to the world, and our common goals with friends. We are writing to you here to request the government turn back and start public conversation on reestablishment of political reform. Please do not imagine that violence or delaying tactics can stop us. The people are alert with hunger strike, and they will come back to join us eventually. Most importantly, cost of losing any youngster is undeniably too high for the SAR government.

The undemocratic government has been a curse to Hong Kong's liberty, or even livelihood of the underprivileged. The ridiculous and ludicrous repression with use of force is playing with fire, regardless our society's future. It is the duty for a leader of a city to cater the public needs and find the way out for political crisis. What Mr Leung doing is just completely the opposite: trying to escape from people's resentment, being indifferent towards the Occupation's reasonable demands, criticising any struggle as useless and meaningless. This arrogant attitude is certainly bullying people with power. Now we are willing to sacrifice for conversation by hunger strike. Please shoulder your responsibility and be sincere to students and all Hong Kong people by starting conversation again.

It is not easy for us to keep up in fierce wind, practicing hunger strike in such freezing weather. But what we believe is that, our hunger strike will tell people the truth. The society will see who are the cruel and inhuman perpetrators or, and who are the adorable dream-seekers. We have to emphasis that reestablishment of political reform is the task of government. As the Chief Executive, you are not allowed to shrink your responsibility. Please agree to talk to us again. Before asking us to stop from the painful hunger strike, please ease the pain for all Hong Kong people from illiberal and repressive lives.

on constitutional reform through illegal and confrontational means is bound to be futile. We hope the students who are undergoing hunger strike could take good care of their health.

The first two steps of the "Five-step" constitutional process on the method for selecting the Chief Executive in 2017 have been completed. The next step is for the HKSAR Government to submit the proposal on constitutional reform to the Legislative Council (LegCo) with a view to securing a majority approval of the LegCo. Therefore, the concept of "withdrawal" does not exist in the constitutional process. In accordance with the decisions of the NPCSC, if the proposal failed to be approved by the LegCo, the method for selecting the Chief Executive in 2012 will continue to be used for selecting the Chief Executive in 2017. Legally, "re-launching the constitutional reform" does not exist either.

As such, the request by some Scholarism members to conduct dialogue with the Government on re-launching the constitutional reform will not and could not be acceded to by the Government for it is impractical and has contravened the legal procedures.

The Government hopes that all sectors of the community could adhere to the Basic Law and the Decisions of the NPCSC to achieve universal suffrage in 2017, so that 5 million eligible voters could for the first time select the Chief Executive by "one person, one vote".

Issued at HKT 19:58

LegCo meeting to continue tomorrow
****
The following is issued on behalf of the Legislative Council Secretariat:

As the business on the agenda of the Legislative Council (LegCo) meeting cannot be finished today (December 3), the President of LegCo, Mr Jasper Tsang has, in accordance with Rule 14(4) of the Rules of Procedure, decided that the Council meeting will resume tomorrow (December 4) at 9am.

Issued at HKT 20:05

DECEMBER 4[51]

HKMA's update on the operation of the banking system and financial market
****

The following is issued on behalf of the Hong Kong Monetary Authority:

According to the reports to the Hong Kong Monetary Authority (HKMA) from banks as at 8am today (December 4), all previously affected bank branches have resumed operation. One branch of one bank would shorten their business hours today. The HKMA has requested banks to resume normal services as soon as circumstances permit. The HKMA would closely monitor the situation in the areas concerned including Admiralty and Mongkok and announce relevant update if necessary. Customers can also pay attention to the relevant announcements by banks.

Issued at HKT 09:35

CJ's speech at St Paul's College Speech Day
****

The following is issued on behalf of the Judiciary:

Following is the speech by the Chief Justice of the Court of Final Appeal, Mr Geoffrey Ma Tao-li, delivered at St Paul's College 163rd Anniversary Speech Day today (December 4):

Dr Cheng, Mr Yuen, distinguished guests. It is a great honour to be asked to say a few words this evening at the School's Speech Day. This is the fifth occasion on which I have had the privilege of being asked to address a school at Speech Day. It gives me particular pleasure to be here; St Paul's College, which was officially founded in 1851, is arguably the oldest school in Hong Kong without any gaps in its history. It has experienced first hand every significant event in Hong Kong's history and its distinguished alumni have often been at the centre of our history as well.

I attended the whole of my secondary schooling in the north of England. The first year I was there happened also to be the last year that class prizes (called Form prizes) were awarded. I still have the prize awarded to me in 1968 - it is a history book, "100 Great Events that Changed the World", covering prehistoric and ancient events right through to what constituted then the modern era. Events such as the origins of Buddhism and Taoism through to the New Deal and the World Wars are covered. One of the

---

[51] http://www.info.gov.hk/gia/general/201412/04.htm

chapters was about the Magna Carta (the Great Charter). In 13th century mediaeval England (at the time of Robin Hood and Ivanhoe), the sovereign ruled without much regard for the rights of anyone else. Under the name of the King, taxes were levied at will and there was no equality before the law. Such courts of law as there were hardly dispensed any justice as we know it today. They were not independent and they did not treat everyone equally. In other words, the rule of law simply did not exist. Judges, or those who pretended to administer justice, applied the law only to the extent that they helped promote the injustices perpetrated by the King. For example, the courts would imprison anyone unable to pay the heavy taxes levied by the King and permit imprisonment without trial. In short, the courts did not administer justice. The words of St Augustine (Note 1) rang true, "Take away justice and what are kingdoms but acts of robbery?" (Note 2)

In 1215, the sovereign in England was King John, (Note 3) who succeeded his brother Richard I (Richard the Lionheart). Taking money from his subjects in the form of taxes or fines, became common. This was what led to romantic legends, such as that of Robin Hood, to circulate. The mistake that King John made was not only to inflict his injustices on poor people but also on those in positions of power, in those days the noblemen or barons. But no one in England was prepared to tolerate injustice on that scale anymore. Having made great sacrifices during the Crusades and then having had a small taste of what justice was supposed to be when Henry II (Note 4) introduced the jury system, the people were in no mood to continue to be subjected to injustices. In the spring of 1215, at the height of the tensions between the King and the barons, the barons marched on London. This resulted in the historic event at Runnymede when the barons produced a charter - the Magna Carta, which had been drafted with the advice of the Archbishop of Canterbury, Archbishop Stephen Langton - for the King to sign.

That document established forever the concepts of equality and justice as we know them today: an independent judiciary administering justice without fear or favour, no one to be punished without a fair trial, punishments to be proportionate to the offence charged, justice was not to be delayed or denied or sold, and other fundamental rights. Most important of all, these rights and liberties applied equally to everyone and would be enforced against anyone, including (or especially) against the King. The charter states, "We grant to all the freemen of our realm, from us and our heirs forever all the under-mentioned liberties to have and to hold for them as our heirs from us and our heirs."

Next year, the 800th anniversary of the signing of Magna Carta is celebrated, with many events taking place in England. I am invited to speak at one such event in London next February. There are celebrations in the USA, for the influence of the principles of Magna Carta on US constitutional law and on its constitution is widely recognised.

So why have I spent so long in making this introduction to the importance of the rule of law in Hong Kong? It is because the underlying principles of the Magna Carta are timeless, as relevant today as they were 800 years ago. There is a concern that the longer an institution has been in existence, that people forget about it and take its importance for granted; worse still, they come not to appreciate its value. Those principles of the Magna Carta I have set out - the independence of the judiciary, equality, respect for fundamental human rights - are fundamental to Hong Kong's well-being. These principles underlie our Basic Law.

The Basic Law, as you will all know from your studies, is Hong Kong's own constitution. Under the Basic Law, the independence of the judiciary and equality are guaranteed. The legal system specified in the Basic Law for Hong Kong is the common law system; thus the link to England, widely regarded as the home of the common law, can readily be seen. The Basic Law also makes reference to international conventions: Article 39 of the Basic Law states, for example, that the International Covenant on Civil and Political Rights (the ICCPR) as applied in Hong Kong shall be in force here. The ICCPR is implemented in Hong Kong under the Hong Kong Bill of Rights Ordinance, (Note 5) which sets out the Bill of Rights for Hong Kong in 23 Articles. The Basic Law and the Bill of Rights set out fundamental rights in Hong Kong:

(1) The right to equality. The right to enjoy rights without distinction of any kind such as race, colour, sex, language, religion, political or other opinion, national or social origin, property birth or other status.

(2) The right to life.

(3) The right not to be subjected to torture or to cruel, inhuman or degrading treatment or punishment.

(4) The right not to be held in slavery or in servitude.

(5) The right not to be subjected to arbitrary arrest or detention.

(6) The right to marry and have a family.

(7) The right to vote and stand for election.

(8) Freedom of speech, of the press and of publication.

(9) Freedom of association, of assembly, of processions and of demonstration.

(10) Freedom to form and join trade unions and to strike.

(11) Freedom from arbitrary arrest or detention.

(12) The right of access to the courts and a fair trial. Within this the important right to institute legal proceedings and seek redress from the courts against acts of the executive authorities.

(13) The right to seek confidential legal advice.

One of the main themes of the Basic Law is continuity. It was important (and this remains important today) that those institutions that had served Hong Kong well and had contributed to its success, should be in place after July 1, 1997. One of those institutions is the rule of law. A community which is governed by laws that respect human rights, a community which respects these rights and the equal entitlement of everyone in the community to enjoy these rights, a community which has an independent judiciary to administer these rights in courts of law - this is a community that has the rule of law.

The existence of the rule of law is of critical importance in any society and Hong Kong is no exception. The enjoyment of those rights - they can be called fundamental human rights - is dependent on their proper recognition and, if necessary, enforcement by the courts. These rights basically recognise the right of every person to enable himself or herself to lead a decent life. Hong Kong is also a major commercial and financial centre in the world. Her success here is to a very large extent dependent on the existence of the rule of law. Most people will tell you that the rule of law is a great advantage that Hong Kong enjoys over many other places.

But Hong Kong is not just about money. It is about seven million people who all want to be able, for themselves and their families, to lead a decent and dignified life. People will have different priorities, different interests and vastly different points of view. The law and the administration of justice by the courts try to achieve a proper balance of these widely divergent interests and points of view. Ultimately, the objective is to ensure that fundamental human rights are properly enforced, and that individual rights and the rights of others in our community are respected. This is the challenge that faces me as Chief Justice and the challenge that faces my colleagues in the courts. Fundamental, however, to the work that the courts and judges do is the knowledge that the community respects the rule of law. I believe our community does respect it.

Respect for the rule of law is respect for society itself and this includes in particular a respect for rights belonging to all members of the community. St Paul's College has as one of its main goals the role of its students in the community, to raise civic awareness and to develop every student into a responsible person in our society. This is truly learning based on mutual respect and trust, and a respect for human rights and justice.

I congratulate all those students who will receive prizes today and your families. I salute the College, its staff and students both past and present for their ethos. And, as we approach what is a happy time of year at Christmas, I wish you all good health and happiness.

Notes:

1. Augustine of Hippo, the influential theologian and the philosopher (354-430).

2. From De Civitate Dei (The City of God) Book IV.

3. He reigned from 1199 to 1216.

4. He reigned from 1154 to 1189.

5. Cap. 383.
Issued at HKT 18:40

LegCo meeting to continue tomorrow
****
The following is issued on behalf of the Legislative Council Secretariat:

As the business on the agenda of the Legislative Council (LegCo) meeting cannot be finished today (December 4), the President of LegCo, Mr Jasper Tsang has, in accordance with Rule 14(4) of the Rules of Procedure, decided that the Council meeting will resume tomorrow (December 5) at 9 am.
\Issued at HKT 20:31

Letter to Bangkok Post to rebut an editorial entitled "A problem of attitude"[52]

Dear Editor,

Your December 3 editorial, entitled "A problem of attitude", mentioned that "[Hong Kong] Police, clearly acting under orders from Beijing, have moved violently against protesters, ..." and "If Hong Kong police are unable to quell the protests in the special region, China has plenty of backup power available." It is a gross mis-representation of Hong Kong's situation.

Under the Basic Law, Hong Kong residents enjoy the freedom of and the right to peaceful assembly, procession and demonstration. However in exercising such rights, they shall not willfully disrupt public order or act in defiance of the law. Protesters of "Occupy Central" willfully cause massive traffic blockage to sever trunk roads and deliberately charge the Police cordon line. They have caused serious road blockage in different areas of Hong Kong, paralyzed the traffic of major trunk roads and deprived many members of the public of normal daily. The rally is an unlawful assembly.

Under the Police Force Ordinance (Cap 232 of Hong Kong Law), it is the duties of the Police Force to take lawful measures for preserving the public peace. As the guardian of public order, Police are duty bound to take resolute enforcement actions with the powers conferred by the law in order to maintain public order and protect public safety.

Operations conducted by the Hong Kong Police Force in relation to the protest activities, being an issue related to the protection of public order and public safety, are entirely within the jurisdiction of the Special Administrative Region Government. The Hong Kong Police Force is a professional law enforcement agent with rich experiences in handling large-scale public order events. It has absolute capability and confidence to handle all affairs taken place in Hong Kong.

The Police endeavour to strike a balance by striving to facilitate the smooth conduct of lawful and peaceful public meetings and processions on one hand, while on the other, minimizing the impact of such events on members of the public and road users, as well as ensuring public order and public safety. The Police will act in accordance with the law under all circumstances and will, in the light of the prevailing circumstances, take decisive measures against any illegal behaviour, breach of peace or public order in a bid to maintain public order and ensure public safety.

The Hong Kong Police Force shall continue to discharge their duties professionally, impartially and in a manner unbiased to neither side when tackling the challenges arising from the current protest activities in Hong Kong.

---

[52] http://www.isd.gov.hk/2017/eng/mr_20141204.html

Yours sincerely,

FONG Ngai

Director

Hong Kong Economic & Trade Office

The Government of the Hong Kong Special Administrative Region

DECEMBER 5[53]

Special arrangements on submission of tenders arising from temporary closure of Government Secretariat Tender Box
****

Owing to the special access arrangements at the Central Government Offices (CGO) in Tamar, the Government Secretariat Tender Box (GSTB) located on the ground floor of the East Wing of CGO is closed for tender deposit temporarily.

All tenders that should originally be deposited into the GSTB are instead requested to be deposited into the Government Logistics Department Tender Box (GLDTB) located on the ground floor of North Point Government Offices at 333 Java Road, North Point. This special arrangement came into effect on September 30 this year and remains in effect until further notice.

Tenderers may wish to check in advance their route to the GLDTB and allow sufficient time to make arrangements to deposit their tenders into the GLDTB before the respective closing time of tenders. Late tenders will not be accepted.

For enquiries, please call 2810 2497 or 2231 5288 between 9am and 6pm from Mondays to Fridays (except public holidays).
Issued at HKT 08:30

HKMA's update on operation of banking system and financial market
****
The following is issued on behalf of the Hong Kong Monetary Authority:

According to the reports to the Hong Kong Monetary Authority (HKMA) from banks as at 8am today (December 5), all previously affected bank branches have resumed operation. One branch of one bank would shorten its business hours today. The HKMA has requested banks to resume normal services as soon as circumstances permit. The HKMA would closely monitor the situation in the areas concerned including Admiralty and Mongkok and announce relevant update if necessary. Customers can also pay attention to the relevant announcements by banks.
Issued at HKT 09:44

---

[53] http://www.info.gov.hk/gia/general/201412/05.htm

DECEMBER 6[54]

SCMA answers media question

****

Following is the transcript of the reply by the Secretary for Constitutional and Mainland Affairs, Mr Raymond Tam, to a question from the media after attending a public function this afternoon (December 6):

Reporter: (on whether it is possible for the Government to have dialogue with the students)

Secretary for Constitutional and Mainland Affairs: I personally would not think that it is the right time to have such a dialogue given the circumstance is as such that it is for the overall and long-term benefit of the whole society that the "Occupy Movement" should end peacefully in the near future. So any dialogue that may procrastinate such a peaceful ending of the "Occupy Movement" would only be counter-productive.

Secondly, I think it is also a very difficult decision by the Government not to enter into such a dialogue because we should not encourage, or we should not accept, certain sectors of the community to use illegal means, to use means that would force the Government to make any concessions or to have hunger strike that would harm their own bodily health to put forward their requests. If the Government would concede to politics or political needs at the moment but sacrifice long-term interests of the overall community, I think the Government is only right to make a very difficult decision and that is not to entertain such a request at this moment in time.

But, as I explained to the media just now, when the "Occupy Movement" would end in the near future, the Government would spare no efforts and we would in the near future launch the second round of public consultation on universal suffrage for selecting the Chief Executive in 2017. And, that consultation would be open to all sectors of the community including the student bodies. So, I believe that will be the only right thing to do.

Issued at HKT 17:23

---

[54] http://www.info.gov.hk/gia/general/201412/06.htm

DECEMBER 9[55] [56]

Opening remarks by Assistant Commissioner of Police at press conference
****

Following are the opening remarks by the Assistant Commissioner of Police (Operations), Mr Cheung Tak-keung, at the press conference today (December 9).

The illegal road occupations have lasted for more than two months, and the daily lives and livelihoods of the general public have been seriously affected. The illegal road occupiers have totally defied the law and order. Their prolonged unlawful assembly and blockage of roads have undermined the rule of law which is a core value of Hong Kong. Different sectors of the community have clearly expressed their views in having the illegal road occupiers to respect the rule of law, to obey court orders and to immediately cease the illegal road occupation so that public order could be restored.

Last week, the Court of First Instance granted an Injunction Order regarding sections of illegally occupied roads in Central and Admiralty and the plaintiffs have completed the relevant procedures. This morning, Police met with the plaintiffs and bailiffs about the execution of the Injunction Order. Police will render full assistance to the bailiffs when necessary in executing the Injunction Order on the public carriageways on Connuaght Road Central, Harcourt Road and Cotton Tree Drive on December 11, that is the coming Thursday.

Police remind those who are still illegally occupying the roads that the court has authorized bailiffs to execute the court order. Any act of obstructing the execution of court order would amount to 'criminal contempt of court'. Police will take resolute actions against anyone who obstructs or violently charges the bailiffs who are executing their duty. Police will also reclaim misappropriated government properties, such as mills barriers and water barriers.

Police have pointed out on many occasions that the assembly at the illegally occupied areas in Admiralty is unlawful. There are radicals and troublemakers mixing with the crowd and the situation has become very complicated. The unlawful assembly in Admiralty is of high risk and Police have to re-open the illegally occupied roads so as to minimize the associated risks.

After assisting bailiffs with the execution of the Injunction Order on Thursday, Police will remove other obstacles on the carriageways and pavements in Admiralty and Central in order to re-open the nearby roads. These include Connuaght Road Central, Harcourt Road, Tim Wa Avenue, Tim Mei Avenue and Gloucester Road. As for the illegally occupied road sections in Causeway Bay, Police will

---

[55] There was no government press releases concerning Occupy Central for December 7 and 8
[56] http://www.info.gov.hk/gia/general/201412/09.htm

remove the obstacles and re-open the relevant roads at an appropriate time.

As a professional law enforcement agency, Police are duty bound to preserve public peace and to protect public safety and public order. As such, apart from complying with the instructions of the Injunction Order on Thursday, Police will also exercise other legal powers conferred by the law to remove obstacles blocking roads in the areas of Central and Admiralty so as to re-open the blocked roads so that the general public can resume their normal daily lives.

Police have been disseminating relevant information to the public through different channels before starting a Police operation, and this includes issuing press releases and statements, holding press briefings or even on-site media briefings. The purpose is to further enhance the transparency of Police operations. We hope that the illegal road occupiers could cooperate with Police so as to avoid unnecessary confrontations.

Police stress that the Injunction Order is a solemn order of the court. I want to remind the illegal occupiers that there would not be much time for them to pack their personal belongings on Thursday. Police once again urge the illegal occupiers to obey the court order, remove obstacles and take away personal belongings and leave in a peaceful and orderly manner so that the blocked roads can be re-opened and public order can be restored as soon as possible.

Police reiterate that we are duty bound to maintain public order and to protect public safety. Police will take resolute actions against anyone who attempts to block other roads or re-occupy roads that have been re-opened.

In the past two months, Police have demonstrated utmost tolerance and restraint in dealing with the illegal occupations as we do not want to see members of the public, particularly students, getting injured during large-scale confrontations. I hope that the illegal road occupiers could leave the area in a peaceful and orderly manner as soon as possible and not to resist or charge at Police with full body armuor or other offensive equipment.

I have noted that there are media reports that some illegal road occupiers had declared they would continue with their illegal occupations and resort to resistance. These radicals even stated that they would obstruct Police enforcement actions with different means such as throwing water bottles and bricks at Police officers. They claim that they need to protect or rescue their peers with violence. There is also a claim by an association that they would go to the illegally occupied areas to protect and support their children.

I need to point out that these statements would only increase the risk of confrontations by creating further resistance and even charging at Police. Under such circumstances, Police have to use necessary force to execute our duties. We are left with no other alternatives but to resort to the minimum use of force if there are confrontations caused by protestors. The so-called 'protection' or 'rescue' that some of the illegal road occupiers proclaimed are only excuses put up by radicals and troublemakers to cover their violent acts of charging and mask their illegal acts of defying the law. These excuses would only mislead others into risk of confrontations. We do not want to see protestors attempting to charge at Police, assault officers or to commit other illegal acts such as forcibly taking away of arrested persons.

The prolonged illegal blockage and occupation of major thoroughfares are undoubtedly unlawful and there is no excuse to obstruct Police enforcement actions. In fact, the current developments of the illegal occupation have completely deviated from the 'peaceful and non-violent' principles as proclaimed by the initiators and organizers of the illegal occupations.

Members of the public could see clearly from media reports and coverage that there are radicals and troublemakers mixing with the protestors illegally occupying the roads. They also incited others to violently charge Police cordon lines at various areas and ignored Police's repeated warnings and display of warning banners. I need to point out that if protestors take heed of Police advice to leave the area without putting up resistance or charging Police cordon lines, Police would not have to use any force.

During the operation and depending upon the behaviors and level of resistance put up by the illegal occupiers, Police will employ the necessary and proportional level of actions and these include the use of minimum level of force. There are stringent guidelines governing the use of force by officers and force will only be used to achieve an intended lawful purpose. Once the intended purpose has been achieved, the use of force will cease. Police will not tolerate any violent acts such as charging Police check lines by radicals and troublemakers and will take resolute actions in executing our statutory duty to protect public safety and public order. I urge members of the public, students in particular, to stay away from radicals and not to be used or incited by others to commit crimes. On Thursday, citizens should avoid going to the illegally occupied roads at Central and Admiralty areas unless it is absolutely necessary.

I hope that the illegal occupiers could leave the areas in a peaceful and orderly manner immediately. If they refuse to leave, Police would disperse them and may effect arrest against anyone who attempts to obstruct Police in execution of duty. I urge protestors not to obstruct Police officers who are taking enforcement actions, or to put up any form of resistance or attempt to violently charge at Police. I repeat that Police will not tolerate any violent acts and will take resolute actions against anyone using violence.

Police would also like to take this opportunity to remind frontline press and media workers to be vigilant of personal safety, particularly in midst of abrupt confrontations and to avoid placing themselves in between radical protestors and Police check lines. We advise the press to bring with them their staff cards or other documents to prove their press identity and to put on easily identifiable clothing or armband etc. Police will facilitate the work of the press as usual at scene and continue to deploy Media Liaison Teams to make proper arrangements.

Police have all along been politically neutral and we will continue to carry out our statutory duties in a fair and impartial manner. As a law enforcement agency, we do have the obligation to restore public order and to re-open blocked roads.

Hong Kong is a civilized and law-abiding society. Regrettably, the prolonged illegal occupations have seriously undermined the rule of law and disrupted public order. I hope that the illegal road occupiers could respect the rule of law, obey court orders, remove obstacles and take away personal belongings and to leave the areas in a peaceful and orderly manner immediately so that the blocked roads could be re-opened and public order be restored.

Issued at HKT 22:29

Letter by the Information Coordinator, Chief Executive's Office to Wall Street Journal in response to an op-ed "Arresting Democracy in Hong Kong"
(Published on 2014-12-09)[57]

On the Selection of Hong Kong's Chief Executive

Regarding David Feith's Dec. 5 op-ed "Arresting Democracy in Hong Kong," it is wrong to state that candidates standing in the 2017 Chief Executive election will be "government-approved." The makeup of the nominating committee has not yet been decided, nor has the voting procedure, including the threshold for primary nominations and the runoffs needed to select two or three candidates.

Second, regarding the Occupy Central organizers' desire to shift debate away from the Basic Law, as described in Mr. Feith's op-ed, it is entirely appropriate to focus debate and discussion on Hong Kong's constitutional document. Any proposal must be consistent with the Basic Law, so we must base all discussions on what is possible within its framework.

Andrew Fung
Information Co-ordinator
Chief Executive's Office
Hong Kong SAR Government

---

[57] http://www.isd.gov.hk/2017/eng/mr_20141209.html

Letter by the Information Coordinator, Chief Executive's Office to South China Morning Post in response to an article "World Must Hold Beijing to Account for Its Actions in HK" (Published on 2014-12-11)[58]

Letter to the Editor

Ambassador Stephen M. Young (retired) says in his article "World Must Hold Beijing to Account for Its Actions in HK" (SCMP 9 December 2014) "We must hold them accountable for their actions to undermine Hong Kong's desire for a representative government whose leaders they can choose themselves."

It is regrettable that Ambassador Young did not make any reference to the Sino-British Joint Declaration or the Basic Law.

On the question of "choice of leaders", Annex 1 of the 1984 Sino-British Joint Declaration states that "The chief executive of the Hong Kong Special Administrative Region shall be selected by election or through consultations held locally and be appointed by the Central People's Government." It is clear that universal suffrage as a method of election was not mentioned in the Joint Declaration. Secondly and equally importantly, whatever the method of election, the elected candidate is subject to appointment by the Central People's Government.

It is Article 45 of the Basic Law, promulgated in 1990 that stipulates universal suffrage: "The ultimate aim is the selection of the Chief Executive by universal suffrage upon nomination by a broadly representative nominating committee in accordance with democratic procedures." So rather than "undermining", it is Beijing that gives Hong Kong people the right to choose their Chief Executive.

The Hong Kong Government and the Central Authorities of China are determined and are following the stipulations of the Basic Law and relevant decisions of the Standing Committee of the National People's Congress, in implementing universal suffrage to elect the head of government for the first time in Hong Kong's history.

9 December 2014
Andrew Fung
Information Coordinator
Government of the Hong Kong Special Administrative Region

---

[58] http://www.isd.gov.hk/2017/eng/mr_20141209a.html

DECEMBER 10[59]

Special arrangements on submission of tenders arising from temporary closure of Government Secretariat Tender Box

****

Owing to the special access arrangements at the Central Government Offices (CGO) in Tamar, the Government Secretariat Tender Box (GSTB) located on the ground floor of the East Wing of CGO is closed for tender deposit temporarily.

All tenders that should originally be deposited into the GSTB are instead requested to be deposited into the Government Logistics Department Tender Box (GLDTB) located on the ground floor of North Point Government Offices at 333 Java Road, North Point. This special arrangement came into effect on September 30 this year and remains in effect until further notice.

Tenderers may wish to check in advance their route to the GLDTB and allow sufficient time to make arrangements to deposit their tenders into the GLDTB before the respective closing time of tenders. Late tenders will not be accepted.

For enquiries, please call 2810 2497 or 2231 5288 between 9am and 6pm from Mondays to Fridays (except public holidays).

Issued at HKT 11:30

Transcript of remarks by CS at media session

****

Following is the transcript of remarks by the Chief Secretary for Administration, Mrs Carrie Lam, at a media session at the Legislative Council Complex today (December 10):

Chief Secretary for Administration: I shall say a few words in English. In light of the actions announced by the Police yesterday evening, I want to make a few appeals. In simple terms, what the Police have announced last evening is they will first assist the plaintiff of the injunction order as well as their agents and the bailiffs to execute the injunction order. That is to remove the obstructions on certain sections of the roads covered by the injunction order in the occupied area in Central and Admiralty, and thereafter the Police will move on to clear other obstructions on other parts of the road with a view to reopening all the affected roads so that we could restore social order as early as possible. And I believe that this is the public expectation as well, because the illegal occupation has gone on for more than two months now.

---

[59] http://www.info.gov.hk/gia/general/201412/10.htm

The several appeals I want to make are: First is I appeal to the protesters who have been illegally occupying our roads to pack up their belongings and to leave the protest sites in the next 20 hours or so. And secondly I want to appeal to parents, teachers, principals and university heads, as well as those who care about the protesters, particularly the students, to contact the protesters and students within today and to persuade them to leave the protest sites. And thirdly I notice that student leaders have sort of invited participants in the early stage of the occupation to return to Admiralty tomorrow. I think this is most undesirable, because once the police operation is under way, and knowing very well that there are some radical elements amongst the protesters, confrontation might become inevitable. So it would not be advisable for more people to come back to Admiralty. For the same reason, the Director of Administration has already informed all the 3,000 staff working in the Tamar headquarters that they do not need to come back to the Tamar headquarters tomorrow.

The fourth appeal is, understandably, despite all the appeals from various quarters, I suspect there would still be protesters who prefer to stay in the protest site tomorrow. So I will appeal to them that they should abide by what they have said all along, and that is to adopt a peaceful, orderly and non-violent approach with a view to avoiding unnecessary confrontation with the Police. And finally I understand that this is a significant incident which our Hong Kong media as well as overseas media will like to report comprehensively throughout the operation. The Police will do all they could to assist media reporting, but I would appeal to media workers to make sure that your identity can be easily identified so as to avoid any unnecessary misunderstanding.

Reporter: Mrs Lam, would you consider any kind of communication, direct or indirect, with the Federation of Students within the next two days, given the development of the whole movement?

Chief Secretary for Administration: I think the important thing now before us is the actions that have been announced by the Police, because this is really in response to public aspiration. Now that the occupation movement has gone on for more than two months, many, many people have said in public and relayed to us their wish that social order should be restored as soon as possible and the blocked roads should be reopened as soon as possible. So this is our first priority for the time being. As far as dialogues with the students are concerned, I have said on several occasions in public that once we launch the second-round public consultations on electoral arrangements for universal suffrage in the selection of the Chief Executive in 2017, I am very happy to meet with all sectors, of course including the student representatives. That message has been conveyed to the students on several occasions.

Issued at HKT 14:10

LCQ2: Police assistance in executing injunction orders in Mong Kok
****

Following is a question by Dr Hon Helena Wong and a reply by the Secretary for Security, Mr Lai Tung-kwok, in the Legislative Council today (December 10):

Question:

It has been reported that late last month, when assisting bailiffs in executing the injunction orders by the court at the occupied areas in Mong Kok and in subsequent operations to disperse the crowd, some police officers abused their powers, which included using excessive force on the occupiers and passers-by, arresting members of the public and reporters indiscriminately, and suppressing freedom of the press. In this connection, will the Government inform this Council:

(1) as it has been reported that during the operations, some police officers assaulted members of the public who were standing on the footpaths which were not covered by the injunction orders, hit their vital body parts (such as the head and the neck) with batons, pushed pedestrians onto the ground, and hurled abuses at the ethnic minority people, whether it has assessed if such behaviours of the police officers were justifiable, violated the Police General Orders (PGO), and reflected that the police officers had lost control of their temper; whether the authorities will make a public apology for this and how they will follow up the matter, as well as how they will prevent the occurrence of similar incidents;

(2) of the Police's justifications for arresting a crew member of a television station and a newspaper reporter respectively on the 25th and 27th of last month; whether the authorities have assessed if such arrests were targeted at individual media organisations and represented hostility towards reporters; as some online media reporters said that they had been obstructed by the Police in making coverage, of the criteria adopted by the Police for dealing with such reporters and the measures in place to ensure that reporters may cover news freely during police operations; given that at least 25 reporters have claimed to have been treated violently by police officers, how the authorities will follow up such cases; and

(3) as it has been reported that during the operations, a large number of police officers concealed their police identification numbers by the reflective vests which they were wearing or removed the numbers from their uniforms so that members of the public would not be able to identify them, whether the authorities have investigated if the police officers had violated the PGO by such acts and their justifications for so

doing; if the investigation results indicate that such acts violated the relevant requirements or were attempts to avoid being complained, whether the authorities will penalise the police officers concerned, and how the authorities will prevent the occurrence of similar incidents?

Reply:

President,

The issue that the Police rendered assistance to bailiffs in enforcing the court's injunction orders and Police's enforcement operations in Mong Kok in end-November was thoroughly discussed at the adjournment debate on December 3 and 4, during which I responded to Members' views in detail. Today, as Dr Hon Helena Wong is raising a further question on the Police's handling of the Mong Kok injunction orders, I would take this opportunity to reiterate that the orders issued by the High Court in relation to the injunction applications concerning the obstruction of certain roads in Mong Kok have given clear directions for the bailiff to request the assistance of the Police where necessary. It is also clearly stated in the court orders that the Police are authorised to arrest and remove any person whom a police officer reasonably believes or suspects to be obstructing or interfering any bailiff in carrying out his or her duties in enforcing the injunction order. The Judge of the Court of First Instance and the two Justices of Appeal of the Court of Appeal, when handling the injunction applications and related applications for leave to appeal respectively, clearly pointed out that the terms of the injunction orders had no bearing on the Police's enforcement power under general law.

I hope that Members will stop directing their criticism only at the Police' ways of rendering assistance in clearing the obstructions and dispersal of crowds in breach of the injunction orders or other laws on that day, instead of choosing not to probe into, or even to the extent of ignoring the consequences of the protesters' disregard of the court's injunction orders and disruption of public order at the time.

In their operations in Mong Kok, the Police discharged their duties in strict compliance with the law. The Police could carry out their duties in accordance with the wording or scope of the injunction orders and enforce the law in accordance with the statutory power conferred upon them under general law, including the Police Force Ordinance (Cap. 232). According to section 10 of the Police Force Ordinance, the duties of the Police Force include taking lawful measures for preserving the public peace; preventing crimes and offences; controlling traffic upon and removing obstructions from public thoroughfares, etc.

I am of the view that the physical scuffles between the Police and the public and even the injuries sustained by both sides during the operations in Mong Kok were by no means a result of the Administration's non-interference. The Police did not, as alleged, curb press freedom and restrict Hong Kong residents' right and freedom of peaceful assembly, procession and demonstration under the Basic Law. As we always stress, members of the public shall not intentionally disrupt public order or take no heed of law and order. The fact that the unlawful "Occupy Central" or the "Occupy Movement" has been dragging on for over two months and full-scale clearance operations are yet to be launched has indicated that the Administration, including the Police, have been handling the incident with greatest tolerance. However, no one should infer that the Police are not enforcing the law. In fact, the Administration has repeatedly stressed that proper actions would be taken by the Police as and when appropriate to restore public order and protect public safety in a resolute manner.

The Administration's reply to Dr Hon Wong's question is as follows:

(1) and (2) Since the re-opening of the blocked roads in Mong Kok, some radical protesters unlawfully assembled at a number of roads in the district in the consecutive nights, trying to block the roads again. On one pretext or another, such as shopping together, picking up dropped money, crossing the road back and forth, waiting for someone else, those protesters caused road blockage, disturbed order and created nuisance to shop business. In an attempt to exhaust police manpower, such protesters deliberately stirred up troubles everywhere by inciting people on the scene to provoke the Police, charge the Police cordon, disrupt social order and obstruct the Police's enforcement actions. The residents, shop owners and road users in the district were in great distress as a result of the incident.

On the few nights immediately following the enforcement of the injunction orders, some radical protesters created chaos by erecting barricades with iron railings and wooden pellets. Worse still, some people confronted police officers on the scene by deliberately throwing miscellaneous items like bamboo poles, water bottles and umbrellas at them. The Police immediately gave advice and warnings against the protesters' acts by broadcasting and displaying of warning banners, pointing out that the hard objects they had been throwing might injure other persons on the spot, including reporters covering the incident and passers-by. Despite the Police had given them ample time to leave, the people at the unlawful assemblies, instead of taking heed of it, continued to scurry around. To avoid aggravation of the situation, the Police had no alternatives but to take resolute actions to disperse the people at the unlawful assemblies and arrested suspected troublemakers in breach of law, with a view to restoring public order and protecting public safety.

As a matter of fact, since the onset of "Occupy Central", the Police have repeatedly stressed that Mong Kok is a high risk area and have also on a number of occasions urged members of the public, particularly students, to refrain from going to the area to avoid unnecessary injuries in crowded and chaotic situation.

The Police have the responsibility to take resolute measures to prevent injury to life and property.

They have very clear guidelines and training as well as strict criteria for the use of force in that the force to be used shall be the minimum force necessary for achieving a lawful purpose. When handling public order events, field commanders shall assess the circumstances on the scene and exercise their professional judgement for appropriate actions, which include using the minimum force required. Prior to the use of force, police officers shall, as far as circumstances permit, give warnings while the person(s) involved shall be given every opportunity, whenever practicable, to obey police orders before force is used.

News coverage by reporters during major police operations is mentioned in Dr Hon Wong's question. I have to stress that the Police always pay great respect to press freedom and attach great importance to their cooperation with the media and that they understand reporters' duty of news coverage. At a meeting with editorial and news department heads of major media organisations on November 28, senior management of the Police Force, while reiterating the Police's notion of respect of press freedom, explained the operational difficulties encountered by Police Officers in the midst of chaos at the scene. They also appealed for mutual understanding and mutual respect between frontline journalists and police officers at the scene.

In fact, emergencies always arise in a split-second during large-scale confrontations. In covering news, reporters must take into account their own safety while at the same time cooperate with the Police to avoid hindrance to the latter. While involving themselves in news coverage of possible large-scale confrontations or chaotic situations, frontline reporters are advised by the Police to wear easily-identifiable clothing and take heed of on-scene police officers' instructions. To facilitate reporters' coverage, the Police shall continue to deploy officers from Media Liaison Team to the scene of large scale police operations in a bid to provide proper coordination and mediation as far as possible. To strengthen cooperation, the Police shall continue to maintain communication with the media and continue to provide them with assistance on the basis of mutual respect and understanding.

In the discharge of duties, the Police are keenly aware of public expectation and the importance of taking enforcement actions in a restrained and professional manner. Throughout "Occupy Central" and the operations in Mong Kok, Police Officers, when confronted with troublemakers' violent charging, deliberate provocations and insults with foul languages, have as a whole demonstrated a high degree of restraint and tolerance. Any persons dissatisfied about the Police's enforcement operations, be they members of the public or reporters, may lodge a complaint and the Complaints Against Police Office (CAPO) shall follow up on such a complaint under a statutory two-tier police complaints handling mechanism, and shall submit its investigation report to the Independent Police Complaints Council for examination in accordance with the statutory requirements under the Independent Police Complaints Council Ordinance (Cap. 604). A total of 235 persons, including two reporters, were arrested by the Police during the operations in Mong Kok in end-November. All arrest cases shall be handled by the Police in a fair, just and impartial manner in accordance with established procedures.

(3) Concerning the uniform of Police Officers on duty, the Police have reminded frontline uniformed officers of the proper donning of uniform. The CAPO shall, upon receipt of any relevant complaints, launch an investigation in a fair and impartial manner.

In fact, as at December 8, CAPO received complaints from 1 952 members of the public about issues in relation to the Police's handling of the "Occupy Central". Of these, 101 cases had been categorised as reportable complaints. Generally speaking, in the event that a complaint case is found to be "substantiated" upon follow-up under the above two-tier police complaints handling mechanism, the officer(s) concerned may be subjected to disciplinary action or more severe punishment, depending on the nature and severity of the case.

Thank you, President.
Issued at HKT 17:11

Transcript of remarks by S for S
****

Following is the transcript of remarks (the opening remarks are an English translation) by the Secretary for Security, Mr Lai Tung-kwok, at a media session after attending the Legislative Council meeting today (December 10):

Secretary for Security: The illegal occupation and road blockage have lasted for some 70 days. The daily lives and livelihood of the general public have been seriously affected. The Government and Police have been exercising the utmost restraint and tolerance towards the matter. Different sectors of the community and most of the general public have expressed their views clearly and strongly that the illegal occupiers should stop the occupation immediately in order to restore social order.

A few days ago, the High Court granted an Injunction Order concerning part of the illegally occupied roads in Admiralty. According to the Court's order, the Police would provide assistance to the bailiffs, where necessary, in enforcing the Injunction Order tomorrow (December 11) to remove the obstacles along Connaught Road Central, Harcourt Road and Cotton Tree Drive.

Police held a press conference last night explaining in detail the objective of, areas covered by and legal basis for their enforcement action. The Police have clearly stated that, apart from the injunction order granted by court, they would also execute their power conferred under the law to remove obstacles in the areas of Central and Admiralty to re-open the blocked roads. As for the illegally occupied road sections in

Causeway Bay, police will remove the obstacles and re-open the relevant roads in due course.

A number of Legislative Council members have just appealed to occupiers to disperse peacefully. I appeal again to those engaged in the unlawful assemblies and road occupations, who are still staying at the occupied areas, to leave peacefully before tomorrow morning. They should stop blocking roads, provoking and obstructing police officers from performing their duties. They should not use any violent acts. Students are advised to leave as soon as possible and stay away from troublemakers. We do not want anyone, including any members of the public or police, to get hurt in the Police operations. The Police will take resolute actions against anyone who obstructs the enforcement of the injunction order, continues to block the roads, charges at police officers, re-occupies re-opened roads or disrupts the public order, with a view to resuming public order and public safety.

I reiterate that the Police have already made due preparations. They are determined and competent in taking enforcement actions to restore traffic and public order in the affected areas.

Reporter: Mr Lai, what are the tactics that the Police will adopt to advise students and protesters? And my second question is, are there any contingency plans ...?

Secretary for Security: As regards the operation details, I am afraid that it is premature to give you a very detailed account, but you will probably know that last night the Police held a press conference and answered questions raised by the press regarding the outline of what they are going to do. Thank you.
Issued at HKT 17:20

LCQ6: Immigration policies
****

Following is a question by Dr Hon Kenneth Chan and a reply by the Secretary for Security, Mr Lai Tung-kwok, in the Legislative Council today (December 10):

Question:

It has been reported that earlier on, a number of members of student bodies as well as members of the public who openly supported the occupation movement were refused entry by mainland border officials when heading for the Mainland, and the Hong Kong and Macao Residents Entry and Exit Permits (commonly known as "home return cards") held by some of them had even been cancelled. A crew member on duty on a plane of a local airline company to Shanghai was also refused entry upon arrival. Moreover, a

Hong Kong journalist was refused entry when he visited the Philippines last month as a tourist, and he thus realised that a number of Hong Kong journalists had been put on a blacklist for entry restriction by the Philippine Government. Regarding Hong Kong residents being refused entry by the immigration authorities of other jurisdictions, will the Government inform this Council:

(1) whether the Government has received, since the start of the occupation movement, any request for assistance from members of the public because they had been refused entry or their home return cards had been cancelled by the mainland authorities; if it has, of the number and nature of such cases, and whether the Government has taken any follow-up action; if it has taken follow-up actions, of the latest progress;

(2) of the details of the follow-up actions taken by the authorities in respect of the aforesaid incident of a Hong Kong journalist being refused entry by the Philippine authorities; and

(3) whether the Government provided any information on Hong Kong residents to the immigration authorities of other jurisdictions in the past three years; if it did, of the reasons, principles and justifications for providing such information, the number of Hong Kong residents involved, and the number of Hong Kong residents who were refused entry by the relevant countries or places as a result?

Reply:

President,

The Government of the Hong Kong Special Administrative Region (HKSARG) attaches importance to the legal rights of Hong Kong residents outside Hong Kong, and will provide practical assistance as necessary. According to international practice, immigration authorities around the world will examine and process the entry of foreigners in accordance with their local laws and prevailing circumstances. We must respect the right of other jurisdictions in exercising immigration control and making decisions in accordance with their laws. We will not, and should not, interfere.

Similarly, Hong Kong and the Mainland have all along maintained respective immigration policies and systems. Immigration authorities of the two places implement immigration policies in accordance with their respective laws. The Mainland authorities respect the HKSARG in implementing our immigration policy according to our laws and we should also respect the Mainland authorities in carrying out their immigration policy according to their laws. In this respect, we also will not interfere.

Our reply to the questions raised by Hon Chan is as follows:

(1) Since the occupying incident, the Security Bureau or Immigration Department has not received any request for assistance from residents for being refused entry by the Mainland authorities or having their Mainland Travel Permit for Hong Kong and Macau Residents cancelled.

(2) Regarding the incident of a Hong Kong journalist being refused entry into the Philippines, the Philippine authorities confirmed the media reports that nine Hong Kong journalists would be refused entry and would not be allowed to enter the Philippines to cover the 2015 Asia-Pacific Economic Cooperation Summit. The HKSARG had received requests from the concerned media organisations, the Hong Kong Journalists Association and Legislative Council member, etc. to follow up the matter with the Philippine authorities. The HKSARG therefore immediately contacted the person concerned via the Assistance to Hong Kong Residents Unit of the Immigration Department to understand the specific circumstances. We had also liaised with the Office of the Commissioner of the Ministry of Foreign Affairs of the People's Republic of China in the Hong Kong Special Administrative Region and met the Consul General of the Philippines to express the views and demands of the concerned organisations and persons regarding the incident. At the meeting, the Consul General of the Philippines undertook to take follow-up action. Thereafter, the Consulate General of the Philippines confirmed that the Philippine immigration authorities had lifted the entry ban on the nine concerned Hong Kong journalists.

(3) Our local law enforcement agencies and law enforcement agencies elsewhere have all along maintained close liaison and co-operation in the combat against cross-border criminal activities. It is of paramount importance to conduct intelligence and professional exchanges on issues such as organised crimes, triads, drugs, commercial crimes, technology crimes, smuggling, using counterfeit travel documents and bogus marriages, etc. for the purpose of preventing and combating crimes together. We do not have the number of Hong Kong residents involved in joint combat actions against cross-border criminal activities. Furthermore, for Hong Kong residents who encounter difficulties or emergencies such as accidents or loss of identity documents outside Hong Kong, the Immigration Department will, subject to their written consent and the actual circumstances and needs, confirm the identities of the Hong Kong residents with the relevant authorities. Practical assistance such as timely processing of travel documents may then be rendered to facilitate their return to Hong Kong.

As mentioned above, immigration authorities around the world will examine and decide whether to grant entry to foreigners in accordance with their local laws and prevailing circumstances. Hong Kong residents who have been refused entry outside Hong Kong are not obliged to, and would not, report the matter to the HKSARG. Separately, according to international practice, immigration authorities will not usually comment on the reason and decision of individual case in detail. We therefore do not have the number of, and information on reasons for, Hong Kong residents being refused entry by other jurisdictions.

Issued at HKT 17:35

Special arrangements for the Legislative Council Complex on December 11
****

The following is issued on behalf of the Legislative Council Secretariat:

As there is no meeting of the Legislative Council (LegCo) or its committees to be held tomorrow (December 11) and out of safety considerations, the Legislative Council Commission has agreed to adopt the following arrangements tomorrow:

(a) no visitor will be admitted into the LegCo Complex between 8am on December 11 and 8am on December 12;

(b) all services to the public, including the Public Complaints Office, guided educational tours, and visits to the LegCo Library, Archives and Children's Corner, will be suspended; and

(c) LegCo Cafeteria will be closed.

Issued at HKT 18:34

Police urge illegal occupiers to leave soonest
****

A Police spokesman said today (December 10) that the illegal road occupations have lasted for more than two months, and have seriously undermined the rule of law and disrupted public order. The daily lives of the general public have also been greatly disrupted. Police urge the illegal road occupiers to respect the rule of law, obey the court order, remove the obstacles and personal belongings, and leave in a peaceful and orderly manner immediately, so that the blocked roads can be re-opened and public order restored.

Police announced yesterday that Police would render full assistance to bailiffs when necessary in executing the Injunction Order on the public carriageways on Connuaght Road Central, Harcourt Road and Cotton Tree Drive tomorrow (December 11). After assisting bailiffs with the execution of the Injunction Order, Police will also exercise other powers conferred by the law to remove obstacles on the carriageways and pavements in Admiralty and Central in order to re-open the nearby roads, including Connaught Road Central, Harcourt Road, Tim Wa Avenue and Gloucester Road. As for the sections of illegally occupied roads in Causeway Bay, Police will remove the obstacles and re-open the roads concerned at an appropriate time.

Police have pointed out on many occasions that the illegal occupation in Admiralty is an unlawful assembly. Thus, it is highly irresponsible for anyone to call on others to return to the illegally occupied areas so as to be arrested. Such act is in fact inciting others to take part in an unlawful assembly. To keep on blocking roads will only greatly disrupt the daily lives of the general public. There are also individuals claiming that they will equip themselves with full body armour or other offensive equipment to put up the so-called 'self-defence', obstruct enforcement actions by throwing water bottles and bricks at Police officers, or resist Police officers violently so as to 'protect' or 'rescue' their peers. Police stress that these are illegal acts, and are only excuses put up by radicals and troublemakers to cover their violent acts and mask their illegal acts of defying the law. These excuses will only mislead others into dangerous confrontations and these acts may constitute the offences of "Obstructing Police Officers", "Assaulting Police Officers", "Disorderly Conduct in Public Place" and "Unlawful Assembly". These proclamations and acts will increase the risk of further confrontations, leading to further resistance and even charging at Police. Under such circumstances, Police are left with no other alternatives but to proportionally escalate the level of use of force to execute our duties. This is not what Police want to see.

If the illegal occupiers take heed of Police advice and leave immediately without committing any illegal acts, putting up resistance or charging Police cordon lines, Police will not have to use any force. Police emphasise that resolute actions will be taken against anyone who obstructs or violently charges the bailiffs and Police officers who are executing their duties. Police will also reclaim government properties misappropriated by illegal occupiers, such as mills barriers and water barriers.

Police urge the illegal occupiers to remove the obstacles, take away personal belongings and leave in a peaceful and orderly manner immediately so that the blocked roads can be re-opened and public order be restored. Police also urge members of the public, students in particular, to distance themselves from the radicals and not be used or incited by them. On the day of Police operation, members of the public should avoid going to the concerned illegally occupied areas.

Police reiterate that if anyone blocks the re-opened roads or other sections of roads, Police are duty bound to take resolute and professional actions to preserve public peace, and to safeguard public order and public safety.

Issued at HKT 19:38

DECEMBER 11[60]

Government statement on illegal occupation
****

In response to the illegal occupation in Central and Admiralty, a Government spokesman said today (December 11) that the illegal occupation has dealt a severe blow to Hong Kong's economy, politics, society and people's livelihood. The police operation in Central and Admiralty today to remove the obstacles and reopen the roads is being conducted smoothly in general. The affected roads in the area will be reopened to traffic as soon as possible. This is what the general public in Hong Kong would like to see.

The Government spokesman said, "The police enforcement action has been both professional and restrained in restoring public order and protecting citizens' rights to use the roads. The Government expresses gratitude to the police officers for their hard work and appeals to occupiers to respect the rule of law and not to re-occupy the roads. The public should abide by the law when expressing their views. Doing so by illegal means should not and could not be accepted by the society and the Government will deal with it in accordance with the law."

Issued at HKT 18:52

Statement by ExCo Non-official Members
****

The following is issued on behalf of the Executive Council Secretariat:

The Non-official Members of the Executive Council (ExCo) noted the Police operation today (December 11) to remove the obstacles and reopen the roads in the occupied areas in Central and Admiralty. Members believe the blocked roads and affected public transport services would soon return to normal and that public order would be restored. Members support the Police's professional, restrained and highly transparent enforcement action which has facilitated a smooth operation in general so far.

The ExCo Non-official Members urge members of the public to express their views on constitutional development through legal means with a view to realising the Hong Kong people's wish to select the Chief Executive by universal suffrage.

Issued at HKT 19:12

---

[60] http://www.info.gov.hk/gia/general/201412/11.htm

LegCo Public Works Subcommittee meeting cancelled

****

The following is issued on behalf of the Legislative Council Secretariat:

The meeting of the Legislative Council Public Works Subcommittee originally scheduled for tomorrow (December 12) at 8.30am has been cancelled.

Issued at HKT 23:18

DECEMBER 12[61]

Opening remarks by Assistant Commissioner of Police at press conference
****

Following are the opening remarks by the Assistant Commissioner of Police (Operations), Mr Cheung Tak-keung, at the press conference yesterday (December 11).

At around 9am on December 11, the plaintiffs and bailiffs executed the Injunction Order on the major carriageways on Connaught Road Central, Harcourt Road and Cotton Tree Drive, and removed four sets of obstacles. The process was generally smooth. Police were on standby in case assistance was required. During the process, the bailiffs did not request the assistance of Police in executing the Injunction Order. The subsequent Police operation to remove obstacles and re-open roads was also carried out smoothly in general.

Unfortunately, at around 8pm on December 11, a Sergeant felt unwell whilst on duty and collapsed suddenly. He is now being treated at the Intensive Care Unit of Ruttonjee Hospital.

At around 1.20pm on December 11, Police conducted an on-site media briefing and informed the public that the operation to remove obstacles and re-open roads would commence after 30 minutes and that people within the occupied area were free to leave before this operation began. When the thirty-minute period was over, Police cordoned the occupied area and set up a Police Operational Area at road sections on Harcourt Road, Tim Mei Avenue and Tim Wa Avenue. By that time, illegal occupiers within the cordoned area were required to comply with Police instructions and leave the area through a designated route, that was by way of Tim Mei Avenue towards the Promenade or Lung Wui Road direction. Police had made it clear that protestors would be asked to present their identity cards for recording their personal particulars and details before they left the area and that Police might pursue criminal liability against them later. After that, Police removed obstacles from the relevant carriageways and pavements, and take actions to disperse or arrest those who refused to leave the area. If anyone put up resistance, Police would have no alternative but to use the minimum and proportional level of force to achieve the lawful purpose. Police urged the illegal road occupiers again to take away their personal belongings and leave the area in a peaceful and orderly manner.

After providing sufficient time for the illegal occupiers to leave the areas on their own, Police cordoned the area at about 2.20pm on December 11 and started to remove the obstacles and re-open roads at Admiralty and Central areas. About two hours later, Police removed 21 sets of obstacles from the areas.

---

[61] http://www.info.gov.hk/gia/general/201412/12.htm

During the process, most of the illegal occupiers did not resort to violence or provocation to resist or obstruct Police enforcement actions. They complied with Police instructions by presenting their identity cards for recording before leaving. A total of 909 people were allowed to leave the area after Police had recorded their personal particulars. Police may pursue criminal liability against them later.

Regrettably, the remaining illegal occupiers refused to leave. Despite numerous Police advice and warnings, they behaved in an uncooperative manner. At about 4.25pm on December 11, Police started arresting those who continued to engage in the unlawful assembly so as to re-open the roads. Police arrested 209 people, including 131 males 78 females, for the offences of 'Unlawful Assembly' and 'Obstructing Police in Execution of Duty'. Police also seized dozens of packs of baking powder, 13 wooden shields, six metal shields and one plastic shield in the occupied areas.

Furthermore, between December 10 night and December 11 afternoon, Police arrested four males, aged between 26 and 35, at different locations for the offences of 'Taking Part in Unauthorised Assembly', 'Inciting Others to Take Part in Unauthorised Assembly' and 'Organising an Unauthorised Assembly'.

Throughout the operation on December 11, Police have been professional and restrained and maintained a high degree of transparency by disseminating relevant information to the public through various channels, including the issue of press statements, arrangement of press conference and on-site briefings on the forthcoming Police actions. In addition, at the request of the Independent Police Complaints Council, Police facilitated the chairman and members of the council to observe the obstacles removal and roads re-opening operation at scene in order to enhance their understanding of Police operation.

At present, miscellaneous items and rubbish on Connaught Road Central, Harcourt Road, Tim Wa Avenue, Tim Mei Avenue, Gloucester Road and Cotton Tree Drive have already been removed. Some of the carriageways have already been re-opened. I believe this is what the general public have longed for and are happy to see.

As for the illegally occupied road sections in Causeway Bay, Police will remove the obstacles and re-open the relevant roads at an appropriate time. Police urge members of the public not to gather or linger at the illegally occupied area in Causeway Bay and to stay away from radicals and troublemakers. Do not be incited to commit any illegal acts. Police have been demonstrating utmost restraints and tolerance to deal with the illegal occupation professionally as we do not want to see anyone getting injured during large-scale confrontations, no matter they are protestors, students in particular, the general public or Police officers.

I need to point out that although roads at Admiralty and Central have already been partially re-opened, past experience indicated that some radicals and troublemakers might scatter to different areas and create chaos in an attempt to block the roads again. I stress that Police are duty bound to maintain public peace and to protect public order and public safety. Police will take resolute actions against anyone who disrupts public order by blocking other roads or roads that have been re-opened. Police have stepped up patrol at relevant locations and will take strict enforcement actions against anyone who plans or attempts to re-occupy other roads or places.

Police have all along been maintaining political neutrality. We will continue to carry out our statutory duties to protect public safety, maintain public order and prevent injury to life and property in a fair and impartial manner. Effective Police enforcement actions are dependent on public co-operation and support. We are very grateful for the support of various sectors of the society towards our operation to remove obstacles and to re-open the roads. I hope that members of the public would continue to support our professional enforcement actions. I trust that you would agree with me that the cooperation between Police and the public are vital in supporting and maintaining our proud tradition of the rule of law and good law and order. I hope that members of the public will abide by the law when expressing their views. If public peace and public order are jeopardised, Police will take resolute action to protect public safety and public order.

Issued at HKT 00:41

Special arrangements on submission of tenders arising from temporary closure of Government Secretariat Tender Box
****

Owing to the special access arrangements at the Central Government Offices (CGO) in Tamar, the Government Secretariat Tender Box (GSTB) located on the ground floor of the East Wing of CGO is closed for tender deposit temporarily.

All tenders that should originally be deposited into the GSTB are instead requested to be deposited into the Government Logistics Department Tender Box (GLDTB) located on the ground floor of North Point Government Offices at 333 Java Road, North Point. This special arrangement came into effect on September 30 this year and remains in effect until further notice.

Tenderers may wish to check in advance their route to the GLDTB and allow sufficient time to make arrangements to deposit their tenders into the GLDTB before the respective closing time of tenders. Late tenders will not be accepted.

For enquiries, please call 2810 2497 or 2231 5288 between 9am and 6pm from Mondays to Fridays (except public holidays).

Issued at HKT 08:30

Transcript of remarks by SHA
****

Following is the transcript of remarks made by the Secretary for Home Affairs, Mr Tsang Tak-sing, after attending the meeting of the Panel on Home Affairs of the Legislative Council this morning (December 12):

Secretary for Home Affairs: The occupation movement has ended after the Police cleared the streets yesterday. The operation which went smoothly. Hong Kong is a civilised society. I hope that in the days ahead, people with different political opinions will stay united and display a sense of cohesion in society. What is most important is to move forward towards our common goal of universal suffrage for our Chief Executive (CE election) in 2017.

Issued at HKT 12:24

Public transport services gradually resumed normal after re-opening of roads
****

The Transport Department (TD) today (December 12) said that the road sections in Central, Admiralty and Wan Chai which were closed while affected by the occupy movement are now re-opened. Bus and minibus routes suspended or diverted earlier due to the road closures are gradually resuming their normal services and original routeings.

Six bus routes which were suspended earlier due to the occupy movement have resumed service while 83 bus routes are also back to their original routeings. Regarding minibus services, 13 routes have resumed normal services and routeings.

The TD reminded members of the public that since some road sections in Causeway Bay are still affected by the occupy movement, Hennessy Road eastbound between Percival Street and Jardine's Bazaar, and Yee Wo Street eastbound between East Point Road and Sugar Street are still closed. This has resulted in the suspension of two bus routes and the diversion or truncation of 53 bus routes. The tram service between Percival Street and Paterson Street is still suspended.

Regarding changes to bus routes, please refer to the following bus companies' websites for details:

For routes of CTB and NWFB: www.nwstbus.com.hk/en/uploadedFiles/OC2014/TAA.htm.

For routes of KMB: www.kmb.hk/en.

As there will be updates on bus services from time to time due to traffic changes, members of the public are advised to pay attention to the latest service arrangements announced by bus companies before starting their journeys.

Issued at HKT 12:54

DECEMBER 13[62]

Opening remarks by Police Chief Superintendent at press conference
****

Following are the opening remarks by the Chief Superintendent of Police Public Relations Branch, Mr Hui Chun-tak, at the press conference today (December 13).

The illegal road occupations have lasted for more than two months. The daily lives and livelihoods of the general public have been seriously disrupted. I hope the illegal road occupiers can respect the rule of law and stop the illegal road occupation at once so that public order can be restored.

As a professional law enforcement agency, Police are duty bound to preserve public peace and protect public safety and public order. On December 11, Police reopened the blocked roads after removing the obstacles in Admiralty and Central.

I need to point out that the assembly within the occupied area in Causeway Bay is unlawful. There were previous outbreaks of confrontations and the illegal occupation there still carries certain risks. The illegal blockage of a section of Yee Wo Street has created serious traffic congestion around Causeway Bay and the nearby shop operators have also been extensively affected. Therefore, Police have to reopen the road so that normal traffic flow can be resumed.

On the coming Monday morning (December 15), Police will exercise legal powers conferred by the law to remove the obstacles in the illegally occupied area on Yee Wo Street, Causeway Bay so as to reopen that section of road. To enhance the transparency of Police operation, we will arrange an on-site media briefing on the forthcoming Police action at around 9.30am that morning. I hope that the illegal road occupiers thereat can cooperate with Police so as to avoid unnecessary confrontation. During the operation, Police will need to set up an operational cordoned area and arrange temporary traffic diversion. We hope that members of the public will follow the instructions of Police officers at scene. Police will facilitate the access of those who work or live on the affected section of road. I appeal to members of the public to avoid going to the illegally occupied area and its vicinity in Causeway Bay on coming Monday morning.

Police Negotiators have been deployed to urge those who are still in the illegally occupied area in Causeway Bay to leave. I now urge the illegal road occupiers to remove the obstacles, take away their personal belongings and leave the occupied area in a peaceful and orderly manner soonest. During the

---

[62] http://www.info.gov.hk/gia/general/201412/13.htm

operation on Monday, there will not be much time for them to pack their personal belongings. Meanwhile, members of the public should avoid gathering or lingering in the illegally occupied area. They should stay away from radicals and troublemakers and not be incited to commit any illegal acts.

If the illegal road occupiers refuse to leave, Police will take actions to disperse them and may effect arrest against those who attempt to obstruct Police in the execution of duty. If protestors at scene do not resort to resistance or violent acts, Police will not need to use any force. We do not want to see anyone getting injured. I urge protestors not to obstruct Police officers in the execution of duties, or put up any forms of resistance or attempt to violently charge at Police. I reiterate that Police will not tolerate any violent acts and will take resolute actions against anyone resorting to violence. I hope the illegal occupiers can take heed of Police advice and leave at once.

Now, I would like to talk about the obstruction of pavements in Mong Kok and Causeway Bay in the past days. Police noted that, since the removal of obstacles from the major thoroughfares in Mong Kok on November 25 and 26, some people had used shopping as an excuse to assemble and cause malicious nuisance to the shops and public transportation in Mong Kok every night. They shouted loudly, rummaged shops, blocked shop access and even interfered with shopkeepers who tried to close the shops.

Protestors continued to gather along various roads in Mong Kok last night (December 12) and in the early morning of today (December 13). They claimed that they were shopping and scattered to different areas including Sai Yeung Choi Street South, Soy Street, Nathan Road and Argyle Street. They obstructed pavements and disturbed business of nearby shops. Police issued numerous advice and warnings and asked them to leave. Regrettably, they refused to comply and continued to yell and scatter around the area.

Subsequently, Police warned the protestors that they were taking part in an unauthorized assembly and warned them to leave the area as soon as possible. However, they refused to comply. In the end, Police arrested seven persons including three males and four females, aged between 16 and 52, in Mong Kok area. Two of them were wanted persons while the remaining five were arrested for 'obstructing Police officer in the execution of duty', 'failure to produce identity card on demand' and 'fighting in a public place'. The cases are now investigated by Mong Kok Police District.

I noted that some people claimed to be shopping and assembled on Yee Wo Street of Causeway Bay in an attempt to block traffic and disrupt public order in the previous two nights. It was obvious that the malicious and disorderly acts of these people caused grave concern for the nearby business operators and the passers-by. Many of the shop operators were forced to tolerate with these disturbing behaviours as they were worried of being targeted by these troublemakers. Some of them chose to close their shops early to avoid chaos. These harassing acts harmed the business of innocent shop operators and the livelihoods of the employees. They also obstructed citizens and visitors who genuinely wanted to shop in the area. This had damaged the image of Hong Kong as an international city. I believe the general public will not tolerate or endorse such harassing and law- breaching acts.

I need to remind the public that these disruptive and harassing acts are not only selfish but may also constitute the offences of 'nuisance in public place', 'unlawful assembly' and 'obstructing Police officer in the execution of duty'.

Police urge these protestors to stop committing these selfish and malicious acts and not to deprive others of their rights and freedom. They should express their opinions in a peaceful and rational manner. It is against the law for anyone to deliberately disrupt public peace or engage in acts that disregard the safety of others. Police will take enforcement actions against such illegal acts.

Police have all along been politically neutral and we will continue to carry out our statutory duties in a fair and impartial manner. As a professional law enforcement agency, we do have the obligation to restore public order and to reopen the blocked roads.

I once again urge the illegal road occupiers in Causeway Bay to respect the rule of law and to cease the illegal occupation immediately so that public order can be restored. Members of the public, students in particular, should stay away from radicals and not be used or incited to commit illegal acts. Police will take resolute enforcement actions against anyone who attempts to illegally block roads that have already been reopened or any other roads.

Issued at HKT 20:11

DECEMBER 14[63]

SJ on constitutional reform

****

Following is the transcript of remarks by the Secretary for Justice, Mr Rimsky Yuen, SC, today (December 14) after attending the opening ceremony of the office of legislators Ms Starry Lee and Dr Elizabeth Quat:

Reporter: The Hong Kong Federation of Students has announced they would continue their movement by asking people to stop paying their rent or to pay late or to pay their taxes late and to write cheques for $6.89 or $68.9. And even the pan-democrats will continue their unco-operation movement and they don't want to participate in the second round of consultation. How do you think you could move forward with this much of opposition?

Secretary for Justice: First of all, I would not agree to any suggestion to act in breach of the law or to cause any further disorder in the society. I always believe that one can attain democracy, including universal suffrage, by using lawful and legal means. I do not see the use of illegal act can be conducive to the achievement of universal suffrage. So I would take this opportunity to appeal to everyone in Hong Kong not to accede to those suggestions by the Hong Kong Federation of Students. I do not think it is a wise act, wise suggestion to follow. In relation to what we are going to do next to achieve a consensus, admittedly it would be a difficult, if not a daunting task. However, as we have been stressing all along, under the decision made on the 31st of August by the Standing Committee of the National People's Congress, there remain rooms within which we can discuss and try to make the entire process, particularly the nomination process, as transparent and as competitive as possible. And by so doing, we believe that at the end of the day, the election, by way of universal suffrage, in 2017, will be a truly competitive one and therefore will be conducive to the attainment of democracy in Hong Kong.

Issued at HKT 16:40

---

[63]http://www.info.gov.hk/gia/general/201412/14.htm

Police urge illegal occupiers in Causeway Bay to leave soonest
****

A Police spokesman said today (December 14) that the illegal road occupations have lasted for some seventy days, and have seriously affected the rule of law and public order. The daily lives of the general public have also been greatly disrupted. Police urge the illegal road occupiers in Causeway Bay to respect the rule of law and immediately cease the illegal occupation so that public order can be restored.

Police announced yesterday that, tomorrow (December 15) morning, Police would exercise other legal powers conferred by the law to remove the obstacles at the illegally occupied road section on Yee Wo Street, Causeway Bay, and to re-open the roads. To further enhance transparency of Police operation, at around 9.30 am tomorrow, Police will arrange an on-site media briefing about forthcoming Police actions. Police hope that the people who are still occupying the road illegally at that time can cooperate with Police so as to avoid unnecessary confrontation.

Police already stated that, during the operation, it would be necessary to set up an operational cordoned area and implement traffic control measures. Police hope that citizens will follow the instructions of Police at scene. Police will facilitate the access of those who work or live near the affected area. Police appeal to members of the public to avoid going to the illegally occupied area and its vicinity in Causeway Bay unless it is necessary during the operation tomorrow (December 15).

Police urge the illegal occupiers to remove the obstacles soonest, to take away their personal belongings and to leave in a peaceful and orderly manner so that the blocked roads can be re-opened. During the operation tomorrow, there will not be much time for them to pack their personal belongings. Meanwhile, members of the public should avoid gathering or lingering in the illegally occupied area. They should stay away from radicals and troublemakers and not be incited to commit any illegal acts.

If the illegal road occupiers refuse to leave, Police will take actions to disperse them and may effect arrest against those who attempt to obstruct Police in the execution of duty. If protestors at scene do not resort to resistance or violent acts, Police will not need to use any force.

As for the harassments of business operators and public transportation in Mong Kok and Causeway Bay by people blocking pavements with the excuse of 'shopping' in the past nights, Police have already pointed out that these acts are not only selfish but may breach the laws of Hong Kong.

In this early morning, some protestors gathered in Mong Kok to obstruct various road sections including Nathan Road and Argyle Street and interfered with the operation of business thereat. Police issued multiple warnings for the protestors to leave. A majority of these people left after Police had recorded their personal details. In the end, Police arrested 20 persons, including 14 males and six females, aged between 15 and 65 for the offences of 'Participating in an Unauthorised Assembly' and 'Obstructing Police Officer in Due Execution of Duty'.

In addition, Police located seven juveniles, including five boys and two girls, aged between 13 and 15, at scene. Police brought them back to station and contacted their parents to pick them up in order to ensure their personal safety.

Police urge the relevant protestors to stop committing these selfish and malicious acts and not to deprive others of their rights and freedom. They should express their opinions in a peaceful and rational manner. It is against the law for anyone to deliberately disrupt public peace or engage in acts that disregard the safety of others. Police will take enforcement actions against such illegal acts. Police are duty bound to maintain public peace and to protect public safety and public order. Police will take professional enforcement actions against anyone who attempts to illegally block roads that have already been reopened or any other roads.

Issued at HKT 18:01

DECEMBER 15[64]

HKMA's update on operation of banking system and financial market
****

The following is issued on behalf of the Hong Kong Monetary Authority:

According to the reports to the Hong Kong Monetary Authority (HKMA) from banks as at 8am today (December 15), one branch of one bank was affected and temporarily closed this morning. The HKMA has requested banks to resume normal services as soon as circumstances permit. Customers should pay attention to the relevant banks' announcements regarding affected branches and ATMs. The HKMA will also publish on its website relevant updates from time to time.
Issued at HKT 09:54

HKMA's update on the operation of the banking system and financial market (2)
****

The following is issued on behalf of the Hong Kong Monetary Authority:

According to the reports to the Hong Kong Monetary Authority from banks as at noon today (December 15), all previously affected bank branches have resumed normal services.
Issued at HKT 15:55

Public transport services resumed normal after re-opening of all roads
****

The Transport Department (TD) today (December 15) said that the road sections in Causeway Bay which were closed while affected by the occupy movement have now been now reopened. Bus routes diverted earlier due to the road closures have resumed their original routeings. The tram service suspended for a long time has also resumed normal service.

Following the re-opening of road sections in Central, Admiralty and Wan Chai last week, the illegally occupied road sections in Causeway Bay, including Hennessy Road eastbound between Percival Street and Jardine's Bazaar, and Yee Wo Street eastbound between East Point Road and Sugar Street, have also been reopened. All road sections which were illegally occupied during the occupy movement are now reopened.

---

http://www.info.gov.hk/gia/general/201412/15.htm[64]

The tram service between Percival Street and Paterson Street which was suspended due to the illegal occupation of Yee Wo Street in Causeway Bay has returned to normal and all tram services have resumed. All bus routes diverted due to the road closures are back to their original routeings.

Issued at HKT 16:06

Opening remarks by Commissioner of Police at press conference
****

Following are the opening remarks by the Commissioner of Police, Mr Tsang Wai-hung, at the press conference today (December 15):

In the past 79 days, the unlawful assemblies and illegal blockage of major thoroughfares have seriously disrupted the public order and undermined the rule of law, which is the cornerstone of Hong Kong's success.

Today, Police opened the last section of illegally blocked road in Causeway Bay and fully restored normal traffic and public order. The Police operation continued to be highly transparent and officers highly professional and restrained.

In order to avoid large scale confrontations and bloodshed, Police have exercised a high degree of tolerance and restraint in the past 79 days to deal with the illegal acts of unlawful assemblies and illegal blockage of major thoroughfares at various locations in Hong Kong.

Police are grateful to members of the public for the support and trust, and ample time given to resolve this crisis. I would also like to express my gratitude to each member of the Force who has remained steadfast, devoted and forbearing at this difficult time and completed the mission of maintaining law and order and safeguarding public safety and public order.

In the past 79 days, Police took resolute actions to stop the violent acts of some protesters and prevent confrontations between the supporters and opponents of the illegal occupation, and protect individuals including the illegal occupiers whose safety was under threat. No matter how complicated or dangerous the situation was, or how onerous the missions were, our officers did their best to ensure public order and public safety. The difficulties and complexity of this operation were unprecedented. The duration of the illegal occupation, the vast number of protesters involved, the mobilisation capability of organisers, as well as factors such as the methods used, the radical acts undertaken by protesters could not all be anticipated.

Police have all along remained tolerant and restrained. However, Police still have to use the minimum level of force when confronted with violent behaviours and chaotic situations mostly on the following nine days including:

September 28

Protesters charged the Police and Police cordon outside the Central Government Offices.

October 3

Persons supporting and opposing the illegal occupation had major confrontation in Mong Kok.

October 15

Illegal occupiers dashed onto Lung Wo Road and occupied the major thoroughfares.

October 17

Illegal occupiers re-occupied the re-opened sections of roads in Mong Kok and charged the Police.

October 18

Illegal occupiers charged the Police and attempted to extend the illegally occupied areas in Mong Kok.

November 19

Protesters stormed the Legislative Council Building and caused wanton damages.

November 25

Illegal occupiers scattered around and attempted to block the roads in Mong Kok and Yau Ma Tei after Police had assisted the execution of Injunction Order in Mong Kok.

November 26

Large groups of illegal occupiers gathered at night and attempted to block the roads from Mong Kok to Tsim Sha Tsui after Police had assisted the execution of Injunction Order in Mong Kok.

November 30

Protesters blockaded the Central Government Offices and charged the Police.

While handling these incidents, Police have to take into account the acts and resistance of the illegal occupiers to decide the necessary and proportional response, including the use of minimum level of force. I stress that Police have strict guidelines on the use of force. Force is used only for the purpose of achieving lawful purpose. When the lawful purpose has been achieved, the use of force will cease. I must also point out that Police will not have to resort to the use of force if the persons involved comply with Police advice and follow the instruction to leave, and do not commit any criminal acts, put up resistance or charge the Police.

As of today (December 15), a total of 955 persons have been arrested for committing various offences relating to the illegal occupation. Police will endeavour to complete the investigations as soon as possible, including arresting other offenders, particularly the principal instigators. Our target is to complete all investigations within three months.

During the confrontations, many police officers and protesters got injured. In this period, a total of 130 police officers were injured and 221 protesters received medical treatment through Police arrangement. Police do not want to see anyone getting injured, whether they are protesters or Police officers. However, in order to stop the violent acts and chaotic situations, Police had no other alternative but to use the minimum level of force. The number of injured officers clearly reflects the danger officers have to face whilst carrying out their duties. On December 11, a Sergeant felt unwell when taking part in the road-reopening operation. He was later found unconscious without heartbeat and was rushed to hospital. At present, he is still in a coma and receiving treatment at the Intensive Care Unit. His condition remains critical. All members of the Force wish him early recovery.

Police are aware of the community's concerns over the illegal occupation and the dissatisfaction expressed by certain members of the public with the Police operations. As at this morning, the Complaints Against Police Office (CAPO) has received complaints from 1,972 complainants, among them, 106 are reportable complaints. Majority of them are allegations of 'Neglect of Duty' and 'Unnecessary Use of Authority'. Only about seven per cent of the complainants, i.e. 137 persons, are the aggrieved parties or directly affected parties. The remaining over 90 per cent are mostly members of the public who lodged complaints after watching media footages, reports or other information on the Internet.

CAPO will investigate and handle all these complaints in accordance with the established procedures in a fair and impartial manner. CAPO has set up three designated special investigation teams to handle these complaints. Observers of Independent Police Complaints Council (IPCC) will participate in observing the investigation process. CAPO will report monthly to the IPCC Serious Complaints Committee on the progress of investigations. CAPO will also submit investigation reports to IPCC for endorsement in accordance with the IPCC Ordinance.

Police understand that members of the public hold different views on how Police have handled the illegal occupation. We have received a lot of complaints, but we have also received many compliments from the public. We will continue to execute our duties impartially in accordance with the law.

I note that, after the blocked roads in Mong Kok and Admiralty were reopened, a number of protesters conducted public meetings and processions in Tsim Sha Tsui, Mong Kok and Causeway Bay by way of the so-called "mobile occupation". These have caused serious nuisance to the local community including the shop operators. Police urge members of the public not to take part in such activities. We will closely monitor the development and take effective actions against any illegal acts according to the law. Police also urge the protesters not to attempt to block the reopened roads, or other sections of roads. Otherwise, we will take immediate and resolute actions to stop these unlawful acts.

Police have all along respected the freedom of speech and freedom of assembly. Members of the public who wish to express their views are advised to do so in a lawful, peaceful and orderly manner and not to undermine the public safety and public order.

Police understand that the public may be concerned about the possible re-occupation of roads and the continuous acts of nuisance by some protesters. In the coming days, Police will strengthen the deployment in various districts to maintain pubic order and safeguard public safety so that all Hong Kong citizens can enjoy the festive season cum Christmas and the New Year.

Issued at HKT 19:53

CE's statement
****

The Chief Executive, Mr C Y Leung, today (December 15) openly appreciated colleagues of various government departments for their efforts in handling the occupy movement:

"Following the end of the occupy movement in Causeway Bay today, all road sections which were illegally occupied during the occupy movement are now fully reopened and all public transport have resumed normal services.

In the past two months or so, colleagues from police, fire services, healthcare, food and environmental hygiene, transport and other departments stayed committed to their work despite tremendous pressure. They made relentless efforts to serve Hong Kong people and minimise the disturbances caused by the occupy movement.

I greatly appreciate colleagues of various departments who have performed their duties and served Hong Kong people with dedications."

Issued at HKT 20:00

DECEMBER 17[65][66]

Special arrangements on submission of tenders arising from temporary closure of Government Secretariat Tender Box
****

Owing to the special access arrangements at the Central Government Offices (CGO) in Tamar, the Government Secretariat Tender Box (GSTB) located on the ground floor of the East Wing of CGO is closed for tender deposit temporarily.

All tenders that should originally be deposited into the GSTB are instead requested to be deposited into the Government Logistics Department Tender Box (GLDTB) located on the ground floor of North Point Government Offices at 333 Java Road, North Point. This special arrangement came into effect on September 30 this year and remains in effect until further notice.

Tenderers may wish to check in advance their route to the GLDTB and allow sufficient time to make arrangements to deposit their tenders into the GLDTB before the respective closing time of tenders. Late tenders will not be accepted.

For enquiries, please call 2810 2497 or 2231 5288 between 9am and 6pm from Mondays to Fridays (except public holidays).

Issued at HKT 11:30

LCQ3: Additional demand for railway services
****

Following is a question by the Hon Tony Tse and a reply by the Secretary for Transport and Housing, Professor Anthony Cheung Bing-leung, in the Legislative Council today (December 17):

Question:

The MTR Corporation Limited (MTRCL) announced last month that the West Island Line (WIL), which is an extension of the MTR Island Line to Kennedy Town, would be partially commissioned at the end of this month, and that the Sai Ying Pun Station of WIL was expected to be ready for use in the first quarter of next year. Some members of the public have expressed the concern that as the train compartments are already very crowded at present, the commissioning of WIL may worsen the situation. In this connection, will the Government inform this Council:

---

[65] There were no government press releases concerning Occupy Central for December 16
[66] http://www.info.gov.hk/gia/general/201412/17.htm

(1) whether it knows, during the period from the beginning of the road occupation on September 28 this year to 15th of this month, the daily average patronage, the respective daily average patronages during the morning and the afternoon peak hours in respect of each railway line (except for the Disneyland Resort Line, and the same exception applies below), as well as the daily average passenger flow at each interchange station; how such figures compare with those for the period from September 1 to 27 this year; whether MTRCL has formulated any measure to alleviate the pressure on its passenger services in the event of occurrences of similar road occupation incidents in future;

(2) whether it knows if MTRCL has assessed the impacts of the commissioning of WIL on the patronage of the various railway lines and the passenger flow at various interchange stations before the end of the road occupation; if MTRCL has assessed, of the outcome and what corresponding measures it has put in place; if MTRCL has not assessed, the reasons for that, and how MTRCL ensures that its passenger services, railway station facilities and manpower resources, etc., are adequate to cope with the increase in patronage; and

(3) given that the road occupation in Admiralty is one of the causes for the delay in the Admiralty Station extension works, whether it knows if MTRCL has assessed how the passenger flow at the Admiralty Station upon the commissioning of WIL at the end of this month will compare with the current figure and with the original estimate for the initial operation stage of WIL respectively; if MTRCL has assessed, of the outcome and the measures to alleviate the crowdedness at the Admiralty Station (especially at the train platforms) before the completion of the extension works for the Station; whether MTRCL has assessed the impacts of offering fare concessions to passengers travelling from the Sheung Wan Station or WIL's HKU Station on the railway patronage and passenger flow (particularly at the Admiralty Station); if MTRCL has not assessed, the reasons for that?

Reply:

Acting President,

My reply to the various parts of the Hon Tony Tse's question is as follows.

The "Occupy Central" movement ended on December 15 this year. During the movement, some roads were occupied and road-based public transport services were affected. MTR heavy rail services recorded an increase in number of passengers during the period. The weekday patronage of MTR heavy rail network from September 1 to December 15 this year is at Annex[67]. The average weekday daily patronage of heavy rail during the first four weeks, the peak period since the beginning of the "Occupy Central" movement (i.e. from September 28 to October 25), was about 5.34 million. This was 10 per cent higher than that from September 1 to 27 (i.e. before the "Occupy Central" movement) of about 4.85 million. But, the average weekday daily patronage of heavy rail during the subsequent seven weeks (i.e. from October 26 to December 15) dropped to about 5.11 million, though still about 5 per cent higher than that before the "Occupy Central" movement.

As there is no gate admission record of passengers using interchange stations (such as interchange to Tsuen Wan Line or Kwun Tong Line at Mong Kok Station), the MTR Corporation Limited (MTRCL) advises that it is unable to provide the passenger flow statistics of interchange stations.

Without compromising railway safety and apart from continuing to run at 2 minutes headway during morning peak hours (normally from 7.15am to about 9.15am), the MTRCL also enhanced train services at other hours as necessary during the "Occupy Central" movement.

Regarding staff deployment, on top of the 2 800 frontline operations staff rostered on duty each day, the MTRCL has deployed about 400 additional staff (including temporary staff and staff from other departments) to strengthen passenger service and handle disruptions due to unforeseen circumstances. Most of them were at stations with higher volume of passenger flow to assist passengers and maintain station order. Having regard to the actual situation, the MTRCL also implemented further passenger flow management measures including maintaining single direction passenger flow at station exits and concourses, limiting number of passengers waiting at platforms, and diverting passengers to less crowded areas of platforms and concourses to ensure smooth train operation and passenger safety.

Further, the MTRCL's Infrastructure Maintenance Rapid Response Unit and Rolling Stock Rapid Response Unit have deployed additional manpower to station at different positions of the railway network strategically. They could be the first on the scene of any equipment failure to start recovery work with a view to minimising impact of any disruption.

Acting President, according to the assessment carried out by the Transport Department (TD) and the MTRCL on the impact of the West Island Line (WIL) to be commissioned at the end of this month, the new patronage brought by the WIL during the morning peak hours will be generated mainly by commuters going northward from Island West to Kowloon or the New Territories areas via the Tsuen Wan Line (TWL) and those heading eastward for Island East via the Island Line (ISL). Currently, passenger movements of the TWL and ISL are mainly southward and westward respectively toward Central in the

---

[67] To view: http://gia.info.gov.hk/general/201412/17/P201412170530_0530_139306.pdf

morning peak hours. Hence, these two major passenger flows go just in the opposite directions. In the evening peak hours, commuters of the WIL also move in the other direction of the major passenger flows of the TWL and ISL. Despite there being an increase brought by the commissioning of the WIL to the overall passenger trips along the ISL, the impact on the passenger flows should not be significant.

WIL passengers can interchange at Central Station for journeys to and from Kowloon via the TWL. This interchange arrangement is no different from the existing one for switching to the TWL at Central Station from Sheung Wan Station or the other way round. As such, the MTRCL expects that the commissioning of the WIL (including concessionary arrangements for passengers) will not significantly affect the interchange passenger flow at the platforms of Admiralty Station. That said, the MTRCL will continue to enhance platform management at Admiralty Station to maintain smooth circulation of passengers, with a view to alleviating crowdedness during peak hours at the station.

To tie in with the commissioning of the WIL, the MTRCL has deployed operating staff to work at the new stations since September this year to undergo relevant training and prepare the stations for operation. In addition, the MTRCL will deploy mobile service teams which are familiarised with the neighbourhood at critical locations such as concourses, platforms and major walkways of the stations to help passengers with direction and other service information during the initial operation of the WIL.

The expansion works at Admiralty Station are underway to tie in with the South Island Line (East) (SIL(E)) works. We have reported the challenges faced by the SIL(E) works and the reasons for progress delay in the paper submitted to the Subcommittee on Matters Relating to Railways of the Legislative Council in November this year. According to the information provided by the MTRCL, the "Occupy Central" movement, though not a major reason for delay, has indeed affected the expansion works at Admiralty Station.

Issued at HKT 14:38

LCQ2: Loss entailed by "Occupy Central"
****

Following is a question by the Hon Chan Hak-kan and a reply by the Secretary for Security, Mr Lai Tung-kwok, in the Legislative Council today (December 17):

Question:

It has been more than two months since the occurrence of the illegal road occupation movement. It has been reported that in the occupied areas, the occupiers put up a lot of publicity materials, generated large quantities of garbage, drew graffiti everywhere and used without permission large quantities of government properties, including mills barriers, water barriers and traffic cones, etc. Some of them even damaged lamp posts and illuminated bollards, removed paving blocks and planter blocks, dismantled the central dividers on roads and vandalised police cars. In this connection, will the Government inform this Council:

(1) whether it has assessed the public expenditure involved in and the number of working hours spent by civil servants on cleaning up the occupied areas and repairing the facilities concerned since the occurrence of the occupation movement, as well as the manpower and expenditure needed for completely restoring the occupied areas to their original form; if it has assessed, of the details;

(2) whether it has compiled statistics on the quantity of government properties that were used without permission or vandalised, and on the costs of purchase and the reprovisioning costs of such properties; if it has, of the details; whether it will recover such losses from the people or groups concerned; if it will, of the details; if it has not compiled such statistics, the reasons for that; and

(3) of the criminal liabilities to be borne by the people who have used government properties without permission or vandalised them; whether it will commence criminal investigations into the use without permission and vandalism of government properties by the occupiers and make arrests accordingly?

Reply:

President,

Following the bailiffs' execution of the court injunction orders in end-November and last week and the Police's clearance of road obstructions, the "Occupy Central" (OC) or the "Occupy Movement", lasting for more than two months, came to a close. Our society has paid a heavy price for the whole movement. There are calls in the community for a clear estimation of the loss suffered by Hong Kong and the price that the public have to pay for the entire OC. In this respect, I would like to thank the Hon Chan Hak-kan for his question. Although focusing on the extent of loss of government property and the reinstatement expenditure, the Hon Chan's question has ushered us to a reflection of a deeper level, i.e. apart from tangible and quantifiable loss such as money, manpower and resources, the severity of the OC's impact on Hong Kong in other respects, including the rule of law, economic activities, society in the state of being torn apart and public distress, and furthermore, the means of future restoration. In this connection, I maintain that all involved parties, particularly the OC instigators and propagators, should ponder hard and account for it.

The Hon Chan's question involves policy areas of different bureaux and departments, including the Transport and Housing Bureau, Development Bureau, Food and Health Bureau, Highways Department, Food and Environmental Hygiene Department, Civil Engineering and Development Department and Hong Kong Police Force. In consultation with relevant bureaux and departments, the Administration provides a consolidated reply as follows:

During the OC, protesters made road obstructions by misappropriating and taking away a huge quantity of public property, including mills barriers, water barriers, pavement railings, litter bins, recycling bins, traffic cones, road signs and so on, in the illegally occupied areas and their vicinity. Drainage covers at both sides of carriageways and pavement tiles were removed without permission while central dividers on roads were dismantled. Apart from making graffiti on places such as road surface, road dividers and footbridges, some protesters erected wooden staircases or railings on road dividers. They also trod on grass and turned over the soil in roadside planters for planting. Some occupiers even damaged traffic lights and dismantled the covers of illuminated bollards and lamp posts, which was an act of suspected abstracting of electricity, and rendered escalators to malfunction by spreading cement on the steps of the escalators. During the entire OC, 32 police cars were vandalised so far. In addition to government property, the glass doors and walls of the Legislative Council Complex were severely smashed and there were misappropriations of or damages to the property of public and private companies, such as bus/minibus stops and railings of bus/minibus companies, luggage trolleys at the Airport Express, trolleys of supermarkets, and tools and materials at construction sites, including fire extinguishers, precast concrete units, hoardings, aggregates, bricks and bamboo poles.

Given that the occupied road surface and public areas as well as locations at which protest materials were placed or posted fall within the purview of a number of government departments, the Administration has removed the obstructions on the roads and their surrounding areas, washed the streets, and inspected public facilities within the illegally occupied areas, etc, through the concerted efforts of relevant departments. Since the roads in illegally occupied areas that covered a larger space, i.e. those in Admiralty, Central and Causeway Bay were not re-opened until very recently, the Administration is, at this point of time, in no position to assess the additional public expenditure and manpower for clearing up the illegally occupied areas and their vicinity as well as restoring and repairing the public facilities in such areas. Nor has it comprehensively assessed the exact degree of damage in those illegally occupied areas and their vicinity. Nevertheless, I can tell you that about 100 truck trips were consumed just for the delivering of cleared rubbish and miscellaneous items upon the re-opening of roads in Central and Admiralty. As the misappropriated or damaged government property items were under different departments, it will take certain resources, time and concerted effort among departments before such districts can be fully reinstated.

President, the authorities concerned will certainly retrieve the government property misappropriated by the occupiers where necessary and pursue such illegal acts in accordance with the law. Taking government property without permission may constitute theft. Under section 9 of the Theft Ordinance (Cap. 210), any person who commits theft shall be guilty of an offence and shall be liable on conviction to imprisonment for ten years. Moreover, damaging government property involves criminal damage and by the same token, a person shall be liable on conviction to imprisonment for 10 years under section 63 of the Crimes Ordinance (Cap. 200).

Furthermore, in accordance with section 4(19) of the Summary Offences Ordinance (Cap. 228) on nuisances committed in public places, any person who without lawful authority or excuse in or near any public place defaces any rock or any roadcutting by carving or otherwise marking thereon any letter, character, figure or device shall be liable to a fine of $500 or to imprisonment for three months. In addition, under section 8(b) of the above Ordinance on other offences against good order, any person who without the consent of the owner or occupier writes upon, soils, defaces or marks any building, wall, fence or paling with chalk or paint or in any other way whatsoever; or wilfully breaks, destroys or damages any part of any building, wall, fence or paling, or any fixture or appendage thereof shall be liable to a fine of $500 or to imprisonment for three months.

President, as I have just pointed out, the OC has entailed great loss to Hong Kong, both tangible and intangible, calling for a serious deliberation on whether similar confrontational and illegal acts should be allowed to go on at the expense of Hong Kong's future. As Secretary for Security, I have to reiterate that the Administration has the responsibility to maintain public order and public safety at all times. Any illegal acts shall definitely be pursued according to the law as long as there is sufficient evidence. Just like the public at large, I hope that the OC will not recur, and that all Hong Kong citizens will, in one spirit and by seeking common ground and accommodating differences, join hands to build a better Hong Kong.

Thank you, President.
Issued at HKT 15:21

DECEMBER 19[68] [69]

Transcript of remarks by S for S after FCC meeting

****

Following is the transcript of remarks made by the Secretary for Security, Mr Lai Tung-kwok, at a media session at Central Government Offices, Tamar, after the Fight Crime Committee meeting this afternoon (December 19):

Reporter: Mr Lai, the occupy protest ended for now but do you expect them to flare up again over the Christmas period? Is the Government going to take any measures to stop that from happening? Secondly, a couple of activists today tried to go to Macau but were denied entry, are you going to follow up on that? Does Macau have a blacklist of Hong Kong activists?

Secretary for Security: Two questions. Let me answer the first question. Christmas holiday is very important and this year we've got at least two days plus two days if I am correct. So we have four days to celebrate this festival. In accordance with our expectation, there will be quite a lot of Hong Kong residents going outdoors to have gatherings and celebrations. The Police will deploy sufficient manpower to facilitate and enable people who come out to celebrate to have a happy time. Anybody who gathers illegally without prior notification to the Police and who breached the law will be handled by the Police promptly. The purpose is to ensure that any protest actions will be properly handled so that people who come out to celebrate will not be adversely affected. Regarding your second question, any jurisdiction has its own power either to admit or to refuse entry of visitors. We respect the decisions of the respective authorities. We have a standard established procedure that any Hong Kong resident who encounters problems outside Hong Kong can make a request for assistance to the Immigration Department. And, if the department receives any such request, the department will handle it in accordance with the established practice.

Issued at HKT 19:50

---

[68] There were no government press releases concerning Occupy Central for December 18
[69] http://www.info.gov.hk/gia/general/201412/19.htm

DECEMBER 23[70] [71]

Police urge no nuisance acts during festive season
****

Police today (December 23) appeal to members of the public to express views in a peaceful and rational manner. They should refrain from conducting public meeting and procession by way of "mobile occupation" and causing nuisance to local community and shops, so that all Hong Kong citizens can enjoy the Christmas and New Year festive season.

Police recently noted that some protesters still gathered and lingered in the vicinity of Mong Kok, Tsim Sha Tsui and Causeway Bay at times, causing obstruction to the roads and adversely affecting business of the shops there. Some netizens also called on people to participate in assemblies or processions at a number of locations before and during the holidays.

Police stress that such malicious acts of nuisance may commit the offences of "taking part in unauthorized assembly", "obstructing Police officer in execution of duty", "disorderly conduct in public place", "unlawful assembly", or "loitering", etc. Police will strengthen deployment in various districts and step up patrol with a view to maintaining public order and safeguarding public safety.

If anyone refuses to comply with Police advice and warning, and deliberately disrupts public order and engages in acts that disregard the safety of others, Police will take resolute enforcement action to stop the unlawful behaviour. Police also urge members of the public, in particular underage youngsters, not to take part in such activities or be incited to commit illegal acts.

Police reiterate that we respect the public's freedoms of expression, speech and assembly. It is the policy of Police to facilitate all lawful and peaceful public events while at the same time ensuring public safety and public order. Members of the public should comply with the laws of Hong Kong and maintain social order when expressing their views.

Issued at HKT 17:56

---

[70] There were no government press releases concerning Occupy Central for December 20-22
[71] http://www.info.gov.hk/gia/general/201412/23.htm

DECEMBER 25[72][73]

Police condemn protesters endangering public order and public safety
****

Protesters gathered on various sections of roads, including Sai Yeung Choi Street South and Nathan Road, in Mong Kok from last night (December 24) to the small hours of today (December 25). They caused chaos and blocked the roads. Police had made repeated public announcements and displayed warning banners at scene to urge them to leave the scene but they refused to comply. Police, with no other alternatives, used the minimum level of force and took resolute actions, including using pepper spray and batons to stop the unlawful acts, and to disperse and arrest the protesters involved.

Police arrested 10 men and two women, aged between 13 and 43, for "assaulting Police officer", "obstructing Police officer in execution of duty", "disorderly conduct in public place", "criminal damage" and "failing to produce proof of identity". Two police officers were injured in the operation.

Police condemned the acts of nuisances of the protesters which disregarded safety of others and seriously endangered public order. Police reiterate that resolute enforcement actions will be taken to preserve public order and safeguard public safety.

Police reiterate that we respect the public's freedoms of expression, speech and assembly. It is the policy of Police to facilitate all lawful and peaceful public events while at the same time ensuring public safety and public order. Members of the public should comply with the laws of Hong Kong and maintain social order when expressing their views. They should refrain from conducting public meeting and procession by way of the so-called "mobile occupation".

Issued at HKT 10:19

---

[72] There were no government press releases concerning Occupy Central for December 24
[73] http://www.info.gov.hk/gia/general/201412/25.htm

DECEMBER 26[74]

Police condemn protesters endangering public order and public safety
****

Protesters gathered on various sections of roads, including Sai Yeung Choi Street South, Nathan Road, Tung Choi Street, Bute Street and Price Edward Road West in Mong Kok from last night (December 25) to the small hours of today (December 26). They blocked the roads and caused chaos and nuisance to the residents nearby. Police had made repeated public announcements and displayed warning banners at scene to urge them to leave the scene. Some people left after Police had recorded their personal details, but others refused to comply. Police, with no other alternatives, took actions to disperse and arrest the protesters involved.

Police arrested 26 men and 11 women, aged between 13 and 76, for "disorderly conduct in public place" and "criminal damage", etc.

Police condemned the acts of nuisances of the protesters which disregarded safety of others and seriously endangered public order. Police reiterate that resolute enforcement actions will be taken to preserve public order and safeguard public safety.

Police reiterate that we respect the public's freedoms of expression, speech and assembly. It is the policy of Police to facilitate all lawful and peaceful public events while at the same time ensuring public safety and public order. Members of the public should comply with the laws of Hong Kong and maintain social order when expressing their views. They should refrain from conducting public meeting and procession by way of the so-called "mobile occupation".

Issued at HKT 09:47

---

[74] http://www.info.gov.hk/gia/general/201412/26.htm

DECEMBER 30[75][76]

Police urge to stop nuisance acts during New Year's Eve and festive season
****

Police noticed that during the Christmas holidays and last weekend, protestors still gathered in the vicinity of Mong Kok, blocking the roads and causing chaos. They not only affected the business of the shops there, but also caused serious nuisance to the residents nearby. A Police spokesman today (December 30) appeal to members of the public to express views in a peaceful, rational and lawful manner and to desist from conducting public meeting and procession by way of so called "mobile occupation", particularly at crowded areas on New Year's Eve, to avoid causing nuisance to local community and shops, so that the public can enjoy a peaceful and joyful New Year's Eve and festive season.

Police arrested 49 persons, aged between 13 and 76, in Mong Kok in the past few days for offences including "assaulting Police officer", "obstructing Police officer in execution of duty", "disorderly conduct in public place" and "criminal damage", etc. Police condemned such malicious acts of nuisance, and will strengthen deployment in various districts during New Year's Eve and the New Year holidays with a view to maintaining public order and safeguarding public safety.

Police emphasise that if anyone refuses to comply with Police advice and warning, and deliberately disrupts public order and engages in acts that disregard the safety of others, Police will take resolute enforcement action to stop the unlawful behaviour. Police also urge members of the public, in particular underage youngsters, not to take part in such activities or be incited to commit illegal acts.

Police reiterate that we respect the public's freedoms of expression, speech and assembly. It is the policy of Police to facilitate all peaceful, rational and lawful public events while at the same time ensuring public safety and public order. Members of the public should comply with the laws of Hong Kong and maintain social order when expressing their views.

Besides, Police noted recent media reports saying that some people alleged they were mistreated by Police officers during unlawful public order events held earlier. Police urged the people concerned to provide information to the Complaints Against Police Office so that we could handle those allegations according to the established procedures in a fair and impartial manner.

Issued at HKT 17:38

---

[75] There were no government press releases concerning Occupy Central for December 27-29
[76] http://www.info.gov.hk/gia/general/201412/30.htm

DECEMBER 31

Letter by the Undersecretary for Security, Mr John Lee, to The Economist to rebut its special report "The world in numbers" (The World in 2015)[77]

Sir -

"The world in numbers" (The World in 2015) says Beijing has relaxed residency rules for mainlanders coming to Hong Kong. This in not true. Under our Basic Law (Article 22), those from other parts of China who wish to settle in Hong Kong must apply for approval. The quota for settlement is determined by the Mainland authorities after consulting the Hong Kong Special Administrative Region Government, and this quota has remained the same since Hong Kong's return to the Mainland in 1997.

John Lee
Undersecretary for Security
Hong Kong Spacial Administrative Region Government

---

[77] http://www.isd.gov.hk/2017/eng/mr_20141231.html

January 1 2015[78]

LCQ15: Tram service during occupy movement
****

Following is a question by the Hon Tony Tse and a written reply by the Acting Secretary for Transport and Housing, Mr Yau Shing-mu, in the Legislative Council today (January 7):

Question:

During the period from September 28 last year to the 15th of last month when the illegal road occupation movement was underway, some parts of the tramway in Admiralty and Causeway Bay were obstructed, resulting in partial suspension of tram service which caused inconvenience to members of the public. In this connection, will the Government inform this Council:

(1) whether Hong Kong Tramways Limited (HKT) requested, during the road occupation movement, the authorities to provide assistance in removing the obstacles on the tramway; if HKT did, of the follow-up actions taken by the authorities;

(2) given the stipulation in section 58 of the Tramway Ordinance (Cap. 107) that any person who wilfully and without lawful excuse interferes with or obstructs any part of the tramway commits an offence, whether the authorities will institute prosecutions against those persons who obstructed the tramway; if they will, of the details;

(3) whether it knows the average daily number of trips and patronage of the tram service during the road occupation movement, and how such figures compare with those in the same period of the year before; and

(4) whether it has made reference to the experience gained from handling the road occupation movement and drawn up contingency measures in the event of an obstruction of the tramway; if it has, of the details of such measures; if not, the reasons for that?

---

[78] http://www.info.gov.hk/gia/general/201501/07.htm

Reply:

President,

During the "Occupy Central" movement, road traffic on Hong Kong Island and in Kowloon was severely affected by extensive road closure and traffic diversion. Owing to the blockage of the tramway by protesters in Central, Admiralty and Causeway Bay, east-west tram service was interrupted and had to be operated in sections. At the worst, tram service between Sheung Wan (Western Market) and Causeway Bay (Victoria Park) and that for the Happy Valley circuit had to be suspended. Following the removal of the obstacles in Causeway Bay by the Police on December 15, 2014, tram service has resumed normal.

My reply to the various parts of the Hon Tony Tse's question is as follows:

(1) and (2) During the "Occupy Central" movement, the Government had been calling on the protesters to leave the illegally occupied road sections. Representatives of the Transport Department (TD), Police, district offices, district councils concerned and transport trades had contacted the protesters and urged them to leave the occupied road sections. Subsequent to the re-opening of Queensway on October 14, 2014, tram service between Kennedy Town and Happy Valley resumed normal. However, service along Yee Wo Street between Percival Street and Causeway Road was still blocked.

The Hong Kong Tramways Limited (HKT) was aware of the sensitivity and complexity of the situation at the time. It requested the Government to deal with the blockage of the tramway at the road section concerned. The Police were very concerned about the protesters' illegal occupation of the tramway and were determined to take resolute enforcement actions. All obstacles at that road section were subsequently cleared on December 15, 2014, with tram service fully resumed on the same day. A total of 17 protesters were arrested that day and the case is still under investigation. The Police are determined to uphold law and order in Hong Kong and will not tolerate illegal actions. The Police will take appropriate enforcement actions to deal with similar situations in future.

Throughout the "Occupy Central" movement, the TD's Emergency Transport Co-ordination Centre maintained close liaison with the HKT. Service adjustments were made having regard to actual circumstances. They included the provision of free circular tram service between Victoria Park and Paterson Street, and free tram transfer service between the eastern and western areas of Hong Kong Island. These adjustments aimed to maintain tram service as far as practicable to minimise inconvenience caused to the passengers. Also, the TD and HKT publicised the latest service information through the media and other channels at appropriate times.

(3) According to the HKT's figures, only short-haul tram service (i.e. trips from Kennedy Town to Sheung Wan, from Shau Kei Wan to Victoria Park, and from Kennedy Town to Happy Valley since the re-opening of the tramway along Queensway) could be maintained during the "Occupy Central" movement. Tram journeys were therefore shorter than normal, resulting in a higher daily average service frequency of about 33 per cent over the same period in 2013. Patronage, however, suffered a serious drop, with the daily average down by around 30 per cent over the same period in 2013.

(4) Government departments have had conducted risk assessments and formulated contingency plans for various major incidents and public activities. In respect of traffic and transport arrangements, the TD will liaise closely with the Police and public transport operators through the Emergency Transport Co-ordination Centre in accordance with the established mechanism. Subject to actual circumstances, the TD will implement appropriate contingency plans, including traffic diversion and adjustments of public transport services, to minimise the impact on the general public. We will also draw lessons from the experience of handling the road blockage during the "Occupy Central" movement.

Issued at HKT 12:00

LCQ4: Official elucidation on the provisions of the Basic Law and related concepts
****

Following is a question by the Hon Claudia Mo and a reply by the Secretary for Constitutional and Mainland Affairs, Mr Raymond Tam, in the Legislative Council today (January 7):

Question:

The "Hong Kong Fact Sheet" ("Fact Sheet") series published by the Information Services Department provides information on various aspects of Hong Kong on a topical basis. The Fact Sheet on the topic of the Basic Law, as published in August 2013, contained the following sentence: the Basic Law "enshrines within a legal document the important concepts of 'one country, two systems', 'a high degree of autonomy' and 'Hong Kong People ruling Hong Kong'", in which "Hong Kong People ruling Hong Kong" was the English rendition of "港人治港". However, in the updated version of December 2014 of this Fact Sheet, the English rendition of "港人治港" has been changed to "Hong Kong People administering Hong Kong", i.e. the word "ruling" has been replaced by the word "administering". Moreover, among the three concepts listed in that sentence, "a high degree of autonomy" has been relegated from the second place to the third place. There are comments that the word "administering" implies that the Government of the Special Administrative Region is merely responsible for implementing the instructions handed down by the Central People's Government and, therefore, the aforesaid changes were made to deliberately play down the importance of "a high degree of autonomy" in Hong Kong's constitutional system. Regarding the official elucidation on the provisions of the Basic Law and related concepts, will the Government inform this Council:

(1) of the justifications for the authorities making the aforesaid changes to the Fact Sheet; the procedures that the authorities are required to follow in amending the official elucidation relating to the contents of the Basic Law, as well as the rank of the officials who make the relevant decisions; whether the authorities have assessed the reaction of members of the public to the aforesaid changes;

(2) whether the authorities last year amended, apart from the aforesaid Fact Sheet, the elucidation on the concepts of "one country, two systems", "a high degree of autonomy", "Hong Kong People ruling Hong Kong", etc. in any other official documents, publications or on government web sites; and

(3) why it is that in the printed version of the aforesaid Fact Sheet, only Article 28(1) of the Basic Law (i.e. "The freedom of the person of Hong Kong residents shall be inviolable") is quoted whereas in the electronic version of the Fact Sheet on the web site of the Constitutional and Mainland Affairs Bureau, Article 28 is quoted in full, i.e. apart from Article 28(1), Article 28(2) (which is "No Hong Kong resident shall be subjected to arbitrary or unlawful arrest, detention or imprisonment. Arbitrary or unlawful search of the body of any resident or deprivation or restriction of the freedom of the person shall be prohibited. Torture of any resident or arbitrary or unlawful deprivation of the life of any resident shall be prohibited") is also quoted; apart from the printed version of the aforesaid Fact Sheet, whether the authorities last year amended the elucidation on any provision of the Basic Law in other official documents, publications or on government web sites?

Reply:

Acting President,

The Preamble of the Basic Law stipulates that the People's Republic of China (PRC) has decided that, upon China's resumption of the exercise of sovereignty over Hong Kong, a Hong Kong Special Administrative Region (HKSAR) will be established in accordance with the provisions of Article 31 of the Constitution of the PRC, and that under the principle of "one country, two systems", the socialist system and policies will not be practised in Hong Kong. In accordance with the Constitution of the PRC, the National People's Congress (NPC) enacted the Basic Law of the HKSAR of the PRC, prescribing the systems to be practised in the HKSAR, in order to ensure the implementation of the basic policies of the PRC regarding Hong Kong.

Article 1 of the Basic Law states that "the Hong Kong Special Administrative Region is an inalienable part of the People's Republic of China". Article 2 of the Basic Law clearly stipulates that "the National People's Congress authorizes the Hong Kong Special Administrative Region to exercise a high degree of autonomy and enjoy executive, legislative and independent judicial power, including that of final adjudication, in accordance with the provisions of this Law". Article 12 of the Basic Law also provides that "the Hong Kong Special Administrative Region shall be a local administrative region of the People's Republic of China, which shall enjoy a high degree of autonomy and come directly under the Central People's Government". Article 5 of the Basic Law stipulates that "the socialist system and policies shall not be practised in the Hong Kong Special Administrative Region, and the previous capitalist system and way of life shall remain unchanged for 50 years". Article 3 of the Basic Law prescribes that "the executive authorities and legislature of the Hong Kong Special Administrative Region shall be composed of permanent residents of Hong Kong in accordance with the relevant provisions of this Law". Many provisions of the Basic Law, including Articles 44, 61 and 55, etc. prescribe respectively that the Chief Executive, principal officials and members of the Executive Council of the HKSAR shall be Chinese citizens who are permanent residents of the Region with no right of abode in any foreign country.

Given the aforementioned articles of the Basic Law, it is evident that "one country, two systems", "Hong Kong people administering Hong Kong" and a high degree of autonomy are being implemented through relevant provisions of the Basic Law.

Our reply to Hon Claudia Mo's question, after consulting the Information Services Department (ISD), is as follows:

(1) Compiled by the ISD, the "Hong Kong Fact Sheets" series aim to provide basic information about Hong Kong on over 60 topics covering government structure, the judiciary, public finance, and financial services, etc. The ISD regularly invites relevant policy bureaux, departments and organisations to assist in

updating and editing the contents of the various "Hong Kong Fact Sheets" topics to reflect the latest information and data, as well as to meet the requirements of word count and typesetting for publication.

When updating the "Hong Kong Fact Sheets", relevant officers of the policy bureaux, departments and organisations will review the contents that are relevant to their purview and provide necessary updates, or add new information, or make editorial refinements.

The recent update of the topical "Hong Kong Fact Sheets - The Basic Law" made some editorial refinements and did not involve revisions of any content and information. In fact, public documents about the policy initiatives of the Constitutional and Mainland Affairs Bureau (CMAB) submitted to the Panel on Constitutional Affairs of the Legislative Council by the Bureau have also adopted the order of "one country, two systems", "Hong Kong people administering Hong Kong" and a high degree of autonomy. As such, the order used in the "Hong Kong Fact Sheets" is not exceptional.

Adopting the translation of "Hong Kong people administering Hong Kong" in the English version of the "Hong Kong Fact Sheets" is for the consistency of word choice. The word was first used in the Hong Kong Yearbook 2007. We have also noted that Clause 1 of Article 22 of the Basic Law reads "...the affairs which the Hong Kong Special Administrative Region administers on its own in accordance with this Law". Besides, the CMAB has also adopted the translation of "Hong Kong people administering Hong Kong" in its replies to the questions on the estimates of expenditure in the Legislative Council.

Mr Acting President, I reiterate that the update of the "Hong Kong Fact Sheets - The Basic Law" is purely based on editorial refinement considerations. It is not intended to and will definitely not affect the provisions and the underlying principles of the Basic Law. The revisions will definitely not affect the PRC's authorisation of the HKSAR to implement the principles of "one country, two systems", "Hong Kong people administering Hong Kong" and a high degree of autonomy in accordance with the Basic Law.

(2) As stated in paragraph (1) of the reply, the HKSAR Government regularly updates and edits various government publications, government websites and other information papers issued by the government. The Basic Law is the constitutional document of the HKSAR. Any update of background information or editorial refinements will not affect the legal effect of the provisions or the underlying principles of the Basic Law.

(3) The full text of the Basic Law includes the Preamble, nine chapters (consists of a total number of 160 articles) and three annexes. In view of space constraints, the "Hong Kong Fact Sheets - The Basic Law" has all along only provided brief introduction on some important provisions of the Basic Law to illustrate the basic policies of the PRC regarding Hong Kong. We have provided the website of the Basic Law in the "Hong Kong Fact Sheets - The Basic Law" for the convenience of readers who wish to view the specific details of the full text of the Basic Law.

In addition, information on the Basic Law posted on CMAB's website contains mainly the background and summaries of provisions of the Basic Law. As the design of the website is more flexible with fewer restrictions in word count, we are able to set out Article 28 of the Basic Law in full on the website.
Issued at HKT 15:16

January 28[79]

LCQ20: Tram service during "Occupy Central" movement
****

　　Following is a question by the Hon Tang Ka-piu and a written reply by the Secretary for Transport and Housing, Professor Anthony Cheung Bing-leung, in the Legislative Council today (January 28):

Question:

　　During the road occupation movement (occupation movement), some parts of the tramway along Yee Wo Street in Causeway Bay were obstructed, resulting in suspension of tram service between the east and west of the Hong Kong Island. Hong Kong Tramways Limited (HKT) has pointed out that the patronage of tram service during that period dropped as compared to previous years, and tram maintenance work was also affected as some of the tramcars could not return to the depot in the Western District. Some tram drivers have pointed out that the incident not only affected tram service but also caused their income to drop. In this connection, will the Government inform this Council whether it knows:

(1) the average daily (i) patronages, (ii) numbers of trips (iii) distances in kilometres travelled, as well as (iv) incomes from tram fares, in respect of the tram service during the three periods from September 1 to 27, September 28 to December 14 and December 15, 2014 till now; how such figures differ from those in the same period of the preceding year in terms of percentage points;

(2) as HKT has pointed out that during the occupation movement, some tramcars were taken out of service for safety reasons as maintenance of them could not be carried out, whether HKT had reduced the number of tram trips as a result; if so, of the number of trips so reduced and the resultant loss in fare income; whether HKT has indicated that it is under pressure to increase fares due to reduction in income;

(3) the respective numbers of tram drivers in each shift, and their average numbers of working hours and hours of overtime work each day during the three periods mentioned in (1); whether HKT had requested some of its staff members to take no pay leave during the occupation movement; and

(4) the additional expenses incurred by HKT for procurement of heavy-duty machines and cables wiring

---

[79] http://www.info.gov.hk/gia/general/201501/28.htm

for the Sai Wan Ho Depot to facilitate tram maintenance work to be carried out there during the occupation movement, and whether HKT has plans to procure more machines for the depot, so as to ensure that tram maintenance work will not be affected by similar incidents in future?

Reply:

President,

During the "Occupy Central" movement, owing to the blockage of the tram track by protesters in Central, Admiralty and Causeway Bay, east-west tram service was interrupted and had to be operated in sections. Following the removal of obstacles in Causeway Bay by the Police on December 15, 2014, tram service has resumed normal.

My reply to the various parts of the Hon Tang Ka-piu's question is as follows:

(1) and (2) According to information provided by the Hong Kong Tramways Limited (HKT), the average daily patronage, service frequency, mileage and fare revenue prior to, during and after the "Occupy Central" movement, and the corresponding year-on-year comparisons, are set out in Annex 1[80]. HKT pointed out that only short-haul tram service (i.e. trips from Kennedy Town to Sheung Wan, from Shau Kei Wan to Victoria Park, and from Kennedy Town to Happy Valley since the re-opening of the tramway along Queensway) could be maintained during the "Occupy Central" movement. Tram journeys were therefore shorter than normal, resulting in a higher daily average service frequency. Yet, patronage and fare revenue, as shown in Annex 1, had both dropped.

According to the HKT, although the company is still under pressure resulting from an increase in operating costs and a decrease in fare revenue, it has no plans to apply to the Government for a fare adjustment at this stage.

(3) According to information provided by the HKT, the average daily number of tram drivers on duty, their basic daily working hours and average daily overtime working hours during the three periods mentioned in Part (1) are set out in Annex 2[81]. The operator advised that there was no change in the basic working hours of the tram drivers during the "Occupy Central" movement. It, however, needed to adjust

---

[80] http://gia.info.gov.hk/general/201501/28/P201501280451_0451_141286.pdf
[81] http://gia.info.gov.hk/general/201501/28/P201501280451_0451_141287.pdf

manpower deployment with certain flexibility in response to partial service disruption. Similar to what would happen under normal situation, the HKT had reminded its staff that they might apply for paid or non-paid leave on their own accord. The operator would consider such applications flexibly. In doing so, the HKT had maintained close communication with its staff, and was appreciative of the understanding and support from the staff side.

(4) According to the HKT, given the need to carry out certain maintenance at the Sai Wan Ho Tram Depot that was essential for maintaining tram service during the "Occupy Central" movement, the operator has installed some equipment at an additional cost of about $200,000. As to whether it would procure more equipment, considerations must be given to the cost-effectiveness to do so and possible impact on the operating costs and tram fares. In case of large-scale incidents and public activities in future, the Transport Department and the HKT will keep in close liaison and implement appropriate contingency measures in the light of the actual situation, with an objective to maintain tram service as far as practicable to minimise the inconvenience caused to the passengers.

Issued at HKT 14:31

May 3[82]

CE's "Letter to Hong Kong" (English only)

****

Following is the "Letter to Hong Kong" by the Chief Executive, Mr C Y Leung, broadcast on Radio Television Hong Kong this morning (May 3):

Dear fellow Hong Kong people,

It is almost two weeks since we released the details of the constitutional development proposal. In about two months - before the summer recess - LegCo members will be asked to vote on it. The result will decide whether the 5 million eligible Hong Kong people will be given the right to vote for the Chief Executive in 2017.

We need more than a simple majority in LegCo to make it happen. To change the election method, the Basic Law requires a two-thirds majority of all LegCo members, or 47 votes. As things now stand, we are short of a few votes.

Over the next few weeks, all members of my political team will be meeting with a wide cross-section of the community to explain the proposal and seek their support. We believe - and the polls tell us - that the majority of the people want to exercise their right under the Basic Law to vote for the Chief Executive in 2017. All eyes are now on LegCo.

If we take this opportunity - that is if we can win over a few more LegCo members - then we can start a new chapter in the constitutional development of Hong Kong. For the first time, we will be able to elect the Chief Executive by one-person, one-vote. This is the historic outcome that I want to see and which I and all my political team will be fighting for.

If the proposal is voted down, at the next Chief Executive election, we would see a repeat of the past election - and that is - 1 200 members of the Election Committee going to the polls, and the rest of Hong Kong watching, on television.

If the proposal is voted down, to re-start the process, everything and everyone will be back to square one. The next Chief Executive, if he agrees, will have to trigger the five-step process again. He would have to secure the approval of the National People's Congress Standing Committee (the NPCSC), again. And lobby LegCo members, again. Are we sure that the next Chief Executive will agree? Are we sure that the then NPCSC will approve? Furthermore, who can say when the next opportunity to start this process will be?

---

[82] http://www.info.gov.hk/gia/general/201505/03.htm

Those who are opposed to the proposals for universal suffrage in 2017 should also remember that it is not just the Chief Executive election that is at stake. We are also talking about the universal suffrage for all LegCo members, since NPCSC has stated that LegCo may be returned by universal suffrage only after implementing universal suffrage for the Chief Executive. If the proposal is rejected, then the earliest time to have universal suffrage for LegCo will be 2024, nine years from now.

It is puzzling why the pan-democrats are pushing back. It is more puzzling why they have not offered any alternative that complies with the Basic Law. They seem to have abandoned civic nomination, which they insisted on having, during the Occupy Central movement. So what are our differences?

Politics is the art of the possible. The NPCSC has the constitutional power under the Basic Law of approving or not approving the change. And no one has seriously suggested that the NPCSC will retract or change their August 31st Decision. The deal is now on the table. If the pan-democrats walk away, will they have something better for the Hong Kong people? Do they seriously think that their proposal will have the support of two-thirds of LegCo members?

Changing election methods is always controversial. The method of electing the Chief Executive was one of the most controversial subjects when the Basic Law was being drafted more than 25 years ago. Many opposed universal suffrage outright. The Basic Law has struck a balance by requiring nomination by a nominating committee before universal suffrage election. The pan-democrats may well think that the NPCSC Decision was too conservative or restrictive. They may want to vote down the proposal. But who is to say that those who had opposed any form of universal suffrage in the first place would not slip back to their original position?

The proposal gives an open nomination system. Anyone who is supported by 120 members of the 1 200 strong Nominating Committee will have the opportunity to face the Committee as a whole for nomination. Anyone nominated will have to face the 5 million eligible voters of Hong Kong. Here I have some experience to share. I took my election to the streets and to the town halls, although my voters were the 1 200 Election Committee members. And the experience is this - once you have to face the people, you cannot ignore their wishes. And that, is democracy.

The proposed change is also not the end-game. The Basic Law doesn't say that this proposed change, or any other after this, is a one-off.

The choice is simple - support a system that allows five million people to vote, or stay with the status quo where only 1 200 people have that right.

I urge everyone in Hong Kong who wants to vote in the next Chief Executive election, to speak up in support of the proposal and make it happen. I also urge the pan-democrats to let it happen.

Issued at HKT 08:45

May 6[83]

LCQ8: Rule of Law

****

Following is a question by Hon Wong Ting-kwong and a written reply by the Secretary for Justice, Mr Rimsky Yuen, SC, in the Legislative Council today (May 6):

Question:

It has been reported that the Hong Kong Ideas Centre carried out a study on the situations and aspirations of young people in Hong Kong, and conducted a random telephone survey between January and March this year with a sample of 1 505 young people aged between 15 and 39. As shown by the findings of the study, over 80% of the respondents considered that abiding by the law was an obligation of every member of the public. However, nearly 40% of the respondents considered that there was nothing wrong to adopt civil disobedience as a means of fighting for justice. In the group of young people aged between 20 and 24, the percentage of respondents agreeing to this view was as high as 47.1%. When asked whether they would take part in a movement similar to the occupation movement should it occur, 25.4% of the respondents indicated that they would. In this connection, will the Government inform this Council:

(1) whether the authorities have studied the impact of the occupation movement on the rule of law in Hong Kong after its conclusion; if they have, of the details; if not, the reasons for that;

(2) as the findings of the aforesaid study showed that the core values to which the respondents attached importance were in the order of freedom from corruption, freedom, justice and the rule of law, with the rule of law receiving the lowest ranking, whether the authorities have studied why young people nowadays attach relatively less importance to the rule of law; and

(3) as nearly 40% of the respondents agreed to fighting for justice by confrontational means, whether the authorities have assessed the impact of this view on the overall development of Hong Kong; how the authorities will enhance the law-abiding awareness of young people?

---

[83] http://www.info.gov.hk/gia/general/201505/06.htm

Reply:

President,

The rule of law is a fundamental core value of the Hong Kong society underpinning its success as well as an important and indispensable pillar of its competitiveness. It is a treasure of our community. Every citizen, including young people, the government and the entire community, irrespective of their position and role, should make every effort to uphold and defend the rule of law, including respecting and complying with court decisions.

Our consolidated reply to the question raised by Hon Wong Ting-kwong is as follows:

Since the "Occupy Movement" had begun, different members of the community have made remarks concerning the rule of law, some of which have distorted the spirit of the rule of law and may have a negative impact on the citizens, including young people. The Hong Kong Special Administrative Region (HKSAR) Government has been paying attention to such a situation.

On the other hand, the Hong Kong and the international communities generally considered that Hong Kong's rule of law and judicial independence were functioning well during the "Occupy Movement", effectively withstanding various challenges and impacts, while their foundations remained unshaken. Indeed, as clearly provided for in the Basic Law, the legal system practised and the independent judicial power and the power of final adjudication enjoyed in Hong Kong are fully protected at the constitutional level.

On November 10, 2014, the Honourable Mr Justice Au of the Court of First Instance of the High Court ruled on the applications for interim injunction concerning the "Occupy Movement". The relevant judgment contained a clear exposition of the concept of the rule of law. The key points include:

(1) The concept of the rule of law must include the notion that every citizen and the government alike should obey and comply with the law.

(2) Even if the defendants are of the view that a court order is wrongly granted, instead of simply disobeying it, they should first comply with it and then seek to challenge that order pursuant to the judicial process. The law cannot allow obedience of its orders to be a matter of individual choice.

(3) It is wrong for any suggestions that the rule of law is not undermined or under challenged if people can freely or intentionally disobey the law first and then accept the legal consequences. The rule of law cannot realistically and effectively operate in a civilised and orderly society on this basis.

(4) The upholding of the rule of law must be built upon, among others, the due administration of justice for the enforcement of court orders and the law.

(5) Worryingly, there have been repeated open suggestions by a number of public figures (including some legally trained individuals) to the public and the protestors and demonstrators en masse to the effect that ex parte injunctions need not to be complied with until they had been determined after an inter partes hearing, and that there is no challenge to the rule of law from merely disobeying civil orders, and that the rule of law is only threatened when there is disobedience of an actual order of committal for contempt of court. These suggestions are wrong and incorrect and would cause the public and the defendants an unwarranted misunderstanding on the concept of the rule of law.

Moreover, when the Court of Appeal dealt with the relevant applications for leave to appeal, it clearly stated that it echoed the above observations made by the Honourable Mr Justice Au.

The Department of Justice (DoJ) welcomes the courts' exposition of the concept of the rule of law. While respecting citizens' rights of peaceful expression of views, the HKSAR Government has been advising citizens, including young people, to abide by the laws of Hong Kong and court orders and respect others' rights when expressing their aspirations. They are also advised to express their views in a rational, peaceful and law abiding manner, or else there would be profound negative impact on Hong Kong.

At the same time, the HKSAR Government has been promoting and publicising the concept of the rule of law to the citizens, including young people, through various channels. These works include:

(1) Apart from actively participating in the "Law Week" organised by the Law Society of Hong Kong on an annual basis, the DoJ also organises the "Prosecution Week" event and "Meet the Community" programme to further enhance citizens' understanding, in particular that of young people, of the criminal justice system, their role therein and their appreciation of the importance of the rule of law through activities such as visits, talks, mock court as well as different types of competitions.

(2) The Government has been working with the Committee on the Promotion of Civic Education to promote civic education outside schools with the focus on the core civic value of "respect and inclusiveness". This seeks to promote the importance of mutual respect and accommodating people with diverse cultural background, different views and perspectives with a view to enhancing social harmony and promoting messages concerning the upholding of the rule of law.

For instance, the Youth Community Legal Information Centre (CLIC) website (youth.clic.org.hk) developed and run by the University of Hong Kong with sponsorship from Home Affairs Bureau was launched in April 2012 to provide information and videos on more than 60 offences and legal issues concerning young people. The contents of the Youth CLIC website have also been converted into teaching packages for Liberal Studies in secondary schools, which are downloadable free of charge from the Youth CLIC website.

(3) For the purposes of upholding the rule of law and maintaining law and order, the Police are committed to raising citizens' law abiding and crime prevention awareness through various channels. Specifically for young people, with the introduction of the Junior Police Call and the Police School Liaison Programme, the Police strengthen communication with young people and students so as to give them an understanding of the role of the Police and the importance of respecting law and order, as well as to help them develop a sense of discipline and positive values. In the light of the development of the Internet and social media in recent years, the Police actively disseminate updated information through the Internet and social media platforms, such as the Police Public Page, Hong Kong Police Mobile Application and Hong Kong Police YouTube Channel, to enhance interaction with young people and raise their awareness in law abiding and crime prevention.

(4) The Education Bureau has strived to promote the spirit of the rule of law among students. To deepen students' understanding of the spirit of the rule of law, the related learning contents are covered in various Key Learning Areas/subjects, including General Studies for primary schools, Life and Society at junior secondary levels and Liberal Studies at senior secondary levels.

In addition, "recognising the importance of the rule of law and respect for human rights" has been accorded as one of the major expected learning outcomes at Key Stage 4 in the Revised Moral and Civic Education Curriculum Framework (2008). Furthermore, in the Basic Education Curriculum Guide (P1–

P6) 2014, schools have been recommended to strengthen their Moral and Civic Education through developing students' positive values, including the spirit of the rule of law.

The Education Bureau has also placed great emphasis on enhancing students' understanding of core values and developing their positive values. The Bureau has recommended that schools adopt daily life events and topics as learning materials to help students hold onto such core values as the rule of law, integrity, freedom and justice in a fast-changing social environment. The Bureau will continue to place emphasis on students' whole person development and offer teachers suitable professional support (e.g. developing learning and teaching resources, organising professional development programmes and creating teachers' networks) to enable them to instil positive values in students through suitable learning experiences that are relevant to their daily lives and can help them cope with the changes they face.

The HKSAR Government will continue with the above work, and is proactively considering ways to enhance this area of work. The DoJ will also continue to steadfastly uphold the rule of law and safeguard judicial independence in Hong Kong.

Issued at HKT 14:32

May 13

LCQ14: Implementation and promotion of Basic Law
****

Following is a question by the Dr Hon Lam Tai-fai and a written reply by the Secretary for Constitutional and Mainland Affairs, Mr Raymond Tam, in the Legislative Council today (May 13):

Question:

This year marks the 25th anniversary of the promulgation of the Basic Law. In connection with the implementation and promotion of the Basic Law, will the Government inform this Council:

(1) whether it has assessed if the Central People's Government (CPG) is satisfied with the implementation of the Basic Law in the Hong Kong Special Administrative Region (SAR); if it has, of the details; if not, the reasons for that;

(2) given that Article 23 of the Basic Law stipulates that SAR shall enact laws on its own to prohibit any act of treason, secession, etc, of the reasons why the SAR Government still has no specific timetable for enacting laws to implement this provision so far; whether it has assessed the risks to national security of not having such laws enacted yet; if it has, of the details; if not, the reasons for that;

(3) whether it has assessed if any foreign forces have attempted to sabotage the effective implementation of the Basic Law since the reunification and hence have affected its efforts to promote constitutional reform and implement universal suffrage for the selection of the Chief Executive (CE), etc; if it has made such an assessment, of the details; if it has not, the reasons for that;

(4) given that a member of Hong Kong deputies to the National People's Congress has earlier proposed that attending national studies courses on the Mainland should be made an entry requirement for prospective teachers, whether the authorities will adopt such a proposal or require teachers to pass a special pre-employment examination on the Basic Law; if they will, of the details; if not, the reasons for that;

(5) whether, prior to CE nominating and reporting to CPG for appointment of principal officials under the accountability system, the authorities will assess such persons' understanding of the Basic Law, establish

a regular mechanism to conduct the relevant assessments or evaluations on them after their assumption of office, and provide them with systematic training in this respect; and

(6) given that some District Council members, Legislative Council Members and Executive Council Members are often alleged to have different understanding of certain provisions of the Basic Law, whether the Government will provide training for them to ensure that they have a consistent understanding of the provisions of the Basic Law; if it will, of the details; if not, the reasons for that?

Reply:

President,

In consultation with the Education Bureau (EDB) and the Security Bureau, our consolidated reply to the questions raised by the Dr Hon Lam is as follows:

The Basic Law of the Hong Kong Special Administrative Region of the People's Republic of China (the Basic Law) is the constitutional document for the Hong Kong Special Administrative Region (HKSAR), enshrining in legal form the basic policies of "one country, two systems", "Hong Kong people administering Hong Kong" and a high degree of autonomy and prescribing the systems practised in the HKSAR. Since the establishment of the HKSAR, the Central Government has been acting in strict accordance with the fundamental principles and policies of "one country, two systems", "Hong Kong people administering Hong Kong" and a high degree of autonomy, as well as the provisions of the Basic Law, to support the Chief Executive and the HKSAR Government in administering Hong Kong in accordance with law. Similarly, the HKSAR Government has also been administering the affairs of Hong Kong in strict accordance with the "one country, two systems" principle and the Basic Law.

As regards the enactment of Article 23 of the Basic Law (BL23), the HKSAR is constitutionally obliged under BL23 to enact laws for national security. The HKSAR Government administers in accordance with the Basic Law. However, we do not have any plan to enact laws in respect of BL23 for the time being.

Constitutional development of Hong Kong is an internal matter for the HKSAR and an internal affair for China, in which foreign governments should not interfere. We hope foreign governments will respect our position. Regarding the question on external forces, the Chief Executive has already responded in various occasions. The HKSAR Government has nothing further to supplement.

The EDB plays an active role in promoting Basic Law education and continues to organise professional development programmes for primary and secondary school teachers in order to enhance teachers' understanding of the concepts and essence of the Basic Law. These courses cover curriculum planning, learning and teaching, use of learning and teaching resources, and knowledge enrichment, and aim to facilitate the implementation of Basic Law education in schools and enhance curriculum leadership and teaching effectiveness. The EDB always respects academic freedom in the aspect of initial teacher training. Teacher Education Institutions (TEIs) design initial teacher training courses in line with the needs of the society, students and the profession. The EDB also communicates with TEIs on matters related to teacher professional development and training, through meetings to ensure their course planning aligned with the needs of policy development. Pre-service teachers may also acquire knowledge of current affairs and development of the country through joining various exchange programmes and activities. In addition, the EDB also produces different learning packages, on-line assessment banks and on-line resources to support student learning of the Basic Law.

The Basic Law Promotion Steering Committee (BLPSC) established by the HKSAR Government in January 1998 provides the steer on the overall programme and strategy for promoting the Basic Law, and coordinates the efforts of Government departments and various sectors in the community in taking forward the Basic Law promotion activities. The BLPSC and its five working groups also organise various promotion activities and invite people from all walks of life to attend these events, in order to enable more in-depth understanding of "one country, two systems" and the Basic Law by different strata and sectors in the society.

Issued at HKT 14:30

June 3 [85]

LCQ20: Illegal occupation of public place
****

Following is a question by the Hon Chan Hak-kan and a written reply by the Secretary for Security, Mr Lai Tung-kwok, in the Legislative Council today (June 3):

Question:

Some members of the public have relayed to me that since the end of the occupation movement late last year, some people have erected unauthorised structures, such as tents, wooden sheds, etc., on the pavements outside the Legislative Council Complex and Central Government Offices. Moreover, the number of such structures is on the increase. They have pointed out that this situation will pose problems to the law and order as well as environmental hygiene. In this connection, will the Government inform this Council:

(1) of the respective numbers of reports and complaints about the aforesaid structures received by the Police from members of the public since December last year, and the nature of such complaints;

(2) whether it has assessed the problems of the law and order as well as environmental hygiene posed by these structures; if it has, of the assessment findings; and

(3) of the reasons why the authorities have not yet cleared these structures; of the legislation based on which the authorities may clear these structures at present; whether there are plans to clear these structures; if there are such plans, of the details?

Reply:

President,

With respect to the Hon Chan Hak-kan's concern over the law and order and environmental hygiene issues caused by the allegedly illegal erection of tents and placement of objects by certain members of the public on the pavements of Tim Mei Avenue and Harcourt Road outside the Legislative Council Complex

---

[85] http://www.info.gov.hk/gia/general/201506/03.htm

(LCC) and Central Government Offices (CGO), the Government's reply is as follows:

(1) and (2) From December 15 last year to May 31 this year, the Police have received over 30 reports involving obstruction caused by the tents, erected structures and other objects on the aforesaid pavements. In respect of law and order, in the same period, a total of four persons concerning three cases were arrested by the Police on the pavements of Tim Mei Avenue and Harcourt Road for suspected common assault and criminal damage. The Police will continue to closely monitor the situation of the aforementioned pavements, maintain law and order, and combat illegal acts.

In the same period, the Food and Environmental Hygiene Department (FEHD) has received 11 complaints on environmental hygiene pertaining to tent erection, odour emission and pest problems on the pavements of Tim Mei Avenue and Harcourt Road. While daily sweeping and refuse collection as well as regular pest control are being conducted on the aforesaid pavements, the FEHD has been unable to carry out routine street-cleansing as usual since last December due to the illegal occupation of certain pavement sections of Tim Mei Avenue and Harcourt Road.

(3) The HKSAR Government respects the public in expressing their views in a lawful and peaceful manner. The Government, at the same time, also has the responsibility to safeguard the public's right of using the roads, as well as to ensure public safety, public order and public health.

The pavements of Tim Mei Avenue and Harcourt Road are a public place and a main access to the CGO and LCC. While expressing their views, members of the public should respect others' right to use these roads and should not illegally occupy public place by means of tents, erected structures or other objects.

From the perspective of law and order, given that most of the tents on the aforesaid pavements are enclosed and that a few of them are indeed very large, it is difficult for passers-by to see from the outside what articles are stored inside the tents, or whether such articles are dangerous, offensive or illegal, and whether any person is lurking inside the tents for any criminal act, thereby causing concern amongst passers-by over their own personal safety. At the same time, some members of the community have already expressed dissatisfaction over the acts of illegally occupying the pavements of Tim Mei Avenue and Harcourt Road. Large-scale illegal occupation of pavements will heighten the risk of confrontation between people of different views at these locations. Besides, a section of the pavement on Tim Mei Avenue outside the CGO is a designated public activity area. Members of the public and the media often have to stand on vehicular access in order to stage demonstrations or cover news as the pavement is occupied by the tents, hence exposing themselves to danger. The above-mentioned various factors will create risks in respect of law and order on relevant pavements.

On environmental hygiene, given that the pavements of Tim Mei Avenue and Harcourt Road outside the LCC and CGO have not been thoroughly cleansed for about half a year, coupled with the hot and humid summer of Hong Kong, the tents, erected structures and other objects currently occupying these pavements may trigger environmental hygiene problems such as mosquito and pest breeding as well as odour emission etc.

The HKSAR Government urges the protesters to remove the tents, erected structures and other objects from the pavements of Tim Mei Avenue and Harcourt Road outside the CGO and LCC, so that members of the public can use these pavements in the normal way. Relevant government departments will continue to closely monitor the situation of the aforesaid pavements, examine necessary follow-up measures and take appropriate law enforcement actions at an appropriate time. It is not appropriate to reveal details at this stage.

Issued at HKT 13:27

LCQ6: Proposals for selecting CE by universal suffrage
****

Following is a question by Dr Hon Kwok Ka-ki and a reply by the Secretary for Constitutional and Mainland Affairs, Mr Raymond Tam, in the Legislative Council today (June 3):

Question:

On April 22 this year, the Government published the Consultation Report and Proposals on the Method for Selecting the Chief Executive by Universal Suffrage. In addressing this Council on that day, the Chief Secretary for Administration pointed out that "after the Chief Executive (CE) is selected by universal suffrage through 'one person, one vote' in 2017, the ultimate aim of the selection of the CE by universal suffrage as prescribed in Article 45 of the Basic Law will have been attained." There are comments that as the pan-democratic Members of the Legislative Council (LegCo) have repeatedly indicated that they will vote against the constitutional reform package proposed by the Government for selecting CE by universal suffrage in 2017, the chance for the passage of the constitutional reform package by this Council is very slim. In this connection, will the Government inform this Council:

(1) whether the Government will, after the constitutional reform package is negatived by this Council, expeditiously restart the "Five-step Process" of constitutional reform regarding the selection of CE by universal suffrage, so as to attain the ultimate aim of the selection of the CE by universal suffrage as prescribed in Article 45 of the Basic Law; if it will, of the specific timetable;

(2) as some members of the public have criticised that the public consultation conducted by the Task Force on Constitutional Development (comprising the Chief Secretary for Administration, the Secretary for Justice and the Secretary for Constitutional and Mainland Affairs) was not comprehensive, ignoring the views of some members of the public, whether the Government has assessed if the three Secretaries of Departments and Director of Bureau should be held politically accountable for the constitutional reform package being negatived by this Council and tender resignation; if it has, of the details; and

(3) given that Article 50 of the Basic Law stipulates that if LegCo refuses to pass a budget or any other important bill introduced by the Government, and if consensus still cannot be reached after consultations, CE may dissolve LegCo, whether CE will dissolve LegCo after the constitutional reform package is negatived by this Council, so as to restart the "Five-step Process" of constitutional reform regarding the selection of CE by universal suffrage?

Reply:

Acting President,

The HKSAR Government published on April 22, 2015 the Consultation Report and Proposals on the Method for Selecting the Chief Executive by Universal Suffrage (Consultation Report and Proposals). The proposals for selecting the Chief Executive (CE) by universal suffrage put forward by the HKSAR Government are constitutional, lawful, fair and reasonable. We sincerely hope that the general public and Members of the Legislative Council (LegCo) would support the proposals, so that five million eligible voters of Hong Kong could select the next CE by universal suffrage through "one person, one vote" in 2017 as scheduled. Our reply to the questions raised by Dr Hon Kwok is as follows:

(1) The HKSAR Government has repeatedly emphasised, and also stated clearly in the Consultation Report and Proposals as well as in the statement made by the Chief Secretary for Administration on April 22 at the LegCo meeting, that according to the Decision of the Standing Committee of the National People's

Congress on Issues Relating to the Selection of the Chief Executive of the Hong Kong Special Administrative Region by Universal Suffrage and on the Method for Forming the Legislative Council of the Hong Kong Special Administrative Region in the Year 2016, if the motion to amend Annex I to the Basic Law concerning the method for the selection of the CE is not endorsed by a two-thirds majority of all the Members of the LegCo, the CE in 2017 would continue to be elected by the 1 200-member Election Committee. Constitutional development will come to a standstill, the aim of selecting the CE by universal suffrage will fall through, and it would then be even more difficult to know when the aim of selecting all the Members of the LegCo by universal suffrage could be achieved. Some people suggest vetoing the proposals so as to restart the "Five-step Process" immediately. However, this is legally infeasible and impracticable in terms of legislative timetable, and hence is an unrealistic proposition. Therefore, the HKSAR Government urges LegCo Members and political parties to demonstrate their courage and determination at this critical moment, act in the overall and long-term interests of Hong Kong, heed the strong aspiration of the majority of Hong Kong people, and support the constitutional development proposals, so that Hong Kong could achieve universal suffrage as scheduled, and allow constitutional development to continue to move forward.

(2) Since the establishment of the Task Force on Constitutional Development (Task Force) led by the Chief Secretary for Administration on October 17, 2013, the HKSAR Government has conducted two rounds of extensive and systematic public consultations on the method for selecting the CE by universal suffrage, and truthfully reflected the views of the public received during the consultation periods. All the written submissions received were uploaded in full to the constitutional development website for public inspection. We absolutely disagree with the unreasonable allegation made by Dr Hon Kwok that the public consultations conducted by the Task Force were "not comprehensive, ignoring the views of some members of the public".

At this moment, the most important task of the HKSAR Government is to strive to secure endorsement of the proposals for selecting the CE by universal suffrage by a two-thirds majority of all the Members of the LegCo, so that five million eligible voters could select the CE by universal suffrage in 2017 through "one person, one vote". The LegCo has an important constitutional role and responsibility in the constitutional development of Hong Kong. I urge all Members to act in the overall and long-term interests of Hong Kong and support the proposals put forward by the HKSAR Government.

(3) The concept of "important bill" under Article 50 of the Basic Law only applies to local legislation. Amendments to the method for selecting the CE are, by nature, amendments to the provisions of

Annex I to the Basic Law, and hence are part of the constitutional arrangements, not amendments to local legislation. Therefore, Article 50 of the Basic Law is not applicable to the amendments to the method for selecting the CE.

Issued at HKT 16:05

June 15[86]

LegCo to vote on Electoral Reform Package to amend method for selection of Chief Executive of HKSAR

****

The following is issued on behalf of the Legislative Council Secretariat:

The Legislative Council (LegCo) will hold a meeting on Wednesday (June 17) at 11am in the Chamber of the LegCo Complex. During the meeting, Members will debate and vote on a motion moved by the Secretary for Constitutional and Mainland Affairs to amend the method for the selection of the Chief Executive of the Hong Kong Special Administrative Region.

The motion states: "Pursuant to Article 7 of Annex I to the Basic Law of the Hong Kong Special Administrative Region of the People's Republic of China, the Interpretation by the Standing Committee of the National People's Congress of Article 7 of Annex I and Article III of Annex II to the Basic Law of the Hong Kong Special Administrative Region of the People's Republic of China of April 6, 2004, and the Decision of the Standing Committee of the National People's Congress on Issues Relating to the Selection of the Chief Executive of the Hong Kong Special Administrative Region by Universal Suffrage and on the Method for Forming the Legislative Council of the Hong Kong Special Administrative Region in the Year 2016 of August 31, 2014, the "(Draft) Amendment to Annex I to the Basic Law of the Hong Kong Special Administrative Region of the People's Republic of China Concerning the Method for the Selection of the Chief Executive of the Hong Kong Special Administrative Region" appended to this Motion is hereby endorsed by this Council by a two-thirds majority of all Members.

Annex

(Draft) Amendment to Annex I to the Basic Law of the Hong Kong Special Administrative Region of the People's Republic of China Concerning the Method for the Selection of the Chief Executive of the Hong Kong Special Administrative Region

---

[86] http://www.info.gov.hk/gia/general/201506/15.htm

1. Starting from 2017, the Chief Executive shall be selected by universal suffrage upon nomination by a broadly representative Nominating Committee in accordance with democratic procedures and appointed by the Central People's Government.

2. The Nominating Committee shall be composed of 1200 members from the following sectors:

Industrial, commercial and financial sectors	300
The professions	300
Labour, social services, religious and other sectors	300
Members of the Legislative Council, representatives of members of the District Councils, representatives of the Heung Yee Kuk, Hong Kong deputies to the National People's Congress, and representatives of Hong Kong members of the National Committee of the Chinese People's Political Consultative Conference	300

The term of office of the Nominating Committee shall be five years. In the event that the office of Chief Executive becomes vacant within the five-year term of office of the Nominating Committee and a by-election is held, the term of office of the new Chief Executive shall be the remainder of the previous Chief Executive.

3. The delimitation of the various sectors of the Nominating Committee, the organizations in each sector eligible to return Nominating Committee members and the number of such members returned by each of these organizations and how to return them shall be prescribed by an electoral law enacted by the Hong

Kong Special Administrative Region in accordance with the principles of democracy and openness.

Corporate bodies in various sectors shall, on their own, elect members to the Nominating Committee, in accordance with the number of seats allocated and the election method as prescribed by the electoral law.

Members of the Nominating Committee shall discharge their duties in their individual capacities.

4. A person seeking nomination by the Nominating Committee may be recommended jointly by not less than 120 members and not more than 240 members of the Nominating Committee. Each member may recommend only one person.

The Nominating Committee shall, from the persons recommended as aforesaid, nominate two to three persons seeking nomination to become Chief Executive candidates by secret ballot. Each Nominating Committee member shall vote for at least two persons, and may at most vote for all persons seeking nomination by the Nominating Committee. Each candidate must have the endorsement of more than half of all the members of the Nominating Committee. The specific nominating method shall be prescribed by the electoral law.

5. All eligible electors of the Hong Kong Special Administrative Region who have registered in accordance with the law shall, from the list of candidates nominated by the Nominating Committee, elect one Chief Executive designate by secret ballot. The specific election method shall be prescribed by the electoral law."

Meanwhile, Chairman of the LegCo Subcommittee on Proposals on the Method for Selecting the Chief Executive in 2017, Mr Tam Yiu-chung, will present the Report of the Subcommittee at the meeting and address the Council on the Report.

Mr Andrew Leung will also move a motion under Rule 49E(2) of the Rules of Procedure. The motion states: "That this Council takes note of Report No. 23/14-15 of the House Committee laid on the Table of the Council on June 17, 2015 in relation to the Mandatory Provident Fund Schemes (Amendment) Ordinance 2015 (Commencement) Notice 2015."

During the meeting, Members will also ask the Administration 22 questions on various policy areas, six of which require oral replies.

The agenda of the above meeting can be obtained via the LegCo Website (www.legco.gov.hk). Please note that the agenda is subject to change, and the latest information about the agenda could be found on the LegCo Website.

Members of the public are welcome to observe the proceedings of the meeting from the public galleries of the Chamber of the LegCo Complex. They may reserve seats by calling 3919 3399 during office hours. Members of the public can also watch or listen the meeting via the "Webcast" system on the LegCo Website.

Issued at HKT 19:33

June 16[87]

Police response on stand-by deployment in LegCo Complex
****

    Police have conducted risk assessment in view of recent incidents and the latest situation. Upon consultation with the Legislative Council (LegCo) Secretariat, Police officers will be deployed into the LegCo Complex for stand-by duties this evening (June 16). This is to ensure that in case of emergencies and on the request of LegCo Secretariat, Police can make a quick and effective response to protect the safety of the LegCo members and staff as well as to enable the smooth proceeding of LegCo meetings. Police will adjust the manpower inside the LegCo Complex according to the prevailing situation to stand ready for any untoward incidents.

    According to Section 19 of the Legislative Council (Powers and Privileges) Ordinance (Cap. 382), anyone who assaults, obstructs or molests any member going to, being within or going from the precincts of the Chamber commits an offence. Police appeal to participants of the public order events not to obstruct any members of the Council while in the execution of their duty to refrain from committing any criminal offence.

    In addition, starting from 11pm today, Police will implement temporary road closure on Tim Wa Avenue. Motorists on Harcourt Road (Eastbound) will not be allowed to turn left into Tim Wa Avenue. Those who destine for Lung Wo Road (Westbound) should use Tim Mei Avenue, via Legislative Council Road and return to original path. There will also be no right turn to Tim Wa Avenue from Lung Wo Road (Eastbound). Motorists who destine for Harcourt Road or Gloucester Road (Eastbound) should use Edinburgh Place or Performing Arts Avenue and return to original path. They are advised to pay attention to the special traffic arrangements and take heed of instructions of the Police on site.

    Police reiterate that we respect the public's freedoms of expression, speech and assembly. It is the policy of Police to facilitate all peaceful and lawful public events in a fair and impartial manner while at the same time ensuring public safety and public order. Members of the public should comply with the laws of Hong Kong and maintain social order when expressing their views.

    Police also remind members of the public who will take part in public events not to believe rumours on the Internet or social media and be incited or used by others to commit violent acts. Should there be any

---
[87] http://www.info.gov.hk/gia/general/201506/16.htm

confrontation, they should protect their own safety, maintain a safe distance from the violent protestors or leave the scene at once so as to give Police enough space to deal with any violent and unlawful acts. If the public spot any suspicious persons or objects, they should inform Police under safety circumstances.

Police will not tolerate any acts endangering public order and public safety. We will take resolute and effective actions against any violent and unlawful activities in order to restore social order.
Issued at HKT 18:22

Transcript of remarks by Chairman of Legislative Council Commission on security arrangements for LegCo Complex
****
The following is issued on behalf of the Legislative Council Secretariat:

Following is the transcript of remarks by Mr Jasper Tsang, Chairman of The Legislative Council Commission, at a media briefing on security arrangements for the Legislative Council Complex at the Legislative Council Complex today (June 16):

The latest risk assessment by the Police indicates that there is a likelihood of the Legislative Council Complex being stormed by radical groups in the next couple of days. At the same time, it has been brought to the attention of our Secretariat that there will be large numbers of people coming from opposing political camps gathering in the precincts of the Complex.

Considering the situation, I have decided to agree to the Police's proposal that we should allow the Police to enter the Complex later today to help ensure the security of the Complex. My two colleagues, ex-officio members of The (Legislative Council) Commission, that is the Chairman and the Deputy Chairman of the House Committee, have concurred. So following our decided procedure, the Secretariat will inform the Police that they can come in and stand by later this evening. Also, the Secretariat will issue the Amber Alert some time later today, not later than midnight. And the corresponding security measures will be enforced.
Issued at HKT 19:32

June 17[88]

LCQ9: Illegal occupation of public place
****

Following is a question by the Hon Jeffrey Lam and a written reply by the Secretary for Security, Mr Lai Tung-kwok, in the Legislative Council today (June 17):

Question:

After the end of the occupation movement late last year, a group of people have set up and lived in the tents, erected study rooms and placed miscellaneous items such as tables and chairs, etc., on the pavements outside the Central Government Offices and the Legislative Council Complex. The number of tents has been increasing in recent months, with the area of pavements occupied expanding as well. It has been reported that cases of theft and indecent assault have occurred in the area. Some members of the public have pointed out that since some people cook food and place a large quantity of wood inside the tents, they are worried about the fire hazards thus caused. They are also worried that the occupation of pavements may turn into a second occupation movement. In this connection, will the Government inform this Council:

(1) whether it has recorded, on a regular basis, the situation of occupation of the aforesaid pavements; if it has, of the details (including a breakdown of the number of tents by size and the number of various types of miscellaneous items); if not, the reasons for that;

(2) whether it has assessed if the worsening of the occupation of the aforesaid pavements will give rise to the following incidents: people who work in the vicinity cannot gain access to their workplaces because of blockage of pavements, and emergency rescue services are even disrupted due to traffic obstruction; if it has, of the details; if not, the reasons for that;

(3) of the number of cases of theft, indecent assault and other crimes that occurred in the aforesaid area since late last year; and

(4) given that some people cook food inside the aforesaid tents, whether the Police have carried out inspections to check if inflammable substances and other dangerous goods are stored in such tents; if the

---

[88] http://www.info.gov.hk/gia/general/201506/17.htm

Police have done so, of the details; if not, the reasons for that?

Reply:

President,

With respect to the Hon Jeffrey Lam's concern over the risk to law and order, safety risk as well as fire risk caused by the allegedly illegal erection of tents and placement of objects by certain members of the public on the pavements outside the Central Government Offices (CGO) and Legislative Council Complex (LCC), the Government's consolidated reply is as follows:

According to Police records, as at June 15 this year, there were in total about 200 tents and erected structures of different sizes, plus other objects such as tables, chairs and potted plants etc., on the above-mentioned pavements. From December 15 last year to June 15 this year, the Police have received over 30 reports involving obstruction caused by the tents, erected structures and other objects on the aforesaid pavements.

The Police have been closely monitoring the situation of the aforementioned pavements with a view to maintaining law and order and combating illegal acts. From December 15 last year to June 15 this year, a total of five persons concerning four cases were arrested by the Police on the aforesaid pavements for suspected common assault, criminal damage and assault occasioning actual bodily harm.

In addition, the Police have found potentially dangerous items at and near the tents on the aforementioned pavements. Such items included wooden planks, metal bars, glass bottles, bricks, crushed rocks and knives etc. Given that large-scale public order events would be held on June 14 and the following few days at the above-mentioned road sections and nearby places, the Police are concerned that those items may pose risk to public safety. Therefore, the Police, after having attempted to get in touch with the owners of those items and made appeals to the persons concerned to remove those items, in the afternoon of June 13 removed those potentially dangerous items which had not yet been taken away to the Central Police Station for safekeeping in order to reduce the risk to public safety. The Police have called on members of the public not to bring any dangerous items to the aforesaid pavements. At the same time, the Police have strengthened patrol of the relevant road sections and will continue to adopt appropriate measures to ensure public safety and public order. The Fire Services Department has also strengthened inspection of those road sections so as to monitor fire risk and make sure that the emergency vehicle access remains free from obstruction.

The Hong Kong Special Administrative Region (HKSAR) Government respects the public in expressing their views in a lawful and peaceful manner. However, the Government at the same time also has the responsibility to safeguard the public's right of using the roads, as well as to ensure public safety, public order and public health.

The pavements outside the CGO and LCC are a public place and a main access to these two important facilities. While expressing their views, members of the public should respect others' right to use these road sections and should not illegally occupy public place by means of tents, erected structures or other objects. The HKSAR Government urges the protesters to remove soon the tents, erected structures and other objects from the aforesaid pavements, so that members of the public can use these pavements in the normal way. Relevant government departments will continue to closely monitor the situation of the aforesaid pavements, examine necessary follow-up measures and take appropriate law enforcement actions at an appropriate time. It is not appropriate to reveal details at this stage.
Issued at HKT 12:08

Police appeal to public meeting participants to express views peacefully and lawfully
****

The public events outside the Legislative Council Complex were generally conducted in an orderly manner today (June 17). Most of the participants exercised restraint and expressed their views peacefully and rationally. However, there were rebukes and scuffles between a small number of participants. They were later separated by Police officers, security staff and marshals of organisers who put the situation under control and maintained order at scene.

Meanwhile, Police arrested a 17-year-old man on a footbridge on Tim Mei Avenue for possession of offensive weapons. The case is being investigated by District Investigation Team of Central District. In the evening, a 46-year-old woman was arrested in Tamar Park for criminal damage. Investigation by District Investigation Team of Western District is underway.

With a view to ensuring public safety and public order, Police will deploy sufficient manpower and make necessary arrangement according to the situation so that the public events can be conducted in a safe and peaceful environment.

Police remind participants of the public events to comply with the law and express their views in a peaceful and rational manner. Police also appeal to them not to commit any violent acts. Should there be any confrontation, they should protect their own safety, maintain a safe distance from the violent protestors or leave the scene at once so as to give Police enough space to deal with any violent and unlawful acts. If the public spot any suspicious persons or objects, they should inform Police under safety circumstances.

Issued at HKT 23:33

June 18[89]

Transcript of remarks by CE at media session (with video)
****

Following is the transcript of remarks by the Chief Executive, Mr C Y Leung, at the question-and-answer session of the media session at the ground floor lobby of the Office of the Chief Executive at Tamar today (June 18):

Reporter: Do you see this veto as any kind of a failure on either your part or your Government? Point number one. And secondly, do you think it closes the door on future communication between the pan-democrats and Beijing?

Chief Executive: Well, we tried our very best and actually we have been trying very hard to provide all kinds of opportunities for all members, including, of course, the pan-democrats, to have constructive dialogues with the Central Authorities in Beijing. But as we can all see in the past 20 months, including the four events that we had provided before the Decision on the 31st of August was made by the NPC (National People's Congress) Standing Committee (NPCSC), not all members of the pan-democratic camp actually rose to the opportunities. But nonetheless, going forward we shall continue to provide such opportunities as and when they are likely to be constructive.

On the question of the efforts on my part, on the part of my team, again it is clear and beyond doubt to members of the community that the Hong Kong Government had tried its very best. Two-thirds majority, a super-majority, is a high threshold. This is as close as we could get to a two-thirds majority, and I think the responsibility is very much on those members who voted against the Government's motion and therefore denying 5 million eligible voters of their democratic rights.

Reporter: ... Central Government will have less trust for the SAR Government and for Hong Kong in general? And you mentioned that you're extremely disappointed with the result. Are you also a little bit disappointed, maybe, towards pro-establishment lawmakers for what they did?

Chief Executive: I think you'll hear from the Central Government about how they see the vote today. On the question of the result, as I said in my opening remarks, of course we are disappointed at the fact that 28 members, which is a minority amongst the 69 or 70 in LegCo, voted against the majority view of the

---

[89] http://www.info.gov.hk/gia/general/201506/18.htm

Hong Kong people. The majority view is very clear over the past 20 months. People want to have universal suffrage, they want to exercise their democratic right to elect the Chief Executive in 2017, and that's been very clear in the various polls conducted, including polls conducted in the past couple of weeks. So of course we are disappointed.

On the question of the relationship between the Central Authorities and the pan-democrats in Hong Kong, Hong Kong Government as in the past will do whatever it can to create opportunities for constructive dialogue between the pan-democrats and other members of the political community in Hong Kong and the Central Authorities in Beijing.

Reporter: Mr Leung, do you have any plans on how to satisfy aspirations for democracy among the people of Hong Kong? Do you still have any plans to satisfy that?

Chief Executive: The democratic aspiration of the Hong Kong people is a legitimate aspiration, but this aspiration can only be satisfied in accordance with the provisions of the Basic Law and the Decision of the National People's Congress Standing Committee, and therefore I appeal to members of the pan-democratic camp not to mislead the Hong Kong people any further into thinking that democratic aspirations in Hong Kong, particularly amongst their followers, could be satisfied or accomplished by ignoring provisions of the Basic Law and Decisions of the NPCSC.

Issued at HKT 18:38

June 19[90]

Opening remarks by CE at media session (with video)
****

Following are the opening remarks by the Chief Executive, Mr C Y Leung, at a media session at the Office of the Chief Executive at Tamar this afternoon (June 19):

In the past 20 months, the Hong Kong community has been inundated with arguments over the issue of constitutional development. Now that the Government's constitutional development proposal has been blocked by ExCo (should be LegCo), it's time for all of us to move on. We should try to forge consensus on various economic and livelihood issues. There are already initiatives in the pipeline that we should work on. The Government attaches great importance to the relationship between the executive and legislature. The Basic Law has defined the respective roles and responsibilities of the executive and legislature. Both should work together to serve the public of Hong Kong.

I and the Government will now make the first move to work together with LegCo to seize the opportunities for developing the economy and addressing livelihood issues. The Government will propose a series of initiatives to the meeting of the Finance Committee of Legislative Council next Friday, including the relief measures in the Budget this year, enhancement of remuneration package for District Council members, construction of rehab centres and a residential care home, adjustment of pay for civil servants according to the 2013 Pay Level Survey and for 2015-16, establishment of a $1 billion recycling fund and a $1.5 billion increase in commitment for the SME funds.

These measures will improve people's livelihood and propel economic growth. The application for funding for establishing the Innovation and Technology Bureau will follow these items. I hope LegCo will respond positively and take care of both economic and livelihood issues. Thank you.
Issued at HKT 15:52

---

[90] http://www.info.gov.hk/gia/general/201506/19.htm

FEBRUARY 9, 2016[91][92]

Police appeal motorists not to drive to Mong Kok
****

As emergency incident occurred in Mong Kok, motorists are advised not to drive to Mong Kok as far as possible.

Issued at HKT 02:34

Police strongly condemn law-breaking behaviours
****

A number of illegal hawking reports were received by the relevant department on a section of Portland Street junction between Shangtung Street and Nelson Street in Mong Kok last night (February 8). Some public officers were obstructed in executing their duties. Police were deployed to the scene as requested for assistance by the relevant department. A large number of people were found gathering on the carriageway and caused serious disturbances to public safety and other road users.

Police gave repeated advice and warnings, to urge them to return to the pavement but they refused to comply and shoved Police officers at scene. To ensure public safety and public order, Police took resolute actions, including using baton and pepper spray, to stop the unlawful violent acts.

During the incident, Police arrested three men, aged 27 to 35, for assaulting police officer and obstructing police officer. In addition, three police officers were injured and were sent to hospital for treatment.

Police strongly condemned the unlawful behaviours of protesters. Police will conduct follow-up investigations and will not rule out the possibility of further arrest action.

Police reiterate that we respect the public's freedoms of expression, speech and assembly. It is the policy of Police to facilitate all lawful and peaceful public events while at the same time ensuring public safety and public order. Resolute enforcement actions will be taken against any illegal acts to preserve public order and safeguard public safety.

Issued at HKT 03:23

---

[91] http://www.info.gov.hk/gia/general/201602/09.htm
[92] While the protest in Mong Kong, for Lunar New Year, were not part of the Occupy Central protests it does show that there is still a underlying distrust of the Hong Kong government that has continued since Occupy Central and its immediate aftermath.

Police appeal to the people at scene in Mong Kok to leave as soon as possible
****

Regarding the chaotic situation and confrontations occurred currently (February 9) in the vicinity of Nathan Road and nearby roads in Mong Kok, and the provocation at Police by the crowd, Police appeal to members of the public to exercise restraint and comply with the instructions of the Police officers. They are also urged to leave the scene as soon as possible.

Police reiterate that any acts endangering public order and public safety will not be tolerated. The Hong Kong community regard that the public should express their views in a rational and peaceful manner. Police will take enforcement actions decisively on law-breaking behaviours.

As emergency incident occurred in Mong Kok, MTR Mong Kok Station exits are temporarily closed until further notice.

Members of the public and motorists are advised not to go to Mong Kok as far as possible.
Issued at HKT 05:58

The Government condemns mob activities
****

Since midnight today (February 9), at least a few hundred mobs have taken part in a riot in Mong Kok, attacking police officers on duty and media covering the incident at the site.

The mobs damaged police cars and public properties, committed acts of arson, threw bricks and other objects at injured police officers who were on the ground, seriously jeopardising the safety of police officers and other people at the site.

A spokesman for the SAR Government strongly condemned such violent acts, and stated that the mobs would be apprehended and brought to justice.
Issued at HKT 09:50

Transcript of remarks by CE and S for S

****

Following is the transcript of remarks by the Chief Executive, Mr C Y Leung, and the Secretary for Security, Mr Lai Tung-kwok, at a media session at the ground floor lobby of the Office of the Chief Executive today (February 9):

Chief Executive: There was a riot in Mong Kok in the early hours of today. A few hundred mobs attacked police officers and the media in Mong Kok. They damaged police cars and public properties, committed acts of arson, threw bricks and other objects at police officers, including those who had already been injured and were lying on the ground, seriously jeopardising the safety of police officers and other people at the site. I believe the public can see for themselves from TV news reports the seriousness of the situation. The SAR Government strongly condemns such violent acts, the police will apprehend the mobs and bring them to justice. Also I send my regards to police officers and members of the media who were injured in the riot.

Reporter: ... and the Police have said that mobs organised that. Do you agree with those ...?

Secretary for Security: As what the Police have said there're indications that they are organised activities. The Police are still investigating the case. They'll take all efforts to arrest those suspects.

Reporter: Was it proper to fire shots here?

Secretary for Security: I think everyone of us have seen what happened on the TV screen. Police officers were knocked down on the ground and were further attacked. So, other police officers have to take all necessary actions to keep the peace.

Reporter: Mr Leung, what would be the direct reason behind the escalating chaos scenes in Hong Kong? Is it the general sense of dissatisfaction towards the Government? Or what would be the reason behind the protests in your ...?

Chief Executive: I think you have to ask those people who appeared to be organisers behind this riot.

Reporter: What about the Government's position? How do you analyse the situation?

Chief Executive: Our position is the same position as the Police, we enforce the laws of Hong Kong.

Issued at HKT 13:09

Statement by ExCo Non-official Members
****

The following is issued on behalf of the Executive Council (ExCo) Secretariat:

In response to the riot in Mong Kok early this morning (February 9), the ExCo Non-official Members issued the following statement:

Non-Official Members of the Executive Council strongly condemn the violent acts occurred in Mong Kok this morning. ?Since midnight today, a few hundred mobs have attacked police officers on duty and media covering the incident at scene. ?The mobs damaged vehicles and public properties, and committed acts of arson, seriously jeopardising the safety of police officers and other people at the site.

The ExCo Non-Official Members?fully support Police enforcement and swift apprehension of the mobs.

Issued at HKT 15:05

Opening remarks by Commissioner of Police at press conference
****

Following are the opening remarks by the Commissioner of Police, Mr Lo Wai-chung, at the press conference today (February 9):

Yesterday evening, a large number of violent radicals maliciously damaged Government properties and Police vehicles, committed acts of arson and attacked police officers on duty as well as media workers covering the incident in Nathan Road, Shantung Street, Nelson Street, Argyle Street and its vicinities in Mong Kok.

Police strongly condemn the unlawful behaviour of the protesters leading to these serious disturbances. In this incident, it was discovered that some people transported supplies by vehicles for use by the violent radicals at scene. Police do not rule out that it was an organised and pre-planned action. Police will conduct follow-up investigations and take enforcement actions. The possibility of further arrest actions cannot be ruled out.

I reiterate that Police have the ability, confidence and determination in handling all unlawful behaviour and will make all efforts to take enforcement actions against those who are responsible. My officers had been working very hard for the last few days at the flower markets to ensure an orderly and peaceful environment for the enjoyment of the public. For last night, they rushed to the scene right after the bus parade event and continued to work until this morning. I salute them and want to thank them all for their perseverance, courage and devotion to duties throughout the period. I also wish to express my gratitude for the support and help from some members of the public and the media at the scene.

The riot originated from an incident in which at about 10pm last night (February 8), a number of hawkers were selling cooked food at a section of Portland Street between Shantung Street and Nelson Street in Mong Kok illegally. Officers of the Food and Environmental Hygiene Department were surrounded, abused and obstructed in executing their duties and therefore requested assistance from Police. Police were then deployed to the scene. A large number of people (over 200) were found gathering on the carriageway. Their presence endangered public safety and other road users.

Police gave repeated advice and warning to the people at the scene, urged them to return to the pavement but they refused to comply and pushed the officers. The radical individuals held self-made weapons and shields to shove the Police officers that led to further confrontations.

The situation escalated and turned into a serious disturbance and subsequently a riot. A large number of violent radicals set fires in various places thereby endangering public safety and public order. Ignoring Police advice, some protesters moved objects to obstruct the carriageways and threw bricks prized from the pavement in order to attack Police officers. To safeguard public safety and public order, Police exercised most restraint as far as possible and used the minimum level of force including using baton and pepper spray, to stop the unlawful violent acts. However, the violent radicals kept throwing hard objects such as bricks, rubbish bins and glass bottles at officers from a short distance. A number of Police officers were injured and sustained head injuries. Some violent radicals also maliciously damaged police vehicles at scene.

Up to this time, nearly 90 police officers sustained injuries and required medical treatment. Some officers were wounded by broken glass and sustained head injuries after being hit by hard objects. The scope of injuries included: bone fractures, lacerations to forehead and face, bleeding nose and other abrasions and bruises. Some media workers who were covering the incident were also injured. Some of our officers remained in hospital for observations or awaiting treatment.

Police have all along exercising great restraint in handling the riot but you have seen from the TV live broadcast, the malicious acts of these rioters. At about 2am, at the junction of Argyle Street and Shanghai Street, rioters attacked a Police officer with hard objects and threatened his life. He fell onto the ground but was kept attacked by the rioters. With no alternative, his Police colleague used his firearm in accordance with the use of force principles to prevent his fellow colleague from being further attacked and also for his own personal safety.

I stress that Police have strict guidelines on the use of force and strictest training for our officers on the use of firearms. The officer made a judgment which he considered correct in accordance with the principles of the use of force and the prevailing circumstances which were presented before him at the scene.

So far, Police have arrested 54 people (including 47 men and 7 women), aged 15 to 70, for unlawful assembly, assaulting police, resisting arrest, disorderly conduct in public place, possession of offensive weapons and obstructing Police officer. Should evidence review, we will consider charging the arrested persons for participating in a riot.

The Hong Kong community does not want to see such violent disturbance, it is particularly saddening to have occurred on first day of the festive Lunar New Year. Police reiterate that we respect the public's right of freedoms of expression but at the same time we have the duty of ensuring public safety and public order as well as protecting the safety of the public and the reporters who are going about their business on the street. Resolute enforcement actions will be taken against any illegal acts to preserve public order and safeguard public safety.

Tonight, there will be the fireworks display in the Victoria Harbour. I appeal to member of the public to take heed of Police officers' instructions and conduct themselves in an orderly fashion at the scene. If suspicious persons or activities are seen, they should call the Police and they should also stay away from disturbances if any during tonight's event.

I repeat, we will absolutely not tolerate any violent behaviour which has crossed the line of law and order. We will take resolute action to interdict such acts and bring those who are responsible to justice. Issued at HKT 19:54

SFH condemns violent acts in Mong Kok
****

　　The Secretary for Food and Health, Dr Ko Wing-man today (February 9) condemned violent acts in Mong Kok.

　　There were hawkers selling cooked food in the section of Portland Street between Shantung Street and Nelson Street in Mong Kok last night (February 8). Hawker control officers of the Food and Environmental Hygiene Department (FEHD) were conducting squad patrol without taking any enforcement action. However, the squad was surrounded, scolded and pushed around by over 50 persons, causing injury to a squad member. During that time, two carts carrying cooked food as well as boiling oil and using flame cooking were also being pushed towards squad members. In the interest of the safety of the members of the squad and the large number of people at the scene, FEHD called for police assistance at about 9.40pm last night.

　　FEHD has all along been tolerant of handling illegal hawking activities. Should illegal hawking involving selling dry goods be found obstructing pedestrian passageways, verbal warning will be given and dispersal action will be taken in normal circumstances. But in view of food safety and environmental hygiene, if illegal hawking of cooked food or restricted food is found, FEHD staff will take enforcement action depending on the situation at the scene.

　　Dr Ko said the Government noted that there had been calls for the establishment of open-air bazaars and night markets in recent years.

　　"From a policy perspective, the Government is committed to formulating a hawker policy which can strike a fine balance. We have reviewed the hawker policy. Since itinerant hawkers usually gather at prime locations when in operation and their carts with goods inevitably obstruct pedestrian flow, and adversely affect environmental hygiene, the conclusion of the review is that the Government will no longer issue new itinerant hawker licences," he said.

　　"As regards setting up open-air hawker bazaars and night markets, we keep an open mind and believe that for the successful operation of such bazaars, the proposals should be district-led so that they can balance different views of the local community. We have to consider the operation of hawking business on the one hand, and address public concerns over environmental hygiene, food safety and obstruction to public passageways on the other. There are mechanism and channels in place to handle the matters. If suitable sites are identified and support from the relevant District Councils are obtained, provided that food safety and environmental hygiene are not compromised, we stand ready to facilitate liaison with relevant government departments," he added.

For setting up open-air hawker bazaars during Chinese New Year, among 18 districts, only one organisation in Sham Shui Po district had submitted proposal to organise a Chinese New Year festive event in 2016 at Maple Street Playground in Sham Shui Po. Sham Shui Po District Office, FEHD, Police, Fire Services Department, Leisure and Cultural Services Department had later discussed the proposal in details.

Dr Ko pointed out that those who sincerely cared about hawkers should adopt a pragmatic attitude and work with the Government and District Councils to strive for a best balanced way of moving forward, rather than taking radical means to achieve their ends as the latter approach of addressing the issue will only be counter-productive. We condemned the violent acts last night and supported our front line staff who steadfastly carry out their duties.

Issued at HKT 21:26

February 11[93]

FHB's statement on handling of illegal hawking activities by FEHD staff on first day of Lunar New Year
****

Regarding the handling of illegal hawking activities by the staff of the Food and Environmental Hygiene Department (FEHD) on the first day of the Lunar New Year (February 8), a spokesman for the Food and Health Bureau today (February 11) issued the following statement:

"Some political parties and student associations issued statements on the riot in Mong Kok, accusing that it was caused by the joint raids of FEHD and the Police against the hawkers, which has led to clashes with the public. We are of the view that such comments are unfounded and would confuse the public.

In fact, in his statement on February 9 and media sessions in the evening of February 9 and the morning of February 10, the Secretary for Food and Health, Dr Ko Wing-man, explained in details the handling of the illegal hawking activities by FEHD in Mong Kok on February 8. He pointed out that hawker control officers of FEHD were conducting general squad patrol. At that time, they did not issue any warning nor take any enforcement action against the hawkers selling cooked food illegally, let alone conducting raids. However, they were already surrounded, scolded and pushed around by over 50 persons, causing injury to a squad member. During that time, two carts carrying cooked food were also being pushed towards squad members. In view of the above clashes and violent acts, and the concerned cooked food stalls involving boiling oil and using flame cooking, as well as in the interest of the safety of the members of the squad and the large number of people at the scene, FEHD called for police assistance at about 9.40pm.

We also note that there were media reports on February 10 quoting hawkers at the site of Mong Kok as saying that they were not being dispersed by FEHD when the above clashes occurred.

The claims by some people that the riot was caused by hawker management are unfair and untrue. We therefore consider it necessary to make clarifications and set the record straight."
Issued at HKT 22:40

---

[93] http://www.info.gov.hk/gia/general/201602/11.htm

February 12[94]

Secretary for Justice on violent acts in Mong Kok
****

Following is the transcript of remarks made by the Secretary for Justice, Mr Rimsky Yuen, SC, at a media session this morning (February 12):

Reporter: Mr Yuen, do you think that this so-called "Fishball Revolution" is a challenge to Hong Kong's rule of law? And secondly, what's the difference between riot and unlawful assembly in legal terms?

Secretary for Justice: I think just to deal with the last question, as I was just saying in Cantonese, riot has been defined quite clearly in the Public Order Ordinance. So if you are interested, you can see the definitions in the Public Order Ordinance yourself.

Back to the first part of your question, you mentioned the expression "Fishball Revolution". If I may also take this opportunity to perhaps clarify a few points. I've seen reports both in Chinese as well as in English and I've seen local and also international media describing this event as "Fishball Revolution" or in similar expressions. And there are also suggestions that the whole incident was caused by the activities of regulating illegal hawking. I'm afraid this may not be a very accurate way of describing the incident. I think you would have recalled (the Secretary for Food and Health) Dr Ko Wing-man has already mentioned and explained in public that in fact on that occasion, it was because of certain colleagues dealing with illegal hawking got injured and that's why they called for police assistance. So it's got nothing to do with the operations concerning illegal hawking. And in any event, as I was stressing earlier in Cantonese, that the court has set it very clearly, including our Court of Final Appeal, that irrespective of your political motive, irrespective of your political opinion, the way to express your views, the way to express your political opinion has to be lawful. And I think everyone would agree that unlawful violence would not be the appropriate way to express one's political demand and political motive.

And therefore I would also make use of this opportunity to make an appeal to everyone in Hong Kong that I think the majority of people in Hong Kong would love to have a peaceful Hong Kong and I don't think anyone in Hong Kong would love to see such kind of violent act. And that's why, as I was saying in Cantonese just now, the Department of Justice takes this matter very seriously. We will work closely with

---

[94] http://www.info.gov.hk/gia/general/201602/12.htm

the Police, we will scrutinise the evidence and we would decide whether there are other charges that we need to consider from now until the 7th of April. As I was saying just now, we do not exclude the possibility that we might need to add further charges to those defendants. Thank you.

Issued at HKT 10:53

Commissioner of Police meets with staff associations
****

The Commissioner of Police, Mr Lo Wai-chung, took the initiative to meet with the four staff associations on the riot in Mong Kok on February 8 and 9 this morning (February 12). During the meeting, Mr Lo listened and responded positively to the aspirations of the staff representatives. He pledged to conduct a full review of the incident and invited staff representatives to take part in the review.

Staff associations assured that they will stay united and work together as always to support the management and to uphold law and order, as well as protect the safety of members of the public.

Issued at HKT 15:22

Heads of disciplinary forces condemn violence and fully support police enforcement
****

The Commissioner of Customs and Excise, Mr Roy Tang; the Director of Immigration, Mr Chan Kwok-ki; the Director of Fire Services, Mr Lai Man-hin; the Commissioner of Correctional Services, Mr Yau Chi-chiu; and the Acting Controller of the Government Flying Service, Mr Trevor Marshall, issued the following statement today (February 12):

We are deeply concerned about the riot that took place in Mong Kok a few days ago. In blatant defiance of the law, the mobs damaged public property, set fires in multiple locations and constantly attacked police officers and journalists at the scene. Such reprehensible behaviour went far beyond what can be accepted by Hong Kong society. As heads of law enforcement departments, we strongly condemn the mobs' violent acts, and do not agree with people putting up excuses for the savage acts in an attempt to shift attention. We fully support the Commissioner of Police, Mr Lo Wai-chung, and all colleagues in the Hong Kong Police Force and appreciate their efforts and contributions in upholding the rule of law and stability in Hong Kong. We extend our deep sympathy to the injured police officers and wish them a speedy recovery. They were injured while maintaining law and order, and deserve our respect. As in the past, the disciplinary forces will stand united and continue to contribute to Hong Kong's law and order and stability.

Issued at HKT 20:23

February 13

Transcript of remarks by S for S
****

Following is the transcript of remarks by the Secretary for Security, Mr Lai Tung-kwok, at a media session after attending a radio interview today (February 13):

Reporter: Mr Lai, Beijing has concluded the unrest in Mong Kok was orchestrated by separatists. Is the Government reaching the same conclusion it was orchestrated by separatists? And also the term " Fishball Revolution" you mentioned in the programme that it was wrong for people to use this term to justify the act, can you elaborate and explain more, please?

Secretary for Security: Yes. We have repeatedly stated in public what we feel about this case. The Police have arrested more than 60 suspects and 39 （should be 40） of them have been charged with riot. So, the position of Hong Kong SAR Government is clear. This is a violent case. And we have to take all possible actions legally to apprehend the culprits and bring them to the court.

Regarding your second part of the question, about the "Fishball Revolution". Firstly, the word "fishball" is totally misplaced. It appears to be that the word "fishball" points to hawkers were selling food and the Government took enforcement actions against them during the incident. This is totally wrong. In fact, at that time, officers from the Food and Environmental Hygiene Department were patrolling there. They were not taking any enforcement actions. I hope that everybody would appreciate that patrolling in order to maintain certain order is essential in view of the local situation. The crowd was there, so many people coming and going around, so we must be present there. There was nothing called enforcement actions. Officers from the Food and Environmental Hygiene Department were surrounded by a group of above 50 persons and one of the officers was hurt. That's why they asked the Police for assistance. So, that's nothing to do about hawkers selling and taking enforcement actions. As regarding "revolution", it implies that all the actions amounting to a riot situation are justifiable. Is it justifiable? I think every Hong Kong residents can reach a conclusion.

Issued at HKT 14:58

February 15[95]

Government's response to proposal for setting up independent commission of inquiry into Mong Kok riot
****

In response to proposal that the SAR Government should set up an independent commission of inquiry headed by a judge to look into the Mong Kok riot, a SAR Government spokesman today (February 15) made the following statement:

The SAR Government does not agree to the proposal. The riot in Mong Kok was a serious violent incident. Criminal investigations by the Police are underway with a view to apprehending all culprits for fair trials and rulings by the court. As such, the SAR Government does not consider it necessary to set up an independent commission of inquiry, headed by a judge, to look into the incident.

It was noted that, following the disturbances in Hong Kong in the 1960s, a commission of inquiry was set up by the government at the time. However, the SAR Government considers it inappropriate to make direct comparisons between the incident and the Mong Kok riot. Hong Kong nowadays enjoys free access to information and is a highly democratic and transparent society. Members of the public are entitled to freedom of speech and can express their opinions and aspirations on social problems and government administration through various channels, including different tiers of councils, consultative bodies or even in the form of peaceful processions, demonstrations and assemblies. Individuals can also seek relief from the court to review the administrative decisions through legal proceedings.

The SAR Government has all along been listening attentively to members of the public and is committed to balancing the interests and needs of all sectors of the community. The SAR Government will continue to improve governance to ensure that policies are geared towards the overall and long-term well-being of Hong Kong. Meanwhile, the SAR Government stresses that the expression of views and demands must not be conducted through illegal and violent acts.
Issued at HKT 20:12

---

[95] http://www.info.gov.hk/gia/general/201602/15.htm

February 17

Expenses limit raised for Chief Executive election
****

The Chief Executive in Council has made the Maximum Amount of Election Expenses (Chief Executive Election) (Amendment) Regulation 2016 under section 45 of the Elections (Corrupt and Illegal Conduct) Ordinance (Cap. 554) yesterday (February 16) to increase the election expenses limit (EEL) for the Chief Executive election. The subsidiary legislation will be published in the Gazette on February 19.

A government spokesman said today (February 17) that after the above subsidiary legislation has come into effect, the EEL for the Chief Executive election will be increased from $13 million to $15.7 million starting from the fifth-term Chief Executive election in March 2017.

"The adjustment of the EEL has taken into account the estimated cumulative inflation rate from 2012 to 2017 (i.e. 19 per cent), as well as the changes in rental levels since the last review exercise," the spokesman said.

The subsidiary legislation will be tabled at the Legislative Council on February 24 for negative vetting. Issued at HKT 11:02

LCQ10: Hong Kong Police Force's integrity management
****

Following is a question by the Hon Leung Yiu-chung and a written reply by the Secretary for Security, Mr Lai Tung-kwok, in the Legislative Council today (February 17):

Question:

Recently, there have been a number of media reports on crime cases allegedly committed by police officers, such as threatening sex workers to provide sex service, colluding with drug traffickers to fabricate false narcotics cases for detection by them, and deceiving public money, etc. Some members of the public have queried that the Police Force has become a hotbed of crime. In this connection, will the Government inform this Council:

---

[96] http://www.info.gov.hk/gia/general/201602/17.htm

(1) over the past five years, of (i) the number of police officers convicted, broken down by type of crimes, (ii) the detection rate of the crime cases in which the suspects were police officers, broken down by type of crimes, and (iii) the number of police officers who were interdicted from duty as they were alleged to have committed crimes (broken down by the remuneration arrangements during their interdiction), the total number of days of interdiction, as well as the total amount of remuneration received by the police officers concerned during their interdiction; if it cannot provide such information, whether it will compile the relevant statistics;

(2) of the mechanism and procedures adopted by the Police for following up the crime cases in which the suspects are police officers; the measures in place to prevent police officers from harbouring their colleagues;

(3) whether a mechanism is currently in place to forestall police officers' committing crimes; if so, whether the Government will establish an independent committee dedicated to reviewing if such a mechanism has rooms for improvement, and studying new measures to prevent the problem of police officers committing crimes from worsening; if it will not, of the reasons for that;

(4) whether the Police will consider covering cases of crimes committed by police officers on its television programme "Police Magazine", so as to alert members of the public to stay vigilant; and

(5) whether it has assessed if the recent incidents of police officers breaking the law deliberately have undermined the credibility of the Police Force, thus constituting a serious social problem; if it has assessed and the outcome is in the affirmative, whether the authorities have examined the roots of the problem and ways to solve the problem at its roots?

Reply:

President,

The Police show zero tolerance to and have no bias towards police officers' behaviour that runs against the law or discipline. Should any individual police officer is suspected of violating the law or discipline, the Police shall handle the case in accordance with the relevant legislation and established procedures in a fair and impartial manner.

In the past five years, a total of 55 police officers were convicted of criminal offences, such as theft, fraud, sexual offences, corruption-related offences and misconduct in public office. During the same period, a total of 133 police officers that were involved in criminal cases were interdicted from duty, of which the lengths of interdiction varied with cases. The Police do not maintain the figures on the amount of salary paid to those officers during the period.

If any police officer is suspected of a criminal offence, the case shall be handled by the Police under sections 13 and 17 of the Police Force Ordinance (the Ordinance) (Cap. 232) to ascertain whether an interdiction is required, and to make arrangements for salary payment during the interdiction period. In the event that a charge in respect of a criminal offence is subsequently pressed against such an officer and that the court has found in criminal proceedings that the charge has been proved, the Police shall make arrangements for cessation of salary or allowance in accordance with section 37(4) of the Ordinance. In addition, section 37(5) of the Ordinance stipulates that if an officer in respect of whom a court has found in criminal proceedings that a charge against him has been proved and whose appeal or other application for review of those proceedings is not allowed or is abandoned or withdrawn, may be, by the Chief Executive or the Commissioner of Police, dismissed without retirement benefits, compulsorily retired with full retirement benefits or reduced retirement benefits or without retirement benefits, reduced or reverted in rank or subjected to a lesser punishment.

The Police understand the public's very high expectation on the standard of conduct and discipline of police officers. To enhance police officers' integrity management, a Force Committee on Integrity Management (FCIM) was set up in 2009. Chaired by the Deputy Commissioner of Police (Management), the FCIM, in addition to providing guidelines and making assessments on major integrity management matters, monitors the effectiveness and promotion of the Force Strategy for Integrity Management. At the formation level, the Police have appointed 45 Chief Superintendents or Senior Superintendents as Formation Integrity Officers.

In 2009, the Police formulated a four-pronged approach of integrity management strategy, namely, "education and integrity culture building", "governance and control", "enforcement and deterrence", and "reintegration and support". In 2010, the Police further developed a series of baseline activities for all officers to participate. A review of relevant activities was completed in 2015, and measures for further enhancement shall be rolled out by phase. Relevant measures include providing scenario-based integrity management training in various training programmes; incorporating integrity management elements into professional examinations and promotion exercises; setting up an "Integrity Management Coordinating Committee" chaired by Chief Superintendent (Complaints and Internal Investigations Branch) thus enhancing the co-ordination of various Formation Integrity Committees and sharing of successful experiences; strengthening training of front-line supervisors on investigations so as to equip them for conducting efficient criminal investigation and disciplinary reviews on cases involving integrity issues; and stepping up the promotion of "Individual Reintegration Plan" in a bid to render more appropriate support and encouragement to the Police officers previously with integrity issues.

By means of the above integrity management strategies, the Police shall continue to alert police officers of the need to maintain a high standard of integrity and discipline at all times, so that the Police shall remain to be an organisation of impeccable integrity.

As for the content of the television programme "Police Magazine", the Police have been disseminating through the programme fight crime messages and fostering Police-public co-operation. In addition to a lively and light-hearted presentation of latest crime trends and crime prevention tips, the programme provides the public with Police updates and enhances their understanding of the law. To this end, the Police shall continue to produce the programme content in the light of prevailing crime trends.

Issued at HKT 15:55

February 24

Statement by DoJ in respect of recent opinions on Mong Kok riot
****

The riot that took place in Mong Kok on February 8 and 9 has attracted much attention. How the court dealt with those criminal cases arising from the incident has also led to considerable discussion. The Department of Justice (DoJ) notices that some recent opinions sought to speculate about judicial officers' political stances, or accused them of being biased or having conflicts of interest.

The rule of law, judicial independence and fundamental rights such as freedom of expression are the core values which the Hong Kong Special Administrative Region (HKSAR) Government endeavours to safeguard. When exercising a particular right or safeguarding a particular core value, one should not lose sight of other rights and core values.

Public order event cases concerning the rights of expression, assembly, procession and demonstration often attract public attention and extensive discussions. The Judiciary is the guardian of the rule of law. The public has the right to express their views on court decisions and related matters within the boundary permitted by the law. Healthy discussions can also promote awareness of the rule of law. As Lord Atkin once remarked in Ambard v AG for Trinidad and Tobago [1936] AC 322, "Justice is not a cloistered virtue: she must be allowed to suffer the scrutiny and the respectful even though outspoken comments of ordinary men."

When expressing views on court rulings, one must also respect the rule of law and judicial independence; otherwise, there might be impact on the rule of law even though one might have acted with the best intentions. Further, one should avoid making comments which might constitute or might be perceived to constitute the exertion of pressure on the courts or individual judges, so as to avoid the risk of prejudicing judicial independence and the healthy development of the rule of law. As a spokesman for the DoJ said in response to media enquiries yesterday (February 23), accusing judicial officers of being biased or speculating about their political inclination in the absence of cogent evidence will not do any good to the maintenance of the HKSAR's judicial independence.

The DoJ will continue to pay attention to the public's views on matters relating to the rule of law including the criminal justice system, and will urge the public to respect judicial independence and the rule of law.

Issued at HKT 19:37

February 28[98]

SAR Government responds to statement by US Congressional-Executive Commission on China
****

In response to media enquiries on the statement issued by the US Congressional-Executive Commission on China about its concern for the trial of student leaders involved in the 2014 illegal occupy Central movement, the Hong Kong Special Administrative Region Government (SAR Government) today (February 28) issued the following statement:

"The SAR Government is committed to upholding the rule of law. Any arrest and prosecution are conducted according to the laws of Hong Kong and those being prosecuted will be tried by the court in an independent, fair and open manner.

The Department of Justice (Department) of the Hong Kong SAR handles all criminal prosecutions independently and free from any interference. When making a prosecutorial decision, the Department does not take into account any political considerations and there is no question of political prosecution whatsoever.

Prosecution and trial in Hong Kong are entirely affairs of the SAR and no foreign governments should intervene. The SAR Government regrets that the US Congressional-Executive Commission on China has openly made comments on cases that are subject of pending legal proceedings. The Commission should respect the legal and judicial system as well as the judicial independence of the Hong Kong SAR. It is inappropriate for the Commission to make any open comment on cases that are subject of pending legal proceedings.
Issued at HKT 22:26

---

[98] http://www.info.gov.hk/gia/general/201602/28.htm

March 2

LCQ5: Mong Kok riot
****

Following is a question by Hon James To and a reply by the Secretary for Security, Mr Lai Tung-kwok, in the Legislative Council today (March 2):

Question:

From the night on the eighth of last month (i.e. the recent Lunar New Year's Day) to the early hours of the following day, the clashes between the Police and members of the public in Mong Kok, allegedly sparked by the authorities' enforcement operations against unlicensed hawkers, eventually turned into a serious disturbance (the incident of clashes in Mong Kok). It has been reported that quite a number of people who participated in the disturbance were outraged by the prevailing political stalemate and the Government's performance in policy implementation. While people from various sectors of the community condemned the use of violence, more than 600 people (including academics, professionals and eminent persons) jointly signed a statement on the fourteenth of last month requesting the Government to set up an independent commission of inquiry to look into the sequence of events and causes of the incident of clashes in Mong Kok, and to put forward suggestions to prevent the recurrence of similar incidents. In response to that request on the following day, the Government stated that the SAR Government did not consider it necessary to set up an independent commission of inquiry, to be headed by a judge, to look into the incident on the grounds, inter alia, that criminal investigations by the Police were underway. In this connection, will the Government inform this Council:

(1) as the authorities decided to set up a commission of inquiry to look into the vessel collision off Lamma Island eight days after the occurrence of the incident, at which time the relevant criminal investigations were still underway, why the authorities do not adopt the same practice and set up a commission of inquiry to look into the incident of clashes in Mong Kok;

(2) whether the authorities have ruled out the possibility that the incident of clashes in Mong Kok was related to the Government's performance in policy implementation, the atmosphere in the community and the political stalemate; if they have, of the justifications for that; and

(3) how the authorities will alleviate the distrust in the current-term Government among some members of the public, and assuage their frustrations about the prevailing social circumstances and political stalemate, in order to prevent public grievances from escalating incessantly, which may lead to the recurrence of similar incidents of clashes?

Reply:

President:

The riot that occurred in the early hours of February 9 this year in Mong Kok was the most serious large-scale mob violence since Hong Kong's return to China. During the incident, a vast number of rioters attacked police officers with self-made weapons and various kinds of hard objects, set fires at various locations and damaged police vehicles. Over 100 persons were injured in the incident. Most of the injured persons were police officers, while several members of the media were also injured.

The HKSAR Government strongly condemns the acts of the rioters. As at yesterday (March 1), the Police have arrested in total 75 persons and prosecuted 48 of them for riot and one person for unlawful assembly. The Police have been making all efforts to investigate and gather evidence with a view to bringing other rioters involved to justice. The Police have also set up a hotline to facilitate provision of information related to the riot by members of the public. The HKSAR Government fully supports the Police in maintaining law and order and pays solemn tribute to the professional and fearless spirit of our police officers, firemen and ambulance personnel who stood fast to their posts in the face of danger to their lives.

After the incident, some groups alleged that the riot was triggered by a raid on hawkers jointly conducted by the Food and Environmental Hygiene Department (FEHD) and the Police in the evening of the first day of the Lunar New Year (February 8), and that it was a matter pertaining to the governance of the HKSAR Government. In response, the Secretary for Food and Health has made prompt clarification that FEHD officers were only conducting general patrol in Mong Kok in the evening in question. They did not issue any warning nor take any enforcement action against the hawkers, let alone conducting a raid. However, they were already surrounded, scolded and pushed around by over 50 persons, causing injury to an officer. Putting the blame of the riot on hawker management policy or the governance of the HKSAR Government is merely an attempt to rationalise the violent acts of the rioters as well as to divert attention.

After the riot, there was an opinion that the HKSAR Government should set up an independent commission of inquiry headed by a judge to conduct investigation. The HKSAR Government does not agree to this proposal.

The Mong Kok riot was a serious violent incident. The top priority of the Police is to conduct criminal investigation with a view to apprehending all culprits for fair trials and rulings by the court. To respond to the challenges ahead, the Police have established a review committee, chaired by Deputy Commissioner of Police (Management), to examine three areas, namely, "operations", "arms, equipment and training" and "support", so as to enhance the safety and professional competency of police officers in the execution of their duties.

The Hon James To mentioned the independent commission of inquiry set up by the HKSAR Government after the vessel collision incident near Lamma Island in October 2012. I have to stress that the collision incident and the Mong Kok riot were two incidents of entirely different nature, with the former being a marine traffic accident which led to serious casualties. The Chief Executive-in-Council decided to set up a commission of inquiry with the aim to ascertain the causes of the accident, consider and evaluate the general conditions of maritime safety concerning passenger vessels and the system of control, and make recommendations for the prevention of the recurrence of similar accidents in future.

On the contrary, the Mong Kok riot was not a traffic accident, but an incident of serious criminal violence by rioters with a collective intention to break the law, involving offences such as riot, unlawful assembly, arson, criminal damage, assaulting police officers and possession of offensive weapon, etc. As such, the most appropriate way of handling the incident is to conduct criminal investigation, which will also look into whether there were persons behind the scene organising and planning the riot, as well as to apprehend the rioters as soon as possible and then initiate prosecution and bring them to court for trial. During the process, the public will come to know the background of the incident and the truth through open trials. Last Friday, the House Committee of the Legislative Council (LegCo) rejected a proposal requesting the LegCo to appoint a select committee to inquire into the incident. Some political and community figures also agree that it may not be necessary to set up a select committee to understand the real causes behind the riot.

It was mentioned that following the disturbances in Hong Kong in the 1960s, a commission of inquiry was set up by the government at the time. The HKSAR Government considers it inappropriate to make direct comparison between the incident and the Mong Kok riot. Hong Kong nowadays enjoys free access to information and is a highly democratic and transparent society. Members of the public are entitled to freedom of speech and can express their opinions and aspirations on various social problems and government administration through various channels, including different tiers of councils, consultative bodies or even in the form of peaceful processions, demonstrations and assemblies etc. Individuals can also seek relief from the court to review administrative decisions of the government through legal proceedings.

While meeting the media on February 16, the Chief Executive stated that, "The current-term HKSAR Government attaches great importance to various issues prevailing in our community. In the area of people's livelihood, we have done a lot and our efforts have delivered results...... Yet no one should resort to unlawful means, let alone violence, in expressing his demands, no matter what difficulties he is confronting in his daily life, and no matter what he thinks of the community."

In the Chief Secretary for Administration's speech during the debate on the motion of thanks to the Policy Address at the LegCo on February 19, she stated that, "There is no perfection in governance; extensive acceptance of public opinion and continual improvement are cornerstone for good governance. However, unsatisfactory governance by the government does not mean that one can portray a heart-breaking violent incident that is shown to the public as 'a revolt against government oppression', 'fighting brutality with violence', or a police-civilian conflict triggered by government tyranny."

The Secretary for Justice also stated on the same day at the LegCo that, "No political ideas or aspirations shall be cited as defence for violent acts."

President, Hong Kong people all along cherish peace and rationality. Openness, diversity, freedom and the rule of law have all along been the core values of Hong Kong. The rioters of the Mong Kok riot claimed to defend "local" characteristics with the stand of "localism", and yet they resorted to violent means that ran totally against the core values of Hong Kong. The Financial Secretary, in the concluding remarks of his Budget speech of February 24, stated that, "What we are facing today is the result of a raft of intricately-related factors...... As long as everyone is willing to set aside short-term political considerations in favour of the long-term overall interests of Hong Kong, we shall have a chance to return to rationality." I believe we all agree that violence is not a solution to problems, but only a trigger for more violence. We should definitely educate our younger generation to embrace peace and rationality and say "no" to violence and hatred.

The HKSAR Government has all along been reviewing its work and services provided to the public and looking for improvement. The HKSAR Government will, as always, listen attentively to the aspirations of all sectors of the community and continue to improve governance to ensure that policies are geared towards the overall and long-term well-being of the public while balancing the interests and needs of various sectors. At the same time, no one should express his or her aspirations through illegal and violent acts.

As the Secretary for Security, I am responsible for protecting public safety and public order of Hong Kong. The reputation of Hong Kong as one of the safest cities in the world is a hard-earned achievement after years of effort by all members of our community. We cannot afford seeing this achievement being devoured. We must curb the spread of violence ideology and make a concerted effort to steer Hong Kong out of the current predicament.

Thank you, President.

Issued at HKT 15:52

COURT INJUCTIONS (MONG KOK)
OCTOBER 20, 2014

HCA 2086/2014

IN THE HIGH COURT OF THE
HONG KONG SPECIAL ADMINISTRATIVE REGION
COURT OF FIRST INSTANCE
ACTION NO 2086 OF 2014

BETWEEN

CHIU LUEN PUBLIC LIGHT BUS   Plaintiff
COMPANY LIMITED (潮聯公共小型巴士有限公司)
    and

PERSONS UNLAWFULLY OCCUPYING   Defendant
OR REMAINING ON THE PUBLIC HIGHWAY NAMELY, THE WESTBOUND
CARRIAGEWAY OF ARGYLE STREET BETWEEN THE JUNCTION OF TUNG
CHOI STREET AND PORTLAND STREET AND/OR OTHER PERSONS HINDERING
OR PREVENTING THE PASSING OR REPASSING OF ARGYLE STREET

HCA 2104/2014
(HCZZ 136/2014)

IN THE HIGH COURT OF THE HONG KONG SPECIAL ADMINISTRATIVE REGION
COURT OF FIRST INSTANCE
ACTION NO 2104 OF 2014
    (INTENDED ACTION NO 136 OF 2014)

BETWEEN

LAI HOI PING (黎海平)　　　　　　　　1st Plaintiff
(suing on his own behalf and on the behalf of all other members of Hong Kong Taxi Association 香港計程車會)

TAM CHUN HUNG (譚駿雄)　2nd Plaintiff
(suing on his own behalf and on the behalf of all other members of Taxi Drivers and Operators Association 的士司機從業員總會)

　　　　　and

PERSONS OCCUPYING PORTIONS OF　　　　Defendants
NATHAN ROAD NEAR TO AND BETWEEN ARGYLE STREET AND DUNDAS STREET
TO PREVENT OR OBSTRUCT NORMAL VEHICULAR TRAFFIC FROM PASSING
AND REPASSING THE OCCUPIED AREAS

Before : Hon Poon J in Chambers (Open to the public)
Date of Hearing : 20 October 2014
Date of Ruling : 20 October 2014

RULING

1.　These two ex parte applications on notice arose out of the recent public demonstrations in the centre of Mongkok as part of the "Occupy Central" Campaign directed against the constitutional development of Hong Kong by way of civil disobedience.

2.　It is the usual practice of the court to hear an ex parte application for injunction (even on notice) in chambers not open to the public. However because of the immense public importance involved in the two applications now before me, I agree with Mr Mok SC for the applicants in one of the applications (HCA 2104/2014) that the hearing should be heard in chambers open to public so that the public is made aware of not only the order that the court is going to make, but also the submissions advanced before the court and the court's reasoning in arriving at its conclusion; although given the nature of the applications, such reasoning is bound to be brief but I hope succinct.

A.   PARTIES

A1.   Parties in HCA 2104/2014

3.   The plaintiffs are Mr Lai Hoi-ping and Mr Tam Chun hung.

4.   Mr Lai is a taxi manager and the chairman of Hong Kong Taxi Association ("HKTA"). Its core function is the management of taxi business in Hong Kong. HKTA has around 400 members, comprising owners and managers of taxis. Each of HKTA's members who is a manager manages 10 to 50 taxis and in the case of Mr Lai, he manages 30 taxis. There are around 2,000 taxis being operated or managed by HKTA's members.

5.   Mr Tam is a committee member and a member of Taxi Drivers and Operators Association ("TDOA"). TDOA has around 10,900 current taxi driver members. About 80 percent of its members are adversely affected by the "Occupy Central" Campaign.

6.   Depending on where the taxi drivers live, some of the taxis mostly operate in Kowloon and some on the Hong Kong side, although they also travel to and from the other side of the Harbour, the New Territories and certain permitted areas of Lantau Island and operate there if required to do so by a customer.

7.   Both Mr Lai and Mr Tam sue on behalf of themselves as well as on behalf of the members of their respective associations.

8.   The defendants are the persons occupying portions of Nathan Road near to and between Argyle Street and Dundas Street to prevent or obstruct normal vehicular traffic from passing and repassing the area occupied. They seek an injunction to restrain the intended defendants from obstructing that portion of Nathan Road near to and between Argyle Street and Dundas Street.

A2.   Parties in HCA 2086/2014

9.   The plaintiff is Chiu Luen Public Light Bus Company Limited ("Chiu Luen").

10.   Chiu Luen is carrying on the business of organising, managing and providing commute routes of public light buses for the purpose of public transportation. It is responsible for organising, managing and providing commute routes of public light buses and receives a management fee of $1,000.00 from the owners of each public light bus. The owners of the public light buses find self-employed drivers to lease and operate the public light buses and the self-employed drivers of the public light buses are required to

pay $1,000.00 per day to lease a public light bus. The drivers of the public light buses act as sole proprietors who drive the light buses along the commute route organised, managed and provided by the plaintiff and receive fares from passengers.

11. Chiu Luen and its predecessor has operated, managed and provided the commute routes from Kwun Tong to Olympic Station in Tai Kok Tsui in a circular manner with 14 stops for over 50 years.

12. The defendants are demonstrators or protestors unlawfully occupying or remaining at the area occupied, that is the westbound carriageway of Argyle Street between the junction of Tung Choi Street and Portland Street in Mongkok. Chiu Luen is seeking an injunction to restrain the defendants from obstructing that passageway.

B. BACKGROUND

13. As I have said, these applications arose of the recent "Occupy Central" Campaign which has spilled over from Hong Kong Island to Mongkok. The events that took place since the Campaign began some 20 days ago have been covered by the media closely and extensively and in a real sense have unfolded before the eyes of the public. So for present purposes, I only need to refer to what has been deposed to in the supporting affirmations, in particular paragraphs 6 to 22 of Mr Lai's affirmation and paragraphs 10 to 15 of Mr Lam Sum-keung's affirmation. Mr Lam is a director of the Chiu Luen. In the interest of time, I shall not repeat what they have said for the purpose of this judgment.

C. DISCUSSION

14. These being ex parte applications for interim injunction, the relevant principles can be found in a recent judgment of Godfrey Lam J in Turbo Top Limited v Lee Cheuk Yan [2013] 3 HKLRD 41 at paragraph 14 :

"The principles applicable in relation to interlocutory injunction are not in dispute. The Court has to see whether there are serious issues to be tried, whether damages would be an adequate remedy for either side, and if damages would not be adequate, where the balance of convenience lies in terms of whether or not to grant an interim injunction pending the trial of the matter. In that balancing exercise [the Court] must take into account the interests of the general public as well even though they are not represented before [the Court]."

C1. Serious question to be tried

15. I first consider if there is a serious question to be tried.

16. The plaintiffs before me are suing the defendants for public nuisance. The law on public nuisance is well settled. In brief, it is a public nuisance to obstruct or hinder the free passage of the public

along a highway by land or water. A private individual has a right of action in respect of a public nuisance if he can prove that he has sustained particular damage other than beyond the general inconvenience and injury suffered by the public, and that the particular damage which he has sustained is direct and substantial. Every person is entitled in law to make reasonable use of highways for the purpose of passing and re passing. The use of a highway for any other purpose, such as standing or sitting on, or placing objects, or playing games on, may well amount to a public nuisance if such use is unreasonable. In an action in public nuisance, once the nuisance is proved and the defendant is shown to have caused it, the legal burden shifts to the defendant to justify or excuse himself. If he fails to do so he will be liable. See Clerk & Lindsell on Torts 20th Edition at paras 21-121; DK Srivastava & AD Tennekone on The Lord of Tort in Hong Kong 3rd Ed paras 22.74, 22.85.

17. In Leung Tsang Hung & Another v The incorporated Owners of Kwok Wing House [2007] 10 HKCFAR 480 at para 12, Ribeiro PJ dealt with the offence of public nuisance. In gist his Lordship said that public nuisance is a common law offence, that it is actionable as a tort by an individual who has been caused particular damage over and above the damage suffered by the public at large. His Lordship identified three elements which constituted the tort of public nuisance :

(1) A state of affairs which endangers the lives, safety, health, property or comfort of the public, or obstructs the public in the exercise or enjoyment of any right that is common to members of the public.

(2) An act or omission committed by the defendants that is causative of particular injury to a member of the public. The injury caused to the plaintiffs must be of a foreseeable type.

(3) The defendants knew or ought to reasonably to have known that his act or omission would result in the likely consequence of a nuisance hazard presenting a real risk of harm to the public.

18. On the evidence before me, I agree with Mr Mok's submissions that a state of affairs has arisen which endangers the comfort and convenience of the property as well as obstructs the public in the exercise of enjoyment of their right to use the areas in question as a two way carriageway for normal vehicular traffic.

19. I also accept his submission that the act of occupying the areas concerned and the erecting of barriers and of obstructions thereat are causative of the blockage of a major road in Kowloon causing serious traffic congestion. That obstruction, in conjunction with the occupation of other major roads on Hong Kong Island side, has substantially deterred potential customers, including tourists, from using taxis as a means of transportation both in Kowloon and Hong Kong Island thereby resulting in substantial loss of taxi drivers and taxi managers. That type of injury is clearly foreseeable.

20. The barriers and other obstruction in the areas concerned has the obvious effect of preventing and obstructing the public, including taxi drivers, from using the occupied areas and such barriers and other

obstruction might even be hazardous to the public, particularly when it is necessary for emergency vehicles to us the occupy areas to reach those requiring their assistance. I accept Mr Mok's submissions that it is within the occupiers knowledge that the acts would result in the likely consequence of a nuisance hazard presenting a real risk of harm to the public.

21. Turning to Mr Wong's clients, I also accept his submissions that the Chiu Luen should be entitled to free passage of the public along the area concerned so that the public light buses in question could make use of the way as part of the route in providing public transportation service to the public. The defendants have created a public nuisance by obstructing and hindering the vehicular movement of the area concerned.

22. I also accept counsel's submissions that in both cases the activities involved give rise to a host of criminal offences under the Public Order Ordinance and the Summary Offences Ordinance.

C2. Adequacy of damages

23. I next consider whether or not damages are a sufficient remedy. I agree with counsel's submissions that damages in the cases before us are not adequate. Injunction is the proper and effective remedy available to the plaintiffs.

C3. Balance of Convenience

24. I now come to the question of balance of convenience. I take into account a number of factors.

C3.1 Balancing the public interest involved

25. The right to use public highway in a lawful and reasonable manner for legitimate purposes is a right commonly enjoyed by all members of the public. No one can possibly claim a monopoly of using the public highway in total disregard of the interests of his fellow citizens, no matter how honourable or noble his cause may be. That is so even if the right to demonstration or assembly as guaranteed by the Basic Law is engaged. It is a question of balancing the competing interests and considering what is reasonable in the overall circumstances of the case.

26. I derive support for that proposition from the judgment of the Court of Final Appeal in Yeung May Wan v HKSAR [2005] 8 HKCFAR 137. The majority of the Court of Final Appeal in that case had this to say :

"42. It is clear that a person who creates an obstruction cannot be said to be acting without lawful excuse if his conduct involves a reasonable use of the highway or public place. The suggestion in some of the earlier reported cases that the public's right to use the highway is limited to the right of passage and repassage and acts incidental or ancillary thereto, is too narrow. It is now established that '...the public have the right to use the public highway for such reasonable and usual activities as are consistent with the general public's primary right to use the highway for purposes of passage and repassage.'

43. Many examples of obstructions which may nevertheless constitute reasonable use of the highway can be found in the two cases..."

And examples are given by the Court of Final Appeal and they went on to say at p157B-D :

"43. ...It seeks to strike a balance between possibly conflicting interests of different users of the highway based on a requirement of reasonableness. Whether any particular instance of obstruction goes beyond what is reasonable is a question of fact and degree depending on all the circumstances, including its extent and duration, the time and place where it occurs and the purpose for which it is done.

44. Where the obstruction in question results from a peaceful demonstration..."

And I stress "peaceful demonstration" :

"44. ...a constitutionally protected right is introduced into the equation. In such cases, it is essential that the protection given by the Basic Law to that right is recognized and given substantial weight when assessing the reasonableness of the obstruction. While the interests of those exercising their right of passage along the highway obviously remain important, and while exercise of the right to demonstrate must not cause an obstruction exceeding the bounds of what is reasonable in the circumstances, such bounds must not be so narrowly defined as to devalue, or unduly impair the ability to exercise, the constitutional right."

In short, a balancing exercise has to be carried out to balance on the one hand the general public's right to use the highway and on the other those who are exercising their right to demonstration or assembly on the highway.

27. Having evaluated the overall circumstances, I think the balance tilts in favor of granting the interim injunction so that the rights enjoyed by the plaintiffs to use the areas occupied can be restored.

C3.2 Possibility that the court order might not be obeyed

28. I next consider the possibility that the court order might not be obeyed. This is a point raised by Mr Mok in the course of his submissions. He drew my attention to the relevant cases in England. One is the English Supreme Court's decision in Secretary of State for the Environment, Food and Rural Affairs v Meier [2009] 1 WLR 2780 at para 17 where Lord Rogers cited South Bucks District Council v Porter [2003] 2 AC 558 :

"32. ...When granting an injunction the court does not contemplate that it will be disobeyed ... Apprehension that a party may disobey an order should not deter the court from making an order otherwise appropriate : there is not one law for the law-abiding and another for the lawless and truculent."

In a similar vein, Lord Neuberger said at paragraph 81 that :

"81. On the other hand, in the same paragraph of his opinion, Lord Bingham also said that '[a]pprehension that a party may disobey an order should not deter the court from making the order otherwise appropriate.' A court may consider it unlikely that it would make an order for sequestration or imprisonment, if an injunction it was being invited to grant were to be breached, but it may none the less properly decide to grant the injunction. Thus, the court may take the view that the defendants are more likely not to be trespass on the claimant's land if an injunction is granted, because of their respect for a court order, or because of their fear of the repercussions of breaching such an order. Or the court may think that an order of imprisonment for breach, while unlikely, would nonetheless be a real possibility, or it may think that a suspended order of imprisonment, in the event of a breach, may well be a deterrent...."

29. As indicated in the course of Mr Mok's submissions, it is the foundation of the rule of law in Hong Kong that a court order is to be obeyed. And I fully expect that that order that I am going to make will be obeyed, even if the defendants disagree with it. If they feel aggrieved by the order, they should come back to court so that the question whether they can continue with their occupation of the areas affected by their activities can be resolved in a peaceful and legal manner with the benefit of mature consideration of the law applicable to their rights and obligations on the one hand, and those of their fellow citizens affected by their activities on the other.

C3.3 Civil Disobedience

30. I next come to the question of civil disobedience because as I have said the "Occupy Central" Campaign is avowedly a form of civil disobedience. The nature of civil disobedience is explained by Lord Hoffmann in R v Jones [2007] 1 AC 136 as follows :

"89. My Lords, civil disobedience on conscientious grounds has a long and honourable history in this country..."

That is in England :

"89. ...People who break the law to affirm their belief in the injustice of a law or government action are sometimes vindicated by history...It is the mark of a civilised community that it can accommodate protests and demonstrations of this kind. But there are conventions which are generally accepted by the law breakers on one side and the law-enforcers on the other. The protesters behave with a sense of proportion and do not cause excessive damage or inconvenience. And they vouch the sincerity of their beliefs by accepting the penalties imposed by the law. The police and prosecutors, on the other hand, behave with restraint and the magistrates impose sentences which take the conscientious motives of the protesters into account...

90. These appeals... and similar cases concerned with controversial activities, such as animal experiments, fox hunting, genetically modified crops, nuclear weapons and the like, suggest the emergence of a

new phenomenon, namely litigation as the continuation of protest by other means. The protesters claim that their honestly held opinion of the legality or dangerous character of the activities in question justifies trespass, causing damage to property or the use of force. By this means they invite the court to adjudicate upon the merits of their opinion and provide themselves with a platform from which to address the media on the subject. They seek to cause expense and, if possible, embarrassment to the prosecution by exorbitant demands for disclosure such as happened in this case.

91. In Hutchinson v Newbury Magistrates' Court (2000) 122 ILR 499, where a protester sought to justify causing damage to a fence at Aldermaston on the ground that she was trying to halt the production of nuclear warheads, Buxton LJ said at p510 :

'[T]here was no immediate and instant need to act as Mrs Hutchinson acted, either [at] the time when she acted or at all : taking into account that there were other means available to her of pursuing the end sought, by drawing attention to the unlawfulness of the activities and if needs be taking legal action in respect of them. In those circumstances, self-help, particularly criminal self-help of the sort indulged in by Mrs Hutchinson, cannot be reasonable.'

92. I respectfully agree. The judge then went on to deal with Mrs Hutchinson's real motive, which ('on express instructions') her counsel had frankly avowed. It was to 'bring the issue of the lawfulness of the Government's policy before a court, preferable a Crown Court.' Buxton LJ said at p510 :

'[I]n terms of the reasonableness of Mrs Hutchinson's acts, this assertion on her part is further fatal to her cause. I simply do not see how it can be reasonable to commit a crime in order to be able to pursue in the subsequent prosecution, arguments about the lawfulness or otherwise of the activities of the victim of that crime.'

93. My Lords, I do not think that it would be inconsistent with our traditional respect for conscientious civil disobedience for your Lordships to say that there will seldom if ever be any arguable legal basis upon which these forensic tactics can be deployed."

31. I am mindful of the fact that I am only dealing with the applications and the evidence before me on an ex parte basis, but on the materials before me when the demonstration in question based on civil disobedience have taken place for so long, in such a scale which has affected so many people and which has the real risk of turning into civil disorder, I do not think the fact that the demonstration is civil disobedience, no matter how noble the underlying cause the participants may consider it to be, can constitute a factor which militates against the granting of an injunction.

C3.4 Possible Defence

32. Finally I come to the question of possible defence. Mr Mok very fairly drew my attention to the possible defence that the defendants may wish to raise, that is, they are exercising their fundamental rights

to freedom of speech, assembly and demonstration as guaranteed under Article 27 of the Basic Law. He drew my attention to what the Court of Final Appeal has said in Yeung May Wan, supra, that is :

(1)   A person who created an obstruction in a public place is not acting without lawful excuse if his conduct involves a reasonable use of the public place; and

(2)   What is reasonable is a question of fact and degree depending on all the circumstances, including its extent and duration, the time and place where it occurs and the purpose for which it is done.

33.   I agree with Mr Mok's submissions that at least on the materials before me the defendant's conduct in the purported exercise to demonstrate has caused an obstruction which is far exceeding the bounds of what is reasonable in light of the length of the demonstration, the extent of the demonstration and the increasingly violent confrontations between the protesters and the police. I also accept his submission that on the evidence before the court the protesters' conduct is disproportionate and any reliance on the fundamental rights to freedom of assembly, demonstration, will unlikely succeed.

D.   CONCLUSION

34.   For the above reasons, subject to the actual wording of the order, I will grant the injunctive relief.

(Jeremy Poon)
Judge of the Court of First Instance
High Court

Mr Tim Wong, instructed by CMK Lawyers, for the plaintiff in HCA 2086/2014

Mr Johnny Mok SC, Mr Jose-Antonio Maurellet and Ms Eva Leung, instructed by Phyllis K Y Kwong & Associates, for the intended 1st and 2nd plaintiffs in HCA 2104/2014 (HCZZ 136/2014)

NOVEMBER 10

HCA 2086/2014

IN THE HIGH COURT OF THE HONG KONG SPECIAL ADMINISTRATIVE REGION
COURT OF FIRST INSTANCE
ACTION NO 2086 OF 2014

BETWEEN

CHIU LUEN PUBLIC LIGHT BUS COMPANY LIMITED (潮聯公共小型巴士有限公司)   Plaintiff

and

PERSONS UNLAWFULLY OCCUPYING OR REMAINING ON THE PUBLIC HIGHWAY NAMELY, THE WESTBOUND CARRIAGEWAY OF ARGYLE STREET BETWEEN THE JUNCTION OF TUNG CHOI STREET AND PORTLAND STREET AND/OR OTHER PERSONS HINDERING OR PREVENTING THE PASSING OR REPASSING OF ARGYLE STREET   1st Defendant

NG TING PONG (吳定邦)   2nd Defendant

FOK WAI PONG DOMINIC   3rd Defendant

CHEN RAYMOND   4th Defendant

HCA 2094/2014

IN THE HIGH COURT OF THE HONG KONG SPECIAL ADMINISTRATIVE REGION
COURT OF FIRST INSTANCE
ACTION NO 2094 OF 2014

_____

BETWEEN

GOLDON INVESTMENT LIMITED   Plaintiff

and

PERSONS WHO ERECTED OR PLACED OR   1st Defendant
MAINTAINED OBSTRUCTIONS OR OTHERWISE DO ANY ACT TO CAUSE
OBSTRUCTION, OR TO PREVENT OR HINDER THE CLEARANCE AND REMOVAL
OF THE OBSTRUCTIONS AT THE ENTRANCES OR EXITS OF CITIC TOWER,
1 TIM MEI AVENUE, CENTRAL, HONG KONG ("CITIC TOWER"),
AND/OR THE VEHICULAR/PEDESTRIAN
PASSAGEWAY AT TIM MEI AVENUE AND/OR LUNG WUI ROAD WHICH BLOCK
VEHICULAR OR PEDESTRIAN ACCESS TO CITIC TOWER

WONG YUEN CHING   2nd Defendant

_____

HCA 2104/2014

IN THE HIGH COURT OF THE HONG KONG SPECIAL ADMINISTRATIVE REGION
COURT OF FIRST INSTANCE
ACTION NO 2104 OF 2014

_____

BETWEEN

LAI HOI PING (黎海平)   1st Plaintiff

(suing on his own behalf and on the behalf of all other members of Hong Kong Taxi Association 香港計程車會)

TAM CHUN HUNG (譚駿雄)   2nd Plaintiff

(suing on his own behalf and on the behalf of all other members of Taxi Drivers and Operators Association 的士司機從業員總會)

and

PERSONS OCCUPYING PORTIONS OF   1st Defendant
NATHAN ROAD NEAR TO AND BETWEEN ARGYLE STREET AND DUNDAS STREET
TO PREVENT OR OBSTRUCT NORMAL VEHICULAR TRAFFIC FROM PASSING
AND REPASSING THE OCCUPIED AREAS

NG TING PONG (吳定邦)   2nd Defendant

FOK WAI PONG DOMINIC   3rd Defendant

CHEN RAYMOND   4th Defendant

Before: Hon Au J in Chambers (Open to the public)
Dates of Hearing: 24 and 27 October 2014
Date of Judgment: 10 November 2014

JUDGMENT

A.   INTRODUCTION

1.   In each these three actions, the plaintiffs obtained an ex parte injunction before Poon J on 20 October 2014 against the respective unnamed defendants. For convenience, I would call the action under

HCA 2094/2014 as the "CITIC Tower Action", under HCA 2086/2014 as the "Taxi Operators Action" and under HCA 2104/2014 the "Minibus Manager Action".

2. The injunctions obtained relate to what is now widely known as the Occupy Central Campaign ("OCC") in Hong Kong directed against the constitutional development of Hong Kong. Under the OCC, mass protestors and demonstrators have since late September occupied parts of a number of major roads on Hong Kong Island and Kowloon. The occupations have been "reinforced" by the protestors and demonstrators in placing and securing various barriers, barricades and objects on these parts of the roads and streets. The result is that vehicular traffic through these parts of the roads and streets has been effectively completely blocked.

3. The defendants in all these actions are the respective unidentified protestors and demonstrators who have occupied the relevant parts of the roads or streets that said to have affected the plaintiffs. In the CITIC Tower Action, the plaintiff (as the owner of CITIC Tower in Admiralty) brought the claim against the defendants on the bases of both private nuisance and public nuisance. In both the Taxi Operators Action and the Minibus Manager Action, the plaintiffs (who said they derive their incomes from the operations or related operations of respectively taxis and minibuses) premised their claims on public nuisance.

4. The ex parte injunction ("the CITIC Tower Injunction") obtained under the CITIC Tower Action is one which effectively restrains the 1st unnamed defendants from (a) obstructing or maintaining obstruction (whether by themselves or through placing objects thereat) at the entrances and exits of CITIC Tower and the vehicular and pedestrian passage at Tim Mei Avenue and Lung Wui Road which block vehicular or pedestrian access to CITIC Tower, and (b) preventing the plaintiff from clearing and removing the obstructions and obstacles presently placed thereat obstructing the said CITIC Tower's entrances and exits, as well as vehicular and pedestrian exits.

5. The ex part injunction obtained under the Taxi Operators Action is effectively to restrain the defendants (either by themselves or by placing objects thereat) from (a) occupying portions of the Nathan Road near and between Argyle Street and Dundas Street ("the Blocked Area") to prevent or obstruct vehicular traffic from passing and re-passing the Blocked Area, and (b) preventing the plaintiffs from removing any such obstructions from the Blocked Area.

6. The ex parte injunction obtained under the Minibus Manager Action is to restrain the defendants (either by themselves or by placing objects thereat) from (a) occupying portion of the westbound carriageway of Argyle Street between the injunction of Tung Choi Street and Portland Street ("the Blocked Way") to prevent or obstruct vehicular traffic from passing and re-passing the Blocked Way, and (b) preventing the plaintiffs from removing any such obstructions placed on or from the Blocked Way.

7. For convenience, I would call these two injunctions collectively the "Mongkok Injunctions" as both the Blocked Area and the Blocked Way are at one of the busiest areas in Mongkok.

8. Before me now are the respective plaintiffs' applications by way of inter partes summons to (a) continue these injunctions, and (b) ask for certain directions to facilitate the enforcement of the injunctions. The latter part of the applications is necessary, say the plaintiffs, as there has been en masse flouting and non-compliance of the ex parte injunctions by the defendants after they have been granted. I would of course return to this when I have to deal with this part of the applications.

9. These applications are opposed at the hearing:

(1) Under the Taxi Operators Action and the Minibus Manager Action, Mr Ng Ting Pong (after obtaining legal aid) and Mr Dominic Fok have appeared (after joined as the 2nd and 3rd defendants respectively) to oppose the continuation of the Mongkok Injunctions. They are respectively represented by Mr Dykes SC (leading Ms Christine Yu) and Ms Gladys Li SC (leading Ms Margaret Ng and Mr Michael Yin). Mr Raymond Chen (as the 3rd defendant) also appeared at the first day of the hearing and asked to be joined as a named defendant to oppose the plaintiffs' applications.

(2) Under the CITIC Tower Action, Ms Wong Yuen Ching has appeared (again after obtaining legal aid) and been joined as the 2nd defendant to oppose the continuation of the CITIC Tower Injunction. She is represented by Mr Manzoni SC (leading Mr Earl Deng).

10. Before I deal with specifically the arguments raised by the parties in these applications, it is important to point out that, in all the three actions, all the opposing defendants have fairly and rightly accepted that the occupations of the concerned areas amount to public nuisance, and none of them argue that a court order (even an ex parte one) need not or should not be complied with.

11. Further, as emphasised by Poon J in his judgment for the ex parte CITIC Tower Injunction, the court as an independent institution in determining the present applications is only and strictly to apply the law and to uphold the rule of law. The political views or considerations behind the OCC are entirely irrelevant to the determination.

B. WHETHER THE INJUNCTIONS SHOULD BE CONTINUED

B1. The applicable principles on the grant of an interlocutory injunction

12. The legal principles governing the grant of an interlocutory injunction are well established and not in dispute. As succinctly and helpfully summarised by G Lam J in Turbo Top Ltd v Lee Cheuk Yan [2013] 3 HKLRD 41 at paragraph 14, the court has to see (a) whether there are serious issues to be tried, (b) whether damages would be an adequate remedy for either side, and if damages would not be adequate for both parties, (c) where the balance of convenience lies in terms of whether or not to grant an interim

injunction pending the trial of the matter. In that balancing exercise, the court must take into account the interests of the general public even though they are not represented before the court.

13. Given that the issues raised in whether the Mongkok Injunctions should be continued are the same, I would first deal with them together before I look at the issues raised in the CITIC Tower Action.

B2. The Mongkok Injunctions

B2.1 Serious issues to be tried – Do the plaintiffs have a proper cause of action

14. As I mentioned above, the plaintiffs for the Mongkok Injunctions brought their claims in public nuisance. As I have also said above, none of the opposing defendants contends that the occupation of the Blocked Area and the Blocked Way do not amount to public nuisance in law. This must be right, as it is well established that the blocking of highway for an unreasonably period of time and extent, which significantly affects and interferes the public's right to use them (as in the present case) amounts to public nuisance. See: Clerk & Lindsell on Torts (20th ed), at paragraphs 21-121; Leung Tsang Hung v The Incorporated Owners of Kwok Wing House [2007] 10 HKCFAR 480 at paragraph 12 per Ribeiro PJ.

15. The principal contentions raised by the 2nd and 3rd defendants under this question have been premised on a number of bases, which I would look at in turn now.

B2.1.1 Do the plaintiffs suffer particular, substantial and direct damage because of the public nuisance

16. It is well established that, as public nuisance results in infringing the general public's rights, generally only (in the case of Hong Kong) the Secretary for Justice ("SJ") can bring a claim in public nuisance for and on behalf of the general public (who has suffered the inconvenience generally by reason of the public nuisance). For a private individual (without joining the SJ in a relator action) to bring a claim in public nuisance, the law requires that he must show that he has suffered a "particular, direct and substantial" injury above and beyond what is suffered by the rest of the public at large: Benjamin v Storr (1874) LR 9 CP 400 at 406-406 per Brett J.

17. In light of this requirement, the fundamental and primary contentions raised by Mr Dykes and Ms Li is that in the present case, the damage said to be suffered by the plaintiffs in both actions do not and cannot be regarded as "particular, substantial and direct" injury to enable them to bring a private claim in public nuisance. As such, the plaintiffs' cause of action is clearly defective without also jointing the SJ as a plaintiff. The claim for an interlocutory injunction must therefore fail.

18. Before I deal with the defendants' arguments in detail, it is convenient to first look at some case law relevant to the question of "particular, substantial and direct" damage in public nuisance.

19. Whether a damage or loss said to be suffered by the plaintiff can be regarded as particular, substantial and direct is essentially a question of fact, and a matter of degree and extent: Jan de Nul v Royale Belge [2000] 2 LLR 700 at paragraph 44 (p 715).

20. In this respect, it is also pertinent to note that it has also been well established that:

(1) The "particular" damage needs not be pecuniary (and thus special) in nature. It may consist of proved general damage, such as inconvenience and delay provided that it is substantial, that it is direct and non-consequential, and that it is appreciably greater in degree than any suffered by the general public: Walsh v Ervin [1952] VLR361 at 371 per Scholl J.

(2) "Substantial" means no more than that the damage suffered is more than trivial: Jan de Nul, supra, at paragraph 44.

(3) It is also not necessary prove that the plaintiff has any injury to property, or has any interest or relationship with any land or building: Benjamin v Storr, supra, at 406; Leung Tsang Hung, supra, at paragraph 13.

21. Further, the authorities show that the requirement of "direct" damage is satisfied not only by one which is immediately caused by or flowed from the nuisance. It also covers those injuries and damage which are caused by or flowed from the nuisance through a chain of events, so long as those events can be regarded as probable events as a result of the nuisance and the chain is not broken by external matters unrelated to the nuisance. It is a question of fact in each case as to whether the damage claimed to be suffered fall within the requisite chain of events. See: Overseas Tankship (UK) Ltd v Miller Steamship Co Pty (Wagon No 2) [1967] 1 AC 617, at 634E-636D per Lord Reid; Gravesham v British Railways Board [1978] 1 Ch 379 at 396F-397C and 398H-399B.

22. I now turn to look at what the plaintiffs say they have suffered as damage and loss in the present case.

23. In the Taxi Operators Action:

(1) The 1st plaintiff (Mr Lai) sues on his own behalf and on behalf of all the other members of Hong Kong Taxi Association (香港計程車會) ("HKTA"). The 2nd plaintiff (Mr Tam) sues also on his own behalf and on behalf of the Taxi Drivers and Operators Association (的士司機從業員總會) ("TDOA").

(2) The core function of the HKTA is to promote the welfare and rights of taxi trade in Hong Kong. There are about 400 members who are taxi owners, taxi owners who are also taxi drivers, or taxi drivers who do not own taxis. Some of these members (about 50 of them) also happen to be taxi managers.

(3) Mr Lai is the Chairman of the HKTA and an owner and taxi driver. He is also a taxi manager himself who manages 30 taxis.

(4) TDOA has about 10,900 members who are taxi drivers. Mr Tam is a member of TDOA (and thus apparently a taxi driver) and occupies the post of committee member.

24. The plaintiffs' evidence of the loss and damage said to be suffered by reason of the public nuisance is essentially this:

(1) Because of the blocking of the Blocked Area, it has led to general traffic blockages and serious road congestions in Kowloon. As a result, a lot of passengers (including tourists) no longer use taxis as their preferred means of transportation. This results in loss of business and income for taxi drivers. By way of example, the average income of a taxi driver has dropped from some $23,800 to about $17,800 per taxi. This also impacts on the income of taxi owners and managers, as the taxi drivers are only willing to pay less as rental for taxis to operate or even not to rent a taxi at all for some days. Not only therefore is that the daily rental of taxi has gone down by $100 per session for the owners (and thus reducing their income), the income of taxi managers has also been reduced as if the taxis are not rented out, a taxi manager would not receive his daily management fee and would have to pay for the idled taxi's parking cost.

(2) Mr Lai personally (suing in his own capacity) as a taxi manager, taxi owner and a driver thus has suffered and would continue to suffer those types of losses. The HKTA members (sued by Mr Lai on their behalf) have suffered and would continue to (if the obstructions of the Blocked Area continues) suffer those types of losses respectively as an owner, owner driver or solely a driver.

(3) Mr Tam personally (suing in his own capacity) as a driver and the TDOA members (who are taxi drivers) (sued by Mr Tam on their behalf) have suffered and would continue to suffer losses in the form of decrease in daily income.

25. In the Minibus Manager Action, the plaintiff is a minibus manager. Its business is to organise, manage and provide commute routes of public light buses (minibuses) for the purposes of public transportation. It is the plaintiff's case that it receives a monthly management fee of $1,000 from the owner of each minibus in return for organising, managing and providing commute routes of them.

26. At present, the plaintiff manages 6 different commute routes across Kowloon. One of them is the circular commute route ("the Olympic Station Route") from Kwun Tung to Olympic Station, which has 14 stops. This route generates the main and strongest source of revenue for the plaintiff. In fact, the other routes managed by the plaintiff are either less profitable or run at a loss.

27. The plaintiff's evidence on its loss and damage caused by the blocking of the Blocked Way is in gist as follows:

(1) Because of the Blocked Way, the minibuses of the Olympic Route have to skip 3 stops (of the 14 stops) from Argyle Street to Olympic Station, namely: the Ladies' Market (Tung Choi Street), Sin Tat Plaza stop, the Tai Kok Tsui Olympic Station, HSBC Public Light Bus Terminus stop and the Tai Kok Tsui, Fuk Tsun Street Olympic Station Public Light Bus Terminus stop.

(2) The skipped 3 stops are amongst the most popular stops for passengers. As a result of the skip, there have been less passengers taking the Olympic Station Route, resulting in reducing the daily trips of that route from 150 times to 100 times.

(3) The earnings of the drivers of that route have similarly therefore been reduced, which in turn results in the drivers reducing the amount of the daily rent they are prepared to pay the minibus owners from $1,000 to $800.

(4) Given the reduced earnings of the owners, which they say is caused by the plaintiff's failure to manage and organise the Olympic Route properly to include all the 14 stops, they have threatened not to pay the plaintiff the management fee unless the plaintiff is to take action by 21 October 2014.

(5) The plaintiff therefore is going to suffer loss in the management fees arising from managing the Olympic Station Route and damage to its long standing reputation as minibus manager as a result of the public nuisance if it continues. The financial impact on the plaintiff if it does lose the income from this route is dire and there is a real risk that it would be wound up eventually.

28. Mr Dykes and Ms Li both submit that the type and kind of loss and damage said to be suffered by these plaintiffs do not and could not amount to particular, substantial and direct damage caused by the Blocked Area or Blocked Way. In particular, counsel says the alleged losses suffered are not direct and immediate enough to bring them within the legal requirements. They are not, it is contended, immediately referable to the Blocked Area or Blocked Way specifically.

29. I am not persuaded by these arguments.

30. Applying the principles relating to "particular, substantial and direct" damage as I have summarised above, as far as I can see:

(1) Those claimed losses and damage are pecuniary in nature, and are clearly something beyond and above what the general public has suffered at large as inconvenience by reason of the nuisance. Thus, they must or at the least arguably come within the meaning of "particular" damage. See: Benjamin v Storr (1874) LR 9 CP 400 at 406-406 per Brett J; Clerk & Lindsell, paragraph 20-181 at p 1371; paragraph 19(1) above.

(2) Those losses and damage must or at least arguably also come within the meaning of "substantial", as they are more than trivial, or not fleeting or evanescent: Benjamin v Storr, at 407; Jan du Nul, supra, at paragraph 44.

31. Insofar as to whether they amount to "direct" damage, it is at least triable that they are as they are the result of a chain of probable events caused by or flowed from the nuisance. It is at least triable that :

(1) It is a probable result of the nuisance in blocking the Blocked Area and Street (which are by themselves under heavy use by vehicles) that there would be serious traffic congestions in other roads and streets in Kowloon generally;

(2) It is also a probable result of the nuisance that frequent or regular road users (including commercial vehicular users) of the Blocked Area and Street would have to divert their route;

(3) It is a probable result of the general traffic congestions and the need by the regular road users of the Blocked Area and Way to avoid them that there would be a serious interference on the business operations of those classes of road users whose businesses (and thus incomes) are dependent upon or related to the carriage of passengers on the roads generally and specifically through the Blocked Area and Way;

(4) It is also a probable result of (if not common sense that) the heavy general traffic congestions caused by the nuisance that at least some passengers would avoid taking public transportations on the roads (including taxis, minibuses and buses) because of the serious and heavy traffic congestions;

(5) It is thus also a probable result of these events that the businesses of these classes of road users (or at least some of them) would be adversely affected with loss of their incomes;

(6) The above chain of events is interlinked and unbroken.

32. In the premises, the plaintiffs have shown at least a triable issue that the types of damage and loss said to have been suffered by them are particular, substantial and direct damage to entitle them to bring the claim in public nuisance against the defendants.

33. I should also mention that it appears also to be Ms Li's contention that, given that this question concerns the locus of the plaintiffs to bring the claims, even for the purpose of deciding whether to continue the interlocutory injunction, the court should not determine it on the basis of whether there is a triable issue only.

34. I am not sure from where Ms Li has derived support for this contention as she has cited no authority in this regard. The principles governing the granting of an interlocutory injunction as summarised above are well established. Whether one calls the challenge based on locus or that the plaintiff lacks some of the necessary elements in constituting their proper cause of action, I see no reason why the same principles should not apply, which is whether the plaintiffs have shown a serious question (on the law or the facts) to be tried on their claims. I therefore do not accept Ms Li's submissions that under this question, it is not sufficient for the plaintiffs to only show a good arguable case.

35. Perhaps what Ms Li really means is this: even taking the plaintiffs' evidence on the type and nature damage they said to have suffered at the highest (thus assuming the evidence is established at trial), as a matter of law, they do not amount to the ones required to entitle them to bring privately a claim in public nuisance. The court should therefore be able to determine conclusively this question even at this stage.

36. On that basis assuming that the evidence before me has been all been proved, for the reasons I have explained above, I would accept that the plaintiffs have satisfied me that the type of damage they

said to have been suffered falls within the meaning of particular, substantial and direct damage, which gives them a good cause of action in public nuisance.

37. Alternatively, if Ms Li argues that my reading of the case law at paragraph 21 above is incorrect, then I would only say that this at least amount to a serious question of law that should be tried.

38. In the premises, I reject the 2nd and 3rd defendants' primary contentions that the plaintiffs' cause of action is defective.

B2.1.2 The plaintiffs in the Taxi Operators Action cannot properly bring a representative action

39. This ground is raised by Mr Dykes. Leading counsel submits that in order to bring a representative action (as Mr Lai and Mr Tam seek also to bring), it must be shown that all the represented persons must share the same or identical interest, and it is not sufficient to show like or similar interest. Mr Dykes therefore says a representative claim in the present case is clearly not permissible as each member of the HKTA and TDOA at the highest suffers or will suffer a different degree of damage and therefore does not share the same interest. He relies on the authority of Preston v Hilton [1920] 55DLR 647 at 653-654 (as followed in Turtle v Toronto [1924] 56 OLR 252 at paragraphs 4 and 57) to support his contentions.

40. This objection can be disposed of for the present purpose shortly:

(1) The decision in Preston was based on Moulton LJ's dicta in Markt & Co Ltd v Knight Steamship Co Ltd [1910] 2 KB 1023 at 1035-1039 (see Preston, at p 654). However, it is at least now arguable if not established that the law on this has since the judgment of Markt moved on, in that the rigid view as expressed by Moulton LJ in excluding a representative action where each of the represented members may have a different degree of interest in the matter is no longer applicable: Irish Shipping Ltd v Commercial Union [1991] 2 QB 206 (CA) at 224B- 227B per Staughton LJ. The rule in the right to bring a representative action is now regarded as a flexible tool of convenience to facilitate the administration of justice: John v Rees [1970] Ch 345 at 370E per Megarry J (as referred to Irish Shipping at 226F-E). The condition that there must be an "interest" shared by all members of the class in a representative action can be satisfied if every member of the class has a separate cause of action in tort: Prudential Assurance Co Ltd v Newman Industries Ltd [1981] Ch 229 at 254-255 per Vinelott J (as referred to in Irish Shipping at 225B-F). See also: Hong Kong White Book 2015, paragraph 15/12/2.

(2) In the present case, it is at least triable on the state of the evidence as to whether each and every member of the HKTA and the TDOA suffers the type of particular and direct loss (as described in the evidence) which would have entitled each of them to bring a separate claim in public nuisance against the defendants. If so, it must be for the benefit of this class and the administration of justice if all these separate claims could be dealt with together in a representative action.

(3)   In the premises, this cannot be a valid objection to the continuation of the interlocutory injunction on the basis that the plaintiffs' claim brought as representative action is not arguably maintainable.

(4)   Further, and in any event, even if (for the sake of argument) Mr Dykes is right in his submissions that Mr Tam and Mr Lai cannot bring the representative action, it must not be forgotten that they also bring the claims in their own respective right. These parts of the claims would not be affected by these submissions at all. If they could maintain their own personal claims, there is no reason why the interlocutory injunction should not be continued (if all the other conditions for continuing the injunction are also satisfied).

41.   I therefore also reject this ground as a basis to oppose the continuation of the Mongkok injunction in the Taxi Operators Action.

B2.1.3 Injunction should not be granted as a matter of principle

42.   Ms Li further argues that, as a matter of principle, an injunctive relief cannot be granted at the suit of a private individual to restrain a public wrong (unless the acts complained of amounts to invade some private rights belonging to him). She says it is so because public nuisance is about infringing the right of the public generally, and an application for an injunction to protect that right should only be made by the SJ for the benefit of the general public. She prays in aid of the authority of Gouriet v UPW [1978] AC 435 at 481 to support her submissions.

43.   With respect, I think there is nothing in this argument.

44.   Relevant for the present purposes, the facts in Gouriet are these: the Post Office Workers Union announced that they would call upon their members not to handle any mails from UK to South Africa to protest against the South African government's then apartheid policy. The threatened actions could well amount to an offence under the various provisions of the Post Office Act and the Telegraph Act. A private citizen (Mr Gouriet) brought a claim against the trade union in public nuisance, seeking an interlocutory injunction to restrain the union from carrying out the threatened acts. Mr Gouriet brought the action in his own name after the Attorney General had refused to bring a relator action at his invitation. The Court of Appeal by majority initially granted the injunction on an urgent basis. The defendants appealed to the House of Lords. The House of Lords allowed the defendants' appeal and concluded that no injunction should be granted as the plaintiff could not maintain a private claim in public nuisance.

45.   It is important to note that this case was decided on the pertinent fact that Mr Gouriet sought to bring a claim in public nuisance purportedly under the right as enjoyed by all members of the public to see that the law be obeyed and to prevent offences from being committed. He was not claiming that he had any special interest in the transmission of mails or messages to South Africa and was likely to suffer any special damage from the non-transmission. See: Gouriet, at p 476B-C.

46. It was, among others, in this context that Lord Wilberforce made the observations at pp 477E and 481F-H relied on by Ms Li as follows:

"A relator action – a type of action which has existed from the earliest times – is one in which the Attorney-General, on the relation of individuals (who may include local authorities or companies) brings an action to assert a public right. It can properly be said to be a fundamental principle of English law that private rights can be asserted by individuals, but that public rights can only be asserted by the Attorney-General as representing the public. In terms of constitutional law, the rights of the public are vested in the Crown, and the Attorney General enforces them as an officer of the Crown. And just as the Attorney-General has in general no power to interfere with the assertion of private rights, so in general no private person has the right of representing the public in the assertion of public rights. If he tries to do so his action can be struck out.

…

These and other examples which can be given show that this jurisdiction – though proved useful on occasions – is one of great delicacy and is one to be used with caution. Further, to apply to the court for an injunction at all against the threat of a criminal offence, may involve a decision of policy with which conflicting considerations may enter. Will the law best be served by preventive action? Will the grant of an injunction exacerbate the situation? (Very relevant this in industrial disputes.) Is the injunction likely to be effective or may it be futile? Will it be better to make it clear that the law will be enforced by prosecution and to appeal to the law-abiding instinct, negotiations, and moderate leadership, rather than provoke people along the road to martyrdom? All these matters – to which Devlin J justly drew attention in Attorney-General v Bastow [1957] 1 QB 514, 519, and the exceptional nature of this civil remedy, point the matter as one essentially for the Attorney General's preliminary discretion. Every known case, so far, has been so dealt with: in no case hitherto has it ever been suggested that an individual can act, though relator actions for public nuisance which may also involve a criminal offence, have been known for 200 years."

47. Under the law of public nuisance as I have discussed above, a private individual (such as Mr Gouriet) who has suffered no special damage above and beyond the one suffered by the general public at large of course cannot bring an action and then to obtain an interlocutory injunction. It is trite that under those circumstances that it is for the AG to bring an claim, and the AG has discretion to decide whether to do so or not, after taking into account of all relevant considerations (some of which as identified by Lord Wilberforce in the quoted passage above).

48. It can therefore be immediately seen that Gouriet is clearly distinguishable from, and thus not applicable to, the present case where a private individual who has shown to have suffered a special damage by reason of the public nuisance. The law has already established that he has a right to bring a private individual claim in public nuisance . There is no doubt that such a personal claim brought in public

nuisance could seek the relief of an interlocutory injunction. There are many instances where an interlocutory injunction was granted.

49. For these reasons, I would also reject any contentions that generally no injunction should be granted in a personal claim in public nuisance.

B2.1.4 Material non-disclosure

50. Mr Dykes also submits that the plaintiffs in these actions are guilty of material non-disclosure, and thus the ex parte injunctions should be set aside.

51. Mr Dykes' submissions in relation to the Taxi Operators Action are as follows.

52. First, counsel says Mr Lai's Affirmation only claims that at least 65% of the HKTA Members operate mainly on the Kowloon side. This, Mr Dykes submits, is not enough as the evidence should disclose what percentage of this 65% members travel across the Blocked Area, as this is the material figure relevant to the question of whether the plaintiffs have suffered particular and substantial damage. Without disclosing this material and relevant figure, the plaintiff is guilty of material non disclosure.

53. I do not agree. The plaintiff's case on particular and substantial and direct damage is advanced upon the basis that all the members suffer loss as a result of the general decrease in passengers by reason of the general traffic congestion over the roads in Kowloon and Hong Kong Island caused by the Blocked Area. It is therefore not material for them to show what percentage of the drivers pass the Blocked Area per se every day.

54. Second, Mr Dykes says Mr Lai's evidence is that the revenue of each taxi has been significantly reduced as a result of the serious road congestions in Kowloon and Hong Kong Island. Counsel submits it is unclear as to how the Blocked Area could have created all these matters since:

(1) As Mr Lai fairly accepted, traffic blockages and serious road congestion occurred in places far away from the Blocked Area, including Hong Kong Island. It must be obvious that such general description cannot prove what damage, if any, was caused specifically by occupation of the Blocked Area alone. The plaintiffs have not produced any evidence in this regard.

(2) There are allegations that rental of taxis and income of taxi drivers have dropped. Notwithstanding these are bare assertions, it is difficult to see how these allegations are caused by occupation of the Blocked Area alone.

(3) Even if it is assumed for the benefit of the plaintiffs that some taxi drivers have been reluctant to provide taxi services since the Occupy Central movement, it is difficult to see the necessary connection between this and occupation of the Blocked Area.

55. Properly understood, Mr Dykes' above submissions relate to how he analyses and disagrees with Mr Lai's evidence in supporting the plaintiffs' case. It has nothing to do with material non-disclosure.

56. I therefore reject Mr Dykes' arguments that the plaintiffs in the Taxi Operators Action are guilty of material non-disclosure.

57. Mr Dykes' submissions on material non-disclosure in the Minibus Manager Action are as follows.

58. First, he says it is misleading for the plaintiff in the Minibus Action to say at length in Mr Lam's affirmation that (a) the Olympic Station Route is the most profitable route and that the other routes are either not as profitable or even making a loss, and (b) the income of the drivers of minibus of the Olympic Station Route has dropped significantly after the occupation of the Blocked Way. This is so since it is Mr Lam's own evidence that the plaintiff receives a fixed monthly management fee of $1,000 from each minibus owner. This income is thus not dependent upon whether the Olympic Station Route is the most profitable of all the routes under the plaintiff's management and whether the income of the drivers has dropped. This evidence is thus introduced to confuse and mislead the court on the effect of the occupation on the plaintiff's financial position.

59. I do not accept that this amounts to material non-disclosure. As I explained above, properly looked at, Mr Lam's evidence is to the effect that because of the drop of the drivers' incomes under the Olympic Station Route as a result of the obstructions of the Blocked Way, they have paid the owners less for the rentals of the minibuses, and the owners then in turn threatened not to pay the plaintiff the management fees. Thus, this part of the evidence is to show that there is a real risk that the plaintiff would suffer serious financial loss (because firstly this route is the most profitable one of all the routes, and secondly that the owners' threat not pay the management fees is a genuine one). This in my view is relevant to the ex parte judge's determination as to whether the plaintiff will suffer a foreseeable loss as a result of the public nuisance. It is also pertinent to note that Mr Lam has in fact expressly and clearly stated in the evidence that the plaintiff receives a fixed monthly fee from each owner. There can be no misleading in the evidence in this respect.

60. Second, Mr Dykes submits that Mr Lam in his affirmation has not said that the plaintiff could not have arranged some of the minibuses to other routes so that the plaintiff can still enjoy the same monthly management fee. It is further submitted that in particular, the plaintiff has not disclosed whether it has rerouted some of the minibuses since the OCC. At the same time, Mr Ng (the 2nd defendant) has filed an affirmation to say that there are no regulatory route restrictions on red minibuses and thus they are free to change route. This amounts to (contended by Mr Dykes) again misleading material non-disclosure to create or exaggerate the situation about the minibus drivers' loss of income.

61. I am equally not convinced by these submissions. First, Mr Lam's affirmation has in fact dealt with the question of rerouting. It is his evidence that although it had considered rerouting the Olympic

Station Route so as to reach at least the end of the Olympic Station stop, this would have resulted in skipping the most popular Mongkok stop and also increased the average commute time by 15 minutes. This is therefore considered to be unworkable . There is no evidence to show what Mr Lam has said is clearly wrong. There is in my view no material non disclosure in this part of the evidence as submitted. Second, the submissions that Mr Lam has not said the minibuses in this route cannot be arranged to join the other routes is also a non-point, in light of the unchallenged evidence that the other routes are either not profitable or even running at a loss which means.

62. Third, Mr Dykes has sought to point out various doubts on Mr Lam's evidence of a signature campaign where various owners' drivers had signed to threaten not to pay the plaintiff's management fees .

63. I must say that even taking those doubts to the highest, Mr Dykes at best can only say that the document produced can be subject to vigorous challenge by way of cross-examination at trial. At this interlocutory stage, this court clearly cannot conclude that the document is not credible and cannot be relied upon. The mere fact that the document can be subject to challenge at trial itself cannot be a proper basis to say that there is material non-disclosure.

64. Finally, it is submitted that Mr Lam's evidence that that the plaintiff would not be able to pay the expenses for October 2014 and could be wound up imminently if the injunction is not granted given the threat of non-payment of the management fees is "a pack of lie or deliberate statement to mislead the court". Mr Dykes in his skeleton at paragraph 16(16) seeks to demonstrate this by providing a critical analysis of the statement of account produced by the plaintiff in support of its case. It is also said that Mr Lam seeks to "create an impression that [the plaintiff] only had a Bank of East Asia Account with a balance of HK$62,212.06" but it appears to have a Bank of China current and savings account as indicated in the statement of accounts.

65. Again, Mr Dykes' submissions taking to the highest only suggest that the plaintiff's case and evidence on the imminent adverse financial impact can be subject to serious challenge at trial. I do not think I can come to any conclusion at this interlocutory stage that this position is "a pack of lie" so as to "mislead the court". As to the existence of the other bank accounts, it is clear that these bank accounts and the balances thereof have been shown in the statement of accounts. The fact that no underlying bank statements have been adduced in my view per se cannot be said to be misleading the court, unless there is now clear evidence (and there is none) to say the figures represented are or cannot be correct. I therefore also reject the contention that there is material non disclosure on this basis.

66. I therefore do not accept that there is material non disclosure on the part of the plaintiff in the Minibus Action.

67. For all the above reasons, I would reject all the 2nd and 3rd defendants' contentions on why the injunction should not be continued on an inter partes basis.

B2.2 Balance of convenience - should the injunction be granted and continued?

68. After rejecting the defendants' above contentions, it is still necessary for me to consider whether I should continue the Mongkok Injunctions as sought on the question of balance of convenience.

69. In this respect, I would simply and respectfully agree and adopt Poon J's analyses as set out in his judgment at paragraphs 15 to 34 (as there are no material changes since then and no opposing defendants have raised any further arguments to say those analyses are inapplicable or inappropriate) and come to the clear view that in the present case the balance of convenience lies obviously in favour of granting and continuing the injunctions.

70. I would further add that, in case I were wrong in the above on the question of material non-disclosure, after setting aside the ex parte injunctions on that basis, I would still have re-granted them on an inter partes basis as I think the circumstances of the case justifies that given the above analyses.

71. I would therefore continue the Mongkok Injunctions in the terms as I have revised at the hearing on 26 October 2014 until trial or further order of the court.

72. I now proceed to consider the applications under the CITIC Tower Action.

B3. The CITIC Tower Injunction

B3.1 Background

73. The relevant background leading in this action is not in any controversy. Relevant for the present purposes, I would generally adopt what has been summarised in the plaintiff's skeleton as follows.

74. CITIC Tower is located at the intersection of Tim Mei Avenue and Lung Wui Road in Admiralty. The vehicular entrance of CITIC Tower which leads to the car parking floors in the building is located at Tim Mei Avenue. Vehicles can enter Tim Mei Avenue either from Lung Wui Road or Harcourt Road. The Emergency Vehicular Access ("EVA") to CITIC Tower is along the building perimeter abutting on Tim Mei Avenue.

75. CITIC Tower's car park comprises of 201 car parking spaces over eight levels. Further, there are loading and unloading bays for lorries and trucks on the lower ground floor level (LG Floor) of the car park. The only point of access to the car park of CITIC Tower and the loading and unloading bays for lorries and trucks is via the ingress and egress point of CITIC Tower at Tim Mei Avenue ("Car Park Entrance").

76. CITIC Tower has five fire exits. Staircase fire exit number 3 ("Fire Exist No 3") serves all floors from 29/F to the ground floor; and staircase fire exit number 4 ("Fire Exit No 4") serves 3/F to the ground floor.

77. The lot on which CITIC Tower is erected is held under Conditions of Sale which contain the Special Conditions that the Plaintiff would provide suitable means of access for the passage of Fire Services personnel and Fire Services appliances, to maintain such means of access, and to keep the same free from obstruction. Further, the plaintiff has a positive obligation to ensure the EVA is kept free from obstruction at all times.

78. From about 28 September 2014 onwards, Tim Mei Avenue and Lung Wui Road were completely obstructed by the 1st defendants, rendering it impossible for motor vehicles to ingress or egress CITIC Tower. The 1st defendants also blocked the EVA as well as Fire Exits No 3 and No 4. The blockages at Lung Wui Road near Performance Arts Avenue and Tim Mei Avenue Eastbound were removed by the Police in the morning of 13 October 2014. However, the blockages at Lung Wui Road and at the entrance of the run-in of the car park and the blockages at Fire Exit No 4 continue to this day. The blockages at Fire Exit No 3 were once removed at around 2:40 pm on 20 October 2014 by firemen . However, the blockage has been later reinstated by the 1st defendants by placing steel barriers across Fire Exit 3 .

79. The 1st defendants' blockage has therefore prevented access to Fire Exit Nos 3 and 4 and. This has exposed the occupants of CITIC Tower to a serious risk of safety as important escape routes have been denied to the occupants. The plaintiff is also exposed to huge potential liability at the suit of the occupants. On 14 October 2014, an elderly lady was trapped in stairway no 3 for about 45 minutes because of the obstruction at Fire Exit No 3. Fortunately, there was no fire or smoke at the time; but blockage of fire exists creates a serious fire hazard.

B3.2   The plaintiff's case on its loss and damage

80. The plaintiff's evidence shows that it would suffer loss and damage by reason of the blockages caused by the 1st defendants as follows.

81. A portion of the car park spaces in CITIC Tower are let on a monthly basis yielding an average of about HK$450,000 a month, while the remaining car park spaces are used for hourly parking, yielding an average of about HK$4,500 per day. The blockage of the Car Park Entrance results in continuous and substantial loss to the Plaintiff.

82. The plaintiff's rental income has from the shops and offices also been adversely affected, but it is much more difficult to quantify this loss. Existing tenants including those whose agreements are coming up for renewal have complained and have raised or are likely to raise demands for reduction in rent. The plaintiff has also faced difficulty in letting out space presently available for letting within the building .

83. As a result of the 1st defendants' blockage of the Car Park Entrance, the disposal of the waste of CITIC Tower has had to go through the office lobby, severely affecting its hygiene and environment. Since the unloading bays at the Car Park Entrance are inaccessible, this also affected utility and delivery vehicles from accessing CITIC Tower for regular repair and maintenance, such repair and maintenance including the effective removal of solid and liquid waste from the pipes and manholes of the property. This poses a health and safety risk to the occupants at CITIC Tower.

84. The increase in manpower necessary for managing CITIC Tower properly in light of the 1st defendants' actions also led to an increase in its operation costs.

85. In summary, the blockages have significantly interfered the plaintiff's use of CITIC Tower. In particular they have completely prevented the Car Park (which offers hourly and monthly parking) from being used and caused and would continue to cause the plaintiff loss in the form of rental income. They have also caused serious potential hazards (in case of fire and any other emergencies) to the people working in and visiting the offices and retail premises within CITIC Tower as the EVA and Fire Exit Nos 3 and 4 are blocked, resulting in exposing the plaintiff to potential and significant liability at the suit of the occupants which may not be covered by insurance.

B3.3 The plaintiff's failed efforts to seek to remove the blockages

86. CITIC Tower is managed by CITIC Tower Property Management Company Limited ("PMC"). Personnel of the plaintiff, PMC and the Building Management Office of CITIC Tower had since 28 September 2014 attempted to negotiate with the 1st defendants, but the 1st defendants had refused to cooperate.

87. PMC also wrote to Kong Wan Fire Station on 11 October 2014 and to Central Police Station on 15 October 2014 to seek the professional assistance of the Fire Services Department and the Police. It would appear that there was little either could do as:

(1) Even though on 11 October 2014 firemen came to CITIC Tower, they said that they could only refer the case to the Police;

(2) PMC had not yet received a response from the Police.

88. The unchallenged evidence also shows that both before obtaining and even after the CITIC Tower Injunction was granted, the plaintiff has attempted a number of times without any success to remove any of the obstacles blocking the above vehicular access to and exits from CITIC Tower, as these attempts had been obstructed by the unidentified defendants. The evidence shows further that, even if the plaintiff managed at times to remove some of the barriers or obstructions, further and even more secured obstructions or barriers would be quickly reinstated by the 1st defendants to maintain the blockages.

B3.4   The 2nd defendant

89.   The 2nd defendant, Ms Wong, is a student of the Institute of Education. She does not claim that she is one of those protestors or demonstrators who have placed, maintained or sought to maintain the blockages near CITIC Tower as described above.

90.   However, since 28 September, she says she has been attending lectures held on Tamar Park as part of the student boycott programme organised by the Federation of Students. Because of the location of Tamar Park, she has to "traverse on Tim Mei Avenue to walk to there from time to time". It is because of that that she asked to be joined in these proceedings to seek to set aside the ex parte injunction (and presumably the continuation of it), as she believes that the inclusion in the descriptions of the 1st defendant and the term of the injunction reference to persons who have "otherwise done any act to cause obstruction" is too wide. This, she complains, would have caught someone like her, who may have only been physically present at the protest site on Tim Mei Avenue from time to time .

91.   She therefore asks the injunction to be set aside or alternatively revised to narrow its scope.

B3.5   Whether the CITIC Tower Injunction should be continued

92.   I now look at whether the injunction should be continued by applying the relevant principles. In this respect, it is important to note that none of the 1st unnamed defendants appears at the hearing to oppose the application, while the 2nd defendant as mentioned above only opposes the injunction on the grounds that the descriptions of the 1st defendants and the scope of the injunction as granted are too wide. I would deal with these objections later, after considering the general principles.

B3.5.1   Serious issues to be tried

93.   The plaintiff's present claim is made in public nuisance and private nuisance.

94.   With the above uncontroversial evidence of the blockages and their effect on CITIC Tower, it is clear that the plaintiff's has a good cause of action in bringing a claim:

(1)   In public nuisance: The obstructions of the roads amount to public nuisance, and the evidence summarised above shows that the plaintiff as a private individual has suffered and would continue to suffer a particular, substantial and direct damage caused by the nuisance. See also paragraphs 19-21 above.

(2)   In private nuisance: The owner of the property adjoining the highway has a common law right of access to the highway which is a private right remediable by an action of private nuisance. See: Marshall v Blackpool Corp [1935] A C 16 at 22 per Lord Atkin; Winfield & Jolowicz, 19th ed, paragraph 15-076; Clerk and Lindsell on Torts, 20th ed, paragraph 20-180.

95.   As I said above, no one is raising any arguments otherwise.

96.   The plaintiff has therefore clearly shown a serious issue to be tried.

B3.5.2 Damages adequate remedy and balance of convenience

97. Damages are unlikely to be a sufficient remedy for the plaintiff as (a) there is nothing to show that the unnamed defendants are in a position to compensate the plaintiff's financial loss, and (b) in any event, damages would not be an adequate remedy for the continuing health and safety hazard posed by the blockages of EVAs, Fire Exits and indirectly by the failure of the plaintiff to carry out necessary repair and maintenance work to pipes and manholes.

98. At the same time, it is unclear what damage the defendants would suffer if the interim injunction is later shown to be wrongly granted. There is no suggestion that the defendants' freedom of expression could not exercised without causing the nuisance in the way as interfering the plaintiff's use of its property.

99. On this basis alone, the injunction should thus be continued.

100. For the sake of argument, even if I have to consider the question of balance of convenience, similarly adopting what Poon J has said in the Taxi Operators Action and the Minibus Manager Action on the question of balance of convenience (as I have adopted at paragraph 69 above), this is a clear case where the balance of convenience weighs in favour of continuing the CITIC Tower Injunction.

101. Thus, subject to further considering the objections now raised by the 2nd defendant (which I would next proceed to), I will continue the CITIC Tower Injunction.

B3.5.3 The 2nd defendant's contentions

102. Mr Manzoni SC for the 2nd defendant raises essentially the following arguments.

103. First, Mr Manzoni submits that the plaintiff should not have proceeded to apply for the injunction on an ex parte basis on 20 October, as there was no material urgency (given that the blockages had been there for weeks) or secrecy to justify it. On that basis alone, says Mr Manzoni, the ex parte injunction should be set aside.

104. Mr Benjamin Yu SC for the plaintiff submits that, the concern of the growing health and safety hazards caused by the blockages, in particular after the plaintiff's failed efforts to negotiate with the protestors and to enlist the assistance of the Fire Services Department and Police to remove some of the blockages, justifies the urgency to make the application on an ex parte basis. Leading counsel also says that the plaintiff was not guilty of any delay as:

(1) The plaintiff had not been sitting on its hands. It had communicated with the 1st defendants repeatedly to try to persuade them to clear or to permit the plaintiff to clear the blockages, and had sought assistance from the Police and Fire Department with no success.

(2) The plaintiff was forced to take legal recourse when it became clear that no other way was available and that the defendants were likely to maintain the indefinite blockages of access to CITIC Tower.

105. I agree with Mr Yu's submissions. In my view, when it comes to the risks of personal safety (as the Fire Exits, EVAs and all the vehicular access to CITIC Tower have been unquestionably blocked) and no one can say or predict when an emergency (such as the breaking out of a fire or someone suffering from an urgent medical condition) may occur, there is justification for urgency for the plaintiff to apply for the injunction on an ex parte basis.

106. In any event, even if I were to set aside the ex parte injunction on the basis as submitted by Mr Manzoni, I would have no hesitation to re grant it on an inter partes basis for the reasons I have set out above.

107. Second, Mr Manzoni argues that the descriptions of the unnamed 1st defendants and the terms of the injunction in including the words "or otherwise done any act to cause obstruction" of the vehicular or pedestrian passage at Tim Mei Avenue or Lung Wui Road which block vehicular or pedestrian access to CITIC Tower are simply too wide. He submits that the descriptions would have caught innocent people, such as the 2nd defendant, who may be doing an entirely lawful act, such as simply crossing Tim Mei Avenue or Lung Wui Road (in particular when at the moment the other nearby pedestrian pathways may have been blocked), or happens also to stop by on the road to talk to someone or pick up something. This is so as the 2nd defendant's said lawful acts of crossing the roads would be caught by the words "to cause obstruction" of Tim Mei Avenue or Lung Wui Road simply by being physically present on the road.

108. With respect, I am unable to accept Mr Manzoni's submissions. The descriptions must be read with common sense and in context. The relevant parts of the descriptions and the terms of the injunction are to restrain the obstructions of Tim Mei Avenue and Lung Wui Road which would prevent vehicular and pedestrian access to CITIC Tower. Those words are clearly and objectively meant to cover only those acts where a person is blocking the vehicular access to and from CITIC Tower through Tim Mei Avenue and Lung Wui Road for such time and extent that is objectively unreasonable. The words could not have objectively understood to include any acts which would only cause a brief period of obstruction of the concerned vehicular and pedestrian access. Thus, the acts of crossing those roads, even with a stopping by to chat or picking up something, clearly and objectively cannot be caught by these words. Any reasonable persons in such circumstances would have moved away or given way to allow vehicular passage to enter into or leave CITIC Tower.

109. Third, Mr Manzoni submits that the terms of the injunction by reference to the entire Tim Avenue and Lung Wui Road are also too wide for an interlocutory injunction, which is granted on the basis of the existence of triable issues on the plaintiff's claim. He submits that, in the circumstances as the present case, in particular where the SJ has not acted to bring a claim for injunction in public nuisance, the court

should strike a balance and only grant an injunction on terms which are least intrusive of effecting interference of the defendants' right: The Mayor Commonality and Citizens of London v Tammy Samede 2012] EWCA (Civ) at paragraph 51.

110. Mr Manzoni however fairly accepts that, under this argument, it is for the 2nd defendant to persuade the court that there is another less intrusive term of the order that (a) would achieve similar effect provided under the original order, and (b) is workable in practice. See Samede, supra, at paragraph 53.

111. Mr Manzoni has provided two alternatives of the scope of the injunction which he says is less intrusive than the original terms of the injunction but would be sufficient to enable the objective of the injunction to allow vehicular access to CITIC Tower. Instead of requiring the clearance of the entire Tim Mei Avenue and the Lung Wui Road as provided under the original terms, these two alternatives effectively provides clearance of part of the south bound lanes (instead of both the south bound and north bound lanes) of Tim Mei Avenue and part of the west bound lane (instead of the entire west bound and east bound lanes) of Lung Wui Road. The two alternatives only differ in whether to include the relevant pedestrian walkway along Lung Wui Road in the injunction as well.

112. Counsel however accepts that for any of these two alternatives to work, it would require the police's coordination to implement a traffic control of a two-way traffic operation over the south bound lane of Tim Mei Avenue and the west bound lane of Lung Wui Road (which are originally under one-way traffic) so that vehicles can come and go along these lanes.

113. I am unable to accept these alternatives as the 2nd defendant has not shown that they are workable in practice. In both alternatives, before having any evidence to say whether it is feasible for the police to implement the two-way traffic operation as verbally suggested by Mr Manzoni at the hearing, the court cannot simply assume that it can and would be done. The court is not in a position to know whether there are any practical or otherwise difficulties in implementing the suggestions.

114. In the premises, I am not persuaded by any of the 2nd defendant's above arguments to say why the injunction should not be continued or that the descriptions of the unnamed defendants and the terms of the injunction should be revised and narrowed.

B3.5.4 Conclusion on the continuation of the CITIC Tower Injunction

115. For all the above reasons, I would continue the CITIC Tower Injunction until trial or further order of the court.

C. DIRECTIONS ON ENFORCEMENT

116. The unchallenged evidence shows that, since the granting of the ex parte injunctions in all three actions by Poon J:

(1) The unnamed defendants en masse (and many of them wearing masks) have refused to comply with (and also in continuing breach of) the court orders by continuing to maintain (and in fact reinforce) the obstructions on the Blocked Area, the Blocked Way and near CITIC Tower;

(2) The unnamed defendants en masse (any many of them wearing masks) have in breach of the court orders prevented the plaintiffs from removing those obstructions;

(3) In relation to the CITIC Tower Injunction, there were public figures who went to CITIC Tower where the blockages are and (in front of the defendants) openly said to the plaintiff's staff who were seeking to enforce the injunction that they should not do anything until the inter partes hearing, on the purported reason that the injunction was only granted on an ex parte basis.

117. In short, the plaintiffs have not been able to enforce the ex parte injunctions, and the unnamed defendants en masse have openly flouted and in continued breach of them.

118. The plaintiffs have therefore all asked this court to make the following directions to facilitate the enforcement of the court orders:

(1) The bailiff do take all reasonable and necessary steps to assist the plaintiff and its agents to effect clearance and removal of the relevant obstructions until further order;

(2) The bailiff be authorised and directed to request the assistance of the Police where necessary;

(3) Any Police officer be authorised to arrest and remove any person who the Police officer reasonably believes or suspects to be in contravention of this order provided that the person to be arrested has been informed of the gist of the terms of the court order and that his action is likely to constitute a breach of the order and that he may be arrested if he does not desist.

119. I would refer the first two directions as "the bailiff directions" and the last one "the police authorisation direction".

C1. The bailiff directions

120. There are no questions that the court could direct bailiffs to assist in the carrying out of court orders. Thus, none of the opposing defendants seek to raise any objections to the bailiff directions.

121. I have no hesitation in granting the bailiff directions in light of the circumstances of the present case as summarised above.

C2. The police authorisation direction

122. I now turn to look at the police authorisation direction.

123. Any person who obstructs the bailiff's performance of his duties would be in criminal contempt of the court:

(1) An intention and act to interfere with or impede the due administration of justice is a criminal contempt: Halsbury's Laws of England, Vol 22, paragraph 5.

(2) Thus, a person who, with knowledge of a court order, and deliberately impedes the bailiff in the due execution of his duties has both the requisite actus reus and mens rea of a criminal contempt as his conduct intentionally and deliberately interferes with or impedes the due administration of justice: AG v Times Newspapers [1992] 1 AC 191 at 208E F, 208H-209B, 216A-D; Dobson v Hastings [1992] Ch 393 at 402D-403D.

(3) It is therefore a criminal contempt to obstruct or impede a bailiff in the execution of his duties: Halsbury's Laws of England, Vol 22, paragraphs 17 and 49.

124. Criminal contempt is a common law offence punishable by imprisonment: Arlidge Eady & Smith on Contempt (4th ed), paragraph 3-67.

125. At the same time, Police are empowered under the Police Force Ordinance (Cap 232) to arrest a person suspected of being guilty of criminal contempt as:

(1) Under s 50(1)(a), it shall be lawful for any police officer to apprehend any person who he reasonably believes will be charged with or whom he reasonably suspects of being guilty of any offence for which a person, among others, may (on a first conviction for that offence) be sentenced for imprisonment;

(2) Under s 10(j), the duties of the police force shall include taking lawful measures for executing summonses, subpoenas, warrants, commitments and other process issued by the courts.

126. In the premises, a police officer is empowered in law to arrest any person who he reasonably believes or suspects of being guilty of criminal contempt (which is publishable by imprisonment on a first conviction) in obstructing or impeding the bailiff in executing his duties in enforcing a court order, such as the injunctions granted herein.

127. Thus, the police authorisation direction is only to re-state what the law has empowered the police to do.

128. The defendants in all three actions however oppose the making of the police authorization direction as sought. They raise the following in principle arguments.

129. First, Mr Dykes and Ms Li both submit that even though they are empowered to do so under the law, the police on the field have a discretion to decide whether or not to make any arrest after taking into account the actual circumstances and perhaps other relevant considerations on the ground. The court should not interfere or fetter such discretion so that the police on the ground can decide what is best to do according to the actual circumstances of the events.

130. This cannot be a valid in principle objection to make the police authorization direction. The term of the direction does not compel or direct the police to make an arrest. It only re-states the position of the

law that that the police are authorised to do so. The direction therefore does not take away or fetter in any way the police's discretion as submitted by Ms Li and Mr Dykes.

131. Second, Mr Manzoni argues that the court has no jurisdiction to make such a direction as it is prohibited from doing so by s 21A(1) of the High Court Ordinance (Cap 4).

132. S 21A provides relevantly as follows:

"(1) Subject to section 21B, a person shall not be arrested or imprisoned to enforce, secure or pursue a civil claim for the payment of money or damages except under an order of Court; and the Court shall have jurisdiction to make such an order for arrest or imprisonment only to enforce, secure or pursue a judgment for the payment of a specified sum of money.

….

(6) This section shall not affect any jurisdiction of the Court to make orders of committal in relation to –

    (a)   contempt of court; or

    (b)   disobedience of a judgment or order of the Court."

133. Mr Manzoni says s 21A(1) therefore provides that the court cannot make an order to effect an arrest in civil claims generally except for the enforcement, securing or pursuance of a judgment for payment of sum.

134. With respect, I do not agree. S 21(A)(1) on its own terms deals with only a civil claim for payment of damages or sum of money. It does not cover or apply to all civil claims generally, such as a claim for an injunction. Further, the police authorization direction relates to authorizing the police to arrest persons suspected for being guilty of a criminal contempt, which is clearly not intended to be covered by s 21(A)(1). In any event, the exceptions provided at s 21A(6) in my view makes this clear.

135. I therefore also reject this submission.

136. Finally, all the represented defendants submit that it is simply not necessary for the court to make such a direction, since if as a matter of law the police are already authorised to so, it is superfluous to include such a direction in the order.

137. However, I am of the firm view that it is necessary to include the direction in light of what have happened after the granting of the ex parte injunction orders. I will explain why.

138. Hong Kong has always adhered to the concept of rule of law. This concept is treasured and has always been jealously guarded by the general public. It is universally regarded that the rule of law is one of Hong Kong's most important foundations that has led to her being a civilised, safe and orderly society.

139. The concept of the rule of law must include and embrace the notion that every resident and the government alike should obey and comply with the law. As said by Hartmann J (as the learned NPJ then

was) in Secretary for Justice v Ocean Technology Ltd (t/a Citizens' Radio) [2010] 1 HKC 456 at paragraph 9, the concept of rule of law means that every resident of Hong Kong are governed by and bound to the operation of the law.

140. Under the rule of law, even if the defendants are of the view that a court order (including an ex parte order) is wrongly granted, instead of simply disobeying it, they should first comply with it but seek to challenge and argue against that order in court under due process and in accordance with the law. As said by Hoffmann LJ (as Lord Hoffmann then was) in Department of Transport v Lush (unreported, 29 July 1993) : "…the law cannot allow obedience of its orders to be a matter of individual choice even on grounds of conscience".

141. It is therefore wrong for any suggestions that the rule of law is not undermined or under challenged if people can freely or intentionally disobey the law first and then accept the consequences of breaking the law. The rule of law cannot realistically and effectively operate in a civilised and orderly society on this basis.

142. The upholding of the rule of law must therefore be built upon, among others, the due administration of justice for the enforcement of court orders and the law. This is also one of reasons why the independence of the Judiciary, and the respect for the dignity and authority of the court are fundamental tenets of the concept of the rule of law.

143. However, recent events relating to these actions have shown that there is a real risk that the due administration of justice and the respect for the authority of the court, and therefore the rule of law in Hong Kong, would be seriously undermined:

(1) As I have mentioned above, the ex parte injunctions, which are valid and proper court orders until set aside, have been openly disobeyed and flouted by the defendants en masse.

(2) Not only that, and worryingly, there have also been repeated open suggestions by a number of public figures (including some legally trained individuals) to the public and the protestors and demonstrators en masse to the effect that ex parte injunctions need not to be complied with until they had been determined after an inter partes hearing, and that there is no challenge to the rule of law from merely disobeying civil orders, and that the rule of law is only threatened when there is disobedience of an actual order of committal for contempt of court. As I have said above, these suggestions, with the greatest respect, are in my view wrong and incorrect and would cause the public and the defendants an unwarranted misunderstanding on the concept of the rule of law.

144. When the rule of law and the due administration of justice are at the risk of being seriously challenged and undermined, as it is now, the court must act and strive to protect and uphold them for the benefit and best interest of the general public.

145. The present circumstances therefore undoubtedly justify and call for the inclusion of the police authorisation direction in these injunction orders. The direction would send a clear message to the defendants that civil court orders should be obeyed and about the serious consequences for breaching them.

146. Further, in MacMillan v Simpson, supra, the court granted an interim injunction prohibiting the defendants (named and unnamed) from engaging in conducts interfering the plaintiff's logging operations at specified locations and barring members of the public from blocking a bridge. The court order also included a provision (similar to the police authorisation direction herein) that "any peace officer [which included police officer] be authorized to arrest and remove any person who the peace officer has reasonable and probable grounds to believe is contravening or has contravened the provisions of this order".

147. On appeal to the Supreme Court of Canada, the defendants challenged, among others, the appropriateness of the inclusion in the order a provision to authorize the police to arrest persons breaching the injunction. In dismissing the appeal and in particular this challenge, McLachlin J (as she then was) observed this at paragraph 41 (p 1069):

"···I observe only that the inclusion of police authorization appears to follow the Canadian practice of ensuring that orders which may affect members of the public clearly spell out the consequences of non-compliance. Members of public need not take the word of the police that the arrest and detention of violators is authorized because this is clearly set out in the order signed by the judge. Viewed thus, the inclusion does not harm and may make the order fairer." (emphasis added)

148. I respectfully adopt McLaughlin J's above observation.

149. As I have emphasised above, the public in general and the defendants in particular appear to be at the risk of misunderstanding the serious consequence (including the serious effect on the rule of law) of disobeying a civil court order. Given that misunderstanding and the en masse open and persistent disobedience of the ex parte orders, there is also the real likelihood that (a) the defendants (which are in large numbers) would continue to seek to disobey the injunction orders and obstruct the bailiffs in carrying out their duties to enforce those orders, and (b) the defendants may well (mistakenly and incorrectly) dispute the police's power to arrest them if they obstruct the due administration of justice in interfering or obstructing the bailiffs in carrying out their duties to enforce the injunctions.

150. In the premises, the police authorisation direction if included in the injunction orders would help to inform the en masse defendants the consequence of any disobedience and confirm the police's power. This would not only make the orders clearer and fairer, but also facilitate the due administration of justice.

151. I have therefore come to the clear conclusion that it is necessary to include the police authorisation direction in all the injunction orders. In light of the circumstances of the present case, I would however revise the direction to the following terms:

"Any police officer be authorised to arrest and remove any person who the police officer reasonably believes or suspects to be obstructing or interfering any bailiff in carrying out his or her duties in enforcing the terms of the injunction order herein, provided that the person to be arrested has been informed of the gist of the terms of this court order and that his action is likely to constitute a breach of the order and obstruction of the administration of justice, and that he may be arrested if he does not desist."

D. CONCLUSION

152. For all the above reasons, I will continue the Mongkok Injunctions (in the terms as I have revised on 27 Oct) and the CITIC Tower Injunction. I would also make the following directions in those orders:

(1) The bailiff do take all reasonable and necessary steps to assist the plaintiff and its agents to effect the clearance and removal of the obstructions [as provided in the respective injunction orders].

(2) The bailiff be authorised and directed to request the assistance of the Police where necessary.

(3) Any police officer be authorised to arrest and remove any person who the police officer reasonably believes or suspects to be obstructing or interfering any bailiff in carrying out his or her duties in enforcing the terms of the injunction order herein, provided that the person to be arrested has been informed of the gist of the terms of this court order and that his action is likely to constitute a breach of the order and obstruction of the administration of justice, and that he may be arrested if he does not desist.

(4) Any person so arrested by the police shall be brought before the court as soon as practicable for further directions.

153. Given that all the respective represented defendants have failed in their opposition to these applications, I further make an order nisi that they should pay the respective plaintiffs' costs of the respective applications, to be taxed if not agreed. There be certificate for two counsel for the plaintiffs in the Taxi Operators Action and the CITIC Tower Action. For the represented defendants who are under legal aid, their own costs be taxed in accordance with legal aid regulations.

154. Lastly, I thank counsel for their assistance.

(Thomas Au)
Judge of the Court of First Instance
High Court

Mr Tim Wong, instructed by CMK Lawyers, for the plaintiff in HCA 2086/2014

Mr Benjamin Yu SC, Mr Victor Dawes and Ms Bianca Yu, instructed by Mayer Brown JSM, for the plaintiff in HCA 2094/2014

Mr Johnny Mok SC, Mr Jose-Antonio Maurellet and Ms Eva Leung, instructed by Phyllis K Y Kwong & Associates, for the 1st and 2nd plaintiffs in HCA 2104/2014

Mr Philip Dykes SC and Ms Christine Yu, assigned by the Director of Legal Aid, instructed by JCC Cheung & Co, for the 2nd defendant in HCA 2086/2014 and HCA 2104/2014

Ms Gladys Li SC, Ms Margaret Ng and Mr Michael Yin, instructed by Daly & Associates, for the 3rd defendant in HCA 2086/2014 and HCA 2104/2014

Mr Charles Manzoni SC and Mr Earl Deng, assigned by the Director of Legal Aid, instructed by Vidler & Co, for the 2nd defendant in HCA 2094/2014

Raymond Chen, in person, present on 24 October 2014, absent on 27 October 2014

Mr Jin Pao, instructed by Department of Justice, for the Secretary of Justice (a non-party)

NOVEMBER 13

HCA 2086/2014

IN THE HIGH COURT OF THE HONG KONG SPECIAL ADMINISTRATIVE REGION
COURT OF FIRST INSTANCE
ACTION NO 2086 OF 2014

BETWEEN

CHIU LUEN PUBLIC LIGHT BUS   Plaintiff
COMPANY LIMITED (潮聯公共小型巴士有限公司)

and

PERSONS UNLAWFULLY OCCUPYING   1st Defendant
OR REMAINING ON THE PUBLIC HIGHWAY NAMELY, THE WESTBOUND
CARRIAGEWAY OF ARGYLE STREET BETWEEN THE JUNCTION OF TUNG
CHOI STREET AND PORTLAND STREET AND/OR OTHER PERSONS HINDERING
OR PREVENTING THE PASSING OR REPASSING OF ARGYLE STREET

       NG TING PONG (吳定邦)   2nd Defendant

       FOK WAI PONG DOMINIC   3rd Defendant

       CHEN RAYMOND   4th Defendant

HCA 2104/2014

IN THE HIGH COURT OF THE HONG KONG SPECIAL ADMINISTRATIVE REGION
COURT OF FIRST INSTANCE

ACTION NO 2104 OF 2014

_____

BETWEEN

LAI HOI PING (黎海平)	1st Plaintiff

(suing on his own behalf and on the behalf of all other members of Hong Kong Taxi Association 香港計程車會)

TAM CHUN HUNG (譚駿雄)	2nd Plaintiff

(suing on his own behalf and on the behalf of all other members of Taxi Drivers and Operators Association 的士司機從業員總會)

and

PERSONS OCCUPYING PORTIONS OF NATHAN ROAD NEAR TO AND BETWEEN ARGYLE STREET AND DUNDAS STREET TO PREVENT OR OBSTRUCT NORMAL VEHICULAR TRAFFIC FROM PASSING AND REPASSING THE OCCUPIED AREAS	1st Defendant
NG TING PONG (吳定邦)	2nd Defendant
FOK WAI PONG DOMINIC	3rd Defendant
CHEN RAYMOND	4th Defendant

_____

Before: Hon Au J in Chambers (Open to the public)
Date of Hearing: 13 November 2014
Date of Decision: 13 November 2014

_____

D E C I S I O N

1. These are the applications by the 2nd and 3rd defendants seeking leave to appeal against the orders I made in the judgment handed down on 10 November 2014 (the "Main Judgment"), and a stay of the orders principally pending appeal.

2. I do not think the intended grounds of appeal raised by them are reasonably arguable with a reasonable prospect of success. I would therefore refuse to grant leave.

3. As the matters are likely to go further, I would only give some brief reasons for my decision.

4. I will deal with Ms Li SC's grounds for the 3rd defendant first as to why I say they are not reasonably arguable.

UNDER HCA 2086/2014

5. Grounds 1 and 2 are in substance a repeat of the 3rd defendant's arguments before this court. For the same reasons I have set out in the Main Judgment, I do not think they bear a reasonable prospect of success for the purpose of the appeal.

6. Ground 3 is a misreading of the judgment. Paragraph 36 must be read together with paragraphs 33-35, which are to deal with the alternative assumption that if it was Ms Li's argument that the court should decide on the question of law on the basis of taking the plaintiff's evidence to the highest. The court in the earlier passages of the judgment has already assessed the plaintiff's evidence to say why, applying the legal principles summarised at paragraphs 19-21 therein, the plaintiff has on the state of the evidence already shown a triable issue of fact on the question of particular, substantial and direct loss. See also paragraph 37 of the Main Judgment.

7. Ground 4 in my view was not formally argued before this court. But in any event, the interim injunction granted will not finally dispose of the action in favour of the plaintiff as submitted. There are still claims for damages and there are also no suggestions that the defendants (or any of them) would not re-obstruct the areas if the plaintiff's claims are eventually dismissed. This question must also be looked at in the context that the defendants have never raised any grounds that they have a legal right to obstruct the blocked areas in the way as the defendants have been doing to exclude other members of the public from using them.

8. Ground 6(1) is unarguable. The right of abatement is not the basis to support the injunction. Ground 6(2) is also not arguable: other than that it was not formally raised before the court, in any event, the plaintiff has said on the evidence that the minibuses could not use the blocked areas, it is for the defendants to show otherwise.

9. Ground 7 is in my view not even a proper ground of appeal. It amounts to no more than saying that the plaintiff's claim has no merits.

10. Ground 8 is effectively a repeat of all the grounds above.

UNDER HCA 2104/2014

11. All the grounds under this action except ground 5 (relating to the right to bring representative actions) are effectively the same as raised in HCA 2086/2014. For the same reasons mentioned above, I find them not to be reasonably arguable. As to ground 5, it is effectively a repeat of the arguments made before this court, and for the reasons I have set out in the Main Judgment, I also find them not reasonably arguable for the intended appeal.

12. I now turn to the 2nd defendant's grounds under both actions as raised by Mr Dykes SC. The grounds under both actions are in substance the same, and with respect, I also find them to be not reasonably arguable for the following brief reasons.

13. For grounds (1) to (7), they are effectively a repeat of the arguments previously advanced before this court. For the same reasons set out in the Main Judgment, I do not find them to be reasonably arguable.

14. For ground (8), the arguments were not previously raised before this court. In any event, I do not find them having a reasonable prospect of success. The procedural provisions in Police Force Ordinance (Cap 232) ("PFO") and the Magistrates Ordinance (Cap 227) referred to by Mr Dykes could not, as a matter of construction, in my view limit the general meaning of "offences" in "any offences… for which a person may (on a first conviction for that offence) be sentenced for imprisonment" of s 50(1)(a) of the PFO as submitted by Mr Dykes.

STAY APPLICATIONS

15. As I would not grant leave to appeal, I also see no basis of staying the orders as asked for by the 2nd and 3rd defendants.

16. Ms Li for the 3rd defendant has apparently also raised a submission (through a skeleton faxed to the court yesterday seeking an urgent stay) that a stay should be granted (presumably generally) on the basis that no directions for substituted service (which would in any event only be relevant to the 1st unnamed defendants, but not the 3rd defendant represented by Ms Li) have been made for the present orders. On my further inquiry today, I understand that Ms Li is contented not to advance this as a formal ground for stay, given the court's indication yesterday that it must be its intention to include the directions

for substituted service as originally contained in the original injunction when the court continued the original injunction, and, as a matter of fact, in the draft orders provided to the court by the plaintiffs, they do include the directions for substituted service.

17. For all these reasons, I would dismiss the 2nd and 3rd defendants' summonses, with costs to the respective plaintiffs to be taxed if not agreed. There be certificate for two counsel for the plaintiffs under HCA 2104/2014. The 2nd and 3rd defendants' own costs be taxed in accordance with legal aid regulations.

(Thomas Au)
Judge of the Court of First Instance
High Court

Mr Tim Wong, instructed by CMK Lawyers, for the plaintiff in HCA 2086/2014

Mr Johnny Mok SC, Mr Jose-Antonio Maurellet and Mr Kerby Lau, instructed by Phyllis K Y Kwong & Associates, for the 1st and 2nd plaintiffs in HCA 2104/2014

Mr Philip Dykes SC and Ms Christine Yu, assigned by the Director of Legal Aid, instructed by JCC Cheung & Co, for the 2nd defendant in HCA 2086/2014 and HCA 2104/2014

Ms Gladys Li SC and Ms Margaret Ng, assigned by the Director of Legal Aid, instructed by Daly & Associates, for the 3rd defendant in HCA 2086/2014

Ms Gladys Li SC, assigned by the Director of Legal Aid, instructed by Daly & Associates, for the 3rd defendant in HCA 2104/2014

Raymond Chen, in person, absent

AUGUST 11, 2015

HCA 2086/2014

IN THE HIGH COURT OF THE HONG KONG SPECIAL ADMINISTRATIVE REGION
COURT OF FIRST INSTANCE
ACTION NO 2086 OF 2014

BETWEEN

CHIU LUEN PUBLIC LIGHT BUS Plaintiff
COMPANY LIMITED (潮聯公共小型巴士有限公司)

and

PERSONS UNLAWFULLY OCCUPYING   1st Defendant
OR REMAINING ON THE PUBLIC HIGHWAY NAMELY, THE WESTBOUND
CARRIAGEWAY OF ARGYLE STREET BETWEEN THE JUNCTION OF TUNG
CHOI STREET AND PORTLAND STREET AND/OR OTHER PERSONS HINDERING
OR PREVENTING THE PASSING OR REPASSING OF ARGYLE STREET

NG TING PONG (吳定邦)   2nd Defendant

FOK WAI PONG DOMINIC   3rd Defendant

CHEN RAYMOND   4th Defendant

HCA 2104/2014

IN THE HIGH COURT OF THE HONG KONG SPECIAL ADMINISTRATIVE REGION
COURT OF FIRST INSTANCE
ACTION NO 2104 OF 2014

BETWEEN

LAI HOI PING (黎海平)　　1st Plaintiff
(suing on his own behalf and on the behalf of all other members of Hong Kong Taxi Association 香港計程車會)

TAM CHUN HUNG (譚駿雄)　2nd Plaintiff
(suing on his own behalf and on the behalf of all other members of Taxi Drivers and Operators Association 的士司機從業員總會)

and

PERSONS OCCUPYING PORTIONS OF　　1st Defendant
NATHAN ROAD NEAR TO AND BETWEEN ARGYLE STREET AND DUNDAS STREET
TO PREVENT OR OBSTRUCT NORMAL VEHICULAR TRAFFIC FROM PASSING
AND REPASSING THE OCCUPIED AREAS

　　　NG TING PONG (吳定邦)　　2nd Defendant

　　　FOK WAI PONG DOMINIC　　3rd Defendant

　　　CHEN RAYMOND　　4th Defendant

Before: Hon Au J in Chambers
Dates of Written Submissions: 29 December 2014, 16, 19, 23 January, and 2 February 2015
Date of Decision on Costs: 13 August 2015

DECISION ON COSTS

A. INTRODUCTION

1. On 10 November 2014, I handed down judgment ("the Judgment") continuing the injunction under these two actions that the plaintiffs obtained on an ex parte basis on 20 October 2014. In the Judgment, I also made an order nisi that costs of the applications to continue the injunction be to the plaintiffs, to be taxed if not agreed, with certificate for two counsel ("the costs order nisi").

2. By summons taken out respectively by the 2nd and 3rd defendants, respectively under these two actions, the 2nd and 3rd defendants seek to vary the costs order nisi to the extent that the costs of the injunction applications be in the cause, or alternatively the plaintiffs' costs be in the cause.

3. It is directed that the summonses be dealt with on papers, and the parties have respectively filed their written submissions.

4. This is the decision on the costs variation applications. This decision should be read together with the Judgment. For convenience, the abbreviations used in the Judgment will be adopted here unless otherwise stated. I will also not repeat herein any of the history and matters that have already been set out in the Judgment.

B. THESE VARIATION APPLICATIONS

B1. The parties' contentions

5. As I said, the 2nd and 3rd defendants (for convenience, collectively "the defendants") ask for the costs of the injunction application to be in the cause or alternatively the plaintiffs' costs be in the cause.

6. The principal submissions made by the defendants in support of the applications can be summarised as follows:

(1) The costs of the interlocutory injunction should normally be costs in the cause, or the successful party's costs in the cause. This is so as normally it would not be just and fair to require the unsuccessful party to bear the costs at that stage when the successful party at the end of the day may lose after substantive determination, meaning that he should never have been entitled to the interlocutory relief in the first place. The position is different if it can be shown that the contesting party has acted improperly or in some way to be penalised. See: King Fung Vacuum Ltd v Toto Toys Ltd [2006] 2 HKLRD 785 at paragraph 27 (applied in Velatel Global Communications Inc v Chinacomm Ltd, unreported, HCA 1978/2011, 8 March 2013 at paragraph 4); Picnic At Ascot v Kalus Degris [2001] FSR 2 at paragraphs 5 16, per Neuberger (as he then was), referring also to Desquenne et Giral UK Ltd v Richardson [2001] FSR 1.

(2) At the same time, post Civil Justice Reform ("CJR"), under Order 62, rules 3(2) and (2A), it is now specifically provided that costs follow the event is not the starting position, but only one of the options, for costs relating to interlocutory application in the court's exercise of discretion in costs.

(3) In the present case, the defendants had not acted improperly or unreasonably in seeking to resist the continuation of the injunction by disputing at least, among others, the locus point. This is particularly so when it is squarely for the plaintiffs to show that they had suffered special damage to bring them within the exception so that they as private individuals had the necessary title to bring a public nuisance claim against the defendants. The issues arising (including legal as well as evidential ones) from this question of title to sue, which were hotly contested at the hearing, were only held by both this court and later the Court of Appeal to be arguable which merited thorough and serious consideration at trial. In the circumstances, there cannot be any justifications to require the defendants to bear the costs now when the issues, which go to the important question of title to sue, would still need to be properly and no doubt heavily contested at trial. In this regard, to highlight that the plaintiffs' claims are not bound to win, the defendants also point to the observations by this court in the Judgment at paragraphs 63 and 65 that the plaintiffs' evidence as to the specific loss and damage said to be suffered by them might well be subject to heavy cross-examination and challenge at trial in light of the defendants' adverse observations raised in their submissions.

7. In resisting these variation applications, the plaintiffs' counsel in substance submit that it is nowadays open to the court to adopt an issue merits approach in deciding costs in interlocutory applications in granting costs to the successful party, including on a forthwith basis. See: Waxman v Li Fei Yu [2013] 6 HKC 424 at paragraphs 3 – 20, per To J; Mendlowitz & Associates Inc v Winner International Group Ltd (unreported, HCA 574/2009, 14 May 2010, per Au J) at paragraphs 29 30; and Midland Business v Lo Man Kui (No 2) [2011] 2 HKLRD 667 at paragraphs 7 – 8, per Lam J (as the learned VP then was).

8. In the present case, the defendants should clearly be aware of the at the least arguable nature of the plaintiffs' case (and thus their title to sue), and under the well established principles governing the grant of interlocutory injunction, the plaintiffs had a clear case for the injunction. It was therefore unreasonable for the defendants to have opposed the continuation of the interlocutory injunction as they did. The costs order nisi was thus rightly and justly made in all the circumstances and the defendants are in fact "lucky" not to be required to pay the costs forthwith.

B2. Court's views

9. It cannot be disputed that costs is in the wide discretion of the court by taking into account all the circumstance of the case. In particular, post CJR, the court should also take into account the underlying objectives set out in Order 1A, rule 1 and the conduct of the parties: see Order 62, rule 5(1). In the context of the wide discretion, in relation to costs in an interlocutory injunction, all the authorities, including Order 62, rules 3(2) and (2A), cited by the parties, show that in the exercise of that discretion, the court could take into account, among others, (a) the consideration that the inherent nature of an interlocutory injunction may make it fair to normally require the unsuccessful party only to bear the costs of the application if the successful party also succeeds in the substantive action; (b) any facts or factors, including the conduct of the parties and the reasonableness of resisting the application, which may render it just to require the unsuccessful part to bear the costs without being dependent upon the final outcome of the action, and even on a forthwith basis. In so exercising its discretion, the court must as usual also take into account all the circumstances pertinent to that particular application, and the underlying objectives of CJR as set out in Order 1A, rule 1.

10. Bearing these principles in mind, and looking at the continuation application globally, I agree that in the present case, the fair and just costs order should be that the plaintiffs' costs be in the cause given in particular the following considerations:

(1) It cannot be said that the defendants had acted improperly to contest the continuation of the injunction, as:

(a) The hearing of continuation application provided the first occasion where the parties could address the question of title to use. It is noted that at the ex parte hearing, the issues of whether the plaintiffs as private individuals could commence these claims in public nuisance had not been mentioned before Poon J.

(b) The legal arguments as to what constitutes special damage to found the title to sue are not straightforward questions, in particular as to what may meet the requirement for "direct" loss. Thus, it also cannot be said that the defendants acted improperly in seeking to resist the injunction by arguing that as matter of legal analysis, the plaintiffs did not come within this requirement.

(2) On the other hand, the defendants were unsuccessful in resisting the continuation application. In this respect, other than the arguments on title to use, both this court and the Court of Appeal (in refusing leave to appeal against the continuation of the interlocutory injunction) observed that (a) all the defendants did not have a legal right to occupy the subject roads in the way they did, and as such they would not suffer any legally recognisable loss or damage if the injunction was later held to be wrongly granted, and (b) the balance of convenience tilted "overwhelmingly" in favour of granting the interlocutory injunction.

In such a context, it would also be unfair to require the plaintiff in any event to bear the costs of their successful application for the continuation of the injunction whatever the outcome of the substantive claims.

11. For these reasons, in my view, the fair and just costs order in the circumstances of the present case should be that the plaintiffs' costs be in the cause.

C. CONCLUSION

12. I will therefore vary the costs order nisi to the extent that costs of the application to continue to the injunction in each of these proceedings be the plaintiffs' costs in the cause, with certificate for two counsel (as the case may be).

13. All the parties seek costs of these applications in their submissions. In my view, the defendants are successful in their applications to vary the costs order nisi. I think it is only just that they should have costs of the variation applications, to be taxed if not agreed, with certificate for two counsel.

(Thomas Au)
Judge of the Court of First Instance
High Court

Mr Tim Wong, instructed by CMK Lawyers, for the plaintiff in HCA 2086/2014

Mr Jose-Antonio Maurellet instructed by Phyllis K Y Kwong & Associates, for the 1st and 2nd plaintiffs in HCA 2104/2014

Mr Philip Dykes SC and Ms Christine Yu, assigned by the Director of Legal Aid, instructed by JCC Cheung & Co, for the 2nd defendant in HCA 2086/2014 and HCA 2104/2014

Ms Gladys Li SC and Ms Margaret Ng and Mr Michael Yin,
assigned by the Director of Legal Aid, instructed by Daly & Associates, for the 3rd defendant in HCA 2086/2014 and 2104/2014

COURT INJUCTIONS (CITIC TOWERS)
OCTOBER 20[99]

HCA 2094/2014

(HCZZ 137/2014)

IN THE HIGH COURT OF THE HONG KONG SPECIAL ADMINISTRATIVE REGION

COURT OF FIRST INSTANCE

ACTION NO 2094 OF 2014

(INTENDED ACTION NO 137 OF 2014)

_____

BETWEEN

GOLDON INVESTMENT LIMITED   Plaintiff

and

PERSONS WHO ERECTED OR PLACED OR   Defendants
MAINTAINED OBSTRUCTIONS OR OTHERWISE DO ANY ACT TO CAUSE
OBSTRUCTION, OR TO PREVENT OR HINDER THE CLEARANCE AND REMOVAL
OF THE OBSTRUCTIONS AT THE ENTRANCES OR EXITS OF CITIC TOWER,
1 TIM MEI AVENUE, CENTRAL, HONG KONG ("CITIC TOWER"),
AND/OR THE VEHICULAR/PEDESTRIAN PASSAGEWAY AT TIM MEI AVENUE
AND/OR LUNG WUI ROAD WHICH BLOCK VEHICULAR OR PEDESTRIAN ACCESS
TO CITIC TOWER

_____

Before : Hon Poon J in Chambers (Open to the public)

Date of Hearing : 20 October 2014

Date of Ruling : 20 October 2014

_____

---

[99] http://legalref.judiciary.gov.hk/lrs/common/search/search_result_detail_frame.jsp?DIS=95377&QS=%2B&TP=JU

RULING

1. This is the third application for interim injunction arising from the recent "Occupy Central" Campaign that I need to deal with this evening.

2. The plaintiff in this application is the owner of Citic Tower located in Admiralty. The fire access, the entrance to the main car park and the emergency vehicular access to the building have all been blocked by the protestors, which triggered the present application.

3. I would simply adopt what I have already said in the earlier judgment (HCA 2086/2014 and HCA 2104/2014, dated 20.10.2014) that I delivered a moment ago, about the proper approach to this type of applications and the law insofar as it is applicable to the present case.

4. There can be no doubt that the plaintiff does have a serious question to be tried on their cause of action based on nuisance against the defendants.

5. On the balance of convenience, the evidence, I think, is overwhelming. The blockage to fire exits, the emergency vehicular access, and indeed the main vehicle access to the building, causes tremendous hazards and risks, which are real, to the safety and well being of the building and its occupiers. An injunction is clearly in order.

6. On the balance of convenience, I would also repeat what I have said in the earlier judgment which is equally applicable here.

7. Perhaps I will just reiterate one particular point. The court is not engaged with any political discussion. The court is not the forum where political views are to be ventilated or argued. The court is only to apply the law and to uphold the rule of law. If the defendants are aggrieved, or feel aggrieved by the injunction that the court is going to make, they can return to court and have the matter properly argued so that their rights and obligations, together with the plaintiff's rights and obligations, can be properly determined in accordance with the law, eschewing any political debate or consideration. After all, this is how the rule of law operates in Hong Kong.

8. Subject to the actual wording of the injunction, I am going to grant the relief.

(Jeremy Poon)
Judge of the Court of First Instance
High Court

Mr Benjamin Yu SC, and Ms Bianca Yu, instructed by Mayer Brown JSM, for the plaintiff

NOVEMBER 10

HCA 2086/2014

IN THE HIGH COURT OF THE HONG KONG SPECIAL ADMINISTRATIVE REGION
COURT OF FIRST INSTANCE
ACTION NO 2086 OF 2014

BETWEEN

CHIU LUEN PUBLIC LIGHT BUS   Plaintiff
COMPANY LIMITED (潮聯公共小型巴士有限公司)

and

PERSONS UNLAWFULLY OCCUPYING   1st Defendant
OR REMAINING ON THE PUBLIC HIGHWAY NAMELY, THE WESTBOUND
CARRIAGEWAY OF ARGYLE STREET BETWEEN THE JUNCTION OF TUNG CHOI STREET
AND PORTLAND STREET AND/OR OTHER PERSONS HINDERING
OR PREVENTING THE PASSING OR
REPASSING OF ARGYLE STREET

NG TING PONG (吳定邦)   2nd Defendant

FOK WAI PONG DOMINIC   3rd Defendant

CHEN RAYMOND   4th Defendant

HCA 2094/2014

IN THE HIGH COURT OF THE HONG KONG SPECIAL ADMINISTRATIVE REGION
COURT OF FIRST INSTANCE
ACTION NO 2094 OF 2014

_____

BETWEEN

GOLDON INVESTMENT LIMITED   Plaintiff

and

PERSONS WHO ERECTED OR PLACED OR   1st Defendant
MAINTAINED OBSTRUCTIONS OR OTHERWISE DO ANY ACT TO CAUSE
OBSTRUCTION, OR TO PREVENT OR HINDER THE CLEARANCE AND REMOVAL
OF THE OBSTRUCTIONS AT THE ENTRANCES OR EXITS OF CITIC TOWER,
1 TIM MEI AVENUE, CENTRAL, HONG KONG ("CITIC TOWER"),
AND/OR THE VEHICULAR/PEDESTRIAN PASSAGEWAY AT TIM MEI AVENUE
AND/OR LUNG WUI ROAD WHICH BLOCK VEHICULAR OR PEDESTRIAN ACCESS
TO CITIC TOWER

WONG YUEN CHING   2nd Defendant

_____

HCA 2104/2014

IN THE HIGH COURT OF THE HONG KONG SPECIAL ADMINISTRATIVE REGION
COURT OF FIRST INSTANCE
ACTION NO 2104 OF 2014

_____

BETWEEN

LAI HOI PING (黎海平)   1st Plaintiff

(suing on his own behalf and on the behalf of all other members of Hong Kong Taxi Association 香港計程車會)

TAM CHUN HUNG (譚駿雄)   2nd Plaintiff

(suing on his own behalf and on the behalf of all other members of Taxi Drivers and Operators Association 的士司機從業員總會)

and

PERSONS OCCUPYING PORTIONS OF   1st Defendant
NATHAN ROAD NEAR TO AND BETWEEN ARGYLE STREET AND DUNDAS STREET TO PREVENT OR OBSTRUCT NORMAL VEHICULAR TRAFFIC FROM PASSING AND REPASSING THE OCCUPIED AREAS

NG TING PONG (吳定邦)   2nd Defendant

FOK WAI PONG DOMINIC   3rd Defendant

CHEN RAYMOND   4th Defendant

Before: Hon Au J in Chambers (Open to the public)

Dates of Hearing: 24 and 27 October 2014

Date of Judgment: 10 November 2014

J U D G M E N T

A. INTRODUCTION

1. In each these three actions, the plaintiffs obtained an ex parte injunction before Poon J on 20 October 2014 against the respective unnamed defendants. For convenience, I would call the action under HCA 2094/2014 as the "CITIC Tower Action", under HCA 2086/2014 as the "Taxi Operators Action" and under HCA 2104/2014 the "Minibus Manager Action".

2. The injunctions obtained relate to what is now widely known as the Occupy Central Campaign ("OCC") in Hong Kong directed against the constitutional development of Hong Kong. Under the OCC, mass protestors and demonstrators have since late September occupied parts of a number of major roads on Hong Kong Island and Kowloon. The occupations have been "reinforced" by the protestors and demonstrators in placing and securing various barriers, barricades and objects on these parts of the roads and streets. The result is that vehicular traffic through these parts of the roads and streets has been effectively completely blocked.

3. The defendants in all these actions are the respective unidentified protestors and demonstrators who have occupied the relevant parts of the roads or streets that said to have affected the plaintiffs. In the CITIC Tower Action, the plaintiff (as the owner of CITIC Tower in Admiralty) brought the claim against the defendants on the bases of both private nuisance and public nuisance. In both the Taxi Operators Action and the Minibus Manager Action, the plaintiffs (who said they derive their incomes from the operations or related operations of respectively taxis and minibuses) premised their claims on public nuisance.

4. The ex parte injunction ("the CITIC Tower Injunction") obtained under the CITIC Tower Action is one which effectively restrains the 1st unnamed defendants from (a) obstructing or maintaining obstruction (whether by themselves or through placing objects thereat) at the entrances and exits of CITIC Tower and the vehicular and pedestrian passage at Tim Mei Avenue and Lung Wui Road which block vehicular or pedestrian access to CITIC Tower, and (b) preventing the plaintiff from clearing and removing the obstructions and obstacles presently placed thereat obstructing the said CITIC Tower's entrances and exits, as well as vehicular and pedestrian exits.

5. The ex part injunction obtained under the Taxi Operators Action is effectively to restrain the defendants (either by themselves or by placing objects thereat) from (a) occupying portions of the Nathan Road near and between Argyle Street and Dundas Street ("the Blocked Area") to prevent or obstruct vehicular traffic from passing and re-passing the Blocked Area, and (b) preventing the plaintiffs from removing any such obstructions from the Blocked Area.

6. The ex parte injunction obtained under the Minibus Manager Action is to restrain the defendants (either by themselves or by placing objects thereat) from (a) occupying portion of the westbound carriageway of Argyle Street between the injunction of Tung Choi Street and Portland Street ("the Blocked

Way") to prevent or obstruct vehicular traffic from passing and re-passing the Blocked Way, and (b) preventing the plaintiffs from removing any such obstructions placed on or from the Blocked Way.

7. For convenience, I would call these two injunctions collectively the "Mongkok Injunctions" as both the Blocked Area and the Blocked Way are at one of the busiest areas in Mongkok.

8. Before me now are the respective plaintiffs' applications by way of inter partes summons to (a) continue these injunctions, and (b) ask for certain directions to facilitate the enforcement of the injunctions. The latter part of the applications is necessary, say the plaintiffs, as there has been en masse flouting and non-compliance of the ex parte injunctions by the defendants after they have been granted. I would of course return to this when I have to deal with this part of the applications.

9. These applications are opposed at the hearing:

(1) Under the Taxi Operators Action and the Minibus Manager Action, Mr Ng Ting Pong (after obtaining legal aid) and Mr Dominic Fok have appeared (after joined as the 2nd and 3rd defendants respectively) to oppose the continuation of the Mongkok Injunctions. They are respectively represented by Mr Dykes SC (leading Ms Christine Yu) and Ms Gladys Li SC (leading Ms Margaret Ng and Mr Michael Yin). Mr Raymond Chen (as the 3rd defendant) also appeared at the first day of the hearing and asked to be joined as a named defendant to oppose the plaintiffs' applications.

(2) Under the CITIC Tower Action, Ms Wong Yuen Ching has appeared (again after obtaining legal aid) and been joined as the 2nd defendant to oppose the continuation of the CITIC Tower Injunction. She is represented by Mr Manzoni SC (leading Mr Earl Deng).

10. Before I deal with specifically the arguments raised by the parties in these applications, it is important to point out that, in all the three actions, all the opposing defendants have fairly and rightly accepted that the occupations of the concerned areas amount to public nuisance, and none of them argue that a court order (even an ex parte one) need not or should not be complied with.

11. Further, as emphasised by Poon J in his judgment for the ex parte CITIC Tower Injunction, the court as an independent institution in determining the present applications is only and strictly to apply the law and to uphold the rule of law. The political views or considerations behind the OCC are entirely irrelevant to the determination.

B. WHETHER THE INJUNCTIONS SHOULD BE CONTINUED

B1. The applicable principles on the grant of an interlocutory injunction

12. The legal principles governing the grant of an interlocutory injunction are well established and not in dispute. As succinctly and helpfully summarised by G Lam J in Turbo Top Ltd v Lee Cheuk Yan [2013] 3 HKLRD 41 at paragraph 14, the court has to see (a) whether there are serious issues to be tried,

(b) whether damages would be an adequate remedy for either side, and if damages would not be adequate for both parties, (c) where the balance of convenience lies in terms of whether or not to grant an interim injunction pending the trial of the matter. In that balancing exercise, the court must take into account the interests of the general public even though they are not represented before the court.

13. Given that the issues raised in whether the Mongkok Injunctions should be continued are the same, I would first deal with them together before I look at the issues raised in the CITIC Tower Action.

B2. The Mongkok Injunctions

B2.1 Serious issues to be tried – Do the plaintiffs have a proper cause of action

14. As I mentioned above, the plaintiffs for the Mongkok Injunctions brought their claims in public nuisance. As I have also said above, none of the opposing defendants contends that the occupation of the Blocked Area and the Blocked Way do not amount to public nuisance in law. This must be right, as it is well established that the blocking of highway for an unreasonably period of time and extent, which significantly affects and interferes the public's right to use them (as in the present case) amounts to public nuisance. See: Clerk & Lindsell on Torts (20th ed), at paragraphs 21-121; Leung Tsang Hung v The Incorporated Owners of Kwok Wing House [2007] 10 HKCFAR 480 at paragraph 12 per Ribeiro PJ.

15. The principal contentions raised by the 2nd and 3rd defendants under this question have been premised on a number of bases, which I would look at in turn now.

B2.1.1 Do the plaintiffs suffer particular, substantial and direct damage because of the public nuisance

16. It is well established that, as public nuisance results in infringing the general public's rights, generally only (in the case of Hong Kong) the Secretary for Justice ("SJ") can bring a claim in public nuisance for and on behalf of the general public (who has suffered the inconvenience generally by reason of the public nuisance). For a private individual (without joining the SJ in a relator action) to bring a claim in public nuisance, the law requires that he must show that he has suffered a "particular, direct and substantial" injury above and beyond what is suffered by the rest of the public at large: Benjamin v Storr (1874) LR 9 CP 400 at 406-406 per Brett J.

17. In light of this requirement, the fundamental and primary contentions raised by Mr Dykes and Ms Li is that in the present case, the damage said to be suffered by the plaintiffs in both actions do not and cannot be regarded as "particular, substantial and direct" injury to enable them to bring a private claim in public nuisance. As such, the plaintiffs' cause of action is clearly defective without also jointing the SJ as a plaintiff. The claim for an interlocutory injunction must therefore fail.

18. Before I deal with the defendants' arguments in detail, it is convenient to first look at some case law relevant to the question of "particular, substantial and direct" damage in public nuisance.

19. Whether a damage or loss said to be suffered by the plaintiff can be regarded as particular, substantial and direct is essentially a question of fact, and a matter of degree and extent: Jan de Nul v Royale Belge [2000] 2 LLR 700 at paragraph 44 (p 715).

20. In this respect, it is also pertinent to note that it has also been well established that:

(1) The "particular" damage needs not be pecuniary (and thus special) in nature. It may consist of proved general damage, such as inconvenience and delay provided that it is substantial, that it is direct and non-consequential, and that it is appreciably greater in degree than any suffered by the general public: Walsh v Ervin [1952] VLR361 at 371 per Scholl J.

(2) "Substantial" means no more than that the damage suffered is more than trivial: Jan de Nul, supra, at paragraph 44.

(3) It is also not necessary prove that the plaintiff has any injury to property, or has any interest or relationship with any land or building: Benjamin v Storr, supra, at 406; Leung Tsang Hung, supra, at paragraph 13.

21. Further, the authorities show that the requirement of "direct" damage is satisfied not only by one which is immediately caused by or flowed from the nuisance. It also covers those injuries and damage which are caused by or flowed from the nuisance through a chain of events, so long as those events can be regarded as probable events as a result of the nuisance and the chain is not broken by external matters unrelated to the nuisance. It is a question of fact in each case as to whether the damage claimed to be suffered fall within the requisite chain of events. See: Overseas Tankship (UK) Ltd v Miller Steamship Co Pty (Wagon No 2) [1967] 1 AC 617, at 634E-636D per Lord Reid; Gravesham v British Railways Board [1978] 1 Ch 379 at 396F-397C and 398H-399B .

22. I now turn to look at what the plaintiffs say they have suffered as damage and loss in the present case.

23. In the Taxi Operators Action:

(1) The 1st plaintiff (Mr Lai) sues on his own behalf and on behalf of all the other members of Hong Kong Taxi Association (香港計程車會) ("HKTA"). The 2nd plaintiff (Mr Tam) sues also on his own behalf and on behalf of the Taxi Drivers and Operators Association (的士司機從業員總會) ("TDOA").

(2) The core function of the HKTA is to promote the welfare and rights of taxi trade in Hong Kong. There are about 400 members who are taxi owners, taxi owners who are also taxi drivers, or taxi drivers who do not own taxis. Some of these members (about 50 of them) also happen to be taxi managers .

(3) Mr Lai is the Chairman of the HKTA and an owner and taxi driver. He is also a taxi manager himself who manages 30 taxis .

(4)   TDOA has about 10,900 members who are taxi drivers. Mr Tam is a member of TDOA (and thus apparently a taxi driver) and occupies the post of committee member.

24.   The plaintiffs' evidence of the loss and damage said to be suffered by reason of the public nuisance is essentially this:

(1)   Because of the blocking of the Blocked Area, it has led to general traffic blockages and serious road congestions in Kowloon. As a result, a lot of passengers (including tourists) no longer use taxis as their preferred means of transportation. This results in loss of business and income for taxi drivers. By way of example, the average income of a taxi driver has dropped from some $23,800 to about $17,800 per taxi. This also impacts on the income of taxi owners and managers, as the taxi drivers are only willing to pay less as rental for taxis to operate or even not to rent a taxi at all for some days. Not only therefore is that the daily rental of taxi has gone down by $100 per session for the owners (and thus reducing their income), the income of taxi managers has also been reduced as if the taxis are not rented out, a taxi manager would not receive his daily management fee and would have to pay for the idled taxi's parking cost.

(2)   Mr Lai personally (suing in his own capacity) as a taxi manager, taxi owner and a driver thus has suffered and would continue to suffer those types of losses. The HKTA members (sued by Mr Lai on their behalf) have suffered and would continue to (if the obstructions of the Blocked Area continues) suffer those types of losses respectively as an owner, owner driver or solely a driver.

(3)   Mr Tam personally (suing in his own capacity) as a driver and the TDOA members (who are taxi drivers) (sued by Mr Tam on their behalf) have suffered and would continue to suffer losses in the form of decrease in daily income.

25.   In the Minibus Manager Action, the plaintiff is a minibus manager. Its business is to organise, manage and provide commute routes of public light buses (minibuses) for the purposes of public transportation. It is the plaintiff's case that it receives a monthly management fee of $1,000 from the owner of each minibus in return for organising, managing and providing commute routes of them.

26.   At present, the plaintiff manages 6 different commute routes across Kowloon. One of them is the circular commute route ("the Olympic Station Route") from Kwun Tung to Olympic Station, which has 14 stops. This route generates the main and strongest source of revenue for the plaintiff. In fact, the other routes managed by the plaintiff are either less profitable or run at a loss.

27.   The plaintiff's evidence on its loss and damage caused by the blocking of the Blocked Way is in gist as follows:

(1)   Because of the Blocked Way, the minibuses of the Olympic Route have to skip 3 stops (of the 14 stops) from Argyle Street to Olympic Station, namely: the Ladies' Market (Tung Choi Street), Sin Tat Plaza stop, the Tai Kok Tsui Olympic Station, HSBC Public Light Bus Terminus stop and the Tai Kok Tsui, Fuk Tsun Street Olympic Station Public Light Bus Terminus stop.

(2) The skipped 3 stops are amongst the most popular stops for passengers. As a result of the skip, there have been less passengers taking the Olympic Station Route, resulting in reducing the daily trips of that route from 150 times to 100 times.

(3) The earnings of the drivers of that route have similarly therefore been reduced, which in turn results in the drivers reducing the amount of the daily rent they are prepared to pay the minibus owners from $1,000 to $800.

(4) Given the reduced earnings of the owners, which they say is caused by the plaintiff's failure to manage and organise the Olympic Route properly to include all the 14 stops, they have threatened not to pay the plaintiff the management fee unless the plaintiff is to take action by 21 October 2014.

(5) The plaintiff therefore is going to suffer loss in the management fees arising from managing the Olympic Station Route and damage to its long standing reputation as minibus manager as a result of the public nuisance if it continues. The financial impact on the plaintiff if it does lose the income from this route is dire and there is a real risk that it would be wound up eventually.

28. Mr Dykes and Ms Li both submit that the type and kind of loss and damage said to be suffered by these plaintiffs do not and could not amount to particular, substantial and direct damage caused by the Blocked Area or Blocked Way. In particular, counsel says the alleged losses suffered are not direct and immediate enough to bring them within the legal requirements. They are not, it is contended, immediately referable to the Blocked Area or Blocked Way specifically.

29. I am not persuaded by these arguments.

30. Applying the principles relating to "particular, substantial and direct" damage as I have summarised above, as far as I can see:

(1) Those claimed losses and damage are pecuniary in nature, and are clearly something beyond and above what the general public has suffered at large as inconvenience by reason of the nuisance. Thus, they must or at the least arguably come within the meaning of "particular" damage. See: Benjamin v Storr (1874) LR 9 CP 400 at 406-406 per Brett J; Clerk & Lindsell, paragraph 20-181 at p 1371; paragraph 19(1) above.

(2) Those losses and damage must or at least arguably also come within the meaning of "substantial", as they are more than trivial, or not fleeting or evanescent: Benjamin v Storr, at 407; Jan du Nul, supra, at paragraph 44.

31. Insofar as to whether they amount to "direct" damage, it is at least triable that they are as they are the result of a chain of probable events caused by or flowed from the nuisance. It is at least triable that:

(1) It is a probable result of the nuisance in blocking the Blocked Area and Street (which are by themselves under heavy use by vehicles) that there would be serious traffic congestions in other roads and streets in Kowloon generally;

(2) It is also a probable result of the nuisance that frequent or regular road users (including commercial vehicular users) of the Blocked Area and Street would have to divert their route;

(3) It is a probable result of the general traffic congestions and the need by the regular road users of the Blocked Area and Way to avoid them that there would be a serious interference on the business operations of those classes of road users whose businesses (and thus incomes) are dependent upon or related to the carriage of passengers on the roads generally and specifically through the Blocked Area and Way;

(4) It is also a probable result of (if not common sense that) the heavy general traffic congestions caused by the nuisance that at least some passengers would avoid taking public transportations on the roads (including taxis, minibuses and buses) because of the serious and heavy traffic congestions;

(5) It is thus also a probable result of these events that the businesses of these classes of road users (or at least some of them) would be adversely affected with loss of their incomes;

(6) The above chain of events is interlinked and unbroken.

32. In the premises, the plaintiffs have shown at least a triable issue that the types of damage and loss said to have been suffered by them are particular, substantial and direct damage to entitle them to bring the claim in public nuisance against the defendants.

33. I should also mention that it appears also to be Ms Li's contention that, given that this question concerns the locus of the plaintiffs to bring the claims, even for the purpose of deciding whether to continue the interlocutory injunction, the court should not determine it on the basis of whether there is a triable issue only.

34. I am not sure from where Ms Li has derived support for this contention as she has cited no authority in this regard. The principles governing the granting of an interlocutory injunction as summarised above are well established. Whether one calls the challenge based on locus or that the plaintiff lacks some of the necessary elements in constituting their proper cause of action, I see no reason why the same principles should not apply, which is whether the plaintiffs have shown a serious question (on the law or the facts) to be tried on their claims. I therefore do not accept Ms Li's submissions that under this question, it is not sufficient for the plaintiffs to only show a good arguable case.

35. Perhaps what Ms Li really means is this: even taking the plaintiffs' evidence on the type and nature damage they said to have suffered at the highest (thus assuming the evidence is established at trial), as a matter of law, they do not amount to the ones required to entitle them to bring privately a claim in public nuisance. The court should therefore be able to determine conclusively this question even at this stage.

36. On that basis assuming that the evidence before me has been all been proved, for the reasons I have explained above, I would accept that the plaintiffs have satisfied me that the type of damage they

said to have been suffered falls within the meaning of particular, substantial and direct damage, which gives them a good cause of action in public nuisance.

37. Alternatively, if Ms Li argues that my reading of the case law at paragraph 21 above is incorrect, then I would only say that this at least amount to a serious question of law that should be tried.

38. In the premises, I reject the 2nd and 3rd defendants' primary contentions that the plaintiffs' cause of action is defective.

B2.1.2 The plaintiffs in the Taxi Operators Action cannot properly bring a representative action

39. This ground is raised by Mr Dykes. Leading counsel submits that in order to bring a representative action (as Mr Lai and Mr Tam seek also to bring), it must be shown that all the represented persons must share the same or identical interest, and it is not sufficient to show like or similar interest. Mr Dykes therefore says a representative claim in the present case is clearly not permissible as each member of the HKTA and TDOA at the highest suffers or will suffer a different degree of damage and therefore does not share the same interest. He relies on the authority of Preston v Hilton [1920] 55DLR 647 at 653-654 (as followed in Turtle v Toronto [1924] 56 OLR 252 at paragraphs 4 and 57) to support his contentions.

40. This objection can be disposed of for the present purpose shortly:

(1) The decision in Preston was based on Moulton LJ's dicta in Markt & Co Ltd v Knight Steamship Co Ltd [1910] 2 KB 1023 at 1035-1039 (see Preston, at p 654). However, it is at least now arguable if not established that the law on this has since the judgment of Markt moved on, in that the rigid view as expressed by Moulton LJ in excluding a representative action where each of the represented members may have a different degree of interest in the matter is no longer applicable: Irish Shipping Ltd v Commercial Union [1991] 2 QB 206 (CA) at 224B- 227B per Staughton LJ. The rule in the right to bring a representative action is now regarded as a flexible tool of convenience to facilitate the administration of justice: John v Rees [1970] Ch 345 at 370E per Megarry J (as referred to Irish Shipping at 226F-E). The condition that there must be an "interest" shared by all members of the class in a representative action can be satisfied if every member of the class has a separate cause of action in tort: Prudential Assurance Co Ltd v Newman Industries Ltd [1981] Ch 229 at 254-255 per Vinelott J (as referred to in Irish Shipping at 225B-F). See also: Hong Kong White Book 2015, paragraph 15/12/2.

(2) In the present case, it is at least triable on the state of the evidence as to whether each and every member of the HKTA and the TDOA suffers the type of particular and direct loss (as described in the evidence) which would have entitled each of them to bring a separate claim in public nuisance against the defendants. If so, it must be for the benefit of this class and the administration of justice if all these separate claims could be dealt with together in a representative action.

(3) In the premises, this cannot be a valid objection to the continuation of the interlocutory injunction on the basis that the plaintiffs' claim brought as representative action is not arguably maintainable.

(4) Further, and in any event, even if (for the sake of argument) Mr Dykes is right in his submissions that Mr Tam and Mr Lai cannot bring the representative action, it must not be forgotten that they also bring the claims in their own respective right. These parts of the claims would not be affected by these submissions at all. If they could maintain their own personal claims, there is no reason why the interlocutory injunction should not be continued (if all the other conditions for continuing the injunction are also satisfied).

41. I therefore also reject this ground as a basis to oppose the continuation of the Mongkok injunction in the Taxi Operators Action.

B2.1.3 Injunction should not be granted as a matter of principle

42. Ms Li further argues that, as a matter of principle, an injunctive relief cannot be granted at the suit of a private individual to restrain a public wrong (unless the acts complained of amounts to invade some private rights belonging to him). She says it is so because public nuisance is about infringing the right of the public generally, and an application for an injunction to protect that right should only be made by the SJ for the benefit of the general public. She prays in aid of the authority of Gouriet v UPW [1978] AC 435 at 481 to support her submissions.

43. With respect, I think there is nothing in this argument.

44. Relevant for the present purposes, the facts in Gouriet are these: the Post Office Workers Union announced that they would call upon their members not to handle any mails from UK to South Africa to protest against the South African government's then apartheid policy. The threatened actions could well amount to an offence under the various provisions of the Post Office Act and the Telegraph Act. A private citizen (Mr Gouriet) brought a claim against the trade union in public nuisance, seeking an interlocutory injunction to restrain the union from carrying out the threatened acts. Mr Gouriet brought the action in his own name after the Attorney General had refused to bring a relator action at his invitation. The Court of Appeal by majority initially granted the injunction on an urgent basis. The defendants appealed to the House of Lords. The House of Lords allowed the defendants' appeal and concluded that no injunction should be granted as the plaintiff could not maintain a private claim in public nuisance.

45. It is important to note that this case was decided on the pertinent fact that Mr Gouriet sought to bring a claim in public nuisance purportedly under the right as enjoyed by all members of the public to see that the law be obeyed and to prevent offences from being committed. He was not claiming that he had any special interest in the transmission of mails or messages to South Africa and was likely to suffer any special damage from the non-transmission. See: Gouriet, at p 476B-C.

46. It was, among others, in this context that Lord Wilberforce made the observations at pp 477E and 481F-H relied on by Ms Li as follows:

"A relator action – a type of action which has existed from the earliest times – is one in which the Attorney-General, on the relation of individuals (who may include local authorities or companies) brings an action to assert a public right. It can properly be said to be a fundamental principle of English law that private rights can be asserted by individuals, but that public rights can only be asserted by the Attorney-General as representing the public. In terms of constitutional law, the rights of the public are vested in the Crown, and the Attorney General enforces them as an officer of the Crown. And just as the Attorney-General has in general no power to interfere with the assertion of private rights, so in general no private person has the right of representing the public in the assertion of public rights. If he tries to do so his action can be struck out.

...

These and other examples which can be given show that this jurisdiction – though proved useful on occasions – is one of great delicacy and is one to be used with caution. Further, to apply to the court for an injunction at all against the threat of a criminal offence, may involve a decision of policy with which conflicting considerations may enter. Will the law best be served by preventive action? Will the grant of an injunction exacerbate the situation? (Very relevant this in industrial disputes.) Is the injunction likely to be effective or may it be futile? Will it be better to make it clear that the law will be enforced by prosecution and to appeal to the law-abiding instinct, negotiations, and moderate leadership, rather than provoke people along the road to martyrdom? All these matters – to which Devlin J justly drew attention in Attorney-General v Bastow [1957] 1 QB 514, 519, and the exceptional nature of this civil remedy, point the matter as one essentially for the Attorney General's preliminary discretion. Every known case, so far, has been so dealt with: in no case hitherto has it ever been suggested that an individual can act, though relator actions for public nuisance which may also involve a criminal offence, have been known for 200 years."

47. Under the law of public nuisance as I have discussed above, a private individual (such as Mr Gouriet) who has suffered no special damage above and beyond the one suffered by the general public at large of course cannot bring an action and then to obtain an interlocutory injunction. It is trite that under those circumstances that it is for the AG to bring an claim, and the AG has discretion to decide whether to do so or not, after taking into account of all relevant considerations (some of which as identified by Lord Wilberforce in the quoted passage above).

48. It can therefore be immediately seen that Gouriet is clearly distinguishable from, and thus not applicable to, the present case where a private individual who has shown to have suffered a special damage by reason of the public nuisance. The law has already established that he has a right to bring a private individual claim in public nuisance . There is no doubt that such a personal claim brought in public

nuisance could seek the relief of an interlocutory injunction. There are many instances where an interlocutory injunction was granted .

49. For these reasons, I would also reject any contentions that generally no injunction should be granted in a personal claim in public nuisance.

B2.1.4 Material non-disclosure

50. Mr Dykes also submits that the plaintiffs in these actions are guilty of material non-disclosure, and thus the ex parte injunctions should be set aside.

51. Mr Dykes' submissions in relation to the Taxi Operators Action are as follows .

52. First, counsel says Mr Lai's Affirmation only claims that at least 65% of the HKTA Members operate mainly on the Kowloon side. This, Mr Dykes submits, is not enough as the evidence should disclose what percentage of this 65% members travel across the Blocked Area, as this is the material figure relevant to the question of whether the plaintiffs have suffered particular and substantial damage. Without disclosing this material and relevant figure, the plaintiff is guilty of material non disclosure.

53. I do not agree. The plaintiff's case on particular and substantial and direct damage is advanced upon the basis that all the members suffer loss as a result of the general decrease in passengers by reason of the general traffic congestion over the roads in Kowloon and Hong Kong Island caused by the Blocked Area. It is therefore not material for them to show what percentage of the drivers pass the Blocked Area per se every day.

54. Second, Mr Dykes says Mr Lai's evidence is that the revenue of each taxi has been significantly reduced as a result of the serious road congestions in Kowloon and Hong Kong Island. Counsel submits it is unclear as to how the Blocked Area could have created all these matters since:

(1) As Mr Lai fairly accepted, traffic blockages and serious road congestion occurred in places far away from the Blocked Area, including Hong Kong Island. It must be obvious that such general description cannot prove what damage, if any, was caused specifically by occupation of the Blocked Area alone. The plaintiffs have not produced any evidence in this regard.

(2) There are allegations that rental of taxis and income of taxi drivers have dropped. Notwithstanding these are bare assertions, it is difficult to see how these allegations are caused by occupation of the Blocked Area alone.

(3) Even if it is assumed for the benefit of the plaintiffs that some taxi drivers have been reluctant to provide taxi services since the Occupy Central movement, it is difficult to see the necessary connection between this and occupation of the Blocked Area.

55. Properly understood, Mr Dykes' above submissions relate to how he analyses and disagrees with Mr Lai's evidence in supporting the plaintiffs' case. It has nothing to do with material non-disclosure.

56. I therefore reject Mr Dykes' arguments that the plaintiffs in the Taxi Operators Action are guilty of material non-disclosure.

57. Mr Dykes' submissions on material non-disclosure in the Minibus Manager Action are as follows.

58. First, he says it is misleading for the plaintiff in the Minibus Action to say at length in Mr Lam's affirmation that (a) the Olympic Station Route is the most profitable route and that the other routes are either not as profitable or even making a loss, and (b) the income of the drivers of minibus of the Olympic Station Route has dropped significantly after the occupation of the Blocked Way. This is so since it is Mr Lam's own evidence that the plaintiff receives a fixed monthly management fee of $1,000 from each minibus owner. This income is thus not dependent upon whether the Olympic Station Route is the most profitable of all the routes under the plaintiff's management and whether the income of the drivers has dropped. This evidence is thus introduced to confuse and mislead the court on the effect of the occupation on the plaintiff's financial position.

59. I do not accept that this amounts to material non-disclosure. As I explained above, properly looked at, Mr Lam's evidence is to the effect that because of the drop of the drivers' incomes under the Olympic Station Route as a result of the obstructions of the Blocked Way, they have paid the owners less for the rentals of the minibuses, and the owners then in turn threatened not to pay the plaintiff the management fees. Thus, this part of the evidence is to show that there is a real risk that the plaintiff would suffer serious financial loss (because firstly this route is the most profitable one of all the routes, and secondly that the owners' threat not pay the management fees is a genuine one). This in my view is relevant to the ex parte judge's determination as to whether the plaintiff will suffer a foreseeable loss as a result of the public nuisance. It is also pertinent to note that Mr Lam has in fact expressly and clearly stated in the evidence that the plaintiff receives a fixed monthly fee from each owner. There can be no misleading in the evidence in this respect.

60. Second, Mr Dykes submits that Mr Lam in his affirmation has not said that the plaintiff could not have arranged some of the minibuses to other routes so that the plaintiff can still enjoy the same monthly management fee. It is further submitted that in particular, the plaintiff has not disclosed whether it has rerouted some of the minibuses since the OCC. At the same time, Mr Ng (the 2nd defendant) has filed an affirmation to say that there are no regulatory route restrictions on red minibuses and thus they are free to change route. This amounts to (contended by Mr Dykes) again misleading material non-disclosure to create or exaggerate the situation about the minibus drivers' loss of income.

61. I am equally not convinced by these submissions. First, Mr Lam's affirmation has in fact dealt with the question of rerouting. It is his evidence that although it had considered rerouting the Olympic

Station Route so as to reach at least the end of the Olympic Station stop, this would have resulted in skipping the most popular Mongkok stop and also increased the average commute time by 15 minutes. This is therefore considered to be unworkable . There is no evidence to show what Mr Lam has said is clearly wrong. There is in my view no material non disclosure in this part of the evidence as submitted. Second, the submissions that Mr Lam has not said the minibuses in this route cannot be arranged to join the other routes is also a non-point, in light of the unchallenged evidence that the other routes are either not profitable or even running at a loss which means.

62. Third, Mr Dykes has sought to point out various doubts on Mr Lam's evidence of a signature campaign where various owners' drivers had signed to threaten not to pay the plaintiff's management fees.

63. I must say that even taking those doubts to the highest, Mr Dykes at best can only say that the document produced can be subject to vigorous challenge by way of cross-examination at trial. At this interlocutory stage, this court clearly cannot conclude that the document is not credible and cannot be relied upon. The mere fact that the document can be subject to challenge at trial itself cannot be a proper basis to say that there is material non-disclosure.

64. Finally, it is submitted that Mr Lam's evidence that that the plaintiff would not be able to pay the expenses for October 2014 and could be wound up imminently if the injunction is not granted given the threat of non-payment of the management fees is "a pack of lie or deliberate statement to mislead the court". Mr Dykes in his skeleton at paragraph 16(16) seeks to demonstrate this by providing a critical analysis of the statement of account produced by the plaintiff in support of its case. It is also said that Mr Lam seeks to "create an impression that [the plaintiff] only had a Bank of East Asia Account with a balance of HK$62,212.06" but it appears to have a Bank of China current and savings account as indicated in the statement of accounts.

65. Again, Mr Dykes' submissions taking to the highest only suggest that the plaintiff's case and evidence on the imminent adverse financial impact can be subject to serious challenge at trial. I do not think I can come to any conclusion at this interlocutory stage that this position is "a pack of lie" so as to "mislead the court". As to the existence of the other bank accounts, it is clear that these bank accounts and the balances thereof have been shown in the statement of accounts. The fact that no underlying bank statements have been adduced in my view per se cannot be said to be misleading the court, unless there is now clear evidence (and there is none) to say the figures represented are or cannot be correct. I therefore also reject the contention that there is material non disclosure on this basis.

66. I therefore do not accept that there is material non disclosure on the part of the plaintiff in the Minibus Action.

67. For all the above reasons, I would reject all the 2nd and 3rd defendants' contentions on why the injunction should not be continued on an inter partes basis.

B2.2 Balance of convenience - should the injunction be granted and continued?

68. After rejecting the defendants' above contentions, it is still necessary for me to consider whether I should continue the Mongkok Injunctions as sought on the question of balance of convenience.

69. In this respect, I would simply and respectfully agree and adopt Poon J's analyses as set out in his judgment at paragraphs 15 to 34 (as there are no material changes since then and no opposing defendants have raised any further arguments to say those analyses are inapplicable or inappropriate) and come to the clear view that in the present case the balance of convenience lies obviously in favour of granting and continuing the injunctions.

70. I would further add that, in case I were wrong in the above on the question of material non-disclosure, after setting aside the ex parte injunctions on that basis, I would still have re-granted them on an inter partes basis as I think the circumstances of the case justifies that given the above analyses.

71. I would therefore continue the Mongkok Injunctions in the terms as I have revised at the hearing on 26 October 2014 until trial or further order of the court.

72. I now proceed to consider the applications under the CITIC Tower Action.

B3. The CITIC Tower Injunction

B3.1 Background

73. The relevant background leading in this action is not in any controversy. Relevant for the present purposes, I would generally adopt what has been summarised in the plaintiff's skeleton as follows.

74. CITIC Tower is located at the intersection of Tim Mei Avenue and Lung Wui Road in Admiralty. The vehicular entrance of CITIC Tower which leads to the car parking floors in the building is located at Tim Mei Avenue. Vehicles can enter Tim Mei Avenue either from Lung Wui Road or Harcourt Road. The Emergency Vehicular Access ("EVA") to CITIC Tower is along the building perimeter abutting on Tim Mei Avenue.

75. CITIC Tower's car park comprises of 201 car parking spaces over eight levels. Further, there are loading and unloading bays for lorries and trucks on the lower ground floor level (LG Floor) of the car park. The only point of access to the car park of CITIC Tower and the loading and unloading bays for lorries and trucks is via the ingress and egress point of CITIC Tower at Tim Mei Avenue ("Car Park Entrance").

76. CITIC Tower has five fire exits. Staircase fire exit number 3 ("Fire Exist No 3") serves all floors from 29/F to the ground floor; and staircase fire exit number 4 ("Fire Exit No 4") serves 3/F to the ground floor.

77. The lot on which CITIC Tower is erected is held under Conditions of Sale which contain the Special Conditions that the Plaintiff would provide suitable means of access for the passage of Fire Services personnel and Fire Services appliances, to maintain such means of access, and to keep the same free from obstruction. Further, the plaintiff has a positive obligation to ensure the EVA is kept free from obstruction at all times.

78. From about 28 September 2014 onwards, Tim Mei Avenue and Lung Wui Road were completely obstructed by the 1st defendants, rendering it impossible for motor vehicles to ingress or egress CITIC Tower. The 1st defendants also blocked the EVA as well as Fire Exits No 3 and No 4. The blockages at Lung Wui Road near Performance Arts Avenue and Tim Mei Avenue Eastbound were removed by the Police in the morning of 13 October 2014. However, the blockages at Lung Wui Road and at the entrance of the run-in of the car park and the blockages at Fire Exit No 4 continue to this day. The blockages at Fire Exit No 3 were once removed at around 2:40 pm on 20 October 2014 by firemen. However, the blockage has been later reinstated by the 1st defendants by placing steel barriers across Fire Exit 3.

79. The 1st defendants' blockage has therefore prevented access to Fire Exit Nos 3 and 4 and. This has exposed the occupants of CITIC Tower to a serious risk of safety as important escape routes have been denied to the occupants. The plaintiff is also exposed to huge potential liability at the suit of the occupants. On 14 October 2014, an elderly lady was trapped in stairway no 3 for about 45 minutes because of the obstruction at Fire Exit No 3. Fortunately, there was no fire or smoke at the time; but blockage of fire exists creates a serious fire hazard.

B3.2   The plaintiff's case on its loss and damage

80. The plaintiff's evidence shows that it would suffer loss and damage by reason of the blockages caused by the 1st defendants as follows.

81. A portion of the car park spaces in CITIC Tower are let on a monthly basis yielding an average of about HK$450,000 a month, while the remaining car park spaces are used for hourly parking, yielding an average of about HK$4,500 per day. The blockage of the Car Park Entrance results in continuous and substantial loss to the Plaintiff.

82. The plaintiff's rental income has from the shops and offices also been adversely affected, but it is much more difficult to quantify this loss. Existing tenants including those whose agreements are coming up for renewal have complained and have raised or are likely to raise demands for reduction in rent. The plaintiff has also faced difficulty in letting out space presently available for letting within the building.

83. As a result of the 1st defendants' blockage of the Car Park Entrance, the disposal of the waste of CITIC Tower has had to go through the office lobby, severely affecting its hygiene and environment. Since the unloading bays at the Car Park Entrance are inaccessible, this also affected utility and delivery vehicles from accessing CITIC Tower for regular repair and maintenance, such repair and maintenance including the effective removal of solid and liquid waste from the pipes and manholes of the property. This poses a health and safety risk to the occupants at CITIC Tower.

84. The increase in manpower necessary for managing CITIC Tower properly in light of the 1st defendants' actions also led to an increase in its operation costs.

85. In summary, the blockages have significantly interfered the plaintiff's use of CITIC Tower. In particular they have completely prevented the Car Park (which offers hourly and monthly parking) from being used and caused and would continue to cause the plaintiff loss in the form of rental income. They have also caused serious potential hazards (in case of fire and any other emergencies) to the people working in and visiting the offices and retail premises within CITIC Tower as the EVA and Fire Exit Nos 3 and 4 are blocked, resulting in exposing the plaintiff to potential and significant liability at the suit of the occupants which may not be covered by insurance.

B3.3 The plaintiff's failed efforts to seek to remove the blockages

86. CITIC Tower is managed by CITIC Tower Property Management Company Limited ("PMC"). Personnel of the plaintiff, PMC and the Building Management Office of CITIC Tower had since 28 September 2014 attempted to negotiate with the 1st defendants, but the 1st defendants had refused to cooperate.

87. PMC also wrote to Kong Wan Fire Station on 11 October 2014 and to Central Police Station on 15 October 2014 to seek the professional assistance of the Fire Services Department and the Police. It would appear that there was little either could do as:

(1) Even though on 11 October 2014 firemen came to CITIC Tower, they said that they could only refer the case to the Police;

(2) PMC had not yet received a response from the Police.

88. The unchallenged evidence also shows that both before obtaining and even after the CITIC Tower Injunction was granted, the plaintiff has attempted a number of times without any success to remove any of the obstacles blocking the above vehicular access to and exits from CITIC Tower, as these attempts had been obstructed by the unidentified defendants. The evidence shows further that, even if the plaintiff managed at times to remove some of the barriers or obstructions, further and even more secured obstructions or barriers would be quickly reinstated by the 1st defendants to maintain the blockages.

B3.4 The 2nd defendant

89. The 2nd defendant, Ms Wong, is a student of the Institute of Education. She does not claim that she is one of those protestors or demonstrators who have placed, maintained or sought to maintain the blockages near CITIC Tower as described above.

90. However, since 28 September, she says she has been attending lectures held on Tamar Park as part of the student boycott programme organised by the Federation of Students. Because of the location of Tamar Park, she has to "traverse on Tim Mei Avenue to walk to there from time to time". It is because of that that she asked to be joined in these proceedings to seek to set aside the ex parte injunction (and presumably the continuation of it), as she believes that the inclusion in the descriptions of the 1st defendant and the term of the injunction reference to persons who have "otherwise done any act to cause obstruction" is too wide. This, she complains, would have caught someone like her, who may have only been physically present at the protest site on Tim Mei Avenue from time to time .

91. She therefore asks the injunction to be set aside or alternatively revised to narrow its scope.

B3.5 Whether the CITIC Tower Injunction should be continued

92. I now look at whether the injunction should be continued by applying the relevant principles. In this respect, it is important to note that none of the 1st unnamed defendants appears at the hearing to oppose the application, while the 2nd defendant as mentioned above only opposes the injunction on the grounds that the descriptions of the 1st defendants and the scope of the injunction as granted are too wide. I would deal with these objections later, after considering the general principles.

B3.5.1 Serious issues to be tried

93. The plaintiff's present claim is made in public nuisance and private nuisance.

94. With the above uncontroversial evidence of the blockages and their effect on CITIC Tower, it is clear that the plaintiff's has a good cause of action in bringing a claim:

(1) In public nuisance: The obstructions of the roads amount to public nuisance, and the evidence summarised above shows that the plaintiff as a private individual has suffered and would continue to suffer a particular, substantial and direct damage caused by the nuisance. See also paragraphs 19-21 above.

(2) In private nuisance: The owner of the property adjoining the highway has a common law right of access to the highway which is a private right remediable by an action of private nuisance. See: Marshall v Blackpool Corp [1935] A C 16 at 22 per Lord Atkin; Winfield & Jolowicz, 19th ed, paragraph 15-076; Clerk and Lindsell on Torts, 20th ed, paragraph 20-180.

95. As I said above, no one is raising any arguments otherwise.

96. The plaintiff has therefore clearly shown a serious issue to be tried.

B3.5.2 Damages adequate remedy and balance of convenience

97. Damages are unlikely to be a sufficient remedy for the plaintiff as (a) there is nothing to show that the unnamed defendants are in a position to compensate the plaintiff's financial loss, and (b) in any event, damages would not be an adequate remedy for the continuing health and safety hazard posed by the blockages of EVAs, Fire Exits and indirectly by the failure of the plaintiff to carry out necessary repair and maintenance work to pipes and manholes.

98. At the same time, it is unclear what damage the defendants would suffer if the interim injunction is later shown to be wrongly granted. There is no suggestion that the defendants' freedom of expression could not exercised without causing the nuisance in the way as interfering the plaintiff's use of its property.

99. On this basis alone, the injunction should thus be continued.

100. For the sake of argument, even if I have to consider the question of balance of convenience, similarly adopting what Poon J has said in the Taxi Operators Action and the Minibus Manager Action on the question of balance of convenience (as I have adopted at paragraph 69 above), this is a clear case where the balance of convenience weighs in favour of continuing the CITIC Tower Injunction.

101. Thus, subject to further considering the objections now raised by the 2nd defendant (which I would next proceed to), I will continue the CITIC Tower Injunction.

B3.5.3 The 2nd defendant's contentions

102. Mr Manzoni SC for the 2nd defendant raises essentially the following arguments.

103. First, Mr Manzoni submits that the plaintiff should not have proceeded to apply for the injunction on an ex parte basis on 20 October, as there was no material urgency (given that the blockages had been there for weeks) or secrecy to justify it. On that basis alone, says Mr Manzoni, the ex parte injunction should be set aside.

104. Mr Benjamin Yu SC for the plaintiff submits that, the concern of the growing health and safety hazards caused by the blockages, in particular after the plaintiff's failed efforts to negotiate with the protestors and to enlist the assistance of the Fire Services Department and Police to remove some of the blockages, justifies the urgency to make the application on an ex parte basis. Leading counsel also says that the plaintiff was not guilty of any delay as:

(1) The plaintiff had not been sitting on its hands. It had communicated with the 1st defendants repeatedly to try to persuade them to clear or to permit the plaintiff to clear the blockages, and had sought assistance from the Police and Fire Department with no success.

(2) The plaintiff was forced to take legal recourse when it became clear that no other way was available and that the defendants were likely to maintain the indefinite blockages of access to CITIC Tower.

105. I agree with Mr Yu's submissions. In my view, when it comes to the risks of personal safety (as the Fire Exits, EVAs and all the vehicular access to CITIC Tower have been unquestionably blocked) and no one can say or predict when an emergency (such as the breaking out of a fire or someone suffering from an urgent medical condition) may occur, there is justification for urgency for the plaintiff to apply for the injunction on an ex parte basis.

106. In any event, even if I were to set aside the ex parte injunction on the basis as submitted by Mr Manzoni, I would have no hesitation to re grant it on an inter partes basis for the reasons I have set out above.

107. Second, Mr Manzoni argues that the descriptions of the unnamed 1st defendants and the terms of the injunction in including the words "or otherwise done any act to cause obstruction" of the vehicular or pedestrian passage at Tim Mei Avenue or Lung Wui Road which block vehicular or pedestrian access to CITIC Tower are simply too wide. He submits that the descriptions would have caught innocent people, such as the 2nd defendant, who may be doing an entirely lawful act, such as simply crossing Tim Mei Avenue or Lung Wui Road (in particular when at the moment the other nearby pedestrian pathways may have been blocked), or happens also to stop by on the road to talk to someone or pick up something. This is so as the 2nd defendant's said lawful acts of crossing the roads would be caught by the words "to cause obstruction" of Tim Mei Avenue or Lung Wui Road simply by being physically present on the road.

108. With respect, I am unable to accept Mr Manzoni's submissions. The descriptions must be read with common sense and in context. The relevant parts of the descriptions and the terms of the injunction are to restrain the obstructions of Tim Mei Avenue and Lung Wui Road which would prevent vehicular and pedestrian access to CITIC Tower. Those words are clearly and objectively meant to cover only those acts where a person is blocking the vehicular access to and from CITIC Tower through Tim Mei Avenue and Lung Wui Road for such time and extent that is objectively unreasonable. The words could not have objectively understood to include any acts which would only cause a brief period of obstruction of the concerned vehicular and pedestrian access. Thus, the acts of crossing those roads, even with a stopping by to chat or picking up something, clearly and objectively cannot be caught by these words. Any reasonable persons in such circumstances would have moved away or given way to allow vehicular passage to enter into or leave CITIC Tower.

109. Third, Mr Manzoni submits that the terms of the injunction by reference to the entire Tim Avenue and Lung Wui Road are also too wide for an interlocutory injunction, which is granted on the basis of the existence of triable issues on the plaintiff's claim. He submits that, in the circumstances as the present case, in particular where the SJ has not acted to bring a claim for injunction in public nuisance, the court

should strike a balance and only grant an injunction on terms which are least intrusive of effecting interference of the defendants' right: The Mayor Commonality and Citizens of London v Tammy Samede 2012] EWCA (Civ) at paragraph 51.

110. Mr Manzoni however fairly accepts that, under this argument, it is for the 2nd defendant to persuade the court that there is another less intrusive term of the order that (a) would achieve similar effect provided under the original order, and (b) is workable in practice. See Samede, supra, at paragraph 53.

111. Mr Manzoni has provided two alternatives of the scope of the injunction which he says is less intrusive than the original terms of the injunction but would be sufficient to enable the objective of the injunction to allow vehicular access to CITIC Tower. Instead of requiring the clearance of the entire Tim Mei Avenue and the Lung Wui Road as provided under the original terms, these two alternatives effectively provides clearance of part of the south bound lanes (instead of both the south bound and north bound lanes) of Tim Mei Avenue and part of the west bound lane (instead of the entire west bound and east bound lanes) of Lung Wui Road. The two alternatives only differ in whether to include the relevant pedestrian walkway along Lung Wui Road in the injunction as well.

112. Counsel however accepts that for any of these two alternatives to work, it would require the police's coordination to implement a traffic control of a two-way traffic operation over the south bound lane of Tim Mei Avenue and the west bound lane of Lung Wui Road (which are originally under one-way traffic) so that vehicles can come and go along these lanes.

113. I am unable to accept these alternatives as the 2nd defendant has not shown that they are workable in practice. In both alternatives, before having any evidence to say whether it is feasible for the police to implement the two-way traffic operation as verbally suggested by Mr Manzoni at the hearing, the court cannot simply assume that it can and would be done. The court is not in a position to know whether there are any practical or otherwise difficulties in implementing the suggestions.

114. In the premises, I am not persuaded by any of the 2nd defendant's above arguments to say why the injunction should not be continued or that the descriptions of the unnamed defendants and the terms of the injunction should be revised and narrowed.

B3.5.4 Conclusion on the continuation of the CITIC Tower Injunction

115. For all the above reasons, I would continue the CITIC Tower Injunction until trial or further order of the court.

C. DIRECTIONS ON ENFORCEMENT

116. The unchallenged evidence shows that, since the granting of the ex parte injunctions in all three actions by Poon J:

(1) The unnamed defendants en masse (and many of them wearing masks) have refused to comply with (and also in continuing breach of) the court orders by continuing to maintain (and in fact reinforce) the obstructions on the Blocked Area, the Blocked Way and near CITIC Tower;

(2) The unnamed defendants en masse (any many of them wearing masks) have in breach of the court orders prevented the plaintiffs from removing those obstructions;

(3) In relation to the CITIC Tower Injunction, there were public figures who went to CITIC Tower where the blockages are and (in front of the defendants) openly said to the plaintiff's staff who were seeking to enforce the injunction that they should not do anything until the inter partes hearing, on the purported reason that the injunction was only granted on an ex parte basis.

117. In short, the plaintiffs have not been able to enforce the ex parte injunctions, and the unnamed defendants en masse have openly flouted and in continued breach of them.

118. The plaintiffs have therefore all asked this court to make the following directions to facilitate the enforcement of the court orders:

(1) The bailiff do take all reasonable and necessary steps to assist the plaintiff and its agents to effect clearance and removal of the relevant obstructions until further order;

(2) The bailiff be authorised and directed to request the assistance of the Police where necessary;

(3) Any Police officer be authorised to arrest and remove any person who the Police officer reasonably believes or suspects to be in contravention of this order provided that the person to be arrested has been informed of the gist of the terms of the court order and that his action is likely to constitute a breach of the order and that he may be arrested if he does not desist.

119. I would refer the first two directions as "the bailiff directions" and the last one "the police authorisation direction".

C1. The bailiff directions

120. There are no questions that the court could direct bailiffs to assist in the carrying out of court orders. Thus, none of the opposing defendants seek to raise any objections to the bailiff directions.

121. I have no hesitation in granting the bailiff directions in light of the circumstances of the present case as summarised above.

C2. The police authorisation direction

122. I now turn to look at the police authorisation direction.

123. Any person who obstructs the bailiff's performance of his duties would be in criminal contempt of the court:

(1) An intention and act to interfere with or impede the due administration of justice is a criminal contempt: Halsbury's Laws of England, Vol 22, paragraph 5.

(2) Thus, a person who, with knowledge of a court order, and deliberately impedes the bailiff in the due execution of his duties has both the requisite actus reus and mens rea of a criminal contempt as his conduct intentionally and deliberately interferes with or impedes the due administration of justice: AG v Times Newspapers [1992] 1 AC 191 at 208E F, 208H-209B, 216A-D; Dobson v Hastings [1992] Ch 393 at 402D-403D.

(3) It is therefore a criminal contempt to obstruct or impede a bailiff in the execution of his duties: Halsbury's Laws of England, Vol 22, paragraphs 17 and 49.

124. Criminal contempt is a common law offence punishable by imprisonment: Arlidge Eady & Smith on Contempt (4th ed), paragraph 3-67.

125. At the same time, Police are empowered under the Police Force Ordinance (Cap 232) to arrest a person suspected of being guilty of criminal contempt as:

(1) Under s 50(1)(a), it shall be lawful for any police officer to apprehend any person who he reasonably believes will be charged with or whom he reasonably suspects of being guilty of any offence for which a person, among others, may (on a first conviction for that offence) be sentenced for imprisonment;

(2) Under s 10(j), the duties of the police force shall include taking lawful measures for executing summonses, subpoenas, warrants, commitments and other process issued by the courts.

126. In the premises, a police officer is empowered in law to arrest any person who he reasonably believes or suspects of being guilty of criminal contempt (which is publishable by imprisonment on a first conviction) in obstructing or impeding the bailiff in executing his duties in enforcing a court order, such as the injunctions granted herein.

127. Thus, the police authorisation direction is only to re-state what the law has empowered the police to do.

128. The defendants in all three actions however oppose the making of the police authorization direction as sought. They raise the following in principle arguments.

129. First, Mr Dykes and Ms Li both submit that even though they are empowered to do so under the law, the police on the field have a discretion to decide whether or not to make any arrest after taking into account the actual circumstances and perhaps other relevant considerations on the ground. The court should not interfere or fetter such discretion so that the police on the ground can decide what is best to do according to the actual circumstances of the events.

130. This cannot be a valid in principle objection to make the police authorization direction. The term of the direction does not compel or direct the police to make an arrest. It only re-states the position of the law that that the police are authorised to do so. The direction therefore does not take away or fetter in any way the police's discretion as submitted by Ms Li and Mr Dykes.

131. Second, Mr Manzoni argues that the court has no jurisdiction to make such a direction as it is prohibited from doing so by s 21A(1) of the High Court Ordinance (Cap 4).

132. S 21A provides relevantly as follows:

"(1) Subject to section 21B, a person shall not be arrested or imprisoned to enforce, secure or pursue a civil claim for the payment of money or damages except under an order of Court; and the Court shall have jurisdiction to make such an order for arrest or imprisonment only to enforce, secure or pursue a judgment for the payment of a specified sum of money.

….

(6) This section shall not affect any jurisdiction of the Court to make orders of committal in relation to –

    (a)   contempt of court; or

    (b)   disobedience of a judgment or order of the Court."

133. Mr Manzoni says s 21A(1) therefore provides that the court cannot make an order to effect an arrest in civil claims generally except for the enforcement, securing or pursuance of a judgment for payment of sum.

134. With respect, I do not agree. S 21(A)(1) on its own terms deals with only a civil claim for payment of damages or sum of money. It does not cover or apply to all civil claims generally, such as a claim for an injunction. Further, the police authorization direction relates to authorizing the police to arrest persons suspected for being guilty of a criminal contempt, which is clearly not intended to be covered by s 21(A)(1). In any event, the exceptions provided at s 21A(6) in my view makes this clear.

135. I therefore also reject this submission.

136. Finally, all the represented defendants submit that it is simply not necessary for the court to make such a direction, since if as a matter of law the police are already authorised to so, it is superfluous to include such a direction in the order.

137. However, I am of the firm view that it is necessary to include the direction in light of what have happened after the granting of the ex parte injunction orders. I will explain why.

138. Hong Kong has always adhered to the concept of rule of law. This concept is treasured and has always been jealously guarded by the general public. It is universally regarded that the rule of law is one of Hong Kong's most important foundations that has led to her being a civilised, safe and orderly society.

139. The concept of the rule of law must include and embrace the notion that every resident and the government alike should obey and comply with the law. As said by Hartmann J (as the learned NPJ then was) in Secretary for Justice v Ocean Technology Ltd (t/a Citizens' Radio) [2010] 1 HKC 456 at paragraph 9, the concept of rule of law means that every resident of Hong Kong are governed by and bound to the operation of the law.

140. Under the rule of law, even if the defendants are of the view that a court order (including an ex parte order) is wrongly granted, instead of simply disobeying it, they should first comply with it but seek to challenge and argue against that order in court under due process and in accordance with the law. As said by Hoffmann LJ (as Lord Hoffmann then was) in Department of Transport v Lush (unreported, 29 July 1993) : "…the law cannot allow obedience of its orders to be a matter of individual choice even on grounds of conscience".

141. It is therefore wrong for any suggestions that the rule of law is not undermined or under challenged if people can freely or intentionally disobey the law first and then accept the consequences of breaking the law. The rule of law cannot realistically and effectively operate in a civilised and orderly society on this basis.

142. The upholding of the rule of law must therefore be built upon, among others, the due administration of justice for the enforcement of court orders and the law. This is also one of reasons why the independence of the Judiciary, and the respect for the dignity and authority of the court are fundamental tenets of the concept of the rule of law.

143. However, recent events relating to these actions have shown that there is a real risk that the due administration of justice and the respect for the authority of the court, and therefore the rule of law in Hong Kong, would be seriously undermined:

(1) As I have mentioned above, the ex parte injunctions, which are valid and proper court orders until set aside, have been openly disobeyed and flouted by the defendants en masse.

(2) Not only that, and worryingly, there have also been repeated open suggestions by a number of public figures (including some legally trained individuals) to the public and the protestors and demonstrators en masse to the effect that ex parte injunctions need not to be complied with until they had been determined after an inter partes hearing, and that there is no challenge to the rule of law from merely disobeying civil orders, and that the rule of law is only threatened when there is disobedience of an actual order of committal for contempt of court. As I have said above, these suggestions, with the greatest respect, are in my view wrong and incorrect and would cause the public and the defendants an unwarranted misunderstanding on the concept of the rule of law.

144. When the rule of law and the due administration of justice are at the risk of being seriously challenged and undermined, as it is now, the court must act and strive to protect and uphold them for the benefit and best interest of the general public.

145. The present circumstances therefore undoubtedly justify and call for the inclusion of the police authorisation direction in these injunction orders. The direction would send a clear message to the defendants that civil court orders should be obeyed and about the serious consequences for breaching them.

146. Further, in MacMillan v Simpson, supra, the court granted an interim injunction prohibiting the defendants (named and unnamed) from engaging in conducts interfering the plaintiff's logging operations at specified locations and barring members of the public from blocking a bridge. The court order also included a provision (similar to the police authorisation direction herein) that "any peace officer [which included police officer] be authorized to arrest and remove any person who the peace officer has reasonable and probable grounds to believe is contravening or has contravened the provisions of this order".

147. On appeal to the Supreme Court of Canada, the defendants challenged, among others, the appropriateness of the inclusion in the order a provision to authorize the police to arrest persons breaching the injunction. In dismissing the appeal and in particular this challenge, McLachlin J (as she then was) observed this at paragraph 41 (p 1069):

"…I observe only that the inclusion of police authorization appears to follow the Canadian practice of ensuring that orders which may affect members of the public clearly spell out the consequences of non-compliance. Members of public need not take the word of the police that the arrest and detention of violators is authorized because this is clearly set out in the order signed by the judge. Viewed thus, the inclusion does not harm and may make the order fairer." (emphasis added)

148. I respectfully adopt McLaughlin J's above observation.

149. As I have emphasised above, the public in general and the defendants in particular appear to be at the risk of misunderstanding the serious consequence (including the serious effect on the rule of law) of disobeying a civil court order. Given that misunderstanding and the en masse open and persistent disobedience of the ex parte orders, there is also the real likelihood that (a) the defendants (which are in large numbers) would continue to seek to disobey the injunction orders and obstruct the bailiffs in carrying out their duties to enforce those orders, and (b) the defendants may well (mistakenly and incorrectly) dispute the police's power to arrest them if they obstruct the due administration of justice in interfering or obstructing the bailiffs in carrying out their duties to enforce the injunctions.

150. In the premises, the police authorisation direction if included in the injunction orders would help to inform the en masse defendants the consequence of any disobedience and confirm the police's power. This would not only make the orders clearer and fairer, but also facilitate the due administration of justice.

151. I have therefore come to the clear conclusion that it is necessary to include the police authorisation direction in all the injunction orders. In light of the circumstances of the present case, I would however revise the direction to the following terms:

"Any police officer be authorised to arrest and remove any person who the police officer reasonably believes or suspects to be obstructing or interfering any bailiff in carrying out his or her duties in enforcing the terms of the injunction order herein, provided that the person to be arrested has been informed of the gist of the terms of this court order and that his action is likely to constitute a breach of the order and obstruction of the administration of justice, and that he may be arrested if he does not desist."

D. CONCLUSION

152. For all the above reasons, I will continue the Mongkok Injunctions (in the terms as I have revised on 27 Oct) and the CITIC Tower Injunction. I would also make the following directions in those orders:

(1) The bailiff do take all reasonable and necessary steps to assist the plaintiff and its agents to effect the clearance and removal of the obstructions [as provided in the respective injunction orders].

(2) The bailiff be authorised and directed to request the assistance of the Police where necessary.

(3) Any police officer be authorised to arrest and remove any person who the police officer reasonably believes or suspects to be obstructing or interfering any bailiff in carrying out his or her duties in enforcing the terms of the injunction order herein, provided that the person to be arrested has been informed of the gist of the terms of this court order and that his action is likely to constitute a breach of the order and obstruction of the administration of justice, and that he may be arrested if he does not desist.

(4) Any person so arrested by the police shall be brought before the court as soon as practicable for further directions.

153. Given that all the respective represented defendants have failed in their opposition to these applications, I further make an order nisi that they should pay the respective plaintiffs' costs of the respective applications, to be taxed if not agreed. There be certificate for two counsel for the plaintiffs in the Taxi Operators Action and the CITIC Tower Action. For the represented defendants who are under legal aid, their own costs be taxed in accordance with legal aid regulations.

154. Lastly, I thank counsel for their assistance.

(Thomas Au)
Judge of the Court of First Instance
High Court

Mr Tim Wong, instructed by CMK Lawyers, for the plaintiff in HCA 2086/2014

Mr Benjamin Yu SC, Mr Victor Dawes and Ms Bianca Yu, instructed by Mayer Brown JSM, for the plaintiff in HCA 2094/2014

Mr Johnny Mok SC, Mr Jose-Antonio Maurellet and Ms Eva Leung, instructed by Phyllis K Y Kwong & Associates, for the 1st and 2nd plaintiffs in HCA 2104/2014

Mr Philip Dykes SC and Ms Christine Yu, assigned by the Director of Legal Aid, instructed by JCC Cheung & Co, for the 2nd defendant in HCA 2086/2014 and HCA 2104/2014

Ms Gladys Li SC, Ms Margaret Ng and Mr Michael Yin, instructed by Daly & Associates, for the 3rd defendant in HCA 2086/2014 and HCA 2104/2014

Mr Charles Manzoni SC and Mr Earl Deng, assigned by the Director of Legal Aid, instructed by Vidler & Co, for the 2nd defendant in HCA 2094/2014

Raymond Chen, in person, present on 24 October 2014, absent on 27 October 2014

Mr Jin Pao, instructed by Department of Justice, for the Secretary of Justice (a non-party)

COURT INJUNCTIONS (ADMIRALTY)
DECEMBER 1

HCA 2222 & 2223 of 2014

HCA 2222 of 2014

IN THE HIGH COURT OF THE HONG KONG SPECIAL ADMINISTRATIVE REGION
COURT OF FIRST INSTANCE
ACTION NO 2222 OF 2014

BETWEEN

KWOON CHUNG MOTORS COMPANY LIMITED   Plaintiff
(冠忠遊覽車有限公司)

and

PERSONS WHO ERECTED OR PLACED OR   1st Defendants
MAINTAINED OBSTRUCTIONS OR OTHERWISE DO ANY ACT TO CAUSE OBSTRUCTIONS,
OR TO PREVENT OR HINDER THE CLEARANCE AND REMOVAL OF THE OBSTRUCTIONS
OR OCCUPYING ON THE PORTION OF CONNAUGHT ROAD CENTRAL
EASTBOUND BETWEEN EDINBURGH PLACE (WESTERN PORTION) AND EDINBURGH
PLACE (EASTERN PORTION) ("SECTION 1") AND/OR THE
PORTION OF HARCOURT ROAD EASTBOUND BETWEEN EDINBURGH PLACE (EASTERN
PORTION) AND COTTON TREE DRIVE ("SECTION 2") AND/OR THE
PORTION OF COTTON TREE DRIVE TOWARDS MID LEVELS ("SECTION 4") (TOGETHER
"THE AREA") TO PREVENT OR OBSTRUCT NORMAL VEHICULAR
TRAFFIC FROM PASSING THE AREA

KWOK CHEUK KIN   2nd Defendant

WONG HO MING   3rd Defendant

HCA 2223 of 2014

IN THE HIGH COURT OF THE HONG KONG SPECIAL ADMINISTRATIVE REGION
COURT OF FIRST INSTANCE
ACTION NO 2223 OF 2014

BETWEEN

ALL CHINA EXPRESS LIMITED   Plaintiff
(跨境全日通有限公司)

and

PERSONS WHO ERECTED OR PLACED OR   1st Defendants
MAINTAINED OBSTRUCTIONS OR OTHERWISE DO ANY ACT TO CAUSE OBSTRUCTIONS, OR TO PREVENT OR HINDER THE CLEARANCE AND REMOVAL OF THE OBSTRUCTIONS OR OCCUPYING ON THE PORTION OF CONNAUGHT ROAD CENTRAL EASTBOUND BETWEEN EDINBURGH PLACE (WESTERN PORTION) AND EDINBURGH PLACE (EASTERN PORTION) ("SECTION 1") AND/OR THE PORTION OF HARCOURT ROAD EASTBOUND BETWEEN EDINBURGH PLACE (EASTERN PORTION) AND COTTON TREE DRIVE ("SECTION 2") AND/OR THE PORTION OF COTTON TREE DRIVE SOUTHBOUND BETWEEN HARCOURT ROAD EASTBOUND AND QUEENSWAY ("SECTION 3") (TOGETHER "THE AREA") TO PREVENT OR OBSTRUCT NORMAL VEHICULAR TRAFFIC FROM PASSING THE AREA

KWOK CHEUK KIN   2nd Defendant

WONG HO MING   3rd Defendant

Before: Hon Au J in Chambers

Dates of Hearing: 11 and 17 November 2014

Date of Judgment: 1 December 2014

JUDGMENT

A.   INTRODUCTION

1.   These are the respective applications by the plaintiff under each of these two actions for an interlocutory injunction against the defendants. The injunctions sought relate to the occupation and blockage by the defendants of portions of Harcourt Road, Connaught Road and some nearby roads in Admiralty. The occupation arises from the occupy central campaign ("the OCC") whereby a large number of unidentified protestors and demonstrators have occupied various parts of the public roads in Hong Kong directed against the constitutional development in Hong Kong.

2.   The plaintiff ("Kwoon Chung") in HCA 2222/2014 is the operator of various school bus services. Relevant to this application is Kwoon Chung's school bus service route ("Route 9") which carries students to and from Pier 3 in Central and the Island School at Borrett Road in the Mid-Levels. For convenience, I would refer to this action as the "Kwoon Chung Action".

3.   The plaintiff ("ACE") in HCA 2223/2014 is the operator of cross-border bus services. Relevant to this application is the Wan Chai cross border route ("the Wan Chai Route"), which carries passengers to and from Wan Chai in Hong Kong to Huanggang Port in Shenzhen in the Mainland. Again for convenience, I would refer to this action as the "ACE Action".

4.   In both actions, it is not disputed that since late September 2014, unidentified protestors and demonstrators (ie, the 1st defendants) have through themselves and by placing various barricades and obstructions occupied and blocked the following parts of the roads near Central and Admiralty:

(1)   The portion of Connaught Road Central eastbound between Edinburgh Place (Western Portion) and Edinburgh Place (Eastern Portion) ("Section 1");

(2)   The portion of Harcourt Road eastbound between Edinburgh Place (Eastern Portion) and Cotton Tree Drive ("Section 2");

(3) The portion of Cotton Tree Drive southbound between Harcourt Road eastbound and Queensway ("Section 3"); and

(4) The portion of Cotton Tree Drive towards the Mid-Levels ("Section 4").

The locations of Sections 1, 2, 3 and 4 are identified respectively in Map A, B, C and D as provided by the plaintiffs. Copies of these Maps are attached to this judgment for reference.

5. There is also no dispute that the said blockages and obstruction of these Sections have completely prevented any vehicular traffic to pass through these areas.

6. It is Kwoon Chung's case that the school bus operating under the Route passes through the area ("the Kwoon Chung Action Area") under Sections 1, 2 and 4 in its usual and normal operation. However, because of the obstruction and blockages of the Kwoon Chung Action Area, the Route 9 school bus has to take a detour in its route ("the Detour Route"). As a result, the travelling distance of the route has increased from 3.9km to 6.2km, thereby also increasing the average travelling time by about 6 minutes.

7. It is ACE's case that normally the cross-border buses under the Wan Chai Route pass through the area ("the ACE Action Area") under Sections 1, 2 and 3. However, because of the blockages of the roads in this area, and the severe general traffic congestions in northern Hong Kong Island (in particular in the area between the Western Harbour Tunnel and Wanchai) resulted from the said blockages, the buses operating under the Wan Chai Route have to take a detour and cancel the drop-off point at Wan Chai MTR station. The detour has caused an increase in the average travelling time of the southbound route of the Wan Chai Route by 10-20 minutes.

8. By way of the respective actions herein, Kwoon Chung and ACE therefore claim against the defendants for damages and injunction in public nuisance.

9. In the present application, Kwoon Chung now asks for an interlocutory injunction to restrain the defendants until trial effectively from:

(1) Continuing to block and occupy the Kwoon Chung Action Area (whether by themselves and/or by placing obstructions thereat) to prevent vehicular access; and

(2) Preventing Kwoon Chung or its authorised agents from removing the obstructions placed in the Kwoon Chung Action Area.

10. Similarly, ACE asks for an interlocutory injunction to restrain the defendants until trial from:

(1) Continuing to block and occupy the ACE Action Area (whether by themselves and/or by placing obstructions thereat) to prevent vehicular access; and

(2) Preventing ACE or its authorised agents from removing the obstructions placed in the ACE Action Area.

11. These applications are opposed by the 2nd and 3rd defendants. They both accept and confirm to the court that they fall within the descriptions of the 1st defendant in each of these actions, in that they have been occupying and obstructing the Kwoon Chung Action and ACE Action Areas.

12. Other than the 2nd and 3rd defendants, none of the 1st defendants turns up in court to oppose the applications.

13. Before I turn to deal with the applications, it is pertinent to note that this court has recently in HCA 2086/2014 and 2104/2014 (collectively, the "Mongkok Injunction Cases") dealt with similar applications for interlocutory injunction against the protestors under the OCC occupying certain parts of the roads in Mongkok. By a judgment dated 10 November 2014 ("the Mongkok Injunctions Judgment"), I continued the injunctions in the Mongkok Injunction Cases. Respectively under HCMP 2975 & 2976/2014, HCMP 3028/2014 and HCMP 3090/2014, the court of appeal has dismissed the various applications for leave to appeal against the Mongkok Injunctions Judgment.

14. As will be seen later, most of the issues raised in the present applications are similar or related to the ones raised in the Mongkok Injunction Cases. Therefore, whenever necessary, I may refer to these court of appeal judgments and the Mongkok Injunction Cases Judgment when I deal with these issues.

B. THESE APPLICATIONS

B1. Applicable principles

15. It is well established that generally in determining whether or not to grant an interlocutory injunction, the court has to see (a) whether there are serious issues to be tried, (b) whether damages would be an adequate remedy for either side, and if damages would not be adequate for both parties, (c) where the balance of convenience lies in terms of whether or not to grant an interim injunction pending the trial of the matter. In that balancing exercise, the court must take into account the interests of the general public even though they are not represented before the court. See: Turbo Top Ltd v Lee Cheuk Yan [2013] 3 HKLRD 41 at paragraph 14 per G Lam J.

16. However, Mr Pun for the 2nd defendant contends in the present cases that the court should not apply the threshold of whether there are serious issues to be tried in determining whether to grant the injunction. This is so, says Mr Pun, as the grant of an injunction in the present cases would or likely to have the effect of finally disposing of the matters. As such, the court should apply the threshold that the plaintiffs need to show that it is very likely that they will succeed at trial. See: Fast-Link Express Ltd v Falcon Express Ltd (unreported, HCA 2040/2005, 30 December 2005, Deputy High Court Judge Carlson) at paragraph 9.

17. Mr Pun also relies on the case of City of Bradford Metropolitan Council v Brown (1987) 19 HLR 16 at 21-22 to support his submissions that, in an application for interim injunction as the present one, the court should at least reach a "provisional" view on the question of whether the plaintiff has the necessary standing to bring the claim.

18. I do not accept these contentions.

19. I have similarly applied the threshold of a serious issue to be tried in the Mongkok Injunction Cases. In dismissing the defendants' respective applications for leave to appeal in those cases, the court of appeal rejected the similar arguments that this court was wrong to adopt the serious issues to be tried threshold in those cases. Thus, the adoption of this threshold in cases which are similar to the present ones has been approved by the court of appeal. See HCMP 2975/2014 at paragraphs 9 to 19 per Cheung CJHC, and HCMP 3028/2014 at paragraphs 8-9 per Lam VP.

20. Further, the court of appeal in dismissing the applications for leave to appeal against the Mongkok Injunctions Judgment also does not accept that City of Bradford Metropolitan Council is an authority to support that a higher threshold than the one of serious issue to be tried should be adopted in an application as the present ones: HCMP3028/2014, supra, at paragraph 9 per Lam VP.

21. For these reasons, I reject Mr Pun's contentions and would adopt the threshold of serious issue to be tried in the present applications as part of the considerations to determine whether to grant the interlocutory injunctions or not.

22. Applying the above principles, I now look at these applications.

B2. Serious questions to be tried

B2.1 A claim in public nuisance by private individuals

23. It is uncontroversial that the occupations and blocking of the Kwoon Chung Action Area and the ACE Blocked Area amount to public nuisance in law.

24. It is also well established that for a private individual (as opposed to the Secretary for Justice) to bring a claim in public nuisance, he has to show that he has suffered by reason of the public nuisance a "particular, substantial and direct" injury or damage, which is above and beyond what has been suffered by the rest of the public at large: Benjamin v Storr (1874) LR 9 CP 400 at 406-406 per Brett J.

25. The question that I have to consider under this head is thus whether there is a serious issue to be tried as to whether each of the plaintiffs has suffered such a particular, substantial and direct damage.

26. As I have said in the Mongkok Injunctions Judgment, in relation to what amounts to a particular, substantial and direct damage in the law of public nuisance, the authorities show that:

(1)   Whether a damage or loss said to be suffered by the plaintiff can be regarded as particular, substantial and direct is essentially a question of fact, and a matter of degree and extent: Jan de Nul v Royale Belge [2000] 2 LLR 700 at paragraph 44 (p 715).

(2)   The "particular" damage needs not be pecuniary (and thus special) in nature. It may consist of proved general damage, such as inconvenience and delay provided that it is substantial, that it is direct and non-consequential, and that it is appreciably greater in degree than any suffered by the general public: Walsh v Ervin [1952] VLR361 at 371 per Scholl J.

(3)   "Substantial" means no more than that the damage suffered is more than trivial: Jan de Nul, supra, at paragraph 44.

(4)   It is also not necessary prove that the plaintiff has any injury to property, or has any interest or relationship with any land or building: Benjamin v Storr, supra, at 406; Leung Tsang Hung v The Incorporated Owner of Kwok Wing House [2007] 10 HKCFAR 480 at paragraph 13 per Ribeiro PJ.

27.   Further, I have also said that the authorities support that the requirement of "direct" damage is satisfied not only by one which is immediately caused by or flowed from the nuisance. It also covers those injuries and damage which are caused by or flowed from the nuisance through a chain of events, so long as those events can be regarded as probable events as a result of the nuisance and the chain is not broken by external matters unrelated to the nuisance. It is a question of fact in each case as to whether the damage claimed to be suffered fall within the requisite chain of events. See: Overseas Tankship (UK) Ltd v Miller Steamship Co Pty (Wagon Mount No 2) [1967] 1 AC 617, at 634E-636D per Lord Reid; Gravesham v British Railways Board [1978] 1 Ch 379 at 396F-397C and 398H-399B.

28.   The court of appeal has held that there are at least a triable issue raised in relation to these legal propositions.

29.   In light of these at least triable legal propositions, I will now examine the plaintiff's respective case on the question of particular, substantial and direct damage.

B2.1.1 The Kwoon Chung Action

30.   In this action, Kwoon Chung's case and evidence on its loss and damage suffered by reason of the blockages can be summarised as follows :

(1)   Given the Detour Route, the school buses under Route 9 have to travel at an increased distance, which has increased the average travelling time by about 6 minutes. Further, the pick-up time at Pier 3 by the school bus has to be moved to 6:30 am, which is 40 minutes earlier than the normal pick-up time.

(2)   As a result, for the month since 6 October 2014 until 31 October 2014, Kwoon Chung has suffered damage in the nature of increased fuel cost at $843.18 and overtime payments to its drivers at $3,750, totalling $4,593.18.

(3) Further, the students and the drivers all have to wake up relatively earlier in order to catch the school buses because of the earlier pick-up time, and thus have suffered inconvenience and hardship.

(4) If continued, Kwoon Chung would also suffer damage to its reputation as a school bus operator and to its good relationship with the affected schools, students and parents.

31. In my view, Kwoon Chung has not raised a triable issue that it has suffered a particular, substantial and direct damage. My reasons are as follows.

32. First, although the pecuniary loss said to be suffered by Kwoon Chung can at least arguably be said to be amounting to "peculiar" and "direct" damage by reason of the public nuisance, I am not satisfied that it can arguably be said that the loss is one which is "substantial". As I mentioned above, what amounts to "substantial" damage for the purpose of enabling a private individual to bring a claim in public nuisance is that the loss must be more than trivial. In the present case, the total pecuniary loss of $4,593.18 cannot be said to be more than trivial. This is in fact accepted by Kwoon Chung itself: Mr James Wong in his affidavit at paragraph 23 accepts that "the monetary damage to the plaintiff … may seem relatively trivial…". In the circumstances, the loss suffered by the plaintiff does not even arguably amount to "substantial" damage as understood in the law of public nuisance.

33. Second, in relation to the suggestion of damage to its reputation or relationship with the schools, students and parents, there is simply no triable evidence to show that Kwoon Chung's said reputation is or is likely to be so damaged. As a matter of common sense, it is obvious that the increased travelling time is caused by the occupation of the affected area by reason of the OCC. That is something beyond Kwoon Chung's control and has nothing to do with its ability and skill in the operation of school buses (and thus its reputation). It would unlikely lead to any damage to its reputation. This is underlined by the lack of evidence to show that the parents, students or schools have been laying the blame on Kwoon Chung. Quite to the contrary, the evidence of various other parents' emails and letters shows that they were aware of the fact that the increased travelling time was caused by the OCC and thus they fully supported Kwoon Chung's intended application for an injunction.

34. Finally, the inconvenience and hardship said to be suffered by the students and the drivers are simply not one suffered by the plaintiff. It cannot be regarded as the plaintiff's damage or injury.

35. For these reasons, I am not satisfied that Kwoon Chung has shown any triable issues that it has suffered a particular, substantial and direct damage as a result of the public nuisance to enable it (as a private individual) to bring a claim in public nuisance.

36. On this basis alone, I would refuse Kwoon Chung's application for an interlocutory injunction.

B2.1.2 The ACE Action

37. ACE's case and evidence on its loss can be summarised as follows :

(1) ACE operate, among others, the cross-border bus services under the Wan Chai Route, where the relevant passenger service licence is held by ACE's wholly owned subsidiary All China Express (Wanchai) Ltd.

(2) Because of the blocking of the ACE Action Area, and the resultant severe general traffic congestions in northern Hong Kong Island caused by the blockages, (a) the average travelling time of the southbound cross-border buses under the Wan Chai Route has increased by about 20.9% (some 10 20 minutes), (b) ACE has to cancel the drop-off point at Wanchai MTR station of the Wan Chai Route, and (c) the buses have not been able to provide on time scheduled services.

(3) Given the significant increase in the travelling time, the cancellation of the Wanchai MTR drop-off point, and that ACE can no longer provide on time services in accordance to the schedule under the Wanchai Route, the number of passengers and the sales turnover of the Wanchai Route have dropped significantly. In particular, the ticket sales of the southbound service have decreased over 17% (in the sum of $691,754) for the period between 29 September and 26 October 2014.

(4) ACE has therefore suffered pecuniary loss. It will also suffer irreparable damage to its business reputation in operating cross-border buses.

38. Since ACE's business derives income or profits from the operation and provision of transport services in Hong Kong, I accept that the above evidence on the said loss of income by reason of road blockages clearly raises a serious issue to be tried as to whether this amounts to a particular, substantial and direct damage under the law of public nuisance. As said by the learned Chief Judge, it is almost a matter of common sense. Moreover, this is a mixed question of law and fact which can and should only be properly resolved at a full trial. See: HCMP 2975/2014, supra, at paragraphs 19 and 20 per Cheung CJHC; also The Mongkok Injunctions Judgment, at paragraphs 30-32.

39. Mr Pun for the 2nd defendant submits that there are authorities to show that a private individual (for the purpose of bringing a claim in public nuisance) must demonstrate that his loss is also above and beyond the class which he or his business belongs to. In other words, if the damage is common to all persons of the same class, then a personal right of action in public nuisance is not maintainable. Counsel relies on Hickey v Electric Reduction Co of Canada (1970) 21 DLR 368 at 371-372 and Ricket v Metropolitan Railway Co (1867) LR 2 HL 175 at 190, 199 to support this proposition. Thus, contended Mr Pun, as ACE's loss is in nature no different from that suffered by everyone in the class of transport service operators in Hong Kong, it has not suffered any particular loss that would entitle it to bring a private claim in public nuisance.

40. Mr Pun also says in determining the meaning of "particular damage over and above the damage suffered by the public at large", the court has to bear in mind the rationale behind this rule. The rationale is to avoid multiplicity of proceedings and to avoid usurping the discretion of the Secretary for Justice

("SJ") whether to take action in the common interest of the public. Mr Pun seeks to find support of these submissions in Wagon Mount No 2, supra, at 635-636, R v Rimmington [2006] 1 AC 459 at paragraph 8 and William's Case (1591) 5 Coke Reports 72 at 73a.

41. For the present purpose of an interlocutory injunction, suffice for me to say that these contentions on class interest and on the rationale to avoid multiplicity of suits only add further facets to the arguments in law and on the facts as to what could satisfy the requirement of a particular, substantial and direct damage in the circumstance of the present case. As I mentioned above, what amounts to a particular, substantial and direct loss is essentially a question of law and fact. In light of the other authorities I have referred to in paragraphs 26 and 27 above, these authorities relied on by the 2nd defendant could not be regarded as determinative in the present case at an interlocutory stage to show that ACE has not suffered a particular, substantial and direct loss.

42. Mr Pun's contentions therefore only show that there is a serious issue to be tried on the different legal propositions relied on by the respective parties made under this question, which should only be determined after mature debates and arguments at trial. See the observations by Cheung CJHC in HCMP2975/2014, supra, at paragraph 19. See also The Mongkok Injunctions Judgment, paragraphs 42-48.

43. As to Mr Pun's argument on the need to avoid usurping SJ's discretion, I will adopt my reasons set out at paragraphs 60-61 below and paragraphs 42-49 of the Mongkok Injunctions Judgment to reject it as a valid basis to say that there is not triable issue on the question of whether ACE's has suffered a particular, substantial and direct loss.

44. For all the above reasons, I reject all of Mr Pun's above contentions and am satisfied that ACE has shown a serious issue to be tried in its claim in public nuisance against the defendants.

45. I now move on to the question of balance of convenience.

B3. Balance of convenience

46. It is in my view clear that the balance of convenience lies in favour of granting the interim injunction. This is because:

(1) Damages are not a sufficient remedy for ACE given that:

(a) there is no suggestion that, if no injunction is granted now, the unidentified 1st defendants and the 2nd and 3rd defendants are in a position to meet the damages after trial;

(b) further, as observed by the learned Chief Judge in HCMP 2975/2014 at paragraph 17, if no interim injunction is granted in the meantime and if ACE succeeds at trial to show particular, substantial and direct damage and a good claim in public nuisance, it will have suffered in the interim further loss and damage, for which damages are also likely to be difficult to assess.

(2) At the same time, the defendants simply have no legal right whatsoever to occupy and block in the way the protestors do the public roads in question. As such, if the interlocutory injunction pending trial is granted but ACE fails at trial in establishing its claim in public nuisance, the defendants will not in the meantime have suffered, by the grant of the injunction, the loss of anything which they have never had a right to in the first place. See: HMCP 2975/2014 at paragraph 12 per Cheung CJHC.

(3) In the premises, the balance of convenience lies overwhelmingly in favour of granting the injunction. It is clearly just and convenient in all the circumstances to grant the injunction. Cf: HCMP 2975/2014 at paragraphs 8-12, 17-22.

47. However, the 2nd and 3rd defendants respectively raise a number of contentions to say why the court should not exercise its discretion to grant the injunction. I will deal with each of them in turn.

48. First, Mr Pun for the 2nd defendant says the plaintiff cannot engage the judiciary in a matter which is effectively a matter of political choice for the Executive. Counsel says the court's equitable jurisdiction should not be exploited as a means to resolve political disputes, especially when the Executive may well have made a deliberate choice to order its law enforcement agents not to take any action against the protestors occupying the concerned areas. He says the police clearly have lawful power to do so but refrained from doing so. There must be, says counsel, good policy reasons for the tolerance of these protestors by the Executive, and it is thus unjust for the plaintiff to invoke the court's equitable jurisdiction to intervene in such a highly sensitive political matter. The court therefore should not exercise its discretion to grant the injunction.

49. Similarly, the 3rd defendant also argues that the occupation and blocking of the roads are conducts arising out of political issues, which should be resolved politically. Thus, the court should not be engaged to revolve what are essentially political problems.

50. I do not accept these contentions.

51. As repeatedly emphasised by the court in the past, in deciding cases, including the present ones, the court would determine them only by applying the law and would not take into account any political considerations. As demonstrated in the analyses above, this is precisely what this court is doing: adjudicating and resolving disputes concerning the parties' legal rights in accordance to the law, and the law alone. The fact that it also happens that there is political underlying to these disputes does not and should not affect the court's role and duty in adjudicating those legal rights. Nor should the court refrain from adjudicating those legal rights in the dispute.

52. As I have said above, it is when looking at the present matter in accordance with the law that the balance of convenience lies overwhelmingly in favour of granting the injunction to address and balance the respective private rights of the parties.

53. In this respect, I would also respectfully refer to Lam VP's observations in HCMP 3028/2014 at paragraph 36 as follows:

"36. We understand there are exceptional political circumstances which gave rise to the unlawful occupation in the present case. But the court has to be involved in this instance because the rights of private citizens protected by the law are said to be threatened and they seek redress from the court. In so doing, they are exercising a constitutional right conferred on them by article 35 of the Basic Law. It is the duty of the court to adjudicate upon and, where justified, give effect to such rights according to law. Even in cases where protesters are pursuing a noble cause which they feel strongly about (and we express no view on the protest in the case before us), this does not give them any right in the eyes of law to trample upon the rights of the others who may or may not agree with their cause. This is an important facet of the rule of law which, as judges, we must uphold."

54. The 2nd and 3rd defendants' above submissions in effect are asking the court to take into account political considerations (ie, the fact that the Executive has, because of possibly various policy and political considerations, so far "tolerated" the protestors' occupations) to determine the legal rights between private parties. This cannot be right.

55. Further and in any event, even if the court is to and can take into account of this fact, I do not think it is a matter that that would tip the overwhelming case in favour of granting the injunction as I have said above.

56. I would therefore reject these contentions as a basis for not granting the injunction.

57. Second, Mr Pun for the 2nd defendant says there is delay on the part of ACE in taking out this application for injunction. In the premises, the court should refuse to exercise discretion to grant it. In support of the contention, counsel relies on Rogers VP's observation in King Fung Vacuum Ltd v Toto Toys Ltd [2006] 2 HKLRD 785 at paragraph 20 as follows:

"20. There has traditionally been a strong requirement when interlocutory injunctions have been sought, that the plaintiff must show that it has acted promptly and without delay. Promptly in the circumstances of interlocutory injunctions has been commonly understood to be a period of six weeks or so of unexplained delay and three months with an explanation given for the delay in making application for an injunction. Since the American Cyanamid decision the importance of irreparable damage in an application for an interlocutory injunction is paramount. If there is no irreparable damage demonstrated then the need for an interlocutory injunction has not been shown. This is important because of the approach that the courts take to interlocutory injunctions. They are not the trial of the action and the court is concerned with whether irreparable damage will occur before a trial can take place. It stands to reason that if a party is prepared to allow matters to proceed and takes no action with respect to matters which have been extant for lengthy periods, it lies ill in their mouth to say that there is likely to be irreparable damage and that is the case here." (Mr Pun's emphasis)

58. It is trite that delay in taking out an interim injunction is one of the factors (albeit sometimes a very weight factor depending on the circumstances of the case) that the court should take into account in deciding how to exercise the discretion. It is however not an absolute bar to the grant of an injunction. The ultimate question is still, after taking into all the circumstances of the case, including the nature and length of any delay in question, whether the court regards it as just to grant the injunction. See also: Abbott GmbH & Co v Pharmareg Consulting Co Ltd [2009] 3 HKLRD 524 at paragraphs 80-95 per Sakhrani J, and the cases cited therein.

59. In the present case, given that (a) the length of the delay is at most about one month or so, and (b) it was unclear in the beginning that the said occupation would last indefinitely as it is now, I do not think it can be said that the delay is a serious one and wholly inexcusable. In the premises, given also that the defendants simply have no legal rights to occupy the roads in the way as they do to completely deprive the rest of public's right to use them, I am still of the clear view that, notwithstanding the delay, this is an overwhelming case that it is just and convenient to grant the injunction.

60. Third, Mr Pun says the court should exercise great caution in deciding whether to grant the injunction sought when it is invoking the assistance of the civil courts in aid of the criminal law. The court should consider, counsel contends, whether the injunction would exacerbate the situation and whether it would likely to be futile as (suggested Mr Pun) the demonstrators may move to other areas not covered by the injunction. He relies on Gouriet v Union of Post Office Workers at 481C-H to support this contention.

61. I am unable to accept Mr Pun's submissions. Similar arguments relying on Gouriet have been raised in the Mongkok Injunction Cases. I have rejected them at paragraphs 42-49 of the Mongkok Injunctions Judgment. I would simply adopt those reasons herein to reject Mr Pun's arguments. Further, Mr Pun's submission that the injunction would likely to be futile as the demonstrators may move to other areas is wholly misplaced. The purpose of the injunction is to prevent the continued occupation and blocking of the ACE Action Area pending trial. Thus, the suggestion that some demonstrators may move to other areas does not thereby render the injunction useless and futile.

62. Fourth, the 3rd defendant submits that in the exercise of its discretion, the court should take into account the defendants' right to demonstration and the fact that they are carrying out "civil disobedience" in occupying the concerned area.

63. I do not think these factors in the circumstances of the present case can constitute a valid basis for not granting the injunction. As fairly accepted by the 3rd defendant, all these rights are not absolute and

are subject to limitation. The court must balance these rights against the public's unquestioned rights to use the roads.

64. In deciding to grant an ex parte injunction in the Mongkok Injunction Cases, Poon J rejected the potential arguments that the right to demonstration and the notion of civil disobedience in occupying the public roads and streets amounted to good bases for not granting the injunction. The learned judge explained his reasons at paragraphs 25-27 and 30-31 of the judgment as follows:

"Balancing the public interest involved

25. The right to use public highway in a lawful and reasonable manner for legitimate purposes is a right commonly enjoyed by all members of the public. No one can possibly claim a monopoly of using the public highway in total disregard of the interests of his fellow citizens, no matter how honourable or noble his cause may be. That is so even if the right to demonstration or assembly as guaranteed by the Basic Law is engaged. It is a question of balancing the competing interests and considering what is reasonable in the overall circumstances of the case.

26. I derive support for that proposition from the judgment of the Court of Final Appeal in Yeung May Wan v HKSAR [2005] 8 HKCFAR 137. The majority of the Court of Final Appeal in that case had this to say :

'42. It is clear that a person who creates an obstruction cannot be said to be acting without lawful excuse if his conduct involves a reasonable use of the highway or public place. The suggestion in some of the earlier reported cases that the public's right to use the highway is limited to the right of passage and repassage and acts incidental or ancillary thereto, is too narrow. It is now established that '...the public have the right to use the public highway for such reasonable and usual activities as are consistent with the general public's primary right to use the highway for purposes of passage and repassage.'

43. Many examples of obstructions which may nevertheless constitute reasonable use of the highway can be found in the two cases...'

And examples are given by the Court of Final Appeal and they went on to say at p157B-D :

'43. …It seeks to strike a balance between possibly conflicting interests of different users of the highway based on a requirement of reasonableness. Whether any particular instance of obstruction goes beyond what is reasonable is a question of fact and degree depending on all the circumstances, including its extent and duration, the time and place where it occurs and the purpose for which it is done.

44. Where the obstruction in question results from a peaceful demonstration...'

And I stress 'peaceful demonstration' :

'44. ...a constitutionally protected right is introduced into the equation. In such cases, it is essential that the protection given by the Basic Law to that right is recognized and given substantial weight when assessing the reasonableness of the obstruction. While the interests of those exercising their right of passage along the highway obviously remain important, and while exercise of the right to demonstrate must not cause an obstruction exceeding the bounds of what is reasonable in the circumstances, such bounds must not be so narrowly defined as to devalue, or unduly impair the ability to exercise, the constitutional right.'

In short, a balancing exercise has to be carried out to balance on the one hand the general public's right to use the highway and on the other those who are exercising their right to demonstration or assembly on the highway.

27. Having evaluated the overall circumstances, I think the balance tilts in favor of granting the interim injunction so that the rights enjoyed by the plaintiffs to use the areas occupied can be restored.

…

Civil Disobedience

30. I next come to the question of civil disobedience because as I have said the "Occupy Central" Campaign is avowedly a form of civil disobedience. The nature of civil disobedience is explained by Lord Hoffmann in R v Jones [2007] 1 AC 136 as follows :

'89. My Lords, civil disobedience on conscientious grounds has a long and honourable history in this country…'

That is in England :

'89. …People who break the law to affirm their belief in the injustice of a law or government action are sometimes vindicated by history… It is the mark of a civilised community that it can accommodate protests and demonstrations of this kind. But there are conventions which are generally accepted by the law breakers on one side and the law-enforcers on the other. The protesters behave with a sense of proportion and do not cause excessive damage or inconvenience. And they vouch the sincerity of their beliefs by accepting the penalties imposed by the law. The police and prosecutors, on the other hand, behave with restraint and the magistrates impose sentences which take the conscientious motives of the protesters into account…

90. These appeals… and similar cases concerned with controversial activities, such as animal experiments, fox hunting, genetically modified crops, nuclear weapons and the like, suggest the emergence of a new phenomenon, namely litigation as the continuation of protest by other means. The protesters claim that their honestly held opinion of the legality or dangerous character of the activities in question justifies trespass, causing damage to property or the use of force. By this means they invite the court to adjudicate upon the merits of their opinion and provide themselves with a platform from which to address the media on the subject. They seek to cause expense and, if possible, embarrassment to the prosecution by exorbitant demands for disclosure such as happened in this case.

91. In Hutchinson v Newbury Magistrates' Court (2000) 122 ILR 499, where a protester sought to justify causing damage to a fence at Aldermaston on the ground that she was trying to halt the production of nuclear warheads, Buxton LJ said at p510 :

'[T]here was no immediate and instant need to act as Mrs Hutchinson acted, either [at] the time when she acted or at all : taking into account that there were other means available to her of pursuing the end sought, by drawing attention to the unlawfulness of the activities and if needs be taking legal action in respect of them. In those circumstances, self-help, particularly criminal self help of the sort indulged in by Mrs Hutchinson, cannot be reasonable.'

92. I respectfully agree. The judge then went on to deal with Mrs Hutchinson's real motive, which ('on express instructions') her counsel had frankly avowed. It was to 'bring the issue of the lawfulness of the Government's policy before a court, preferable a Crown Court.' Buxton LJ said at p510 :

'[I]n terms of the reasonableness of Mrs Hutchinson's acts, this assertion on her part is further fatal to her cause. I simply do not see how it can be reasonable to commit a crime in order to be able to pursue in the subsequent prosecution, arguments about the lawfulness or otherwise of the activities of the victim of that crime.'

93. My Lords, I do not think that it would be inconsistent with our traditional respect for conscientious civil disobedience for your Lordships to say that there will seldom if ever be any arguable legal basis upon which these forensic tactics can be deployed."

31. I am mindful of the fact that I am only dealing with the applications and the evidence before me on an ex parte basis, but on the materials before me when the demonstration in question based on civil disobedience have taken place for so long, in such a scale which has affected so many people and which has the real risk of turning into civil disorder, I do not think the fact that the demonstration is civil disobedience, no matter how noble the underlying cause the participants may consider it to be, can constitute a factor which militates against the granting of an injunction."

65. I respectfully agree with Poon J's above reasons and would adopt the same herein to reject the 3rd defendant's above contentions as a ground to oppose the granting of the interim injunction in the present case.

66. Finally, the 3rd defendant also says the police have so far not been able to "clear" the ACE Action Area. He further says it may well be that the police lack the necessary resources to carry out the task. If so, the court should not (contended the 3rd defendant) grant the injunction unless the plaintiff can satisfy this court how it would be able to effectively enforce the injunction (if granted).

67. I must reject this submission. It amounts to no more than saying that the court should not grant the injunction as it would not be complied with. This cannot be right. Court orders are expected to be

and should be obeyed. Therefore, as a matter of principle, it cannot be a proper reason not to grant an injunction because of the concern that it may not be complied with. For this, again I would further respectfully adopt Poon J's observations at paragraph 28-29 of his judgment in the Mongkok Injunction Cases as follows:

"28. I next consider the possibility that the court order might not be obeyed. This is a point raised by Mr Mok [counsel for the plaintiffs] in the course of his submissions. He drew my attention to the relevant cases in England. One is the English Supreme Court's decision in Secretary of State for the Environment, Food and Rural Affairs v Meier [2009] 1 WLR 2780 at para 17 where Lord Rogers cited South Bucks District Council v Porter [2003] 2 AC 558 :

"32. …When granting an injunction the court does not contemplate that it will be disobeyed ... Apprehension that a party may disobey an order should not deter the court from making an order otherwise appropriate : there is not one law for the law-abiding and another for the lawless and truculent."

In a similar vein, Lord Neuberger said at paragraph 81 that :

"81. On the other hand, in the same paragraph of his opinion, Lord Bingham also said that '[a]pprehension that a party may disobey an order should not deter the court from making the order otherwise appropriate.' A court may consider it unlikely that it would make an order for sequestration or imprisonment, if an injunction it was being invited to grant were to be breached, but it may none the less properly decide to grant the injunction. Thus, the court may take the view that the defendants are more likely not to be trespass on the claimant's land if an injunction is granted, because of their respect for a court order, or because of their fear of the repercussions of breaching such an order. Or the court may think that an order of imprisonment for breach, while unlikely, would nonetheless be a real possibility, or it may think that a suspended order of imprisonment, in the event of a breach, may well be a deterrent…."

29. As indicated in the course of Mr Mok's submissions, it is the foundation of the rule of law in Hong Kong that a court order is to be obeyed. And I fully expect that that order that I am going to make will be obeyed, even if the defendants disagree with it. If they feel aggrieved by the order, they should come back to court so that the question whether they can continue with their occupation of the areas affected by their activities can be resolved in a peaceful and legal manner with the benefit of mature consideration of the law applicable to their rights and obligations on the one hand, and those of their fellow citizens affected by their activities on the other.

68. In the premises, I reject all of the 2nd and 3rd defendants' above contentions as to why the court should not grant of the interlocutory injunction. As I said above, the balance of convenience overwhelmingly supports the grant of the interim injunction as sought by ACE.

C. CONCLUSION AND THE TERMS OF THE INJUNCTION

69. For the above reasons, I would reject Kwoon Chung's application but allow ACE's application for an interlocutory injunction.

70. ACE has provided to this court a draft order which is in the following terms:

(1) The defendants and each of them be restrained until trial or a further order made by the court, whether by themselves or agent or servant or howsoever from doing, causing, authorising, permitting the doing of, any of the following acts, namely:

(a) Occupying portions of Connaught Road Central Eastbound between Edinburgh Place (Western Portion) and Edinburgh Place (Eastern Portion) (ie, "Section 1" which is more particularly coloured red and marked on the Plan Y attached hereto) and/or the portion of Harcourt Road Eastbound between Edinburgh Place (Eastern Portion) and Cotton Tree Drive (ie, "Section 2" which is more particularly coloured red and marked on the Plan Y attached hereto) and/or the portion of Cotton Tree Drive Southbound between Harcourt Road Eastbound and Queensway (ie, "Section 3" which is more particularly coloured red and marked on the Plan Y attached hereto) (together referred to as "the ACE Action Area") to prevent or obstruct normal vehicular traffic from passing the ACE Action Area;

(b) Erecting, placing, maintaining, building or otherwise set up tents, canopies, barriers, barricades or other structures obstacles or obstruction, or doing any other act, to prevent or obstruct vehicular traffic from passing the ACE Action Area; or

(c) Obstructing or preventing or interfering with, or doing any other act which deters, the plaintiff through it agents properly authorized in writing from or in dismantling or removing barriers and other obstacles and obstruction in or from the ACE Action Area.

(2) Leave to serve the Order herein on the 1st defendants by advertising the Order in one Chinese and one English newspaper circulating in Hong Kong; and placing the Order (with a Chinese translation of the same) in clear plastic envelopes and attached to a board or post, or other prominent location in the Area (with the permission of the Police or another government authority); together with a Notice (in Chinese and English) notifying the 1st defendants that they can obtain copies of the Order, the inter parte summons, Writ of Summons, and supporting affirmation by applying to the Plaintiff's solicitors at an identified address during normal office hours, upon payment of the usual photocopying charges.

(3) Liberty to apply.

71. Plan Y attached to the draft order is one which effectively comprises of Map A, B and C as attached to this judgment. However, I am not satisfied that the descriptions in the draft order together with Plan Y provide sufficient precision as to the locations and delineations of Sections 1, 2 and 3 as covered by the injunction for the purpose of enforcement. As such, I direct that the parties shall appear before this

court on 4 December at 2:30pm whereby ACE shall provide to this court a revised plan with sufficient particulars and/or landmark references (eg, such as lamppost numbers) to identify with sufficient precision the location and delineations of Sections 1, 2 and 3.

72. Further, to avoid any doubt and to facilitate the potential enforcement of the injunction, I would also include in the order a direction that, when requested by the plaintiff, the bailiff do take all reasonable and necessary steps to assist the plaintiff and its agents (properly authorised in writing) to effect the clearance and removal of the obstructions as provided in the injunction, and that the bailiff be authorised to request the assistance of the police where necessary.

73. In this respect, I would repeat what I have said in the Mongkok Injunctions Judgment in that, under the law, a person who, with knowledge of a court order, and deliberately impedes the bailiff in the due execution of his duties is liable for criminal contempt as his conduct intentionally and deliberately interferes with or impedes the due administration of justice. Under the Police Force Ordinance (Cap 232), a police officer has power to arrest any person who he reasonably believes or suspects of being guilty of criminal contempt. In other words, the police have always been empowered under the law to arrest anyone who is reasonably suspected of committing an act of criminal contempt. This power is not dependent on whether the court has made a direction to that effect or not.

74. Finally, as to costs, I would make an order nisi that (a) costs of ACE's application be to the ACE to be taxed if not agreed, with certificate for two counsel, (b) costs of Kwoon Chung's application be to the 2nd and 3rd defendants, to be taxed if not agreed, and (c) the 2nd defendant's own costs in both actions be taxed in accordance with legal aid regulations. This order shall become absolute 14 days from today unless any of the parties applies to vary it by summons.

(Thomas Au)
Judge of the Court of First Instance
High Court

Mr Warren Chan SC, Mr Jose-Antonio Maurellet and Ms Patricia Lam, instructed by Paul W Tse, for the plaintiffs

Mr Hectar Pun and Mr Jeffrey Tam, instructed by Ho Tse Wai, Philip Li & Partners, assigned by the Director of Legal Aid, for the 2nd defendant

The 3rd defendant appeared in person on 17 November 2014

DECEMBER 1

HCA 2222 & 2223 of 2014

HCA 2222 of 2014

IN THE HIGH COURT OF THE HONG KONG SPECIAL ADMINISTRATIVE REGION
COURT OF FIRST INSTANCE
ACTION NO 2222 OF 2014

BETWEEN

KWOON CHUNG MOTORS COMPANY LIMITED   Plaintiff
(冠忠遊覽車有限公司)

and

PERSONS WHO ERECTED OR PLACED OR 1st Defendants
MAINTAINED OBSTRUCTIONS OR OTHERWISE DO ANY ACT TO CAUSE OBSTRUCTIONS,
OR TO PREVENT OR HINDER THE CLEARANCE AND REMOVAL OF THE OBSTRUCTIONS
OR OCCUPYING ON THE PORTION OF CONNAUGHT ROAD CENTRAL
EASTBOUND BETWEEN EDINBURGH PLACE (WESTERN PORTION) AND EDINBURGH
PLACE (EASTERN PORTION) ("SECTION 1") AND/OR THE
PORTION OF HARCOURT ROAD EASTBOUND BETWEEN EDINBURGH PLACE (EASTERN
PORTION) AND COTTON TREE DRIVE ("SECTION 2") AND/OR THE PORTION OF COTTON
TREE DRIVE TOWARDS MID LEVELS ("SECTION 4") (TOGETHER "THE AREA") TO
PREVENT OR OBSTRUCT NORMAL VEHICULAR TRAFFIC FROM PASSING THE AREA

KWOK CHEUK KIN   2nd Defendant

WONG HO MING   3rd Defendant

HCA 2223 of 2014

IN THE HIGH COURT OF THE HONG KONG SPECIAL ADMINISTRATIVE REGION
COURT OF FIRST INSTANCE
ACTION NO 2223 OF 2014

BETWEEN

ALL CHINA EXPRESS LIMITED   Plaintiff
(跨境全日通有限公司)

and

PERSONS WHO ERECTED OR PLACED OR   1st Defendants
MAINTAINED OBSTRUCTIONS OR OTHERWISE DO ANY ACT TO CAUSE OBSTRUCTIONS, OR TO PREVENT OR HINDER THE CLEARANCE AND REMOVAL OF THE OBSTRUCTIONS OR OCCUPYING ON THE PORTION OF CONNAUGHT ROAD CENTRAL EASTBOUND BETWEEN EDINBURGH PLACE (WESTERN PORTION) AND EDINBURGH PLACE (EASTERN PORTION) ("SECTION 1") AND/OR THE PORTION OF HARCOURT ROAD EASTBOUND BETWEEN EDINBURGH PLACE (EASTERN PORTION) AND COTTON TREE DRIVE ("SECTION 2") AND/OR THE PORTION OF COTTON TREE DRIVE SOUTHBOUND BETWEEN HARCOURT ROAD EASTBOUND AND QUEENSWAY ("SECTION 3") (TOGETHER "THE AREA") TO PREVENT OR OBSTRUCT NORMAL VEHICULAR TRAFFIC FROM PASSING THE AREA

KWOK CHEUK KIN   2nd Defendant

WONG HO MING   3rd Defendant

Before: Hon Au J in Chambers

Dates of Hearing: 11 and 17 November 2014

Date of Judgment: 1 December 2014

JUDGMENT

A. INTRODUCTION

1. These are the respective applications by the plaintiff under each of these two actions for an interlocutory injunction against the defendants. The injunctions sought relate to the occupation and blockage by the defendants of portions of Harcourt Road, Connaught Road and some nearby roads in Admiralty. The occupation arises from the occupy central campaign ("the OCC") whereby a large number of unidentified protestors and demonstrators have occupied various parts of the public roads in Hong Kong directed against the constitutional development in Hong Kong.

2. The plaintiff ("Kwoon Chung") in HCA 2222/2014 is the operator of various school bus services. Relevant to this application is Kwoon Chung's school bus service route ("Route 9") which carries students to and from Pier 3 in Central and the Island School at Borrett Road in the Mid-Levels. For convenience, I would refer to this action as the "Kwoon Chung Action".

3. The plaintiff ("ACE") in HCA 2223/2014 is the operator of cross-border bus services. Relevant to this application is the Wan Chai cross border route ("the Wan Chai Route"), which carries passengers to and from Wan Chai in Hong Kong to Huanggang Port in Shenzhen in the Mainland. Again for convenience, I would refer to this action as the "ACE Action".

4. In both actions, it is not disputed that since late September 2014, unidentified protestors and demonstrators (ie, the 1st defendants) have through themselves and by placing various barricades and obstructions occupied and blocked the following parts of the roads near Central and Admiralty:

(1) The portion of Connaught Road Central eastbound between Edinburgh Place (Western Portion) and Edinburgh Place (Eastern Portion) ("Section 1");

(2) The portion of Harcourt Road eastbound between Edinburgh Place (Eastern Portion) and Cotton Tree Drive ("Section 2");

(3) The portion of Cotton Tree Drive southbound between Harcourt Road eastbound and Queensway ("Section 3"); and

(4) The portion of Cotton Tree Drive towards the Mid-Levels ("Section 4").

The locations of Sections 1, 2, 3 and 4 are identified respectively in Map A, B, C and D as provided by the plaintiffs. Copies of these Maps are attached to this judgment for reference.

5. There is also no dispute that the said blockages and obstruction of these Sections have completely prevented any vehicular traffic to pass through these areas.

6. It is Kwoon Chung's case that the school bus operating under the Route passes through the area ("the Kwoon Chung Action Area") under Sections 1, 2 and 4 in its usual and normal operation. However, because of the obstruction and blockages of the Kwoon Chung Action Area, the Route 9 school bus has to take a detour in its route ("the Detour Route"). As a result, the travelling distance of the route has increased from 3.9km to 6.2km, thereby also increasing the average travelling time by about 6 minutes.

7. It is ACE's case that normally the cross-border buses under the Wan Chai Route pass through the area ("the ACE Action Area") under Sections 1, 2 and 3. However, because of the blockages of the roads in this area, and the severe general traffic congestions in northern Hong Kong Island (in particular in the area between the Western Harbour Tunnel and Wanchai) resulted from the said blockages, the buses operating under the Wan Chai Route have to take a detour and cancel the drop-off point at Wan Chai MTR station. The detour has caused an increase in the average travelling time of the southbound route of the Wan Chai Route by 10-20 minutes.

8. By way of the respective actions herein, Kwoon Chung and ACE therefore claim against the defendants for damages and injunction in public nuisance.

9. In the present application, Kwoon Chung now asks for an interlocutory injunction to restrain the defendants until trial effectively from:

(1) Continuing to block and occupy the Kwoon Chung Action Area (whether by themselves and/or by placing obstructions thereat) to prevent vehicular access; and

(2) Preventing Kwoon Chung or its authorised agents from removing the obstructions placed in the Kwoon Chung Action Area.

10. Similarly, ACE asks for an interlocutory injunction to restrain the defendants until trial from:

(1) Continuing to block and occupy the ACE Action Area (whether by themselves and/or by placing obstructions thereat) to prevent vehicular access; and

(2) Preventing ACE or its authorised agents from removing the obstructions placed in the ACE Action Area.

11. These applications are opposed by the 2nd and 3rd defendants. They both accept and confirm to the court that they fall within the descriptions of the 1st defendant in each of these actions, in that they have been occupying and obstructing the Kwoon Chung Action and ACE Action Areas.

12. Other than the 2nd and 3rd defendants, none of the 1st defendants turns up in court to oppose the applications.

13. Before I turn to deal with the applications, it is pertinent to note that this court has recently in HCA 2086/2014 and 2104/2014 (collectively, the "Mongkok Injunction Cases") dealt with similar applications for interlocutory injunction against the protestors under the OCC occupying certain parts of the roads in Mongkok. By a judgment dated 10 November 2014 ("the Mongkok Injunctions Judgment"), I continued the injunctions in the Mongkok Injunction Cases. Respectively under HCMP 2975 & 2976/2014, HCMP 3028/2014 and HCMP 3090/2014, the court of appeal has dismissed the various applications for leave to appeal against the Mongkok Injunctions Judgment.

14. As will be seen later, most of the issues raised in the present applications are similar or related to the ones raised in the Mongkok Injunction Cases. Therefore, whenever necessary, I may refer to these court of appeal judgments and the Mongkok Injunction Cases Judgment when I deal with these issues.

B. THESE APPLICATIONS

B1. Applicable principles

15. It is well established that generally in determining whether or not to grant an interlocutory injunction, the court has to see (a) whether there are serious issues to be tried, (b) whether damages would be an adequate remedy for either side, and if damages would not be adequate for both parties, (c) where the balance of convenience lies in terms of whether or not to grant an interim injunction pending the trial of the matter. In that balancing exercise, the court must take into account the interests of the general public even though they are not represented before the court. See: Turbo Top Ltd v Lee Cheuk Yan [2013] 3 HKLRD 41 at paragraph 14 per G Lam J.

16. However, Mr Pun for the 2nd defendant contends in the present cases that the court should not apply the threshold of whether there are serious issues to be tried in determining whether to grant the injunction. This is so, says Mr Pun, as the grant of an injunction in the present cases would or likely to have the effect of finally disposing of the matters. As such, the court should apply the threshold that the plaintiffs need to show that it is very likely that they will succeed at trial. See: Fast-Link Express Ltd v Falcon Express Ltd (unreported, HCA 2040/2005, 30 December 2005, Deputy High Court Judge Carlson) at paragraph 9.

17. Mr Pun also relies on the case of City of Bradford Metropolitan Council v Brown (1987) 19 HLR 16 at 21-22 to support his submissions that, in an application for interim injunction as the present one, the court should at least reach a "provisional" view on the question of whether the plaintiff has the necessary standing to bring the claim.

18. I do not accept these contentions.

19. I have similarly applied the threshold of a serious issue to be tried in the Mongkok Injunction Cases. In dismissing the defendants' respective applications for leave to appeal in those cases, the court of appeal rejected the similar arguments that this court was wrong to adopt the serious issues to be tried threshold in those cases. Thus, the adoption of this threshold in cases which are similar to the present ones has been approved by the court of appeal. See HCMP 2975/2014 at paragraphs 9 to 19 per Cheung CJHC, and HCMP 3028/2014 at paragraphs 8-9 per Lam VP.

20. Further, the court of appeal in dismissing the applications for leave to appeal against the Mongkok Injunctions Judgment also does not accept that City of Bradford Metropolitan Council is an authority to support that a higher threshold than the one of serious issue to be tried should be adopted in an application as the present ones: HCMP3028/2014, supra, at paragraph 9 per Lam VP.

21. For these reasons, I reject Mr Pun's contentions and would adopt the threshold of serious issue to be tried in the present applications as part of the considerations to determine whether to grant the interlocutory injunctions or not.

22. Applying the above principles, I now look at these applications.

B2.   Serious questions to be tried

B2.1 A claim in public nuisance by private individuals

23. It is uncontroversial that the occupations and blocking of the Kwoon Chung Action Area and the ACE Blocked Area amount to public nuisance in law.

24. It is also well established that for a private individual (as opposed to the Secretary for Justice) to bring a claim in public nuisance, he has to show that he has suffered by reason of the public nuisance a "particular, substantial and direct" injury or damage, which is above and beyond what has been suffered by the rest of the public at large: Benjamin v Storr (1874) LR 9 CP 400 at 406-406 per Brett J.

25. The question that I have to consider under this head is thus whether there is a serious issue to be tried as to whether each of the plaintiffs has suffered such a particular, substantial and direct damage.

26. As I have said in the Mongkok Injunctions Judgment, in relation to what amounts to a particular, substantial and direct damage in the law of public nuisance, the authorities show that:

(1) Whether a damage or loss said to be suffered by the plaintiff can be regarded as particular, substantial and direct is essentially a question of fact, and a matter of degree and extent: Jan de Nul v Royale Belge [2000] 2 LLR 700 at paragraph 44 (p 715).

(2) The "particular" damage needs not be pecuniary (and thus special) in nature. It may consist of proved general damage, such as inconvenience and delay provided that it is substantial, that it is direct

and non-consequential, and that it is appreciably greater in degree than any suffered by the general public: Walsh v Ervin [1952] VLR361 at 371 per Scholl J.

(3) "Substantial" means no more than that the damage suffered is more than trivial: Jan de Nul, supra, at paragraph 44.

(4) It is also not necessary prove that the plaintiff has any injury to property, or has any interest or relationship with any land or building: Benjamin v Storr, supra, at 406; Leung Tsang Hung v The Incorporated Owner of Kwok Wing House [2007] 10 HKCFAR 480 at paragraph 13 per Ribeiro PJ.

27. Further, I have also said that the authorities support that the requirement of "direct" damage is satisfied not only by one which is immediately caused by or flowed from the nuisance. It also covers those injuries and damage which are caused by or flowed from the nuisance through a chain of events, so long as those events can be regarded as probable events as a result of the nuisance and the chain is not broken by external matters unrelated to the nuisance. It is a question of fact in each case as to whether the damage claimed to be suffered fall within the requisite chain of events. See: Overseas Tankship (UK) Ltd v Miller Steamship Co Pty (Wagon Mount No 2) [1967] 1 AC 617, at 634E-636D per Lord Reid; Gravesham v British Railways Board [1978] 1 Ch 379 at 396F-397C and 398H-399B.

28. The court of appeal has held that there are at least a triable issue raised in relation to these legal propositions .

29. In light of these at least triable legal propositions, I will now examine the plaintiff's respective case on the question of particular, substantial and direct damage.

B2.1.1 The Kwoon Chung Action

30. In this action, Kwoon Chung's case and evidence on its loss and damage suffered by reason of the blockages can be summarised as follows :

(1) Given the Detour Route, the school buses under Route 9 have to travel at an increased distance, which has increased the average travelling time by about 6 minutes. Further, the pick-up time at Pier 3 by the school bus has to be moved to 6:30 am, which is 40 minutes earlier than the normal pick-up time.

(2) As a result, for the month since 6 October 2014 until 31 October 2014, Kwoon Chung has suffered damage in the nature of increased fuel cost at $843.18 and overtime payments to its drivers at $3,750, totalling $4,593.18.

(3) Further, the students and the drivers all have to wake up relatively earlier in order to catch the school buses because of the earlier pick-up time, and thus have suffered inconvenience and hardship.

(4) If continued, Kwoon Chung would also suffer damage to its reputation as a school bus operator and to its good relationship with the affected schools, students and parents.

31. In my view, Kwoon Chung has not raised a triable issue that it has suffered a particular, substantial and direct damage. My reasons are as follows.

32. First, although the pecuniary loss said to be suffered by Kwoon Chung can at least arguably be said to be amounting to "peculiar" and "direct" damage by reason of the public nuisance, I am not satisfied that it can arguably be said that the loss is one which is "substantial". As I mentioned above, what amounts to "substantial" damage for the purpose of enabling a private individual to bring a claim in public nuisance is that the loss must be more than trivial. In the present case, the total pecuniary loss of $4,593.18 cannot be said to be more than trivial. This is in fact accepted by Kwoon Chung itself: Mr James Wong in his affidavit at paragraph 23 accepts that "the monetary damage to the plaintiff ... may seem relatively trivial...". In the circumstances, the loss suffered by the plaintiff does not even arguably amount to "substantial" damage as understood in the law of public nuisance.

33. Second, in relation to the suggestion of damage to its reputation or relationship with the schools, students and parents, there is simply no triable evidence to show that Kwoon Chung's said reputation is or is likely to be so damaged. As a matter of common sense, it is obvious that the increased travelling time is caused by the occupation of the affected area by reason of the OCC. That is something beyond Kwoon Chung's control and has nothing to do with its ability and skill in the operation of school buses (and thus its reputation). It would unlikely lead to any damage to its reputation. This is underlined by the lack of evidence to show that the parents, students or schools have been laying the blame on Kwoon Chung. Quite to the contrary, the evidence of various other parents' emails and letters shows that they were aware of the fact that the increased travelling time was caused by the OCC and thus they fully supported Kwoon Chung's intended application for an injunction.

34. Finally, the inconvenience and hardship said to be suffered by the students and the drivers are simply not one suffered by the plaintiff. It cannot be regarded as the plaintiff's damage or injury.

35. For these reasons, I am not satisfied that Kwoon Chung has shown any triable issues that it has suffered a particular, substantial and direct damage as a result of the public nuisance to enable it (as a private individual) to bring a claim in public nuisance.

36. On this basis alone, I would refuse Kwoon Chung's application for an interlocutory injunction.

B2.1.2 The ACE Action

37. ACE's case and evidence on its loss can be summarised as follows :

(1) ACE operate, among others, the cross-border bus services under the Wan Chai Route, where the relevant passenger service licence is held by ACE's wholly owned subsidiary All China Express (Wanchai) Ltd.

(2) Because of the blocking of the ACE Action Area, and the resultant severe general traffic congestions in northern Hong Kong Island caused by the blockages, (a) the average travelling time of the southbound cross-border buses under the Wan Chai Route has increased by about 20.9% (some 10 20 minutes), (b) ACE has to cancel the drop-off point at Wanchai MTR station of the Wan Chai Route, and (c) the buses have not been able to provide on time scheduled services.

(3) Given the significant increase in the travelling time, the cancellation of the Wanchai MTR drop-off point, and that ACE can no longer provide on time services in accordance to the schedule under the Wanchai Route, the number of passengers and the sales turnover of the Wanchai Route have dropped significantly. In particular, the ticket sales of the southbound service have decreased over 17% (in the sum of $691,754) for the period between 29 September and 26 October 2014.

(4) ACE has therefore suffered pecuniary loss. It will also suffer irreparable damage to its business reputation in operating cross-border buses.

38. Since ACE's business derives income or profits from the operation and provision of transport services in Hong Kong, I accept that the above evidence on the said loss of income by reason of road blockages clearly raises a serious issue to be tried as to whether this amounts to a particular, substantial and direct damage under the law of public nuisance. As said by the learned Chief Judge, it is almost a matter of common sense. Moreover, this is a mixed question of law and fact which can and should only be properly resolved at a full trial. See: HCMP 2975/2014, supra, at paragraphs 19 and 20 per Cheung CJHC; also The Mongkok Injunctions Judgment, at paragraphs 30-32.

39. Mr Pun for the 2nd defendant submits that there are authorities to show that a private individual (for the purpose of bringing a claim in public nuisance) must demonstrate that his loss is also above and beyond the class which he or his business belongs to. In other words, if the damage is common to all persons of the same class, then a personal right of action in public nuisance is not maintainable. Counsel relies on Hickey v Electric Reduction Co of Canada (1970) 21 DLR 368 at 371-372 and Ricket v Metropolitan Railway Co (1867) LR 2 HL 175 at 190, 199 to support this proposition. Thus, contended Mr Pun, as ACE's loss is in nature no different from that suffered by everyone in the class of transport service operators in Hong Kong, it has not suffered any particular loss that would entitle it to bring a private claim in public nuisance.

40. Mr Pun also says in determining the meaning of "particular damage over and above the damage suffered by the public at large", the court has to bear in mind the rationale behind this rule. The rationale is to avoid multiplicity of proceedings and to avoid usurping the discretion of the Secretary for Justice

("SJ") whether to take action in the common interest of the public. Mr Pun seeks to find support of these submissions in Wagon Mount No 2, supra, at 635-636, R v Rimmington [2006] 1 AC 459 at paragraph 8 and William's Case (1591) 5 Coke Reports 72 at 73a.

41. For the present purpose of an interlocutory injunction, suffice for me to say that these contentions on class interest and on the rationale to avoid multiplicity of suits only add further facets to the arguments in law and on the facts as to what could satisfy the requirement of a particular, substantial and direct damage in the circumstance of the present case. As I mentioned above, what amounts to a particular, substantial and direct loss is essentially a question of law and fact. In light of the other authorities I have referred to in paragraphs 26 and 27 above, these authorities relied on by the 2nd defendant could not be regarded as determinative in the present case at an interlocutory stage to show that ACE has not suffered a particular, substantial and direct loss.

42. Mr Pun's contentions therefore only show that there is a serious issue to be tried on the different legal propositions relied on by the respective parties made under this question, which should only be determined after mature debates and arguments at trial. See the observations by Cheung CJHC in HCMP2975/2014, supra, at paragraph 19. See also The Mongkok Injunctions Judgment, paragraphs 42-48.

43. As to Mr Pun's argument on the need to avoid usurping SJ's discretion, I will adopt my reasons set out at paragraphs 60-61 below and paragraphs 42-49 of the Mongkok Injunctions Judgment to reject it as a valid basis to say that there is not triable issue on the question of whether ACE's has suffered a particular, substantial and direct loss.

44. For all the above reasons, I reject all of Mr Pun's above contentions and am satisfied that ACE has shown a serious issue to be tried in its claim in public nuisance against the defendants.

45. I now move on to the question of balance of convenience.

B3. Balance of convenience

46. It is in my view clear that the balance of convenience lies in favour of granting the interim injunction. This is because:

(1) Damages are not a sufficient remedy for ACE given that:

(a) there is no suggestion that, if no injunction is granted now, the unidentified 1st defendants and the 2nd and 3rd defendants are in a position to meet the damages after trial;

(b) further, as observed by the learned Chief Judge in HCMP 2975/2014 at paragraph 17, if no interim injunction is granted in the meantime and if ACE succeeds at trial to show particular, substantial and direct damage and a good claim in public nuisance, it will have suffered in the interim further loss and damage, for which damages are also likely to be difficult to assess.

(2) At the same time, the defendants simply have no legal right whatsoever to occupy and block in the way the protestors do the public roads in question. As such, if the interlocutory injunction pending trial is granted but ACE fails at trial in establishing its claim in public nuisance, the defendants will not in the meantime have suffered, by the grant of the injunction, the loss of anything which they have never had a right to in the first place. See: HMCP 2975/2014 at paragraph 12 per Cheung CJHC.

(3) In the premises, the balance of convenience lies overwhelmingly in favour of granting the injunction. It is clearly just and convenient in all the circumstances to grant the injunction. Cf: HCMP 2975/2014 at paragraphs 8-12, 17-22.

47. However, the 2nd and 3rd defendants respectively raise a number of contentions to say why the court should not exercise its discretion to grant the injunction. I will deal with each of them in turn.

48. First, Mr Pun for the 2nd defendant says the plaintiff cannot engage the judiciary in a matter which is effectively a matter of political choice for the Executive. Counsel says the court's equitable jurisdiction should not be exploited as a means to resolve political disputes, especially when the Executive may well have made a deliberate choice to order its law enforcement agents not to take any action against the protestors occupying the concerned areas. He says the police clearly have lawful power to do so but refrained from doing so. There must be, says counsel, good policy reasons for the tolerance of these protestors by the Executive, and it is thus unjust for the plaintiff to invoke the court's equitable jurisdiction to intervene in such a highly sensitive political matter. The court therefore should not exercise its discretion to grant the injunction.

49. Similarly, the 3rd defendant also argues that the occupation and blocking of the roads are conducts arising out of political issues, which should be resolved politically. Thus, the court should not be engaged to revolve what are essentially political problems.

50. I do not accept these contentions.

51. As repeatedly emphasised by the court in the past, in deciding cases, including the present ones, the court would determine them only by applying the law and would not take into account any political considerations. As demonstrated in the analyses above, this is precisely what this court is doing: adjudicating and resolving disputes concerning the parties' legal rights in accordance to the law, and the law alone. The fact that it also happens that there is political underlying to these disputes does not and should not affect the court's role and duty in adjudicating those legal rights. Nor should the court refrain from adjudicating those legal rights in the dispute.

52. As I have said above, it is when looking at the present matter in accordance with the law that the balance of convenience lies overwhelmingly in favour of granting the injunction to address and balance the respective private rights of the parties.

53. In this respect, I would also respectfully refer to Lam VP's observations in HCMP 3028/2014 at paragraph 36 as follows:

"36. We understand there are exceptional political circumstances which gave rise to the unlawful occupation in the present case. But the court has to be involved in this instance because the rights of private citizens protected by the law are said to be threatened and they seek redress from the court. In so doing, they are exercising a constitutional right conferred on them by article 35 of the Basic Law. It is the duty of the court to adjudicate upon and, where justified, give effect to such rights according to law. Even in cases where protesters are pursuing a noble cause which they feel strongly about (and we express no view on the protest in the case before us), this does not give them any right in the eyes of law to trample upon the rights of the others who may or may not agree with their cause. This is an important facet of the rule of law which, as judges, we must uphold."

54. The 2nd and 3rd defendants' above submissions in effect are asking the court to take into account political considerations (ie, the fact that the Executive has, because of possibly various policy and political considerations, so far "tolerated" the protestors' occupations) to determine the legal rights between private parties. This cannot be right.

55. Further and in any event, even if the court is to and can take into account of this fact, I do not think it is a matter that that would tip the overwhelming case in favour of granting the injunction as I have said above.

56. I would therefore reject these contentions as a basis for not granting the injunction.

57. Second, Mr Pun for the 2nd defendant says there is delay on the part of ACE in taking out this application for injunction. In the premises, the court should refuse to exercise discretion to grant it. In support of the contention, counsel relies on Rogers VP's observation in King Fung Vacuum Ltd v Toto Toys Ltd [2006] 2 HKLRD 785 at paragraph 20 as follows:

"20. There has traditionally been a strong requirement when interlocutory injunctions have been sought, that the plaintiff must show that it has acted promptly and without delay. Promptly in the circumstances of interlocutory injunctions has been commonly understood to be a period of six weeks or so of unexplained delay and three months with an explanation given for the delay in making application for an injunction. Since the American Cyanamid decision the importance of irreparable damage in an application for an interlocutory injunction is paramount. If there is no irreparable damage demonstrated then the need for an interlocutory injunction has not been shown. This is important because of the approach that the courts take to interlocutory injunctions. They are not the trial of the action and the court is concerned with whether irreparable damage will occur before a trial can take place. It stands to reason that if a party is prepared to allow matters to proceed and takes no action with respect to matters which have been extant for lengthy periods, it lies ill in their mouth to say that there is likely to be irreparable damage and that is the case here." (Mr Pun's emphasis)

58. It is trite that delay in taking out an interim injunction is one of the factors (albeit sometimes a very weight factor depending on the circumstances of the case) that the court should take into account in deciding how to exercise the discretion. It is however not an absolute bar to the grant of an injunction. The ultimate question is still, after taking into all the circumstances of the case, including the nature and length of any delay in question, whether the court regards it as just to grant the injunction. See also: Abbott GmbH & Co v Pharmareg Consulting Co Ltd [2009] 3 HKLRD 524 at paragraphs 80-95 per Sakhrani J, and the cases cited therein.

59. In the present case, given that (a) the length of the delay is at most about one month or so, and (b) it was unclear in the beginning that the said occupation would last indefinitely as it is now, I do not think it can be said that the delay is a serious one and wholly inexcusable. In the premises, given also that the defendants simply have no legal rights to occupy the roads in the way as they do to completely deprive the rest of public's right to use them, I am still of the clear view that, notwithstanding the delay, this is an overwhelming case that it is just and convenient to grant the injunction.

60. Third, Mr Pun says the court should exercise great caution in deciding whether to grant the injunction sought when it is invoking the assistance of the civil courts in aid of the criminal law. The court should consider, counsel contends, whether the injunction would exacerbate the situation and whether it would likely to be futile as (suggested Mr Pun) the demonstrators may move to other areas not covered by the injunction. He relies on Gouriet v Union of Post Office Workers at 481C-H to support this contention.

61. I am unable to accept Mr Pun's submissions. Similar arguments relying on Gouriet have been raised in the Mongkok Injunction Cases. I have rejected them at paragraphs 42-49 of the Mongkok Injunctions Judgment. I would simply adopt those reasons herein to reject Mr Pun's arguments. Further, Mr Pun's submission that the injunction would likely to be futile as the demonstrators may move to other areas is wholly misplaced. The purpose of the injunction is to prevent the continued occupation and blocking of the ACE Action Area pending trial. Thus, the suggestion that some demonstrators may move to other areas does not thereby render the injunction useless and futile.

62. Fourth, the 3rd defendant submits that in the exercise of its discretion, the court should take into account the defendants' right to demonstration and the fact that they are carrying out "civil disobedience" in occupying the concerned area.

63. I do not think these factors in the circumstances of the present case can constitute a valid basis for not granting the injunction. As fairly accepted by the 3rd defendant, all these rights are not absolute and

are subject to limitation. The court must balance these rights against the public's unquestioned rights to use the roads.

64. In deciding to grant an ex parte injunction in the Mongkok Injunction Cases, Poon J rejected the potential arguments that the right to demonstration and the notion of civil disobedience in occupying the public roads and streets amounted to good bases for not granting the injunction. The learned judge explained his reasons at paragraphs 25-27 and 30-31 of the judgment as follows:

"Balancing the public interest involved

25. The right to use public highway in a lawful and reasonable manner for legitimate purposes is a right commonly enjoyed by all members of the public. No one can possibly claim a monopoly of using the public highway in total disregard of the interests of his fellow citizens, no matter how honourable or noble his cause may be. That is so even if the right to demonstration or assembly as guaranteed by the Basic Law is engaged. It is a question of balancing the competing interests and considering what is reasonable in the overall circumstances of the case.

26. I derive support for that proposition from the judgment of the Court of Final Appeal in Yeung May Wan v HKSAR [2005] 8 HKCFAR 137. The majority of the Court of Final Appeal in that case had this to say :

'42. It is clear that a person who creates an obstruction cannot be said to be acting without lawful excuse if his conduct involves a reasonable use of the highway or public place. The suggestion in some of the earlier reported cases that the public's right to use the highway is limited to the right of passage and repassage and acts incidental or ancillary thereto, is too narrow. It is now established that '...the public have the right to use the public highway for such reasonable and usual activities as are consistent with the general public's primary right to use the highway for purposes of passage and repassage.'

43. Many examples of obstructions which may nevertheless constitute reasonable use of the highway can be found in the two cases...'

And examples are given by the Court of Final Appeal and they went on to say at p157B-D :

'43. ...It seeks to strike a balance between possibly conflicting interests of different users of the highway based on a requirement of reasonableness. Whether any particular instance of obstruction goes beyond what is reasonable is a question of fact and degree depending on all the circumstances, including its extent and duration, the time and place where it occurs and the purpose for which it is done.

44. Where the obstruction in question results from a peaceful demonstration...'

And I stress 'peaceful demonstration' :

'44. ...a constitutionally protected right is introduced into the equation. In such cases, it is essential that the protection given by the Basic Law to that right is recognized and given substantial weight when assessing the reasonableness of the obstruction. While the interests of those exercising their right of passage along the highway obviously remain important, and while exercise of the right to demonstrate must not cause an obstruction exceeding the bounds of what is reasonable in the circumstances, such bounds must not be so narrowly defined as to devalue, or unduly impair the ability to exercise, the constitutional right.'

In short, a balancing exercise has to be carried out to balance on the one hand the general public's right to use the highway and on the other those who are exercising their right to demonstration or assembly on the highway.

27. Having evaluated the overall circumstances, I think the balance tilts in favor of granting the interim injunction so that the rights enjoyed by the plaintiffs to use the areas occupied can be restored.

...

Civil Disobedience

30. I next come to the question of civil disobedience because as I have said the "Occupy Central" Campaign is avowedly a form of civil disobedience. The nature of civil disobedience is explained by Lord Hoffmann in R v Jones [2007] 1 AC 136 as follows :

'89. My Lords, civil disobedience on conscientious grounds has a long and honourable history in this country...'

That is in England :

'89. ...People who break the law to affirm their belief in the injustice of a law or government action are sometimes vindicated by history... It is the mark of a civilised community that it can accommodate protests and demonstrations of this kind. But there are conventions which are generally accepted by the law breakers on one side and the law-enforcers on the other. The protesters behave with a sense of proportion and do not cause excessive damage or inconvenience. And they vouch the sincerity of their beliefs by accepting the penalties imposed by the law. The police and prosecutors, on the other hand, behave with restraint and the magistrates impose sentences which take the conscientious motives of the protesters into account...

90. These appeals... and similar cases concerned with controversial activities, such as animal experiments, fox hunting, genetically modified crops, nuclear weapons and the like, suggest the emergence of a new phenomenon, namely litigation as the continuation of protest by other means. The protesters claim that their honestly held opinion of the legality or dangerous character of the activities in question justifies trespass, causing damage to property or the use of force. By this means they invite the court to adjudicate upon the merits of their opinion and provide themselves with a platform from which to address the media on the subject. They seek to cause expense and, if possible, embarrassment to the prosecution by exorbitant demands for disclosure such as happened in this case.

91. In Hutchinson v Newbury Magistrates' Court (2000) I22 ILR 499, where a protester sought to justify causing damage to a fence at Aldermaston on the ground that she was trying to halt the production of nuclear warheads, Buxton LJ said at p510 :

'[T]here was no immediate and instant need to act as Mrs Hutchinson acted, either [at] the time when she acted or at all : taking into account that there were other means available to her of pursuing the end sought, by drawing attention to the unlawfulness of the activities and if needs be taking legal action in respect of them. In those circumstances, self-help, particularly criminal self help of the sort indulged in by Mrs Hutchinson, cannot be reasonable.'

92. I respectfully agree. The judge then went on to deal with Mrs Hutchinson's real motive, which ('on express instructions') her counsel had frankly avowed. It was to 'bring the issue of the lawfulness of the Government's policy before a court, preferable a Crown Court.' Buxton LJ said at p510 :

'[I]n terms of the reasonableness of Mrs Hutchinson's acts, this assertion on her part is further fatal to her cause. I simply do not see how it can be reasonable to commit a crime in order to be able to pursue in the subsequent prosecution, arguments about the lawfulness or otherwise of the activities of the victim of that crime.'

93. My Lords, I do not think that it would be inconsistent with our traditional respect for conscientious civil disobedience for your Lordships to say that there will seldom if ever be any arguable legal basis upon which these forensic tactics can be deployed."

31. I am mindful of the fact that I am only dealing with the applications and the evidence before me on an ex parte basis, but on the materials before me when the demonstration in question based on civil disobedience have taken place for so long, in such a scale which has affected so many people and which has the real risk of turning into civil disorder, I do not think the fact that the demonstration is civil disobedience, no matter how noble the underlying cause the participants may consider it to be, can constitute a factor which militates against the granting of an injunction."

65. I respectfully agree with Poon J's above reasons and would adopt the same herein to reject the 3rd defendant's above contentions as a ground to oppose the granting of the interim injunction in the present case.

66. Finally, the 3rd defendant also says the police have so far not been able to "clear" the ACE Action Area. He further says it may well be that the police lack the necessary resources to carry out the task. If so, the court should not (contended the 3rd defendant) grant the injunction unless the plaintiff can satisfy this court how it would be able to effectively enforce the injunction (if granted).

67. I must reject this submission. It amounts to no more than saying that the court should not grant the injunction as it would not be complied with. This cannot be right. Court orders are expected to be

and should be obeyed. Therefore, as a matter of principle, it cannot be a proper reason not to grant an injunction because of the concern that it may not be complied with. For this, again I would further respectfully adopt Poon J's observations at paragraph 28-29 of his judgment in the Mongkok Injunction Cases as follows:

"28. I next consider the possibility that the court order might not be obeyed. This is a point raised by Mr Mok [counsel for the plaintiffs] in the course of his submissions. He drew my attention to the relevant cases in England. One is the English Supreme Court's decision in Secretary of State for the Environment, Food and Rural Affairs v Meier [2009] 1 WLR 2780 at para 17 where Lord Rogers cited South Bucks District Council v Porter [2003] 2 AC 558 :

"32. ...When granting an injunction the court does not contemplate that it will be disobeyed ... Apprehension that a party may disobey an order should not deter the court from making an order otherwise appropriate : there is not one law for the law-abiding and another for the lawless and truculent."

In a similar vein, Lord Neuberger said at paragraph 81 that :

"81. On the other hand, in the same paragraph of his opinion, Lord Bingham also said that '[a]pprehension that a party may disobey an order should not deter the court from making the order otherwise appropriate.' A court may consider it unlikely that it would make an order for sequestration or imprisonment, if an injunction it was being invited to grant were to be breached, but it may none the less properly decide to grant the injunction. Thus, the court may take the view that the defendants are more likely not to be trespass on the claimant's land if an injunction is granted, because of their respect for a court order, or because of their fear of the repercussions of breaching such an order. Or the court may think that an order of imprisonment for breach, while unlikely, would nonetheless be a real possibility, or it may think that a suspended order of imprisonment, in the event of a breach, may well be a deterrent...."

29. As indicated in the course of Mr Mok's submissions, it is the foundation of the rule of law in Hong Kong that a court order is to be obeyed. And I fully expect that that order that I am going to make will be obeyed, even if the defendants disagree with it. If they feel aggrieved by the order, they should come back to court so that the question whether they can continue with their occupation of the areas affected by their activities can be resolved in a peaceful and legal manner with the benefit of mature consideration of the law applicable to their rights and obligations on the one hand, and those of their fellow citizens affected by their activities on the other.

68. In the premises, I reject all of the 2nd and 3rd defendants' above contentions as to why the court should not grant of the interlocutory injunction. As I said above, the balance of convenience overwhelmingly supports the grant of the interim injunction as sought by ACE.

C.   CONCLUSION AND THE TERMS OF THE INJUNCTION

69. For the above reasons, I would reject Kwoon Chung's application but allow ACE's application for an interlocutory injunction.

70. ACE has provided to this court a draft order which is in the following terms:

(1) The defendants and each of them be restrained until trial or a further order made by the court, whether by themselves or agent or servant or howsoever from doing, causing, authorising, permitting the doing of, any of the following acts, namely:

(a) Occupying portions of Connaught Road Central Eastbound between Edinburgh Place (Western Portion) and Edinburgh Place (Eastern Portion) (ie, "Section 1" which is more particularly coloured red and marked on the Plan Y attached hereto) and/or the portion of Harcourt Road Eastbound between Edinburgh Place (Eastern Portion) and Cotton Tree Drive (ie, "Section 2" which is more particularly coloured red and marked on the Plan Y attached hereto) and/or the portion of Cotton Tree Drive Southbound between Harcourt Road Eastbound and Queensway (ie, "Section 3" which is more particularly coloured red and marked on the Plan Y attached hereto) (together referred to as "the ACE Action Area") to prevent or obstruct normal vehicular traffic from passing the ACE Action Area;

(b) Erecting, placing, maintaining, building or otherwise set up tents, canopies, barriers, barricades or other structures obstacles or obstruction, or doing any other act, to prevent or obstruct vehicular traffic from passing the ACE Action Area; or

(c) Obstructing or preventing or interfering with, or doing any other act which deters, the plaintiff through it agents properly authorized in writing from or in dismantling or removing barriers and other obstacles and obstruction in or from the ACE Action Area.

(2) Leave to serve the Order herein on the 1st defendants by advertising the Order in one Chinese and one English newspaper circulating in Hong Kong; and placing the Order (with a Chinese translation of the same) in clear plastic envelopes and attached to a board or post, or other prominent location in the Area (with the permission of the Police or another government authority); together with a Notice (in Chinese and English) notifying the 1st defendants that they can obtain copies of the Order, the inter parte summons, Writ of Summons, and supporting affirmation by applying to the Plaintiff's solicitors at an identified address during normal office hours, upon payment of the usual photocopying charges.

(3) Liberty to apply.

71. Plan Y attached to the draft order is one which effectively comprises of Map A, B and C as attached to this judgment. However, I am not satisfied that the descriptions in the draft order together with Plan Y provide sufficient precision as to the locations and delineations of Sections 1, 2 and 3 as covered by the injunction for the purpose of enforcement. As such, I direct that the parties shall appear before this court on 4 December at 2:30pm whereby ACE shall provide to this court a revised plan with sufficient

particulars and/or landmark references (eg, such as lamppost numbers) to identify with sufficient precision the location and delineations of Sections 1, 2 and 3.

72. Further, to avoid any doubt and to facilitate the potential enforcement of the injunction, I would also include in the order a direction that, when requested by the plaintiff, the bailiff do take all reasonable and necessary steps to assist the plaintiff and its agents (properly authorised in writing) to effect the clearance and removal of the obstructions as provided in the injunction, and that the bailiff be authorised to request the assistance of the police where necessary.

73. In this respect, I would repeat what I have said in the Mongkok Injunctions Judgment in that, under the law, a person who, with knowledge of a court order, and deliberately impedes the bailiff in the due execution of his duties is liable for criminal contempt as his conduct intentionally and deliberately interferes with or impedes the due administration of justice. Under the Police Force Ordinance (Cap 232), a police officer has power to arrest any person who he reasonably believes or suspects of being guilty of criminal contempt. In other words, the police have always been empowered under the law to arrest anyone who is reasonably suspected of committing an act of criminal contempt. This power is not dependent on whether the court has made a direction to that effect or not.

74. Finally, as to costs, I would make an order nisi that (a) costs of ACE's application be to the ACE to be taxed if not agreed, with certificate for two counsel, (b) costs of Kwoon Chung's application be to the 2nd and 3rd defendants, to be taxed if not agreed, and (c) the 2nd defendant's own costs in both actions be taxed in accordance with legal aid regulations. This order shall become absolute 14 days from today unless any of the parties applies to vary it by summons.

(Thomas Au)
Judge of the Court of First Instance
High Court

Mr Warren Chan SC, Mr Jose-Antonio Maurellet and Ms Patricia Lam, instructed by Paul W Tse, for the plaintiffs

Mr Hectar Pun and Mr Jeffrey Tam, instructed by Ho Tse Wai, Philip Li & Partners, assigned by the Director of Legal Aid, for the 2nd defendant

The 3rd defendant appeared in person on 17 November 2014

US-China Economic and Security Review Commission Report

SECTION 4: HONG KONG[101]

Introduction

This section examines the controversy over implementing electoral reform in Hong Kong's 2017 chief executive election and the resulting pro-democracy protests; China's increasing military presence in Hong Kong; and Hong Kong's declining freedom of the press. It is based on briefings by foreign government officials, meetings with subject matter experts, and independent research. The section concludes with a discussion of the implications of China's growing interference in Hong Kong's political development for the United States. At the time of writing (October 29, 2014), events surrounding Hong Kong's electoral reform process were still developing.

Controversy over Electoral Reform

Throughout the reporting year, debate surrounding how to elect Hong Kong's next chief executive in 2017 reflected a broader struggle regarding China's role in Hong Kong's political development. China's "basic policies" concerning Hong Kong are outlined in the 1984 Sino-British Joint Declaration, a legally binding international treaty that dictated the terms of Hong Kong's handover from the United Kingdom in 1997. In the Joint Declaration, China granted Hong Kong a "high degree of autonomy," and promised that "Hong Kong will retain its current lifestyle and legal, social, and economic systems until at least the year 2047," while China would administer Hong Kong's defense and foreign affairs in accordance with the "one country, two systems" policy. The Joint Declaration also established that Hong Kong's chief executive will be appointed by China's central government "on the basis of the results of elections or consultations to be held locally."

Hong Kong's mini-constitution, the Basic Law, serves to legally implement China's obligations under the Joint Declaration. The Basic Law holds that the "ultimate aim" for the development of Hong Kong's electoral system is to select the chief executive "by universal suffrage upon nomination by a broadly representative nominating committee in accordance with democratic procedures.' In the reporting year, Hong Kong's government advanced the electoral reform process to achieve the goal of implementing universal suffrage in the 2017 chief executive election. Pro-democracy

---

[101] To view original report: http://origin.www.uscc.gov/sites/default/files/Annual_Report/Chapters/Chapter%203%3B%20Section%204%20Hong%20Kong.pdf. Original endnotes are not included. Asterisks, used in the original text, have been converted to footnotes.

advocates in Hong Kong supported not just expansion of suffrage to all Hong Kong's voters, but also relaxation of nominating requirements for potential candidates. While Beijing's decision on Hong Kong's electoral reform allows all eligible voters to participate in the next chief executive election, it proposes a nominating mechanism that will likely impede democratic candidates from standing for election. This violates commitments made in the Basic Law to uphold election by "democratic procedures."

Electoral Reform Framework Proposed by Beijing

On August 31, 2014, China's National People's Congress (NPC) issued a decision that set new parameters for electing Hong Kong's next chief executive. NPC's ruling declared that in 2017 the chief executive may be elected by universal suffrage by the city's 5 million eligible voters. While implementing universal suffrage is considered a milestone for Hong Kong's political development, the NPC's decision—hailed by Beijing as "historic progress" —ironically limits the choice of candidates that voters will have if Beijing's proposal is approved by Hong Kong's Legislative Council (LegCo).

Currently, to be nominated, a potential chief executive candidate must be supported by no fewer than 150 members (or 12.5 percent) of the 1,200-member election committee, which since Hong Kong's handover has also been responsible for electing the chief executive. While election committee membership has expanded from 400 members in the first chief executive election to 1,200 members in the 2012 election, election committee members represent a mere 1.3 percent of Hong Kong's registered voter population.[102] Moreover, election committee members are exclusively selected from four major "sectors" (see Figure 1). With strong business and political ties to mainland China, many members are local elites seeking to gain favor with Beijing. One member of LegCo estimated that nearly 80 percent of election committee members are controlled by Beijing. As a result of its small size and bias, the current nominating mechanism cannot reasonably be considered "broadly representative" as required by the Basic Law.

---

[102] As of July 25, 2014, Hong Kong's registered voters numbered 3,507,786. Hong Kong SAR's Voter Registration Bureau, "Voter Registration Statistics," July 25, 2014. *http: // www.voter registration.gov.hk/eng/statistic2014.html#1.*

Figure 1: Composition of the Election Committee
(Selected Subsectors)

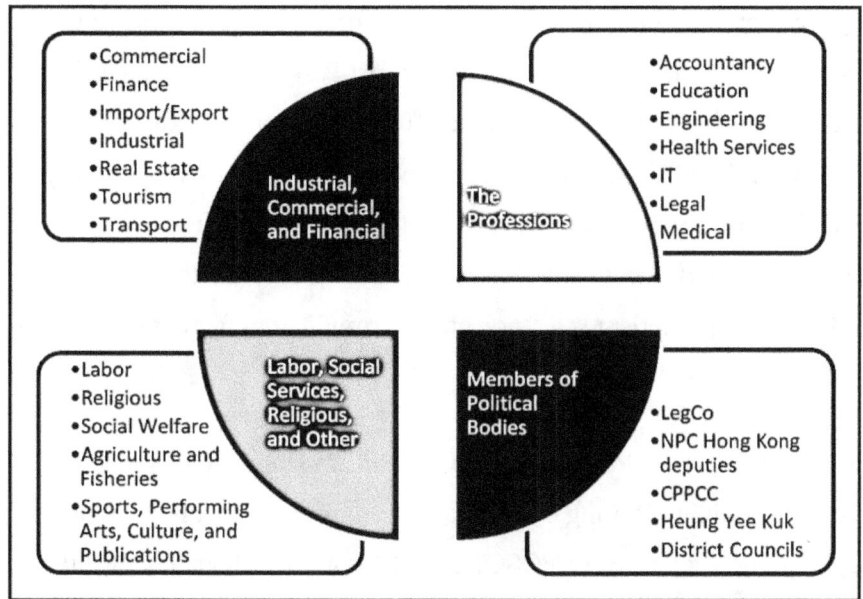

Source: Hong Kong SAR Government, "Let's Talk and Achieve Universal Suffrage," December 2013, pp. 55–56. *http://www.2017.gov.hk/filemanager/template/en/doc/Con☐Doc☐e (FINAL)☐with☐ cover.pdf.*

Implementing universal suffrage in the 2017 election will improve upon the current election configuration in which only a miniscule fraction of Hong Kong's voters can participate, but Beijing's proposed framework for nominating chief executive candidates is more restrictive than the current mechanism. According to the NPC, only two or three candidates may be nominated to stand for election in 2017. Each candidate must be supported by more than 50 percent of the nominating committee, compared with 12.5 percent in the 2012 election. Beijing announced that the 2017 nominating committee shall be formed "in accordance with the number of members, composition, and formation method of the Election Committee," such that the new nominating committee is expected to maintain the same pro-Beijing bias as the current election committee. Democracy advocates in Hong Kong worry that, though all eligible voters would have the opportunity to participate in the next chief executive election if Beijing's proposed framework is approved, the proposed nominating mechanism rules out the possibility of "genuine" democratic election because voters will only be able to choose among two or three Beijing-approved candidates. Beijing's proposal also stipulates that the chief executive must be a "patriot" who "loves the country and loves Hong Kong." In remarks made in 1984 regarding the transfer of Hong Kong's sovereignty to

China under the "one country, two systems" policy, former Chinese leader Deng Xiaoping [103] identified a "patriot" as "one who respects the Chinese nation, sincerely supports the motherland's resumption of sovereignty over Hong Kong, and wishes not to impair Hong Kong's prosperity and stability." In contrast, Beijing's current interpretation of the term "patriot" suggests that Hong Kong's next chief executive should be loyal to the Chinese Communist Party (CCP). In an article published by state-run media outlet *Global Times* on September 10, 2014, Chen Xiankui, a professor of Marxism at the Renmin University of China, wrote that "love of party and love of country are one and the same in modern China," implying that loyalty to the CCP is requisite for patriotism. Hu Xijin, editor-in-chief of the *Global Times,* likewise argued on September 3 that separation of love of the Party from the concept of patriotism is a "poisonous arrow" fired by those with "ulterior motives" seeking to undermine China's unity.

Beijing's conflation of loving the country with loving the Party extends to Hong Kong's administrators. During a press conference explaining Beijing's electoral reform proposal, Li Fei, deputy secretary-general of the NPC Standing Committee (NPCSC), stated "it goes without saying" that chief executive candidates must love both the country and the Party. After democracy advocates in Hong Kong reacted angrily toward the patriotism requirement, NPCSC chairman Zhang Dejiang reportedly said the next chief executive "doesn't have to love the Communist Party, or uphold the Communist Party," according to Michael Tien, deputy chairman of a small, pro-Beijing political party in Hong Kong. Zhang clarified that candidates "can't be against the Communist Party and one- party rule." It is unclear whether conflicting views on patriotism among government officials are due to "ideological divergence" within the CCP or rhetorical confusion.

While the "one country, two systems" principle and the Basic Law stipulate that the chief executive is "accountable" to both the Chinese and Hong Kong governments, nowhere does the law mandate that the chief executive must be a patriot or loyal to the CCP. Likewise, according to Deng Xiaoping's original explanation of the "one country, two systems" policy, Hong Kong's leader need not "be in favor of China's socialist system," but only "love the motherland and Hong Kong." However, in a strongly-worded white paper on the implementation of the "one country, two systems" policy in Hong Kong issued on June 10, 2014, China's State Council Information Office reasserted the central government's position on how the policy applies to Hong Kong's administrators. The white paper, a high-level document intended to explain Beijing's policies to foreign audiences, addressed what Beijing considers the "many wrong views" surrounding Hong

---

[103] Though Deng never assumed the position of Communist Party Chairman, he held a working majority in the party's leadership, and was considered China's de facto ruler from the late 1970s through 1997.

Kong's political development that stem from ''confused'' and ''lopsided'' understanding of the ''one country, two systems'' principle.[104]

China's White Paper on the Practice of "One Country, Two Systems"

> - *Hong Kong's Autonomy:* The white paper emphasized that Beijing maintains ''overall jurisdiction'' over Hong Kong, and that the ''high degree of autonomy'' guaranteed in Hong Kong's Basic Law is derived ''solely from the authorization by the central leadership.'' The State Council asserted that, for Hong Kong, ''there is no such thing called 'residual power.''' In accordance with the ''one country, two systems'' principle, the existence and preservation of Hong Kong's capitalist system ''is subordinate to and derived from 'one country'.''
> - *Universal Suffrage:* The white paper proclaimed Beijing's commitment to implementing a conditional form of universal suffrage in the 2017 chief executive election, which ''must serve the country's sovereignty, security and development interests'' and ''tally with Hong Kong's actual conditions.'' Any system of universal suffrage ''must conform to HKSAR's [Hong Kong Special Administrative Region] legal status as a local administrative region directly under the central government'' and in ''accord with'' relevant NPCSC resolutions.
> - *Mandatory Patriotism:* The white paper asserted that ''loyalty'' and ''loving the country'' are ''basic political requirements for Hong Kong's administrators.'' This assertion echoed claims made by Chinese officials throughout the reporting year that the next chief executive of Hong Kong should abide by the principle of ''love the country, love Hong Kong'' and should not oppose nor confront China's central government.
>
> The barristers of the Hong Kong Bar Association (HKBA) have argued the requirement that Hong Kong's chief executive love China is ''highly questionable as a matter of law'' and ''cannot possibly be a reasonable restriction'' as it contradicts articles in the Basic Law that guarantee the right to stand for election in keeping with ''democratic procedures.'' Moreover, the HKBA has also argued that the categorization of Hong Kong's judges and judicial officers as ''Hong Kong's administrators'' upon whom a political requirement is imposed, as stated in the white paper, would send the

---

[104] China has in the past issued white papers on Xinjiang (2003, 2009), Taiwan (1993, 2000), and several papers on separatist threats in Tibet. Open Source Center, *Hong Kong: White Paper Reaffirms China's Predominance Over Political Reform*, August 25, 2014. ID: CHR20140825 61421053.

> message that Hong Kong's courts are "part of the machinery of the Government and sing in unison with it."
>
> - *Foreign Intervention:* The white paper warned of "outside forces" that are attempting to "use Hong Kong to interfere in China's domestic affairs," and called on readers to "prevent and repel the attempt made by a very small number of people who act in collusion with outside forces" from interfering with Beijing's interpretation of "one country, two systems" in Hong Kong. Chinese state-run media and Chinese officials warned that Western-backed "color revolutions" and "street politics" bring not democracy but chaos comparable to that in Ukraine and the Middle East

While the existing system has twice allowed democrats to run,[105] requiring potential chief executive candidates to satisfy Beijing's standards of patriotism and earn approval from a largely pro-Beijing nominating committee makes it unlikely that a democratic candidate will be nominated, marking a "colossal step backwards" in Hong Kong's political development, according to former head of Hong Kong's civil service Anson Chan. As such, Beijing's proposal appears to conflict with Article 45 of the Basic Law, which calls for election by universal suffrage in accordance with "democratic procedures." Activists argue that Beijing's proposal also violates Article 25 of the International Covenant on Civil and Political Rights (ICCPR) as established by the United Nations Human Rights Council, which stipulates:

Every citizen shall have the right and the opportunity, without any of the distinctions mentioned in article 2 and without unreasonable restrictions:

> *(a) To take part in the conduct of public affairs, directly or through freely chosen representatives;*
>
> *(b) To vote and to be elected at genuine periodic elections which shall be by universal and equal suffrage and shall be held by secret ballot, guaranteeing the free expression of the will of the electors;*
>
> *(c) To have access, on general terms of equality, to public service in his country.*

---

[105] The two pro-democracy (or, "pan-democrat") chief executive candidates who stood for election in the past are Civic Party legislator Alan Leong Kah-kit in 2007 and Democratic Party legislator Albert Ho Chun-yan in 2012. Li Xueying, "China Insists on Right to Choose Candidates for Hong Kong Leader," *Straits Times*, August 31, 2014. http://www.straitstimes.com/news/asia/east-asia/story/china-insists-right-choose-candidates-hong-kong-leader-xinhua-20140831.

Article 39 of the Basic Law states that the ICCPR "shall remain in force and shall be implemented through the laws" in Hong Kong. Therefore, any nominating mechanism that impedes certain candidates from standing election based on political affiliation is inconsistent with Article 39 and Article 45 of the Basic Law.

Considered by some scholars to be "the worst outcome imaginable," Beijing's plan for Hong Kong's next chief executive election may also be designed to shut down aspirations for democracy in the Mainland. Larry Diamond, founding co-editor of the *Journal of Democracy* and senior fellow at Stanford University's Hoover Institution, said that the "Iranian-style rigged system" proposed by China offers no progress toward democracy, and is "not even an effort to gesture toward democracy." Hu Jia, a prominent Chinese dissident in Beijing, believes that, as Hong Kong is a "mirror for people on the Mainland," "the outcome of this battle for democracy will also determine future battles for democracy for all of China." By offering only "fake" democracy, Beijing may be sending a message to Tibet, Xinjiang, and even Taiwan that political change must ascribe to Beijing's rules.

There are few remaining options for rectifying Hong Kong's electoral system before changes to the 2017 electoral method are finalized. A proposal based on Beijing's framework will not be adopted unless it is approved by two-thirds majority in LegCo. If the proposal is not approved, Hong Kong will maintain its current electoral system under which the largely pro-Beijing election committee would choose the chief executive in 2017. All 27 pan-democratic LegCo members (of 70 total members) vowed to veto a final proposal that is based on Beijing's framework, but NPCSC Deputy Secretary-General Li Fei said that it would be a "big step back- wards" if LegCo did not approve the plan. Another possibility is that the formation of the nominating committee, yet undetermined, will not be as closely modeled on that of the election committee as expected. If the electoral base of the nominating committee were expanded, democratic candidates might still have a chance of being nominated. Regardless of which electoral configuration is chosen by Hong Kong, the NPCSC has the final say on any changes to the Basic Law, including changes to electoral methods.

Some analysts believe that Beijing's display of control over Hong Kong's political reform may reflect the central government's perception that Hong Kong's economic importance to China is declining. According to a report issued on August 27, 2014, by Trigger Trend, a Guangzhou-based research firm, Hong Kong is becoming a "mere second-tier city" in China. Based on comparisons of Hong Kong's annual gross domestic product (GDP) growth with that of major regional cities in

China, the report concluded that Guangzhou, Shenzhen, and Tianjin will overtake Hong Kong in terms of GDP by 2017, while inland cities including Chongqing, Chengdu, and Wuhan will catch up by 2022. Hong Kong has long been the gate- way to foreign investment in China, and is consistently ranked near-top in global competitiveness by international organizations.[106] However, if China accomplishes its lofty economic reform goals to internationalize the renminbi, liberalize its capital account, and re- form the banking system, Hong Kong's role as a middleman in facilitating capital flows into China may shrink, according to the Chinese Academy of Social Sciences, a government think tank. China is only obligated to maintain Hong Kong's status as a market economy until 2047 in accordance with the Sino-British Joint Declaration; if the two economies are less integrated at that time, Hong Kong's designation as a market economy is susceptible to change.

International Response to Beijing's Proposed Electoral Reform Framework

In July 2014, the United Kingdom (UK) parliament's Foreign Affairs Committee (FAC) launched an inquiry into the UK's relations with Hong Kong 30 years after the signing of the Joint Declaration. The inquiry aims to determine whether Britain and China are "living up" to commitments made to preserve residents' lifestyle, rights, freedoms, and social system for 50 years after the handover. Lord Chris Patten, the last colonial governor of Hong Kong, believes that the United Kingdom has a "continuing moral and political obligation" to ensure that China keeps the commitments it made. The inquiry has been met with suspicion and fierce opposition from Chinese officials, who call for it to be can celled as it interferes in China's internal affairs. Liu Xiaoming, Chinese ambassador to Britain, warned FAC chairman Richard Ottaway that the inquiry does not "serve the prosperity and stability of Hong Kong, or the healthy development of China-UK relations," and that it "will ultimately harm the interests of Britain." In response to Beijing's election framework proposal the U.S. Department of State warned that Hong Kong's stability and prosperity are dependent on maintaining the city's status as "an open society with the highest possible degree of autonomy and governed by rule of law." After U.S. national security advisor Susan Rice met with top Chinese officials in early September 2014, U.S. officials said "the ability for people of Hong Kong to choose their leadership based on the will of voters" is fundamental, and while Beijing's proposal is one step of the electoral reform process, "there's further to go." Following the eruption of pro-democracy protests in Hong Kong in late September 2014, White House Press

---

[106] In 2014, Hong Kong ranked second by the World Bank in ease of doing business; fourth by the International Institute for Management Development in world competitiveness; and first by The Heritage Foundation in economic freedom.

Secretary Josh Earnest said the legitimacy of the chief executive would be diminished if voters were not given "a genuine choice of candidates that are representative of the peoples' and the voters' will." When U.S. Secretary of State John Kerry addressed the electoral decision protests in a meeting with Chinese Foreign Minister Wang Yi in Washington, DC, on October 1, 2014, Mr. Wang insisted that "Hong Kong affairs are China's internal affairs," and that "illegal acts that violate public order" will not be tolerated. Hua Chunying, spokesperson for China's Ministry of Foreign Affairs, reaffirmed that China "firmly opposes external forces sup- porting illegal activities, such as the [democracy campaign known as the] Occupy Central movement," and is "opposed to any foreign and external interference in China's internal affairs by any country." President Obama is expected to raise the issue with Chinese President Xi Jinping in November.

Hong Kong's Democratic Movement

The people of Hong Kong remained politically active throughout the year, as demonstrated by the high volume of protests held. Notably, on June 4, 2014, the 25th anniversary of the Tiananmen Square massacre, more than 100,000 Hong Kong residents gathered to commemorate the victims of China's crackdown on peaceful student protest. The largest since 1989, the vigil mirrored growing discontent among some Hong Kong residents with China's historical attempts to restrict civil liberties. On July 1, 2014, the 17th anniversary of Hong Kong's handover, democracy advocates peacefully participated in one of the largest marches in Hong Kong's history, from Victoria Park through the Central business district. Estimates of attendance vary widely: police said that the number of marchers peaked at just over 98,000, while the University of Hong Kong and *South China Morning Post* estimated the total was closer to 150,000. Pro-democracy group Civil Human Rights Front, organizer of the march, estimated that 510,000 people marched during the eight-hour demonstration.

Intense political campaigning in the lead-up to the central government's decision on electoral reform in 2017 spurred reactions from groups across the political spectrum. Democracy advocates drew wide support from students, middle-class voters, independent media,[107] and members of the city's judiciary. The most prominent pro-democracy force, known as Occupy Central with Love and Peace (Occupy Central), is a civil disobedience campaign organized in 2013 to advocate for democratic elections in Hong Kong. Since its inception, Occupy Central has widely publicized that

---

[107] In this section, independent media refers to media sources that retain a high degree of free- dom from political intervention and commercial influence, and promote democracy and freedom of speech in Hong Kong. "Hong Kong In-Media," Multiple Journalism. *http://www. multiplejournalism.org/case/hong-kong-in-mediai-e-a-c-c-a-e-i.*

10,000 of its participants will occupy Hong Kong's Central business district, effectively blocking access to government offices and buildings that operate there, unless Beijing accepts sufficiently democratic elections in Hong Kong.

Both Hong Kong and Chinese authorities expressed disdain for the Occupy Central movement. Current Chief Executive Leung Chun-ying (CY Leung) and Chinese Vice President Li Yuanchao denounced the movement as illegal, and threatened that carrying out any protests would "delay universal suffrage." On August, 17, 2014, protesters supporting Beijing's view and estimated to number between 88,000 and 111,000 marched through the city to express their opposition to Occupy Central, which they claimed would disrupt peace and prosperity in Hong Kong. Amid allegations that marchers were bribed to attend, one Chinese-language news source reported that the Federation of Hong Kong Shenzhen Associations might have arranged for as many as 20,000 people to march in ex- change for $38 and a free lunch.

Occupy Central also attracted criticism from multinational companies. The Big Four global accounting companies (Ernst & Young, KPMG, Deloitte Touche Tohmatsu, and PricewaterhouseCoopers) jointly issued advertisements in three Chinese-language newspapers stating their opposition to Occupy Central, warning that it threatens rule of law and disrupts business with multinational clients. After pulling valuable advertisements from pro-democracy news outlets (see "Declining Freedom of the Press," later in this section), British bank HSBC urged investors to sell stock in Hong Kong companies citing "negative news flows" regarding Occupy Central that could serve to "sour relations with China and . . . hurt the economy."

Leading up to Hong Kong's annual July 1 march marking the region's 1997 handover, Occupy Central organized an unofficial citywide referendum on three electoral reform proposals, all of which advocated some form of public nomination (see Table 1). Nearly 800,000 Hong Kong residents, or 22.4 percent of registered voters, participated in the referendum. Of the three proposals, about 42 percent of voters backed that of the Alliance for True Democracy, which gives nomination privileges to the public, political parties, and nominating committee members. Nearly 90 percent of voters wanted LegCo to veto any government proposal that does not allow for genuine fair nomination of chief executive candidates. Public nomination has since been ruled out by the Chinese government, arguing that the Basic Law mandates nomination by a "broadly representative" nominating committee.

Table 1: Referendum Proposals for Chief Executive Nomination

Proposal Originator	Supporters	Nomination Requirements
Alliance for True Democracy	Democratic and Civic parties; 26 pro-democracy legislators (of 27 total); Joseph Cheng (convener).	Candidates require either support of at least 1 percent of registered voters; endorsement from political parties that have won at least 5 percent of votes in the previous legislative election; or, direct election by nominating committee.
Scholarism and Hong Kong Federation of Students	Civic Party; Joshua Wong (convener).	Candidates require support of at least 1 percent of registered voters.
People Power	2 legislators; Wong Yuk-man and Albert Chan (conveners).	Candidates are nominated by the public, LegCo members, and district council members.

Voter turnout surpassed expectations despite ''one of the largest cyberattacks in history'' temporarily shutting down the voting website. Matthew Prince, chief executive of online security firm CloudFlare, explained that the distributed denial-of-service (DDoS) attacks on the voting site, considered to be among the ''most sophisticated'' DDoS attacks ever seen, shut down the site by hijacking computers scattered across the world with malware or viruses and using them to send requests to the site in extremely rapid succession. According to Young Wo-sang, poll IT advisor and convener of the Internet Society of Hong Kong's security and privacy working group, 30 to 40 percent of the 10 billion DDoS attacks came from IP addresses registered to mainland firms in Hong Kong.

In the week leading up to the National Day holiday, which celebrates China's founding, on October 1, 2014, public dissatisfaction with Beijing's electoral reform proposal broke out in waves of protest throughout Hong Kong. On September 22, thousands of Hong Kong university students commenced a five-day strike by boycotting classes and demanding ''genuine'' electoral choice. The Hong Kong Federation of Students, organizer of the boycott, estimated that 13,000 of Hong Kong's 78,000 undergraduate students attended a democracy rally originating at the Chinese University of Hong Kong on September 22. By Friday, September 26, university students were joined by approximately 1,500 grade school students outside the home of CY Leung where they demanded to discuss Hong Kong's democratic future with him. Receiving no response, a group of about one hundred protestors gathered near the government headquarters. Some attempted to breach a barricaded area known as Civic Square that was blocked by police, who used pepper spray and arrested some protesters.

With participants estimated to number close to 200,000,85 protests continued to escalate into the early morning of September 28, when riot police fired 87 cans of tear gas at protesters in order to clear the swelling crowds from the business district roadways. Cheung Tak-keung, assistant commissioner of Hong Kong police, said police had ''no alternative'' but to fire tear gas—considered a tactic of ''minimum force''—to control crowds. One day later, inspired by ''the courage of the students and members of the public in their spontaneous decision to stay'' despite police action, Occupy Central organizers announced the movement's official commencement ahead of schedule to join student protests. The protesters— now comprising Occupy Central, the students, and other supporters—adopted the moniker ''Umbrella Revolution'' to describe the movement, as many demonstrators used umbrellas to shield themselves from pepper spray and tear gas.

After riot police were withdrawn on September 29, protesters continued demonstrating through National Day on October 1. Some protesters, including Occupy Central co-founder Benny Tai Yiuting and organizers of the Hong Kong Federation of Students, demanded that Mr. Leung step down. While removing Mr. Leung from office would placate protesters' demands in the short-term without obstructing Beijing's plan for electoral reform, any new leader to take office before Beijing's reforms are implemented would be selected by the electoral method currently in place. On October 2, the Communist Party newspaper *People's Daily* reported that the central government would continue ''unswervingly'' to support Mr. Leung. Public criticism of Mr. Leung intensified, however, following revelations of his failure to disclose payments he received totaling $6.4 million from an Australian engineering company during his term as chief executive. According to Mr. Leung's statement, he is not required by Hong Kong law to disclose the payments.

In reaction to the Umbrella Revolution protests, Hong Kong Chief Secretary Carrie Lam said on September 29 that further government discussions on political reform would be postponed until the Hong Kong government could "re-examine the situation and find a better time to introduce the next round of consultations." Mr. Leung said that protesters should not expect the NPC to reconsider or reverse their ruling on Hong Kong's electoral reform because "the Chinese government won't give in to threats asserted through illegal activity." An advisor to Mr. Leung indicated that the Hong Kong government's strategy for handling the protests was to "wait and patiently deal with the crisis . . . to resolve it peacefully," but an editorial published in the *People's Daily* on October 2 threatened that the "consequences will be unimaginable" for protesters, who "incited the masses, paralyzed transportation, disrupted businesses, stirred up conflict, and interfered with the daily lives of Hong Kong people," and accused Occupy Central of obstructing Hong Kong's "smooth transition to democracy."

With no clear resolution in sight, demonstrations over Beijing's decision continued through October in the face of pressure from police, the public, and violent gangs. Starting October 3 and continuing sporadically throughout the protests, gangs suspected of having links to the Triads, an organized crime group, infiltrated crowds supporting and opposing the Occupy Central protests, provoking violence among peaceful demonstrations in the Mong Kok district. According to police superintendent Dan Ng Wai-hon, up to 200 suspected gangsters, of whom more than 40 were arrested in connection with the October 3–4 attacks for fighting and illegal gathering, "were well-organized and came with a purpose," though police are still investigating their exact motives. On October 15, clashes between protesters and police over the removal of barricades to resume traffic flow resulted in the beating of a handcuffed protester by seven police officers, who were later suspended.

Following the cancellation of two previously scheduled negotiations, Hong Kong government officials met with five student leaders on October 21 to discuss their perspectives on electoral re- form. In response to students' concerns that the Hong Kong government's July 2014 report to Beijing on popular political views misled the NPC and influenced its proposed guidelines, Chief Secretary Lam conceded that the government was willing to submit a new report to Beijing acknowledging the popular discontent stirred up by the NPC's electoral reform decision. The students and other protesters intend to continue demonstrating until their demands for an open nominating process are met, but Mr. Leung reiterated that the Hong Kong government "cannot make something that is not in the Basic Law possible," and "the Central Authorities. . . will not retract the decision of the

Standing Committee." At the time of writing (October 29, 2014), student protesters and government officials remained deadlocked over Beijing's decision.

Macau and Taiwan Follow Hong Kong

Inspired by Occupy Central's June referendum, democracy activists in Macau held their own informal referendum from August 24–30, 2014, to determine whether residents support universal suffrage in the 2019 chief executive election. Only hours after the referendum began on August 24, police arrested five participants, including poll organizer Jason Chao, on charges of "qualified disobedience," and started shutting down polling stations. Despite heavy police interference, nearly 9,000 residents cast their votes through an online polling website similar to that used in Hong Kong's referendum. The results of the poll showed that 89 percent of participants do not trust the current chief executive, Fernando Chui, and that 95 percent of participants support universal suffrage in the 2019 chief executive election. Chief Executive Chui was re-elected to office on August 31 by a 400-member pro-China election committee. He was the only candidate.

For Taiwan, the reform outcome in Hong Kong serves as a warning that, if Taiwan were reunified with China, Beijing would not likely adhere to its promise to protect Taiwan's civil liberties. In 1982, the NPC made a constitutional provision for reunifying Taiwan with China as a special administrative region under the "one country, two systems" principle, exactly like Hong Kong. Under this provision, "Taiwan's current social and economic systems [would] remain unchanged, its way of life [would] not change, and its economic and cultural ties with foreign countries [would] not change." On September 26, 2014, President Xi reaffirmed China's "firm and unwavering stance" that the best way to reunify Taiwan with China would be under the "one country, two systems" framework. Alan D. Romberg, director of the East Asia program at public policy think tank the Stimson Center, argued that China's strongly-worded white paper on the application of the "one country, two systems" policy in Hong Kong strengthened the case for Taiwanese independence as Hong Kong's "high degree of autonomy" has come under threat.

Democracy advocates in Hong Kong and Taiwan have become more engaged under the shared threat of China's control. Activists in Hong Kong and Taiwan have supported each other throughout both Hong Kong's democratic movement and Taiwan's Sunflower Movement, in which participants occupied the Legislative Yuan in March and April 2014 to protest the Cross-Strait Services Trade Agreement (see Chapter 3, Section 3, "Taiwan," for fuller treatment of Taiwan and the Sunflower Movement). Taiwan's main political parties, typically fiercely divided, similarly expressed regret at Beijing's decision to limit electoral reform in Hong Kong. President Ma Ying-jeou expressed a "high degree of concern and support for [the] Hong Kong people's continuing fight" for democratic progress, while a spokesman from rival Democratic Progressive Party said that Beijing's decision "casts a shadow over the process of democratization."

Following the breakout of Umbrella Revolution protests in response to Beijing's decision, President Ma reaffirmed that he "fully understand[s] and support[s] Hong Kong residents' demand for free nomination and election of Hong Kong's chief executive, and urge[s] the Mainland authorities to listen carefully to the voices of Hong Kong residents and handle the matter in a peaceful and cautious manner." On Taiwan's National Day, October 10, President Ma reiterated his strong support not just for Hong Kong's democratic movement, but for the Mainland's as well, stating "now is the most appropriate time for mainland China to move toward constitutional democracy."

China's Increasing Military Presence in Hong Kong

Heightened activity by the People's Liberation Army (PLA) in Hong Kong throughout the reporting year alarmed Hong Kong pro- democracy advocates and media, as well as international observers. Under Article 14 of the Basic Law and in accordance with the "one country, two systems" policy, China's central government is responsible for the defense of Hong Kong. As such, the PLA's Hong Kong garrison is tasked with the following functions to "vigorously safeguard China's sovereignty and territorial integrity":

1. To guard against and resist aggression, and to guarantee Hong Kong's security;
2. To shoulder the responsibility of defense and patrol duty;
3. To take charge of military installations;
4. To undertake relevant foreign military affairs.

One indicator that Chinese military presence in Hong Kong will continue to expand is the Hong Kong Town Planning Board's unanimous approval on February 14, 2014, to rezone an area of public space measuring 2,970 square meters along the waterfront of Victoria Harbor where a Chinese military port is being constructed. The establishment of the "Central Military Dock" (CMD) was originally provisioned in 1994 under the Sino-British Defense Land Agreement (DLA), and its construction is now near completion. Government officials said that the CMD would be used for "conducting military training, berthing military vessels, running ceremonial activities and carrying out pier maintenance," though the dock will be open to the public when not in use.

Public objections to the CMD construction plan were significant; during the public consultation period, only 0.1 percent of about 19,000 comments favored the plan. One of the most contentious points was the Town Planning Board's decision to rezone the area from "open space" to "military use." Opponents of the CMD argue the rezoning not only disrupts public access to the waterfront promenade,[108] but ensures that public access and law enforcement in that area fall under the discretion of the commander of the PLA garrison rather than the Hong Kong police. While Annex III of the DLA guaranteed that the "Hong Kong Government will leave free 150 meters of the eventual permanent waterfront . . . for the construction of a military dock after 1997," it did not stipulate that zoning should be altered in any way.

In protest of the CMD construction plans, four activists forced their way into garrison headquarters on December 26, 2013, calling for the PLA to "get out" of Hong Kong.[109] In a move widely perceived as retaliatory, the PLA staged its first air-and-sea drill of 2014 in Victoria Harbor less than one month after the protests. The January 24, 2014, drill was carried out by two frigates and three helicopters, and was intended to make the PLA "more familiar with the air-and-sea situation of Hong Kong and improve its ability to handle emergency situations," according to state media. Ni Lexiong, a naval expert and professor of Political Science and Law at Shanghai University, contended the drill was "aimed at warning the public that Hong Kong could continue to enjoy a certain level of freedom, but should not challenge the central government's political authority, with military means being Beijing's last step to maintain Hong Kong's prosperity and stability."

The CMD is the 19th military site in Hong Kong transferred from the British Army to the PLA as a Military Installations Closed Area (MICA), 18 of which currently cover an area totaling 2,700 hectares (27 square kilometers).128 Hong Kong's Garrison Law stipulates that all restricted access military zones must be defined by the garrison "in conjunction with" the Hong Kong government, while the "locations and boundaries" of such zones shall be declared by the Hong Kong government. However, an undisclosed PLA radar station and compound atop Hong Kong's tallest mountain, Tai Mo Shan, was discovered in July 2014. The military and security publication *Jane's*

---

[108] When the CMD section of the promenade is closed for military use, the public can use a pedestrian walkway to the south of the dock area. Hong Kong Security Bureau, e-mail exchange with Commission staff, October 17, 2014.

[109] The four activists were subsequently arrested and convicted for breach of the Public Order Ordinance. Hong Kong Security Bureau, e-mail exchange with Commission staff, October 17, 2014

Defense Weekly reported the station is likely an electronic and signals intelligence (ELINT/SIGINT) facility, though the PLA refused to confirm, citing "military secrecy." The facility is behind fences that restrict public access. Dr. Kenneth Chan Ka-lok, a LegCo member of the Civic Party, supported conducting a judicial review over the garrison's non-disclosure of the construction and use of the facility because "the public has no knowledge about this and [LegCo] cannot find anything about it from documents filed to the legislature." With regard to the compound, which is not listed among Hong Kong's 19 designated military sites (including the CMD), Dr. Chan said the PLA "should follow the Garrison Law provisions to designate the place as a military site with restricted public access."

On July 1, 2014, the same day as the annual march marking Hong Kong's handover, the PLA opened three military bases for public viewing of the barracks. The garrison displayed several new pieces of military equipment during the "open day":

- Small arms: Type 11 pistol, Type 06 (QSW06) silenced pistol, and Type 10 (QBU10) antimateriel rifle
- The garrison's first two Type 056 Jingda-class corvettes: Huizhou (596) and Qinzhou (597)
- Logistics vehicles: Dong Feng EQ2102J-based trucks135

New equipment is often first tested by the garrison before being introduced more widely into PLA service. Among the previously used pieces of equipment displayed was a Z–9WA helicopter armed with two 23mm cannons.

Some Hong Kong commentators believe that the central government could deploy garrison forces to quell democracy protests and that recent increases in military activity are in part meant to intimidate protesters. For example, during "counter-terrorism" drills open to the public that were conducted on July 1, PLA soldiers at the bases were seen carrying riot shields and pepper spray for the first time. While the garrison "does not interfere in Hong Kong affairs," the Hong Kong government may by law request assistance from the garrison as necessary "in the maintenance of public order and in disaster relief." Further, if the NPCSC decides that Hong Kong is in a state of emergency which "by reason of turmoil . . . endangers national unity or security and is beyond the control of the [Hong Kong] government," the central government in Beijing "may issue an order applying the relevant national laws" at its own discretion.

Alan Hoo, chairman of the Basic Law committee and a Hong Kong delegate to the Chinese People's Political Consultative Conference (CPPCC), likened the Occupy Central movement to recent terrorist attacks in Kunming and Xi'an, and claimed that Occupy Central threatens China's national security. According to Hoo, Occupy Central not only justifies PLA intervention under a state of emergency, but also "fosters the legislation of Basic Law Article 23," which mandates:

The Hong Kong Special Administrative Region shall enact laws on its own to prohibit any act of treason, secession, sedition, subversion against the Central People's Government, or theft of state secrets, to prohibit foreign political organizations or bodies from conducting political activities in the Region, and to prohibit political organizations or bodies of the Region from establishing ties with foreign political organizations or bodies.

`In 2003, an anti-subversion bill proposed under Article 23 was shelved after 500,000 Hong Kong residents protested its implementation.144 Earlier this year, mainland academics insisted that Hong Kong temporarily adopt Beijing's national security laws until its own Article 23 legislation is passed. Jasper Tsang Yok-sing, president of the LegCo, said that such a proposal is not consistent with Article 23 of the Basic Law, which stipulates that Hong Kong's government should enact its own laws to handle subversion against the central government.

Declining Freedom of the Press

The reporting year was considered "the darkest for press freedom for several decades" by the Hong Kong Journalists Association (HKJA), as demonstrated by the region's continued fall in global press freedom rankings (see Figure 2). According to Freedom House, a U.S.-based independent watchdog organization that ranks countries by press freedom indices, violence against journalists and pressure from mainland China were two factors that contributed to the downward trend in Hong Kong's press freedom dating back to 2004.

Likewise, Reporters Without Borders' 2014 world press freedom index indicated that "growing subjugation" of the Hong Kong administration and media to China's central government is "increasingly compromising media pluralism."

Figure 2: Hong Kong's Global Press Freedom Ranking

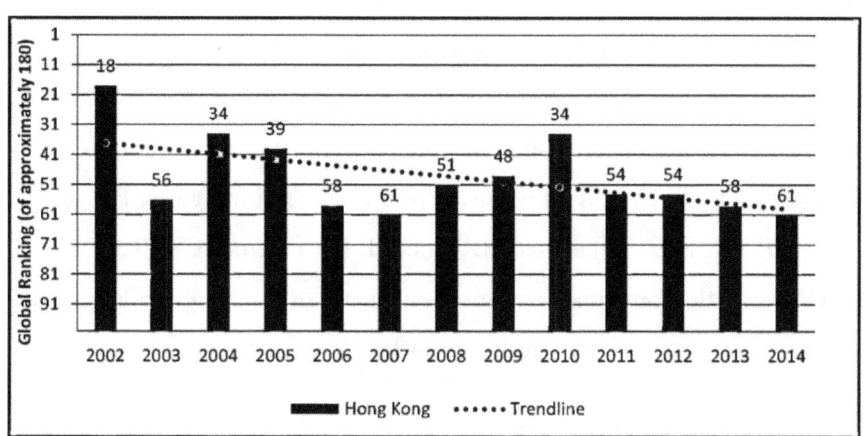

Source: "Freedom of the Press," Reporters Without Borders, 2002–2014. *http://en.rsf.org/*.

Self-censorship on the part of reporters and media outlets alike remained prevalent in Hong Kong in the reporting year. According to a report from the Committee to Protect Journalists, more than half of Hong Kong's media owners hold political appointments in two of China's main political bodies, the NPC and the CPPCC, including Charles Ho of the Sing Tao news group; Richard Li (son of Li Ka-shing, commonly referred to as the richest person in Asia) of Now TV and the *Hong Kong Economic Journal*; and Peter Woo of i-Cable television. As a result, political considerations tend to overshadow objective reporting. According to a 2012 survey of journalists conducted by the HKJA, nearly 40 percent of respondents said that "they or their supervisors had recently played down information unfavorable to China's central government, advertisers, media owners, or the local government."

In the run-up to the 2017 election, the role of the press in determining Hong Kong's democratic future has become even more critical. Members of the press and media outlets perceived as hostile to Beijing's interpretation of "one country, two systems" continued to suffer professional and physical attacks, exemplified by the plight of one of Hong Kong's few remaining independent newspapers, *Ming Pao*. In January 2014, *Ming Pao* announced the abrupt dismissal of its chief editor, Kevin Lau Chun-to, after nearly two years on the job. Though *Ming Pao* claimed Mr. Lau was simply moving to a new position, journalists and scholars speculated that Mr. Lau's removal was retaliation for *Ming Pao's* criticism of government policies and its revelation of the political scandals that derailed 2012 pro-Beijing chief executive candidate Henry Tang under Mr. Lau's tenure. *Ming Pao* also partnered with the Consortium of Investigative Journalists in January 2014 to publish an investigation into the overseas tax-haven accounts of Chinese officials.

Out of concern for the preservation of Hong Kong's press freedom, more than 90 percent of *Ming Pao's* editorial staff petitioned the paper to cite reasons for Mr. Lau's dismissal, while hundreds of protesters gathered outside *Ming Pao's* offices calling for media independence. Rallies for press freedom continued throughout February 2014, when popular radio host Lee Wai-ling, who is known for her Beijing-critical commentary, was dismissed without explanation by Commercial Radio Hong Kong (CRHK), one of Hong Kong's two commercial radio broadcasting companies. To continue broadcasting, CRHK must apply to extend its license, issued by the Hong Kong Broadcasting Authority, by August 25, 2015. It is an ''open secret,'' according to former CRHK broadcasting director Cheung Man-yee, that outspoken program hosts are often forced to leave due to government pressure when a broadcasting company is applying for license renewal.

On February 26, less than two months after his dismissal, Mr. Lau was critically injured by a knife-wielding assailant in Hong Kong's Sai Wan Ho neighborhood. Prompted by the belief that the attack (and previous attacks on journalists) was initiated by pro-Beijing assailants in an effort to threaten free media, nearly 10,000 protesters took to the streets on March 2, 2014, in support of Hong Kong's press freedom, carrying banners reading ''They Can't Kill Us All.'' Two suspects found in southern China's Guangdong Province were charged with Mr. Lau's assault, and admitted that, as members of Hong Kong triad gang Shui Fong, they were each paid approximately $130,000 to harm but not kill Mr. Lau and then go into hiding on the Mainland. Hong Kong Police Commissioner Andy Tsang Wai-hung said that the attack had ''nothing to do with press freedom,'' but that the assailants were merely hired hitmen. Less than one month after Mr. Lau's attack, two Hong Kong media executives were attacked by four assailants with metal bars, an act condemned by the HKJA as another sign of Hong Kong's deteriorating press freedom.

History of Attacks on Journalists in Hong Kong

- *March 2014:* Lam Kin-ming and Lei Lun-han, executives with a new publication, *The Hong Kong Morning News*, were assaulted by four assailants with metal pipes.
- *February 2014:* Kevin Lau Chun-to, former chief editor of the investigative newspaper *Ming Pao*, was badly injured by a knife-wielding assailant.
- *July 2013:* Sze Wing-ching, founder of free Hong Kong daily *am730*, had his car window smashed by two men as he was driving in downtown Hong Kong.
- *June 2013:* A car was rammed into the gates of the residence of Jimmy Lai, founder of the pro-democracy Next Media Group, and an ax and machete were left behind at the scene.
- *June 2013:* Chen Ping, publisher of the political weekly *iSun Affairs*, was beaten by two men wielding batons.
- *July 2008:* Jimmy Lai and pro-democracy leader Martin Lee were the targets of a failed assassination attempt.
- *November 2005:* A small homemade bomb was sent to *Ming Pao's* editorial offices along with a threatening letter, injuring one female employee.
- *August 1998:* Albert Cheng, host of talk radio's popular "Tea-cup in a Tempest" program, was slashed with carving knives on his way to work and seriously wounded.

Source: Isabella Steger, "Thousands Take to the Streets to Support Hong Kong Press Freedom," *Wall Street Journal*, March 2, 2014. *http://online.wsj.com/news/articles/SB10001424052702304585004579414611826771446.*

Beijing continued to exert political and economic pressure on businesses that advertise in pro-democracy media sources, further suppressing Hong Kong's press freedom. Hong Kong's Next Media Limited (Next Media), the publisher of the outspoken paper *Apple Daily*, was reportedly boycotted by its two biggest advertisers at the instruction of China's central government. According to Next Media executive Mark Simon, HSBC and Standard Chartered banks were pressured by the central government's liaison office in Hong Kong into ending their long-held advertising relationships with *Apple Daily* in September 2013. Mr. Simon reported that prior to the boycott, the two banks spent approximately $3.8 million on advertisements in *Apple Daily* annually. In addition to the losses incurred by the banks' boycotts, Next Media reported that additional advertising boycotts on the part of Beijing-dependent firms cost the company at least $26 million annually, or 10 percent of its present value.

Manipulation of media advertising by the central government is likely retaliation for the independent media's outspoken pro-democracy stance. Jimmy Lai, owner of Next Media and the "most powerful critic of the Chinese Communist Party in Hong Kong," has been an outspoken political activist since the 1989 Tiananmen Square massacre. Under his leadership, Next Media released an online animated video mocking Bloomberg's alleged self-censorship—based on commercial interests—to axe a story on the private wealth of Communist party elites in October 2013. Bloomberg later denied the allegations. Next Media and *Apple Daily* also face the threat of cyber attacks in retaliation for critical reporting. In the days leading up to Occupy Central's unofficial referendum on June 20, *Apple Daily's* website was flooded by more than 10 billion DDoS attacks in a 24-hour period, many originating from IP addresses in China and Russia. *Apple Daily* suspected that the attacks were "carried out by hackers from China, trying to suppress Hong Kong people's determination to fight for democracy and to attack the pro-universal suffrage Next Media group."

Independent media suffered another blow on July 26, 2014, when popular pro-democracy news website House News unexpectedly announced its closure, citing intense political pressure. Tony Tsoi Tung-ho, House News co-founder and outspoken supporter of Occupy Central, explained his fear of the political atmosphere in a note he posted on the site:

Hong Kong has changed. To act as a normal citizen, a normal media outlet and to do something right for society is becoming difficult, or even terrifying—not that you feel alienated, but fearful. The ongoing political struggle makes people very anxious—many democrats are tracked and smeared. Their past records have been dug up. A sense of White Terror [110] lingers in society and I feel the pressure as well.

Mr. Tsoi also noted that the popular news aggregator site was not profitable because advertisement revenues were disproportionately low. House News co-founder Leung Man-tao explained that "many big companies don't place advertisements on our website because of our critical stance towards the government and Beijing." In his shutdown announcement, Mr. Tsoi claimed that Hong Kong's tense political atmosphere and "abnormal society" have twisted the market, forcing House News to abandon its core democratic stance.

---

[110] The term "white terror" also refers to a period from 1949 to 1987 when several thousand perceived opponents (Communist or pro-Taiwanese independence) of Chinese Nationalist Party leader Chiang Kai-shek were incarcerated and executed in Taiwan. Many victims were intellectual and social elite.

Implications for the United States

In accordance with the United States-Hong Kong Policy Act of 1992, the United States supports Hong Kong's high degree of autonomy. Beijing's interpretation of the ''one country, two systems'' policy and infringement on civil liberties guaranteed to Hong Kong in the Sino-British Joint Declaration not only undermine Hong Kong's high degree of autonomy, but also reflect the Chinese government's failure to comply with international commitments. Moreover, Beijing's application of ''one country, two systems'' in Hong Kong holds ominous implications for Taiwan if it were to be reunified with China under the same framework. The United States shares with Hong Kong an interest in upholding democratic values, human rights, rule of law, independent journalism, and open and fair market competition, all of which are essential for Hong Kong's continued prosperity and development as an international financial center.

Conclusions

- China's central government has put forth a framework for the election of Hong Kong's next chief executive in 2017 that effectively excludes democratic candidates from nomination and allows Beijing to control the outcome. This proposal conflicts with standards set forth in Hong Kong's Basic Law and the International Convention on Civil and Political Rights, and runs counter to international commitments made by China in the 1984 Sino-UK Joint Declaration to preserve Hong Kong's ''high degree of autonomy'' and way of life for 50 years following its 1997 handover from the United Kingdom.
- Increased Chinese military activity in Hong Kong signals China's determined presence there and serves to intimidate pro-democracy activists from participating in the Occupy Central movement and other peaceful movements out of fear of military retaliation.
- Increased infringement on Hong Kong's press freedom, particularly in the forms of violence against journalists and political pressure on advertisers, threatens the media's ability to serve as a watchdog. The steady erosion of press freedom is a worrying trend that has worsened over the last ten years, and appears to be targeted at outspoken pro-democracy media.

US Congressional-Executive Commission on China[111]

VI. Developments in Hong Kong and Macau

Hong Kong

During the Commission's 2015 reporting year, massive pro- democracy demonstrations ("Occupy Central" or the "Umbrella Movement") took place from September through December 2014, drawing attention to ongoing tensions over Hong Kong's debate on electoral reform and Hong Kong's autonomy from the Chinese central government under the "one country, two systems" approach. The Commission observed developments raising concerns that the Chinese and Hong Kong governments may have infringed on the rights of the people of Hong Kong, including in the areas of political participation and democratic reform, press freedom, and freedom of assembly.

UNIVERSAL SUFFRAGE AND AUTONOMY

Hong Kong's Basic Law guarantees freedom of speech, religion, and assembly; promises Hong Kong a "high degree of autonomy"; and affirms the International Covenant on Civil and Political Rights (ICCPR) applies to Hong Kong. The Basic Law also states that its "ultimate aim" is the election of Hong Kong's Chief Executive (CE) "by universal suffrage upon nomination by a broadly representative nominating committee in accordance with democratic procedures" and of the Legislative Council (LegCo) "by universal suffrage." The CE is currently chosen by a 1,200-member Election Committee, largely consisting of members elected in functional constituencies made up of professionals, corporations, religious and social organizations, and trade and business interest groups. Forty LegCo members are elected directly by voters and 30 by functional constituencies. The electors of many functional constituencies, however, reportedly have close ties to or are supportive of the Chinese government.

Despite committing in principle to allow Hong Kong voters to elect the CE by universal suffrage in 2017, the Chinese government's framework for electoral reform restricts the ability of voters to nominate CE candidates for election. Under this framework, laid out in an August 31, 2014, decision by the National People's Congress Standing Committee (NPCSC), a 1,200-person Nominating Committee (NC), formed similarly to the Election Committee, would select two

---

[111] http://www.cecc.gov/publications/annual-reports/2015-annual-report

to three candidates, each of whom would ultimately require approval by a majority of NC members. Voters would then choose from among these two to three candidates in the CE election. The current Election Committee is dominated by members supportive of the central government. The Hong Kong government announced that any potential reforms would be in "strict conformity" with the NPCSC decision. Pro-democratic legislators pledged to veto any bill adhering to the NPCSC decision, which some described as "fake universal suffrage," and demanded the NPCSC withdraw or revise its decision.

On June 18, 2015, the LegCo voted down the Hong Kong government's electoral reform proposal. All 27 pro-democratic legislators and 1 pro-Beijing legislator voted against the proposal, denying the measure the two-thirds majority required for passage. Because the reform proposal was defeated, future elections, including the 2017 CE and 2016 LegCo elections, will continue to use the current electoral methods. The Hong Kong government rejected calls to restart the electoral reform process, saying that doing so would be "legally infeasible and impracticable."

FALL 2014 PRO-DEMOCRACY DEMONSTRATIONS

International rights non-governmental organizations (NGOs), domestic and international media organizations, and other observers expressed concern over aspects of the Hong Kong government and police response to massive pro-democracy demonstrations in fall 2014, citing threats to the rights of the people of Hong Kong to the freedoms of speech, assembly, and association guaranteed under the Basic Law and international law.

Pro-democratic activists called for protests against the NPCSC's August 31 decision. The "Occupy Central with Love and Peace" protest group initially called for limited duration civil disobedience demonstrations to begin on a holiday. A separate university student class boycott culminated in hundreds of activists attempting to occupy a courtyard outside government headquarters on September 26 and 27, 2014. Thousands of people gathered near government headquarters to support the students. On September 28, police fired tear gas and pepper spray on crowds that had occupied a major thoroughfare near government headquarters, prompting tens of thousands of people to join the demonstration over the next few days and occupy additional major streets in areas beyond the initially planned Central District. Protesters remained encamped at three separate protest sites until the Hong Kong government enforced a civil court order to clear the majority of protesters in November and December.

During the largely non-violent demonstrations, there were reports of violence between police, protesters, and counter-protesters. Some observers reported police at times used "excessive" or "unjustifiable" force against protesters, journalists, and onlookers.

In one incident, police officers were filmed kicking a handcuffed activist. The police officers involved were immediately suspended and later arrested on suspicion of assault. Observers also reported several instances of protesters attacking police, including one instance on December 1 in which protesters reportedly beat a police officer unconscious. Journalists' organizations said that in some instances, police witnessed counter-protesters attacking pro- democracy demonstrators, but did not protect them or promptly arrest the attackers. Hong Kong police and a police watchdog body received over 2,000 complaints regarding police conduct during the demonstrations and began investigating the complaints.

Journalists, media organizations, and NGOs reported dozens of incidents of attacks and threats against journalists covering the demonstrations. Media organizations reported several instances of police intimidating, threatening, or using "unnecessary force" against reporters covering the protests, even when reporters displayed press credentials. Pro-democracy media websites suffered numerous cyberattacks during the demonstrations.

Hong Kong police reportedly selectively enforced the law, arresting pro-democracy advocates and demonstrators as a form of harassment and "political prosecution." Police arrested more than 40 protesters, activists, and legislators for unauthorized assemblies, but released them without charge, reserving the right to prosecute them later. In one instance, police charged four prominent protest leaders in July 2015 with obstructing police officers at a non-violent June 2014 protest against the central government.

One of the protesters said the timing of the charges was meant to
"deter [them] from further political protests," while another described it as "white terror." The lawyer of one of the protesters said police were holding out the threat of additional prosecution against activists and protesters, including for actions and events over a year in the past, in order to forestall future demonstrations. Police reportedly interpreted Hong Kong's Crimes Ordinance broadly to justify ordering the removal of online content encouraging participation in the fall 2014 demonstrations, characterized by police as "incit[ing] others on the Internet to commit illegal acts." Critics worried that by exploiting the Ordinance's ambiguous language (regarding "access to [a] computer with criminal or dishonest intent") to arrest some activists, police may be "criminalizing legitimate, protected speech."

Protesters and pro-democracy activists reported sustained harassment and intimidation during and after the demonstrations, including hacking of their email accounts or phones, by groups reportedly connected to the Chinese government. Sources reported Chinese intelligence services hired former Hong Kong police officers to surveil people perceived to oppose the Chinese government, including pro-democratic legislators.

Some protesters and activists were unable to travel to mainland

China or Macau due to their participation in the demonstrations.

In November, Chinese authorities prevented three student protest leaders from flying to Beijing municipality to meet Chinese officials. Pro-democracy advocates claimed the Chinese and Hong Kong governments had assembled "blacklists" of activists banned from entering mainland China.

PRESS FREEDOM

This past year, continuing pressure from the Chinese and Hong Kong governments, including pressure to self-censor, and violence and intimidation reportedly resulted in further deterioration of Hong Kong's press freedom. Reporters Without Borders lowered Hong Kong's ranking from 61st to 70th out of 180 countries in its 2015 press freedom index. Nearly 90 percent of journalists surveyed by a journalists' union believed press freedom in Hong Kong worsened over the last year. Journalists at some publications reported editorial interference resulting in self-censorship and punishment. After TVB News aired a video reporting the beating of a handcuffed activist by several police officers, an editor temporarily deleted the video's voiceover, later altering it to cast doubt on police use of force. TVB management reportedly punished several journalists who signed a petition condemning the editorial change. Two of the punished editors and several other journalists resigned, claiming dissatisfaction with TVB management. In February 2015, journalists at newspaper Ming Pao protested after the editor-in-chief unilaterally decided to downplay a report on the violent suppression of the 1989 Tiananmen protests.

The Hong Kong and Chinese central governments reportedly pressured journalists to give favorable coverage to opponents of the pro-democracy demonstrations. Many media owners have commercial interests in mainland China and connections to the Chinese government. Pro-democracy media organizations reportedly faced difficulties operating without support from government or business patrons. Pro-democracy media company Next Media and its journalists have been the targets of repeated attacks, threats, and harassment. In January 2015, attackers firebombed Next Media publication Apple Daily's headquarters and the home of its prominent pro-democratic publisher.

Macau

POLITICAL AND PRESS FREEDOMS

Although Macau's Basic Law does not mention "universal suffrage," it ensures the applicability of the International Covenant on Civil and Political Rights (ICCPR) in Macau. During the

Commission's 2015 reporting year, Macau did not make progress toward "an electoral system based on universal and equal suffrage. ." in line with the ICCPR, and no steps were taken to withdraw the reservation to Article 25(b) of the ICCPR, as repeatedly recommended by the UN Human Rights Committee. Macau's Legislative Assembly voted against discussing electoral reform to further democratize its elections, with some lawmakers saying Macau's political development depends on central government decisions. A December 2014 opinion survey indicated that 60 percent of Macau residents supported universal suffrage for Chief Executive elections. Civil society activists in Macau reported intimidation from the Macau and Chinese governments meant to pressure activists to "tone down" their activities, reportedly because of fear of pro-democratic unrest in Hong Kong spreading to Macau. The Macau Journalists Association reportedly received anonymous complaints from reporters at public broadcaster Teledifusão de Macau that self-censorship had worsened.

This past year, Macau authorities blocked some Hong Kong journalists, activists, and others from entering the territory for political reasons. Citing threats to internal security, Macau immigration authorities refused to allow several Hong Kong reporters to enter Macau to report on Chinese President and Communist Party General Secretary Xi Jinping's visit in December 2014. A prominent pro-democratic Hong Kong legislator protested after authorities barred her from entering Macau "for security reasons" while she was on vacation in January 2015. Macau's Secretary for Security denied that the Macau government had a "blacklist" banning certain people from entering Macau.

CORRUPTION AND MACAU'S AUTONOMY

During the Commission's 2015 reporting year, the Macau government expanded coordination with Chinese authorities, in part to fight financial crimes connected to Macau's gambling industry and to cooperate with the central government's anticorruption campaign. Macau continued to be a center for violations of mainland China's currency controls, in part through fraudulent use of UnionPay bank cards at mainland-registered point-of-sale terminals. From January to March 2015, illegal UnionPay transactions in Macau totaled MOP 260 million (US$32.5 million). Macau's gambling regulator requires gaming operators to report "high value transactions" of MOP 500,000 (US$62,000) or greater, a reporting threshold higher than international anti-money laundering standards.

To combat the use of UnionPay bank cards in evading mainland China's capital controls, in November 2014, the Monetary Authority of Macau announced plans to create a "reciprocal surveillance mechanism" providing the Chinese Ministry of Public Security access to UnionPay money transfer data in Macau. Macau's Com- mission Against Corruption said in April 2015 that Macau authorities would cooperate with Chinese authorities in "fugitive manhunt and asset recovery activities." Officials from the Central Commission for Discipline Inspection reportedly are stationed in the central government's Macau liaison office as part of the central government's campaign against corruption.

Macau officials held talks with Chinese authorities in February on potential regulations governing transfer of offenders or suspects to mainland China. The UN Human Rights Committee reiterated its concern that implementation of these regulations must ensure offenders' protection under the ICCPR. In July, mainland anticorruption authorities reportedly worked with Macau law enforcement officials to detain a fugitive corruption suspect in Macau, returning him to Guangdong province. Some Macau legal experts criticized Macau authorities, referring to two previous rulings from Macau's highest court holding that, due to the lack of an ex- tradition agreement between Macau and mainland China, Macau authorities were not permitted to detain individuals wanted for ex- tradition to mainland China.

ABOUT THE EDITOR

Guy Breshears was born in Spokane, Washington, USA. He received both his BAE in Social Science Education and MA in History from Eastern Washington University in Cheney, Washington, USA. He is an educational professional and has taught at the primary and secondary levels both in the US and Hong Kong. With an interest in the advancement of knowledge, understanding and preservation of historical events and places he has lectured teachers and students about the importance of being appreciative of the past and why it is important to study and preserve it. He currently lives in Hong Kong with his wife and can often been seen walking around obscure places of Hong Kong looking for traces of history.

www.ingramcontent.com/pod-product-compliance
Lightning Source LLC
Chambersburg PA
CBHW082019300426
44117CB00015B/2274